Live Well

Foundations of High School Health

HUMAN KINETICS

Library of Congress Cataloging-in-Publication Data

Names: McConnell, Karen E., 1969- author. | Farrar, Terri D., author. | Corbin, Charles B., author.
Title: Live well : foundations of high school health / Karen E. McConnell, Pacific Lutheran University, Terri D. Farrar, Pacific Lutheran University, Charles B. Corbin, Arizona State University, Professor Emeritus.
Description: First. | Champaign, IL : Human Kinetics, [2024] | Includes index.
Identifiers: LCCN 2022044360 (print) | LCCN 2022044361 (ebook) | ISBN 9781718218062 (hardback) | ISBN 9781718218086 (epub)
Subjects: LCSH: Health. | Well-being.
Classification: LCC RA776 .M133 2024 (print) | LCC RA776 (ebook) | DDC 613--dc23/eng/20221114
LC record available at https://lccn.loc.gov/2022044360
LC ebook record available at https://lccn.loc.gov/2022044361

ISBN: 978-1-7182-1806-2 (print)

Copyright © 2024 by Human Kinetics, Inc.

Human Kinetics supports copyright. Copyright fuels scientific and artistic endeavor, encourages authors to create new works, and promotes free speech. Thank you for buying an authorized edition of this work and for complying with copyright laws by not reproducing, scanning, or distributing any part of it in any form without written permission from the publisher. You are supporting authors and allowing Human Kinetics to continue to publish works that increase the knowledge, enhance the performance, and improve the lives of people all over the world.

To report suspected copyright infringement of content published by Human Kinetics, contact us at **permissions@hkusa.com**. To request permission to legally reuse content published by Human Kinetics, please refer to the information at **https://US.Human-Kinetics.com/pages/permissions-information**.

Permission notices for material reprinted in this book from other sources can be found on pages 713-716.

The web addresses cited in this text were current as of April 2022, unless otherwise noted.

Acquisitions Editor: Bethany J. Bentley
Developmental Editor: Melissa Feld
Managing Editor: Derek Campbell
Copyeditor: Amy Pavelich
Indexer: Michael Ferreira
Permissions Manager: Laurel Mitchell
Senior Graphic Designer: Nancy Rasmus
Cover Designer: Keri Evans
Cover Design Specialist: Susan Rothermel Allen
Photographs (cover): kali9/E+/Getty Images (front cover); SDI Productions/E+/Getty Images (back cover, left), skynesher/E+/Getty Images (back cover, right)
Photographs (interior): © Human Kinetics, unless otherwise noted
Photo Asset Manager: Laura Fitch
Photo Production Manager: Jason Allen
Senior Art Manager: Kelly Hendren
Art Style Development: Joanne Brummet
Illustrations: © Human Kinetics, unless otherwise noted
Printer: Walsworth

Printed in the United States of America   1 2 3 4 5 6 7 8 9 10 WPC 28 27 26 25 24 23

The paper in this book was manufactured using responsible forestry methods.

Human Kinetics	*United States and International*	*Canada*
1607 N. Market Street	Website: **US.HumanKinetics.com**	Website: **Canada.HumanKinetics.com**
Champaign, IL 61820	Email: info@hkusa.com	Email: info@hkcanada.com
USA	Phone: 1-800-747-4457	

E8937

Contents in Brief

UNIT I Foundations of Living Well

1	Understanding My Health	3
2	Personal and Consumer Health	63
3	Health Equity and Public Health	109

UNIT II Eating Well and Being Physically Active

4	Food and Your Health	141
5	Managing Good Nutrition	197
6	Staying Active and Healthy	245

UNIT III Your Emotional, Mental, and Social Well-Being

7	Emotional Wellness	289
8	Mental Health	337
9	Relationships and Social Health	373

UNIT IV Destructive and Damaging Behaviors

10	Violence and Conflict	419
11	Alcohol	471
12	Tobacco and E-Cigarettes	509
13	Legal and Illicit Drugs	547

UNIT V Protecting Yourself and the Environment

14	Injury Prevention, Safety, and First Aid	595
15	Environmental Health	645

Contents

Editorial Review Board   ix
Features   xi
To the Student   xiii

UNIT I Foundations of Living Well

1 Understanding My Health   3

LESSON 1.1   Exploring Health and Wellness   5
LESSON 1.2   Developing Skills for Healthy Living   13
LESSON 1.3   My Immune System   26
LESSON 1.4   Communicable Diseases   37
LESSON 1.5   Noncommunicable Diseases   49

2 Personal and Consumer Health   63

LESSON 2.1   Personal Health Habits   65
LESSON 2.2   Healthy Vision and Hearing   79
LESSON 2.3   Healthy Sleep and Rest   88
LESSON 2.4   Being a Healthy Consumer   95

3 Health Equity and Public Health   109

LESSON 3.1   Understanding Health Equity   111
LESSON 3.2   Disability and Inclusion   119
LESSON 3.3   Public Health   127

UNIT II Eating Well and Being Physically Active

4 Food and Your Health   141

LESSON 4.1   Understanding Foods and Nutrients   143
LESSON 4.2   Energy Balance, Hunger, and Appetite   154
LESSON 4.3   Tips and Tools for Eating Well   163
LESSON 4.4   The Digestive and Urinary Systems   172
LESSON 4.5   Making Healthy Nutrition Decisions   182

5 Managing Good Nutrition   197

LESSON 5.1   Eating Well Across the Lifespan   199
LESSON 5.2   Food Access and Safety   209
LESSON 5.3   Maintaining a Healthy Weight   217
LESSON 5.4   Your Body Image   225
LESSON 5.5   Your Nutrition Plan   235

Contents

6 Staying Active and Healthy — 245

- LESSON 6.1 Being Physically Active and Physically Fit   247
- LESSON 6.2 Health-Related and Skill-Related Fitness Components   254
- LESSON 6.3 Preparing for Physical Activity   267
- LESSON 6.4 Fitness Planning   275

UNIT III Your Emotional, Mental, and Social Well-Being

7 Emotional Wellness — 289

- LESSON 7.1 Your Emotional Health   291
- LESSON 7.2 Building Self-Awareness   302
- LESSON 7.3 Developing Emotional Health and Mental Toughness   310
- LESSON 7.4 Recognizing and Managing Stress   318
- LESSON 7.5 Understanding Grief and Loss   326

8 Mental Health — 337

- LESSON 8.1 Understanding and Treating Mental Disorders   339
- LESSON 8.2 Anxiety and Anxiety Disorders   348
- LESSON 8.3 Depression and Mood Disorders   356
- LESSON 8.4 Self-Harm and Suicide   363

9 Relationships and Social Health — 373

- LESSON 9.1 Relationships and Communication Skills   375
- LESSON 9.2 Family Relationships   384
- LESSON 9.3 Friendships   393
- LESSON 9.4 Dating Relationships   400

UNIT IV Destructive and Damaging Behaviors

10 Violence and Conflict — 419

- LESSON 10.1 Understanding Violent Behavior   421
- LESSON 10.2 Anger, Aggression, and Conflict   430
- LESSON 10.3 Bullying and Hazing   437
- LESSON 10.4 Violence, Weapons, and Gangs   447
- LESSON 10.5 Relationships and Violence   455

11 Alcohol — 471

- LESSON 11.1 Alcohol Use, Effects, and Consequences 473
- LESSON 11.2 Influences and Alcohol 488
- LESSON 11.3 Treating Alcohol Use Disorders 497

12 Tobacco and E-Cigarettes — 509

- LESSON 12.1 Tobacco Products and Vaping 511
- LESSON 12.2 Regulations and Influences on Tobacco Product Use 525
- LESSON 12.3 Avoiding and Quitting Tobacco Product Use 535

13 Legal and Illicit Drugs — 547

- LESSON 13.1 Over-the-Counter and Prescription Drugs 549
- LESSON 13.2 Illicit Drugs 559
- LESSON 13.3 Influences on the Use of Drugs 573
- LESSON 13.4 Prevention, Treatment, and Being Drug-Free 581

UNIT V Protecting Yourself and the Environment

14 Injury Prevention, Safety, and First Aid — 595

- LESSON 14.1 Injury Prevention and Safety at Home 597
- LESSON 14.2 Safety in the Community 607
- LESSON 14.3 Safety Online 620
- LESSON 14.4 First Aid and Emergency Procedures 626

15 Environmental Health — 645

- LESSON 15.1 Air, Water, and Noise Pollution 647
- LESSON 15.2 Chemicals, the Environment, and Your Health 658
- LESSON 15.3 Conservation and Living Green 665

Appendix 677
Glossary/Glosario 687
Credits 713
Index 717

Editorial Review Board

Human Kinetics gratefully acknowledges the high school health educators who reviewed selected chapters from this textbook:

Dakota Berg
  Milwaukee High School of the Arts, Milwaukee County, Wisconsin

Dusty Lovejoy
  Hueneme High School, Oxnard, California

Eddie Mattison
  Parkway Schools, St. Louis, Missouri

Chantella Moore
  Lakewood High School, Pinellas County, Florida

Amy C. Reid, EdD
  Milwaukee School of Languages, Milwaukee, Wisconsin

Carlye Satterwhite
  Des Moines Public Schools, Polk County, Iowa

Shannan Tyson
  Seminole High School, Pinellas County, Florida

We also extend our sincere gratitude to ancillary contributor Rebecca L.H. Parker (Renton School District, Renton, Washington), who provided valuable feedback on this manuscript.

About the Edition

Live Well: Foundations of High School Health is adapted from *Live Well: Comprehensive High School Health* by veteran health educators Karen E. McConnell, Terri D. Farrar, and Charles B. Corbin (Human Kinetics, 2024).

Features

Career Connection
Health Educator   22
Patient Advocate   101
Nurse Practitioner   133
Gastroenterologist   179
Food Scientist   237
Personal Trainer   264
Mortician   332
School Counselor   360
Marriage and Family Therapist   390
Social Worker   434
Substance Abuse Counselor   501
Cancer Researcher   521
Social and Human Services Assistant   586
Meteorologist   602

Case Study
Dola's Diabetes Discovery   54
Cara and Natalie's Contrasting Realities   116
Arianna's Acne   69
Dante's Energy Drink Dilemma   151
Maria's Struggle   232
Leo's Story   367
Faiza's Solution   492
Lamar's Music Habit   655

Diversity Matters
Living With a Disability   124
Religion and Food   160
Asher's Challenge   352
Influence of Culture   490

STEM in Health
Vaccinations   33
Laser Eye Surgery   85
Phytochemicals   190
Genetically Modified Foods   215
Wearable Technology   281
Virtual Reality   343
The Breathalyzer   478
Automated External Defibrillator   629
Water Treatment   654

Understanding My Health
My Well-Being   4
My Self-Care   64
How Healthy Is My School?   110
Is My Diet Healthy?   142
What Influences My Eating Behaviors?   198
How Physically Active Am I?   246
My Emotional Health   290
My Anxiety and Emotions   338
Is My Relationship Healthy or Unhealthy?   374
My Knowledge of Anger and Conflict   420
What Do I Know About Alcohol?   472
What Do I Know About Tobacco Products?   510
What Do I Know About Legal and Illicit Drugs?   548
How Prepared Am I for an Emergency?   596
How Environmentally Aware Am I?   646

To the Student

Health is not something you can just read about. To really understand how to take care of your health, you need to *think* about what you read, organize the information in ways that you *understand*, and *apply* it in ways that help you learn *how* to be healthy. This book presents you with essential health information, and it also provides different ways for you to think about and apply that information as you develop your health skills. Knowing how to use this book and all of its features will help improve your knowledge and your skills—and will help you learn more quickly and more effectively. We invite you to join us on a tour of the book so that you can take advantage of the opportunities you will find in a typical unit, chapter, and lesson.

Start With the Unit Opener

1. Note the unit number and title.
2. Look at the chapters in the unit. Think about why the chapters listed might be grouped together. Consider what things you are excited to learn about.

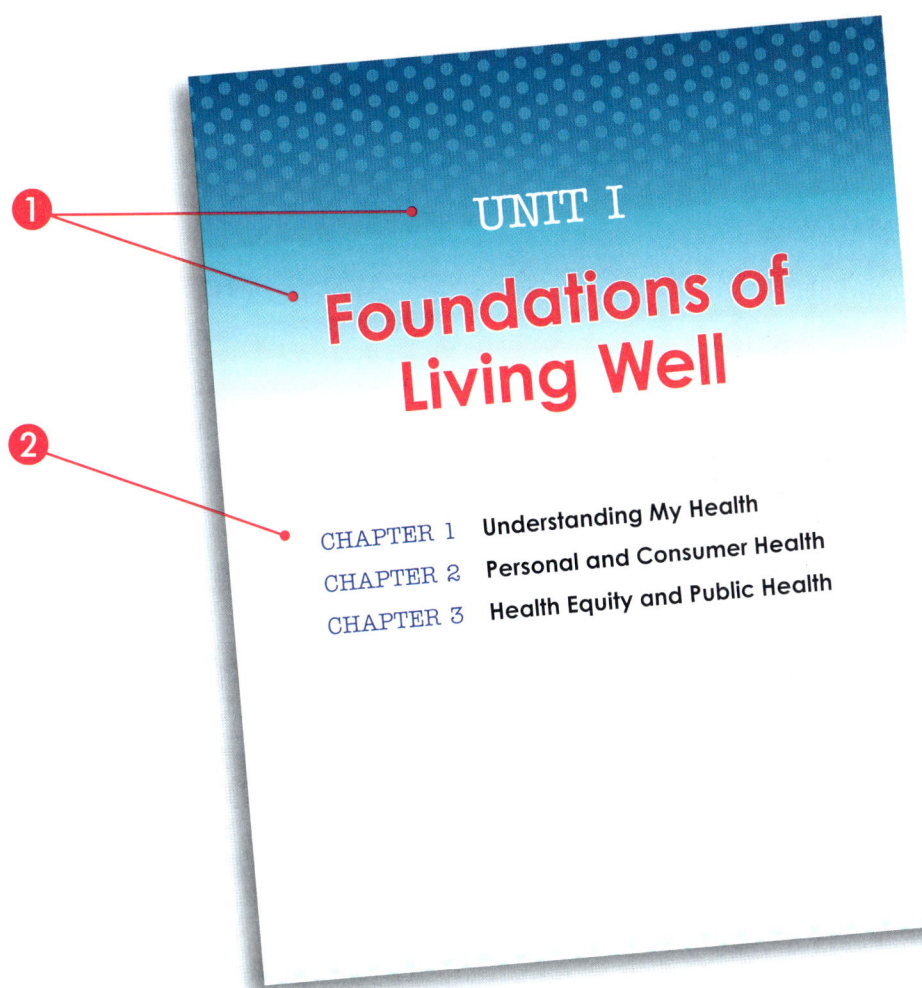

To the Student

Engage With the Chapter Opener

1. Note the chapter number and title, and review the lessons that are part of the chapter. Think about what you may know about each lesson and what questions you have.
2. Read the opening paragraph to help you better understand what the unit is about.
3. Finally, without writing in your book, complete the Understanding My Health self-assessment. Spend some time thinking about your answers and how the information in the unit relates to you personally. Your teacher might provide you with a separate copy to record your answers.

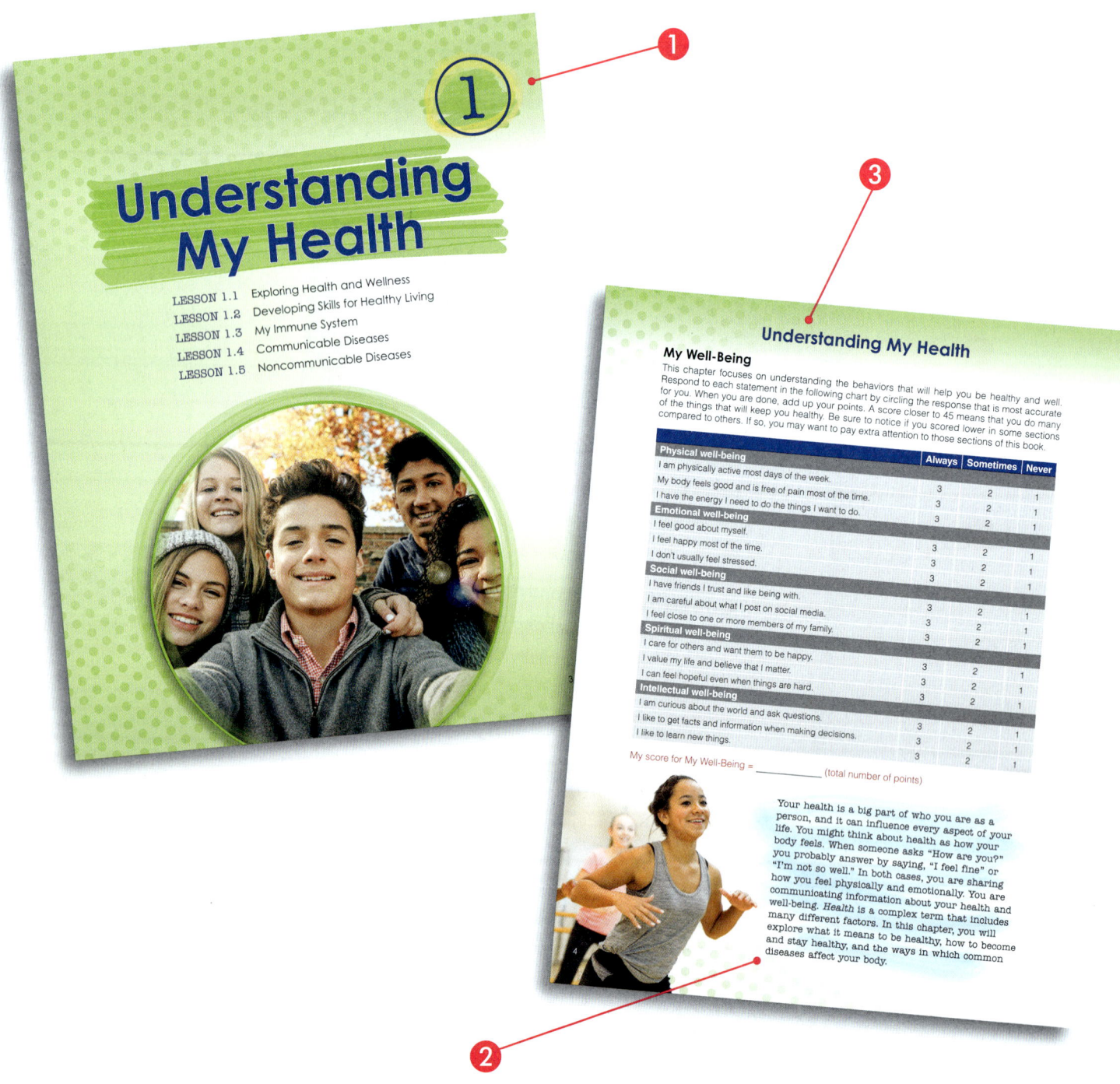

Focus In on the Lesson Opener

1. Note the lesson number and title.
2. Read each Term to Learn and try to define the terms you think you know.
3. Read The Big Picture to get a better sense of what this particular lesson will focus on.
4. Review the Learning Targets to better understand what you should learn as you read the lesson.
5. Write a response to the Write About It question in your notes.
6. Use the Note-Taking Guide your teacher provides to help you organize your thinking and to check your understanding as you read through the chapter.

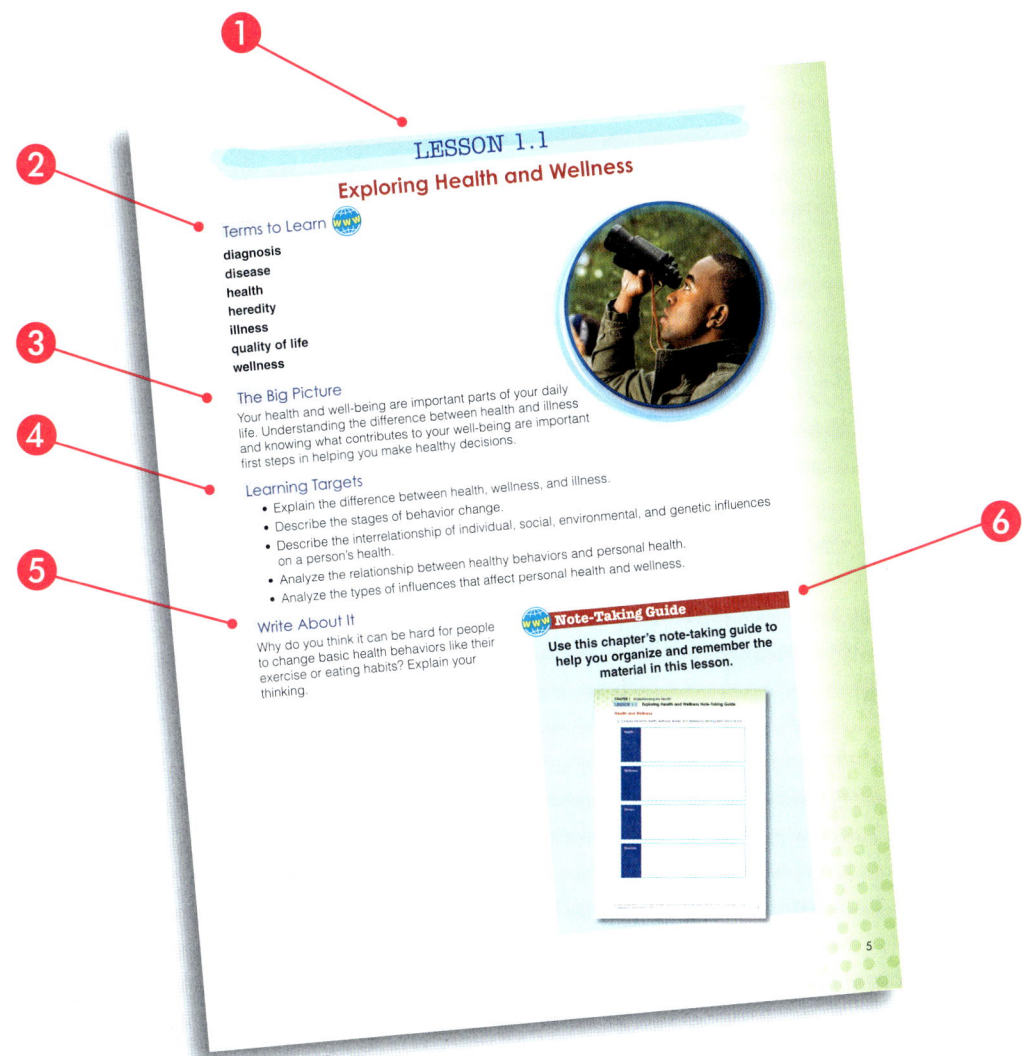

To the Student

Read the Lesson Including All of the Figures and Features

1. Each lesson begins with a story. Reflect on the questions or think about how the story relates to you before moving on.
2. Read the lesson one section at a time. Pause between sections to make sure you understand the concepts and vocabulary in each section.
3. Be sure to read the information that is part of the figures and the captions that appear with the images.
4. Consider the Healthy Living Tip. Is this something you can do?
5. Focus in on any special features like Diversity Matters, Career Connection, or STEM in Health. Think about how the feature relates to the lesson and to you personally. If a question is asked, stop and take a minute to reflect on the question.

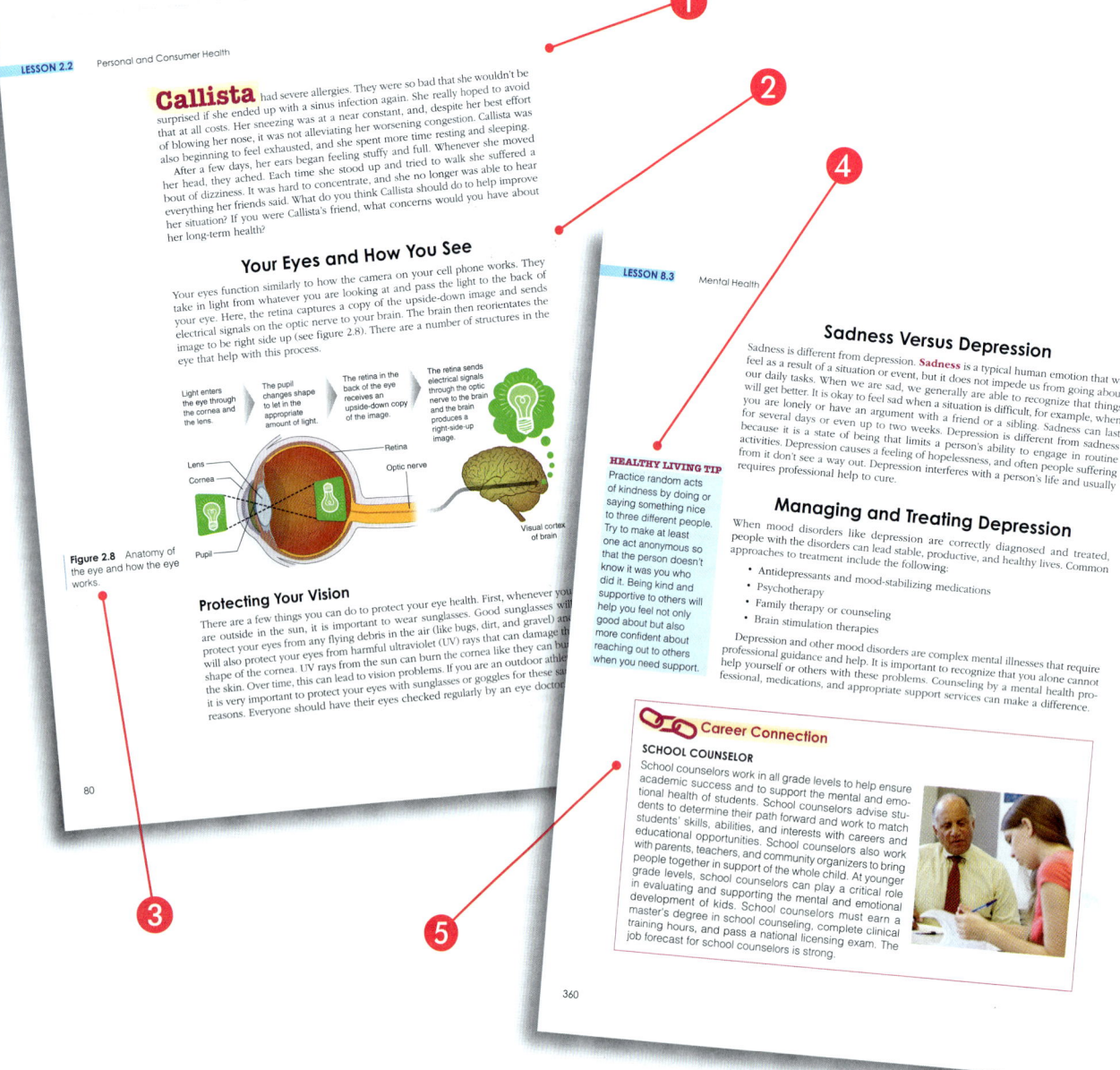

Practice Your Health Skills

1. Complete the Skill-Building Challenge. You may do this on your own in your notes, or your teacher could assign it to you on a worksheet.
2. Consider each of the Healthy Living Skills and select one or more to try on your own as a way to test your ability to apply the information you have read in the lesson.

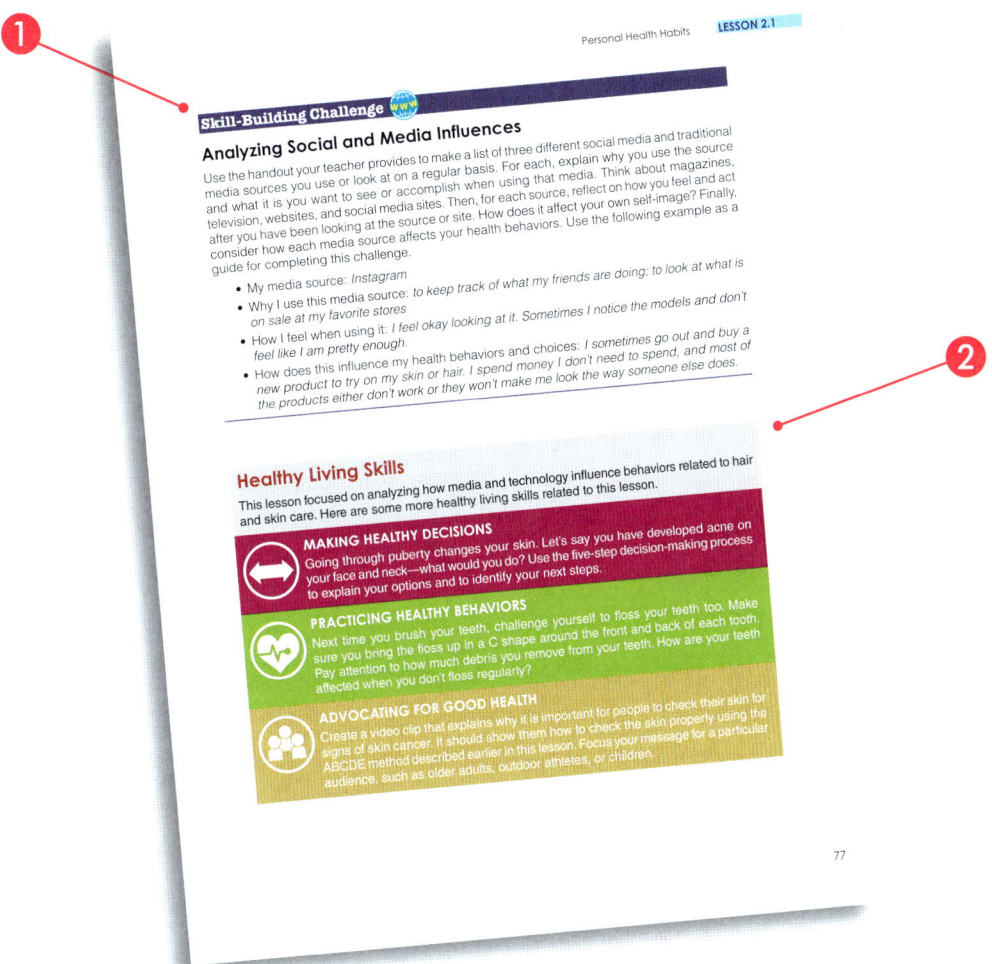

To the Student

Review What You Have Learned

1. Read through the Lesson Summary statements slowly. Try to recall additional details or information related to each statement.
2. Complete the Reviewing Concepts and Vocabulary. Consider defining each vocabulary word you see or use as an additional review.
3. Challenge yourself with the Thinking Critically question. These questions should be harder to answer and may require you to review what you have read.
4. Participate in the Take It Home activity if your teacher assigns it to you or if it is something you want to do. Even if you don't do the challenge, think about what the benefits of doing it might be.

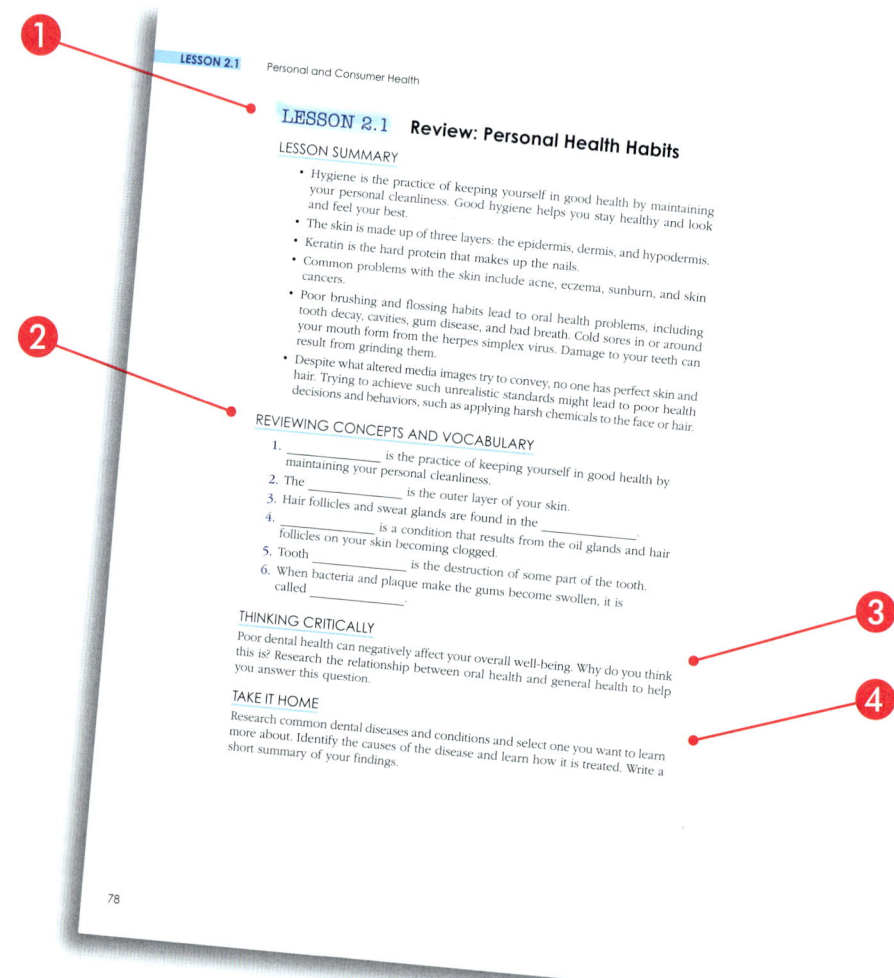

Bring It All Together in the Chapter Review

1. Put your learning from this chapter into action with the Action Plan. This is where you get to decide how you want to challenge yourself to be healthier. You don't just want to complete the Action Plan—you want to try to make the changes in your life. Consider telling a family member or classmate about your plan so that they can help you stay on track.

2. Use the questions in the Test Your Knowledge section to test how well you remember and understand the information you learned in the chapter.

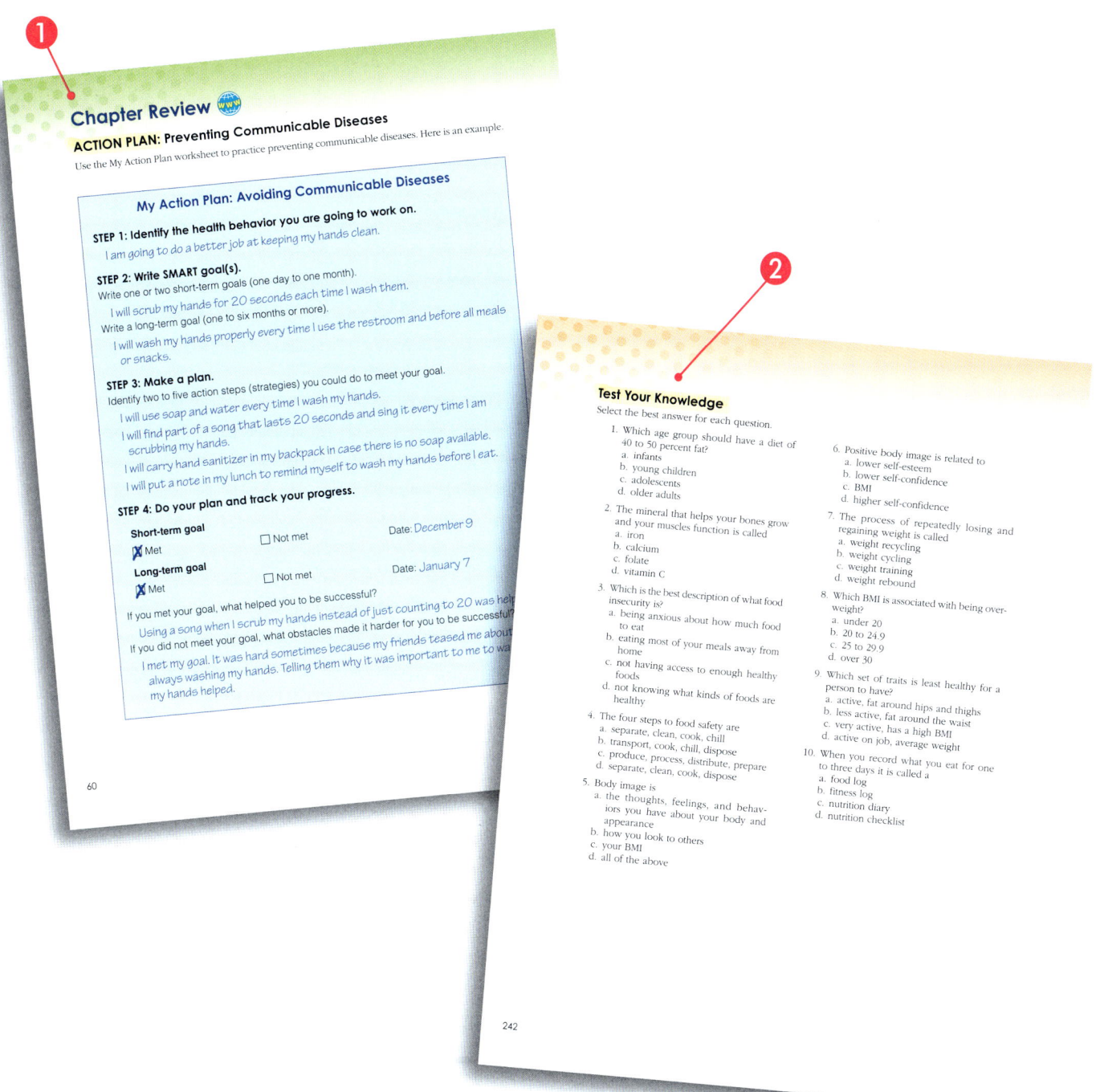

To the Student

Expanding Your Knowledge and Skills

1. The end of each chapter provides an idea for a class project. Read through the project to understand what it is about. Think about why the project is important and how it might help you and your community be healthier. Complete the project with your classmates if your teacher assigns it to you.

2. Each chapter also includes a challenge that lets you connect what you learn in health class to another subject you study in school. It may be reading, writing, math, or science. Complete Cross-Curricular Connections as a way to test your academic abilities.

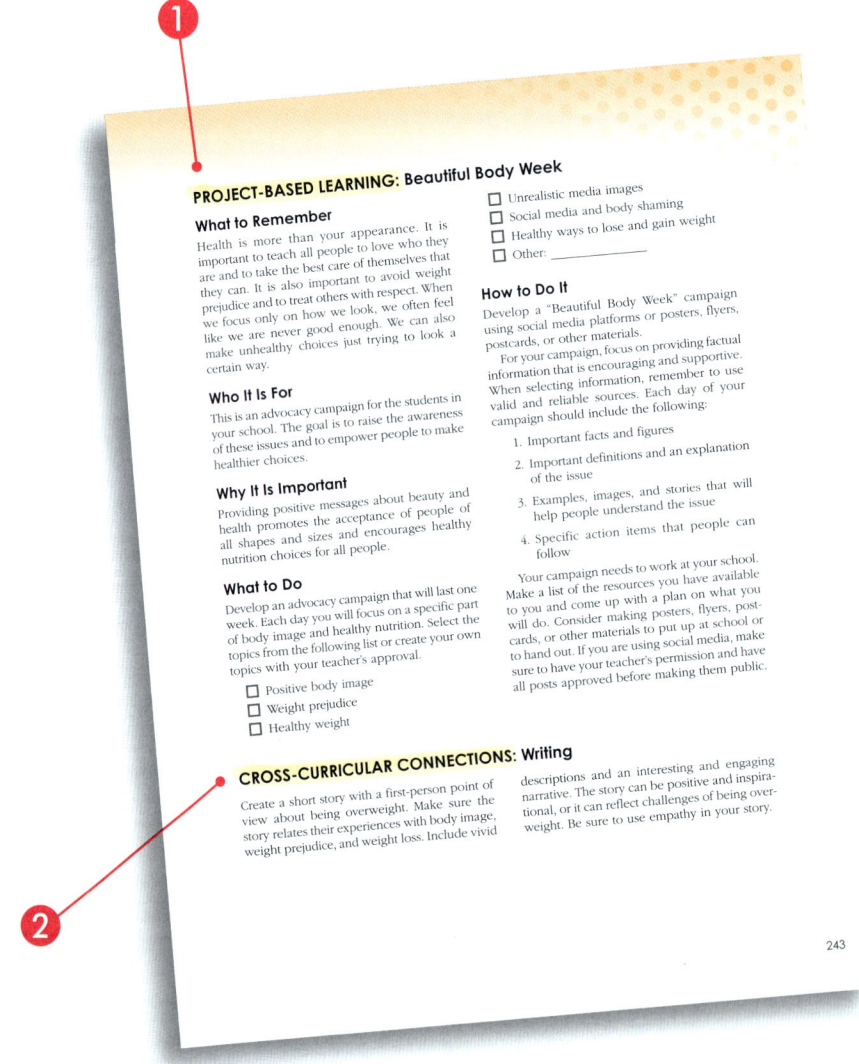

UNIT I

Foundations of Living Well

CHAPTER 1   **Understanding My Health**

CHAPTER 2   **Personal and Consumer Health**

CHAPTER 3   **Health Equity and Public Health**

Understanding My Health

LESSON 1.1   Exploring Health and Wellness
LESSON 1.2   Developing Skills for Healthy Living
LESSON 1.3   My Immune System
LESSON 1.4   Communicable Diseases
LESSON 1.5   Noncommunicable Diseases

Understanding My Health

My Well-Being

This chapter focuses on understanding the behaviors that will help you be healthy and well. Respond to each statement in the following chart by circling the response that is most accurate for you. When you are done, add up your points. A score closer to 45 means that you do many of the things that will keep you healthy. Be sure to notice if you scored lower in some sections compared to others. If so, you may want to pay extra attention to those sections of this book.

	Always	Sometimes	Never
Physical well-being			
I am physically active most days of the week.	3	2	1
My body feels good and is free of pain most of the time.	3	2	1
I have the energy I need to do the things I want to do.	3	2	1
Emotional well-being			
I feel good about myself.	3	2	1
I feel happy most of the time.	3	2	1
I don't usually feel stressed.	3	2	1
Social well-being			
I have friends I trust and like being with.	3	2	1
I am careful about what I post on social media.	3	2	1
I feel close to one or more members of my family.	3	2	1
Spiritual well-being			
I care for others and want them to be happy.	3	2	1
I value my life and believe that I matter.	3	2	1
I can feel hopeful even when things are hard.	3	2	1
Intellectual well-being			
I am curious about the world and ask questions.	3	2	1
I like to get facts and information when making decisions.	3	2	1
I like to learn new things.	3	2	1

My score for My Well-Being = _____ (total number of points)

Your health is a big part of who you are as a person, and it can influence every aspect of your life. You might think about health as how your body feels. When someone asks "How are you?" you probably answer by saying, "I feel fine" or "I'm not so well." In both cases, you are sharing how you feel physically and emotionally. You are communicating information about your health and well-being. *Health* is a complex term that includes many different factors. In this chapter, you will explore what it means to be healthy, how to become and stay healthy, and the ways in which common diseases affect your body.

LESSON 1.1
Exploring Health and Wellness

Terms to Learn
diagnosis
disease
health
heredity
illness
quality of life
wellness

The Big Picture
Your health and well-being are important parts of your daily life. Understanding the difference between health and illness and knowing what contributes to your well-being are important first steps in helping you make healthy decisions.

Learning Targets
- Explain the difference between health, wellness, and illness.
- Describe the stages of behavior change.
- Describe the interrelationship of individual, social, environmental, and genetic influences on a person's health.
- Analyze the relationship between healthy behaviors and personal health.
- Analyze the types of influences that affect personal health and wellness.

Write About It
Why do you think it can be hard for people to change basic health behaviors like their exercise or eating habits? Explain your thinking.

Note-Taking Guide
Use this chapter's note-taking guide to help you organize and remember the material in this lesson.

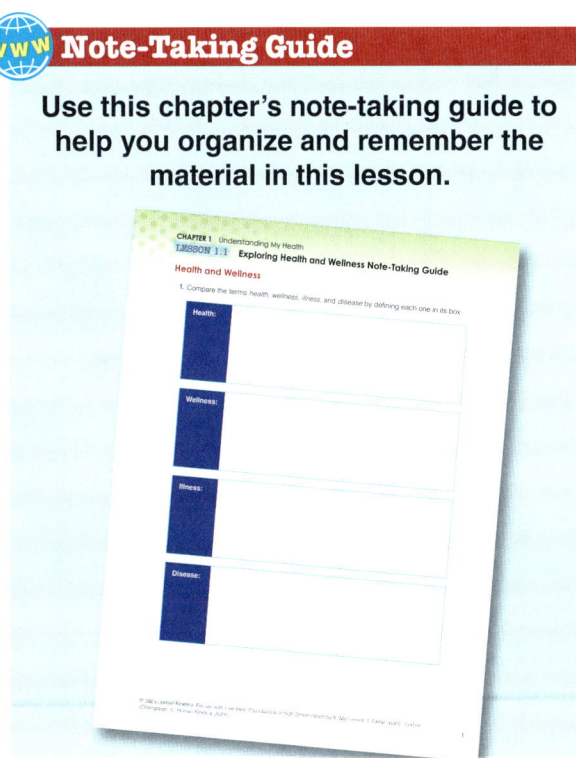

LESSON 1.1   Understanding My Health

Marcus is a quiet person. He is a good student and an accomplished musician. The other students in band admire Marcus's work ethic and sense of humor. He always seems able to empathize with others and make difficult situations a little easier to deal with. Marcus has a strong circle of friends, and they love to spend time together playing music and practicing dance moves. Even though Marcus appears happy and people are drawn to his personality, his friends are unaware of the struggles he has.

Marcus has a large family and doesn't get along with most of his siblings. He spends a lot of time alone and rarely sees his parents, who both work two jobs to support the family. Sometimes he doesn't sleep much because he feels anxious about his situation, and he never has friends over to the house because he is afraid of what they might think. The family rarely eats meals together. Marcus usually eats alone or with friends at school, and he has a pretty poor diet. He has no interest in sports and doesn't exercise. Two of his brothers are always smoking in the house, and that bothers him too.

Which factors have a positive impact on Marcus's health? Which behaviors can Marcus change in order to become healthier?

> **HEALTHY LIVING TIP**
> Each day write down something you did that benefited each part of your wellness: spiritual, social, emotional, physical, and intellectual.

Health and Wellness

In 1947, the World Health Organization (WHO) issued a statement indicating that **health** is more than freedom from disease or illness. This recognition led to a more comprehensive definition of health, which now includes wellness. Not being sick doesn't mean you are well. **Wellness** (see figure 1.1) is the positive component of health that includes having a positive sense of personal well-being and quality of life (i.e., satisfaction with your current life status). Adopting healthy lifestyles enhances health and wellness.

Social
Having lots of friends and social media likes isn't all that matters; you want to find meaningful connections and be able to adapt to different social situations easily.

Physical
This allows you to do more than just get around your school or carry around your school bag; you can bounce back from being sick, cope with stress, and recover from injury.

Intellectual
This helps you do well in school, and it also means you can engage in creative activities that express who you are.

Spiritual
This connects you to a sense of purpose and helps you live an authentic life, and it also builds your empathy for others who might have different beliefs than you do.

Emotional
Not only does this affect how you feel, it allows you to connect with others, manage stress, solve complex problems, and deal more easily with changes.

Figure 1.1 The five components of wellness.

Illness and Disease

Everyone gets sick from time to time. **Illness** is a general word we use to describe feeling unwell or not being fully healthy. A person may feel unwell for many reasons. For example, not getting enough sleep and eating poorly often lead to feelings of tiredness, irritability, and even nausea. Stress and anxiety are other examples that have a negative impact on our health. However, we can also feel ill because we have a disease. A **disease** is something that causes the body to function improperly. During a physical exam, a doctor uses a process to determine the nature of the disease to make a **diagnosis**. Some diseases, such as the common cold, are generally not that dangerous. Other diseases, such as cancer, are very complex and can be life threatening.

Influences on Health and Wellness

Many factors influence health and wellness (see figure 1.2), so making behavior modifications is challenging for people. When something has a strong influence on your health, we call it a *determinant*. Determinants can be individual, genetic, environmental, social, or lifestyle related. Determinants also interact with each other in ways that can affect health differently for different groups of people.

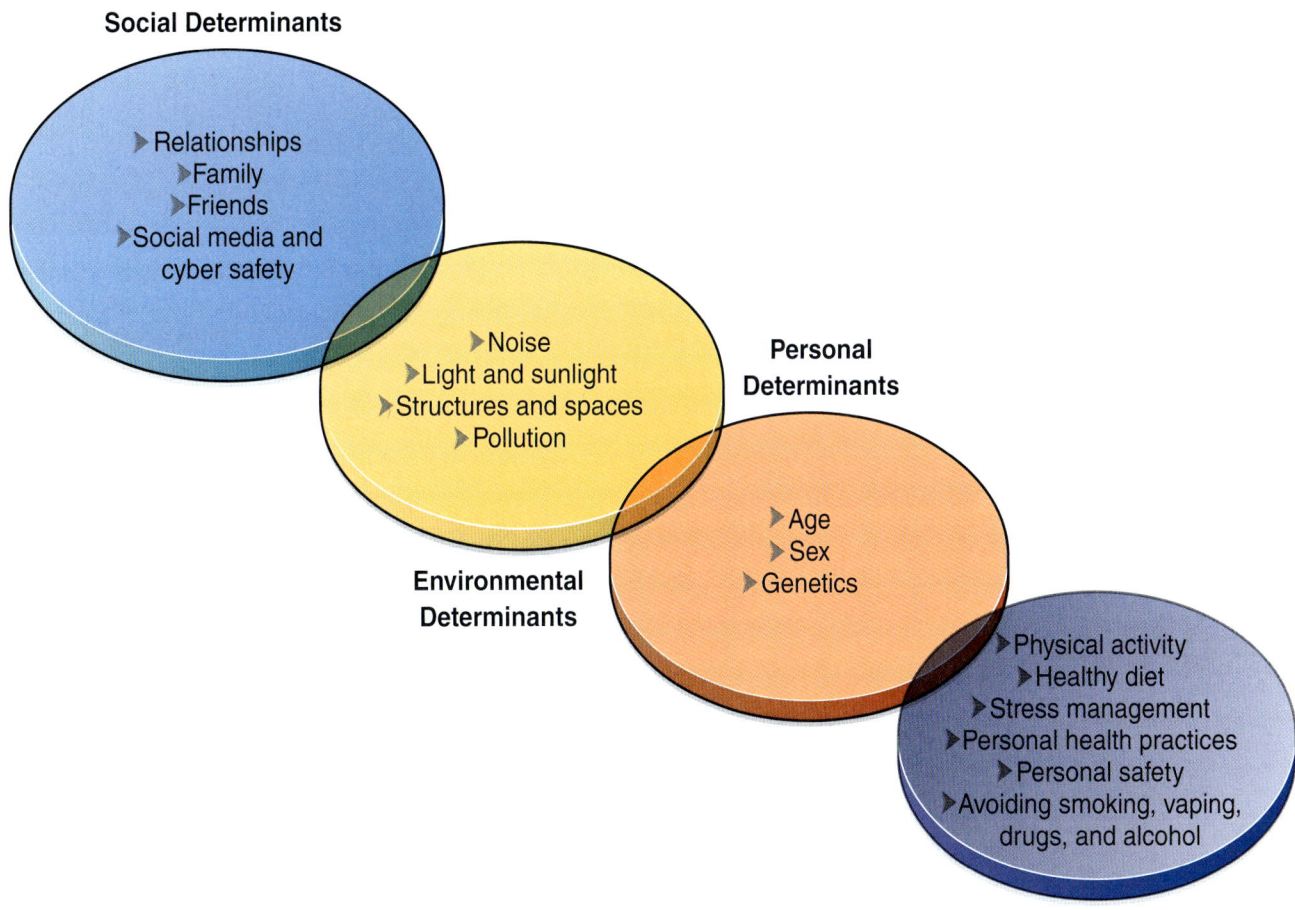

Figure 1.2 Determinants of health.

Individual Determinants

Among the factors that affect our health, there are some we simply cannot control. For example, you did not get to decide your **heredity**, the genes you inherited from your parents. Heredity, age, and sex are examples of individual determinants that influence health. As we age, our risk for disease and disability increases. Heredity contributes to a person's chance of developing certain diseases, ranging from common heart disease and cancers to much rarer forms. Even sex plays a role in our health. On average, women live four to five years longer than men in the United States. Even though you can't control these things, you can learn to understand their influences and make choices that are best for you given your personal circumstances.

Environmental Determinants

Environmental factors are another kind of determinant that affects your health. Loud noises, for example, may damage your hearing. Strong sunlight may be harmful to your eyes or cause skin cancer, and pollution may lead to or worsen asthma. The access you have to healthy food, recreational spaces, and exercise facilities and spaces can also influence your health.

Social Determinants

The people around you are part of your social environment. Those closest to you influence decisions you make and actions you take. For example, if you hang out with friends who avoid risky behaviors like vaping, smoking, and consuming alcohol, you are less likely to do those things too. If your friends like to be physically active and eat well, you are more likely to participate in those healthy behaviors.

Healthy Lifestyle Determinants

Living a healthy lifestyle reduces your risk of dying young or early. In fact, 60 percent of all deaths in the United States could be delayed by living a healthy lifestyle. We also know that healthy lifestyle choices improve the quality of a person's life. Your **quality of life** is the measure of how healthy, happy, and fulfilling your daily life is. Making healthy choices provides many benefits: It increases your energy levels, allows you to have fuller experiences of the world, improves your mood, and brings greater stability in your emotional well-being. You can make several lifestyle choices that will lead to a longer, healthier, and happier life.

Heredity

We all inherit different characteristics from our birth parents. Heredity is the passing of characteristics from parent to child. Hair and eye color, skin color, height, and body type, as well as some health conditions or health risks, make up our heredity. Genes, which largely determine heredity, carry the information our bodies use to create all of our individual traits and characteristics. The way in which your genes are organized and sequenced makes you different from every other person. The study of genes, including their influence on our health, is called *genetics*.

Healthy lifestyle choices include

- getting regular physical activity on all or most days of the week,
- eating a well-balanced diet of many fruits and vegetables and little or no sugar and salt,
- managing stress and anxiety,
- getting regular and adequate sleep,
- practicing good hygiene and personal health,
- avoiding dangerous situations and maintaining boundaries (including online), and
- avoiding tobacco, vape products, alcohol, and drugs.

When you practice healthy lifestyle choices, you will find a wide range of benefits:

- *Increased energy.* Getting regular physical activity and adequate sleep and eating a nutritious diet will help you feel more energetic.
- *Improved emotional stability.* Managing stress, adhering to a sound sleep regimen, and avoiding harmful substances (alcohol, tobacco, drugs) will make you feel happier more often and give you a better outlook on life.
- *Enhanced learning.* Being well rested, eating a balanced diet, and getting plenty of regular physical activity will position you for having the best learning experiences.
- *Heightened confidence.* Taking care of yourself will help you feel your best and significantly boost your self-confidence in a range of settings and situations.
- *Elevated goals and aspirations.* Modeling how to manage emotions and stress, plan and commit to healthy behaviors, and maintain boundaries (both on- and offline) at an early age will promote self-management skills for the future and contribute to long-term success.

Understanding Behavior Change

Our health and wellness are directly related to our choices and behaviors. Fortunately, we know that health behaviors can be changed. We also know that changes often occur in stages rather than all at once. There are five stages of health behavior change, ranging from precontemplation to maintenance (see figure 1.3). The goal is to move from lower stages to higher stages and, ultimately, reach stage five.

Figure 1.3 Stages of health behavior.

Stage 1: Precontemplation
You have no intention to change the behavior.

Stage 2: Contemplation
You acknowledge an intention to change the behavior.

Stage 3: Preparation
You actively plan to change the behavior.

Stage 4: Action
You change the behavior.

Stage 5: Maintenance
You sustain the behavior change for at least six months.

In stage 1, a person refuses to recognize that change is necessary. For example, a smoker may deny the need to stop smoking. The person might say, "I have no intention to stop." A person at stage 2 has thought about making a change but has not taken steps to implement it. This person might say, "I'm thinking about stopping." At stage 3, a person has not only thought about changing but also taken steps toward making the change. In the example shown in the figure, the person might download an app that explains steps to quitting and provides supports for their efforts.

By the time a person reaches stage 4, they have already made some changes but still need to make more. The person in figure 1.3 might have cut down the number of cigarettes per day or even stopped smoking for a few days. At stage 5, a person has made a definitive change and is sticking with it. For example, they might have stopped smoking for six months or more. This stage is often referred to as maintenance because the person is adopting the healthy behavior on a regular basis.

It would be nice if people who want to change health behaviors could always move quickly from stage 1 to stage 5. But this is not always the case. For example, smokers who quit (reach maintenance) often do not find success right away. For some smokers, it takes several tries over a period of many months. Others move through the stages more quickly. Regardless of how long it takes, people often move from a low stage to a higher stage and then fall back to a lower stage. Then they try again, each time moving to a higher stage. Of course, there are exceptions, but gradual change is most common. The stages have been used to help people improve all sorts of health behaviors, including eating patterns, physical activity, adoption of personal health habits, and avoidance of destructive habits other than smoking. Understanding how behavior change works can help you better appreciate the struggles and challenges you may face when trying to change your own behaviors.

Skill-Building Challenge

Analyzing Influences on Your Wellness

What are some of the influences on your wellness, and how important are they to you? Spend time thinking about influences related to family, peers, media, technology, community, values, and culture. Remember that wellness is not only being free from disease but also actively making healthy choices in all areas of your life.

Once you've identified as many influences as you can, write at least three of them, in order of greatest to least influence, for each category of wellness in the following list. For example, if reading books stimulates your intellectual curiosity, you would write "books" under "Intellectual." After completing the list, reflect on the category of influence that has the most significant impact on you. Explain your reasoning for choosing that particular category.

Wellness {
- PHYSICAL
- EMOTIONAL
- SOCIAL
- SPIRITUAL
- INTELLECTUAL

Healthy Living Skills

This lesson focused on recognizing influences on your health and wellness. Here are some additional ways in which you can develop healthy living skills related to this lesson.

HEALTHY COMMUNICATION

This chapter identifies five benefits of making healthy decisions. Create and write down a poem or rap that could be used to communicate these benefits to your peers. Be as accurate and thorough as possible and use only appropriate language and ideas. Prepare to share your work with the class.

SETTING HEALTHY GOALS

Set one goal for tomorrow that will improve one part of your wellness. For example, you might walk to school for your physical wellness or spend one hour reading instead of being on social media for your intellectual wellness. Write your goal down on a small piece of paper and carry it with you throughout the day to serve as a reminder.

MAKING HEALTHY DECISIONS

Use the stages of change to tell a realistic story about someone who is trying to change a health behavior. Make sure the person in your story experiences all of the stages. Think about what might influence the person's behavior and try to predict how that person might be able to respond to those influences when trying to progress through the stages.

LESSON 1.1 Review: Exploring Health and Wellness

LESSON SUMMARY

- Health is the state of being free of illness or disease; emotions, social connections, and sense of purpose in life are also part of health.
- Wellness is the positive component of health.
- *Illness* is a general word we use to describe feeling unwell or not being fully healthy.
- Individual influences on health include heredity, age, and sex.
- People are more at risk for illness as they age.
- *Heredity* refers to the characteristics you inherit from your birth parents. Our heredity is largely determined by our genes. Genetics is the study of genes.
- People move through different stages when trying to change health behaviors.
- Environmental influences include air and noise pollution and overexposure to sunlight.
- Your social environment also affects your health. Here, your friends and family are particularly influential.
- Having a healthy lifestyle helps you to feel your best, have more energy, feel happier, learn better, and achieve your goals and aspirations.
- Your quality of life is a measure of how healthy, happy, and fulfilling your daily life is.

REVIEWING CONCEPTS AND VOCABULARY

1. When someone is free of disease, we say that they are _____.
2. The five components of _____ are physical, emotional, social, spiritual, and intellectual.
3. When someone is not feeling well, we usually say that person has a(n) _____.
4. A(n) _____ is the process a medical professional uses to determine the nature of a disease.
5. The third stage in the stages of change model is _____.
6. _____ is the passing of characteristics from parent to child.
7. When you have a healthy, happy, and fulfilling life, we say that you have a good _____ of life.
8. A(n) _____ causes the body to not function correctly.

THINKING CRITICALLY

How do you think the influences on your health will change as you age? Think about life in decades (10-year periods such as ages 20-29). For each decade, describe what you think the biggest influences on a person's health would be at that age. Explain your response.

TAKE IT HOME

Give the wellness questionnaire from the start of this chapter to someone in your family or household. Explain what each component of wellness means and ask them about what influences their wellness. How do their influences compare to yours?

LESSON 1.2
Developing Skills for Healthy Living

Terms to Learn
advocacy
community
habit
health literacy
long-term goals
plain language
reliable information
short-term goals
valid information

The Big Picture
Imagine if a surgeon learned all about the human body by memorizing details in a book but never practiced the necessary skills to actually perform a surgery. What if no one ever showed the surgeon how to make a clean incision, stop a vessel from bleeding, or stitch up the incision? Do you think the surgeon would be successful performing the surgery? Learning health skills is not that different. To be as healthy as possible, you need both knowledge and skills.

Learning Targets
- Explain what health literacy is and why it is important.
- Explain each of the eight health skills.
- Explain the difference between reliable and valid health information.
- Describe advocacy using a real-world example related to health.
- Apply effective verbal communication skills to enhance health.

Write About It
How difficult or easy is it for you to say "no" when a friend wants you to do something unhealthy or risky like drinking alcohol, vaping, or texting while driving? Why do you think it is easy or hard for you? Explain your answer using an example from your own life if possible.

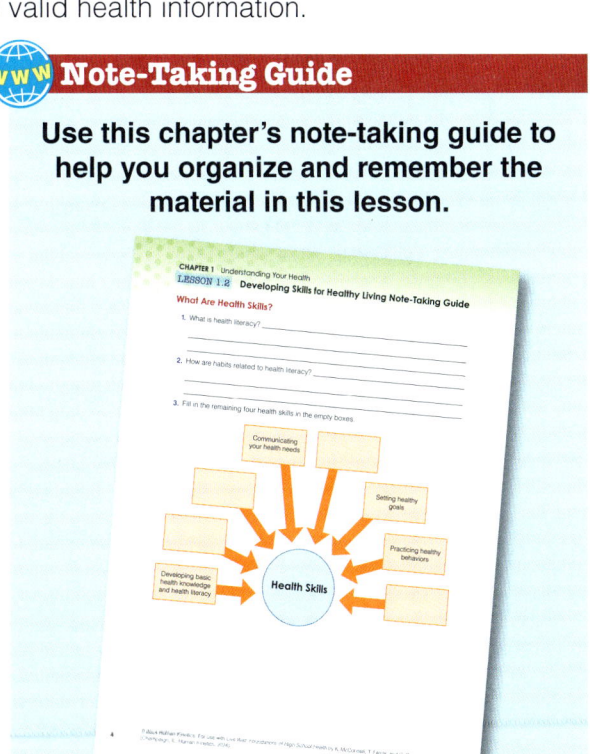

Note-Taking Guide

Use this chapter's note-taking guide to help you organize and remember the material in this lesson.

13

LESSON 1.2   Understanding My Health

Prisha always got the highest grades in her classes. She was really good at memorizing information and understanding concepts. Even though she knew a lot, Prisha wasn't that healthy. She struggled to eat a well-balanced diet and hardly ever got any exercise. Last year, it seemed like she almost always had a cold. When her friend Scott asked her about why she wasn't taking better care of herself, she said, "I know everything I need to know about health. Besides, it's not like I'm sick or anything." Scott knew that his friend had a lot of knowledge, but he didn't understand why Prisha couldn't actually be healthier. He considered this and realized that Prisha might not know how to make healthy decisions or set healthy goals. He also realized that Prisha wasn't very good at communicating how she felt. In fact, it seemed like she had a lot to learn about the skills she needed to use her knowledge and to practice healthy behaviors. Where could Prisha learn better health skills?

What Are Health Skills?

Of all the subjects you learn in school, health may be the most important when it comes to your day-to-day life. Your health decisions are a part of your daily life, the quality of your life, and the longevity of your life. Almost every decision you make or behavior you do each day can affect your health in some way.

A person with good **health literacy** can find and understand basic health information and then use that information to make smart health decisions. Learning to be healthy begins with developing health literacy. This book helps you learn basic health information and gives you opportunities to develop your health literacy skills. Developing basic health skills allows you to put your knowledge into practice. Over time, the skills you practice can become healthy habits. A **habit** is something you do automatically, without really thinking about it.

This lesson introduces basic health skills, each presented with a skill cue, that are referenced in later lessons.

HEALTHY LIVING SKILLS
- ☐ Developing basic health knowledge and health literacy
- ☐ Analyzing what influences your health behaviors
- ☐ Accessing valid and reliable health information and resources
- ☐ Communicating your health needs
- ☐ Making healthy decisions
- ☐ Setting healthy goals
- ☐ Practicing healthy behaviors
- ☐ Advocating for good health for yourself and others

Developing Basic Health Knowledge and Health Literacy

Finding health information is not hard. In fact, the Internet seems filled with varying opinions about every health topic imaginable. Many websites claim to provide health information. Social media influencers often promote untested health plans or products for profit-driven reasons rather than for their audience's best interests. It is easy to get confused, overwhelmed, and taken advantage of if you don't understand some basic facts about your health. Finding, processing, and understanding credible health information for making informed decisions about your health is how you develop health literacy (see figure 1.4). The following Health Knowledge Skill Cues are referenced in later lessons.

A person with health literacy can
- Process health information
- Obtain health information
- Understand health information
- Identify and choose health services
- Make appropriate health decisions

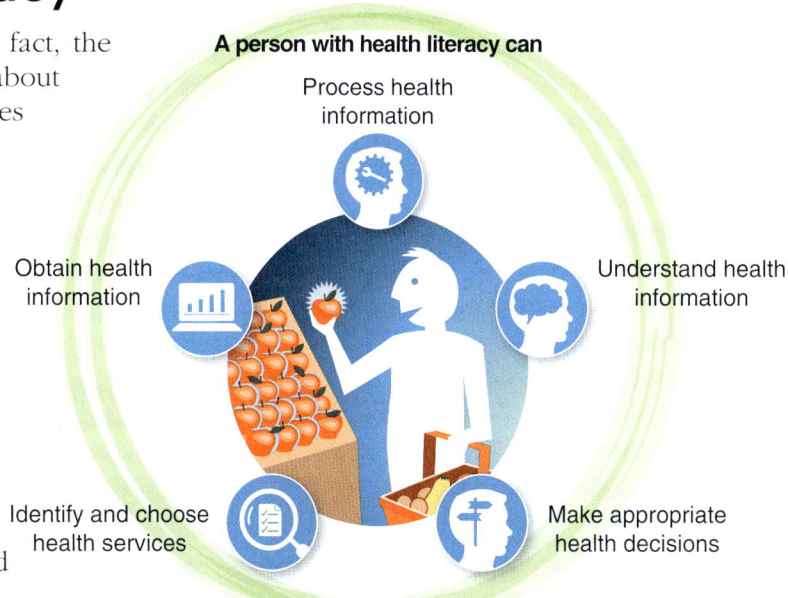

Figure 1.4 The characteristics of health literacy.

Analyzing What Influences Your Health Behaviors

Have you ever wondered: *Why do I do certain things? What makes me want to eat the way I do? Why (or why not) am I active? What makes me feel sad or frustrated? How do my family and friends influence my behaviors? How do advertisements affect my decisions about what I buy or how I expect others to behave?* The reality is that we are all influenced by other people and other things all the time (see figure 1.5). It is very difficult to change our own behaviors or choices if we don't know what makes us do something in the first place. Identifying influences and evaluating their impact is a critical health skill that will help you make healthy choices. The Analyzing Influences Skill Cues shown here will be referenced in later lessons.

Figure 1.5 What influences your health behaviors?

Analyzing Influences Skill Cues

Identify the influence → Evaluate the influence → Make a positive choice/Protect from negative influence

Accessing Valid and Reliable Health Information and Resources

Not everything on the Internet or on social media is good information. Learning how to find and evaluate health information and resources takes time and practice. The information you find should be both valid and reliable. **Valid information** is logical and factually accurate. **Reliable information** is consistent (similar) across sources and is dependable. The Accessing Information Skill Cues shown here will be referenced in later lessons.

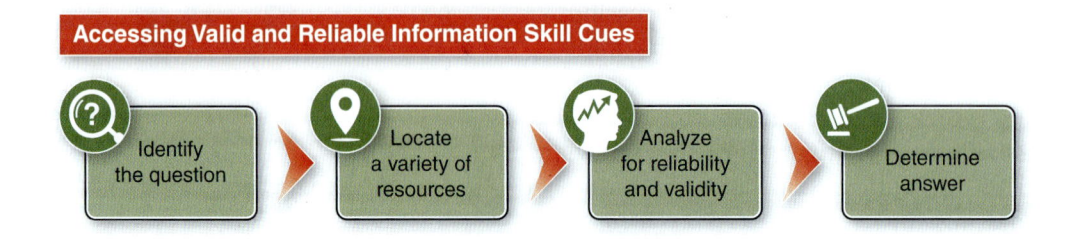

Accessing Valid and Reliable Information Skill Cues

Identify the question → Locate a variety of resources → Analyze for reliability and validity → Determine answer

Valid and Reliable Websites

Most people look for health information online. The quality of online information, however, varies. Some websites are meticulously designed to provide facts and accurate information. Other sites have one purpose, which is selling products and services, and many may not use accurate facts or information. You may notice that websites have different letters attached to their address. These codes are called *top-level domains*. The type of code a website uses provides a clue to the type of information you may find.

Types of Web Domains

.gov for government use only
There are some very accurate and reliable government websites that provide health information. Examples include the National Institutes of Health at www.nih.gov and the Centers for Disease Control and Prevention at www.cdc.gov.

.edu for use by educational institutions
If you have a school website, it uses this domain. Colleges and universities also use .edu.

.org for individual or organizational use
These websites require you to carefully evaluate information. Many sites using this domain provide accurate health information. The American Heart Association at www.heart.org is one example.

.com for commercial use
Be careful of these domain websites, which often are trying to sell you a product or service and may not tell you the full truth. Some .com sites do provide health information, but they rely on advertising to pay for their sites. Companies that sell medicines and drugs often help pay for these health information sites, and they may influence what information is included.

.net for use only by network providers
These sites normally don't provide any health information.

.biz for businesses
These sites are often for small businesses. Generally, they won't be providing health information, but they may be providing a service like massage, personal training, or counseling.

Checklist for Evaluating Health Websites

You can use the following checklist to help you evaluate all types of websites.

- Who publishes the site?
  - Consider the domain and what it might suggest. Start with .gov, .edu, or .org sites.
- What is the purpose of the site?
  - Is it to sell a product? To provide information? To gather information? Try to get basic information first from sites that are not selling a product or service.
- What type of information is on the site?
  - Does the site use data that comes from research? Look for sites that provide data and tell you where the data comes from.

- Is the information reviewed by experts?
  - If there is health information on the site, who is the author? Does the site provide information about who wrote or reviewed the information? Use sites that tell you who wrote the information and what credentials they have.
- Is the information current?
  - Not all old information is bad, especially basic information that does not change much. Still, our knowledge about diseases, treatments, genetics, and other topics related to health is changing quickly. Try to find sites that keep their information up to date. Using information from the Internet that is not older than five years is a good rule to follow.

The Accessing Valid and Reliable Websites Skill Cues shown here will be referenced in later lessons.

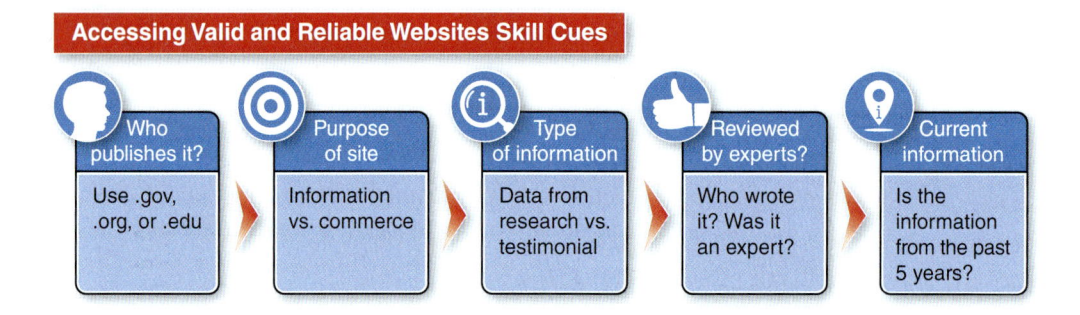

Accessing Valid and Reliable Websites Skill Cues

Who publishes it?	Purpose of site	Type of information	Reviewed by experts?	Current information
Use .gov, .org, or .edu	Information vs. commerce	Data from research vs. testimonial	Who wrote it? Was it an expert?	Is the information from the past 5 years?

Communicating Your Health Needs

Your communication skills influence your health behaviors in many ways. You may need to communicate about how you feel to your parent or guardian, or when you are at a medical clinic. You may also need to communicate what you want or need in a way that gets others to listen and understand. Sometimes communication helps us avoid or manage conflict, and other times it helps us to build relationships. The Communication Skill Cues shown here will be referenced in later lessons.

Communication Skill Cues

Identify communication skill → Follow the skill steps → Have a healthy outcome

A variety of communication skills can help you make healthy decisions (figure 1.6). How you communicate will be different based on the situation you are in and what you are trying to achieve. Part of communicating your needs is identifying which communication skill you need in a given situation. For example, when your opinion differs from that of your parents or guardians, using several communication skills may help you and them understand each other's perspective. It is important to recognize that you can learn new ways to communicate and continue improving your communication skills throughout your life.

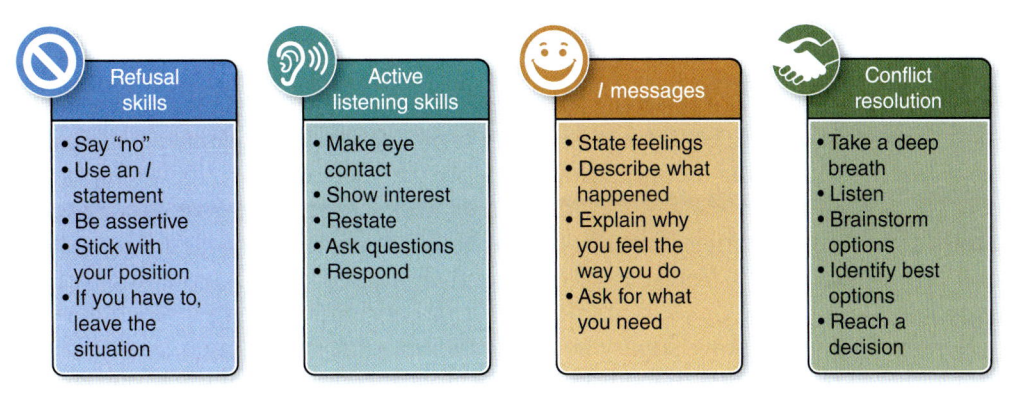

Developing Skills for Healthy Living **LESSON 1.2**

Refusal skills	Active listening skills	I messages	Conflict resolution
• Say "no" • Use an I statement • Be assertive • Stick with your position • If you have to, leave the situation	• Make eye contact • Show interest • Restate • Ask questions • Respond	• State feelings • Describe what happened • Explain why you feel the way you do • Ask for what you need	• Take a deep breath • Listen • Brainstorm options • Identify best options • Reach a decision

Figure 1.6 The four types of communication skills.

Making Healthy Decisions

You make decisions that affect your health every day (see figure 1.7). For example, you decide what to eat, whether you'll exercise, when to go to sleep, and how you will respond if you are offered alcohol or drugs. Some of the decisions you make will seem pretty easy. Deciding between apple slices and potato chips at lunch is not that hard if you are trying to make a healthy choice. Other decisions require more thought. It isn't always easy to decide not to do something potentially dangerous when all of your friends are doing it. It can also be difficult to make a decision that requires hard work or effort, like starting an exercise program.

Your knowledge about health will influence some decisions, like when to see a doctor. Your friends and family will influence others, like what you eat or whether you choose to vape. Some decisions are connected to your personal values and beliefs, and others may be influenced by your culture and traditions. No matter what influences your decisions, there are some steps you can practice that will help you make healthier decisions that you can feel good about. The Decision-Making Skill Cues shown here will referenced in later lessons.

Decisions

- **Wants** — Things you would like to have but that are not essential to survive
- **Priorities** — Things that you value and want to put first
- **Needs** — Things you must have, like air, shelter, food, and water
- **Attitude** — Feelings you have toward things
- **Values** — Things that are important to you

Figure 1.7 What influences your decision making?

Decision-Making Skill Cues

Understand the problem → Gather information and know your options → Know the consequences → Make a decision → Think about your choice

LESSON 1.2   Understanding My Health

Setting Healthy Goals

We often set goals in our life to motivate our behavior or to help us achieve something important. Setting goals for your health is no different. If a person wants to give up smoking or drinking alcohol, they probably can't just quit. It may be important for that person to set some short-term goals and a long-term goal. **Short-term goals** create smaller targets that can be reached in a shorter amount of time—often one day to one month. You may have several short-term goals, depending on the situation. **Long-term goals** will take one to six months or longer to achieve. If you want to quit drinking sugary soda, you might start by setting a goal to drink less soda each day. Eventually, you may be able to go a full day without having any. Finally, you may be able to quit drinking soda completely. Goals can also be categorized as outcome (final result) or process (how you are doing something) goals. Many long-term goals are outcome goals because their focus is on the final behavior or result you want to achieve. For example, you may have an outcome goal to quit drinking soda altogether. Many short-term goals are process goals, meaning that the goal is about a step you will take on your way to your final outcome. Reducing how often you drink soda from twice per day to once per day and then to once every other day and so on is a process goal. However, it is possible to have a short-term outcome goal or a long-term process goal.

Before setting any health goals, it is a good idea to reflect on where you are now with the behavior you want to modify. The process of evaluating your own behaviors and actions is called a *self-assessment*. Self-assessments help you gauge where you are and think more clearly about where you want to go.

When creating goals, you should practice using SMART goals, which are *s*pecific, *m*easurable, *a*chievable, *r*ealistic, and *t*imely (see figure 1.8). You will get better at setting SMART goals the more you practice. It is important to remember that your goals should reflect your values and priorities. It can be very difficult to achieve a goal that someone else set or that you don't believe in. The Goal-Setting Skill Cues shown here will be referenced in later lessons.

Goal-Setting Skill Cues

Identify a SMART goal → Make an action plan → Monitor your progress → Reflect and refine

SMART Goal

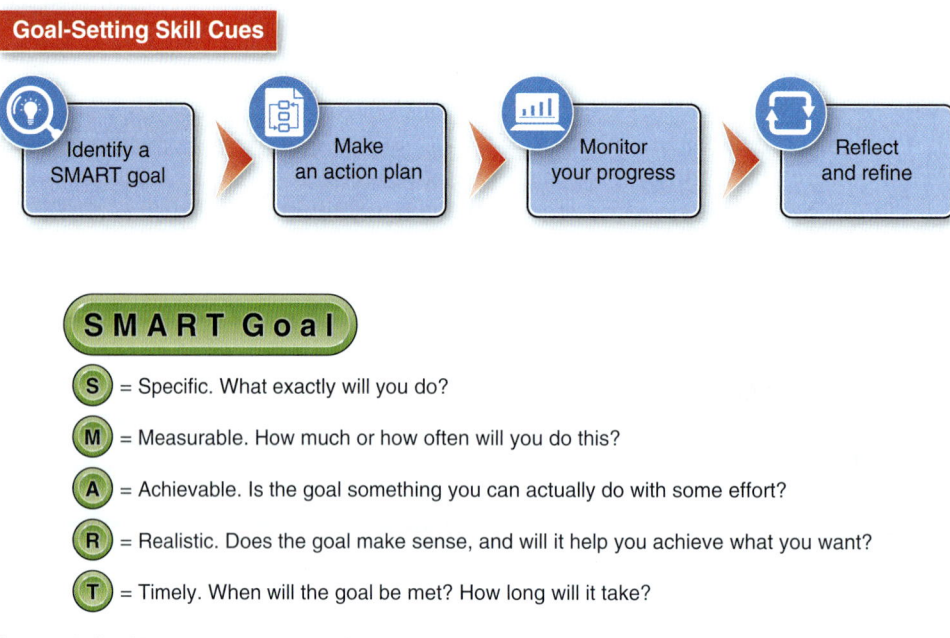

- **S** = Specific. What exactly will you do?
- **M** = Measurable. How much or how often will you do this?
- **A** = Achievable. Is the goal something you can actually do with some effort?
- **R** = Realistic. Does the goal make sense, and will it help you achieve what you want?
- **T** = Timely. When will the goal be met? How long will it take?

Figure 1.8 When creating goals, you should practice using SMART goals.

Developing Skills for Healthy Living **LESSON 1.2**

Practicing Healthy Behaviors

Being healthy is something you must do on a daily basis. It is not enough to just think about being healthy or talk about how you want to be healthy. Health is a series of choices and actions you make every day. To become healthier, you must practice being healthy, which ultimately leads to establishing healthy habits over the long term. It is important to distinguish good habits, like exercising and getting enough sleep, from bad ones, like overexercising or using drugs (see figure 1.9).

Examples of Healthy Habits
- Being physically active
- Eating plenty of fruits and vegetables
- Getting enough quality sleep
- Being supportive and kind to others
- Being mindful and self-aware
- Drinking water

Examples of Unhealthy Habits
- Smoking (including e-cigarettes)
- Using drugs
- Being sedentary
- Excessive drinking
- Being aggressive toward others
- Drinking energy drinks

When you are ready to change a health behavior, start by identifying the behavior and then making a checklist of what you need to do to accomplish that behavior. Once you've begun practicing the behavior, keep track of your progress and reflect on how well you are doing it. The Practicing Healthy Behaviors Skill Cues shown here will be referenced in later lessons.

Figure 1.9 Habits can be healthy or unhealthy.

Practicing Healthy Behaviors Skill Cues

Identify the behavior → Make a checklist → Monitor your progress → Reflect on your progress

HEALTHY LIVING TIP
Carry your own water bottle to school to help you drink plenty of water throughout the day. Make sure the bottle is full when you leave for school and try to drink all the water before you get back home.

21

LESSON 1.2 Understanding My Health

Advocating for Good Health for Yourself and Others

Part of being healthy is learning how to advocate for yourself and others. **Advocacy** is the act or process of supporting or promoting a cause or an issue. Advocacy requires an ability to organize your thoughts and to communicate effectively. The Advocacy Skill Cues shown here will be referenced in later lessons.

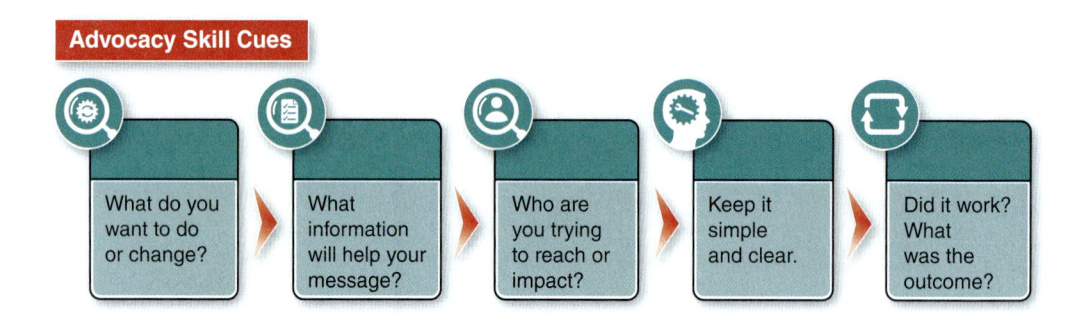

Advocacy Skill Cues

| What do you want to do or change? | What information will help your message? | Who are you trying to reach or impact? | Keep it simple and clear. | Did it work? What was the outcome? |

Advocating for Your Personal Health

Supporting your own health is a form of advocacy. It is important to communicate your needs clearly. For example, you have the opportunity to advocate for your needs at doctor's appointments by being prepared for your visit. One way to achieve this is by bringing a written list of your symptoms that indicates how long you have had them and describes what actions you've already taken to improve your health. Asking questions such as "What else can I do to feel better?" or "Are there any treatments that might help me?" is another way to advocate for your personal health.

Career Connection

HEALTH EDUCATOR

A person who teaches people about behaviors that promote wellness is called a *health educator*. Health educators design and create strategies that help people and communities improve their health behaviors. They also educate people about basic health skills. Health educators generally work full time in a variety of settings, including hospitals, nonprofit organizations, government, doctors' offices, private businesses, and educational institutions. Some health educators hold teaching credentials and also serve as teachers. Other health educators who work with the public can hold a CHES certification, which stands for *certified health education specialist*. To qualify for this certification, you must have a college degree in health education and pass a national certification exam.

Advocating for Family Members and Others

Throughout your life, you will also find a desire to support the needs of others. You may have a close relative or friend who experiences a health issue and needs someone to advocate for them. For someone with a more serious health issue, attending medical appointments with them may be crucial. Being diagnosed, feeling unwell, or being confused and overwhelmed during a consultation can disrupt a person's ability to process the information they receive from a medical professional. By listening, taking notes, and asking questions to clarify information, you are being a good advocate on your relative or friend's behalf.

Advocating for Your Community

If you are concerned with the health of your community, you may become involved in community advocacy. A **community** is any group of people who share common characteristics or interests. Examples of communities include your town or city, your neighborhood, your school, and your cultural groups. Communities might also exist around health topics or issues. For example, the people in a cancer support group are a type of community.

Advocating for the concerns of a community is often more formal than advocating for individual people. You may participate in an organized rally at your state capitol supporting a proposed law, a public gathering designed to raise awareness on a topic, or a social media campaign designed to raise money for a community health issue or cause. Figure 1.10 provides steps to follow that can help you learn to be a more effective community advocate.

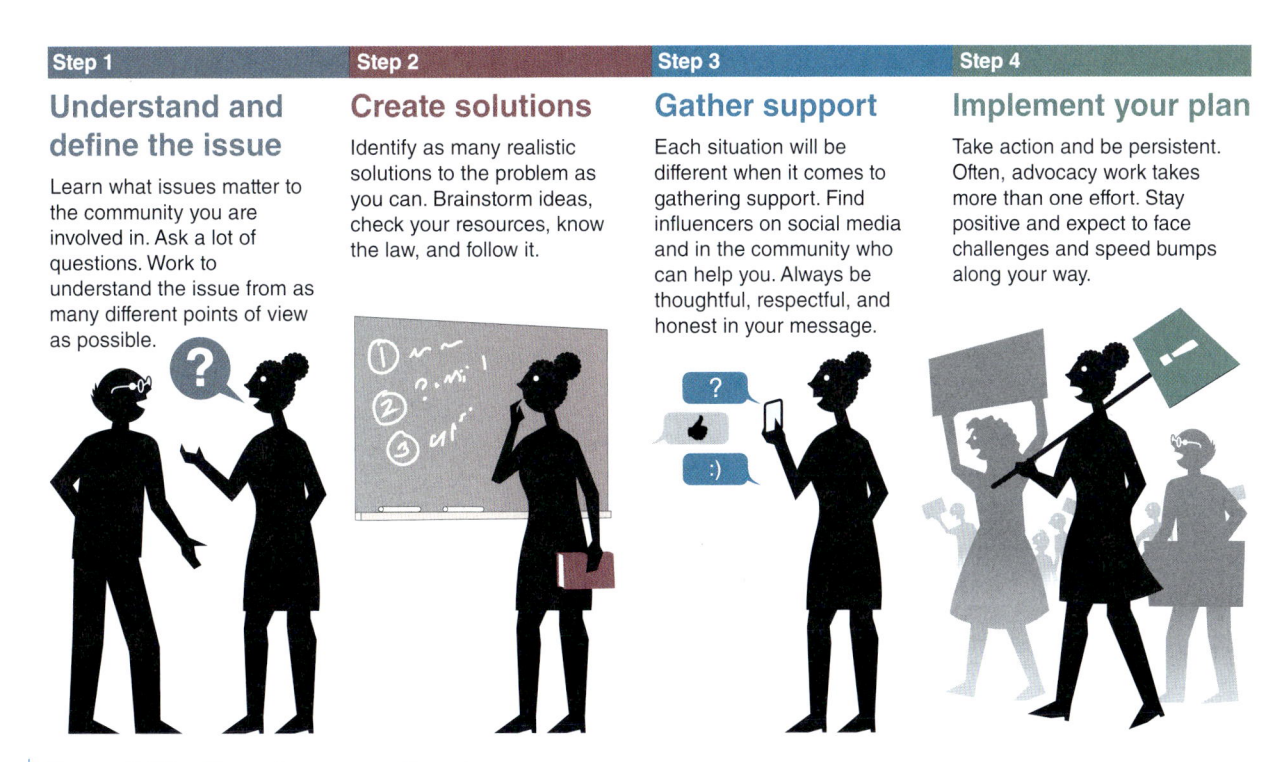

Step 1	Step 2	Step 3	Step 4
Understand and define the issue	**Create solutions**	**Gather support**	**Implement your plan**
Learn what issues matter to the community you are involved in. Ask a lot of questions. Work to understand the issue from as many different points of view as possible.	Identify as many realistic solutions to the problem as you can. Brainstorm ideas, check your resources, know the law, and follow it.	Each situation will be different when it comes to gathering support. Find influencers on social media and in the community who can help you. Always be thoughtful, respectful, and honest in your message.	Take action and be persistent. Often, advocacy work takes more than one effort. Stay positive and expect to face challenges and speed bumps along your way.

Figure 1.10 Steps to community advocacy.

LESSON 1.2 Understanding My Health

Skill-Building Challenge

Healthy Communication

We can help others develop their health literacy by communicating health information in clear ways. Using **plain language** is a strategy for making written and oral information easier for a given population to understand on the first reading. It is one important tool for improving health literacy, and communicators should consider the audience receiving the information. A document using plain language is one in which people can find what they need, understand what they find, and make a good decision based on what they know.

Key elements of plain language include

- organizing information so that the most important points come first,
- breaking complex information into understandable chunks or parts, and
- using simple language and either avoiding or defining technical terms.

TASK

Conduct some research on the concept of wellness. Read through a few different reliable sources of information and gather some facts about what wellness is, why it is important, and what we can do to improve it. Once you have gathered the information, create a brochure or handout that presents the information in plain language. Focus on the key elements of plain language.

Healthy Living Skills

This lesson taught you about healthy living skills. Here are some more ways you can develop healthy living skills related to this lesson.

ANALYZING INFLUENCES

Your culture and its traditions influence what you know and believe about health. Develop a list of six ways that your culture influences your health beliefs. Compare your list with two or three other classmates and discuss similarities and differences. Then compare and contrast your lists to determine common categories or types of cultural influences on health.

MAKING HEALTHY DECISIONS

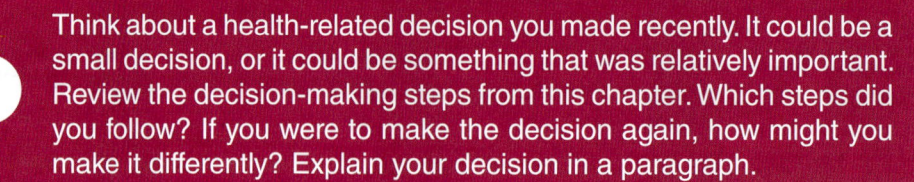

Think about a health-related decision you made recently. It could be a small decision, or it could be something that was relatively important. Review the decision-making steps from this chapter. Which steps did you follow? If you were to make the decision again, how might you make it differently? Explain your decision in a paragraph.

LESSON 1.2 Review: Developing Skills for Healthy Living

LESSON SUMMARY

- Health literacy is the ability to find and understand basic health information and use that information to make well-informed health decisions.
- Major influences on health include family, culture, peers, school, community, media, norms and expectations, values and beliefs, policies, rules, and laws.
- The eight health skills are (1) developing basic health knowledge, (2) analyzing and understanding what influences your health behaviors, (3) accessing valid and reliable health information and resources, (4) communicating your health needs, (5) making healthy decisions, (6) setting healthy goals, (7) practicing healthy behaviors, and (8) being an advocate for good health for yourself and others.
- Valid information is logical and factually accurate. Reliable information is similar across sources and is dependable.
- Advocacy is the act or process of supporting or promoting a cause or an issue.

REVIEWING CONCEPTS AND VOCABULARY

1. A(n) _____ is something you do automatically without really thinking about it.
2. The first step in making a healthy decision is to _____ the problem.
3. A small goal that you wanted to achieve in two weeks would be a _____-term goal.
4. A SMART goal is specific, _____, attainable, realistic, and _____.
5. Web domains using .gov, .edu, and _____ often provide accurate health information.
6. A community is any group of people who share common characteristics or _____.
7. Valid information is information that is _____ and factually accurate.

THINKING CRITICALLY

Select the one healthy living skill that you think is the most important. Write a short speech that convinces others why your skill choice is the most important. Include three supporting details or facts to defend your point of view.

TAKE IT HOME

Explain the eight skills for healthy living to a parent or guardian and discuss how family influences each skill. Together, identify one skill that your family wants to work on, set a SMART goal to help you reach your goal, and make an agreement with other family members to support each other in reaching your goal.

LESSON 1.3
My Immune System

Terms to Learn
allergen
antibodies
bacteria
human immunodeficiency virus (HIV)
immune system
immunization
pathogen
virus

The Big Picture
Have you ever wondered why you get some colds or viruses that go around school but not others? What keeps you from getting sick or ill? The reality is germs are all around us. Although most germs are harmless, some do cause illness, and people are exposed to potential illnesses on a daily basis. Fortunately our bodies are designed to keep us safe from these dangers, and most of the time, our immune systems are able to keep us healthy.

Learning Targets
- Identify the major organs and tissues of the immune system and explain their primary functions.
- Explain what a pathogen is and provide two examples.
- Explain how the immune system responds to pathogens.
- Describe four different problems the immune system could have.
- Explain how HIV affects your immune system.
- Explain how vaccinations work to help your immune system fight off known pathogens.
- Access and analyze the validity of information about immune disorders.

Note-Taking Guide
Use this chapter's note-taking guide to help you organize and remember the material in this lesson.

Write About It
When was the last time you were really sick? What type of illness did you have? What factors might have affected your body's ability to fight off your illness? What did you do to try to feel better and to get healthy again?

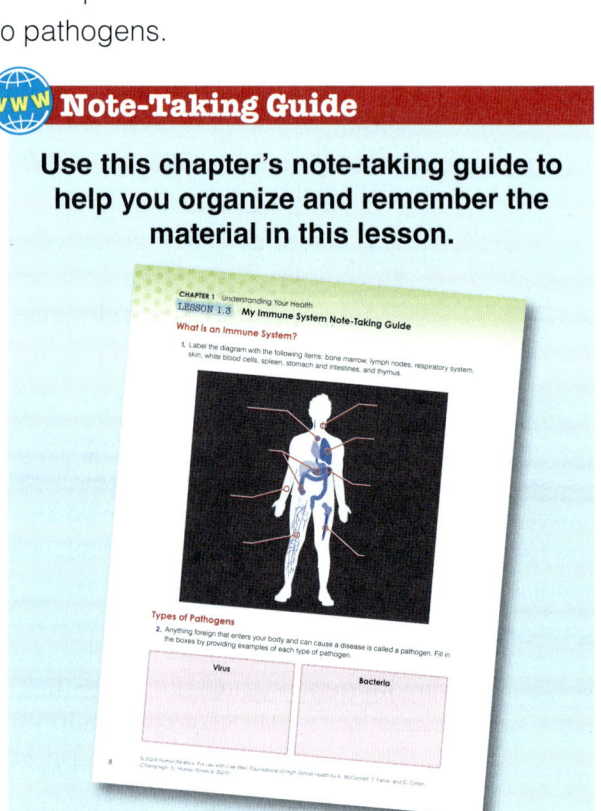

My Immune System LESSON 1.3

Connor wasn't feeling very well. He felt like he had a cold that wasn't going away. He hated being sick because it meant he couldn't go to school, practice for the upcoming basketball game, or see friends on the weekend. So he pretended to be fine most of the time, but it was exhausting. His friends started giving him a hard time because he was always sniffling and sneezing. His dad told him he needed to rest up and drink plenty of fluids, even suggesting that Connor take a day off to fight this bug, but Connor just thought his dad was being overprotective. Despite his fatigue, which only seemed to be increasing in intensity, Connor forced himself to go to basketball practice after school. The big game was on Thursday night, and he and his teammates planned to celebrate their current winning streak over pizza later that weekend. His immune system was already overburdened, and Connor's choices weren't helping matters.

Understanding how your immune system works and ways to take care of it will help you make healthy choices. What behaviors might have contributed to Connor's illness? What might Connor have done differently to help shorten his illness and protect others from getting sick?

What Is an Immune System?

Your **immune system** is your body's defense system. Think of it like a complex army of soldiers actively working to protect your body from invaders. The immune system is made up of cells, tissues, and organs that work together to destroy invaders. These include your bone marrow, lymph nodes, respiratory and digestive systems, skin, white blood cells, spleen, and thymus. Figure 1.11 describes primary functions for each component. For example, the spleen is responsible for filtering out bacteria and viruses in your blood.

Thymus
An organ in your throat that helps make a specialized army of cells to attack invaders

Stomach and intestines
The acid in your stomach kills some bacteria, and your intestines make substances that can attack invaders

Skin
The skin acts as a barrier against all kinds of invaders

White blood cells
These attack invading cells like viruses and bacteria that don't belong

Lymph nodes
These small clusters of cells recognize invaders and work to get rid of them

Respiratory system
The mucus and cells inside your throat and lungs work to trap invaders

Spleen
An organ near your stomach and lungs that filters out the bacteria and viruses in your blood that the rest of your immune system has attacked

Bone marrow
Inside your bones you make white blood cells that protect you from invaders

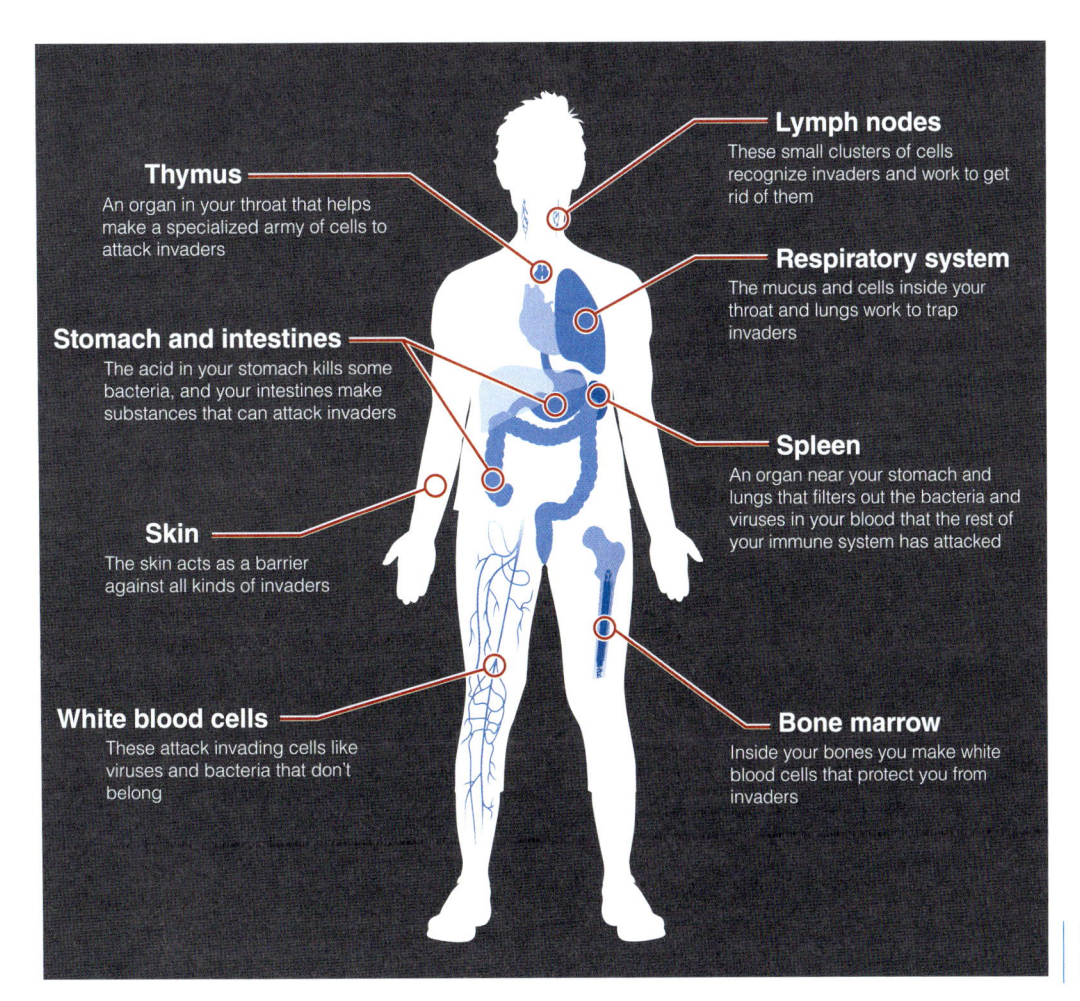

Figure 1.11 The immune system.

LESSON 1.3 Understanding My Health

Types of Pathogens

Anything foreign that enters your body and can cause a disease is a **pathogen**. Different types of pathogens can make you sick, and you will read more about them in lesson 1.4. Two examples of pathogens are viruses and bacteria. **Viruses** are very small bundles of infectious materials that get inside your cells and then multiply. **Bacteria** are single-celled organisms found in the environment that can carry disease. Viruses and bacteria are the most common causes of disease in people (see figure 1.12).

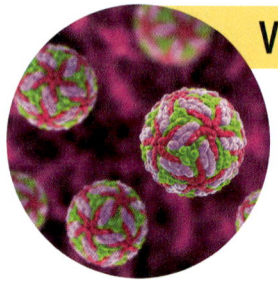

Viruses

Viruses are small bundles of material that get inside your cells and multiply.

Examples: hepatitis A and B, human papillomavirus (HPV), human immunodeficiency virus (HIV), influenza (flu), measles, polio, and rabies

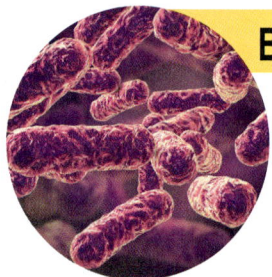

Bacteria

Bacteria are single-cell organisms found in the environment that can carry disease.

Examples: Lyme disease, tuberculosis, syphilis, strep throat, and salmonella

Figure 1.12 Comparing viruses and bacteria.

Keeping Invaders Out and Launching an Attack

Your body has several methods for keeping pathogens out. For example, you can try to prevent them from getting into your body at all, or you can attack them and try to kill them if they do get in. All of the ways in which you protect yourself from pathogens make up your immune response.

Immune Barriers

Your skin acts as a very effective barrier. Under normal circumstances, viruses and bacteria won't get into your blood if your skin is healthy. Getting a cut or scrape or having a crack in your skin breaks this barrier. When this happens, invaders can get into the blood.

Your throat and digestive system also help keep dangerous pathogens out of your body. Mucus in your nose and throat can capture viruses and bacteria. You get rid of some of these invaders when you cough, blow your nose, or sneeze. Saliva and stomach acid can also kill some pathogens that might be in your food.

My Immune System LESSON 1.3

Immune Response

If an invader gets past one of these barriers, the body activates its immune response (see figure 1.13). Different types of white blood cells begin destroying the pathogen. As this happens, certain white blood cells then travel around your body signaling a warning to other cells of the danger. Your body also remembers past invaders and recognizes them immediately if they enter the body again. The cells that carry this knowledge are called **antibodies**. In other words, once you've had a specific illness, your body now has the antibodies needed for destroying the same invader the next time it shows up. When you have a specific set of antibodies in your system, you are said to be immune from whatever invader is threatening you. This process is also why **immunizations**, or preventative shots, work.

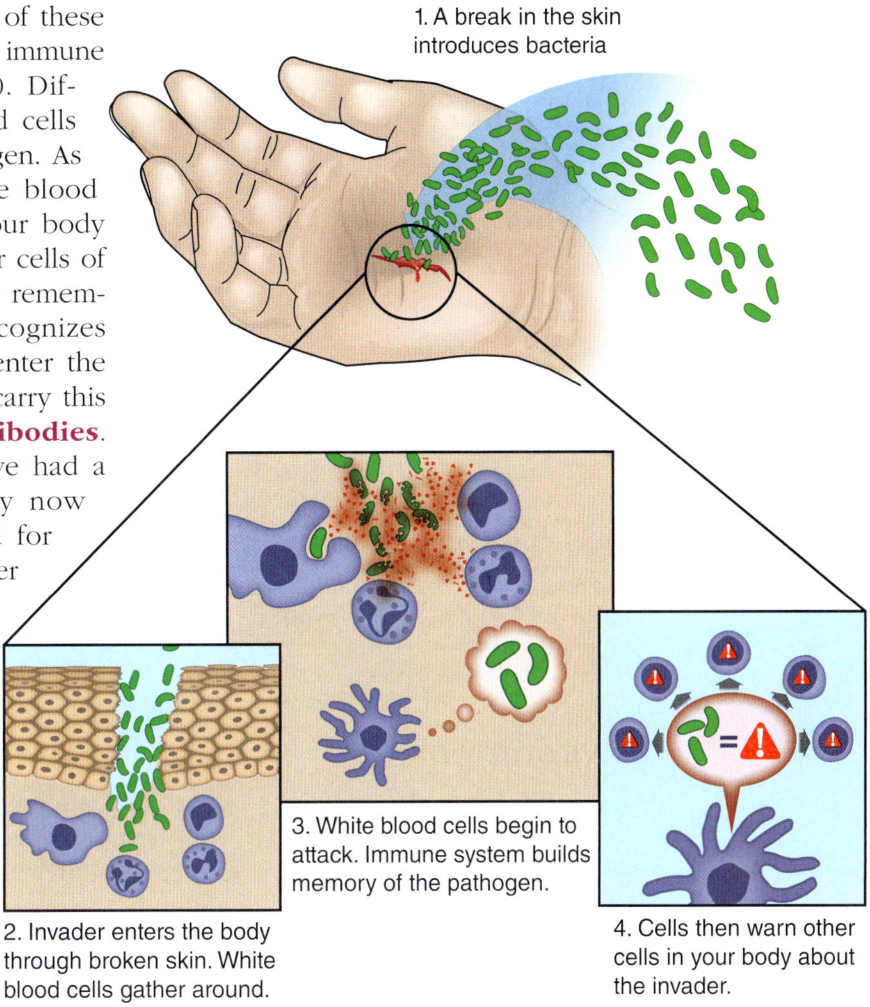

1. A break in the skin introduces bacteria

2. Invader enters the body through broken skin. White blood cells gather around.

3. White blood cells begin to attack. Immune system builds memory of the pathogen.

4. Cells then warn other cells in your body about the invader.

Figure 1.13 Your immune response.

Keeping the Immune System Healthy

Your immune system is complex, and it functions best when you keep your body healthy and strong. Do the following to keep your immune system healthy:

- Eat foods rich in vitamins and minerals, like fruits and vegetables and whole grains.
- Get at least 30 minutes of exercise most days of the week.
- Get 8 to 10 hours of sleep every night.
- Wash your hands regularly.
- Keep up with your immunizations.
- Keep your weight healthy.
- Don't drink alcohol.
- Don't smoke or vape.
- Manage your stress through relaxation, exercise, and social support.

HEALTHY LIVING TIP

Learn about your immunization history. Ask a parent or guardian what immunizations you have had and when you had them. Keep a record as part of your personal health history.

What Influences Your Immune System?

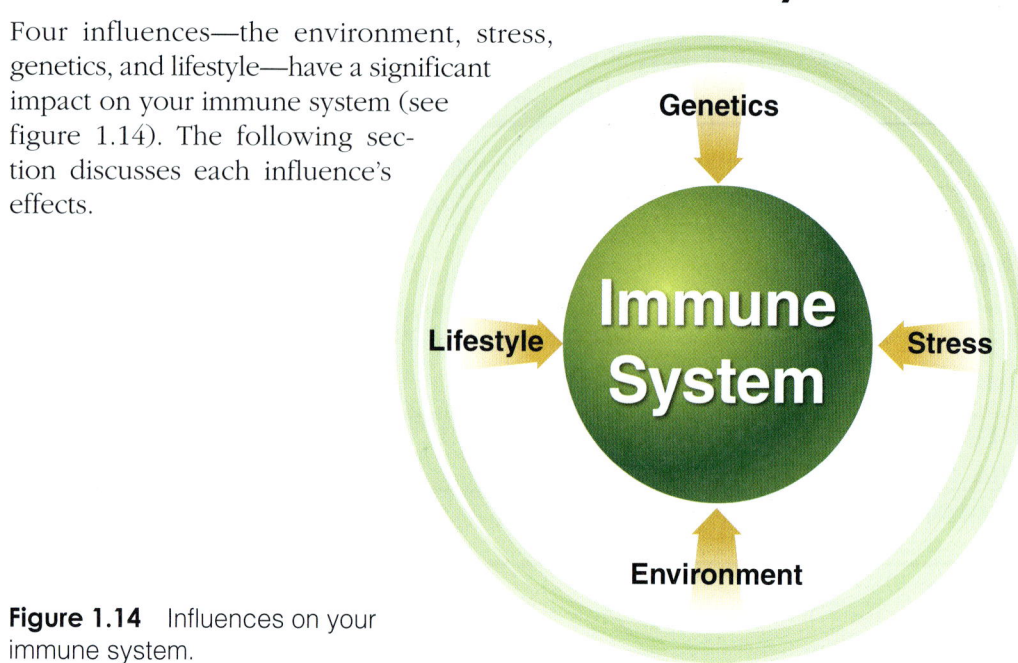

Four influences—the environment, stress, genetics, and lifestyle—have a significant impact on your immune system (see figure 1.14). The following section discusses each influence's effects.

Figure 1.14 Influences on your immune system.

Environment

Your immune system functions by building a memory base. Each time you are exposed to a potential pathogen, your immune system copies and remembers it. Therefore, the environment you live in also affects your immune system. Some researchers have suggested that children who are exposed to more germs in their environment develop healthier immune systems later in life. For example, kids who grow up with pets may build more protection from diseases than kids who don't. The environment can also have a negative influence. For example, people living in a city with heavy air pollution have a higher likelihood to develop asthma.

Stress

People respond differently to stress. When you are under a lot of pressure or are feeling anxious, your immune system may also suffer. Stress can cause your heart to beat fast, and it can raise your blood pressure. The hormones you release when under stress can also weaken your immune response. Stress can also upset digestion, making it less likely that you will eat healthy. All of these things increase your risk for disease (see figure 1.15). When you feel really stressed, you may also be more likely to engage in negative behaviors, like not getting enough sleep, having a poor diet, and not engaging in physical activity.

Genetics

Genetics influences how strong your immune system is and how well your body responds to different pathogens. Your genetic makeup also affects your likelihood of getting diseases of the immune system like autoimmune disorders.

My Immune System   **LESSON 1.3**

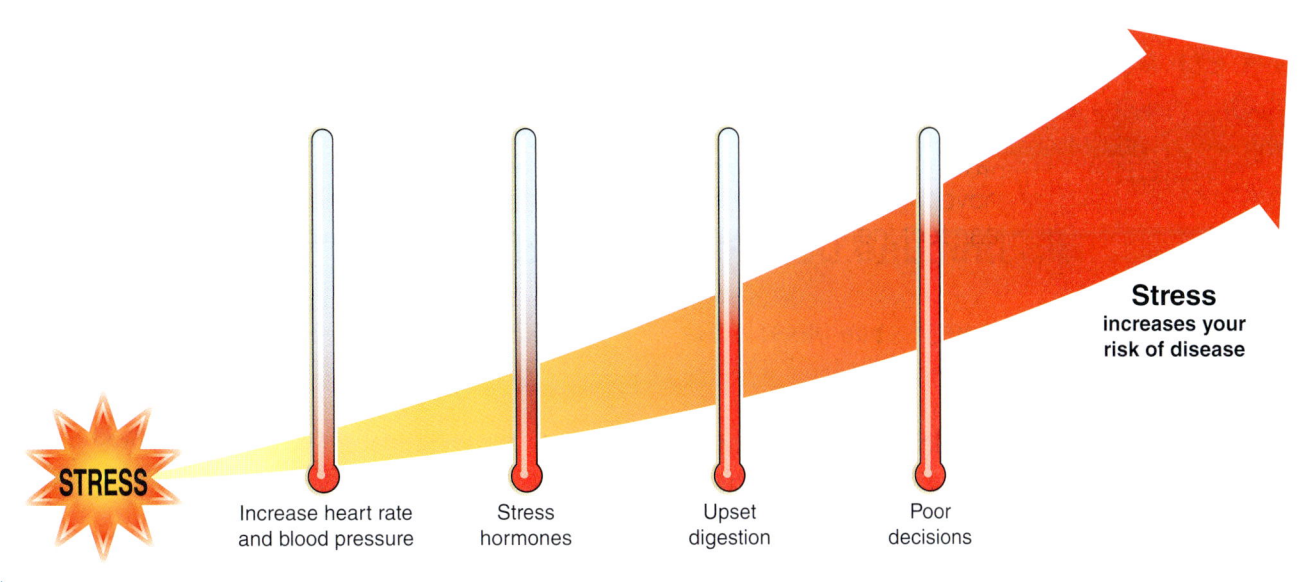

Figure 1.15 Increased stress can interfere with a healthy immune response.

(Stress → Increase heart rate and blood pressure → Stress hormones → Upset digestion → Poor decisions → Stress increases your risk of disease)

Lifestyle

Your immune system responds to living a healthy lifestyle just like other systems in your body do. Frequent exercise, a healthy diet, and adequate sleep all improve your immune system so it functions at its best. Making poor lifestyle choices like using tobacco or drinking alcohol harms your immune response and makes it harder to fight off diseases.

Human Immunodeficiency Virus

Human immunodeficiency virus, or **HIV**, is an aggressive virus that attacks the immune system. People with HIV spread it through certain body fluids like blood or semen. People contract HIV by having unprotected sex or sharing used needles related to drug use. Mothers with HIV may also pass it to their unborn child. HIV destroys so many healthy immune cells that the body can no longer fight off simple infections or diseases. When a person has HIV, their immune system is weakened and they are prone to other infections or cancers. If left untreated, HIV may lead to acquired immunodeficiency syndrome (AIDS).

Prior to the 1990s, most people with HIV died from AIDS, but advancements in medicine have made it possible for people to live with HIV. While this is a significant achievement, it is still important for people who are sexually active to be tested regularly for HIV even if they use protection. Diagnosing and treating the disease early is critical to health and survival. According to the National Institutes of Health, AIDS is the sixth leading cause of death among young people ages 25 to 44.

HIV and AIDS

HIV – Human Immunodeficiency Virus
a virus that attacks the immune system

AIDS – Acquired Immunodeficiency Syndrome
a medical condition that makes the immune system too weak to fight off infections

31

LESSON 1.3 Understanding My Health

Problems With the Immune System

Sometimes your immune system can experience problems of its own. Common problems with the immune system are explained in the next section.

Immune Deficiency Disorders

An immune deficiency disorder happens when your immune system does not make enough white blood cells to attack invading pathogens. Leukopenia is a disorder in which you have a low white blood cell count. When this happens, you are at a higher risk of getting a disease like cancer. You may also become more seriously ill from common diseases like a flu. You can be born with a deficiency or you can get it from a pathogen like a virus. Medical procedures, such as treating cancer with chemotherapy, can also cause immune deficiency.

Autoimmune Disorders

Autoimmune disorders happen when a person's immune system attacks part of its own body rather than the invader it should be attacking, as shown in figure 1.16.

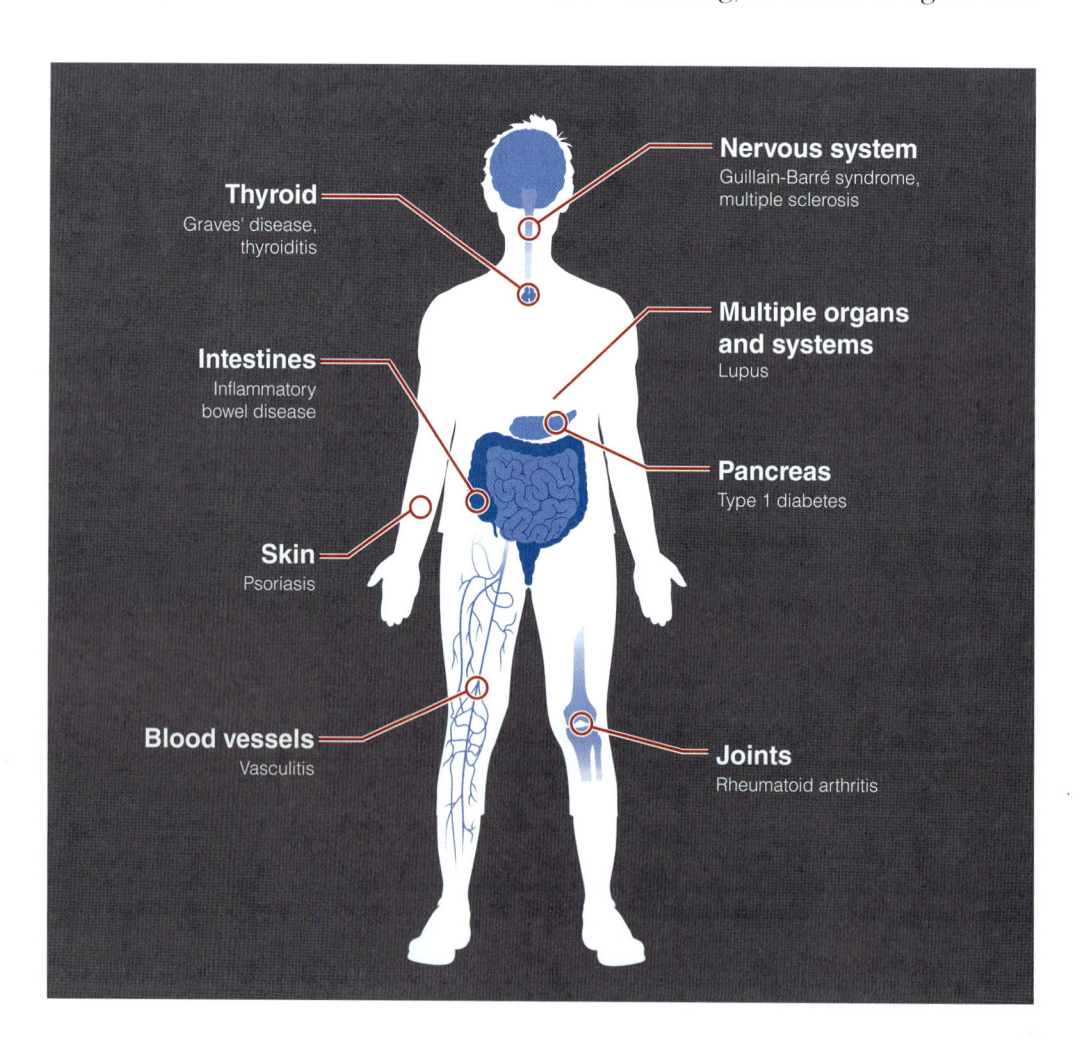

Figure 1.16 Organs and systems affected by autoimmune diseases.

Allergies

Allergies occur when the body becomes hypersensitive to something in the environment and there is a damaging immune response by the body as a result. An **allergen** causes people to develop an allergy. Common allergens include dust mites, pet dander (skin and hair), weeds and grasses, mold, and pollen. Allergies are typically treated with over-the-counter pills or nasal sprays. Serious allergies may require a prescription medication or an injection. Some people have allergies that cause more severe reactions and can be deadly, such as swelling of the throat and airway constriction from being stung by a bee. People can also be allergic to foods, such as peanuts, shellfish, wheat, milk, or eggs.

Lymphoma

Lymphoma is an umbrella term for cancer of the immune system. There are different several kinds of lymphoma, and treatments and survival rates vary by type. Symptoms of lymphoma include

- painless swelling of lymph nodes in your neck, armpits, or groin,
- persistent fatigue,
- fever,
- night sweats,
- shortness of breath, and
- unexplained weight loss.

STEM in Health

VACCINATIONS

Hearing the word *vaccine* probably makes you think about the shots you get at the doctor's office. Some vaccines are administered only once in your lifetime, while others require a dosage once or twice a year. Vaccines come in various forms. Most are administered via injection, but some can be inhaled or ingested. Vaccines have a dead or weakened version of a virus that your body then uses to initiate its own immune response to kill the invader. Getting a vaccine initiates the process of immunization during which your body produces antibodies (memories) that will protect you from future exposure. Another way to think about it is vaccines give your body the opportunity to build up its own defense system in preparation for future attacks. Vaccines are crucial to public health because they help prevent the spread of some diseases. A person who is not immunized against a disease can spread the disease to infants and children who are not yet old enough to safely receive their own vaccinations. That is why most schools have vaccine requirements before students may attend them.

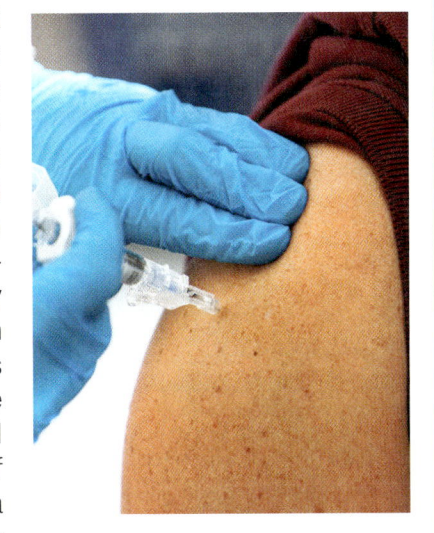

LESSON 1.3 Understanding My Health

Skill-Building Challenge

Accessing Reliable Information

In this lesson, you read about different problems you can have with your immune system. Pick a disease identified in this lesson and conduct more research on the topic.

There are several reputable websites you can explore to learn more about the immune system. For instance, the National Institutes of Health (NIH) and the Centers for Disease Control and Prevention (CDC) provide basic information on immune disorders and diseases. Part of learning how to find accurate information is identifying the key terms you will use in your search. Stick to single words and specific phrases whenever possible. Once the results come up, don't limit yourself to just the top result. Focus on .gov and .org sites that you think might provide reliable information.

Use the following search terms:

- Immune system
- Immune disorders
- Autoimmune disorders
- Allergies
- Lymphoma
- HIV

For your research, find two different sources of information. Remember to use the checklist provided to analyze the validity of your sources. After conducting your research, create a fact sheet about your disease. Include information that addresses these questions: How common is the disease? Who is most likely to get the disease and why? Which factors might have an impact on the disease? What are the current treatments for the disease?

Evaluate your sources:

- ☐ Who publishes the site?
- ☐ What is the purpose of the site?
- ☐ What types of evidence are there on the site?
- ☐ Is the information reviewed by experts?
- ☐ Is the information current (less than five years ago)?

My Immune System LESSON 1.3

Healthy Living Skills

In this chapter, you focused on accessing valid and reliable information. Here are some more ways you can develop healthy living skills related to this lesson.

ANALYZING INFLUENCES
Make a list of determinants, both positive and negative, that might be affecting your immune system. Place a star next to the two determinants you think you have the most control over. Are they positive or negative influences? Should you do anything to change them? If so, what?

HEALTHY COMMUNICATION
Will suffers from several allergies, and some of his peers at school make fun of him for it. He is always blowing his nose and sneezing. In the spring and summer, he has an especially difficult time being outside because he is allergic to grass and most trees. He most often opts to stay inside during lunch, and most kids think of him as a loner. What would you say to the people who tease him to help them better understand Will's situation? Write out a script and practice it with a friend.

PRACTICING HEALTHY BEHAVIORS
Select one of the strategies from this lesson for maintaining a healthy immune system. To the best of your ability, practice that behavior consistently for one week while tracking your progress. Write a self-reflection rating how well you did and describe how practicing the behavior made you feel.

ADVOCATING FOR GOOD HEALTH
Using the information you gathered from this lesson's Skill-Building Challenge activity, become an advocate for someone who lives with a disease:
- Develop a short story based on a fictional character who lives with the disease you just researched.
- Defend your character's choices by highlighting their point of view and experiences.
- Include details about the everyday challenges your character faces and how they strive to overcome them.
- Make sure your story helps the reader understand the challenges the person faces in daily life.

LESSON 1.3 Review: My Immune System

LESSON SUMMARY

- The immune system is made up of bone marrow, lymph nodes, respiratory and digestive systems, skin, white blood cells, the spleen, and the thymus.
- A pathogen is a foreign invader that enters the body and can cause disease. Examples include bacteria and viruses.
- Your immune system attacks foreign invaders and creates antibodies (memories) of that attack in order to help you fight off the same (or similar) invaders in the future.
- To keep your immune system healthy, eat healthy foods, get regular exercise, sleep at least eight hours each night, wash your hands regularly, get vaccinated, keep a healthy weight, avoid alcohol and tobacco, and manage your stress.
- Autoimmune disorders, such as HIV, weaken the immune system and occur when the immune system attacks itself instead of a pathogen. Allergies can also develop when the immune system reacts to something normally not dangerous. Cancers also can affect the immune system.
- Immunizations use weakened or dead versions of diseases to trigger the immune response and help the body create antibodies that provide future protection from the disease.

REVIEWING CONCEPTS AND VOCABULARY

1. Anything foreign that enters your body is called a(n) _____.
2. A(n) _____ is a very small bundle of infectious materials that gets inside your cells and then multiplies.
3. _____ are single-celled organisms found in the environment that can carry disease.
4. The organ that filters out pathogens in your blood is called your _____.
5. Your immune response includes having your _____ blood cells attack invaders.
6. A(n) _____ initiates the process of immunization.
7. A(n) _____ is something in the environment that causes you to have an immune system response.
8. Your _____ acts as an important barrier that protects you from pathogens.

THINKING CRITICALLY

The immune system is a complex system that carries out many tasks. Draw a diagram that shows how the immune system works to fight off pathogens. Label your diagram using appropriate terms.

TAKE IT HOME

Share with your family members what you have learned about the immune system. Find out whether members of your family have any autoimmune diseases or allergies. If so, ask questions to better understand what the disease or condition is like and how it affects that person's life. Document your results and write a short (one-half to one page) summary of your findings. If no one in your family or household has a known autoimmune disorder, research common symptoms associated with an autoimmune disorder of your choosing and write a summary explaining how you think those symptoms would impact a person's day-to-day life.

LESSON 1.4
Communicable Diseases

Terms to Learn
contagious
fungi
protozoan
symptom
toxins
universal precautions

The Big Picture
Before advances in medical care, the most common causes of death were from contagious diseases like the flu. Even though we can prevent or successfully treat many of these types of diseases today, they are still common and can emerge suddenly like COVID-19 did in 2019. In fact, over 10 million children and 30 million adults get the flu each year. Learning about these diseases and taking action to prevent them will help keep you healthy.

Learning Targets
- Explain what an infectious disease is.
- Compare the different methods of transmitting an infectious disease.
- Identify actions you can take to keep from getting an infectious disease.
- Identify common symptoms of an infectious disease.
- Explain what personal protective equipment is and how it can help reduce disease transmission.
- Demonstrate assertive communication to reduce health risk.

Write About It
How does regular hand washing protect you and others against the spread of some infectious diseases? How might you be exposed to a disease if someone else doesn't wash their hands regularly?

Note-Taking Guide
Use this chapter's note-taking guide to help you organize and remember the material in this lesson.

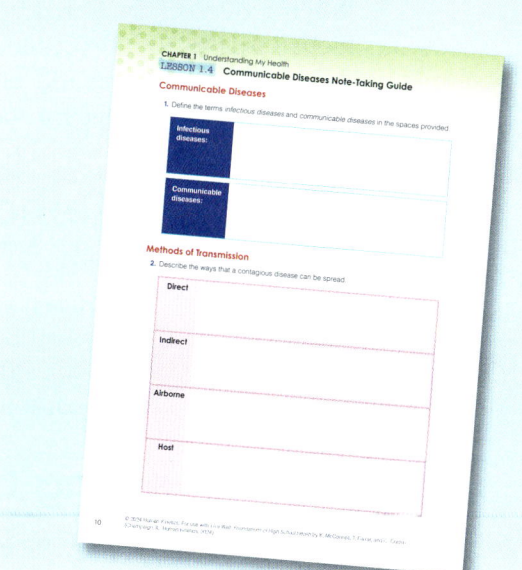

LESSON 1.4 Understanding My Health

Jeremy just got a body piercing. He knew his parents wouldn't approve of him getting a piercing before finishing high school, so he didn't tell them. The problem was Jeremy wasn't quite 18, the minimum age to get a piercing without parental consent. He and his two friends found a parlor that didn't require a parent to be present or for Jeremy to show proof of his age. Jeremy lied and told the owner that he was 18 and a student at the local college. As the owner was setting up, Jeremy began to notice that the place wasn't quite as clean as he would have liked. Still, he wanted to do it. The process was short but painful, but Jeremy didn't complain. Soon the skin all around the piercing began to get red and bumpy.

The following day, the area was swollen and oozing. It was painful and didn't seem normal. Jeremy decided to tell his parents even though he knew he was probably going to be grounded. They took him to the doctor and found out he had an infection. The doctor explained that some piercing facilities don't clean their piercing guns or hands like they should, and that can introduce bacteria—not the good kind—into the body. Fortunately, the doctor was able to use antibiotics to get Jeremy's infection under control, which eliminated the potential for disease and scarring of tissue. Did Jeremy make a healthy decision when he got his piercing? How could he have made a healthier decision?

Communicable Diseases

When a disease can spread between people it is said to be **contagious**. Contagious diseases are also called *communicable diseases*. Learning about the ways these diseases spread and how your body works to fight them off will provide you helpful knowledge for staying healthier and reducing your risk of getting sick.

Methods of Transmission

Pathogens are spread through a variety of ways, including direct and indirect contact, airborne transmission, and hosts like mosquitoes (see figure 1.17). Some pathogens use just one method of transmission; HIV, for example, is spread through direct contact only. Animals that carry diseases like rabies can pass the disease by biting a person. Other pathogens can use more than one method of transmission.

Preventing Communicable Diseases

It is very important to protect yourself from contagious diseases. Luckily, there are many simple ways you can take to stay safe, including the following:

Direct Contact

Direct contact occurs from kissing, sharing straws, exchanging bodily fluids through sexual contact, or even being treated with dental or medical equipment that has not been properly sterilized.

Indirect Contact

Indirect contact occurs when you touch an object such as a cell phone, computer keyboard, doorknob, or other surface where a pathogen may be found.

Airborne Transmission

Airborne transmission occurs when a pathogen is found in small droplets of water in the air, such as when an infected person sneezes, speaks, or breathes heavily.

Host Transmission

Coming in contact with an infected animal, being bitten by an insect carrying a pathogen, or eating infected foods could cause an infectious disease.

Figure 1.17 Methods of transmission: direct contact, indirect contact, airborne transmission, and host transmission.

- Wash your hands with soap and water.
- Cover your nose and mouth with a tissue or your arm when sneezing.
- Get vaccinated.
- Stay home if you are sick.
- Prepare food safely.
- Abstain from sexual activity.
- Don't share personal items like spoons or cups.
- Keep your environment clean, especially surfaces in the kitchen and bathroom.
- Wash clothing, towels, and bedding regularly.
- Use bug repellent when spending time outdoors.
- Wear appropriate protective equipment during outbreaks of airborne pathogens (see figure 1.18).

Figure 1.18 Personal protective equipment can help keep you and others safe from contagious diseases and may be essential during epidemics and pandemics.

Universal Precautions

To prevent communicable diseases that are found in the blood and other body fluids, health care workers are required to take **universal precautions**. They do this by wearing protective clothing such as gowns, masks, goggles, and gloves whenever there is a possibility of coming into contact with a person's blood. Whenever handling needles and other sharps, it's important to wear gloves in order to protect yourself from getting punctured. Sharps, whether at home or in a health care setting, must always be properly disposed of in containers that are approved by your state's health department. This helps protect local waste workers, housekeepers, janitors, and public workers from potentially getting infections.

Symptoms of Communicable Diseases

If you get a communicable disease, you will usually show symptoms. A **symptom** is a sign that tells you something is not right. Symptoms vary among diseases. Some of the most common symptoms of communicable diseases are shown in the following list:

- Runny nose
- Coughing
- Sneezing
- Upset stomach
- Vomiting
- Diarrhea
- Sore throat
- Headache
- Fever

Common Communicable Diseases

Communicable disease are caused by bacteria, viruses, fungi, protozoa, or other types of pathogens.

Bacterial Infections

It can seem intimidating when you think about how bacteria are everywhere. Fortunately, most bacteria are harmless to your health. Some bacteria are dangerous because they give off **toxins**, which are poisonous substances. To date, we know of about 100 bacteria that are harmful to people.

Strep throat is one of the most common bacterial diseases that teenagers get. Strep bacteria invade the nose and throat, and symptoms of the illness include sore throat, swollen lymph nodes on the sides of the neck, headache, and fever (see figure 1.19). Other common bacterial infections include Lyme disease, bacterial meningitis, and tuberculosis. Most bacterial diseases are treated with antibiotics, a prescription drug that kills the bacteria.

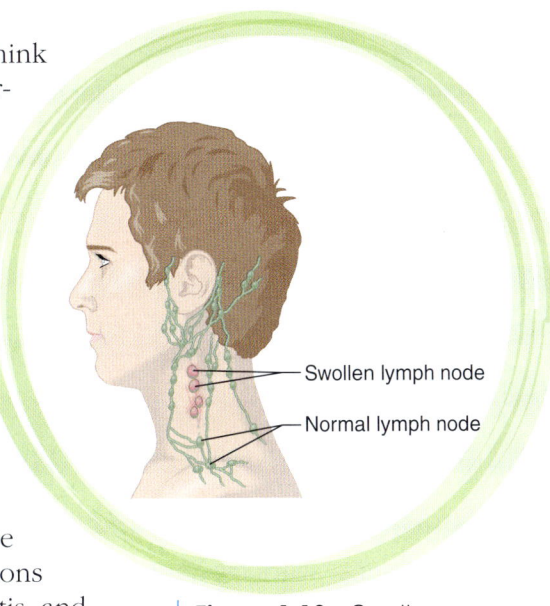

Figure 1.19 Swollen lymph nodes are one symptom of strep throat.

Viral Infections

Viruses are the smallest of all the invaders and can only multiply within a living cell. Once they've entered the cell, viruses take over its reproductive cycle and ultimately cause cell damage or death. As a teenager, the most common viral infections you might encounter include flu and cold, mononucleosis, and conjunctivitis. Viruses can be transmitted in a variety of ways and can attack different systems and organs of the body. A few of the most common viruses are described in figure 1.20.

Flu and Cold

The influenza virus, or flu, is a common viral infection that attacks the upper respiratory system. You can catch the flu by breathing in airborne droplets containing the virus or by coming in contact with a contaminated surface. Symptoms of the

LESSON 1.4 Understanding My Health

Respiratory
Viruses that attack the nasal passage, throat, and lungs
Common symptoms include runny nose, cough, sneeze, fever, and achiness
Examples include the flu, the common cold, and SARS (severe acute respiratory syndrome)
Typically spread by airborne transmission

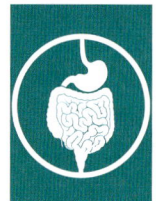

Digestive
Viruses that attack the stomach and intestines
Common symptoms include diarrhea, vomiting, and nausea
Examples include norovirus and rotovirus
Typically spread by host contamination (food)

Skin
Viruses that attack the skin's outer or deeper layers
Common symptoms include a rash or skin sores
Examples include measles, rubella, and smallpox as well as warts and herpes
Spread through all forms of transmission, most often by airborne transmission or direct contact

Hepatic
Viruses that attack the liver
May not have symptoms or may show a range of symptoms like fatigue, jaundice, and weight loss
Examples include all forms of hepatitis
Spread through direct contact

Neurologic
Viruses that attack the nervous system
Common symptoms include fever, confusion, seizures, and coordination problems
Examples include polio, meningitis, and rabies
Spread by host contamination or direct contact; may also be caused by bacteria

Circulatory
Viruses that attack the circulatory system
Common symptoms include high fever, internal bleeding, and weakness
Examples include Ebola and yellow fever
Spread by host contamination or direct contact

Figure 1.20 Some common types of viral infections.

flu include a high fever, sore throat, headache, and cough. A serious case of the flu can be dangerous, especially for infants and older adults. Flu accounts for as many as 30,000 annual deaths in the United States. In recent years, flu vaccinations have become more common because they may keep you from getting the flu or prevent you from getting a serious case of it.

Many people confuse a cold with the flu. Most colds last only three to seven days, as opposed to a flu, which may last 10 days or more. Despite a high number of over-the-counter remedies available, there is no cure for the common cold. In fact, viral infections of all types have no known cure. The best way to treat a cold or the flu is to rest, eat a well-balanced diet, and drink plenty of fluids. Over-the-counter and prescription medications can help ease the discomfort that symptoms of flu and colds cause.

Mononucleosis

Mononucleosis, or mono, is another very common virus. It is sometimes referred to as *the kissing disease* because it can spread through saliva. You can also get mono by sharing lip gloss, toothbrushes, and beverages with infected people. Symptoms include sore throat (often on one side of the throat), fever, swollen lymph glands, loss of appetite, and fatigue. It is also possible to have no symptoms when you have mono. If you think you might have mono, see a medical professional.

Conjunctivitis

Conjunctivitis, also called *pink eye*, is a viral or bacterial infection of the eye (see figure 1.21). The eye becomes very itchy and gets a pink or red appearance when tissue covering the eye gets infected and swollen. In most cases, treatment for pink eye involves antibiotic eye drops. Conjunctivitis is a highly transmissible virus, so it's important not to touch your eye. Otherwise, the virus could be on your hand when you touch other people or surfaces. It could even spread to your other eye!

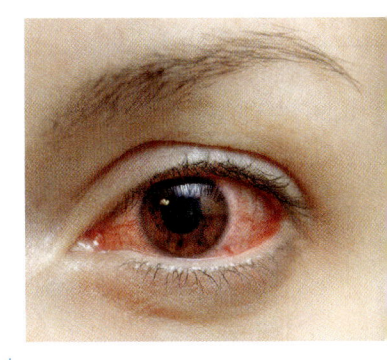

Figure 1.21 Conjunctivitis, also called *pink eye*, is a viral or bacterial infection of the eye.

Fungal Infections

Fungi are single- or multicelled, plantlike organisms that thrive in warm, humid environments. Yeasts, molds, and mushrooms are examples of fungi. About half of all known fungi are dangerous to humans. The most typical ways a fungus can cause infection is by landing directly on the skin (surface infection) or by being inhaled into the lungs (internal infection). It also can be ingested if moldy food is eaten. A fungus attacks the body by releasing enzymes that digest or dissolve your cells.

Athlete's foot is an example of a commonly known fungal infection (see figure 1.22). It begins like other fungal infections when a small amount of the fungus lands on the skin and multiplies in the warm, moist environment of the sock and shoe. You are more likely to get athlete's foot if you wear closed-toed shoes, sweat often, have wet feet for long periods of time, or get a nail or skin infection on the foot. To prevent athlete's foot, be sure to change shoes and socks often, allow

Global Pandemics

Any disease that exists widely over an entire country or is widespread throughout the world is considered to be a pandemic. In December 2019, a novel (new) form of human coronavirus, later named COVID-19, emerged across the globe. The virus, transmitted via airborne transmission, became a global pandemic in just a matter of months. COVID-19 is considered highly contagious. Symptoms of the virus include fever, persistent cough, difficulty breathing, chills, muscle pain, sore throat, and loss of senses such as taste and smell. Many people who contract the virus do not show any symptoms and are considered asymptomatic.

COVID-19 can cause severe respiratory distress and can be deadly. Populations at greatest risk for developing severe symptoms of or dying from COVID-19 include older people and others who have compromised immune systems or other underlying medical conditions, such as diabetes, asthma, or high blood pressure. Vaccinations have been developed to help prevent the spread and resurgence of COVID-19. Like other forms of viruses, COVID-19 has also mutated over time, creating the need for developing new and updated vaccinations and continuing certain precautions to help reduce the spread.

LESSON 1.4   Understanding My Health

HEALTHY LIVING TIP
Wash your feet when you are in the shower and bring a clean pair of socks to wear after participating in sports or other physical activities at school.

shoes to dry and air out, and wash and dry your feet thoroughly every day. It is also a good idea not to share shoes or socks with others.

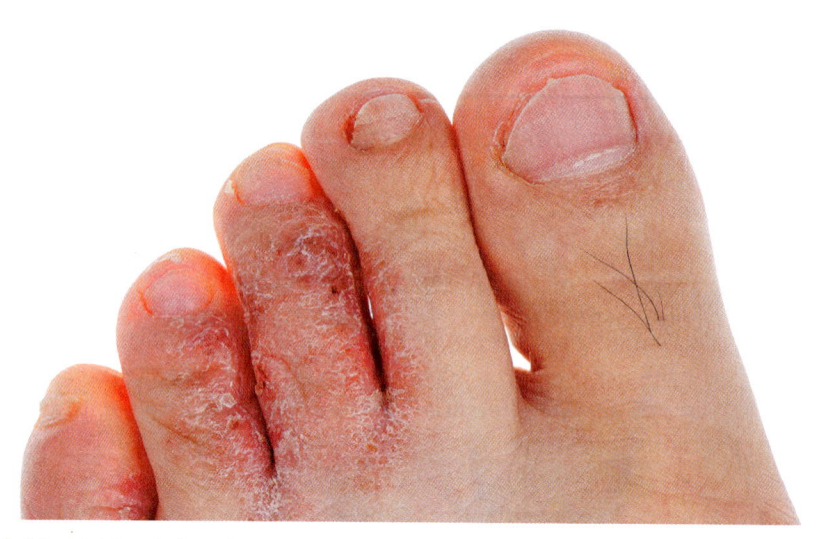

Figure 1.22 Athlete's foot is an example of a commonly known fungal infection.

Disease Risks of Getting a Tattoo

Tattoos are popular among teenagers and adults. It is estimated that 38 percent of adults in the United States have one or more tattoos. The process of getting a tattoo involves breaking the skin with a needle and injecting small amounts of ink under the skin. This means that you will bleed and are at risk for getting an infection like hepatitis, or for having a reaction to toxic substances in the ink. If you choose to get a tattoo in the future, keep a few things in mind and see a medical professional if you experience any rash, swelling, or draining of pus.

- Take a parent or guardian with you if you are under 18.
- Only go to a tattoo business that is approved and registered by your local government and where the tattoo artists are licensed.
- Inspect the facility for general cleanliness, including signs of blood spatter or sloppy equipment handling.
- Ask where the ink is from and ask to see the bottle of ink that will be used. Ink should be specific for tattoo use. Ask if anyone has reported reactions to the ink the artist is using and ask the artist if they have used the ink on themselves.
- Seek out a tattoo business that uses one-time use kits (single-use needles and supplies). Look for a proper sharps container to see whether needles are being properly disposed of.
- Make sure the tattoo artist uses sterile gloves at all times.

Caring for Body Piercings

Like tattoos, body piercings are also popular. Ear piercing has a long history of being socially acceptable, and other body piercings, such as tongue, nose, and navel (belly button), are becoming more common. Piercings take time to heal and can produce potentially dangerous complications. For example, a navel piercing can take up to nine months to heal and can result in infection and scar tissue. Some piercings around the eyes and nose can also cause nerve damage, and a tongue piercing that becomes swollen can interfere with breathing. It is important to keep a new body piercing clean by avoiding hot tubs, rivers, lakes, and other bodies of water while the piercing is healing. Always avoid picking at or rubbing a new piercing, and be sure to wash your hands before cleaning the area. The site should be cleaned at least twice a day using saline (salt water).

Protozoan Infections

A **protozoan** is a large single-celled organism that moves through your body in search of food. It attacks by releasing enzymes or toxins that destroy or damage cells. Malaria is a protozoan that attacks the red blood cells. Malaria is transmitted by mosquitoes and is common in parts of Africa and many tropical locations. In the late 1940s and early 1950s, malaria-carrying mosquitoes were eliminated in the United States. Cases of malaria are rare in the United States today and are typically seen only in people who have traveled to a country with a malaria outbreak.

Other Types of Pathogens

Infectious diseases can also be caused by lice, mites, and some worms. For example, the trichina worm lives in the muscle tissue of pigs and some other animals. If a person consumes meat from these animals that is not properly cooked, the worm can invade the person's body. The best prevention against pathogens in food and meat products is to ensure that all food is properly handled (cleaned, separated, and stored safely) and that meat is fully cooked at appropriate temperatures.

Vector-Borne Illnesses

Vector-borne illnesses are caused by mosquitoes, ticks, and fleas that spread pathogens. Where you live determines which vector-borne disease may be most prevalent in your area. Throughout the United States, the most common mosquito-borne diseases are the West Nile virus and malaria; the most common tickborne diseases are spotted fever rickettsiosis and Lyme disease.

Some vector-borne illnesses cause long-term symptoms and can be passed from mother to fetus. To protect yourself, wear long-sleeved shirts and pants, use an EPA-registered insect repellant containing DEET, stay out of tall grasses and bushes, and check your skin and scalp after being outside. Symptoms of vector-borne illnesses vary but may include the following:

LESSON 1.4 Understanding My Health

- Fever
- Chills
- Headache
- Skin rash
- Nausea
- Difficulty breathing
- Racing heartbeat
- Vomiting
- Swelling of lips, tongue, or face

Always clean any bite with soap and water and rub the area with alcohol. Carefully remove ticks with tweezers. Always see a physician if you show symptoms like rash, swelling, vomiting, or other signs of communicable disease.

Skill-Building Challenge

Communicating Well to Keep Yourself and Others Healthy

Sometimes we need to defend what we know is right and what we know will keep those around us healthy. You may not want to miss out on a practice or game or a lunch date with friends if you are sick, but avoiding these activities until you are healthy again is the right choice to make for everyone's health—including your own. One of the best ways to defend or promote (i.e., advocate for) something is to be assertive.

Being assertive can boost your self-esteem and earn the respect of others, but it takes practice. To gain others' confidence in your mission relies on your ability to be mindful of other people's points of view and feelings as well as to respect their opinions, which may differ from yours. When you feel passionate about something, it's important to avoid becoming aggressive. Aggression communicates to others that you're being unreasonable and inconsiderate. In other words, whatever you're advocating for will not win over anyone through brute force. Being assertive in a nonhostile way is easier for some than it is for others. Luckily we can all strive to learn or improve our assertiveness skills.

Think of a time when you had to defend your choices about your own health. For example, perhaps you chose to miss out on something you wanted to do, or maybe there was a time when, you now realize, you should have been making better, more careful decisions. Write a short script that demonstrates how to use assertive communication to express yourself in that scenario.

TIPS FOR COMMUNICATING ASSERTIVELY

- *Use I statements.* I statements use the word "I" instead of "you" or "them". I statements speak from your personal point of view. If you refer to yourself, others won't think you are blaming them for something. For example, instead of saying "You are so impatient; just wait a second," you could say "I really would like to stop and wash my hands. I'll only be a minute."

- *Practice saying no.* Be direct but also polite. Consider saying something like "No, I can't do that."

- *Practice what you want to say.* Communicating something difficult or uncomfortable is much easier when you have practiced it first.

- *Watch your body language.* You want to stand upright and appear strong without pointing your finger or leaning into someone. Try to keep yourself from making an angry or frustrated face.

- *Check your emotions.* Being angry or frustrated can get in the way of being assertive. If a situation makes you feel angry, wait before you discuss it if you can. If you do feel angry when trying to be assertive, take deep breaths and take a short pause before talking. Always remember to think about how the other person might be feeling.

Healthy Living Skills

In this chapter, you focused on healthy communication. Here are some more ways you can develop healthy living skills related to this lesson.

ANALYZING INFLUENCES

Do you think you are influenced by technology when it comes to making decisions about your health? If you aren't feeling well, do you or other people you know ever research symptoms online and use the information to decide what to do? Do you think using technology like this would help you stay healthier or make it harder to be healthy? Explain your response.

ACCESSING INFORMATION

Conduct research on ways to prevent communicable diseases. Create a checklist of all the behaviors and actions you found. With a partner, combine your lists to form one comprehensive checklist. Remember to follow the guidelines for evaluating websites as you do your research.

MAKING HEALTHY DECISIONS

Liam noticed his sore throat was worsening and his cough becoming more frequent, but he didn't say anything to anyone. The e-gaming team he belonged to was playing in a big tournament over the weekend, and he didn't want to miss it. Liam was uncertain about what to do. Using the steps to a healthy decision, help Liam arrive at making a conscientious decision about what he should do. Write out each step in the process as you go.

SETTING HEALTHY GOALS

Set a short-term SMART goal that will help you avoid getting a communicable disease. Write your goal using the SMART format.

ADVOCATING FOR GOOD HEALTH

You can promote good health by being a positive role model. Help others at your school learn the importance of handwashing by always washing your own hands after using the restroom, before eating, and after blowing your nose.

ACCESSING INFORMATION

Conduct research on the vector-borne illnesses in your area. On your phone, download pictures of the mosquitoes and ticks that may bite you. Make a list of resources you can use to protect yourself from being bitten. Create another list of the symptoms you should look for in the event you or someone else is bitten. Be sure to include treatment items in your hiking or camping gear.

LESSON 1.4 Review: Communicable Diseases

LESSON SUMMARY

- Pathogens such as bacteria, viruses, fungi, and protozoa cause communicable diseases.
- Communicable diseases are transmitted in different ways, including direct and indirect contact, airborne transmission, and contact with a host carrier like a mosquito.
- Preventive measures that help reduce transmission of communicable diseases include washing hands with soap and warm water, covering your nose and mouth with a tissue or your arm instead of your hands when sneezing, and getting vaccinated.
- One of the most important things you can do to stay healthy is to wash your hands regularly.

REVIEWING CONCEPTS AND VOCABULARY

1. A disease that spreads from one person to another is called a(n) _____ disease.
2. Communicable diseases are spread by _____ transmission when someone sneezes or coughs without covering their nose and mouth.
3. When nurses wear gowns, masks, and gloves, they are using _____ to help prevent the direct spread of disease.
4. Some bacteria can give off poisonous substances known as _____.
5. A(n) _____ of conjunctivitis includes an itchy, red eye.
6. Athlete's foot is an example of a disease cause by a(n) _____.
7. _____ illnesses are caused by mosquitoes, ticks, and fleas that spread pathogens.

THINKING CRITICALLY

Have you ever used hand sanitizer? How do hand sanitizers work? Conduct research on the effectiveness of hand sanitizers compared to proper hand washing. Consider your results as well as the convenience and access of both methods. Write a brief set of recommendations for each method that people should follow under different circumstances.

TAKE IT HOME

Use sticky notes to create reminders about the various ways to prevent infectious disease. Post the sticky notes around your home in areas where infectious disease are most likely to spread, such as bathrooms, kitchens, and handrails.

LESSON 1.5
Noncommunicable Diseases

Terms to Learn

Alzheimer's disease
arteriosclerosis
arthritis
atherosclerosis
cancer
cardiovascular disease
chronic disease
coronary heart disease
dementia
diabetes
heart attack
hypertension
lung disease
noncommunicable disease
osteoporosis
peripheral artery disease
stroke

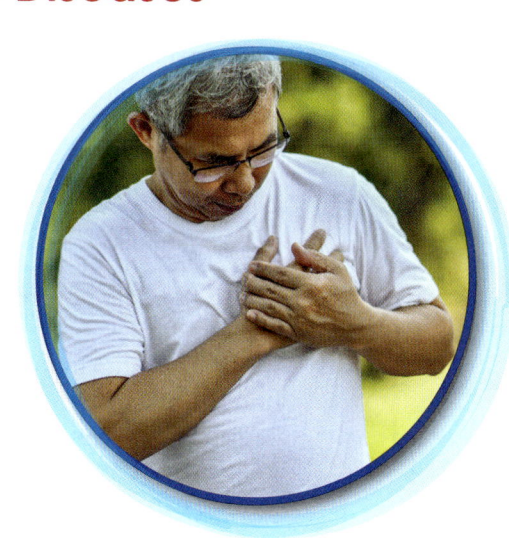

The Big Picture

Most people in the United States will become ill or die from diseases that aren't passed from one person to another. In fact, seven of the 10 leading causes of death in the United States are noncommunicable diseases. Cancer, diabetes, and heart disease are examples of diseases that can be significantly influenced by the choices you make now and throughout your life.

Learning Targets

- Define what a noncommunicable disease is and give four examples.
- Explain why most noncommunicable diseases are also chronic diseases.
- Identify five behaviors that can contribute to a person's risk of noncommunicable diseases.
- Identify the signs of a heart attack.
- Explain what a behavior contract is and how it helps people take responsibility for personal health behaviors.

Write About It

What do you know about heart disease, cancer, or diabetes? Do you know anyone with any of these diseases? Make a list of things you know about each of these diseases.

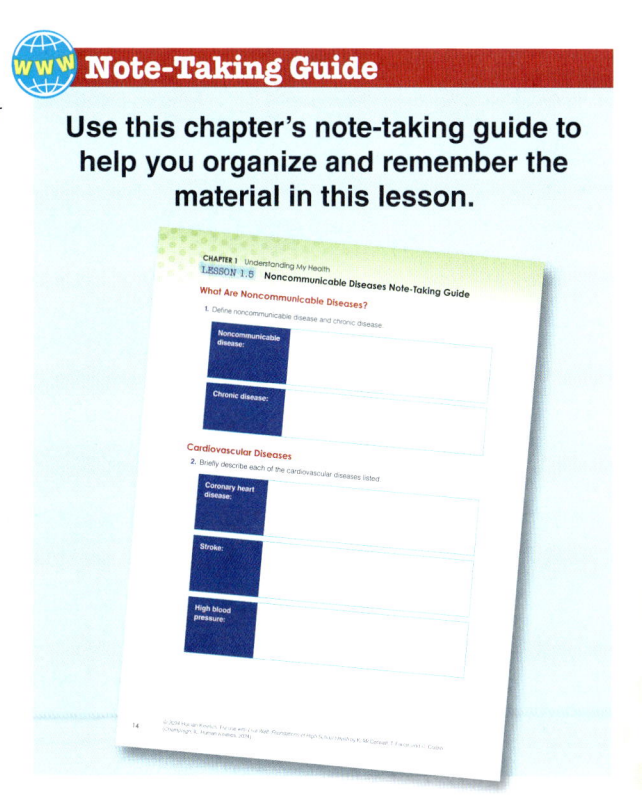

Note-Taking Guide

Use this chapter's note-taking guide to help you organize and remember the material in this lesson.

LESSON 1.5   Understanding My Health

Kai is an outgoing guy who is active and enjoys being outside. He especially loves to hang at the skateboard park near his house, and lately, he's been on a consistent streak with improving his tricks. Unfortunately, Kai has asthma and always has to carry his inhaler with him. Two irritating things about having asthma are that he can't have any pets at home and his mom is always making him clean up his room.

Kai can keep his asthma under control most of the time, and he knows how to use his inhaler properly. At the skateboard park, he sometimes feels an attack coming, especially if he doesn't take enough breaks or if there is a lot of pollution in the air. It's hard for Kai because he wants to skate as much as his friends do, but he knows that the combination of physical activity and air pollution makes skating riskier for him. His closest friends understand that his asthma is not contagious, and they are supportive of him. A good example is how Jason always makes sure Kai has his inhaler on him when they head out to the park. What precautions does Kai make to take care of his health? In what ways are his friends supportive of his health?

What Are Noncommunicable Diseases?

HEALTHY LIVING TIP
Whenever you can, take the stairs instead of the elevator or escalator when you are in a building that has more than one story. By always choosing to take the stairs, you will benefit from getting more physical activity into your daily life as well as creating a healthy habit.

Noncommunicable diseases are diseases that cannot be transmitted from person to person (see figure 1.23) and often result from a combination of genetics and lifestyle factors. Many noncommunicable diseases are chronic. A **chronic disease** lasts three months or longer. Most people in the United States will develop one or more chronic diseases. Cancer, high blood pressure, diabetes, and arthritis are chronic, noncommunicable diseases that also happen to be the most common causes of death in the United States.

Common Noncommunicable Diseases

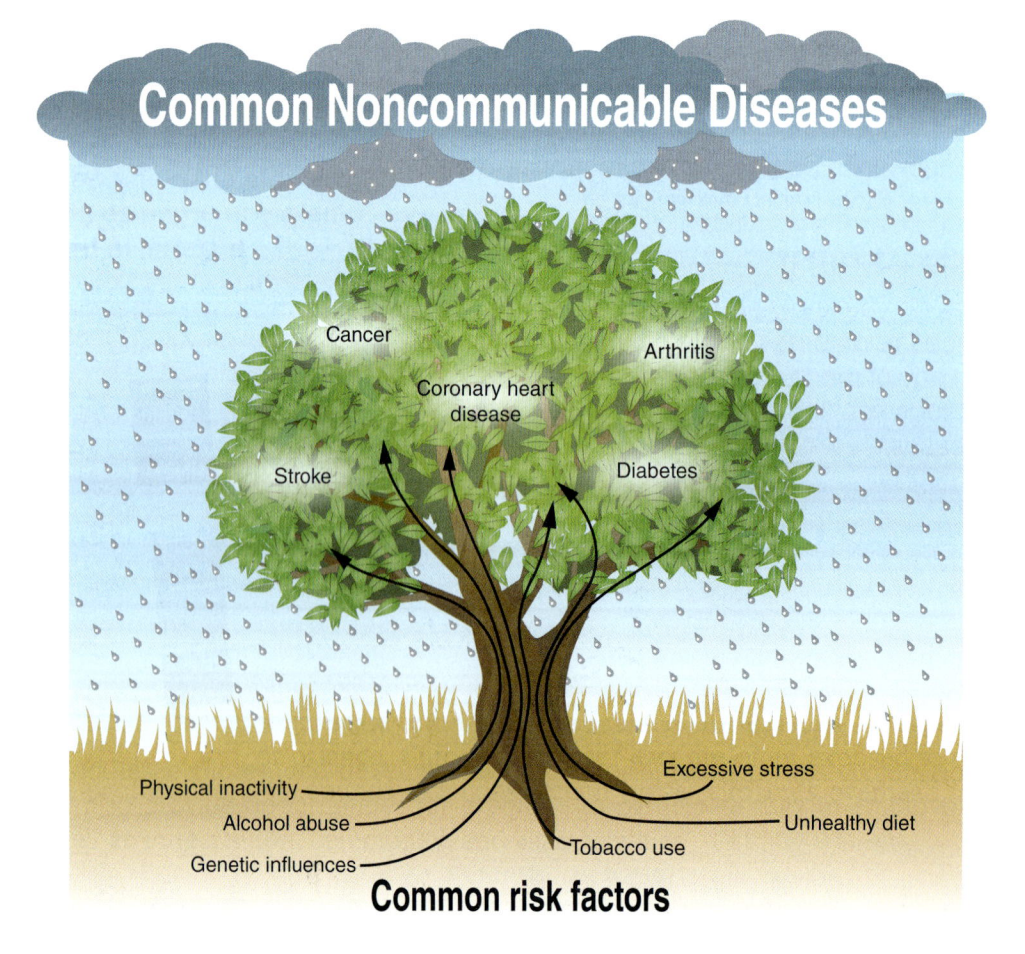

- Cancer
- Arthritis
- Coronary heart disease
- Stroke
- Diabetes

Common risk factors

- Physical inactivity
- Alcohol abuse
- Genetic influences
- Tobacco use
- Excessive stress
- Unhealthy diet

Figure 1.23 Noncommunicable diseases and risk factors.

Cardiovascular Diseases

Cardiovascular disease (CVD) is a term used to describe a number of chronic diseases that affect the cardiorespiratory system (heart, lungs, and blood vessels). One in four Americans has one or more cardiovascular disease; in fact, these diseases account for 60 percent of all global deaths.

Coronary Heart Disease

Coronary heart disease, the most common form of CVD, occurs when the arteries in your heart become clogged or hardened. When this condition arises, your blood is no longer able to deliver oxygen to other areas of your body. Clogged arteries, or **atherosclerosis**, results from eating a diet high in fats, not getting enough exercise, smoking, or being obese. **Arteriosclerosis** occurs when arteries lose their flexibility and become hardened and rigid. Although it is part of the aging process for everyone, maintaining a healthy lifestyle can help prevent it from becoming life threatening. Both types of CVD can lead to **heart attack**. Heart attacks occur when the heart experiences a deficient (not enough) level of blood, which causes a small part of the heart tissue to die from a lack of oxygen (see figure 1.24).

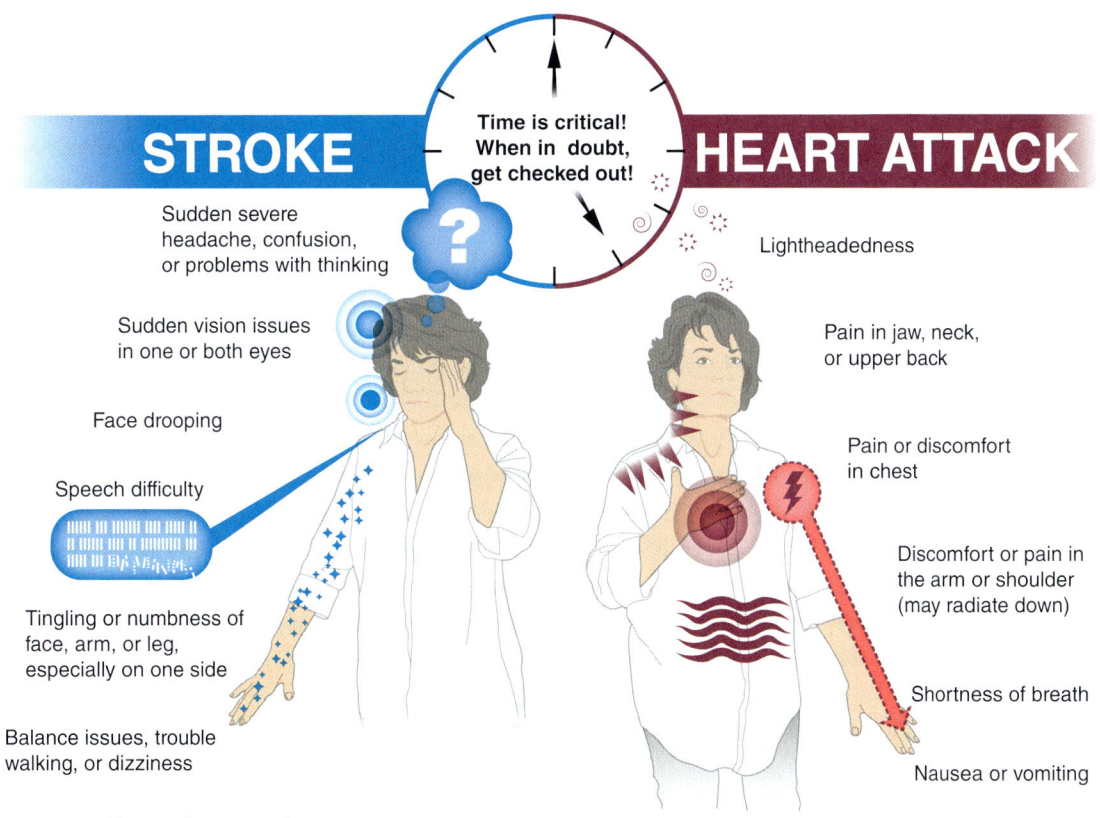

STROKE — Time is critical! When in doubt, get checked out! — **HEART ATTACK**

- Sudden severe headache, confusion, or problems with thinking
- Sudden vision issues in one or both eyes
- Face drooping
- Speech difficulty
- Tingling or numbness of face, arm, or leg, especially on one side
- Balance issues, trouble walking, or dizziness

- Lightheadedness
- Pain in jaw, neck, or upper back
- Pain or discomfort in chest
- Discomfort or pain in the arm or shoulder (may radiate down)
- Shortness of breath
- Nausea or vomiting

For stroke, remember the acronym BE FAST:
- **B** - Balance. Ask if they feel dizzy or off balance. Are they having trouble sitting or standing up?
- **E** - Eyes. Ask if their vision is normal for them. Are they having trouble seeing?
- **F** - Face. Ask the person to smile. Does the face droop to one side?
- **A** - Arms. Ask the person to raise both arms. Does one arm drift or not move?
- **S** - Speech. Ask the person to repeat a simple phrase. Is their speech slurred or hard to understand?
- **T** - Time. If you spot any of these symptoms, call 911 immediately.

Figure 1.24 Signs of heart attack and stroke.

Stroke and Peripheral Artery Disease

The brain requires blood and oxygen to function. Similar to the heart, a small part of your brain will die if it does not get enough blood. When this happens, it is called a **stroke**. Strokes are a serious condition that can cause disability in speech or movement as well as cause death. Figure 1.24 shows signs and symptoms for spotting a stroke.

The arteries that transport blood to other parts of the body are also at risk of getting clogged. **Peripheral artery disease** is when your arms and legs don't get enough blood. You may experience leg pain, muscle aches, poor nail or hair growth, a coldness in one leg or arm compared to the other, or sores and wounds on the toes that don't heal properly.

High Blood Pressure

High blood pressure, or **hypertension**, is another form of CVD. Each time your heart beats, it moves blood through your arteries. When that blood has too much force, it can damage the blood vessels. Think about a garden hose that is running water; it probably doesn't spray very far even if it is fully on. If you cover part of that same stream of water with your thumb, it sprays a lot farther. This is because the pressure has gone up. That is analogous with what happens inside your body when arteries become partially clogged. People with high blood pressure have higher than normal amounts of force in their arteries.

The causes of high blood pressure aren't always known, but certain factors increase your risk: being overweight, smoking, not getting enough exercise, and eating too much salt. Poorly managed stress can also contribute to high blood pressure. People with high blood pressure often experience no symptoms, and the only way to discover it is by taking a blood pressure test. A person with high blood pressure is more likely to get coronary heart disease or have a stroke. While these are the most common forms of cardiovascular diseases, many other forms also exist.

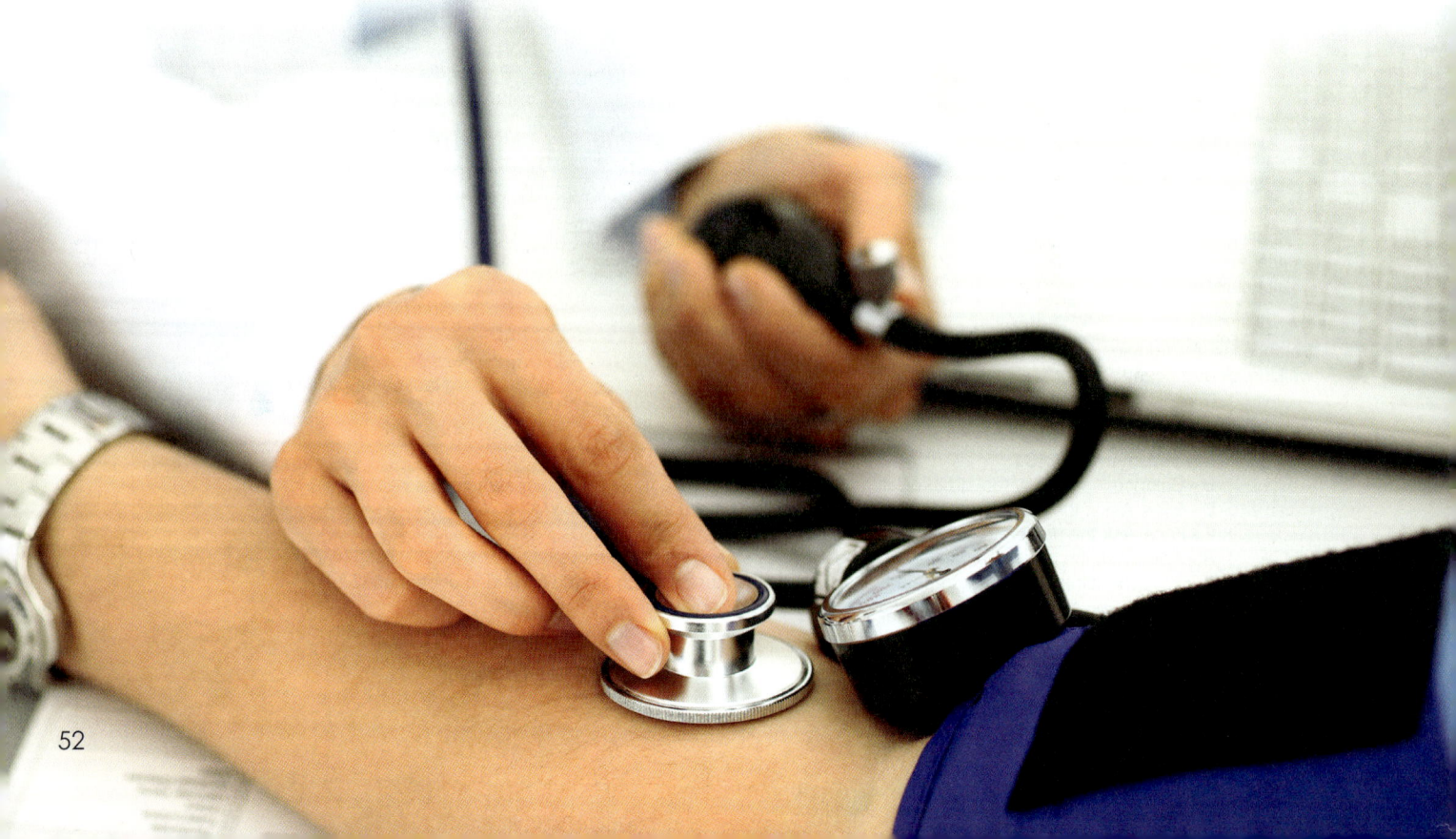

Diabetes

Diabetes is a chronic disease related to having too much sugar (glucose) in the blood. Normally your body can use blood sugar for fuel as long as the sugar can get into your cells. Insulin, which is a type of hormone, acts like a key that allows the sugar to enter the cells. When a person's pancreas no longer is able to produce enough insulin, or if their body can't use the insulin correctly, that person develops diabetes.

There are three types of diabetes (see figure 1.25). In type 1 diabetes, the body does not produce insulin. Type 2 diabetes occurs when the body is either unable to use the insulin it makes or incapable of making enough insulin to keep up with the body's demand. In both cases, the cells aren't able to get the energy they need from the blood. Some women experience gestational diabetes when they are pregnant. While it is a temporary form of diabetes, it can be dangerous if left untreated. According to the American Diabetes Association, about 8 percent of Americans, including 1 in every 400 children, have a form of diabetes.

	Definition	Symptoms	Treatment
Type 1	Body unable to produce its own insulin	• Excessive thirst • Weight loss • Frequent urination	• Monitor blood sugar • Take insulin • Regular medical checkups
Type 2	Body unable to produce enough of its own insulin	• May not have any or may look like type 1 • Associated with obesity and unhealthy lifestyle choices	• Exercise • Medication • Carefully monitored diet
Gestational	High blood sugar levels during pregnancy	• Typically none • Usually diagnosed during routine prenatal exams	• Exercise • Medication • Carefully monitored diet

Figure 1.25 Symptoms and treatments for the different types of diabetes.

Cancers

Cancer is the uncontrolled growth of abnormal cells and can occur anywhere in the body. Prostate, lung, and colon cancers are the most common forms of cancer among men in the United States. Breast, colon, and lung cancers are the most common forms among U.S. women. Children and adolescents can get cancer too. Lymphomas (cancers in the immune system) and leukemias (cancers of the blood) are among the most common forms that children get. Skin cancer is also prevalent in the U.S. population. Your risk of skin cancer increases if you don't protect your skin from sun damage every day.

Cancer symptoms vary among the different types of cancer. It is important to pay attention to how your body normally functions and to make note if something

LESSON 1.5 Understanding My Health

CASE STUDY

Dola's Diabetes Discovery

Dola was having a hard time at school. She had always been a little heavier than most of her friends, and she sometimes heard other kids make fun of her weight behind her back. The women in Dola's family were all a little curvy, and they celebrated their full figures. She never felt like she had to be on a diet, and no one gave that much thought to exercising. Dola and her mom liked to walk their dog, Kona, and they did take him around the neighborhood a few nights a week. The family liked to eat the traditional foods that her parents grew up on, like fried shrimp and meatloaf, but they also were good about eating salads and vegetables with meals. Dola liked desserts, and her parents spoiled her with cookies, candies, and ice cream.

Dola never thought she'd get sick. She figured diabetes was for older people. Lately, though, she had been feeling tired and low on energy. She started having more frequent headaches and was feeling thirsty a lot. She was even losing a little bit of weight. One day at school she felt confused and disoriented and threw up in the restroom. Her friend ran to the school nurse's office to get help. It turned out that Dola had type 2 diabetes.

Think About It

1. What do you know about type 2 diabetes? Is it a disease that young people can get?
2. Which factor(s) in Dola's life might have contributed to her diabetes?
3. Why is it important to get help if a friend is as sick as Dola was at school? Where would you go to get help if someone at school were sick?

---

changes. Changes to bowel habits, wounds that don't heal, moles on your skin that change shape, unexplained weight loss, and a persistent cough that won't go away are some common signs of cancers. See table 1.1 for a list of common types of cancer and their risk factors.

The treatment and survival rates from cancer depend on the type of cancer. Survival also depends on how advanced the cancer is at the time it is diagnosed. Discovering cancer early through regular physical exams and screenings is critical. Regular self-screening for breast and testicular cancers are an important part of self-care and are described in lesson 2.1. Advances in medicine are resulting in better survival rates for many types of cancers. Lifestyle factors such as smoking, physical inactivity, consuming a diet high in fat, and being overexposed to the sun are known risk factors for developing cancer. Cancers are the second leading cause of death in the United States, accounting for over half a million deaths per year.

Osteoporosis

Osteoporosis is a chronic disease during which the bones weaken. One out of every five women in the United States over the age of 50 develops osteoporosis. Osteoporosis is dangerous because it can lead to broken bones like hip fractures. You can get osteoporosis from not making enough new bone or from breaking

TABLE 1.1 **Common Types of Cancer in the United States**

Type of cancer	Description	Risk factors
Breast	Multiple types exist. This is the most commonly diagnosed cancer among women; men may also get it.	Increasing age, early first menstrual period, family history of breast or uterine cancer, being overweight, physical inactivity, high alcohol consumption, genetics
Colon	This cancer attacks the colon or rectum. It is the third most common type of cancer among women and the second most common among men.	Family history of colon cancer, history of polyps, being over the age of 50, smoking, high-fat diet
Leukemia	This is cancer of the bone marrow and blood cells. Multiple types exist, including some that are most common among children.	Genetics, exposure to radiation, smoking, certain related disorders and diseases
Lung	This is the leading cause of cancer deaths among both men and women.	Tobacco smoke, pollution, family history, asbestos and radon exposure, being over age 65
Melanoma	This is a skin cancer caused by excessive sun exposure.	Accumulated sun exposure or tanning bed, severe sunburns that blister (especially before age 18)
Prostate	This cancer attacks the male prostate gland and is the leading cause of cancer among men.	Being over age 65, family history of prostate cancer, being African American, genetics

down the bone that you have. In both cases, a diet low in calcium and vitamin D puts you at risk. Smoking, eating disorders that result in becoming underweight, and being sedentary also increase your risk of osteoporosis.

Caucasian women are at highest risk for the disease, but men and women of all races and ethnicities can get it. Teenagers who suffer from eating disorders like anorexia nervosa may also develop osteoporosis. This is very dangerous because this period of adolescence is a crucial time for proper bone development. You can make choices to help prevent osteoporosis now and in your future. Avoiding nicotine, doing regular vigorous aerobic activity and weight-bearing activity, and eating an adequate and well-balanced diet can help prevent osteoporosis later in life.

Arthritis

Arthritis occurs when joints of the body experience swelling and damage. More than 100 different types of arthritis and related joint conditions exist. Lifestyle and genetics contribute to developing arthritis. While arthritis is commonly thought of as a disease affecting older adults, 1 in every 250 U.S. children under the age of 18 has some variation of the disease. Juvenile rheumatoid arthritis (JRA) is the most common among those under 18. Stiffness, swelling, and joint pain are common symptoms of arthritis. Exercise, proper diet, physical therapy, and medications can all help manage the disease. In some cases, joint replacement surgery may be needed. Due to the many types of arthritis, it is important to be diagnosed by a medical professional to know the best treatment options.

LESSON 1.5   Understanding My Health

Lung Disease

Lung disease includes a variety of conditions that affect the lungs and a person's ability to breathe in and use oxygen. Lung disease is the third most common cause of death in the United States. Asthma, an inflammation of the lungs, is a common lung disease. Nearly 1 in 10 U.S. children has it. Asthma causes spasms of the lung tissue, which makes a person wheeze and have difficulty breathing. Keeping a clean environment, especially a clean sleeping space, is important for avoiding an asthma attack. Staying healthy and avoiding cold air, dust, mold, and pet dander can also help. Asthma can be managed with proper medications, and people with the condition can lead normal lives. Many other forms of lung disease exist, including the following:

- Chronic obstructed pulmonary disease (COPD) involves difficulty in exhaling air from the lungs. Air gets trapped, causing coughing or damage to the tissue. Emphysema and bronchitis are both forms of COPD.
- Pneumonia and tuberculosis are bacterial infections in the lungs.
- Lung cancer is one of the most common cancers in the United States and is most commonly associated with smoking.

How to help someone during an asthma attack.

- ☐ Help the person to sit up straight and remain calm.
- ☐ Have the person take one puff of their inhaler once every 30 to 60 seconds, up to 10 minutes.
- ☐ If the attack worsens, call 911. If help takes more than 15 minutes to arrive, additional puffs of the inhaler can be used.

Alzheimer's and Dementia

Dementia refers to a loss of brain function over time. It can affect memory, judgment, behavior, thinking, and language. Most forms of dementia are permanent. **Alzheimer's disease** is the most common form of dementia. Genetics is one influence on Alzheimer's. It is also more common among women, older people, and those with a history of high blood pressure or head trauma. Alzheimer's affects over five million people in the United States.

When a loved one has dementia, they rely on the care of others to do basic daily tasks. This care often comes from close family and friends who aren't trained to help. Caring for someone who is dependent on others can be difficult. The physical, emotional, and financial strains on caregivers can also put their own overall health at risk.

Behavior Contracts

As you have read, your lifestyle choices play a large role in your risk for disease. Developing the habits necessary for staying healthy throughout your life requires practicing healthy behaviors now. Behaviors can be very hard to change. It is common for people to try to start a new healthy behavior only to quit. When it comes to making the commitment to change a behavior for the long-term, it helps to create a personalized behavior contract.

A behavior contract is an agreement you make with yourself or someone else, like a friend, coach, or teacher, to change a specific health behavior. Contracts usually include your goals, a date when you will complete your goals, a plan or strategy to help you meet your goals, and a reward you will give yourself or will be given when you reach your goal. Behavior contracts help you move your long- and short-term goals into action. Research shows that using a contract can help you stick with your plan. A behavior contract is usually signed by yourself and someone else. Having someone else sign your contract helps you to be more accountable to the actions described in the contract. The person who signed it can also provide social support and can help you stick with your plan.

LESSON 1.5 Understanding My Health

Skill-Building Challenge

Creating a Behavior Contract

Think about the behaviors that help to prevent noncommunicable diseases. Select one that you struggle to do and complete the following contract to help you make a change. Share your thoughts with a classmate and help each other to create SMART goals and the steps you will need to follow to meet your goals.

1. I, _____, have decided to change the following health behavior: _____.
2. My goal is to _____. (insert SMART goal)
3. I will achieve my goal by _____. (insert date)
4. I want to change this behavior because _____.
5. I think it will be hard to change this behavior because _____.
6. The specific steps or actions I will take to help me meet my goal are _____.
7. If I achieve my goal, I will reward myself by _____.
8. I will review this contract on _____. (insert a future date)

Signature _____

Witness _____

Healthy Living Skills

This lesson focused on practicing healthy behaviors. Here are some more ways you can develop healthy living skills related to this lesson.

ANALYZING INFLUENCES

Do you try to protect your skin from sun damage? How do your friends influence your sun protection habits? How could a person's friends and peers influence them to use or not use sunscreen or skin protection? What can you and your friends agree to do differently in order to prevent skin cancer?

ACCESSING INFORMATION

Sunscreen products provide different levels of protection from the sun. Go to the website of the Skin Cancer Foundation or another website that is focused on skin cancer education. Research prevention information, including what makes a sunscreen effective. Find information about how much sunscreen you should wear and how often you should apply it. Keep track of your findings by taking notes.

LESSON 1.5 Review: Noncommunicable Diseases

LESSON SUMMARY

- Noncommunicable diseases, including cancer, diabetes, cardiovascular disease, osteoporosis, arthritis, dementia, and Alzheimer's disease, cannot be transmitted from person to person.
- A chronic disease lasts three months or longer. Most noncommunicable diseases are chronic because they are related to lifestyle factors, genetics, and aging.
- Your risk for developing a noncommunicable disease increases if you are inactive, eat an unhealthy diet, use tobacco, abuse alcohol, or are under a lot of stress.
- The signs of a heart attack include chest discomfort; pain or discomfort in one or both arms, the back, neck, jaw, or stomach; shortness of breath; and cold sweat, nausea, or lightheadedness.
- Signs of a stroke include sudden severe headache; vision issues; drooping face; speech difficulty; tingling or numbness of face, arm, hand, or leg; and balance issues or dizziness.
- A behavior contract is an agreement you make with yourself to change a specific health behavior. Using a contract helps you to stick to your plan and achieve your goals.

REVIEWING CONCEPTS AND VOCABULARY

1. _____ diseases cannot be transmitted from person to person.
2. Behaviors that help you prevent noncommunicable diseases include eating a healthy diet, avoiding alcohol and tobacco, managing stress, and getting regular _____.
3. Coronary _____ disease occurs when your arteries become clogged or hardened.
4. _____ is a condition when the pressure inside your arteries is too high.
5. _____ is a disease that weakens the bones over time.
6. Alzheimer's is a form of _____.
7. When abnormal cells in the body multiply, it is called _____.

THINKING CRITICALLY

Sometimes cities, counties, or states add an additional sales tax to foods that are considered unhealthy. These taxes are designed to discourage people from buying foods or beverages that are bad for them. For example, some states charge more sales tax on a can of soda than they do on a bottle of water. Other states charge an additional tax on bags of chips or candy. Do you think these types of public health policies can actually change people's behaviors? Why or why not?

TAKE IT HOME

Interview a parent or guardian to find out whether anyone in your family has a chronic disease. Learn what you can about that person's lifestyle and how they manage their disease.

Chapter Review

ACTION PLAN: Preventing Communicable Diseases

Use the My Action Plan worksheet to practice preventing communicable diseases. Here is an example.

My Action Plan: Avoiding Communicable Diseases

STEP 1: Identify the health behavior you are going to work on.

> I am going to do a better job at keeping my hands clean.

STEP 2: Write SMART goal(s).

Write one or two short-term goals (one day to one month).

> I will scrub my hands for 20 seconds each time I wash them.

Write a long-term goal (one to six months or more).

> I will wash my hands properly every time I use the restroom and before all meals or snacks.

STEP 3: Make a plan.

Identify two to five action steps (strategies) you could do to meet your goal.

> I will use soap and water every time I wash my hands.
>
> I will find part of a song that lasts 20 seconds and sing it every time I am scrubbing my hands.
>
> I will carry hand sanitizer in my backpack in case there is no soap available.
>
> I will put a note in my lunch to remind myself to wash my hands before I eat.

STEP 4: Do your plan and track your progress.

Short-term goal

☒ Met ☐ Not met Date: December 9

Long-term goal

☒ Met ☐ Not met Date: January 7

If you met your goal, what helped you to be successful?

> Using a song when I scrub my hands instead of just counting to 20 was helpful.

If you did not meet your goal, what obstacles made it harder for you to be successful?

> I met my goal. It was hard sometimes because my friends teased me about always washing my hands. Telling them why it was important to me to wash my hands helped.

Test Your Knowledge

Select the best answer for each question.

1. One of the five components of wellness is
   a. intellectual health
   b. popularity
   c. genetics
   d. disability

2. Which of the following is one of the five stages of change?
   a. consideration
   b. anticipation
   c. action
   d. evaluation

3. _____ is the passing of characteristics from parent to child.
   a. Heredity
   b. Ancestry
   c. Disability
   d. Wellness

4. Which type of website is most likely to be a good source of health information?
   a. .net
   b. .biz
   c. .com
   d. .gov

5. A pathogen is a(n)
   a. white blood cell
   b. red blood cell
   c. antibody
   d. foreign invader

6. Dust mites, pet dander (skin and hair), weeds, and grasses are examples of common
   a. viruses
   b. bacteria
   c. allergens
   d. diseases

7. Which is an example of a communicable disease?
   a. flu
   b. diabetes
   c. cancer
   d. arthritis

8. Which is an example of a common communicable disease among kids and teens?
   a. coronary heart disease
   b. stroke
   c. arthritis
   d. mononucleosis

9. A(n) _____ disease lasts three months or longer.
   a. acute
   b. infectious
   c. contagious
   d. chronic

10. A chronic disease that makes the bones weak and brittle is
    a. arthritis
    b. lymphoma
    c. osteoporosis
    d. atherosclerosis

PROJECT-BASED LEARNING: School Wellness Test and Promotion Campaign

What to Remember

Wellness has five dimensions. The five dimensions are intellectual, social, mental and emotional, spiritual, and physical. A person who has good wellness tries to be as healthy as they can be in all five areas. To help promote good wellness at your school, remember to follow the five steps to community advocacy.

Step 1: Identify the healthy behavior or outcome you want to address.

Step 2: Support your message with facts.

Step 3: Find a healthy, positive, or good reason to do the behavior or work toward the outcome.

Step 4: Identify the people or groups of people that might most benefit from your message.

Step 5: Create your message using the format that works best for the group you want to help.

Who It Is For
The students in your school

Why It Is Important
This will help you learn about the areas of wellness and to help your peers understand what parts of wellness they should try to improve.

What to Do
Find out what areas of wellness your peers score better on, and which ones they score lower on. Then create an educational brochure, website, or blog to help them improve a lower-scoring area of wellness.

How to Do It

Step 1: Find out how well your school is. Give the My Well-Being questionnaire from the beginning of this chapter to students in your school. Break up into teams and decide which students each team will focus on in order to avoid duplicate results. Tell people not to put their name on the questionnaire, and don't look at responses until you have collected all the questionnaires. This will help protect people's privacy.

Step 2: As a group, compile all your results by finding an average score for each area of wellness on the questionnaire.

Step 3: Make a bar graph showing the average response for each area of wellness. A visual example is provided here.

Step 4: Based on the results of your graph, put together an informational brochure, a website, or a blog that educates your classmates about that area of wellness. If your bar chart is like the example shown, you would probably choose social wellness to focus on because it had the lowest scores. Use the Steps to Community Advocacy to help you build your project.

Wellness Score

Physical	Social	Emotional	Spiritual	Intellectual
7	4	5	6	6

CROSS-CURRICULAR CONNECTIONS: Language Arts

Conduct some research on the value and importance of goal setting. Write a position paper that defends the importance of goal setting when it comes to promoting or maintaining good health. Include facts from your research in your writing. When doing your research and writing, think about the following questions: Why is goal setting important? What does goal setting help with? What makes goal setting effective? How is goal setting used when it comes to changing health behaviors?

Personal and Consumer Health

LESSON 2.1 Personal Health Habits
LESSON 2.2 Healthy Vision and Hearing
LESSON 2.3 Healthy Sleep and Rest
LESSON 2.4 Being a Healthy Consumer

Understanding My Health

My Self-Care

In this chapter, you will learn about basic personal hygiene and self-care. Take this quiz to help you assess your current hygiene and self-care habits. Put a check in the Yes column if you do the behavior regularly or in the No column if you do not. The more Yes responses you have, the better your understanding of personal hygiene and self-care is.

Hygiene and self-care behavior	Yes	No
I wash my face, body, and hair regularly.		
I brush my teeth two times each day.		
I floss my teeth once a day.		
I am careful not to listen to music or other audio too loud.		
I take regular breaks from looking at a screen (phone, tablet, computer, TV).		
I wake up and go to bed at a similar time each day.		
I avoid using social media or playing video games right before bed.		
I feel rested and ready to go when I wake up in the morning.		
I know my medical history.		
I have a doctor or medical professional I see regularly.		

My score for My Self-Care = _____ (total number of Yes answers)

Your body is like most everything else in life—it needs to be taken care of if it is to function at its best. Keeping yourself clean, paying attention to how you treat your eyes and ears, and getting plenty of good quality sleep are key to maintaining your body's function. It is also important to know when health concerns require medical attention and how to find the medical care you need.

LESSON 2.1
Personal Health Habits

Terms to Learn

acne
bruxism
cavity
cold sores
dermis
eczema
enamel
epidermis
gingivitis
halitosis
hygiene
hypodermis
keratin
tooth decay

The Big Picture

Your skin, hair, nails, and teeth are often the first things other people notice about you. When you are healthy and are taking good care of yourself, people might notice that your skin glows and that your hair is soft and shiny or that your smile is bright. They also might see that your nails are well groomed and clean. The personal health habits you follow will help you stay, look, and feel healthy now and into the future.

Learning Targets

- Define what hygiene is and explain why it is important.
- Understand the anatomy of the skin, hair, and nails.
- Identify common problems with skin, hair, nails, and teeth.
- Evaluate the effects media have on our decisions about skin and hair care.

Write About It

Have you ever used technology to enhance the look of your hair or skin on an image? If so, describe the situation and explain what you were trying to achieve. If you haven't used technology in this way, why do you think you haven't? Is it something you might consider doing in the future?

Note-Taking Guide

Use this chapter's note-taking guide to help you organize and remember the material in this lesson.

LESSON 2.1 Personal and Consumer Health

Daniel's mom works three jobs just to pay the bills, and his brother works after school to help her out. Sometimes their house has the lights or water cut off when they can't pay the bill. Daniel knows he can't always shower or brush his teeth before school, or he can't really see how he looks if things are dark. Even though he usually has clean clothes and splashes water on his face once he gets to school, he worries that his friends will think he smells or won't want to hang around him if he looks dirty.

Daniel's best friend gives him gum to chew in the morning when he hasn't been able to brush his teeth, and it helps him feel a little better about the situation. Recently Daniel started growing his hair out so that he could just put it in a pony tail and not worry about it. It is hard because he doesn't really know what to do and he doesn't want his mom or brother to feel bad about things. How are Daniel's environment and circumstances contributing to the health of his hair, skin, and teeth? What advice could you offer Daniel to help him manage his situation a little easier?

Developing Good Hygiene

It is important to practice good hygiene if you want to stay healthy. **Hygiene** is the practice of keeping yourself in good health by maintaining your personal cleanliness. Brushing your teeth, washing your face and hands, showering, and trimming your toenails are all examples of ways you maintain your hygiene.

Your Skin

Your skin is the largest organ you have. It plays an important role in keeping you healthy because it provides a barrier to all sorts of pathogens in the environment. Skin also helps to protect every other organ in your body and to keep your body temperature normal.

Personal Health Habits **LESSON 2.1**

The skin comprises three layers: the epidermis, dermis, and hypodermis (see figure 2.1). The **epidermis**, or outer layer, functions to protect you from the environment. It also contains melanin, the cells that give skin its color.

The middle layer, or **dermis**, has several functions. It contains the hairs that you see on your skin. Their follicles (roots) determine whether your hair is curly or straight, thick or thin, and light or dark. The dermis produces oil that serves as a protectant of the hair and skin. The dermis also houses your sweat glands, blood vessels, and nerves. Two proteins found within the dermis layer—collagen and elastin—help the skin stay flexible and strong. As you age, you don't make as many of these proteins. That's why skin wrinkles as you get older.

The innermost layer of skin is the **hypodermis**. This layer consists of blood vessels, fat, and more nerves. It connects the skin to the muscles and bones underneath.

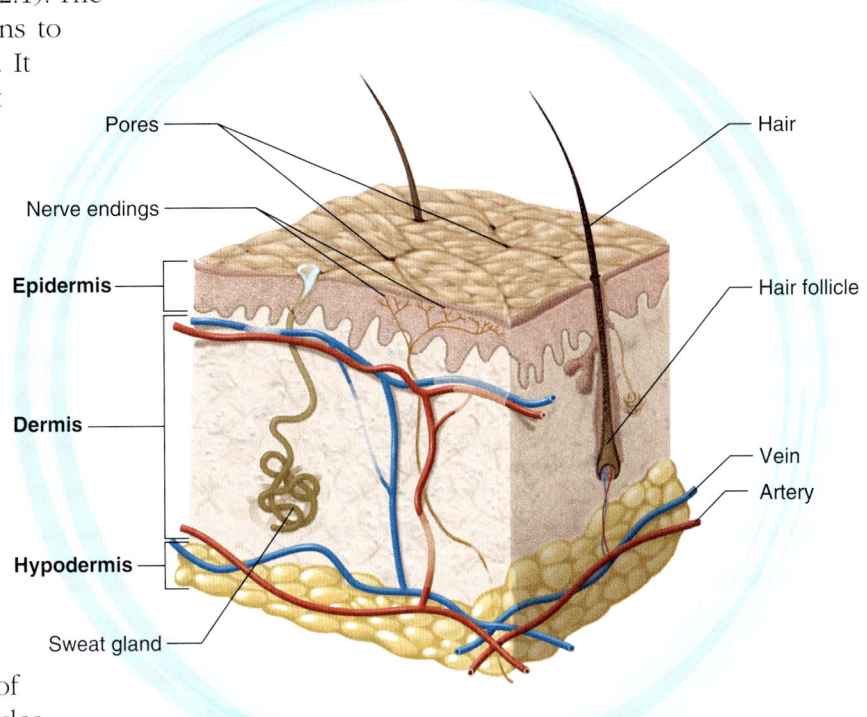

Figure 2.1 Layers of the skin.

Caring for Your Skin

Your skin is a part of your body, and it responds to the choices you make. Following a good skin care regimen is important. Skin is healthiest when you drink plenty of water, eat a healthy diet, and get regular physical activity. On the other hand, smoking, being exposed to too much sunlight, and experiencing a lot of stress make the skin less healthy.

HEALTHY LIVING TIP
Wear SPF 15 or higher sunscreen on your face and ears every day, even if you don't think you will be outside often.

Recognizing and Treating Common Skin Problems

Everyone will experience skin problems or skin irritations at some point in their life. Skin issues can occur for numerous reasons aside from hygiene habit. Environmental circumstances, exposure to irritants and chemicals, aging processes, and side effects from medicines and medical treatments all play roles in causing skin conditions. Sometimes the appearance of the skin can also serve as a clue that other medical conditions like hepatitis might be present. Most skin problems are temporary and can be treated. The next section describes a few of the most common skin conditions.

Acne

Acne is a condition that affects your skin's oil glands and hair follicles. These glands make oil, and they push dead skin cells to the surface of the skin. The mixture of oil and dead skin cells sometimes forms a plug. When this happens, the area can become infected and form a pimple. Acne is a collection of pimples that mostly occurs on the face, neck, back, chest, and shoulders. The best way to prevent and treat pimples is to keep the skin clean. Acne is most likely to result from hormone changes during puberty combined with personal hygiene practices. Acne is not, however, the result of commonly misunderstood causes such as caffeine and chocolate. Washing your face two times a day with warm water and gentle soap can help prevent acne. If you have severe acne, it is a good idea to see a dermatologist. Both over-the-counter (OTC) and prescription medications may help treat acne.

Acne Medication

Over-the-counter acne medicines typically include one of the following active ingredients.

- *Benzoyl peroxide.* This ingredient kills the bacteria that cause acne and helps remove excess oil that can clog pores. With concentrations ranging from 2.5 to 10 percent, possible side effects can include dry skin, scaling, burning, redness, and stinging. Use care when applying these products because they can bleach your hair and clothing. If your skin shows irritation, select a product with a lower concentration.
- *Salicylic acid.* This ingredient helps prevent pores from becoming plugged but can cause mild stinging and skin irritation. Products that contain salicylic acid are available in strengths from 0.5 to 5 percent.
- *Alpha hydroxy acids.* Glycolic acid and lactic acid are the two acids found in OTC medication. They treat acne by helping to remove dead skin cells and by reducing inflammation. They can also stimulate the growth of new, smoother skin. These products can help the overall appearance of skin.

When choosing an acne product, consider the following information from the Centers for Disease Control and Prevention (CDC).

The acne product that's best for you depends on many factors, including your skin type, the type and severity of your acne, and your skin care preferences. Here are some general guidelines for choosing and using acne products:

- *Begin with benzoyl peroxide.* If you're not sure which acne product to buy, start with one that contains benzoyl peroxide. It is effective and often well tolerated.
- *Start with lower strength acne products.* This can help minimize redness, dry skin, and other skin problems. If the product doesn't seem to help, gradually select products with higher concentrations.
- *Use products with different active ingredients to treat stubborn acne.* Acne ingredients work in different ways, and using more than one can be helpful. Try one at night and another in the morning.
- *Be patient.* Treating acne with acne products takes time and patience. It may take two or three months of daily use for a result to be seen.

Personal Health Habits **LESSON 2.1**

CASE STUDY

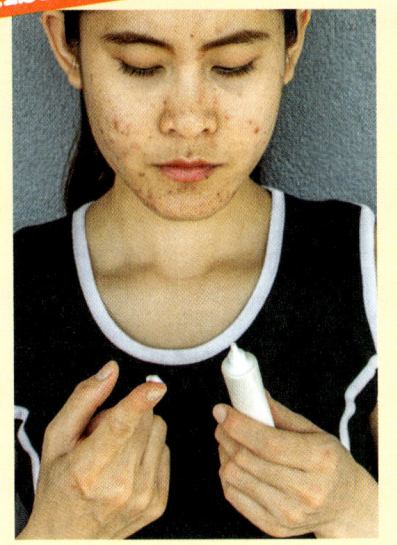

Arianna's Acne

Arianna has always been quite comfortable in her own skin. As a young girl, she loved to play outside and didn't mind getting dirty or sweaty. She has always been athletic and isn't afraid of getting bruised or scraped when she is practicing or competing. Arianna recently started wearing makeup, and it is making her face break out more than usual. Arianna is bothered by her pimples.

Lately Arianna has been trying out over-the-counter medicines to prevent pimples. She's seen blogs and social media posts that have tips on how to use makeup to hide acne cream and pimples. Arianna doesn't have a lot of money to spend on her makeup or various acne remedies, and she knows some of the cheap stuff she uses probably makes things worse. Arianna just really hates the way her pimples look. She knows that she can use apps to change how her skin looks in the pictures she posts on social media, or that she can just angle herself differently in the picture to look a little better. In fact, it seems like hiding imperfections on social media is what everyone does, and it's no big deal. Arianna is self-conscious at school, though, because she knows people will see her true self and worries that they will notice how different she looks from her social media image. Arianna really wishes she could just get rid of the make up and be more natural in her appearance.

Think About It

1. How are the school community, technology, and her peers influencing Arianna's health behaviors?
2. What are two things Arianna could do to feel better about her circumstances? Why do you think Arianna feels like she can't go to school without makeup on?
3. What could you say to Arianna to provide her with the support she needs so that she feels less anxious?

Eczema

Eczema is also called *dermatitis* (see figure 2.2). A majority of the different types of eczema causes dry, itchy skin and rashes either on the face, inside the elbows and behind the knees, or on the hands and feet. Eczema is not contagious. The cause is not known, but most doctors believe it is a result of both genetic and environmental factors. Eczema may get better or worse over time, but it is often a long-term condition. Treatments may include medicines, skin creams, light therapy, and good skin care.

Sunburn

Sunburns will make the skin turn red and hot to the touch. They typically fade on their own after a few days. If you are sunburned too often, it can cause dry or wrinkled skin, dark spots, rough spots, and skin cancers, such as melanoma. It is important to stay out of the sun and to protect your skin from the sun by wearing protective gear, clothing, and sunscreen when you are outside.

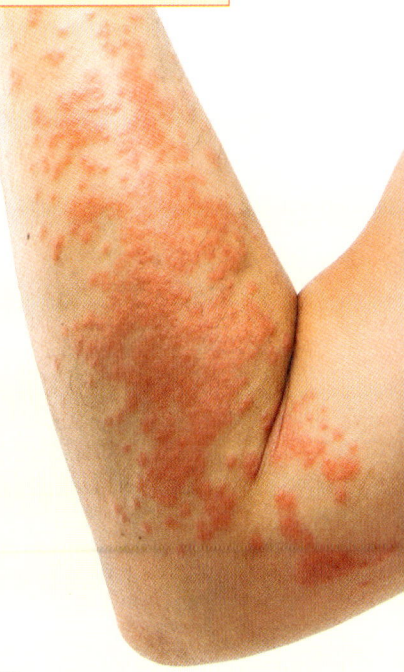

Figure 2.2 Eczema rash on the arm.

LESSON 2.1 Personal and Consumer Health

Preventing and Detecting Skin Cancer

Skin cancer (melanoma) is the most common cancer in the United States. Sun exposure is the leading cause of skin cancer. Only half of all teens report using sunscreen on a regular basis, and 80 percent believe that tan skin makes people look healthier. Unfortunately, sun exposure is especially risky for teenagers because the body is growing, and the cells are rapidly multiplying. Over the long term, tanning can also cause the skin to lose its elastic quality. This means that the skin will wrinkle. Sun spots or uneven skin tone can also occur. It is important to inspect your skin regularly for changes that might suggest skin cancer. When doing a skin check, be sure to check all visible parts of your skin along with your scalp, armpits, spaces between fingers and toes, and genitals and use the ABCDE method (see figure 2.3). To prevent skin cancer and to keep your skin looking as healthy as possible, you should also follow these recommendations from the CDC.

- Seek shade, especially in the middle of the day.
- Wear clothing that covers and protects your skin, such as hats, long sleeves, and long pants. This includes looking for lightweight and breathable fabrics that are specially treated to keep dangerous rays from hitting your skin.
- Wear a hat with a wide brim to protect your neck, ears, and face.
- Wear sunglasses that block UVA (long wave) and UVB (short wave) sun rays.
- Use sunscreen with a sun protection factor (SPF) of at least 15.
- Avoid tanning indoors or outdoors.

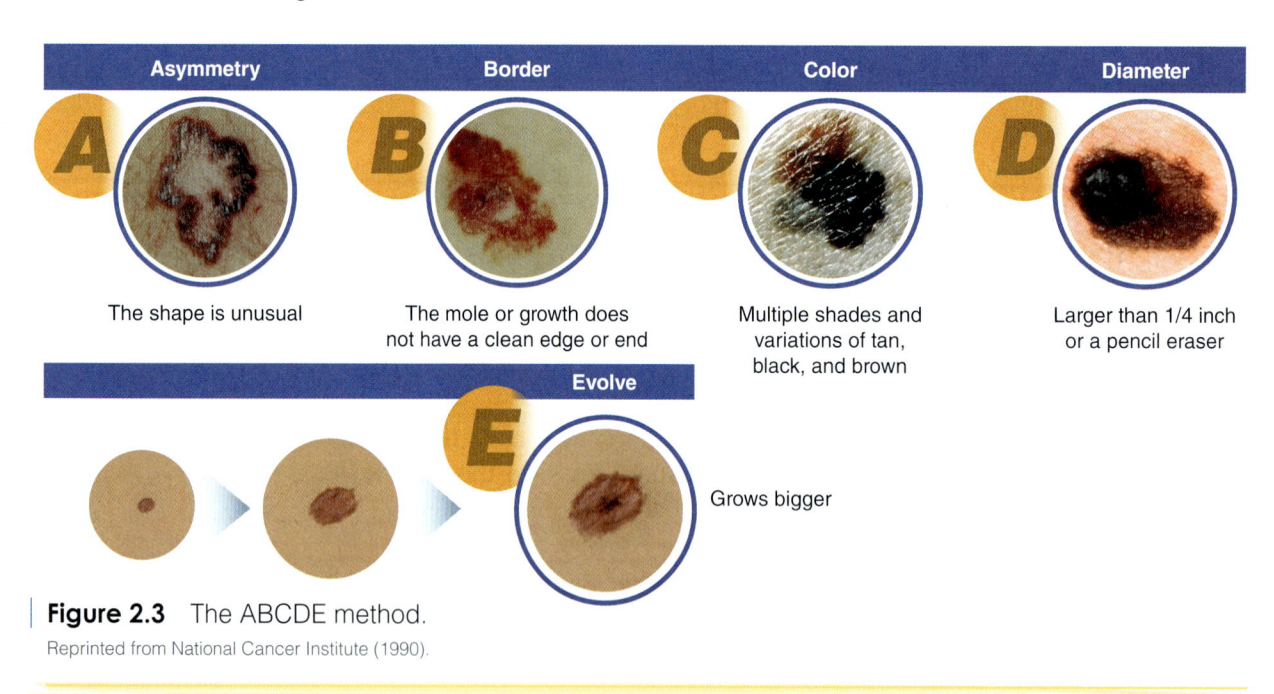

Asymmetry	Border	Color	Diameter
A	B	C	D
The shape is unusual	The mole or growth does not have a clean edge or end	Multiple shades and variations of tan, black, and brown	Larger than 1/4 inch or a pencil eraser

Evolve — E — Grows bigger

Figure 2.3 The ABCDE method.
Reprinted from National Cancer Institute (1990).

Your Hair and Nails

Did you know that the average person has five million hairs on their body? Hair grows all over your body except on your lips, palms, and the soles of your feet. Your hair will grow about half an inch in one month. Most hair grows for up to

Personal Health Habits **LESSON 2.1**

six years, and then it falls out and is replaced by new hair. Hair helps keep you warm and protects openings like the eyes, ears, and nose from small particles in the air.

Your nails are made up of **keratin**, a hard form of protein. Healthy nails are usually smooth and consistent in color. When the nails become discolored or have big pits on them, it can be a sign of other diseases like lung, heart, kidney, and liver diseases. It is normal to sometimes get white spots or to have vertical ridges on your nails. Keeping your nails clean, dry, and trimmed can help you avoid some problems. Be careful not to remove the cuticle (the skin at the base of each nail), because that can cause infection.

Preventing Hair and Nail Problems

Keep your hair and nails healthy through regular bathing and washing and by eating a nutrient rich diet high in vitamins E, A, and C; zinc; biotin; omega 3; protein; iron; and fiber. Even with healthy habits, most people will experience one or more problems with their hair and nails during their lifetime. Hair and nail problems can signal a more systemic issue in the body, so always talk to your doctor if you experience a problem. Figure 2.4 highlights common hair and nail problems.

HAIR

Head lice
(small insects that live in the hair on the scalp or body; highly contagious)

Hair loss
(also called alopecia; can happen to either gender; caused by autoimmune disease)

Dandruff
(redness, itching, and flaking of the scalp; can be worse in winter or with stress; can be treated with medicated shampoo)

NAILS

Bacterial and fungal infections
(caused by bacteria entering the skin near a nail that has been bitten, chewed, cut, or damaged)

Ingrown nails
(the nail grows into the flesh instead of over it; can be caused by cutting nails too short)

Warts
(small, rough, hard growths on the skin; caused by a virus)

Figure 2.4 You are likely to experience one or more of these common hair or nail problems in your lifetime.

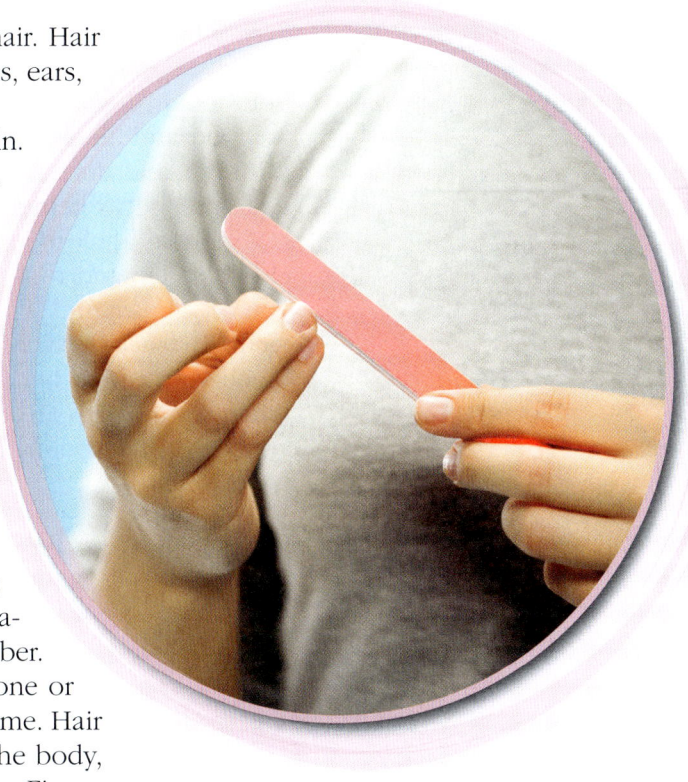

71

LESSON 2.1 Personal and Consumer Health

HEALTHY LIVING TIP
Carry floss sticks, toothpicks, or soft-tipped dental picks in your backpack and use them after lunch to remove food debris that might have gotten stuck in your teeth.

Your Mouth and Teeth

Your mouth is also called your *oral cavity*. It provides an opening into the body for food and air. Your mouth is home to several organs, including the tongue, salivary gland ducts, and teeth (see figure 2.5). The movements of your tongue, lips, and cheeks help you produce sounds and speech.

A normal adult mouth has 32 teeth. Teeth comprise three different parts: the crown, neck, and root (see figure 2.6). The crown is the visible outside part of your tooth. **Enamel** is a hard, white substance made of calcium that protects your teeth. The neck connects the crown to the root of the tooth. The root contains blood vessels and nerves and connects the tooth to the jaw. Sometimes people think that teeth are dead or are pieces of exposed bones. The reality is that teeth are complex, living organs like the rest of your body.

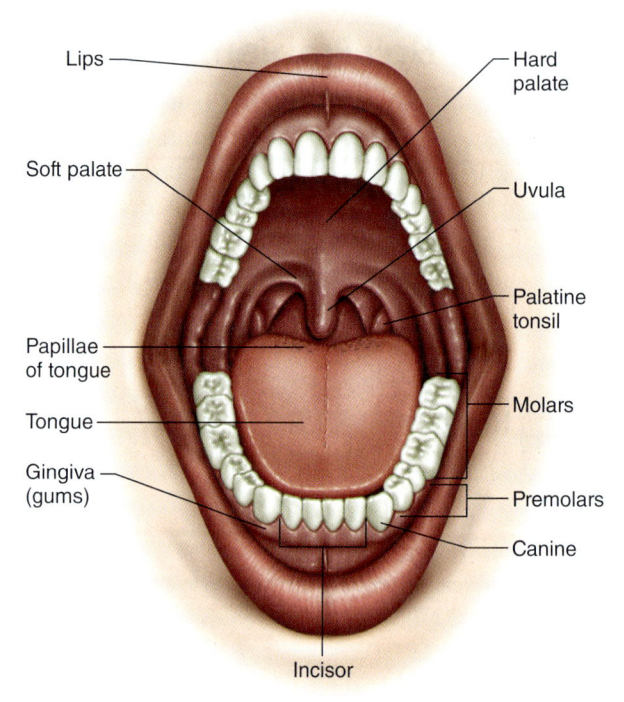

Figure 2.5 Anatomy of the mouth.

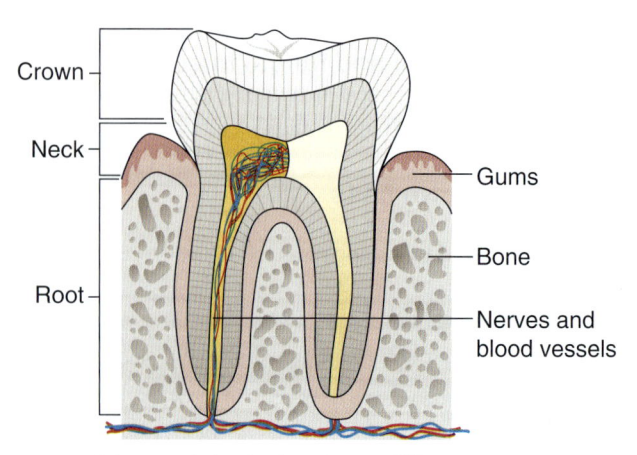

Figure 2.6 Anatomy of the tooth includes three different parts: the crown, neck, and root.

Caring for Your Mouth and Teeth

When it comes to your mouth and teeth, the most important things you can do are to regularly brush and floss your teeth. Brushing twice a day with a soft bristle brush and flossing every day will help remove food debris and bacteria from your teeth. This will keep the teeth from becoming damaged. Caring for your teeth will also help them stay healthy longer. As you get older, you may lose one or more teeth if they become damaged. When this happens, quality of life can go down because eating, drinking, and communicating become more difficult.

Common Problems With the Mouth and Teeth

Most people will experience some sort of problem with their oral health in their lifetime. If any problem you experience causes you pain or discomfort, you should see a dentist right away.

Crooked or Crowded Teeth

Crooked teeth may only be a cosmetic (appearance) concern, or they may actually prevent someone from chewing food properly. If your teeth are not aligned properly, you may also experience pain in the jaw, or you may get frequent headaches. Crooked teeth can also make hygiene practices like flossing more difficult.

When your wisdom teeth begin to grow in (around ages 18 to 20), you may experience crowding in your mouth. This means that there simply isn't enough room for all of the teeth to fit in without twisting or overlapping. Crowding often leads to wisdom teeth becoming impacted (unable to grow) or needing to be pulled after they have come in to allow enough space for the other teeth. Removing the wisdom teeth is a common procedure that does not negatively affect the function of the mouth.

Tooth Decay

Tooth decay is the destruction of some part of the tooth and can affect the outer layer and inner part of the tooth. Decay occurs when foods containing carbohydrates, such as bread, cereal, milk, soda, fruit, and candy, are left on the teeth. Normal bacteria that live in the mouth digest these foods, turning them into acids. The acids combine with bacteria, food debris, and saliva to form plaque. This plaque is a colorless, sticky film that coats the tooth and dissolves the protective enamel on the tooth. Plaque that sits on the tooth causes a hole, or **cavity**. Cavities left untreated become painful and will eventually kill the tooth.

Gum Disease

The soft tissue around your teeth—your gums—helps to protect the root of the tooth and to keep your teeth in place. Gum disease occurs when plaque and tartar build up on the teeth. Bacteria in the plaque make the gums become swollen. This inflammation is called **gingivitis**.

Cold Sores

Cold sores are small blisters that occur on and around your lips or sometimes in your mouth. The herpes simplex virus (HSV) causes this common infection. Blisters can appear in groups and form small patches. After a blister breaks, its interior fluid leaks out and dries up, causing a flaky crust. Cold sores usually heal in two to four weeks without leaving a scar. Cold sores are contagious and can be spread by close contact such as kissing. There's no cure for HSV infection, and the blisters may return. Taking an antiviral medication can help cold sores heal more quickly and may reduce how often they return.

Bad Breath

Bad breath is also called **halitosis**. A variety of hygiene factors or common diseases that can lead to halitosis include

- food in teeth,
- smoking or tobacco use,
- poor dental hygiene,
- dry mouth,
- medications,
- infections,
- chronic sinus infection, and
- metabolic diseases such as diabetes.

Personal Health Habits — LESSON 2.1

Teeth Grinding

People with **bruxism** clench their jaw while awake, grind their teeth in their sleep, or do a combination of both. Stress and anxiety are common causes of this condition. Your dentist can help determine if you have bruxism by looking at the wear pattern of your teeth. Symptoms of tooth grinding include

- flattened, fractured, chipped, or loose teeth;
- worn tooth enamel, exposing deeper layers of your tooth;
- increased tooth pain or sensitivity;
- tired or tight jaw muscles;
- jaw, neck, or face pain or soreness;
- pain that feels like an earache; and
- dull headache.

Visiting the Dentist

Many people don't enjoy visits to the dentist. Fear of pain or needles, anxiety about not being able to breathe, and jaw and neck discomfort are common concerns, and sometimes they get in the way of good oral health care. It is recommended that you visit a dentist every six months for a deep cleaning and a checkup. Dentists have access to specialized tools that remove plaque and tartar in areas that you can't remove yourself. The dentist can also inspect your gums to make sure they are healthy. Your dentist may also X-ray your teeth to find cavities before they cause any significant damage.

If you are afraid of seeing the dentist, it is important to talk to your parent or guardian and to your dentist when you arrive for an appointment. Many dentists can provide a variety of ways to make your visit a pain-free experience. Some dental offices even provide entertainment like televisions on the ceiling that you can watch and listen to on headphones during your cleaning or dental procedure. Oral health care is critical to overall health. It is important to work toward overcoming any fears or barriers you may have so that you can get the dental care you need.

Analyzing Influences: Beauty, Media, and Technology

Today's technology allows us to change photos of people in a lot of ways. When you see a photo in a magazine or on social media, it is difficult to know how realistic the image is. Almost all media images have been changed to look more attractive or appealing. Hair and skin are two of the most commonly altered parts of photos.

75

LESSON 2.1 Personal and Consumer Health

Skin
- All pores, pimples, freckles, and imperfections are removed and skin is given a "glow."
- Body hair on women is often removed.
- A tan or realistic-looking facial hair (for men) is added to the photo.

Features
- Noses, eyes, and lips can all be altered to make them bigger or smaller.
- Digital alterations can even make the shape of the face appear thinner, longer, or rounder.

Hair
- The color, length, and thickness of hair can be adjusted or changed.
- Hair can also be made to look shinier and healthier than it is.

Eyes: Enlarged, color altered, lines under eyes removed
Eyebrows: Shape and color altered
Hair: Lengthened, color altered, flyaways eliminated
Lips: Color altered, shape thickened
Face: Thinned, jaw line altered
Blouse: Wrinkles removed, color altered

Eyes: Enlarged, lines under eyes removed
Skin: Tone evened out, imperfections removed
Teeth: Whitened
Face: Jaw line widened, nose thinned

Before / After

Figure 2.7 The various ways images are altered.

It is important to understand that technology makes it incredibly easy for the media to portray unrealistic images of models and celebrities with flawless skin and ultra-shiny, fantastically thick hair (see figure 2.7). Simply put, these altered images are just part of the business. However, it is easy to fall into a cycle fixating on our own insecurities against these models of perfection. It's important to remember that even the people in the pictures do not actually look the way they appear.

It's important to be aware of the ways in which the steady stream of unrealistic images can influence your health behaviors toward your hair and skin. For example, you might feel pressure to use chemical peels on your face to try to create smoother skin, but they may actually cause irritation, create a rash, or even result in scarring. Hair dyes used for adding color or highlights to hair can dry out and split the hair. In addition, using these products exposes you to harsh and toxic chemicals that can irritate your skin, eyes, and lungs.

Personal Health Habits **LESSON 2.1**

Skill-Building Challenge

Analyzing Social and Media Influences

Use the handout your teacher provides to make a list of three different social media and traditional media sources you use or look at on a regular basis. For each, explain why you use the source and what it is you want to see or accomplish when using that media. Think about magazines, television, websites, and social media sites. Then, for each source, reflect on how you feel and act after you have been looking at the source or site. How does it affect your own self-image? Finally, consider how each media source affects your health behaviors. Use the following example as a guide for completing this challenge.

- My media source: *Instagram*
- Why I use this media source: *to keep track of what my friends are doing; to look at what is on sale at my favorite stores*
- How I feel when using it: *I feel okay looking at it. Sometimes I notice the models and don't feel like I am pretty enough.*
- How does this influence my health behaviors and choices: *I sometimes go out and buy a new product to try on my skin or hair. I spend money I don't need to spend, and most of the products either don't work or they won't make me look the way someone else does.*

Healthy Living Skills

This lesson focused on analyzing how media and technology influence behaviors related to hair and skin care. Here are some more healthy living skills related to this lesson.

MAKING HEALTHY DECISIONS
Going through puberty changes your skin. Let's say you have developed acne on your face and neck—what would you do? Use the five-step decision-making process to explain your options and to identify your next steps.

PRACTICING HEALTHY BEHAVIORS
Next time you brush your teeth, challenge yourself to floss your teeth too. Make sure you bring the floss up in a C shape around the front and back of each tooth. Pay attention to how much debris you remove from your teeth. How are your teeth affected when you don't floss regularly?

ADVOCATING FOR GOOD HEALTH
Create a video clip that explains why it is important for people to check their skin for signs of skin cancer. It should show them how to check the skin properly using the ABCDE method described earlier in this lesson. Focus your message for a particular audience, such as older adults, outdoor athletes, or children.

LESSON 2.1 Personal and Consumer Health

LESSON 2.1 Review: Personal Health Habits

LESSON SUMMARY

- Hygiene is the practice of keeping yourself in good health by maintaining your personal cleanliness. Good hygiene helps you stay healthy and look and feel your best.
- The skin is made up of three layers: the epidermis, dermis, and hypodermis.
- Keratin is the hard protein that makes up the nails.
- Common problems with the skin include acne, eczema, sunburn, and skin cancers.
- Poor brushing and flossing habits lead to oral health problems, including tooth decay, cavities, gum disease, and bad breath. Cold sores in or around your mouth form from the herpes simplex virus. Damage to your teeth can result from grinding them.
- Despite what altered media images try to convey, no one has perfect skin and hair. Trying to achieve such unrealistic standards might lead to poor health decisions and behaviors, such as applying harsh chemicals to the face or hair.

REVIEWING CONCEPTS AND VOCABULARY

1. _____ is the practice of keeping yourself in good health by maintaining your personal cleanliness.
2. The _____ is the outer layer of your skin.
3. Hair follicles and sweat glands are found in the _____.
4. _____ is a condition that results from the oil glands and hair follicles on your skin becoming clogged.
5. Tooth _____ is the destruction of some part of the tooth.
6. When bacteria and plaque make the gums become swollen, it is called _____.

THINKING CRITICALLY

Poor dental health can negatively affect your overall well-being. Why do you think this is? Research the relationship between oral health and general health to help you answer this question.

TAKE IT HOME

Research common dental diseases and conditions and select one you want to learn more about. Identify the causes of the disease and learn how it is treated. Write a short summary of your findings.

LESSON 2.2
Healthy Vision and Hearing

Terms to Learn

conductive hearing loss
empathy
equilibrium
farsightedness
nearsightedness
sensorineural hearing loss
social norm
tinnitus

The Big Picture

The world is full of beautiful images and sounds. Have you ever wondered how your eyes work or how it is you are able to hear the sounds around you? Vision and hearing are two of our most important senses. When we lose the ability to see or hear properly, we miss out on some of the most amazing parts of life. Believe it or not, the habits you develop now might affect how well you can see and hear later in life.

Learning Targets

- Explain how vision works.
- Compare nearsightedness and farsightedness.
- Describe what eye strain is and explain how to help reduce it.
- Analyze how earbuds and headphones might contribute to hearing loss.
- Analyze how perception of norms influence vision and hearing behaviors.

Write About It

How many hours did you spend wearing earbuds or headphones this week? How many hours did you spend looking at a screen (your phone, television, tablet, computer)? How do you think these behaviors affect the long-term health of your eyes and ears?

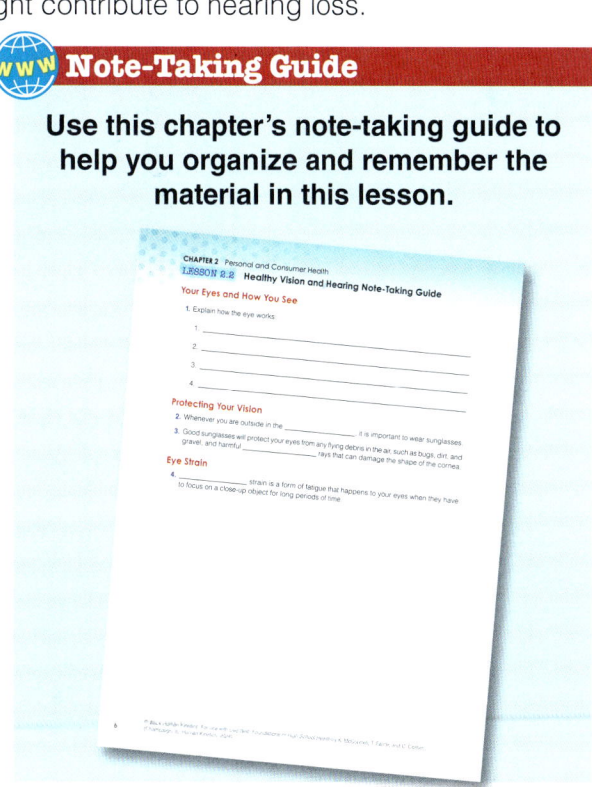

Note-Taking Guide

Use this chapter's note-taking guide to help you organize and remember the material in this lesson.

LESSON 2.2   Personal and Consumer Health

Callista had severe allergies. They were so bad that she wouldn't be surprised if she ended up with a sinus infection again. She really hoped to avoid that at all costs. Her sneezing was at a near constant, and, despite her best effort of blowing her nose, it was not alleviating her worsening congestion. Callista was also beginning to feel exhausted, and she spent more time resting and sleeping.

After a few days, her ears began feeling stuffy and full. Whenever she moved her head, they ached. Each time she stood up and tried to walk she suffered a bout of dizziness. It was hard to concentrate, and she no longer was able to hear everything her friends said. What do you think Callista should do to help improve her situation? If you were Callista's friend, what concerns would you have about her long-term health?

Your Eyes and How You See

Your eyes function similarly to how the camera on your cell phone works. They take in light from whatever you are looking at and pass the light to the back of your eye. Here, the retina captures a copy of the upside-down image and sends electrical signals on the optic nerve to your brain. The brain then reorientates the image to be right side up (see figure 2.8). There are a number of structures in the eye that help with this process.

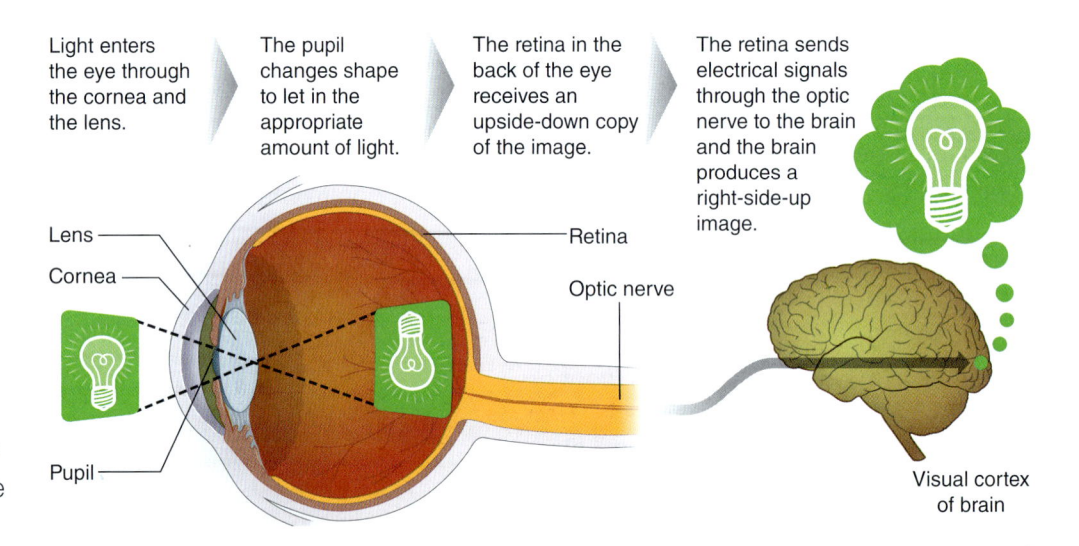

Figure 2.8 Anatomy of the eye and how the eye works.

Light enters the eye through the cornea and the lens.

The pupil changes shape to let in the appropriate amount of light.

The retina in the back of the eye receives an upside-down copy of the image.

The retina sends electrical signals through the optic nerve to the brain and the brain produces a right-side-up image.

Lens
Cornea
Retina
Optic nerve
Pupil
Visual cortex of brain

Protecting Your Vision

There are a few things you can do to protect your eye health. First, whenever you are outside in the sun, it is important to wear sunglasses. Good sunglasses will protect your eyes from any flying debris in the air (like bugs, dirt, and gravel) and will also protect your eyes from harmful ultraviolet (UV) rays that can damage the shape of the cornea. UV rays from the sun can burn the cornea like they can burn the skin. Over time, this can lead to vision problems. If you are an outdoor athlete, it is very important to protect your eyes with sunglasses or goggles for these same reasons. Everyone should have their eyes checked regularly by an eye doctor.

Eye Strain

It is common for people to spend as many as nine or more hours each day looking at a screen. This can cause eye strain. Eye strain is a form of fatigue that happens to your eyes when they have to focus on a close-up object for long periods of time. The best treatment for eye strain is to cut back on the hours of screen time you have each day and to avoid long periods of screen time without a rest.

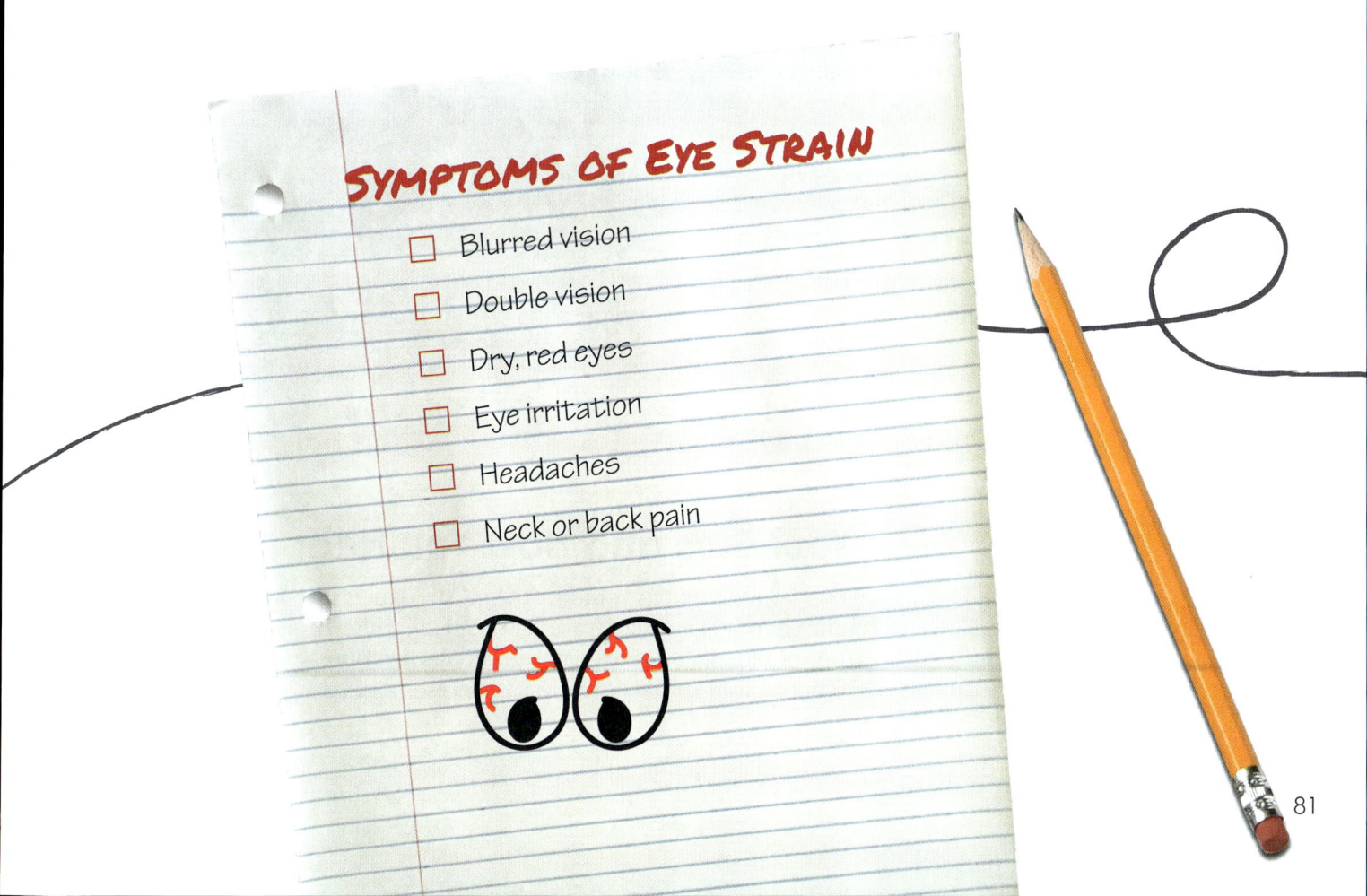

Symptoms of Eye Strain

- ☐ Blurred vision
- ☐ Double vision
- ☐ Dry, red eyes
- ☐ Eye irritation
- ☐ Headaches
- ☐ Neck or back pain

LESSON 2.2   Personal and Consumer Health

> **HEALTHY LIVING TIP**
>
> If you use a tablet, phone, or computer often, follow the 20-20-20 rule to help reduce eye strain: Look away from the screen every 20 minutes and focus on something about 20 feet (6 m) away for about 20 seconds.

Common Problems With Vision

As a younger person, you are less likely to experience common eye problems that affect your vision. As you age, however, it is more likely that you will experience at least one of them. Vision problems can also be genetic: You are more likely to experience a problem if one or both parents have vision issues. Figure 2.9 describes common vision problems, including **nearsightedness** and **farsightedness**.

Nearsightedness
Nearsightedness is also called *myopia*. Nearsighted people can see objects that are up close clearly but have a harder time seeing objects at a distance. This happens when the light entering the eye is focused in front of the retina instead of directly on it.

Farsightedness
Farsightedness is also known as *hyperopia*. In this condition, light focuses behind the retina, making objects that are up close difficult to see clearly.

Astigmatism
Astigmatism occurs when the light is focused unevenly on the retina, making objects appear blurry or distorted.

Presbyopia
Presbyopia happens when the lens of the eye stiffens. Light isn't focused as well, and it becomes harder to see objects up close. Many older adults experience presbyopia and use glasses to read.

Color Blindness
Color blindness is a color vision deficiency that keeps a person from seeing colors in the way most people do. The most common form is red-green color blindness, followed by blue-yellow. People with color blindness have difficulty seeing the differences between these colors.

Red or Bloodshot Eyes
Red or bloodshot eyes occur because the eye surface is covered in blood vessels that expand when they're irritated or infected. Eye drops and rest can help relieve red eyes.

Night Blindness
Night blindness means that a person has a hard time seeing in the dark. A lack of vitamin A in your diet, nearsightedness, or other eye conditions can contribute to night blindness.

Figure 2.9 Common vision problems.

Your Ears and How You Hear

Your hearing allows you to listen to your favorite music, dance, talk to your friends, and listen to natural sounds like ocean waves and rainfall. It also helps you maintain your **equilibrium**, or balance. Unfortunately, our ears are often exposed to very loud or uncomfortable sounds like construction noise, airplanes overhead, and traffic. We even subject ourselves to loud and dangerous sounds on purpose when we wear headphones for playing games, listening to music, or talking with friends.

Your ears are very complex organs (see figure 2.10) that help you take in sound waves from the environment and convert them into things you recognize. The outer ear, or pinna, is the large part of your ear that other people see. It helps to gather sound waves that then pass through the ear canal. The ear canal produces earwax; it also makes the sound waves 60 times louder so that you can hear them.

Your eardrum vibrates the sound waves into the middle ear, where three small bones further vibrate the sound waves into the cochlea in the inner ear. The cochlea is a spiral tube that resembles a very small seashell. It is covered in nerve cells that convert the vibrations into nervous impulses. These impulses travel down the auditory nerve to the brain, where you interpret the impulses as sounds. You also have small, semicircular canals in the inner ear that contain fluid. These canals use the fluid to help you maintain your balance.

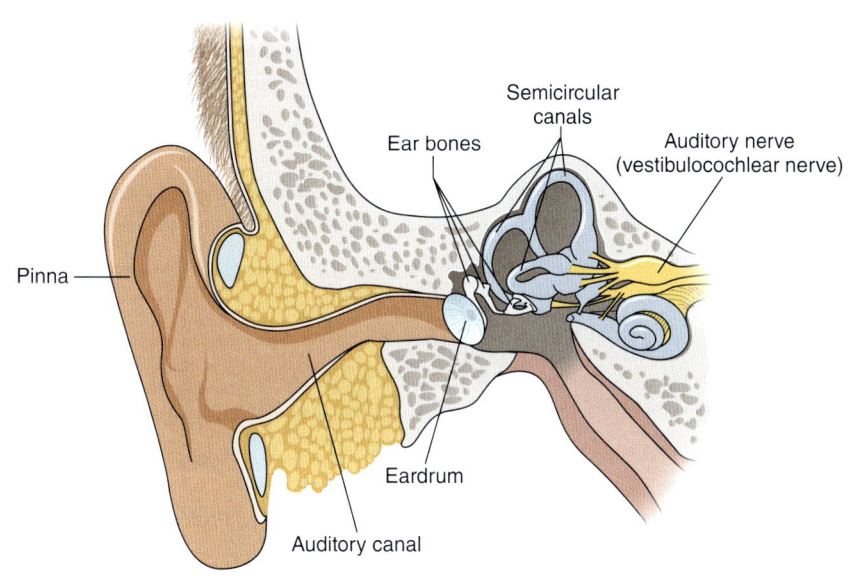

Figure 2.10 Anatomy of the ear.

Protecting Your Hearing

If you lose all or part of your hearing, it is unlikely that you will ever get it back. Most hearing loss is permanent. Hearing aids can help restore some hearing in many situations. Protecting your hearing is important for limiting the chances of experiencing hearing loss. For example, to avoid very high levels of noise at places like concert venues, construction sites, and tarmacs, you can wear small earplugs that lower the decibels of certain frequency sounds while still allowing you to hear normal human conversation. Noise-canceling earphones work in a similar way while allowing you to listen to sound through them. When using any earphone or earbud, it is critical not to listen at a high volume (more than 85 decibels). Even a one-time exposure to loud noise can damage the ear and result in some hearing loss.

It is also important not to stick objects into the ears, because you might puncture or damage the eardrum. This includes cotton-tipped swabs. You should only try to clean the outside of your ears yourself. Your regular medical exams will include inspection of your ears for earwax or signs of infection. If either is present, there are safe medicines that can be used to clean and heal the ear.

Common Problems With Hearing

There are a few common ear problems that affect hearing.

Hearing Loss

The most serious ear-related health issue is permanent hearing loss. Damage to the eardrum (a rupture or tear) that prevents sound from being transmitted into the inner ear is called **conductive hearing loss**. **Sensorineural hearing loss** is another example of permanent hearing loss that occurs when the auditory nerve itself is damaged. This blocks sound information from the inner ear from being passed to the brain properly. Either type of hearing loss can be mild, moderate, severe, or profound (see figure 2.11). Hearing loss can come on suddenly or develop over time.

Mild Hearing Loss
A person with mild hearing loss may hear some speech sounds, but soft sounds are harder to hear.

Moderate Hearing Loss
A person with moderate hearing loss may hear very little or no speech when another person is talking at a normal level.

Severe Hearing Loss
A person with severe hearing loss will hear no speech when a person is talking at a normal level and only some loud sounds.

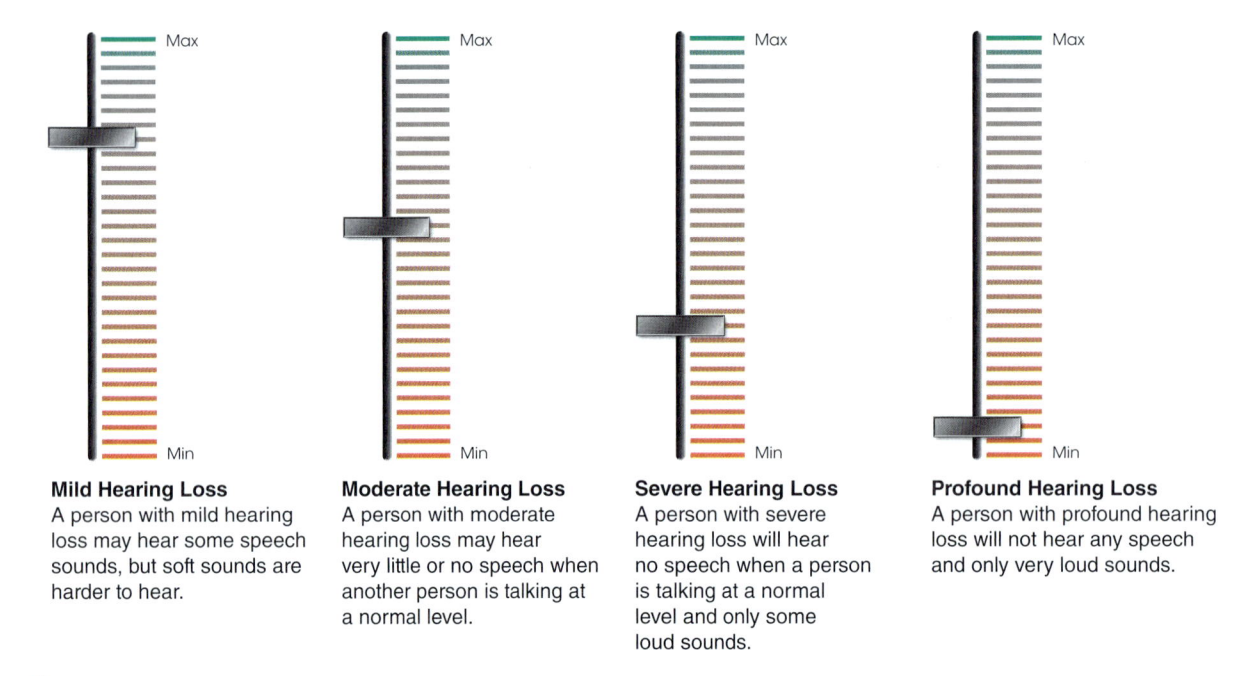

Profound Hearing Loss
A person with profound hearing loss will not hear any speech and only very loud sounds.

Figure 2.11 Degrees of hearing loss.

People who experience hearing loss can use hearing aids to help amplify sounds in their ears. Due to technological advances, today's hearing aids are sleek and hardly noticeable—some are so small that they can fit inside the ear. Hearing aids are also equipped with smart technology that can be controlled through a cell phone. In severe hearing loss or deafness, a person may be fitted with a cochlear implant. These devices are placed inside the ear and head to directly stimulate the auditory nerve. Hearing through a cochlear implant is different from normal hearing and takes time for a person to learn. However, implants allow people to recognize warning signals, understand other sounds in the environment, and understand speech in person or over the phone.

Tinnitus

Tinnitus is another common hearing problem described as a ringing, buzzing, or other sound present in the ear(s). Most people experience some ringing in the ears at some point in their lives. Tinnitus can be caused by damage to some part of the middle or inner ear or by hearing loss itself. Chronic, ongoing tinnitus occurs in about 1 in every 22 people, or 4.5 percent of the U.S. population. Unfortunately, most tinnitus cannot be cured. Treatments include learning coping strategies and using noise suppression techniques such as white noise devices to reduce the discomfort and frustration tinnitus can cause.

Social Norms and Hearing and Visual Behaviors

Most people don't seem to go anywhere without their cell phone. It is very common for people to have earbuds in one or both ears most of the day. It is also common for people to use their phone to listen to music, watch videos, and play games. When a behavior is so common in a society that it is considered standard or expected, we call it a **social norm**. Social norms act like unofficial rules or laws. Social norms influence our behaviors so we can fit into or identify with a particular social group.

When it comes to our eye and ear health, we might not always make the healthiest choice if we don't think it fits in with social norms. For example, it may not be acceptable to wear glasses or protective earplugs in some social groups. These social norms may keep people from wanting to talk about, protect themselves against, or seek help for vision or hearing problems.

We can help limit social norms that are harmful by developing empathy for others. **Empathy** is the ability to understand and appreciate the feelings and emotions of others. If your social norms dictate that glasses aren't stylish, you are less likely to empathize with someone who wears glasses. No one likes being excluded or ridiculed. Considering what an experience is like for someone else can help you improve your empathy skills.

STEM in Health

LASER EYE SURGERY

LASER stands for **l**ight **a**mplification by **s**timulated **e**mission of **r**adiation. Lasers are a common part of your everyday life. They are used for cutting, engraving, and marking a wide range of surfaces and products. They are also used in medical surgeries such as laser eye surgery. Essentially, a laser is a very concentrated energy source in the form of photons, or light. A laser is quite different from a traditional light source like a flashlight. The light in a laser is all one specific wavelength (or color) and highly organized (meaning that energy is all produced at one time), and it releases all of its energy in one direction.

Advances in laser technology have led to the use of lasers for a variety of health issues including surgeries, hair removal, and corrective eye surgeries. For correcting vision, doctors use the laser energy to reshape the curvature of the eye. By changing the shape of the cornea, the laser alters the way light rays enter the eye. This type of surgery is very quick, and most people have improved vision within one week. The eye itself can take up to six months to recover fully from the surgery.

LESSON 2.2   Personal and Consumer Health

Skill-Building Challenge

Analyzing Social Norms on Vision and Hearing Behaviors

Use the handout your teacher provides to analyze how technology, media, and social norms might influence your vision and hearing behaviors. Often we want to fit in, so we make choices based on a desire to be liked or to be popular, even when those choices might negatively affect our health. On the handout, fill in the outer area of the rectangle with as many influences or social norms as you can think of. In the inside of the rectangle, write a short paragraph about how these influences affect your behaviors.

Healthy Living Skills

This lesson focused on analyzing how social norms affect our vision and hearing behaviors. Here are some more ways you can develop healthy living skills related to this lesson.

HEALTHY COMMUNICATION

Work with a team to develop a series of five short messages designed to get others to reduce listening volume when wearing earbuds or headphones. Gather facts about the dangers of listening at a high volume when using a device and develop five short (30 seconds each), catchy video clips to spread your message. End each clip with the phrase "Take the Pledge." Each team member then shows at least one of the clips to 10 other people. Ask viewers to sign off on a sheet of paper (a pledge) if they are willing to try reducing their listening volume. Regroup with your team members and determine the percentage of viewers who added their signature. If the percentage is less than half the viewers, discuss with your team what you could have done differently to make your messaging more effective.

LESSON 2.2 Review: Healthy Vision and Hearing

LESSON SUMMARY

- The eyes take in light from whatever you are looking at and pass the light to the back of your eye. The retina in the back of your eye captures a copy of the upside-down image and then sends electrical signals to your brain. The brain turns the image right side up.
- Nearsighted people can see objects that are up close clearly but have a harder time seeing objects in the distance. In farsighted people, light focuses behind the retina, and objects that are up close are hard to see clearly.
- Eye strain is a form of fatigue that happens when your eyes have to focus on a close-up object for long periods of time. The best treatment for eye strain is to cut back on the hours of screen time you have each day and to avoid long periods of screen time without a rest.
- Your ears gather sound waves from the environment. The eardrum vibrates the sound into the cochlea, which converts the vibrations to electric impulses that are sent to your brain. The brain makes sense of the information in the form of sounds.
- Mild hearing loss can make some speech sounds hard to hear; with moderate hearing loss, a person may hear very little or no speech when another person is talking at a normal level; with severe hearing loss, no speech will be heard when a person is talking at a normal level; and with profound hearing loss, a person will not hear any speech and will only hear very loud sounds.
- Common societal behaviors that are considered standard, or expected, are social norms, which may influence our decisions about whether or not to wear glasses, or how often to wear earbuds and listen to loud music.

REVIEWING CONCEPTS AND VOCABULARY

1. When objects look blurry up close, it is called _____.
2. A person with _____ can't see objects that are far away.
3. Another name for _____ is balance.
4. A standard, or expected, behavior in a group of people is called a social _____.
5. _____ hearing loss is due to damage to the auditory nerve.
6. A ringing, buzzing, or other sound present in the ear(s) is called _____.

THINKING CRITICALLY

Many teenagers listen to music and other media through headphones, and often listen at dangerous levels. Imagine you could look into the future and saw that you would go deaf later in life. What would you say to yourself? Write a letter to yourself from the perspective of your older self. Give your current self the best advice you can to help prevent hearing loss later.

TAKE IT HOME

Talk to someone in your life who spends a lot of time in front of a screen, like a sibling who watches too much TV, a cousin who plays video games for hours every day, or a parent or guardian who works in front of a computer all day. Write down five important points that may help them change their behavior. Then practice your advocacy skills with them by sharing what you know.

LESSON 2.3
Healthy Sleep and Rest

Terms to Learn

good quality sleep
insomnia
sleep debt
sleep-deprived
unconscious

The Big Picture

Getting enough quality sleep and rest is one of the most important health behaviors you can have. Sleep is critical to the human body. When we are well rested, our body functions at its best. When we don't get enough sleep, we can have trouble in every part of our lives. How well you sleep affects how well you learn, how you feel, how your body functions and fights off disease, how well you interact with others, and how your body grows and develops. Developing healthy habits around sleep and rest is essential for having a good quality of life.

Learning Targets

- Explain why sleep is important.
- Explain how much sleep you need at different stages of life.
- Explain common sleep problems.
- Describe ways to help improve how well you sleep.
- Assess your sleep habits and develop a plan to improve your sleep quality.

Write About It

How many hours of sleep did you get last night? What helps you get a good night's sleep? What makes it harder for you to sleep?

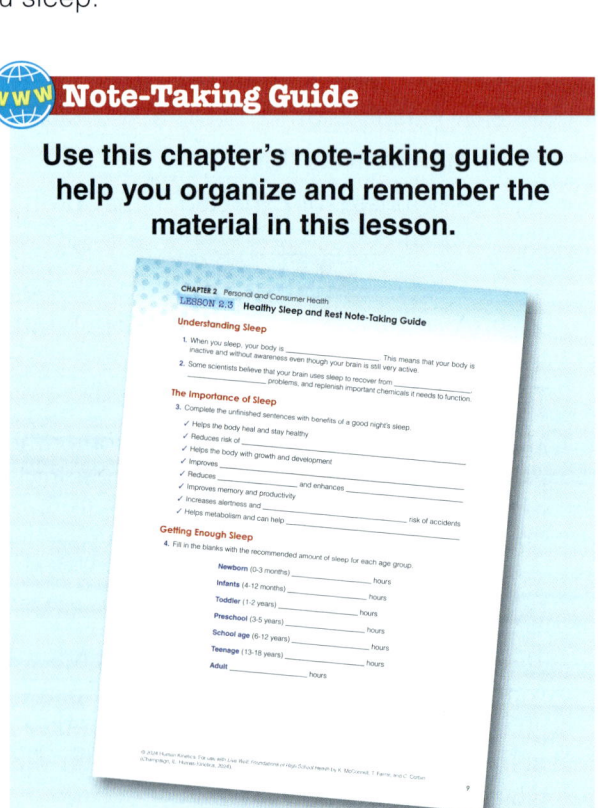

Note-Taking Guide

Use this chapter's note-taking guide to help you organize and remember the material in this lesson.

Healthy Sleep and Rest **LESSON 2.3**

Wully has a robust and busy life. She takes her studies seriously and loves gaming. She hopes to get an esport scholarship to college one day. Each day after school, she goes to her parents' restaurant, where she does her homework at one of the tables and then helps out in the kitchen until her dad brings her home. Most nights, she isn't even home until dinner time. Wully's friends are active on social media and gaming sites, and she usually spends the rest of her evening in her room messaging friends and gaming. She and her two friends usually video chat to say goodnight, and often stay up past midnight laughing and talking. She is up early in the morning to take care of her two younger siblings and get them ready for school. Do you think Wully gets enough sleep? How might Wully's sleeping patterns affect her? This lesson explains why sleep is important to your overall health and well-being.

Understanding Sleep

When you sleep, your brain is still very active, but your body is **unconscious**, meaning it is inactive and without awareness. Some scientists believe that your brain uses sleep to recover from stress, solve problems, and replenish important chemicals it needs in order to function. The truth is, we don't fully understand everything that happens when we sleep. There are five stages of sleep that have been studied (see figure 2.12). We cycle through the stages every 90 to 110 minutes when we are sleeping.

Stage 1
First 5-10 minutes.
Drifting in and out of sleep.
Easily awakened.

Stage 2
Lasts about 15-20 minutes.
Body temperature begins to drop.
Breathing slows down.

Stage 3
Blood pressure lowers.
Brain wave activity changes.
Start of deep sleep.

Stage 4
Lasts about 30 minutes.
Deep sleep.
Muscles are very relaxed.

Stage 5
Dream stage.
Brain activity increases.
Eyes move rapidly.
Heart rate increases and breathing is rapid and shallow.

Figure 2.12 The five stages of sleep.

LESSON 2.3 Personal and Consumer Health

The Importance of Sleep

Even if we don't know exactly what happens in our brains during sleep, we do know what happens to our functioning if we don't sleep enough. Sleep is critically important to our physical and emotional well-being.

Benefits of a Good Night's Sleep

- Helps the body heal and stay healthy
- Reduces risk of heart attack, stroke, and cancer
- Helps the body with growth and development
- Improves alertness and concentration
- Reduces depression and enhances mood
- Improves memory and productivity
- Increases alertness and reduces risk of accidents
- Helps metabolism and regulates weight

Getting Enough Sleep

Everyone's need for sleep will vary some, and your needs will differ depending on your age. Teenagers need a lot of sleep to support growth and maturation. Table 2.1 shows guidelines to help you know how much sleep per day is recommended at different stages of life.

TABLE 2.1 **Sleep Recommendations**

Stage of life	Amount of recommended sleep
Newborn (0-3 months)	14-17 hours
Infant (4-12 months)	12-16 hours
Toddler (1-2 years)	11-14 hours
Preschool (3-5 years)	10-13 hours
School age (6-12 years)	9-12 hours
Teenage (13-18 years)	8-10 hours
Adult	7 or more hours

What Happens When You Don't Sleep Enough or Don't Sleep Well?

Good quality sleep is sleep that is long enough and is peaceful and deep. Good quality sleep doesn't just help you feel your best, it also protects you from health conditions, diseases, and other challenges to good health. Research shows that 73 percent of high school students don't get enough sleep. Poor sleep can contribute to various health issues (see figure 2.13).

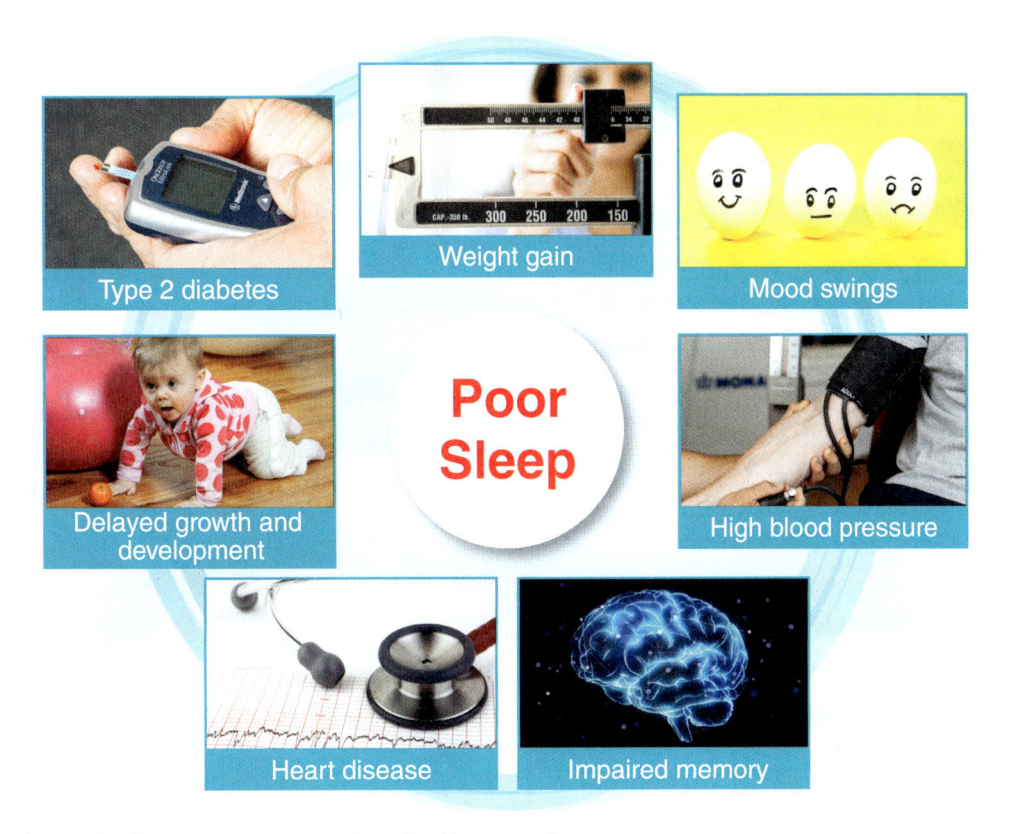

Figure 2.13 Problems associated with poor sleep.

Common Sleep Problems

It is not unusual to have problems sleeping now and then. Stress, anxiety, or excitement can sometimes keep us awake or disturb our sleep. Almost everyone experiences an occasional disruption to sleep. Other problems such as **insomnia**, which happens when you are not able to fall asleep or sleep through the night almost every night, result in long-term disruptions to sleep. If your sleep is disrupted night after night, you become **sleep-deprived**. When you are unable to make up for lost sleep over time, your body develops a **sleep debt**. Eventually your judgment, focus, and overall function will suffer. Sleep problems include

- bed-wetting,
- insomnia,
- nightmares,
- sleepwalking,
- sleep apnea (stopping breathing for short periods of time during sleep), and
- narcolepsy (falling asleep suddenly during the day).

HEALTHY LIVING TIP

Keeping a journal can help you work through the day's events and improve the quality of your sleep. Write about your day for five minutes each night before bed to see whether it helps you feel calmer and more peaceful before you try to sleep.

Self-Management for Good Sleep

Because getting enough good quality sleep is important, you should plan for sleep just like you do for other important parts of your life. If you struggle with falling asleep or staying asleep, developing a sleep routine that consists of nightly rituals before going to bed may be useful. For example, your routine may start with turning off all technology and writing in a journal or reading for 15 minutes before turning in. Washing your face and brushing your teeth or using particular relaxation and breathing techniques are examples of simple and more focused rituals you can engage in before going to bed. Below are some good tools and suggestions that might help you sleep your best. Consider including some of these in your sleep routine.

Things You Should Do Every Day

- *Take naps.* Short naps can help improve mood, alertness, and performance.
- *Get regular exercise.* Daily exercise helps you sleep longer and deeper.
- *Get natural light during the day.* Natural light helps your biological clock work at its best.

Things You Should Do When Preparing to Sleep

- *Set and follow a sleep schedule.* Going to bed at the same time each night and getting up at the same time in the morning helps your body get into a routine and makes it easier to sleep.
- *Avoid stimulants (caffeine, screen time) before bed.* Caffeine and screen time can keep you awake and make it harder to fall asleep at night.
- *Relax before bed.* Doing something relaxing before bed, like taking a bath or reading a book, can help you fall asleep more easily.
- *Create a quality sleeping environment (temperature, darkness, quiet, comfort).* You will sleep best in a cool, dark, quiet space that is comfortable.

Skill-Building Challenge

Developing Self-Management for Good Sleep

In order to get good quality sleep, you need to manage your own behaviors and create a plan. The following steps can help you make your plan. Once you've made your plan, monitor your behaviors every day for one week and decide whether your plan is working or not.

STEP 1: Evaluate your current sleep patterns.

How many hours do you sleep each night? If you are not sure, take your best guess.

What is the quality of your sleep? Do you wake up often? Do you have a hard time falling asleep? Do you wake up tired from not getting enough sleep?

STEP 2: Write out a goal related to your sleep.

Do you want to sleep more hours each night? Do you want to sleep better (not wake up or toss and turn)? Do you want to fall asleep faster? Remember to make your goal SMART.

STEP 3: Identify and write down three to five things you could do to help you reach your goal.

STEP 4: Monitor your progress toward your goal and decide whether you need to make any changes.

STEP 5: Reflect on your progress and refine your goal as needed.

Healthy Living Skills

This lesson focused on self-management for good sleep. Here are some more ways you can develop healthy living skills related to this lesson.

HEALTHY COMMUNICATION

Create a poem, rap, or song that explains why sleep is important to health. Include at least three benefits of sleep and at least two health consequences of poor sleep. Be sure to provide tips for how to improve the quality of your sleep. The information you include should be accurate and make sense. Be creative and write in a style that will appeal to an older audience of people closer to the age of your parents or guardians.

ADVOCATING FOR GOOD HEALTH

Create a brochure that you could hand out at school that provides tips and tools for getting good quality sleep. Include information about why getting enough quality sleep is important. Make sure your brochure is factually accurate and appeals to your peer group.

LESSON 2.3 Review: Healthy Sleep and Rest

LESSON SUMMARY

- Sleep is important to our physical and mental well-being because it helps the body heal and stay healthy; reduces the risk of heart attack, stroke, and cancer; and helps the body with growth and development.
- Good quality sleep improves your alertness and concentration, reduces depression, and enhances mood. It can also improve memory, increase alertness, and help you control your weight.
- The amount of sleep you need each day will vary over the years. Newborns need 14 to 17 hours and infants need 12 to 16. As you grow, the number of hours goes down slightly (toddlers: 11 to 14; preschoolers: 10 to 13; school-age: 9 to 12; teenagers: 8 to 10; adults: 7 or more).
- Common sleep problems include bed-wetting, insomnia, nightmares, sleep-walking, sleep apnea, and narcolepsy.
- You can improve the quality of your sleep by setting and following a sleep schedule; avoiding caffeine and screen time before bed; relaxing before bed; and creating a cool, dark, and quiet sleeping environment that is comfortable.

REVIEWING CONCEPTS AND VOCABULARY

1. It is important that you get good _____ sleep each night.
2. If a person does not get enough sleep each night, they may become sleep-_____.
3. A(n) _____ happens when someone does not get enough sleep night after night.
4. The inability to fall asleep or stay asleep is called _____.
5. To help you sleep, you should avoid consuming any _____ before bed.
6. When you sleep, your body is _____, or inactive and without awareness.

THINKING CRITICALLY

Many high school and college students stay up late or pull an "all-nighter" when preparing for important exams or assessments. Do you think this is a smart decision? Do you think the benefits of studying all night outweigh the impact of not getting any sleep? Explain your thinking using appropriate terminology and facts.

TAKE IT HOME

Talk to a family member in your home about the importance of creating a sleep routine and a good sleeping environment. Look at the environment that person sleeps in and offer suggestions on how to improve their sleep routine and their sleeping environment.

LESSON 2.4
Being a Healthy Consumer

Terms to Learn
active ingredient
assertive
consumer
health care consumer
health care system
hospital
pharmacy
preventive screening
self-care

The Big Picture
You will use health care products and services throughout your life. In order to make choices that are best for you, it is important to understand how to be a healthy consumer.

Learning Targets
- Explain how engaging in self-care behaviors can affect long-term health.
- Identify six things that are part of your medical history.
- Analyze the relationship between having health insurance and access to medical care.
- Demonstrate the use of *I* statements when using assertive communication.

Write About It
If you experienced a significant injury or were concerned you might have a serious health issue, how confident are you that you know where to go for help? Provide three examples of potential health issues a teenager might face and identify where that person might go for help.

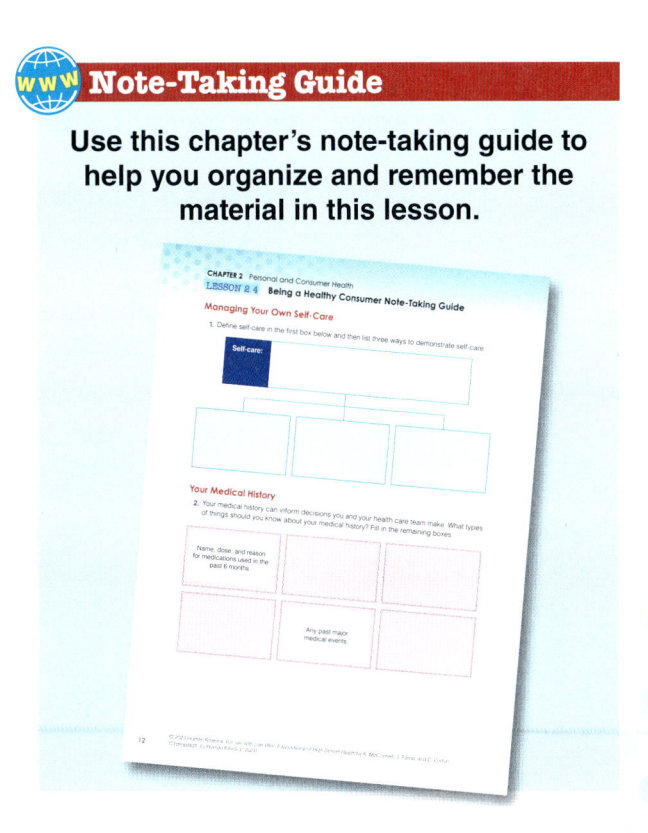

Note-Taking Guide
Use this chapter's note-taking guide to help you organize and remember the material in this lesson.

LESSON 2.4   Personal and Consumer Health

Mara's dad struggled with memory loss and needed her assistance to get seen by the doctor. Mara didn't know who his doctor was or anything about his insurance. When she asked her dad for this information, he eventually recalled the doctor's name, but he couldn't remember anything else about how to reach him. She searched through her dad's phone and finally found the doctor's name.

Upon arriving at the medical facility, the registration associate told Mara's dad that he needed to present his insurance card in order to be seen. This caused a lot of stress and anxiety for Mara and her dad. Mara had to call her mom and ask if she knew the information or had a copy of the card. Luckily, her mom was able to text a photo of the card which detailed his medical ID number and the type of coverage he had. After providing his proof of insurance, she was handed two long forms and was told to fill out both questionnaires for the doctor to review. Mara didn't know most of the answers to the questions about her dad's medical history, so she called both her mom (again) and sister. Between the three of them, they were able to answer most of the questions. Would you know where to find your insurance information in an emergency? Do you know your own medical history and the medical history of your immediate family?

Managing Your Own Self-Care

Most people don't run to the hospital or see their doctor every time they sneeze or feel a little sick. A large part of being a good health care consumer is knowing when you need to seek help or when you can engage in **self-care**, which involves all the decisions you make and the actions you take to maintain your health. Self-care includes knowing how to make basic consumer decisions for items like over-the-counter medicines and first aid supplies. It also involves performing regular self-screening for skin, breast, and testicular cancers. Knowing how to access medical care and following medical advice after seeing a health care professional are important parts of your long-term self-care. If you don't establish good self-care habits, you are likely to become sick more often or to end up with a serious illness.

Your Medical History

Keeping track of your medical history is crucial for taking care of yourself, being a good health care consumer, and providing the background history necessary for you and your health care team to make informed decisions. In some cases, your medical history can also be the key to solving challenging health problems.

Know Your Medical History

- The name, dose, and reason for taking any medications you have used in the past six months
- A list of all over-the-counter medicines, vitamins, or supplements you have used in the past six months
- Any known allergies to medications
- All shots (vaccinations) you have had
- Any past major medical events you have had (such as surgery or hospitalization)
- Your family history of heart disease, cancer, and other diseases (if you know it)

Routine Medical Screens

Getting regular physical exams and medical screenings is one of the most important self-care practices you can have. It is recommended that everyone over two years old see their doctor once a year for a basic exam. In these exams, the doctor will check your vital signs (like heart rate and blood pressure). They will also examine your ears, skin, nails, and eyes. Your height, weight, and reflexes are checked, and laboratory tests of your blood may be ordered. As you get older, additional screenings are necessary to detect diseases such as cancer. **Preventive screening** is a medical test administered to patients to check for early signs of disease. Mammograms and colonoscopy exams are examples of these types of preventive screenings.

Self-Examinations

Performing regular skin checks (see figure 2.3), such as looking for signs of skin cancer, is an example of a self-examination. Breast self-exams and testicular self-exams are also regular self-examinations you should do. Most self-exams should be done every 30 days. By performing regular self-exams, you can catch changes early, which also leads to early detection of disease. Early detection and treatment of cancers typically result in a better outcome and longer survival.

Being a Health Care Consumer

A **consumer** is someone who uses a product or service. We are all consumers. When you use medical services, buy a health-related product, select a physician or other medical professional, or go to the dentist, you are being a **health care consumer**. Chances are you haven't had to make major medical decisions for yourself yet or had to decide who your health care providers will be. Even though you may not engage in very much health care consumerism now, learning basic consumer skills will help you be a healthy consumer later. A big part of both self-care and being a good health consumer is your ability to select and buy appropriate health care products.

Finding Products

Many of the health care products you need can be found in drugstores and in large grocery stores and department stores. Personal care products like shampoo and toothpaste as well as a variety of first aid products are typically available. Many of these stores also have an in-store **pharmacy**, which sells legal prescription and OTC drugs. A pharmacist will answer your questions and help you find the product that is best for your situation.

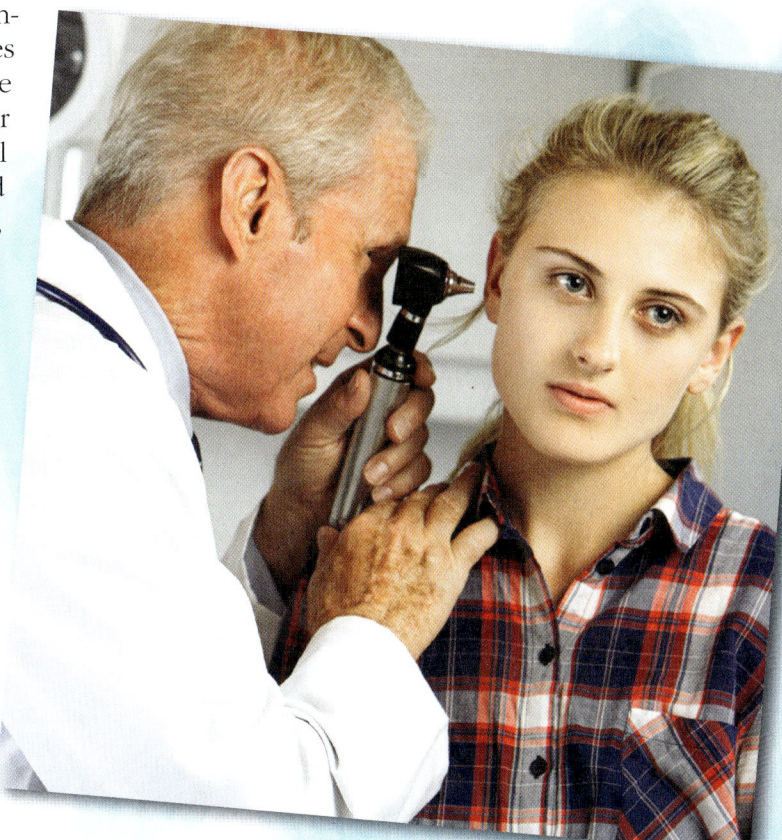

There are also many online retailers and drugstores that can provide the same products. Keep in mind that online sites may use tricks and expensive advertisements to get you to buy their products. Individual testimonials and reviews may be untruthful or inaccurate. Even when shopping online, you should be able to see and use the information from a product label to make a purchasing decision, and you should comparison shop.

Product Labels

Most of us are familiar with the idea of food labels. When you study nutrition, you learn to read food labels and to use them to make good nutrition decisions. Other products such as personal care, sunscreen, insect repellent, and antibiotic creams also have labels that show important information.

The label lists the ingredients and how much of each is in the product, the total amount of the product that is in the container, and the recommended dosage or amount to use at one time. With many health-related products, the label also identifies the amount of an active ingredient the product has. The **active ingredient** is the chemical or drug in a product responsible for the desired effect. All of these are important pieces of information. By comparing the amount of active ingredients found in different antibiotic creams, for example, you can figure out which brand has the most active ingredients for the lowest price.

Self-care and health care product labels can also contain a wide variety of other symbols to help you make consumer decisions that line up with your personal values. For example, the leaping bunny logo is an internationally recognized symbol that indicates the product is cruelty-free and does not contain animal by-products.

Comparison Shopping

Ecommerce, or online shopping, has become significant among consumers, but whether you shop online or in traditional brick-and-mortar stores, you still can learn to comparison shop. For example, if you are looking for sunscreen, spend time comparing your options. Consider the price, total amount of product, and percentage of active ingredients. You want to get more product and more active ingredients for the price you are paying.

There may be other factors to consider based on your situation. You can compare the inactive ingredients for differences in the product, and you can also consider how the product is packaged and used. For example, you might want a spray-on sunscreen or you might want one that is designed to hold up to water or sweat. Perhaps you also are concerned about ethical issues such as whether animals were harmed in developing and testing the product. In the end, consider your options and make an informed decision that lines up with your needs and your priorities.

U.S. Health Care System

A **health care system** is the organization of people, institutions, and resources that deliver health care services to meet the health needs of target populations. The type of health insurance a person has can affect the access and care they receive. Understanding the basics about health insurance and the health care system can help you navigate services more effectively.

Health Insurance

Most Americans have some form of health insurance (public, private, or a combination of both) with a majority of people being covered by private insurance plans through their employers. Health insurance provides financial coverage to people for all or some medical related expenses for a monthly fee, or premium. Government-funded programs, such as Medicaid and Medicare, provide health care coverage to some vulnerable population groups. The government also publicly funds coverage through Indian Health Services and the military. See table 2.2 for common types of health insurance.

TABLE 2.2 **Common Types of Health Insurance Plans**

Plan	Description
Managed care	These plans provide access to a specific, limited set of medical professionals and services. You are required to pay additional costs if you see an unapproved, or out-of-network, provider.
Fee for service	Although you have the option to see any medical professional you want, these plans require you to pay on average 20 percent of all medical bills out of pocket (by yourself).
Health maintenance organization (HMO)	An HMO provides care directly to those they insure. Typically, a primary care physician coordinates all of your care.
Preferred provider organization (PPO)	Similar to a fee for service plan, PPOs use an approved network of providers which have pre-negotiated costs. You can self-refer to specialists without using a primary care physician, but you will pay more money as a result.
Point of service	These plans provide a combination of HMO and PPO services that allows you to use a primary care physician, both in or out of network. Costs vary depending on the specifics of the plan.

Private Health Insurance

Over half of Americans have private health insurance that is often offered through their employer. In most cases, both the employer and the employee pay a monthly fee, or premium, into a private system. In exchange, they receive access to designated health care providers and the approved services they offer. Plans differ with some paying for all costs associated with certain medical services and others paying only a portion of those costs. This means that even the privately insured can experience significant health care costs when serious medical situations arise. Most insurance plans have an annual out-of-pocket limit—a maximum amount a person needs to pay each year in addition to their premium. Knowing your out-of-pocket insurance limit and working to save money to cover the expenses you may incur is an important part of being a smart health care consumer. People without insurance coverage through an employer or spouse have the option to buy into private insurance plans through the Affordable Care Act.

Public Health Insurance

Public, or government, health insurance works in a similar way to private insurance, the difference being a person pays into a government account and has access to facilities and services that accept payment from these plans. Medicare, Medicaid, the Veterans Health Administration, the Children's Health Insurance Plan, and the Indian Health Service are examples of public health insurance. Public insurance often provides access to fewer health care services, but those on public health care plans often have fewer to no additional expenses for their care.

Primary Care Physician

Most people, regardless of their insurance plan, will want a primary care physician. A primary care physician is a medical doctor who is trained to prevent, diagnose, and treat a wide range of illnesses and injuries in the general population. Primary care physicians provide comprehensive care, which means they can address chronic, long-term conditions like diabetes mellitus as well as acute or immediate problems like a cold, flu, allergic reactions, or an injury.

School Health Clinics

Many schools have a nurse or other health care professional who works onsite in an office at the school. School health clinics or centers can serve as a medical home for school-age children and young adults. School clinics are necessary because they provide vaccinations, routine physicals, and emergency care. It is important to know whether your school has a school health clinic and whether your parents or guardians approve of you using their services.

Other Clinics, Centers, and Hospitals

The health care system includes a variety of other centers, clinics, and hospitals. Clinics and centers can include a wide range of services, from general medical care to specialized disease care like cancer care, or they may focus on preventive and rehabilitation services like physical therapy, nutrition, and wellness services. An urgent care clinic provides same-day services to people experiencing non-life-threatening emergencies. A **hospital** is an institution that provides advanced

---

HEALTHY LIVING TIP

Create an emergency contact card to keep in your backpack or bag. Start by writing down the name and contact information of your parent or guardian, then add the name of your primary doctor and their contact information.

Career Connection

PATIENT ADVOCATE

Today's health care system is complex and often challenging for patients and families to navigate insurance and care options. Patient advocates serve as care coordinators who help patients and their families understand all aspects of care. These roles include responding to complaints about patients' grievances; serving as a liaison between patients, providers, and insurers; moving a family member into a long-term care facility; and identifying resources and services so that patients get the appropriate level of care they need and have access to those services. People who have excellent communication and organizational skills are perfect candidates for being patient advocates. Many patient advocates work in hospitals and care facilities. This career path typically requires a college or university degree in an area related to health care services (or health care administration) and optional board certification.

medical care and surgical treatments. Most hospitals also have emergency rooms for handling urgent, life-threatening emergencies.

Consumer Rights and Responsibilities

As a health care consumer, you have some responsibilities as well as some rights. It is important to keep these in mind when you are unhappy about a health care service or product.

You have a responsibility to

- be honest and forthcoming with health care providers,
- provide an accurate and complete medical history, and
- ask questions when you are confused or if you have a concern.

You have the right to

- receive accurate and easily understood information,
- choose health care providers,
- seek emergency care whenever needed,
- participate in your medical decisions,
- be treated with respect,
- be provided with nondiscriminatory care,
- have confidentiality of your medical information and care, and
- be given a fair, fast, and objective review of complaints against a provider or facility.

101

Using Assertive Communication

There may be times when you are not satisfied with the medical care you receive. In this situation, it is important that you speak up in a respectful and effective way. Advocating for your rights or needs requires being an effective communicator. To achieve this, you need to express yourself with an **assertive**—confident but not offensive—tone. Assertive communication is not the same as aggressive or passive communication. Aggressive communication shows that you don't respect the others' perspective. Passive communication, on the other hand, prevents you from expressing your own wants, needs, or expectations effectively. It also allows others to define some or all of these things for you. One of the best ways to learn assertive communication is to practice using *I* statements. When you frame your concerns in this way, others are more likely to respond without becoming defensive or offended. This helps to move the conversation forward.

To help you learn to be assertive, practice using a basic sentence structure that follows these four steps:

1. Begin by sharing what you feel: *I feel* . . .
2. Be specific about what is making you feel that way: *when* . . .
3. Explain why you feel the way you do: *because* . . .
4. Be clear about what you need: *I need* . . .

For example, "*I feel* confused *when* you talk *because* I can't understand the words you use. *I need* you to talk more slowly and use simpler words."

Skill-Building Challenge

Making a Consumer Complaint

Imagine that after using the acne cream you bought at the local drug store, the cream actually worsened your complexion and made your face dry and flaky the next day. You continued using the cream, but after three days, your acne hadn't improved and your skin still felt dry. The package claimed that it could clear up pimples in 24 hours.

Now think about what you would say if you had the chance to talk to the maker of the acne cream. Begin by explaining what happened to you when you used the product. Then use the assertiveness technique in this chapter to help you express your concerns. You may want to write out a script before you practice. Practice making your complaint to a classmate.

Healthy Living Skills

This lesson focused on assertive communication. Here are some more ways you can develop healthy living skills related to this lesson.

ANALYZING INFLUENCES
Make a list of what affects your access to, and use of, health care services. Pay special attention to community, family, and cultural influences. Identify each influence as having a potentially positive or negative impact on your health and explain your reasoning.

ACCESSING INFORMATION
Research the health care services that are available in your school and surrounding community. Make a list of the name of the facility and the types of services it provides. Include a phone number or website address for each service on your list. Share your list with a family member or friend.

MAKING HEALTHY DECISIONS
Go to your local grocery store or drugstore and compare two different brands of toothpaste that claim to whiten your teeth. Decide which toothpaste is a better buy for you and explain why.

LESSON 2.4 Review: Being a Healthy Consumer

LESSON SUMMARY

- Self-care involves all the decisions you make and the actions you take to maintain your health. If you don't learn good self-care habits, you are likely to become sicker more often or to end up with a serious illness.
- Your medical history is a record of your medical conditions and treatments. It can include the medications you have used in the last six months; the over-the-counter medicines, vitamins, or supplements you have used in the last six months; your known allergies to medications; your vaccinations record; any major medical events you've had (like surgery or hospitalization); and your family history of heart disease, cancer, and other diseases (if you know it).
- Most people find health care services through their primary care physician. A primary care physician is a medical doctor who is trained to prevent, diagnose, and treat a wide range of illnesses and injuries in the general population. The type of health care you receive and the costs you have as a result will vary depending on if you have health insurance and the type of insurance you have.
- It is important to communicate your health care needs. Being assertive means communicating your feelings and needs directly without offending others. Assertive communication is good, especially when you need to stand up for yourself, your rights, or your needs.

LESSON 2.4 — Personal and Consumer Health

REVIEWING CONCEPTS AND VOCABULARY

1. A(n) _____ is someone who uses a product or service.
2. _____ involves all the decisions you make and the actions you take to maintain your health.
3. If you have questions about prescription or over-the-counter drugs, you should talk to a(n) _____.
4. The _____ ingredient is what causes the effect in a product.
5. Medical tests that are administered to check for early signs of disease are called _____.
6. By communicating your feelings and needs directly without offending others you are being _____.
7. A(n) _____ is a medical doctor who is trained to prevent, diagnose, and treat a wide range of illnesses and injuries in the general population.

THINKING CRITICALLY

Medical information can be confusing. What would you do if you did not understand something that the doctor was telling you, especially if it involved a treatment they wanted you to get? What responsibility do you have in this situation? How would you communicate your concern with the medical professional?

TAKE IT HOME

Ask your parent or guardian if they can help you make a medical history for yourself. You may need to find old records from past medical visits to help you. Look over the list of items that are part of a medical history and include the ones that apply to you. Make sure to put a current date on your history and leave some empty space to add to it over time.

Chapter Review

ACTION PLAN: Personal Health Habits

Use the My Action Plan worksheet to set goals for your personal health behaviors. An example follows.

My Action Plan: Keeping My Eyes Healthy

STEP 1: Identify the health behavior you are going to work on.

> I am going to protect myself from eye strain by following the 20-20-20 rule any time I look at a screen.

STEP 2: Write SMART goal(s).

Write one or two short-term goals (one day to one month long).

> I will remember to follow the 20-20-20 rule at least half of the time when I am using a screen.

Write a long-term goal (one to six months or more).

> I will follow the 20-20-20 rule every time I am using a screen.

STEP 3: Make a plan.

Identify two to five action steps (strategies) you could do to meet your goal.

> I will put a note by my computer to remind me to follow the rule.
>
> I will use a timer or an app to remind me to rest my eyes when I have been using my screen for too long.
>
> I will find a song verse that I can sing to myself whenever I am looking away from the screen to help me rest my eyes for a full 20 seconds.

STEP 4: Execute your plan and track your progress.

Short-term goal

☒ Met   ☐ Not met   Date: *April 4*

Long-term goal

☐ Met   ☒ Not met   Date: _____

If you met your goal(s), what helped you to be successful?

> Using a note by my computer helped me to rest my eyes when I was studying.

If you did not meet your goal, what made it harder for you to be successful?

> I didn't meet my long-term goal. It was hard to remember to take regular breaks. I couldn't find an app that was easy to use on my phone and had a hard time keeping track of my breaks.

Test Your Knowledge

Select the best answer for each question.

1. Brushing your teeth, washing your face and hands, showering, and trimming your toenails are all examples of
   a. hygiene
   b. consumer health
   c. first aid
   d. contagious disease

2. When the hair follicles on your skin become clogged and infected, you will develop
   a. sunburn
   b. eczema
   c. acne
   d. skin cancer

3. Which of the following might suggest that a mole could be skin cancer?
   a. It stays the same color.
   b. It gets smaller.
   c. It has an unusual shape.
   d. It has a clean edge.

4. Bad breath is called
   a. gingivitis
   b. cold sores
   c. halitosis
   d. tooth decay

5. Blurred vision, double vision, dry eyes, and eye irritation may be signs of
   a. farsightedness
   b. nearsightedness
   c. astigmatism
   d. eye strain

6. When a behavior is so common in a society or group that it is considered standard, or expected, we call it a
   a. social status
   b. social norm
   c. common law
   d. coincidence

7. How many hours of sleep does a teenager need each night?
   a. 14 to 17
   b. 11 to 14
   c. 9 to 12
   d. 8 to 10

8. To help you sleep better at night you should
   a. exercise during the day
   b. set and follow a sleep schedule
   c. relax before bed
   d. all of the above

9. Getting enough good quality sleep each night will help you
   a. maintain alertness and concentration
   b. reduce depression and enhance mood
   c. improve memory and increase alertness
   d. all of the above

10. Which of the following is a consumer right?
    a. getting accurate and easily understood information
    b. being treated with respect
    c. participating in your medical decisions
    d. all of the above

PROJECT-BASED LEARNING: Finding Local Health Resources Project

What to Remember
Being a good health care consumer requires you to find and evaluate products and services.

Who It Is For
The students in your school

Why It Is Important
It is important to help others understand how to find and use health resources. When people can access the information, services, and care they need, the whole community benefits.

What to Do
Research available resources in your community related to the topics covered in this chapter and use your information to help others learn about what resources exist.

How to Do It

1. Form teams of students so that you have at least one team for each of the following focus areas.
   - Oral health
   - Vision
   - Hearing
   - Skin, hair, and nail health
   - Sleep

2. Conduct an online search that will allow you to create a list of as many community resources as you can that provide products or services related to your focus area. Consider medical and health care providers in your area as well as local drugstores and pharmacies that might sell products related to your focus area. Make sure your class agrees on what you are considering your community to be. You might look for services and products within a certain number of miles of your school, or within a neighborhood or town limit. Make sure you consider services at school too. Consider asking other teachers, parents, and adults for recommendations on what to include in your resource list.

3. For each community resource you find, include the address or location, contact information (like a phone number or website address), and a brief description of what services or related products might be available.

4. Type up your resource list and all the required information. Ask your teacher whether they want you to follow a particular format.

5. Share your resources with the other teams and work to create one master list of community resources. If your school has access to websites for you to use, consider making a website that shows off all your information. Finalize your list or website and share it with your school nurse or a doctor.

CROSS-CURRICULAR CONNECTIONS: Math

Read the following scenario and use your math skills to answer the questions about buying personal health care products.

Jolita needs to purchase a few products from the community pharmacy. The total bill for 4 tubes of toothpaste, 4 bottles of shampoo, and 1 jar of lotion is $32. The total bill for 7 tubes of toothpaste, 4 bottles of shampoo, and 1 jar of lotion is $43.25. Calculate the cost of each item if a jar of lotion costs $0.75 more than a bottle of shampoo.

Health Equity and Public Health

3

LESSON 3.1   Understanding Health Equity
LESSON 3.2   Disability and Inclusion
LESSON 3.3   Public Health

Understanding My Health

How Healthy Is My School?

School health services are an important part of public health. This self-assessment asks questions about your school environment and health services. Respond to each statement in the assessment by selecting the response that is most accurate for you. When you are done, add up your points. The closer your score is to 18 the more likely your school is a positive public health influence for you, other students, and your community.

My school . . .	Yes (2 points)	No (0 points)
Has a no-tolerance policy for harassment or bullying		
Has an emergency plan and conducts emergency drills regularly		
Provides a safe and supervised physical environment		
Has a no-tolerance policy for tobacco, alcohol, and drugs on campus		
Has at least one full-time nurse on campus		
Is accessible to those who use wheelchairs or walkers		
Provides counseling and mental health services		
Provides physical education and after-school sports and physical activities		
Provides healthy food options that are affordable and accessible		

My score for How Healthy Is My School? = _____ (total number of points)

This chapter addresses the ways in which differing social and economic factors influence our access to health-related services and how those differences ultimately affect the health of communities and individuals. It includes information on the laws and services that protect and provide for people with disabilities, and it introduces community and public health services that seek to create more equitable health and wellness opportunities.

LESSON 3.1
Understanding Health Equity

Terms to Learn
health disparities
health equity
socioecological model

The Big Picture
Health is a complex idea. Individually we can make decisions that will affect our health every day. We are also influenced by social and economic factors that can make attaining good health relatively harder or easier. Understanding how social and economic factors influence the health outcomes of individuals and communities is essential for being an informed citizen and health advocate.

Learning Targets
- Explain what health equity is.
- Compare and contrast the concepts of equity and equality.
- Describe five major social and economic influences on health.
- Define health disparities and explain how they relate to health equity.

Write About It
Do you think you have the same access to services and opportunities as other people you know when it comes to things that might influence your health? Explain your response.

Note-Taking Guide
Use this chapter's note-taking guide to help you organize and remember the material in this lesson.

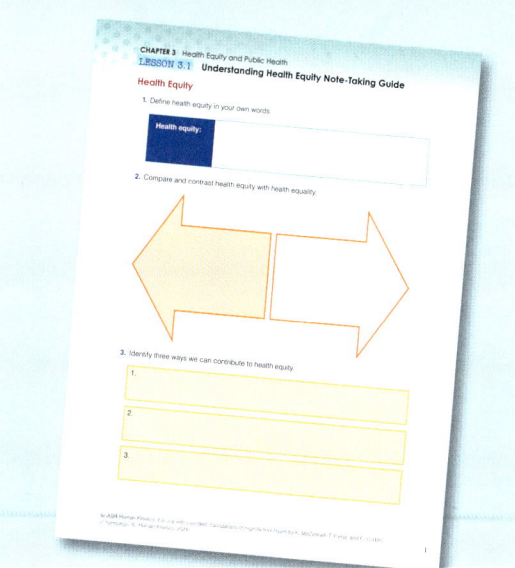

111

LESSON 3.1 Health Equity and Public Health

Damon plays pickup basketball games at the park near his house just about every day. It's usually with a mix of kids from school and a few from the neighborhood, but Damon doesn't know them well enough to hang out together. A while ago, he got some cool high-tops from his uncle, but they've started to wear out, and his feet hurt a lot. Damon lives with his mom and is an only child. She works two jobs, so he doesn't really see her much. It's easy to feel lonely.

Damon wishes he could stay out longer, but he knows it's not safe to be on the court much past five o'clock. His neighborhood is pretty run down, and gang activity has become rampant at night. Damon feels alienated from his friends—many have started using drugs because their community doesn't have anything to offer. There are no boys and girls clubs. What most people take for granted—a nearby grocery store—is not a reality in Damon's community. Most people here get their food from the convenience store attached to the gas station. A lot of them are overweight because they don't eat well, and sometimes his neighbors will tease him for being fit.

Damon likes to play hard and is competitive, but the possibility of getting injured stresses him out all the time. As far as he can tell, there isn't a hospital anywhere nearby. Even if there were, his mom doesn't have medical insurance and can't afford for him to get sick or injured. Of the few times they did go to the doctor, he could tell that the clinic was old and the equipment outdated. It made him wonder whether the medical care he was getting was any good. In what ways is Damon's health possibly influenced by things he can't personally control?

Health Equity

Health equity occurs when everyone has the opportunity to attain full health and wellness, and no one is disadvantaged because of their social position or other socially defined circumstance. Health equity is not the same as equality. *Equity* refers to providing all people equal access and opportunity to achieve good health and quality of life. Equality is not a realistic health goal in most cases because it would mean that all people end up with the same health status or outcome. Since health is complex and influenced by both personal factors and by circumstances, it makes better sense to promote health equity.

Health equity is essential to building a productive and vibrant community and society. Achieving health equity as a society requires that we pay attention to, and do something about, a wide range of related issues and circumstances, such as the following:

- *Creating a culture of health.* This means creating a common understanding and shared systems that allow good health and well-being to flourish for all people. There is a shared value and belief that all people have the right to good health.
- *Attending to the source of health inequities.* This means creating access to safe, affordable housing and quality, affordable health care; eliminating unsafe working conditions and reducing the incidence of poverty-level wages; and providing access to high-quality, free education.
- *Measuring the effect that socioeconomic factors have on health outcomes.* Social factors that are closely tied to economic factors have enormous impacts on a person's health and well-being. Figure 3.1 shows the core social and economic determinants of health.

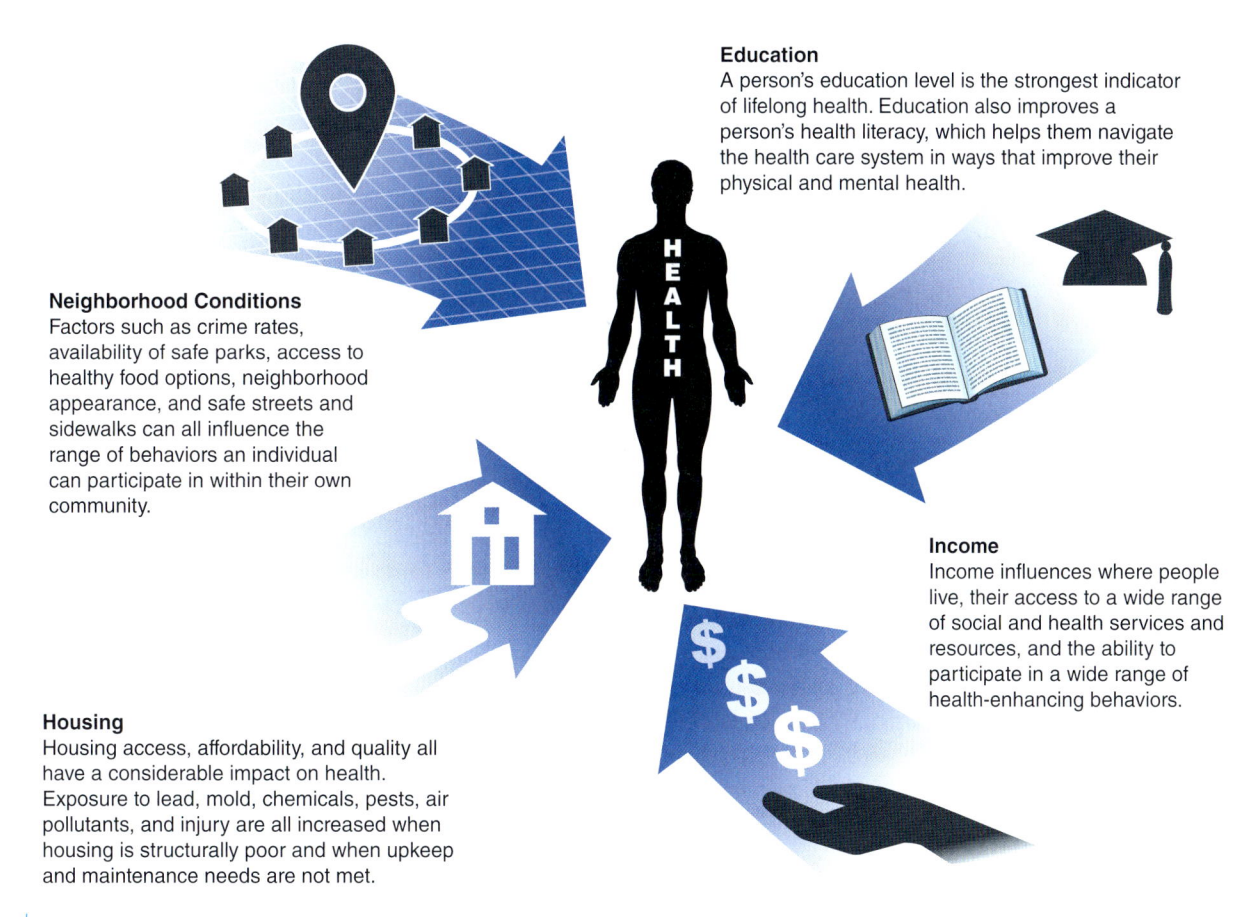

Education
A person's education level is the strongest indicator of lifelong health. Education also improves a person's health literacy, which helps them navigate the health care system in ways that improve their physical and mental health.

Neighborhood Conditions
Factors such as crime rates, availability of safe parks, access to healthy food options, neighborhood appearance, and safe streets and sidewalks can all influence the range of behaviors an individual can participate in within their own community.

Income
Income influences where people live, their access to a wide range of social and health services and resources, and the ability to participate in a wide range of health-enhancing behaviors.

Housing
Housing access, affordability, and quality all have a considerable impact on health. Exposure to lead, mold, chemicals, pests, air pollutants, and injury are all increased when housing is structurally poor and when upkeep and maintenance needs are not met.

Figure 3.1 Social and economic determinants of health.

LESSON 3.1 Health Equity and Public Health

> **HEALTHY LIVING TIP**
> Learn about the free and reduced-cost health services that exist at your school or local health department. Take advantage of those services when and if you need them.

Socioecological Model of Health

While all of us can take responsibility for our individual health choices, not everyone has similar experiences related to the wide range of other factors that have impacts on our health and well-being. The **socioecological model** of health provides a way for us to think about both the individual factors that influence health and also those things we may not personally control that can influence our health (see figure 3.2). For example, when thinking about how health equity issues influence a person's nutrition and physical activity, we could consider differences people might experience related to

- individual behaviors, preferences, and choices regarding diet, gardening and cooking, sports and physical activity, and personal income and socioeconomic status;
- interpersonal influences such as peer pressures, family dietary habits and practices, access to youth sport experiences and the quality of those experiences, and social expectations on weight and eating;
- community influences, including access to farmer's markets, accessible trails and parks, availability of healthy convenience food options, community events that support healthy living, and neighborhood crime and safety concerns;
- organizational influences such as school meal access and quality, recess and physical education policies, access to free community centers, sports and activities, neighborhood grocery store access and food supply, work and school policies related to eating and having active breaks, travel and uniform requirements for youth sport participation, and ease of access to reliable emergency care services; and
- policy influences such as access to government-assisted food programs, taxes on junk foods or soft drinks, food labeling regulations, government agricultural subsidies that influence access and affordability of specific foods, and community planning and tax-based support for developing and maintaining parks and recreation and public lands.

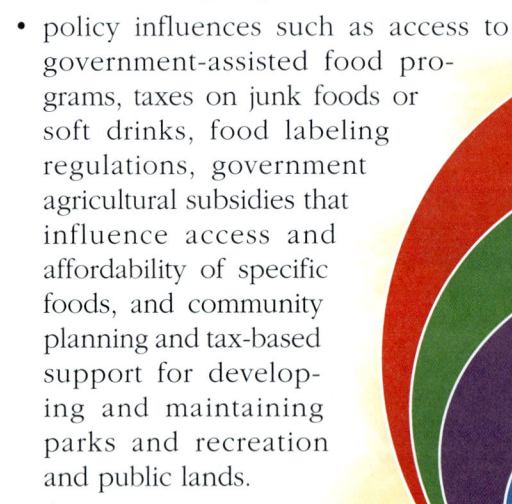

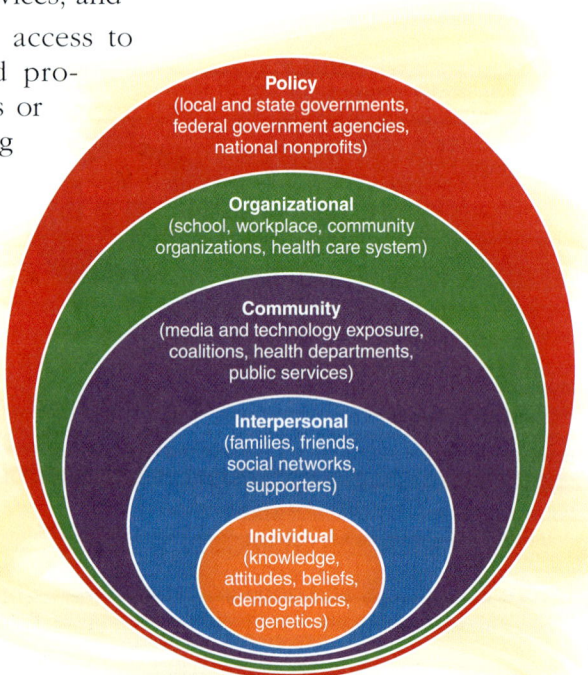

Figure 3.2 Socioecological model of health.

Health Disparities

The goal of health equity is to reduce or eliminate actual **health disparities**. These are preventable differences in health status that are closely linked with social, economic, and environmental disadvantages. Health disparities occur across socioeconomic status, age, geography, language, sex, and disability status. Differences also occur within groups. For example, Hispanic health disparities differ based on time in the country and primary language spoken. In other groups, differences within subgroups exist, such as among Asian Americans and Native American nations.

The following examples are health disparities in the United States:

- **Infant mortality.** Babies born to Black women in the United States are more than two times as likely to die as babies born to white women.
- **Cancer.** People with lower incomes and education levels are more likely to get cancer and to die from it compared to their more affluent peers.
- **Dementia.** Black people have the highest risk for dementia and are twice as likely as white people to develop Alzheimer's disease.
- **Binge drinking.** Young white men are more likely than other groups to binge drink (five or more alcoholic drinks in a two-hour period).

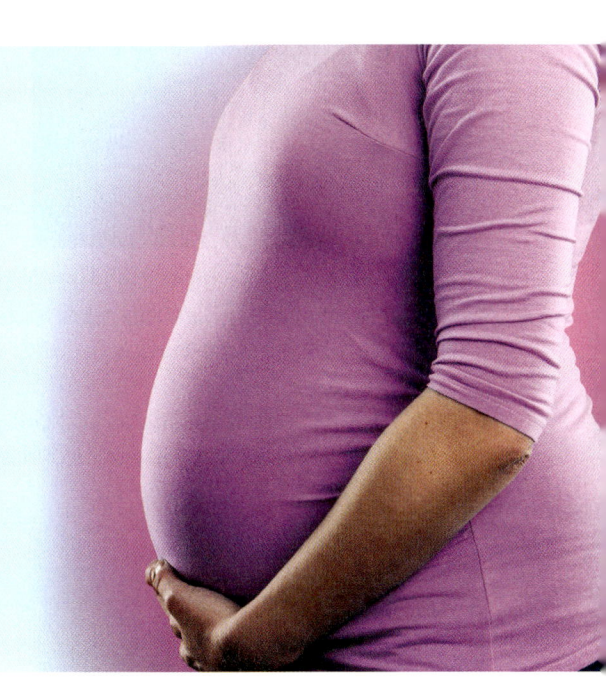

Health disparities affect people at the individual, family, and community levels and can persist across generations. Families can easily slip into the low-income class if a parent becomes too sick to work. Unemployment and low-paying jobs reduce a person's likelihood to have access to health insurance. Between the high cost of living and unaffordable health care options in the United States, many people feel no other choice than to give up medical care. They go to work despite injury or illness because their low-paying jobs don't provide them with paid sick leave. As a result, low-income earners are at higher risk for developing a debilitating health condition that impedes their ability to work. Children from impoverished families are also less likely to persist in school or to go to college and may remain in poverty.

A mother's health and well-being before and during pregnancy also have a major impact on her baby's health. Chronic stress, smoking, consumption of alcohol during pregnancy, and poor prenatal nutrition all contribute to the increased chance of having a preterm baby. Babies born too early are at greater risk for developing serious health issues later in life, including having preterm babies themselves. As a result, generations can continue to suffer similar health disparities as those who came before them.

LESSON 3.1   Health Equity and Public Health

CASE STUDY

Cara and Natalie's Contrasting Realities

Cara

My name is Cara. I live in rural Tennessee. My family has lived in the same community for as long as I know. My great-grandma came here from Mississippi, and all of my relatives have stayed nearby. Our township is small. We have one corner store and a post office. There's a doctor who comes to town and makes house calls once a week, but the nearest hospital is 40 miles (60 km) away, and the closest pharmacy is in the next town over.

People in town use a lot of family recipes to help with things like colds, flu, or small injuries, and most folks just don't bother going to see a doctor unless it is really serious. When I was young, I broke my wrist. We tore up an old pillow case and used a board from the shed to splint it. It healed up, but my wrist is a bit crooked, and I can't move it as well as the other side. It's hard to type or write. I tried to get a job to help out, but working the cash register was too painful. I live with my mom and dad, grandparents, and three siblings in our two-bedroom house. My dad works odd jobs to earn money, but mom has a disability from an accident and can't work anymore. We only have one car, so someone has to drive Dad to and from work each day. I miss a lot of school because I miss the bus if my dad is running late.

Natalie

My name is Natalie. I live in Anaheim, California, with my parents and younger brother. My dad is a teacher, and my mom runs an insurance company. I've had the same family doctor my whole life, and I've never really been that sick. We have great health insurance, so no one worries too much. I did break my ankle once when I was playing in a soccer game, but I can't even remember that really. I wore a cast and had a few weeks of physical therapy.

I love where I live and have lots of friends. We use rideshares and sometimes take the bus to go wherever we want. Between my soccer club, swim team, and trips to the beach, it seems like there is always something to do. My parents gave me a cell phone, so I feel safe and connected all of the time. I have some cousins in town, but the rest of the family lives in other places. We go to visit my grandparents in Arizona every Christmas, and we all took a trip to Hawaii last year. I have a job working at a local fast food chain, but I don't need to work too many hours. My parents want me to focus on school and sports so that I can get into a private college and join a team.

Think About It

1. How do Cara and Natalie's circumstances differ, and how do these factors affect health equity?
2. What socioeconomic influences affect Cara and Natalie in their current circumstances?
3. How might these influences continue to affect their health later in life?

Eliminating Health Disparities

Government policies and efforts designed to reduce health disparities focus on designated priority populations and marginalized groups. When an individual or group is marginalized, it means a system or circumstance has overlooked them or left them out, and they may become disadvantaged as a result. Marginalized groups and priority populations relative to public health services often include people of color, low-income populations, women, children and adolescents, older adults, individuals with specialized health care needs, and individuals living in rural and inner-city areas. These priority designations intersect in meaningful ways. For example, the disparities seen among children of color living in low-income, urban neighborhoods may differ from those of older adults with special health care needs who live in rural areas. For this reason, there is no single approach that will work to eliminate all health inequities and disparities. Addressing disparities in health and health care is important to improving the nation's overall health, workforce, and economic prosperity.

Skill-Building Challenge

Analyzing Influences

Use the socioecological model to analyze determinants on your health. Explain how individual, interpersonal, community, organizational, and policy influences affect your health status related to each of the following:

- My physical activity
- My diet
- My mental health
- My social health

When you are finished, reflect on the following questions:

- Which influence has the greatest impact on your physical activity?
- Which influence on your diet is the most difficult to change?
- What could you do to improve the interpersonal influences on your mental health?
- How does your community influence your social health?

Healthy Living Skills

This lesson focused on analyzing influences on your health. Here are some more healthy living skills related to this lesson.

ADVOCATING FOR GOOD HEALTH

Consider the geographic area you live in and identify a neighborhood, town, or community nearby that has a very different reality than yours when it comes to socioecological impacts on health. Explain how your community and the community you chose differ in terms of health equity. Determine what public health services exist in the two communities. Consider any other differences you might be aware of as well (for example, housing, parks, and education; access and availability of hospitals and medical services). Write a short letter that could be sent to a local or state government official advocating for more health equity between your community and the one you selected (for example, a city councilperson or a state representative).

LESSON 3.1 Review: Understanding Health Equity

LESSON SUMMARY

- Health equity occurs when everyone has the opportunity to attain full health and wellness, and no one is disadvantaged because of their social position or other socially defined circumstance.
- Several social and economic factors influence health equity including education, income, and housing and neighborhood conditions.
- The socioecological model of health provides a way for us to think about the individual, interpersonal, community, organizational, and policy influences that affect our health and our opportunities for health equity.
- Health disparities are actual differences in health status or are the outcomes that can occur due to inequities.

REVIEWING CONCEPTS AND VOCABULARY

1. Health _____ is achieved when no one is disadvantaged due to their social position or circumstances.
2. Creating a(n) _____ of health means there is a shared value and belief that all people have the right to good health.
3. A person's _____ level is the number one predictor of their life-long health.
4. Crime rates, availability of safe parks, access to healthy food options, neighborhood appearance, and safe streets and sidewalks are examples of _____ conditions that might influence a person's health.
5. The goal of health equity is to reduce or eliminate actual health _____, or differences in health status.

THINKING CRITICALLY

Marginalized groups often experience poorer health than others due to bias and discrimination. Why might life circumstances affect health outcomes? Explain your response.

TAKE IT HOME

Talk to a parent or guardian about how community and organizations might be influencing their health and the health of the family. Identify the influences as positive or negative.

LESSON 3.2
Disability and Inclusion

Terms to Learn
disability
disability inclusion
impairment
reasonable accommodation
universal design

The Big Picture
One in four adults, or 61 million Americans, lives with some form of disability. Disabilities are even more common as we age. They influence the health and quality of life for individuals and the larger society, and attending to the rights and needs of individuals with disabilities is a public health issue. The health of a community benefits when all individuals in that community are able to reach their full potential. Learning important concepts such as reasonable accommodations and universal design can help you to be inclusive of those with disabilities.

Learning Targets
- Compare and contrast disabilities and impairments.
- Describe what reasonable accommodations are and explain why they are important.
- Analyze how universal design improves environments, products, and services.

Write About It
When was the last time you interacted with a person who had a visible disability? Did you feel confident and comfortable in your ability to communicate effectively? Describe the situation.

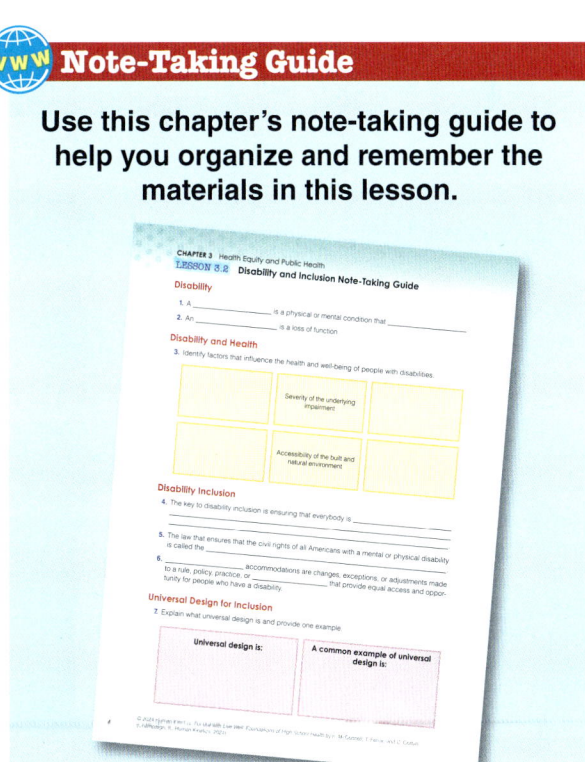

Note-Taking Guide
Use this chapter's note-taking guide to help you organize and remember the materials in this lesson.

LESSON 3.2   Health Equity and Public Health

Manaia is visually impaired. He loves to listen to music and go to the local pool with his family. He is outgoing, happy, and friendly. His sister Maddie plays on a youth soccer team. Manaia always liked trying to pass the ball with her in their yard growing up, but he never had the opportunity to play.

When he got to middle school, he found out that there was a Unified soccer team at the school, and he was excited to join. He was a little nervous because he never learned the rules of the game, and he was not sure if he would be able to see the ball well enough to kick it accurately. When he got to the first practice, he learned that the game was played with a bright yellow ball and that the goals were a little larger than usual. His teammates would also call his name if the ball was coming his way. Manaia realized that he loved playing and even scored a couple of goals. He loves playing soccer because he feels included and no one on his team makes him feel like he is different. He hates it when people assume he isn't capable of being smart or athletic or when they feel sorry for him. He wishes the whole world were as welcoming and supportive as his soccer team is. What do you think it would be like to live with a disability? What parts of Manaia's story can you relate to? Why?

Disability

Unlike disease or illness, a **disability** is a physical or mental condition that limits a person's movements, senses, or activities. There are a wide range of disabilities, and two people with the same disability can be affected in very different ways. Some disabilities are visible to others, while some are hidden or not as visibly apparent. Disabilities can be intellectual, emotional, or physical. Some disabilities are present at birth, like Down syndrome. Others are related to development, like autism spectrum disorder and attention deficit hyperactivity disorder. Finally, disabilities caused by trauma or illness can occur at any time in life.

An **impairment** is the loss of function that occurs with a disability. Impairments affect a wide variety of functions (see figure 3.3).

LESSON 3.2 — Disability and Inclusion

Type of impairment	How to help when interacting with an impaired person
Visual impairments include complete blindness and other problems seeing. Disease, trauma, or genetics may cause visual impairments.	• Avoid startling the person. • Speak clearly and use clear descriptions when talking. • Remember, the person cannot see where you are pointing or looking. • Do not touch the person without permission.
Emotional impairments can include a wide range of conditions (read more in the chapters on mental and emotional health). Some emotional impairments are serious, and some can result in dangerous behaviors.	Use a calm, steady approach to interactions.
Hearing impairments are somewhat common, especially as people get older.	• Stand where the person can see you in case they are able to read your lips. • Speak slowly and clearly and do not shout.
Mobility impairments make it hard or impossible to move some part or parts of the body. Diseases, birth defects, and trauma can all cause mobility impairments.	• When an individual with a physical impairment is in a wheelchair, squat down when speaking to them. • Be patient and move only as quickly as the individual with the mobility impairment can.
Cognitive impairments impact how a person processes information. There are a wide range of these impairments. Individuals with dementia, brain injury, or Down syndrome have cognitive impairments.	Be patient and be willing to repeat yourself when interacting with individuals who have cognitive impairments.

Figure 3.3 Common types of impairments.

Disability and Health

People with disabilities can lead long, healthy, and productive lives. Yet, disabilities can result in significant disadvantages when it comes to health. For example, adults with disabilities are three times more likely to have heart disease, stroke, type 2 diabetes, or cancer than adults without disabilities. Several factors can influence the health and well-being of a person who has a disability:

- Severity of the underlying impairment
- Level of independence with activities of daily living
- Social, political, and cultural influences and expectations
- Accessibility of the built and natural environment
- Access to assistive technology, devices, and services
- Degree of family and community support and engagement

Disability Inclusion

People with disabilities are entitled to the same rights and opportunities as everyone else in the population. **Disability inclusion** involves understanding the relationship between the way people function and how they are able to participate in society and then making appropriate adjustments as a result. The key to inclusion is ensuring that everybody is afforded equal opportunities to participate in all aspects of life to the best of their abilities and desires. From a legal perspective, the Americans With Disabilities Act (ADA) ensures the civil rights of all Americans with a mental or physical disability—including disabilities that emerge from a chronic disease such as cancer or diabetes. The ADA guarantees equal opportunity in employment, public services, public transportation, public accommodations, and communication. A similar law, the Individuals With Disabilities Education Act, ensures equal opportunity in education.

Accommodations

We can provide opportunities for people with disabilities by guaranteeing reasonable accommodations that help people overcome the limitations they may face. **Reasonable accommodations** are changes, exceptions, or adjustments made to a rule, policy, practice, or service that provide equal access and opportunity for people who have a disability. The need can vary even among people with the same type of impairment. The following lists examples of accommodations:

- Installing a ramp or modifying a restroom or public facility
- Providing screen reader software for workers or students
- Using videophones to facilitate communications with deaf individuals
- Providing sign language interpreters or closed captioning in class, at meetings, or at events
- Modifying a policy to allow a service animal in a business or school setting
- Adjusting work schedules to allow employees with chronic medical conditions to go to medical appointments and complete their work at alternate times or locations

Accommodations can be physical, mental or emotional, academic, religious, or related to employment and are often mandated by law. They provide opportunities for all people to learn and apply knowledge, engage in daily tasks like self-care and domestic chores, and develop meaningful social relationships. Accommodations also provide opportunities for everyone to participate fully in employment as well as in recreation, community, and civic activities.

HEALTHY LIVING TIP

Volunteer with Special Olympics or another local organization that offers adapted sports and activities for people with disabilities.

Universal Design for Inclusion

Another approach to inclusion is implementing **universal design** (UD). This means creating and designing maximally accessible, understandable, and useful environments—or any buildings, products, or services within an environment—for all people regardless of their age, size, ability, or disability. An example of UD that we encounter every day is a curb cut or ramp at intersections and sidewalk corners. This simple design not only allows people with a range of physical abilities to navigate moving through a city or neighborhood safely and easily but also assists those who might be biking, pushing a stroller, or running.

Having its roots in the field of architecture, universal design now extends across an array of social sectors, including information technology and education. By applying UD principles to our designs, we are able to provide a greater quality of life for all people (see figure 3.4).

UD Principles

1 Equitable use
The design is useful and marketable to people with diverse abilities.

2 Flexibility in use
The design accommodates a wide range of individual preferences and abilities.

3 Simple and intuitive use
Use of the design is easy to understand, regardless of the user's experience, knowledge, language skills, or current concentration level.

4 Perceptible information
The design communicates necessary information effectively to the user, regardless of ambient conditions or the user's sensory abilities.

5 Tolerance for error
The design minimizes hazards and the adverse consequences of accidental or unintended actions.

6 Low physical effort
The design can be used efficiently and comfortably and with minimal fatigue.

7 Size and space for approach and use
Appropriate size and space are provided for approach, reach, manipulation, and use regardless of the user's body size, posture, or mobility.

Figure 3.4 Seven principles of universal design.

LESSON 3.2   Health Equity and Public Health

Diversity Matters

Living With a Disability

Jess was born with spina bifida and has to use leg braces and a walker. If the path is clear, she can get around just fine; even outside, she moves with ease as long as there are ramps and sidewalk cutouts. As a young child, she didn't face many difficulties related to her disability because her parents homeschooled her and she was able to play and interact with her older siblings. Now that her siblings have gone off to college, though, Jess's parents have decided to end the homeschooling and send her to public high school.

Jess was excited about the idea at first, but that soon gave way to anxieties she never had to experience before. Since she can't drive herself, she has to take the bus to school. It involves having someone to lift her up and down the steps because the bus isn't equipped with a lift system. Jess has to keep her walker folded up as she walks down the aisle. This means she has to use the back of the seats to stabilize herself. It's rough. The other kids basically ignore her, but a handful do tease her. It makes her self-conscious about how long it takes to get to an open seat. Jess hates riding the bus.

Once she is at school, things are a little better. Most of the classrooms are easy to get to, and her teachers assigned her the desk closest to the door, which helps. Jess's friend Andy carries her books for her sometimes, and people usually give her enough space to walk in the hallways. Still, Jess doesn't have many friends, and most people seem to think she different. Aside from how she walks, Jess knows she's a typical teenager and just wishes the other kids would get to know her better.

What accommodations could help Jess with getting to and from school? In what ways do you relate to Jess's story? What might it be like for you if you had a disability that impeded your mobility?

Disability and Inclusion **LESSON 3.2**

Skill-Building Challenge

Accessing Reliable Information

Select one of the mobility disabilities listed below.

- ☐ Amputation
- ☐ Paralysis
- ☐ Cerebral palsy
- ☐ Stroke
- ☐ Multiple sclerosis
- ☐ Muscular dystrophy
- ☐ Arthritis
- ☐ Spinal cord injury

Research the disability using information from at least three different sources. Use the Accessing Valid and Reliable Information Skill Cues for finding valid and reliable sources. Write a summary of your findings and be sure to include the following information:

- A description of the condition or disability and how it affects mobility and independence
- Statistics related to the disability, including differences by sex, age, or race that might exist
- Accommodations that may be needed to support the health equity and quality of life of the person with the condition or disability
- Common misunderstandings people may have about the condition or disability

Healthy Living Skills

This lesson taught you about accessing reliable information. Here is one more way you can develop healthy living skills related to this lesson.

HEALTHY COMMUNICATION
Imagine a situation where you might be interacting with someone who is deaf or hard of hearing and role-play how you would interact. Be sure to understand what is and isn't beneficial when communicating with that person. Repeat the process for someone who is blind or has a visual impairment.

LESSON 3.2 Review: Disability and Inclusion

LESSON SUMMARY

- A disability is unlike a disease or an illness. A person with a disability has some loss of function somewhere in their body.
- Impairments, which are losses in function that occur with a disability, can be visual, audial, mobility, cognitive, or emotional.
- Many factors can influence the health and well-being of a person with a disability such as severity of the impairment, level of independence a person maintains, social and cultural influences, accessibility of environment and technology, and the degree of support the person has.
- Disability inclusion is a process of first determining the relationship between the way a person functions and their ability to participate in society and then making a reasonable accommodation, or appropriate adjustment to the system, to address a person's need.
- Universal design is the process of creating and designing an environment (or the products, services, or spaces within) so that all people can access, understand, and use it to the greatest possible degree.

REVIEWING CONCEPTS AND VOCABULARY

1. A person with a(n) _____ has some loss of function somewhere in the body.
2. A(n) _____ is the loss of function that results from a disability.
3. Factors that can influence the health of individuals with disabilities include the degree of _____ the person has from others.
4. The Americans with Disabilities Act ensures that people with disabilities receive _____ accommodations.
5. _____ design is the creation and design of an environment and the products and services in it that are used by the most people to the greatest degree possible.

THINKING CRITICALLY

Analyze your environment from the perspective of someone who uses a wheelchair, someone who is blind, and someone who has limited use of their hands (cannot do small movements easily). Make a list of activities that would prove to be challenging for each person and propose as many reasonable accommodations as possible to assist them.

TAKE IT HOME

Search your home to find a product (e.g., a remote control) or design element (e.g., a doorknob or lock) that would be difficult for some segments of the population to use. Come up with a new design for the product, or create a new product, that is more universally accessible. Review the seven principles of universal design when creating your design. Explain your design in writing and include diagrams or images as needed.

LESSON 3.3
Public Health

Terms to Learn
community health
epidemiologists
pandemic
primary prevention
public health
secondary prevention
tertiary prevention

The Big Picture
Have you ever wondered who inspects your local restaurants for cleanliness? Who tracks outbreaks of illnesses like measles? Who makes decisions about which vaccinations you were required to get to attend school? These are all public and community health issues. Learning what resources are available to you and others in your community is an important step in becoming and staying healthy.

Learning Targets
- Use examples to explain public and community health services.
- Explain how public health influences you individually.
- Describe two careers related to public health.
- Compare and contrast the three different levels of prevention.
- Advocate for public health services.

Write About It
What health services do you think should be available at your school? Identify and explain at least two different ideas.

Note-Taking Guide
Use this chapter's note-taking guide to help you organize and remember the material in this lesson.

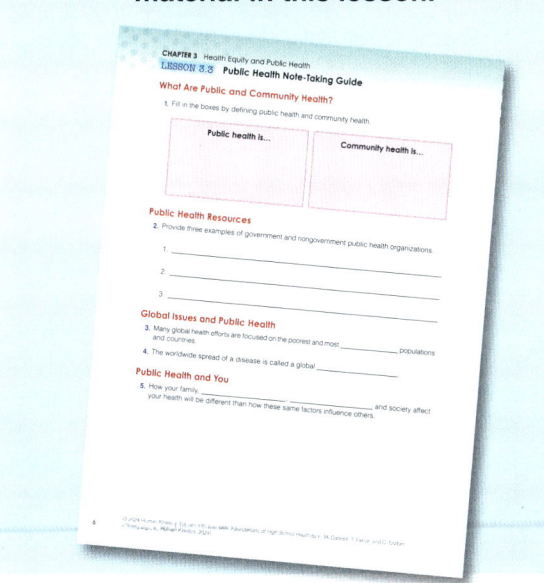

127

LESSON 3.3 Health Equity and Public Health

Luis grew up in Mexico and then moved to the United States when he was 14 years old. He never had vaccinations because he was homeschooled as a kid. He was told that he would not be admitted to a public high school until he received all of his vaccinations. Worse yet, his parents didn't have health insurance, and they couldn't afford for Luis or his brothers to get the shots.

Fortunately, the school nurse suggested that Luis and his family visit the local public health clinic. The clinic offered free vaccinations to children under 16 and provided other medical services at reduced prices. Luis was grateful for the service and was excited to start at his new school. What types of services do you think Luis experienced when he visited the public health clinic?

What Are Public and Community Health?

Public health is the art and science of protecting and improving the health of individuals and large populations. Public health happens at the national, regional, state, and local levels. **Community health** is a term often used to describe public health efforts that focus on a particular group of people in a specific geographic area like a neighborhood, town, or country. This lesson uses the term *public health* to include both community and public health efforts. Public health involves a wide range of activities including the following:

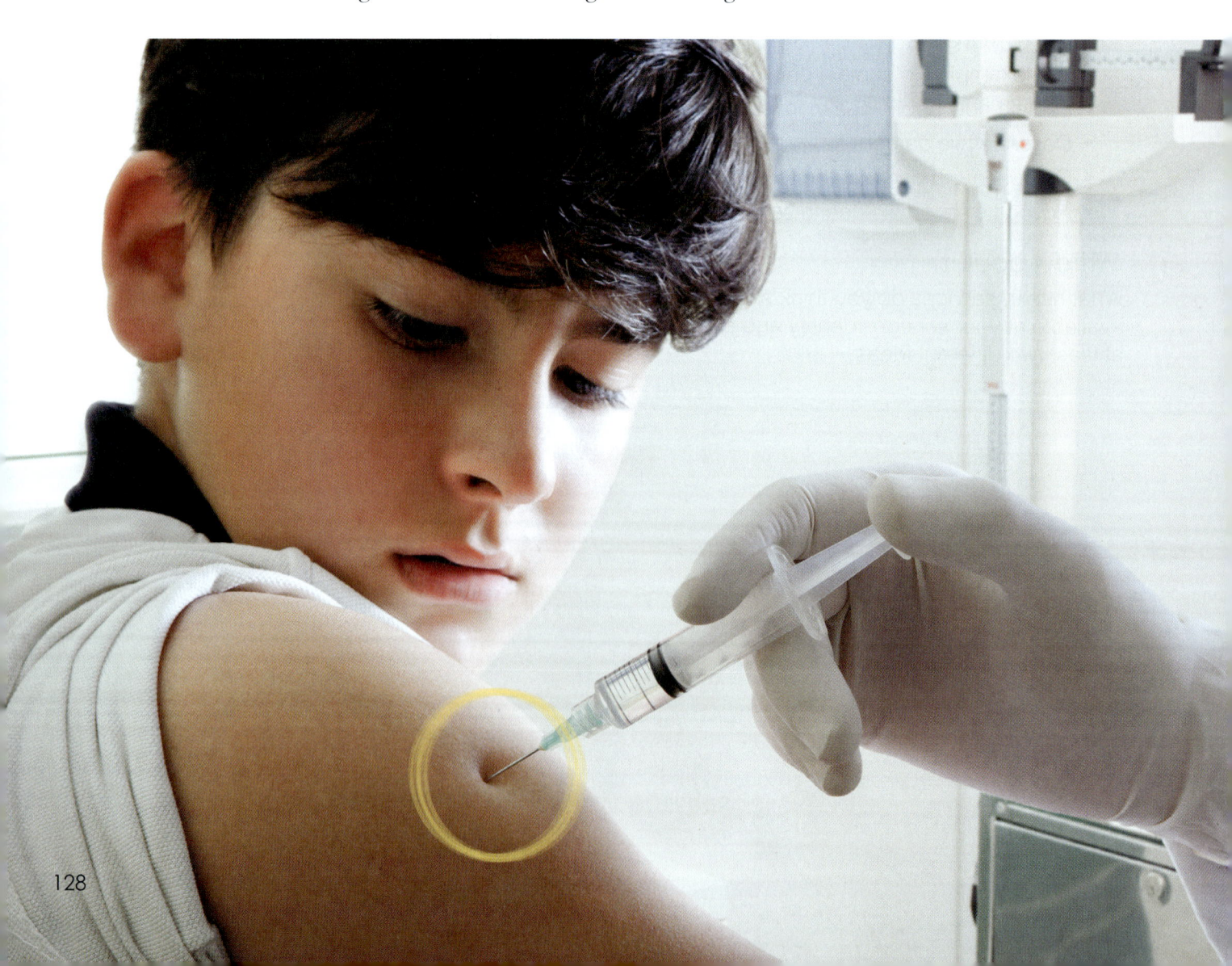

- Educating people through public service announcements, educational websites, community safety, and first aid classes
- Investigating outbreaks of diseases carried in the food supply, like salmonella, and contagious disease outbreaks, like COVID-19
- Monitoring communities by tracking rates of injury, illness, and disease in a community
- Developing policies such as establishing public no-smoking zones and identifying required vaccinations needed for school attendance
- Enforcing laws for things like food handling and serving laws in restaurants or policing convenience stores to make sure they aren't selling alcohol or tobacco products to minors
- Conducting research to establish connections between behaviors and noncommunicable diseases or between pollution and cancer risk
- Responding to disasters by organizing assistance to survivors after a natural disaster, like a hurricane, or a violent event, like a mass shooting or terrorist attack
- Providing preventative services such as free or reduced-cost vaccination clinics or cancer screenings
- Providing accessible services such as free treatment for drug addiction and mental health counseling or building and operating community-use sport complexes or fitness facilities

Public Health Resources

Public health resources exist at different levels and provide different services. The major government provider of public health oversight in the United States is the Centers for Disease Control and Prevention, or the CDC. The CDC is part of the Department of Health and Human Services. The CDC website maintains current, factually accurate public health information on a wide range of topics. Other government and nongovernment agencies also provide public health services (see table 3.1). Government agencies include state and local health departments, which are vital to community health. Nongovernment agencies such as the American Red Cross also play a vital role in public health.

TABLE 3.1 Examples of Government and Nongovernment Public Health Organizations

Government agencies	Nongovernment agencies
Centers for Disease Control and Prevention	World Health Organization
Health and Human Services	American Public Health Organization
National Institutes of Health	Doctors Without Borders
Indian Health Services	World Bank
Food and Drug Administration	The Carter Center
Division of Adolescent and School Health	Bill and Melinda Gates Foundation
State health departments	American Red Cross
Local health departments	National Kidney Foundation
City health departments	

LESSON 3.3 Health Equity and Public Health

School Health Services

Public schools are active members of public and community health. Schools provide free and reduced breakfast and lunch programs that are essential to providing adequate nutrition to a large number of underserved children. Schools may also provide nursing services that include free vaccinations as well as mental health counseling services. Curriculum in schools, including both health and physical education, can also play a vital role in the overall health knowledge and health behaviors of students.

> **HEALTHY LIVING TIP**
>
> Research locations you hope or plan to travel to someday and find out what public health issues might affect your travel. Consider vaccination requirements for entering the country as well as health risks associated with being at the location. Make a list of items to travel with and keep it in a location where you will think to look for it when packing for a trip.

Global Issues and Public Health

Global public health examines the issues that cross borders and affect the health of people around the world. It most often focuses on preventing illness and disease, but it can also include traditional areas of medicine and rehabilitation (see figure 3.5). Many global health efforts are concentrated on the poorest and most underserved populations and countries.

Global health is important because societies have become mobile. When people travel to other countries, their vulnerability to the diseases and risks in that country can have major consequences upon their return home. Some diseases and threats they may have encountered can travel back with them, putting local communities at risk. For example, influenza and coronavirus are highly contagious diseases that can easily travel with people across the globe. Just one person who is sick can infect a new region of the world. When this happens, a global **pandemic**, or worldwide spread of a disease, can occur.

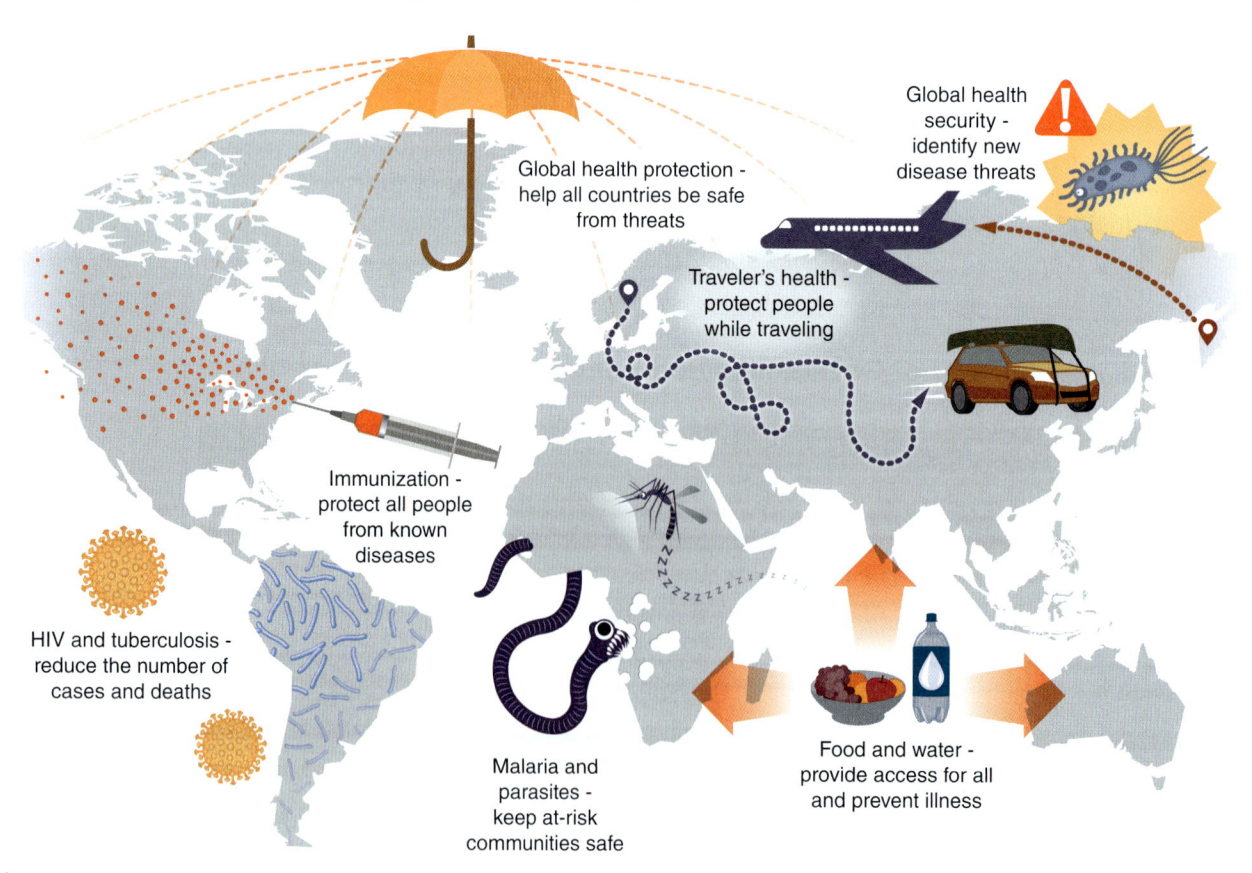

Figure 3.5 Major global health issues.

Public Health and You

Public health is a big idea that may seem unrelated to your personal health. As the socioecological model shows, your individual health is not only a function of the actions you take. It is also affected by the people around you, the community you live in, the society you live in, and the policy and rules that govern it. For example, your diet is a function of the choices you make, but these choices are affected or directed by the food you have access to, how safely you can store or prepare food, the preferences of others who might be providing your food, the influence that culture and social expectations and rules have on your food options, and even laws that might make buying certain foods easier or more difficult. It is impossible for your health not to be influenced by what is happening around you.

When you are thinking about the health of other individuals, it is important to remember that they are also influenced by these factors. How your family, friends, community, and society affect your health may be very different from how these same factors influence others (see figure 3.6).

Figure 3.6 As an individual, you are surrounded by public health influences.

Health Promotion and Prevention

Another way to view public health efforts is through the lens of health promotion and disease prevention. Public health efforts fall into three categories based on the type of prevention they seek: primary, secondary, and tertiary (see figure 3.7). **Primary prevention** includes actions and services that reduce risk and avoid health problems—for example, efforts to keep underage people from drinking. **Secondary prevention** involves recognizing risks for (or beginnings of) problems and intervening before serious illness or effects arise. One example is an educational program aimed at college students who engage in social drinking; the goal is to help young people understand the risks of drinking and avoid becoming alcoholics.

LESSON 3.3 — Health Equity and Public Health

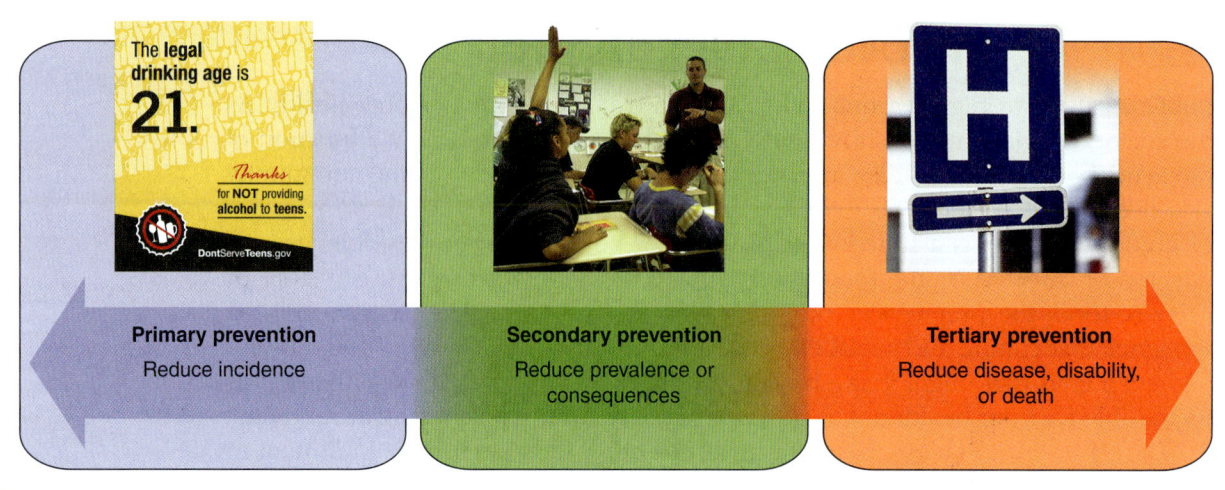

Figure 3.7 Levels of prevention in public health.

Primary prevention — Reduce incidence
Secondary prevention — Reduce prevalence or consequences
Tertiary prevention — Reduce disease, disability, or death

Finally, **tertiary prevention** is best thought of as the prevention of death. It involves treatment and rehabilitation of a person who is already sick, such as someone who's being treated for liver damage due to a lifetime of alcohol abuse. As you might expect, public health efforts are most effective at the primary and secondary levels of prevention.

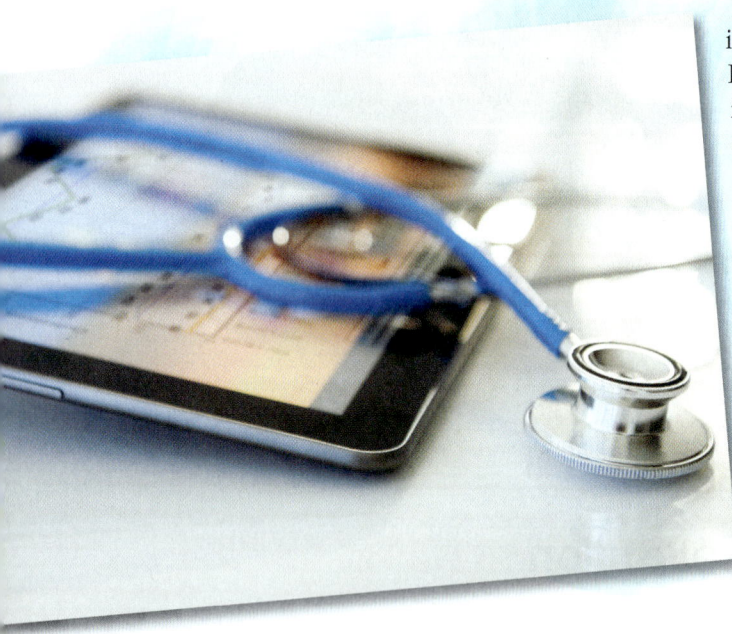

One major public health goal is to reduce both the incidence and the prevalence of disease and disability. Incidence refers to the number of new cases that occur in a year. Prevalence refers to the number of existing cases. **Epidemiologists** are public health workers who track and study both the incidence and the prevalence of diseases, disabilities, and related health behaviors. Tracking the incidence rate of a communicable disease, for example, can help public health officials determine whether there is an epidemic—a widespread occurrence of an infectious disease in a community at a particular time.

Following the prevalence of a disease over time can also help officials determine how effective public health interventions are. For example, studying how positive health behaviors (e.g., healthy eating and regular physical activity) affect disease rates and quality of life can help us better understand and promote the benefits associated with these behaviors.

HEALTHY LIVING TIP
Donate your time to a local charity that is devoted to a public health cause. Helping others through charity work has been shown to benefit a person's overall health.

Careers in Public and Community Health

Health care is the largest employment category in the United States. Health care includes providers like doctors, dentists, and nurses. Public and community health workers are also part of the health care industry. Jobs in public and community health are wide ranging, and most require at minimum an undergraduate college degree, while others require graduate education (see table 3.2).

TABLE 3.2 Examples of Careers in Public and Community Health

Career	Description	Requirements
Epidemiologist	Researches and investigates patterns of disease	Typically at least a master's degree in public health or a related field
Social worker	Provides counseling and assistance to people in need (e.g., children, veterans, older adults, people experiencing homelessness)	A minimum of a bachelor's degree from an accredited social work program
Public health nurse	Focuses on working to improve the health of a specific group or community	A minimum of a bachelor's degree in nursing
Microbiologist	Researches microorganisms with the goal of developing drugs to fight infectious diseases	A bachelor's degree in microbiology to enter the field and a PhD to work as a researcher or at a college or university
Public health educator	Provides education to a community in order to promote health or prevent the spread of disease	A minimum of a bachelor's degree in health education or public health
Public health analyst	Gathers and tracks data about public health activities and programs to determine their effectiveness	A minimum of a bachelor's degree in public health, health analytics, or a related field
Health inspector	Ensures that state laws and sanitary codes are followed in a community	Varied pathways including on-the-job training (technicians) and a bachelor's degree in occupational health and safety (specialists)

Career Connection

NURSE PRACTITIONER

Nurse practitioners (NPs) are licensed medical professionals who manage people's health conditions and are a vital part of public health services. The majority of NPs work as family nurse practitioners. This means that they provide general care and often give vaccinations and treat infectious diseases. Nurse practitioners can specialize by the type of patient they see. For example, they may work only with children or only with older adults. NPs may also specialize in areas of medicine like dermatology (skin), cardiovascular health, and oncology (cancer treatment). Most NPs have a graduate degree in nursing. The first steps to becoming a NP are to graduate from high school and then attend a four-year college before going to graduate school.

LESSON 3.3   Health Equity and Public Health

Skill-Building Challenge

Accessing Community Health Resources

Find three to five online resources in your community that relate to community and public health. Write down the name of the resource and describe what services each resource provides. Record a phone number, an email address, or a web address for each resource. A few major categories are provided to help you get ideas of what to look for.

- Public health department for the city or county you live in
- Public health department for the state you live in
- Local chapters of the American Red Cross or the American Heart Association
- County hospitals
- Women's and children's health clinics
- Health clinic at your school or school district
- Social and health services department for the city or county you live in
- Catholic or other church-related health services in your community
- Community and senior recreation or wellness centers in your city or town

Share your list of resources with your classmates. As a class, create one comprehensive and organized list of resources. Develop a brochure, flyer, or web page that you can provide to your school counselor and nurse as a resource.

Healthy Living Skills

This lesson focused on accessing valid and reliable information. Here is one more way you can develop healthy living skills related to this lesson.

ANALYZING INFLUENCES

Research your school's rules and policies about health by talking to school administrators and your school nurse to identify which ones exist. Consider things like vaccination requirements, physical and health education requirements, food services, counseling services, tobacco and vaping policies, antibullying rules, and recycling and other environmental health policies. Explain how each rule and policy might influence your personal health and well-being.

LESSON 3.3 Review: Public Health

LESSON SUMMARY

- Public health is the art and science of protecting and improving the health of individuals and large populations. Public health happens at the national, regional, state, and local levels.
- Community health is a form of public health that is focused on a particular group of people or geographic area.
- Global public health examines the issues that cross borders and affect the health of people worldwide.
- Your individual health is affected by the people around you, the community you live in, the society you live in, and the policy and rules that govern it.
- Public and community health services seek to reduce the incidence (number of new cases) and prevalence (total number of cases) of disease in the population through primary (preventing occurrence), secondary (preventing severity), and tertiary (preventing death) prevention.
- Many job opportunities related to public health exist. Social worker, public health educator, and health inspector are a few examples.

REVIEWING CONCEPTS AND VOCABULARY

1. Public health seeks to protect and improve the health of individuals and _____.
2. _____ health focuses on a segment of people or specific area.
3. The _____ of a disease is the number of new cases of the disease over a specified time period.
4. Issues that cross international borders and affect the health of people around the world are a part of _____ public health.
5. When you do something to prevent a disease from ever starting, you are engaged in _____ prevention.
6. The worldwide spread of a disease is called a(n) _____.

THINKING CRITICALLY

We know that people who have more education generally have better health. Why do you think that is the case? Provide as many reasons as you can think of and use specific examples when you can.

TAKE IT HOME

Research a global health issue. Start by visiting the website of the World Health Organization to help you identify an issue of particular interest. Gather information and report the types of actions being taken to help reduce or eliminate the disease, threat, or condition.

Chapter Review

ACTION PLAN: Improving My Understanding of Health Equity

Use the My Action Plan worksheet to practice understanding the challenges of having a disability. Here is an example.

My Action Plan: Health Equity

STEP 1: Identify the health behavior you are going to work on.

I want to learn more about different disabilities and understand how they affect people.

STEP 2: Write SMART goal(s).

Write one or two short-term goals (one day to one month long).

I will identify six common disabilities and research basic information about each.

Write a long-term goal (one to six months or more).

I will interview at least one person with one of the disabilities I identified to better understand how the disability affects their life.

STEP 3: Make a plan.

Identify at least two to five action steps (strategies) you could do to meet your goal.

Research the most common disabilities in the United States to inform my selection.

Find at least three valid websites to inform my learning on each disability.

Identify people I know who might have a disability.

Talk to friends and family members to see what experiences they have had with people with disabilities at work, at school, or in the family.

Create questions to ask someone about living with a disability.

STEP 4: Execute your plan and track your progress.

Short-term goal

☒ Met   ☐ Not met   Date: *December 1*

Long-term goal

☒ Met   ☐ Not met   Date: *April 30*

If you met your goal, what helped you to be successful?

I was able to research six different disabilities using the skills I learned in health class.

If you did not meet your goal, what things made it harder for you to be successful?

I was uncomfortable interviewing someone I didn't know who had a disability. I interviewed a close family member instead.

Test Your Knowledge

Select the best answer for each question.

1. When everyone has the opportunity to attain full health and wellness, it is called
   a. health equality
   b. health equity
   c. health disparity
   d. health socioeconomics

2. Two of the social and economic determinants of health are
   a. education and ethnicity
   b. genetics and education
   c. genetics and ethnicity
   d. education and income

3. A preventable difference in health status that is closely linked with social, economic, and environmental disadvantages is called a
   a. socioeconomic determinant
   b. policy influence
   c. health disparity
   d. reasonable accommodation

4. A person who has some loss of function somewhere in the body has a
   a. disability
   b. disease
   c. disparity
   d. none of the above

5. Providing a sign language interpreter at a public lecture or event if people with hearing loss are present is an example of a
   a. responsible action
   b. reasonable accommodation
   c. reasonable restitution
   d. disparity correction

6. Developing new products, services, or spaces so that they can be used efficiently and effectively by all people is called
   a. universal equity
   b. equity design
   c. universal design
   d. equality in action

7. Which of the following is the art and science of protecting and improving the health of individuals and large populations?
   a. health science
   b. epidemiology
   c. health education
   d. public health

8. The worldwide spread of a disease is called a(n)
   a. emergent disease
   b. pandemic
   c. epidemiologic situation
   d. disease disaster

9. An educational campaign that tries to keep teens from starting vaping is an example of
   a. a primary prevention effort
   b. a secondary prevention effort
   c. a tertiary prevention effort
   d. none of the above

10. The term used to describe the number of new cases of a disease in a population is
    a. epidemiology
    b. prevalence
    c. pandemic
    d. incidence

PROJECT-BASED LEARNING: Advocating for the Public Health of Your School

What to Remember

School health and local public health services are a major part of a community's public health. Oftentimes a young person's only access to health care services is at school or at a local public health office or clinic. Having equitable access to critical health services is an important part of creating a healthy community.

Who It Is For

Your school community

Why It Is Important

Learning how to advocate for the public health needs of yourself and others is an important health skill that can help promote better health and inclusion for all.

What to Do

Understand and define a health equity issue in your school or community. Develop a realistic solution, gather support for your idea, and take action on your plan.

How to Do It

Develop your campaign by using the steps to community advocacy to advocate for needed public health services in your community or school.

Step 1: Understand and define the issue. As a class, begin by identifying public health needs that students in your school might have. Focus on underserved populations in order to improve health equity. Begin by brainstorming as many needs as you can as a class. Conduct online research of the public health services in your local community and school that are available to teenagers your age and create a list of those services. You may also want to conduct a survey at your school to gather more information about the health services people need or would benefit from. Use all of your information to create a comprehensive list. Try to organize your list in a logical way by type, populations served, or another appropriate organizational framework. Talk through the list and consider which types of services might be missing or underrepresented based on the needs you identified.

Step 2: Create solutions. Brainstorm as many different public health services as you can think of that would benefit the population groups and needs you identified in the first step. Be specific and offer concrete suggestions. Discuss the strengths and weaknesses of each idea and select one to advocate for. Write a summary of your idea that describes the community need and how the proposed resource might help. Conduct any additional fact gathering you need to as you write your summary.

Step 3: Gather support. Gather signatures from other students, teachers, and administrators in the school who support your idea.

Step 4: Take action. Write a letter, organize a public meeting, or meet with school or local officials to share your concerns and ideas. Stay positive in your message and be respectful of others who might challenge your idea.

Reflect on Your Work

Did the campaign work? What worked best? Which part wasn't as successful? What did you learn about the public and community health needs of your peers while doing the project? What did you learn about yourself and your ability to work with others on complex challenges?

CROSS-CURRICULAR CONNECTION: Math

Public health data is often described using statistics. Create a graph to illustrate the following data and then interpret the graph you create. Identify two conclusions from the graph.

U.S. Deaths per 100,000 People by Ethnic Group and Sex in 2018

Ethnic group	Male	Female
Non-Hispanic white	1,121	1,056
Non-Hispanic Black	869	735
American Indian and Native Alaskan	807	615
Asian and Pacific Islander	394	340
Hispanic	373	309

UNIT II

Eating Well and Being Physically Active

CHAPTER 4   Food and Your Health

CHAPTER 5   Managing Good Nutrition

CHAPTER 6   Staying Active and Healthy

Food and Your Health

4

LESSON 4.1   Understanding Foods and Nutrients
LESSON 4.2   Energy Balance, Hunger, and Appetite
LESSON 4.3   Tips and Tools for Eating Well
LESSON 4.4   The Digestive and Urinary Systems
LESSON 4.5   Making Healthy Nutrition Decisions

Understanding My Health

Is My Diet Healthy?

In order to help you make good dietary choices, you need to first understand your current habits. Complete the following self-assessment to help you understand your choices so that you can consider changing them if needed. Answer each question in the following chart by selecting the response that is most accurate for you. When you are done, add up your points. The closer you are to 30 points, the healthier your diet is.

	Always	Sometimes	Never
I eat at least 5 servings of fruits and vegetables each day.	3	2	1
I eat whole grain bread instead of white bread.	3	2	1
I avoid fried foods like chips, fries, and fried meat.	3	2	1
I choose meat substitutes like nuts, beans, and seeds or choose leaner meats like chicken, fish, and turkey.	3	2	1
I choose healthy fats like fish, nuts, and avocados.	3	2	1
I drink at least 8 cups (64 ounces) of water each day.	3	2	1
I don't drink soda or energy drinks that contain sugar and caffeine.	3	2	1
I eat only until I am satisfied and avoid overeating.	3	2	1
I limit processed baked goods like cakes, muffins, and sweet breads.	3	2	1
I eat a healthy breakfast every day.	3	2	1

My score for Is My Diet Healthy? = _____ (total number of points)

Food is fuel for your body. Just as a car needs gas or your cell phone needs power to run, your body needs food to function. The types of foods you eat will determine how well your body works, performs, and ages. The habits you create as a young adult will have an impact on your nutrition choices throughout your life. This means that making good food choices and building healthy nutrition habits now is extra important.

LESSON 4.1

Understanding Foods and Nutrients

Terms to Learn

- caffeine
- calories
- carbohydrates
- complete proteins
- empty-calorie food
- fats
- fiber
- incomplete proteins
- minerals
- multigrain
- nonnutritious drinks
- nutrients
- nutritious drinks
- protein
- vitamins
- water
- whole foods
- whole grain

The Big Picture

The foods you eat give you important nutrients. These nutrients will affect your health and well-being. Understanding the nutrients that make up the food you eat allows you to make healthy changes to your diet and can help you achieve a lifetime of healthy eating.

Learning Targets

- Explain how nutrients affect your overall health.
- Describe the importance of each nutrient category and provide examples of foods for each.
- Identify and defend the benefits of drinking enough water each day.
- Explain how sugary drinks and energy drinks might influence your health.
- Use communication skills to increase water consumption and improve the health of others.

Write About It

What do you drink when you are thirsty, and how do you decide what to drink? Explain your answer using three different circumstances and situations.

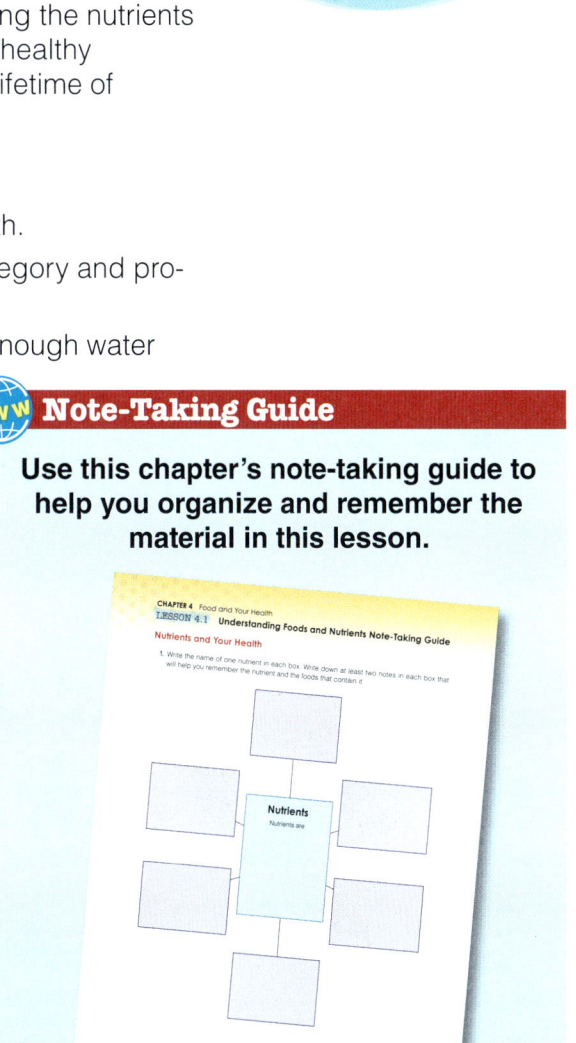

Note-Taking Guide

Use this chapter's note-taking guide to help you organize and remember the material in this lesson.

LESSON 4.1 Food and Your Health

Jemma is a typical kid who likes to eat candy, chips, and soda. She doesn't think too much about her food choices and usually just picks whatever is quickest and most convenient. Her mom, grandma, and older sister all struggle with their weight. Jemma's sister has type 2 diabetes, and her grandma is recovering from a recent stroke. Jemma doesn't really see the connection between her diet, how her family eats, and the diseases her sister and grandma have. Her mom just calls it "bad luck" and regularly says, "We all just die someday anyway." How do you think Jemma's health will be influenced by her family? Do you think she is likely to become overweight and to have health complications later in life?

Nutrients and Your Health

Food gives your body energy and nutrients. **Nutrients** are the substances found in food that your body needs to survive. You can think of nutrients like parts of a computer. Each part does a different job, and together they make the computer work. The nutrients you consume each day keep you healthy, help you perform your best, and give you the energy you need to move. The nutrients you need to be healthy are grouped into six categories (see figure 4.1).

How you eat not only affects how you feel today but also can contribute to the start of diseases that might harm you later in life. Heart disease and type 2 diabetes are two diseases that are commonly linked to eating habits. No single choice causes these diseases to happen. The habits you create over time will either help protect you or make you more likely to get the disease. No one eats a "perfect" diet. The key is to make the best choices you can every day, day after day.

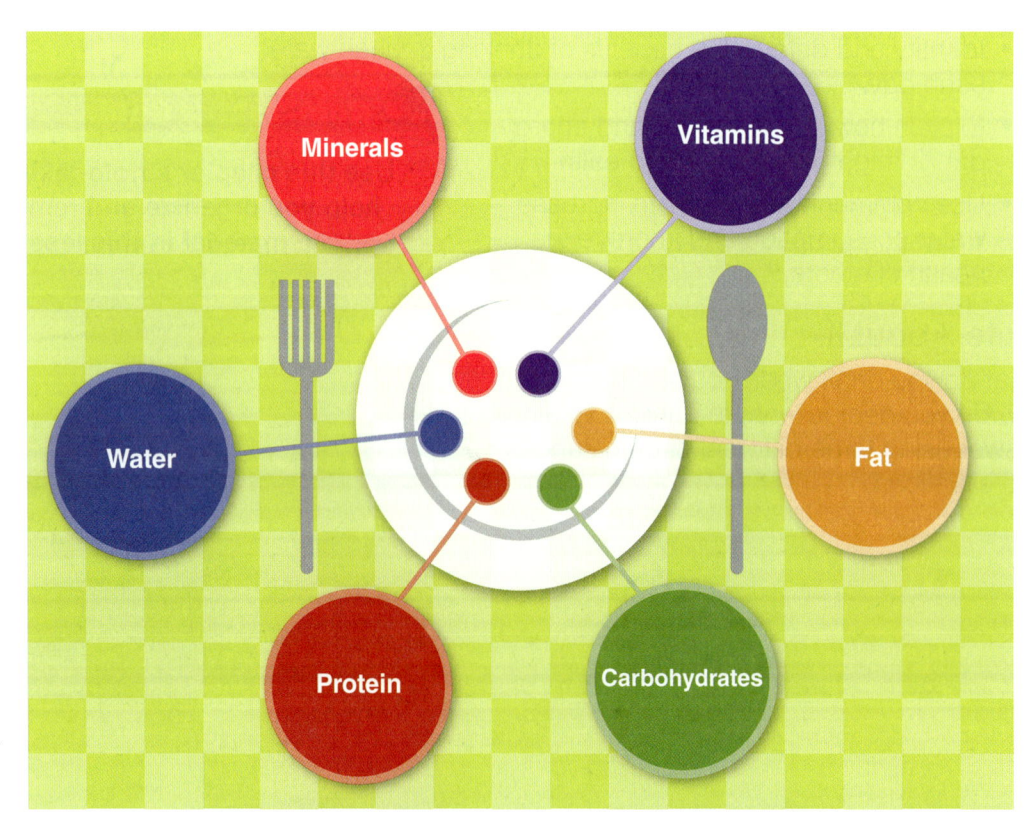

Figure 4.1 The six categories of nutrients you need to be healthy.

Understanding Foods and Nutrients **LESSON 4.1**

Energy Nutrients and Foods

Calories are the form of energy found in food. All foods contain energy in the form of calories. It is important to eat enough calories and to eat the right types of the nutrients to stay healthy. The nutrients that give us calories are carbohydrates, fats, and proteins. It is important to get the right balance of these nutrients every day (see figure 4.2).

Carbohydrates

Carbohydrates are the main source of energy for your body. Simple carbohydrates, also called simple sugars, are found in foods like fruits and milk. Other foods, like bread, pasta, potatoes, and rice, contain complex carbohydrates, called starches. All carbohydrates have the same number of calories by weight (4 calories per gram). Carbohydrates often have a bad reputation. The fact is that there are many healthy carbohydrates that are essential for life. All fruits and vegetables are considered carbohydrates, as are healthy grains like wheat, bulgur, amaranth, and quinoa.

Healthy carbohydrates contain fiber. **Fiber** is found in plant foods like fruits and vegetables. Fiber is hard for your body to digest. When fiber travels through your digestive system, it helps to clear out things like cholesterol that may be bad for your health. Proper amounts of fiber in the diet are linked to lower rates of diseases like heart disease and some forms of cancer. In general, you will get more fiber from foods that are whole, like an apple, and less fiber from foods that are processed or changed, like applesauce (see figure 4.3). Foods that have not been changed are called **whole foods**. Grains that have not had fiber removed from them are called **whole grain**. **Multigrain** foods are those made from two or more grains. Grains typically used for whole and multigrain foods include barley, flax, millet, oat, and wheat (see figure 4.4).

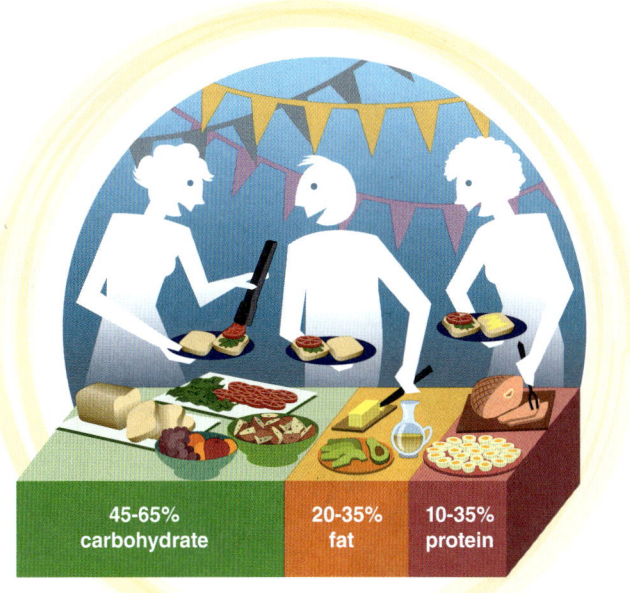

45-65% carbohydrate 20-35% fat 10-35% protein

Figure 4.2 Percentage of calories recommended daily by the USDA for carbohydrate, protein, and fat.

HEALTHY LIVING TIP

When you eat a sandwich, select whole grain and multigrain bread instead of white bread. If you are looking for a healthy snack, try it toasted, with all natural (no sugar added) peanut butter or avocado on top.

Apples have lots of fiber in their skins.

High fiber

Low fiber

Applesauce is made by taking the skin off and removing much of the fiber.

Figure 4.3 Processing foods reduces their fiber content.

145

Figure 4.4 A wide variety of whole grains are part of a healthy diet.

Fats

Fats are the greasy part of foods and are another source of energy in food. Some fats are better for you than others. In general, a fat from a plant is healthier than a fat from an animal, so eating avocados or using olive oil is healthier than eating bacon. Getting the right amount of healthy fats is important to your health (see figure 4.5). Fats are used to make hormones and serve as carriers for other substances in the blood. Fat that is stored as body fat also helps to protect your organs and provides you with insulation to keep your body warm.

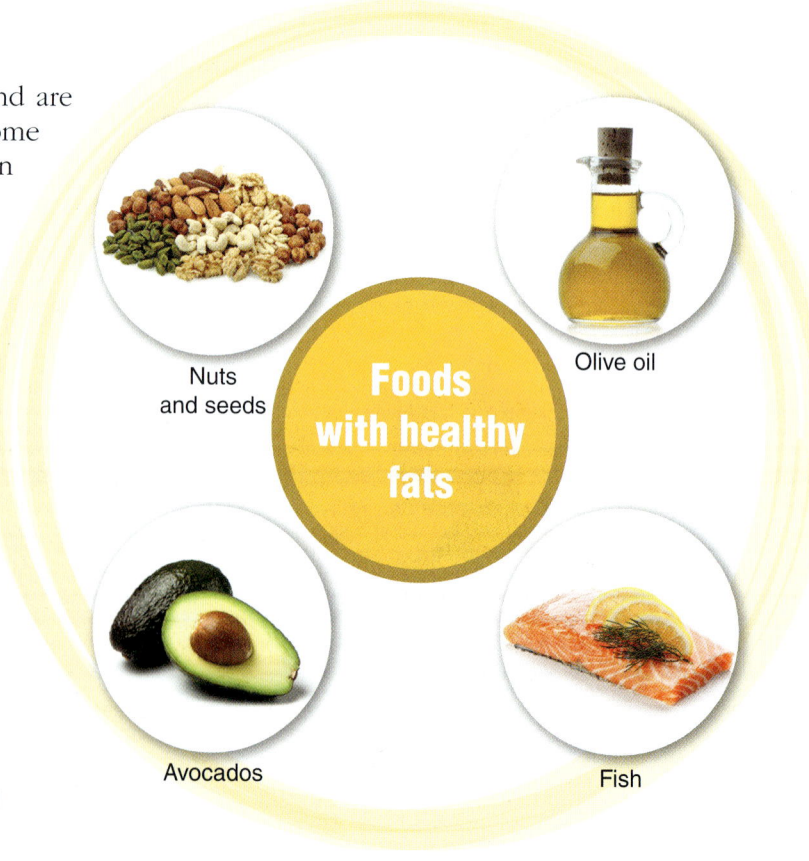

Figure 4.5 Healthy fats can be found in a variety of foods.

Proteins

Another source of calories in your diet is **protein**, the substance found in food that provides calories and helps build and repair tissues. Like carbohydrates, proteins have four calories per gram. The proteins you eat are like building blocks. Some foods have all the building blocks you need. These foods are called **complete proteins**. Animal products like eggs, meat, and cheese are examples of complete proteins. Other foods are missing one or more building blocks, so they are called **incomplete proteins**. Vegetables, beans, seeds, and grains also have proteins in them (see figure 4.6). You can eat plant foods in combinations, like rice and beans or peanut butter on whole grain bread, and get a full set of protein building blocks from them.

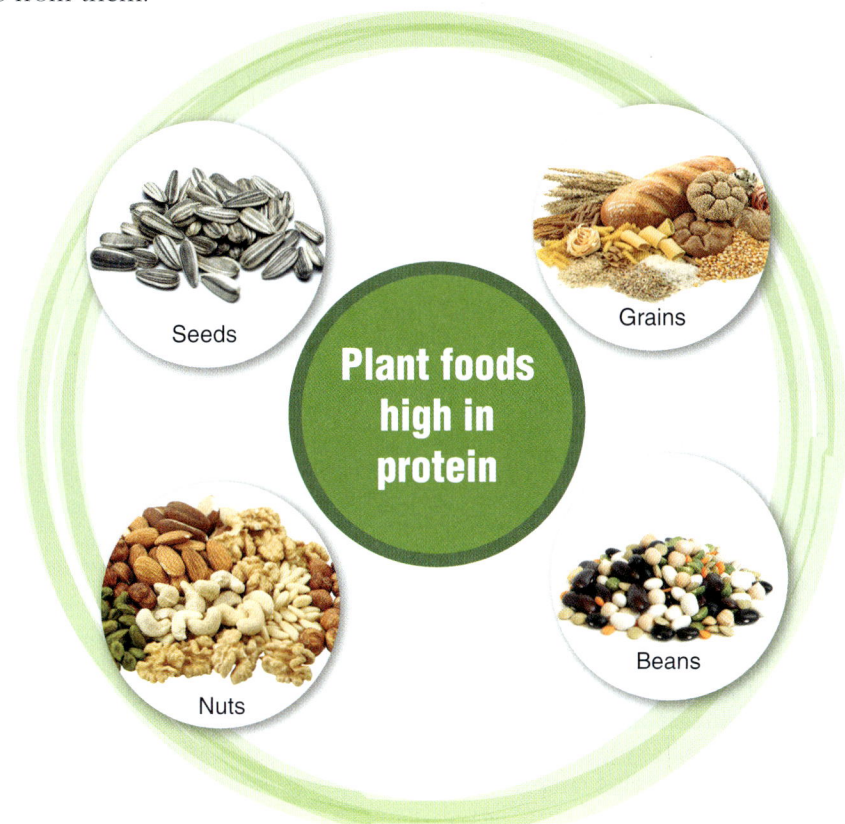

Plant foods high in protein
- Seeds
- Grains
- Beans
- Nuts

Figure 4.6 You can find proteins in plant foods.

Vitamins and Minerals

Vitamins and **minerals** are small substances found in foods that are essential for life. Each vitamin and mineral has a unique role in maintaining overall health (see tables 4.1 and 4.2). Vitamins and minerals have no calories, so they don't give you any food energy. Instead, these nutrients work more like helpers so your body can create the chemical reactions needed to get the energy out of the carbohydrates, fats, and proteins that you eat. The Recommended Daily Allowance, or RDA, is how much of a specific vitamin or mineral your body needs each day.

When you don't get enough of a needed vitamin or mineral, you may experience a deficiency. For example, a lack of iron in the diet can cause anemia; a lack of calcium and vitamin D can contribute to bone loss or osteoporosis. Vitamins and minerals can also be dangerous in higher amounts or can interfere with medications

LESSON 4.1 Food and Your Health

TABLE 4.1 Vitamin Functions and Food Sources

Vitamin	Function	Food sources
B1 (thiamine)	Helps release energy from carbohydrate	Pork, organ meat, legumes, greens
B2 (riboflavin)	Helps break down carbohydrate and protein	Meat, milk products, eggs, green and yellow vegetables
B6 (pyridoxine)	Helps break down protein and glucose	Yeast, nuts, beans, liver, fish, rice
B12 (cobalamin)	Aids formation of nucleic and amino acids	Meat, milk products, eggs, fish
Biotin	Aids formation of amino, nucleic, and fatty acids and glycogen	Eggs, liver, yeast
Folacin (folic acid)	Helps build DNA and protein	Yeast, wheat germ, liver, greens
Pantothenic acid	Involved in reactions with carbohydrate and protein	Most unprocessed foods
Niacin	Helps release energy from carbohydrate and protein	Milk, meat, whole grain or enriched cereals, legumes
C (ascorbic acid)	Aids formation of hormones, bone tissue, and collagen	Fruits, tomatoes, potatoes, green leafy vegetables
A (retinol)	Helps produce normal mucus and is part of a chemical necessary for vision	Butter, margarine, liver, eggs, green or yellow vegetables
D	Aids absorption of calcium and phosphorus	Liver, fortified milk, fatty fish
E (tocopherol)	Prevents damage to cell membranes and vitamin A	Vegetable oils
K	Aids blood clotting	Leafy vegetables

TABLE 4.2 Mineral Functions and Food Sources

Mineral	Function	Food sources
Calcium	Builds and maintains teeth and bones; helps blood clot; helps nerves and muscles function	Cheese, milk, dark green vegetables, sardines, legumes
Iron	Helps transfer oxygen in red blood cells and other cells	Liver, red meat, dark green vegetables, shellfish, whole grain cereals
Magnesium	Aids breakdown of glucose and protein; regulates body fluids	Green vegetables, grains, nuts, beans, yeast
Phosphorus	Builds and maintains teeth and bones; helps release energy from nutrients	Meat, poultry, fish, eggs, legumes, milk products
Potassium	Regulates fluid balance in cells; helps nerves function	Oranges, bananas, meat, bran, potatoes, dried beans
Sodium	Regulates internal water balance; helps nerves function	Most foods, table salt
Zinc	Helps transport carbon dioxide; helps wounds heal	Meat, shellfish, whole grains, milk, legumes

Understanding Foods and Nutrients **LESSON 4.1**

or medical treatments. For example, some vitamins will dissolve in water and can be easily removed from the body through urine. Others require fat in order to be dissolved and stored. These fat soluble vitamins (A, D, E, and K) can become dangerous in large quantities. Because of the dangers that some vitamins and minerals may cause, it is important to talk to a medical professional about taking any vitamin or mineral supplement that exceeds the established RDAs.

Water and Other Beverages

The last type of nutrient is water. **Water** is a tasteless liquid essential for life. Without water, you could not carry any of the other nutrients around in your body. In fact, your body is made up mostly of water. People need 9 to 14 cups of fluids each day. Some of these fluids can come from eating fruits and vegetables, but it is recommended that you drink at least six to eight cups of water every day to meet your body's needs. Water should be the main fluid in your diet. Coffee, sport drinks, and energy drinks can have unnecessary or even dangerous levels of sugar and caffeine. Water also helps keep your body at a constant temperature. If you are playing or exercising outside during hot weather, you may need as many as four more cups of water that day. See figure 4.7 for the benefits of drinking water.

Benefits of drinking 64 ounces (8 cups) of water each day

- Keeps your eyes, brain, blood, kidneys, and lungs healthy
- Keeps your skin looking healthy and reduces your chance of getting pimples
- Helps your muscles function for sports and activities
- Helps with maintaining a healthy body weight
- Carries important nutrients through your body

Figure 4.7 There are many benefits to drinking water.

A healthy diet replaces nonnutritious drinks such as soda with nutritious drinks such as milk.

Drinks High in Sugar

It may be tempting to drink liquids other than water. The problem with many of these other drinks is that they are high in sugar. If you drink soda, that is probably the biggest source of added sugar in your diet. Drinks high in sugar, sodium (salt), or caffeine are not healthy choices for getting the water you need.

Sugar can cause cavities in your teeth, add to health problems like type 2 diabetes, and cause you to gain weight. Sugar has calories but lacks vitamins and minerals. When a food has no real nutrition value but still gives you calories, we call it an **empty-calorie food**. Empty-calorie drinks are called **nonnutritious drinks**. They not only give you calories with no vitamins or minerals but also sometimes prevent you from eating other, healthier foods like fruits and vegetables. Sodas and alcoholic beverages like beer, wine, and mixed drinks add a large number of calories to a person's diet. Consuming nonnutritious drinks is a major contributor to becoming overweight for many people.

Analyzing Energy Drinks

Many drinks are high in caffeine and other things that make you feel like you have energy. **Caffeine** is a stimulant that affects your nervous system. If you are a typical teenager, the chances are high that you have tried energy drinks (see figure 4.8). Feeling

Energy Drink	Iced Coffee	Soda
160mg caffeine	**120mg** caffeine	**34mg** caffeine

Figure 4.8 Most energy drinks have more caffeine than coffee, tea, or soda.

LESSON 4.1 Understanding Foods and Nutrients

CASE STUDY

Dante's Energy Drink Dilemma

Dante feels like he is always struggling to have energy at school. He can't seem to focus or to pay attention to his teachers during instruction. In math class, his head is almost always on the desk, and he knows he is not doing very well. In Spanish class, Dante sits in the back of the class and hopes his teacher won't notice that he is having a hard time concentrating.

Most mornings, Dante is running late for school and doesn't eat breakfast. He hates school lunch because his friends don't think it's cool to eat in the cafeteria. Most days he doesn't have much money, so he just grabs what he can from home or at the convenience store he passes on his way to school. Usually all he can afford is a candy bar or some packaged pastries. Every once in a while, he can splurge on a corn dog or some chicken strips.

One of Dante's friends gave him an energy drink to help boost his energy at school. After drinking it, Dante noticed that his heart started beating really fast and he was sweating in class. For a while, he thought he was having a heart attack or some sort of anxiety attack. Even with the energy drink and feeling more alert, he had a hard time concentrating in his math class. Once his body calmed down, he felt pretty good for a while, but then he crashed even harder than before. He didn't feel well at all later that day. Dante decided he might try a different energy drink next time.

Think About It

1. Do you think it was a good idea for Dante to use an energy drink to boost his energy in school? Why or why not?
2. How could Dante use his diet choices to improve his energy throughout the day?
3. What could you say to try to convince Dante to make a healthier choice for lunch? What could his friends do to help support him?

---

your heart beat fast or seeing your hands shake when you try to write are signs that your body is not handling the caffeine well. Energy drinks can also give you anxiety or cause you to sleep poorly. These drinks can be dangerous. Young people who drink a lot of energy drinks or who drink them during athletic practices or workouts put themselves at risk for serious medical problems.

If you want something to drink other than water, look for **nutritious drinks**, which give you essential nutrients like vitamins, minerals, and carbohydrates. These drinks help meet your nutrient needs without added sugars and caffeine, and they provide the body with a more natural energy source. Low-fat milk and 100 percent fruit juices are healthier options than sodas and energy drinks.

LESSON 4.1   Food and Your Health

Skill-Building Challenge

Communicating the Benefits of Drinking Water

Persuasion is a way of communicating that tries to convince the listener to agree with a point of view. One way we use persuasion in health is to develop public service announcements, or PSAs, which are generally 20 to 30 seconds long. There are four steps to creating a clear PSA.

1. *Identify the issue.* Ask yourself: What do I want to convince others to believe?
2. *Hook your audience.* Ask yourself: Who am I speaking to, and what can I say that will grab their attention and get them to listen?
3. *Know your facts.* Ask yourself: What facts, statistics, or truths can I use to get the person to believe my message?
4. *Be straightforward.* Ask yourself: What is the most direct way I can deliver my message?

Create a 20- to 30-second PSA that addresses the importance of making healthy beverage choices and avoiding unhealthy ones. Follow the steps identified and include at least four benefits of choosing healthy beverages in your PSA. Perform your PSA in front of the class.

1. My issue is: _____

2. My hook is: _____

3. Facts that support my point of view are: _____

4. The most direct way I can deliver my message is: _____

Healthy Living Skills

This lesson includes an activity on using persuasive communication to advocate good health. Here are some more ways you can develop healthy living skills related to this lesson.

ACCESSING INFORMATION

Conduct online research about the risks of taking too many vitamins and minerals. Identify which vitamins and minerals are dangerous in higher amounts and what might happen if someone gets too many of these nutrients. Find at least three different sources and evaluate the validity and reliability of the information you find.

MAKING HEALTHY DECISIONS

Investigate all the food options available to you at school, including vending machines, snack bars, and the cafeteria. From three options, select healthy food choices that are nutrient dense (high in vitamins, minerals, and fiber) and that limit salt, sugar, and unhealthy fat. Write down these healthy choices and select them next time you are getting food at school. After eating them, reflect on what made the food choices healthy and how eating them made you feel.

LESSON 4.1 Review: Understanding Foods and Nutrients

LESSON SUMMARY

- The nutrients you eat affect how well your body functions each day. Eating healthy carbohydrates, fats, and proteins and drinking plenty of water helps you to stay healthy and avoid many chronic diseases such as type 2 diabetes and heart disease.
- The six classifications of nutrients include carbohydrates (fruits, vegetables, and grains), fats (oils, butter, and cream), proteins (meats, dairy, nuts, and vegetables), vitamins and minerals (which are found in all whole foods), and water.
- You should drink 9 to 14 cups of fluids each day, which should include six to eight cups of water.
- Choosing drinks with added sugar can be very dangerous to your health. Sugar can cause cavities in your teeth, add to health problems like type 2 diabetes, and cause you to gain weight.
- Energy drinks are also a dangerous choice because they contain high levels of caffeine and other stimulants. Energy drinks can also give you anxiety or cause you to sleep poorly.

REVIEWING CONCEPTS AND VOCABULARY

1. _____ are the form of energy found in food.
2. _____ are the substances found in food that your body needs to survive.
3. Healthy carbohydrates contain _____, which is found in plant foods like fruits and vegetables.
4. _____ are substances found in food that provide calories and help build and repair tissue.
5. _____ is a tasteless liquid that is essential for life.
6. _____ and _____ are small substances found in foods that are essential for life.
7. A drink that has no real nutrition value but still gives you calories is a(n) _____.

THINKING CRITICALLY

Your friend doesn't like to eat any kind of vegetable except processed potatoes in chips and French fries, which they eat at least once a day. What could you tell your friend about the benefits of eating vegetables? What could you tell them about their habit of eating chips and fries? Identify three ways they might get more fresh vegetables into their diet. Write a two-paragraph persuasive response.

TAKE IT HOME

Tell the people you live with that you are trying to promote drinking water instead of sugary drinks, and why. Write a benefit on at least six cards or sticky notes that you place in key locations in your home where they will serve as good reminders for your family. After three days, ask your family members whether the notes helped them to drink more water.

LESSON 4.2
Energy Balance, Hunger, and Appetite

Terms to Learn
appetite
daily energy need
deficiency
energy balance
hunger
metabolic rate
negative energy balance
positive energy balance
satiated

The Big Picture
Your body works to keep the calories you eat in balance with the calories you use each day. When you are out of balance, it can harm your health. Understanding how much energy your body needs to function helps you know how much to eat. You also need to consider both what makes you want to eat (even if you are not hungry) and what affects your food choices. Once you grasp these issues, you can move down the path to making healthier food decisions.

Learning Targets
- Explain the concept of energy balance.
- Explain how energy balance relates to health.
- Identify how many calories are recommended each day for boys and girls aged 14 to 18.
- Compare hunger and appetite and explain what makes them different.
- Identify and explain the major influences on appetite.

Write About It
What does it feel like to be hungry? Have you ever eaten something even though you weren't hungry? What influenced you to eat when you weren't hungry?

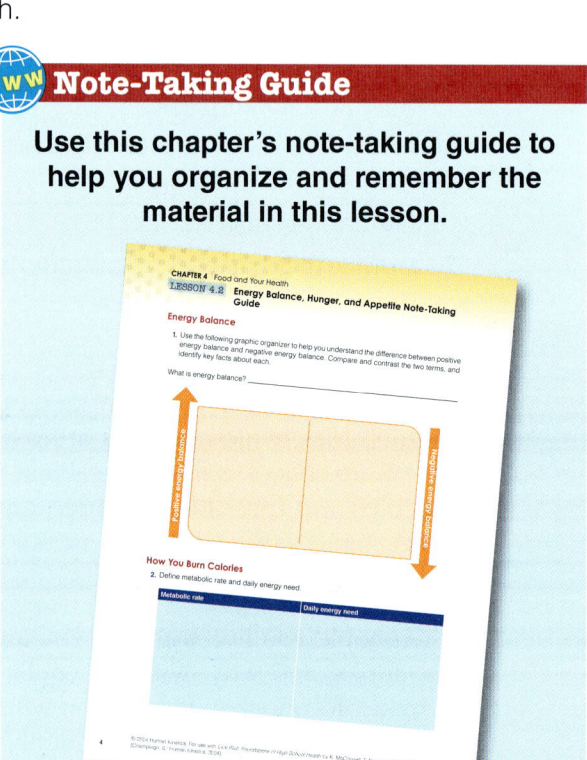

Note-Taking Guide

Use this chapter's note-taking guide to help you organize and remember the material in this lesson.

Energy Balance, Hunger, and Appetite LESSON 4.2

Raina loves to eat, especially at family gatherings and holiday events. Sometimes she finds herself eating because it is what other people are doing; other times, it is simply because everything smells so good and it is hard to resist. Her friend Siri never seems tempted by the sight or smell of food or by what other people around her are doing. Siri just says, "I'm not hungry," and that seems to be it. When they were both at a swim party last week, Siri didn't eat anything because she had just had lunch not that long before. Raina, on the other hand, ate a hotdog and some ice cream even though she didn't feel hungry at all. Why are Raina and Siri so different when it comes to their eating behaviors? What might be influencing each of them?

Energy Balance

From the time you were born, your body has known when it was hungry and when it was full. As a baby, you would cry to signal that you were hungry. When being fed, you would simply stop eating or spit out food when you were satisfied. The human body wants to control its own energy balance. Unfortunately, several factors influence our eating habits as we grow and age. Some of these influences are powerful enough to make us eat when we are full or stop eating when we are still hungry.

Energy balance is the relationship between the calories (energy) you eat and the calories (energy) you burn off (see figure 4.9). The human body functions best when the amount we eat is similar to the amount we use. If you eat more than you use, you have too many calories in your body. This is called **positive energy balance**, and weight gain can occur when you eat more food than you use. When you burn off more than you eat, your body does not have enough energy, resulting in **negative energy balance**. People may experience weight loss when this occurs.

Energy in   Energy out

Figure 4.9 Energy balance.

How You Burn Calories

You burn energy in three main ways (see figure 4.10). First, you need to keep your body alive by having your brain, heart, blood, and lungs working properly. You burn a lot of calories each day just surviving. Your **metabolic rate** is the number of calories you burn to keep your basic body functions working. Genetics, body size, muscle mass, and sex are some of the factors that influence metabolic rate (see figure 4.11).

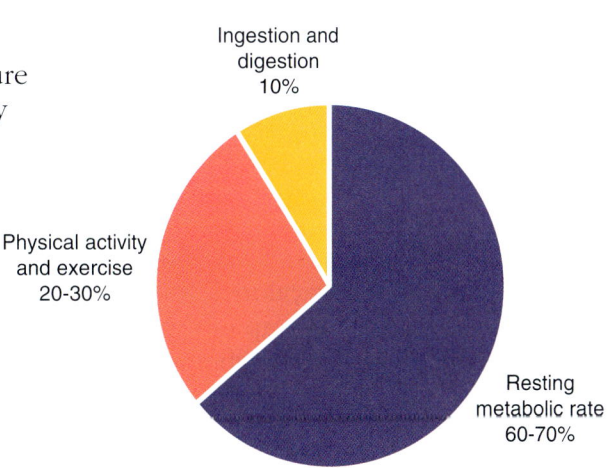

Figure 4.10 Contributors to daily energy expenditure.

Ingestion and digestion 10%

Physical activity and exercise 20-30%

Resting metabolic rate 60-70%

155

LESSON 4.2   Food and Your Health

You also use calories when you ingest and digest food. A small amount of the energy you eat every day is used for this purpose. In other words, your body has to use some of the calories you eat each day helping you get those nutrients to the rest of your body.

The third main way you use calories every day is in physical activity and movement. Whenever you use a muscle to move, you are burning calories. In fact, movement is the way you can most influence your metabolic rate. You will burn more calories when you engage in regular physical activity and exercise. You will also develop stronger muscles and a stronger heart.

Factors that increase metabolic rate
- Lean body mass
- Physical activity and exercise
- Growth and development
- Being male
- Height (overall size)
- Stress
- Digestion

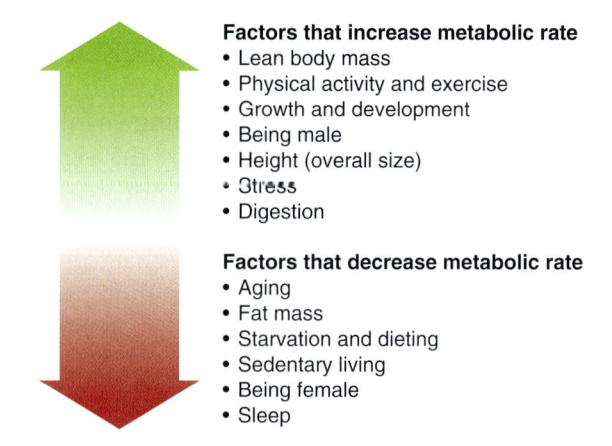

Factors that decrease metabolic rate
- Aging
- Fat mass
- Starvation and dieting
- Sedentary living
- Being female
- Sleep

Figure 4.11 Your level of daily physical activity influences how many calories you need each day.

Daily Energy Need

You need a set number of calories each day to stay healthy. Your **daily energy need** is the number of calories you need each day (see table 4.3). Remember that calories are a form of energy; without them, you don't have the fuel you need to move, think, and function. Not everyone needs the same number of calories each day. Some people need more because they are taller or bigger or have more muscle. Others need more because they are active. We also need more calories when we are growing.

Guidelines can help you know how many calories you need to eat. Eating more calories than you need each day can lead to weight gain over time. If the extra calories include unhealthy fats, salt, and sugar, you will also be more likely to get a disease like type 2 diabetes. If you don't eat enough calories each day, you may either lose weight or not grow and gain weight the way you should. A **deficiency**, also known as malnutrition, occurs when you don't get enough food. This means you also no longer get enough essential nutrients like vitamins and minerals. Deficiencies can lead to brittle hair and nails, weakened bones, and poor night vision.

Determining Your Caloric Need

It is important to eat enough calories without overeating. You may need to set a goal to eat more calories if you are active in sports, or you may need to work on eating fewer calories if you spend your time playing video games or doing other sedentary activities. Table 4.3 will help you determine a starting place for how many calories you need each day. Determine how active you are and adjust the calories up or down slightly if needed. The number of calories you eat each day should be about the same as the amount you use.

Follow these steps to help you set a goal for your daily caloric needs.

- Write down the recommended range of calories you need based on your sex and age using table 4.3.
- If you do not engage in much physical activity each day, choose the bottom number of the range.
- For light to moderate activity up to 30 minutes on most days, choose a number in the middle of the range.
- If you do more than 30 minutes of moderate or vigorous activity most days (like sports practice, dance, or cheer practice), choose the top of the range.

Remember that because each person is different, these are estimated ranges that may need to be adjusted over time. Table 4.3 Energy Needs Across the Life Span

Age (years)	Calories per day (sedentary → active*)
Children 2-3	1,000 → 1,400
Females	
4-8	1,200 → 2,000
9-13	1,400 → 2,200
14-18	1,800 → 2,400
19-30	2,000 → 2,400
31-50	1,800 → 2,200
51+	1,600 → 2,200
Males	
4-8	1,200 → 2,000
9-13	1,600 → 2,600
14-18	2,000 → 3,200
19-30	2,600 → 3,000
31-50	2,400 → 3,000
51+	2,200 → 2,800

Active means doing daily activity equivalent to walking three miles at three to five miles per hour (4.8 kilometers at 4.8 to 8 kilometers per hour).

From U.S. Department of Agriculture 2020.

Understanding Your Hunger

Many factors influence how much you eat and what you eat. Some internal body functions make you want to eat or stop eating. Your blood and brain can keep track of the energy that is in your body. When nutrients in blood are low, the brain signals to the body that it is time to eat. You may feel your stomach growling, or you may feel low on energy. The communication inside your body that tells you when to eat is your **hunger** (see figure 4.12). It is your body's drive to eat. Your hunger is influenced by your hormones, what and when you eat, your level of physical activity, and even your genetics. After you eat, your body knows that nutrients are available and tells your brain that you are satisfied so that you will stop eating. When you are **satiated**, it means that your body is full and your hunger is satisfied.

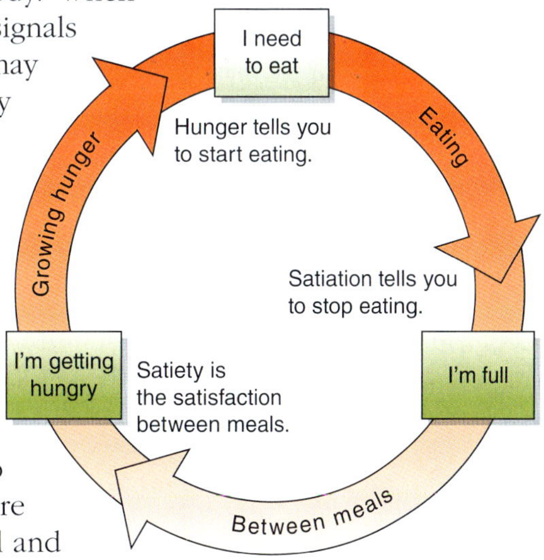

Figure 4.12 Hunger, satiation, and satiety are cues that tell you when to start and stop eating.

LESSON 4.2   Food and Your Health

Understanding Your Appetite

Appetite is the desire to eat. Your desire to eat depends on several factors, including smell and sight of food, a special event like a holiday or birthday, the friends you hang out with, your mood, your family and cultural traditions, and the advertisements you see. Appetite can make you want to eat even if you are not feeling hungry. It can also keep you from wanting to eat despite your body being hungry.

Influences on Your Appetite

Think about what it is like to smell fresh bread baking or garlic cooking. Does it make you want to eat when you pass by? What about if you are feeling lonely or sad? Do you find yourself wanting certain foods? Does your family have traditions that center around a certain meal or type of food? Have you ever gone to a fast food restaurant or ordered something because of a commercial or ad you saw? These are just some of the many different factors that influence appetite (see figure 4.13).

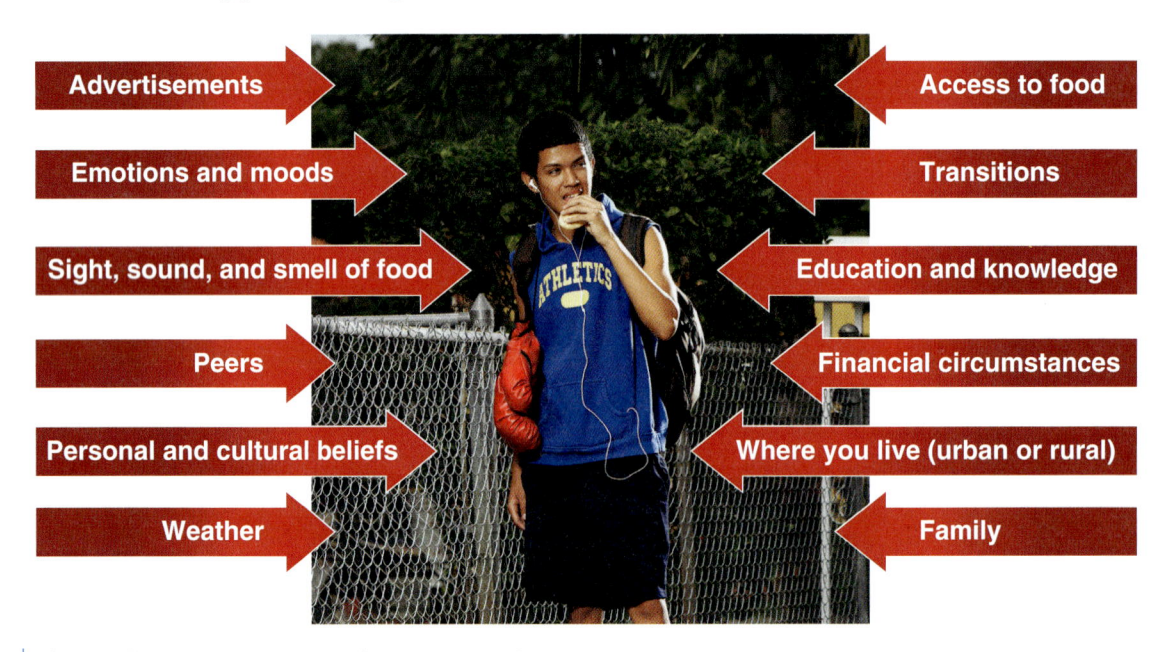

Figure 4.13 Factors that influence appetite.

Factors shown: Advertisements, Emotions and moods, Sight, sound, and smell of food, Peers, Personal and cultural beliefs, Weather, Access to food, Transitions, Education and knowledge, Financial circumstances, Where you live (urban or rural), Family.

Peers

Your peers have a significant influence on your appetite and food choices, especially when you are at school or away from home. For example, you might tend to avoid greasy and fried foods because they upset your stomach. If you have friends who love fried or greasy foods, though, you are more likely to eat those foods even at the risk of developing a stomach ache. The pressure to fit in and belong may alter your choices in food as well as affect your behavior. Finding friends who will eat healthy and support your healthy choices is important to helping you eat a healthy diet.

Family

When you are a teen, your family may influence your food choices more than anything else. Chances are you don't decide on the family menu or do the grocery shopping or the cooking in your family. You may be limited by what is given to you or what you have access to at home. Studies show that parents' and guardians' eating habits affect their children's eating

Energy Balance, Hunger, and Appetite **LESSON 4.2**

habits. If you live in a home that makes healthy food choices, this is good news. If you live in a home that can't afford enough food or buys and prepares unhealthy foods, this is harder. Talking with your parent or guardian about your desire to eat healthy and encouraging healthier choices at home is important.

Personal and Cultural Beliefs

You may have personal convictions about what is or isn't appropriate to eat. For example, you might choose to be vegetarian for ethical reasons. Your personal beliefs affect your food choices. Cultural beliefs about who is responsible for making food, how many meals (and how much food) should be eaten in a day, and what times are appropriate for eating food also affect our appetites and food choices (see figure 4.14). Insects may be a common source of protein in some cultures, but in the United States, much of the population would find the very idea of eating insects unusual. What cultural foods and traditions have you experienced?

HEALTHY LIVING TIP
Help make the grocery list at your home. Include items like fresh fruits and vegetables on the list and then eat those as snacks throughout the day.

Figure 4.14 Different cultures have different food traditions.

159

Diversity Matters

Religion and Food

A person's religious beliefs affect the values and the traditions they follow. As a result, religion influences diet. People follow the food rules and guidelines of their religious tradition differently. Some are strict followers, and others select some traditions to follow on holidays or special events only. For example, most Hindus are vegetarians all the time. Meat and eggs represent life, and the Hindu faith respects all life (human and animal). In the Muslim faith, followers will fast (not eat at all) from sunrise to sunset every day for a month during Ramadan, and in the Roman Catholic tradition, meat is not eaten on Fridays during Lent.

School and Community

You spend a lot of hours at school. Access to food, food options, and pressure to eat a certain way are all part of school influences on what you eat. Schools are required to follow some federal guidelines when it comes to the foods they serve or provide access to. Even with some rules in place, it is still possible to make unhealthy choices at school. For example, if you eat low-fat tortilla chips for lunch every day, you are likely not getting enough fruits or vegetables in your diet and may be getting too much sodium. If the school environment does not offer healthy choices that appeal to you, think about bringing a lunch from home. Eating in the cafeteria rather than getting fast food and choosing salads, vegetables, and foods that have not been fried are also better choices.

Analyzing Influences: Targeting Teens in the Media

Studies have shown that teens who spend more than two hours watching commercial TV are more likely to eat unhealthy foods. Similarly, teens who view Internet ads are more likely to be or become overweight or obese. Companies market toward specific populations. For example, many fast food companies have created specific advertisements that target Black youth and Latino youth. What do you think about being the target of ads that try to get you to make less healthy eating choices? Do you think you are influenced by these ads? Why or why not?

Energy Balance, Hunger, and Appetite **LESSON 4.2**

Skill-Building Challenge

What Influences Your Eating?

Think about who and what influences your food choices. Identify four influences and explain how they change your food choices. An example is provided.

Influence:

My mom and grandma

This influence:

- [x] Helps me eat healthier
- [ ] Does not help me eat healthier

Explain how this influence affects you.

My mom and grandma are both vegetarians. They fix a lot of meals that have vegetables. I wouldn't get as many if I made my own food.

Influence: _____

This influence:

- [ ] Helps me eat healthier
- [ ] Does not help me eat healthier

Explain how this influence affects you.

_____
_____
_____
_____
_____
_____
_____

Healthy Living Skills

This lesson focused on learning to recognize and analyze influences on your diet. Here is one more way you can develop healthy living skills related to this lesson.

HEALTHY COMMUNICATION

How would you help a younger student understand the ways that media might influence their food choices? Identify three ways the media tries to influence the ways kids eat, and use real-world or realistic examples to illustrate your thoughts.

161

LESSON 4.2 Food and Your Health

LESSON 4.2 Review: Energy Balance, Hunger, and Appetite

LESSON SUMMARY

- Energy balance is the relationship between the calories (energy) you eat and the calories (energy) you burn off. It is best to stay in balance.
- When you eat too many calories compared to how many you use, you may gain weight. When you don't eat enough to fuel your activities, you may lose weight. You can develop health problems from eating too much or too little.
- Girls aged 14 to 18 need between 1,800 and 2,400 calories every day. Boys aged 14 to 18 need between 2,200 and 3,200 calories every day.
- Many factors influence what you choose to eat and how much you choose to eat. Internal signals from your body are your hunger. Your hormones, how often you eat, what you eat, and how much exercise you do influence your hunger.
- Your desire to eat is your appetite. Family, peers, culture, media, and the environment can all influence your food choices, habits, and preferences. Learning to recognize what influences your food choices can help you make healthier decisions.

REVIEWING CONCEPTS AND VOCABULARY

1. If you eat more calories than you use, you have a(n) _____ energy balance.
2. If you burn off more calories than you eat, you have a(n) _____ energy balance.
3. The number of calories you burn to keep your basic body functions working is called your _____.
4. When you don't get enough of a needed nutrient, we call it a(n) _____.
5. The communication inside your body that tells you when to eat and when to stop is your _____.
6. _____ is the desire to eat.
7. The number of calories you need each day is called your _____.

THINKING CRITICALLY

Malik goes to baseball games with his family almost every weekend, and you've noticed that he always gets a chili dog with fries no matter what time the game is or whether he has recently eaten. Other families in the stands also bring popcorn, chips, and other snacks. Malik never wants to be rude, so he always takes the snacks when offered. Why do you think Malik is in this habit? What advice could you give him to help him think about his choices? Write your response in one to two paragraphs.

TAKE IT HOME

Draw a picture or create a simple infographic (a collection of images with minimal text that gives an easy-to-understand overview of a topic) that shows how your family influences your appetite and the choices you make when you eat. Think about ethnic, cultural, and religious traditions as well as where you live and what access you have to foods. Use labels and headers to help explain your work. Discuss your infographic with your family to see whether they have anything to add.

LESSON 4.3
Tips and Tools for Eating Well

Terms to Learn
adequacy
balance
biased information
diet
Dietary Guidelines for Americans
dietitian
moderation
MyPlate
nutrition facts label
variety

The Big Picture
A healthy diet can come in many forms if it follows a few basic key ideas like balance, variety, moderation, and adequacy, and if it follows general guidelines for calorie and nutrient intake.

Learning Targets
- Explain the four keys to a healthy diet.
- Explain what biased information is.
- Demonstrate the ability to read a nutrition facts label.
- Explain how to use MyPlate to plan a healthy diet.
- Demonstrate how to access valid and reliable nutrition information.

Write About It
How often do you read a food label when you are choosing what to eat? Have you ever asked to see the nutrition information when eating at a restaurant? Why do you think you do or do not use these tools to help you make decisions?

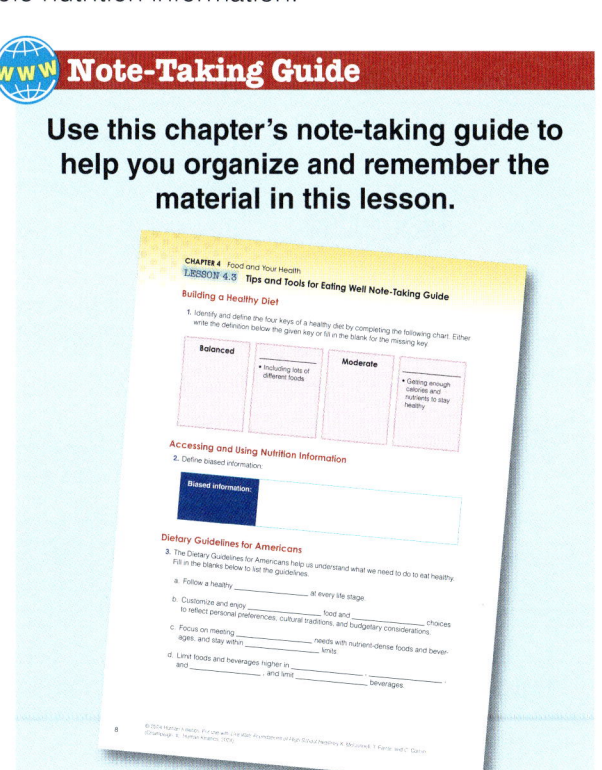

Note-Taking Guide
Use this chapter's note-taking guide to help you organize and remember the material in this lesson.

LESSON 4.3 Food and Your Health

Samantha is always looking for information about how to eat. Her friends tease her because she seems to change her beliefs and her diet all the time. Last year, she was eating paleo because she thought eating lots of meat and protein was the best choice. Now Sam is a vegetarian. She used to avoid all bread and potatoes too, but now she eats potatoes all the time since she doesn't eat meat. Yesterday she told her friend Raul that she is thinking about adding cold-water fish to her diet because she heard fish oil is healthy. Raul just shook his head and asked Sam, "Why don't you just eat a balanced diet?" Have you ever noticed that nutrition advice doesn't always make sense? Who do you think has a healthier understanding of nutrition, Sam or Raul? Learning how to find trustworthy nutrition information is important.

Building a Healthy Diet

There is more than one way to eat healthy. You and your friends may like different types of foods and may eat meals that seem different from each other. The combinations of nutrients you eat and the way you eat is called your **diet**. While your diet may differ from that of your friends, some things are common to all healthy diets. You can think of **balance**, **variety**, **moderation**, and **adequacy** as the four keys to unlocking a healthy diet (see figure 4.15).

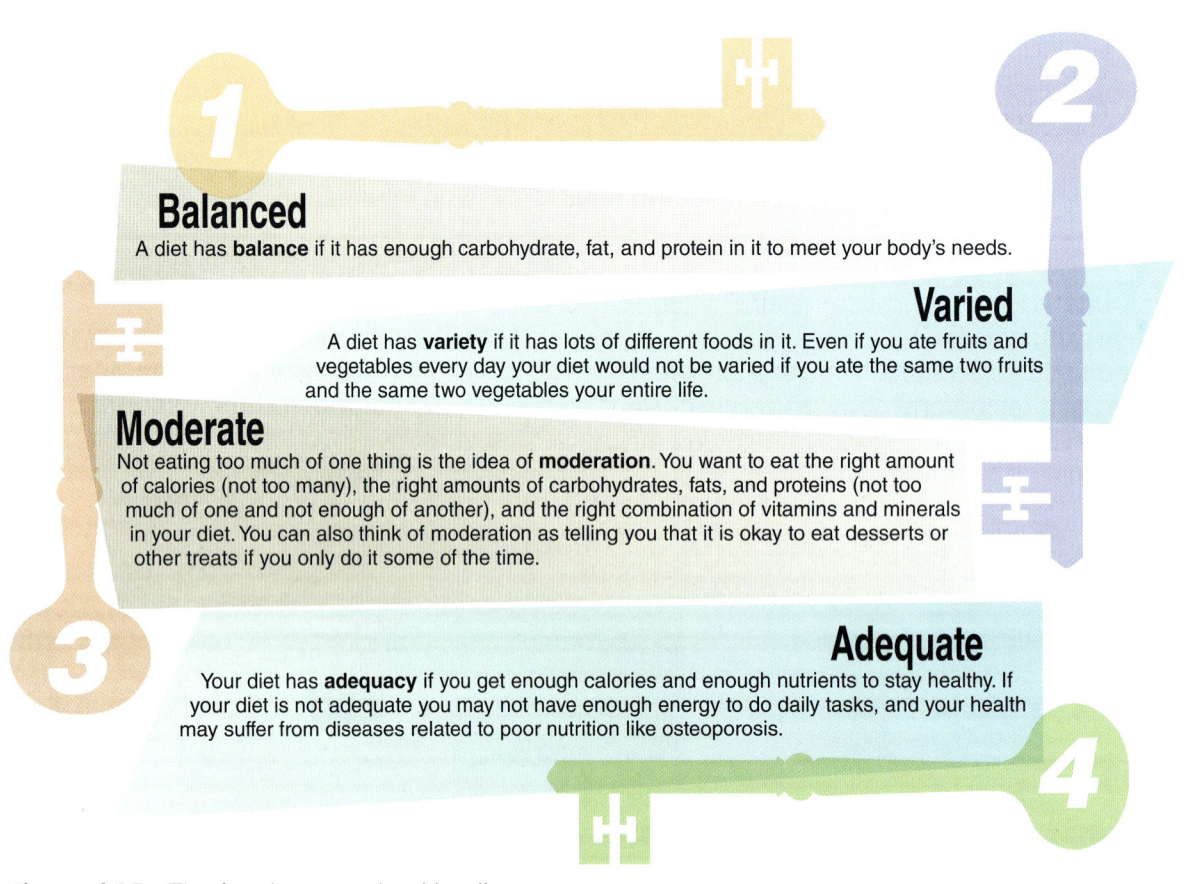

Balanced
A diet has **balance** if it has enough carbohydrate, fat, and protein in it to meet your body's needs.

Varied
A diet has **variety** if it has lots of different foods in it. Even if you ate fruits and vegetables every day your diet would not be varied if you ate the same two fruits and the same two vegetables your entire life.

Moderate
Not eating too much of one thing is the idea of **moderation**. You want to eat the right amount of calories (not too many), the right amounts of carbohydrates, fats, and proteins (not too much of one and not enough of another), and the right combination of vitamins and minerals in your diet. You can also think of moderation as telling you that it is okay to eat desserts or other treats if you only do it some of the time.

Adequate
Your diet has **adequacy** if you get enough calories and enough nutrients to stay healthy. If your diet is not adequate you may not have enough energy to do daily tasks, and your health may suffer from diseases related to poor nutrition like osteoporosis.

Figure 4.15 The four keys to a healthy diet.

Accessing and Using Nutrition Information

The Internet is filled with information about nutrition, some of which is biased or wrong. **Biased information** is based on feelings and opinions more than on facts alone. Biased information sometimes uses only part of a fact and does not tell you the full story. Several websites want to sell you products like vitamin and mineral supplements and often misuse information to get you to buy the product. These profit-driven websites are more interested in making money than in helping you be healthy. However, there are other sources of information that provide more valid and reliable information.

Dietary Guidelines for Americans

The **Dietary Guidelines for Americans** help us understand what we need to do to eat healthy (see figure 4.16). These guidelines are based on research and are updated every five years:

1. Follow a healthy dietary pattern at every life stage.
2. Customize and enjoy nutrient-dense food and beverage choices to reflect personal preferences, cultural traditions, and budgetary considerations.
3. Focus on meeting food group needs with nutrient-dense foods and beverages, and stay within calorie limits.
4. Limit foods and beverages higher in added sugars, saturated fat, and sodium, and limit alcoholic beverages.

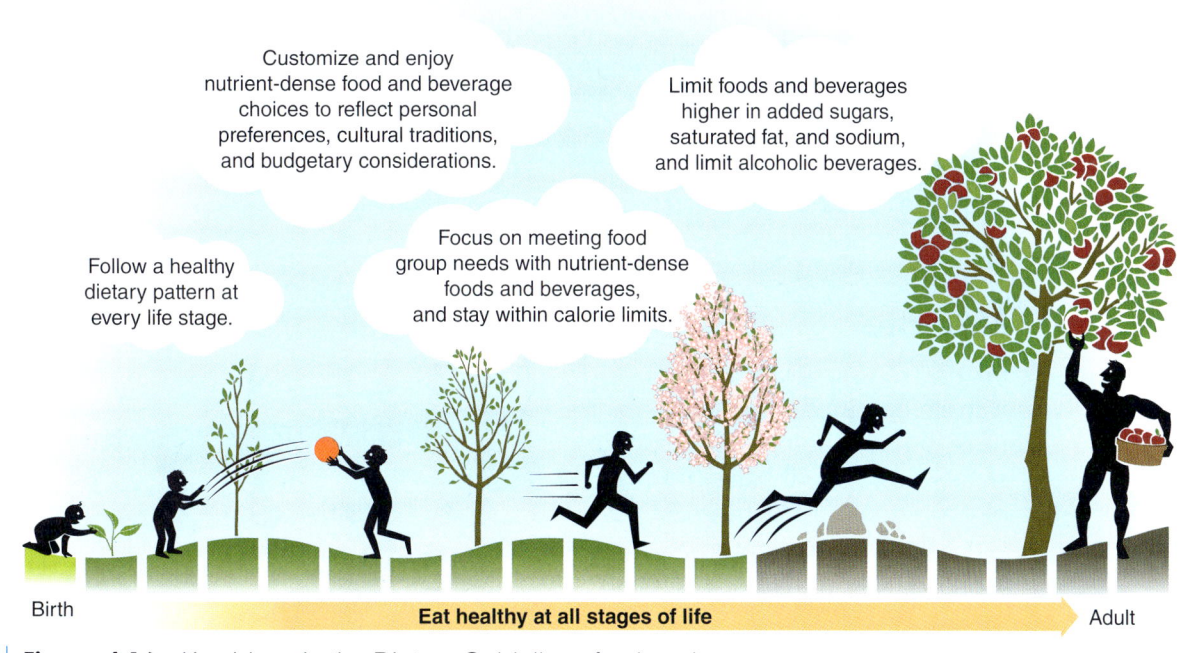

Figure 4.16 Key ideas in the Dietary Guidelines for Americans.

Reading Food Labels

Another great tool you can use to choose healthy foods is the **nutrition facts label**, which is found on all food products. This label provides you with important nutrition information (see figure 4.17).

LESSON 4.3 Food and Your Health

Serving size
Shows how much of this food is normally eaten. The serving size is not a recommendation. It is designed to be realistic. You can use this section to compare similar products.

% Daily Value (%DV)
Shows how much each nutrient listed contributes to the daily diet. In general, 5% DV or less of a nutrient per serving is considered low, and 20% is considered high. For example, this product is high in fiber, which is good.

Vitamin D and potassium are also required on the label because many Americans do not get the recommended amounts.

Nutrition Facts
4 servings per container
Serving size 1 1/2 cup (208g)

Amount per serving
Calories 240

	% Daily Value*
Total Fat 4g	5%
Saturated Fat 1.5g	8%
Trans Fat 0g	
Cholesterol 5mg	2%
Sodium 430mg	19%
Total Carbohydrate 46g	17%
Dietary Fiber 7g	25%
Total Sugars 4g	
Includes 2g Added Sugars	
Protein 11g	
Vitamin D 2mcg	10%
Calcium 260mg	20%
Iron 6mg	35%
Potassium 240mg	6%

* The % Daily Value (DV) tells you how much a nutrient in a serving of food contributes to a daily diet. 2,000 calories a day is used for general nutrition advice.

Ingredients list
The list of ingredients is not part of the Nutrition Facts label, but it is also a helpful tool. Ingredients are listed by weight. So, the ingredient that is most common in the food by weight is listed first. Some people use the ingredients list as a way to eat a "clean" diet. A clean diet is one with as few added chemicals and preservatives as possible.

Servings per container
Shows the total number of servings in the entire food package or container. Some packages are single servings—meaning they have only one serving in the bag, box, or can. Other products have lots of servings in the container.

Calories
Tells you how many total calories is in one serving of the food. Remember, if there is more than one serving in the container and you eat the whole container, you have eaten more calories than is shown here.

All labels are required to tell you the amount of added sugars in the product.

Added sugars are sugars added to foods during processing or packaging. Try not to have more than 10% of your total daily calories come from added sugars.

| **Figure 4.17** The nutrition facts label is a valid source of nutrition information.

HEALTHY LIVING TIP
Use the Start Simple with MyPlate app to help you set simple goals for healthy eating. Track your progress on your goals and use the app to get tips and motivation when making food decisions.

MyPlate

MyPlate is a graphic tool and website designed to help you make healthy food choices. The graphic shows how a well-balanced plate of food looks (see figure 4.18). Half of the plate comprises fruits and vegetables. Grains and protein sources make up the other half of the plate. Dairy is represented by the glass of milk alongside the plate. Try using this tool with the following tips to help you plan a balanced, nutritious meal.

Make half your plate fruits and vegetables. Choose whole fruits—fresh, frozen, dried, or canned in 100 percent juice. Enjoy fruit with meals, as snacks, or as a dessert. Vary your veggies—choose a variety of colorful vegetables prepared in healthful ways: steamed, sautéed, roasted, or raw.

Make half your grains whole. Look for whole grains listed first or second on the ingredients list. Try oatmeal, popcorn, whole grain bread, and brown rice. Limit grain-based desserts and snacks, such as cakes, cookies, and pastries.

Vary your protein routine. Mix up your protein foods to include seafood, beans and peas, unsalted nuts and seeds, soy products, eggs, and lean meats and poultry. Try main dishes made with beans or seafood like tuna salad or bean chili.

Choose low-fat or fat-free milk, yogurt, and soy beverages (soymilk) to cut back on saturated fat. Replace sour cream, cream, and regular cheese with low-fat yogurt, milk, and cheese.

Drink water instead of sugary drinks.

Limit sodium, fat, and added sugar. Use the nutrition facts label and ingredients list to limit items high in sodium, unsaturated fat, and added sugar.

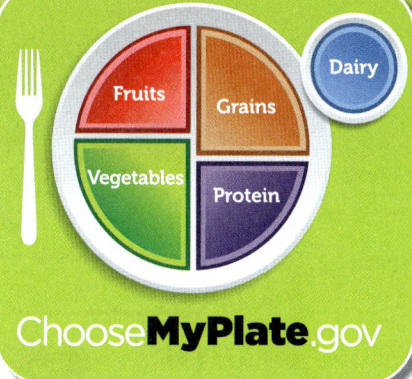

Figure 4.18 The MyPlate graphic along with tips.

LESSON 4.3   Food and Your Health

MyPlate also includes information about how much of each food group to eat. The amount you need from each food group depends on how many calories you need each day. Figure 4.19 shows how to use MyPlate tips and the MyPlate Plan to balance your calories and get the right types of foods.

Dairy

1,600 calorie diet = 3 cups of dairy
1,800 calorie diet = 3 cups of dairy
1 cup from the dairy group counts as:

- 1 cup milk; or
- 1 cup yogurt; or
- 1 cup fortified soy beverage; or
- 1 1/2 ounces natural cheese or
   2 ounces processed cheese

Grains

1,600 calorie diet = 5 ounces of grains
1,800 calorie diet = 6 ounces of grains
1 ounce from the grains group counts as:

- 1 slice bread; or
- 1 ounce ready-to-eat cereal; or
- 1/2 cup cooked rice, pasta, or cereal

Protein foods

1,600 calorie diet = 5 ounces of protein
1,800 calorie diet = 5 ounces of protein
1 ounce from the protein group counts as:

- 1 ounce cooked/canned lean meats, poultry, or seafood; or
- 1 egg; or
- 1 Tbsp peanut butter; or
- 1/4 cup cooked beans or peas; or
- 1/2 ounce nuts or seeds

Fruit

1,600 calorie diet = 1 1/2 cups from the fruit group
1,800 calorie diet = 1 1/2 cups from the fruit group
1 cup from the fruit group counts as:

- 1 cup raw, frozen, or cooked/canned fruit; or
- 1/2 cup dried fruit; or
- 1 cup 100% fruit juice

Vegetables

1,600 calorie diet = 2 cups from the vegetable group
1,800 calorie diet = 2 1/2 cups from the vegetable group
1 cup from the vegetable group counts as:

- 1 cup raw or cooked/canned vegetables; or
- 2 cups leafy salad greens; or
- 1 cup 100% vegetable juice

Figure 4.19 MyPlate Plan: The daily recommended amounts for each food group and examples of different foods.

Other Sources of Nutrition Information

Just as some online sources of information may not be accurate, some people who provide nutrition advice may not be correct either. A **dietitian** is a nutrition expert who has completed their university education in nutrition and has a professional license. Seek out a licensed dietitian for nutrition guidance when you can.

Some people call themselves nutritionists. A nutritionist is someone who claims to have knowledge in nutrition. They are not always educated about, or trained in, nutrition. Be careful when asking for nutrition advice from nutritionists, personal trainers, or others who are not dietitians. When getting nutrition advice from others, find out whether they have had college or university classes in nutrition. Be careful taking nutrition advice from anyone who is trying to sell you a diet product or service. They may be more interested in making money than in actually helping you. Medical doctors, school nurses, and health and physical education teachers are other reliable sources of nutrition information.

Skill-Building Challenge

Accessing Valid Nutrition Information

Since there is so much bad nutrition information available to you, it is important to learn how to find information that is accurate. You could go see a dietitian, but not everyone can afford to pay for nutrition advice. Instead, we often get our information online. Learning where to go for the best information is important.

Conduct online research on the following types of diets and answer the questions provided. Make sure the sources you identify are valid and reliable.

LACTO-OVO VEGETARIAN

1. What is a lacto-ovo vegetarian?
2. Plan a lacto-ovo vegetarian diet for one day. Be sure the diet you plan demonstrates balance, variety, moderation, and adequacy.

VEGAN

1. What is a vegan diet?
2. What are the primary nutritional concerns about vegan diets when it comes to providing a balanced and varied diet?
3. Modify your lacto-ovo vegetarian diet to a vegan diet. Be sure that it demonstrates balance, variety, moderation, and adequacy.

PESCO-VEGETARIAN

1. How does a pesco-vegetarian differ from a vegan or lacto-ovo vegetarian?
2. Are there any known health benefits or risks to this type of diet?

LESSON 4.3 Food and Your Health

Healthy Living Skills

This lesson focused on learning to access valid and reliable information on your diet. Here are some more ways you can develop healthy living skills related to this lesson.

ANALYZING INFLUENCES
Learning to eat a healthy diet includes knowing how much to eat. Portion size refers to how much food you eat at one time. For example, based on the nutrition facts label, a whole bag of potato chips may be six or seven servings. If you eat the whole bag at one time, you are consuming a large portion size. Are you influenced by the recommended serving size of a food when you are eating? Do you look at the nutrition facts label when choosing foods? Why or why not? Write your response in one paragraph.

HEALTHY COMMUNICATION
Create a poem, song, story, or rap that explains what MyPlate is and how it can help you eat a more balanced diet. Use examples of foods in your work that can help explain your points and that are realistic to your financial, social, family, and cultural circumstances.

MAKING HEALTHY DECISIONS
Compare the nutrition facts labels of two packaged foods or snacks that you like to eat. Choose the food that you think is healthier for you and write down three reasons for your choice. The next time you are deciding between the two foods or snacks, remember this analysis and use it to make a healthier choice.

ADVOCATING FOR GOOD HEALTH
Create a series of social media posts that demonstrate the four keys to a healthy diet. Tag your posts according to the key they represent (e.g., #eatvariety or #bebalanced).

LESSON 4.3 Review: Tips and Tools for Eating Well

LESSON SUMMARY

- A healthy diet is balanced (has enough carbohydrate, fat, and protein to meet your body's needs), varied (has lots of different foods in it), moderate (does not include too much of any one nutrient or food), and adequate (has enough calories and enough nutrients to keep you healthy).
- Biased information is based on feelings and opinions more than on facts.
- Use the serving size, servings per container, calories, percent daily values (%DV), and added sodium and sugar on a nutrition facts label to help you make a healthy choice.
- The MyPlate graphic shows how a well-balanced plate of food looks. MyPlate also provides you with the amount of each food group you should eat based on your age, sex, and activity level.
- Registered dietitians are the best source of accurate nutrition information.

REVIEWING CONCEPTS AND VOCABULARY

1. The combinations of nutrients you eat and the way you eat is called your _____.
2. A diet that has enough carbohydrate, fat, and protein in it to meet your body's needs has _____.
3. A diet has _____ if it has lots of different foods in it.
4. A diet has _____ if it gives you enough calories.
5. The _____ provides information such as how much added sugar is in a food product.
6. The percent daily value shows how much each _____ listed contributes to the daily diet.
7. A licensed _____ provides expert guidance about nutrition.

THINKING CRITICALLY

You and your classmates have been asked to visit a class at the local elementary school to explain what MyPlate is and to help kids younger than you to understand how to use it to help them eat a healthier diet. Outline the key points you would make to the class and then write three questions you could ask the young students to see whether they understood your message.

TAKE IT HOME

Look at the foods in your kitchen or pantry at home. Pick out three boxed, canned, or packaged foods and use the nutrition facts label to compare the calories, fat, sodium, and added sugar in each item. Decide which of the foods is the healthiest for you and your family. Explain your findings to a sibling, parent, or guardian.

LESSON 4.4
The Digestive and Urinary Systems

Terms to Learn

- absorption
- bile
- chyme
- digestion
- elimination
- esophagus
- gastroenterologist
- gut health
- kidney dialysis
- kidney disease
- large intestine
- prebiotics
- probiotics
- small intestine
- stomach

The Big Picture

In order to understand how food gets from your plate to the cells in your body, you need to know about the digestive system. When this system is functioning well, you probably don't give it much thought. But when it is not, you may experience a wide range of problems that can be physically, socially, and emotionally uncomfortable. Learning to take care of this system can help you benefit from the nutrition choices you make.

Learning Targets

- Explain how the organs of the digestive system work together to get nutrients out of food and to the body.
- Identify the main organs and functions of the urinary system.
- Explain common problems associated with the digestive system.
- Describe what prebiotics and probiotics are and explain how they relate to gut health.
- Explain the long-term risks of poor kidney health.
- Describe how to maintain good digestive and urinary health.

Write About It

Which common digestive problems do you think most people experience at some point in their lives? Describe a time you experienced one of these problems. What did you do to feel better?

Note-Taking Guide

Use this chapter's note-taking guide to help you organize and remember the material in this lesson.

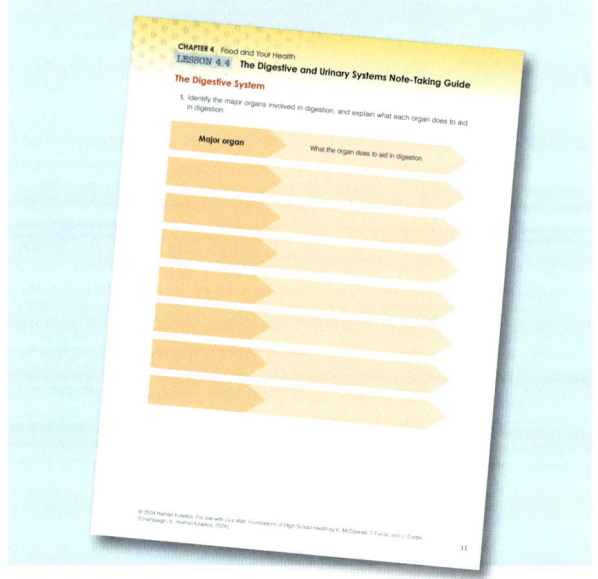

The Digestive and Urinary Systems   **LESSON 4.4**

Kenyan experiences anxiety whenever he has to give a class presentation. It physically manifests itself in his stomach, where he feels sharp pains in his gut that come and go. Lately they've become much more frequent. The pain gets worse when he doesn't eat, which happens a lot when he's anxious. Eating only intensifies the cramps. Kenyan learned about ulcers in a unit in health class and has started to wonder if he's developed them. When he told his grandma what was wrong, she worried it was something more serious and made an appointment for Kenyan to see the doctor. What do you think might be happening with Kenyan?

The Digestive System

You cannot live without food for very long. Food gives your body the nourishment it needs to survive and to thrive. Usually we think about how food tastes or smells, or we are aware that we feel full and content after eating. We don't typically think about what happens to food after we chew it and swallow it. The reality is that your body has just begun the work of digesting your food when you finish eating. The digestive system is the group of organs that break down the food you eat and get it to the cells for fuel (see figure 4.20).

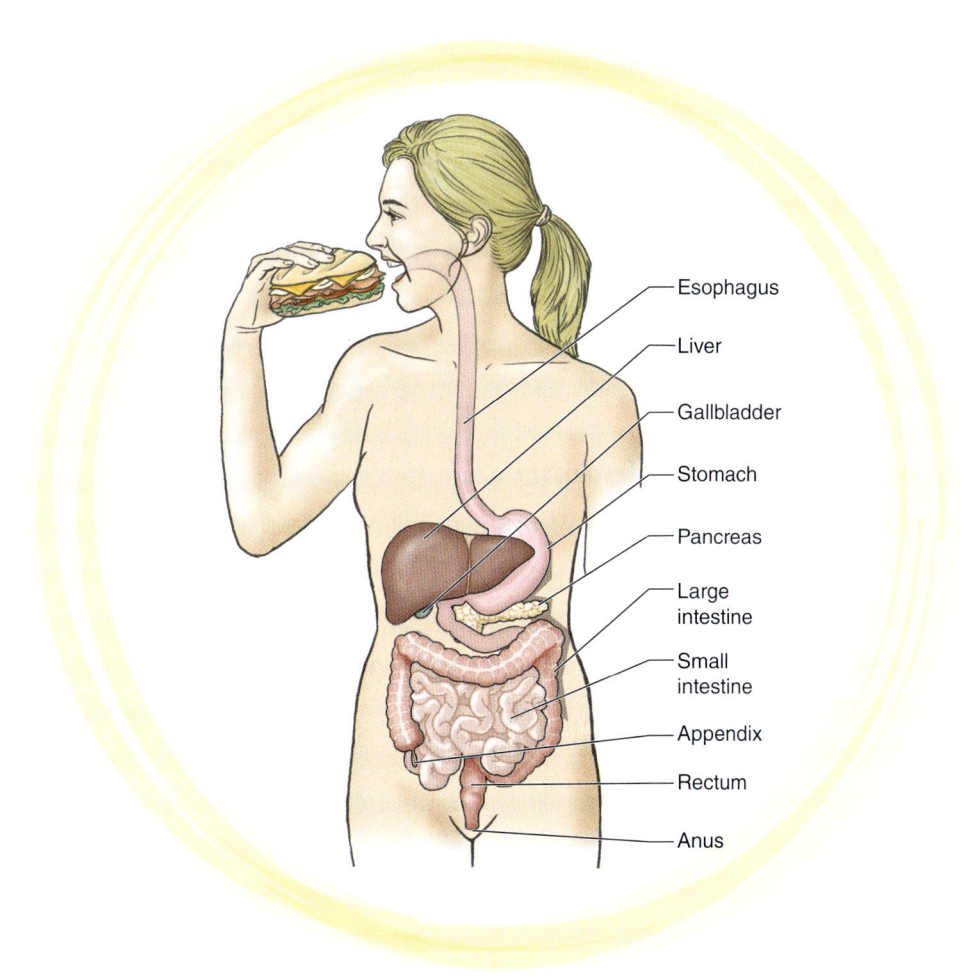

Figure 4.20 The organs that comprise the digestive system.

173

LESSON 4.4   Food and Your Health

How Digestion Works

Digestion is a complex process that involves many organs and actions. This system is involved in **digestion**, **absorption**, and **elimination** (see figure 4.21).

Digestion
Mechanical and chemical breakdown of food

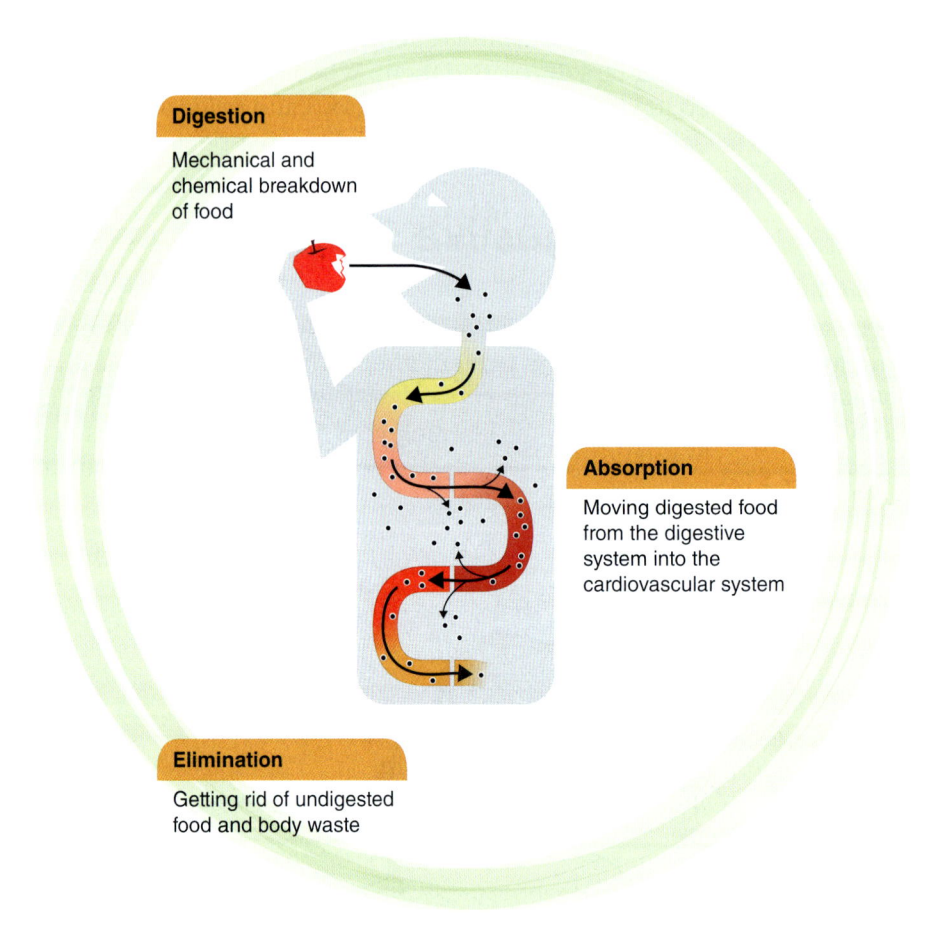

Absorption
Moving digested food from the digestive system into the cardiovascular system

Elimination
Getting rid of undigested food and body waste

Figure 4.21 The digestive functions.

Chewing and Swallowing

Digestion begins with the mechanical breakdown of food: chewing. When you chew your food, your teeth break the food into smaller pieces and prepare them for swallowing. Your salivary glands produce saliva, which begins to break down some carbohydrates and helps to moisten the food. Your tongue helps move food around inside the mouth and helps with swallowing your food safely and properly. Once swallowed, food travels down the **esophagus**, a muscular tube that is about 10 inches (25 cm) long. The esophagus uses small muscle contractions to help move the food toward the stomach. After food enters the stomach, a small valve at the base of the esophagus closes to prevent food from traveling back up.

Mixing, Storing, and Moving Food

The **stomach** is a hollow organ that functions like a small sack. Your stomach mixes foods with gastric juices like hydrochloric acid and pepsin. These juices begin the process of chemically breaking down the food you eat. The stomach can also act like a temporary storage vessel for the broken-down food. Eventually,

The Digestive and Urinary Systems   **LESSON 4.4**

the stomach will release the **chyme**, or partially digested and mixed-up food, into your small intestine.

Your pancreas, liver, and gallbladder also contribute to the chemical digestion of your food. The liver makes **bile**, a yellow-green fluid that helps you break down and absorb the fat from food. Bile is stored in the gallbladder and is released as the food you've eaten leaves the stomach and heads to the small intestine.

Absorbing Nutrients

The **small intestine** is where most of the actual work of the digestive process occurs (see figure 4.22). The small intestine is 20 to 23 feet (6 to 7 m) long and an inch (about 3 cm) in diameter. It has three different parts: the duodenum, the jejunum, and the ilium. About 90 percent of all nutrients are absorbed as food travels through the small intestine. In addition to being quite long, the small intestine's interior surface is covered in small projections called villi, which create more surface area for absorption to occur.

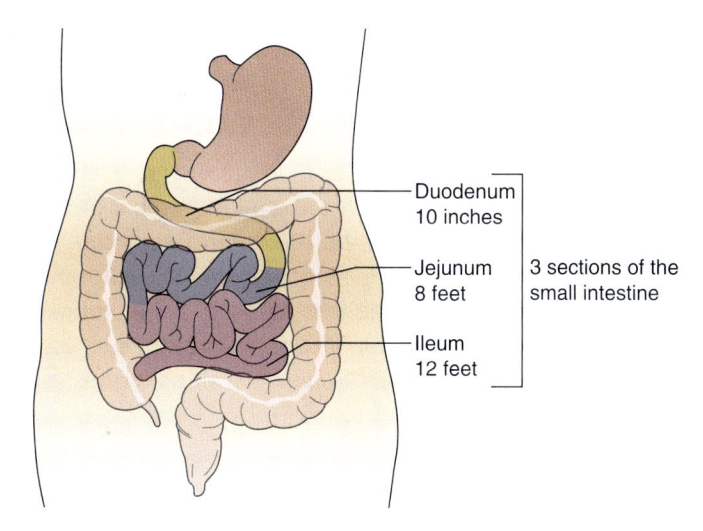

Figure 4.22 The small intestine.

Absorbing Water and Eliminating Waste

Once the food has passed through the small intestine, the body begins to prepare what is left for removal. The **large intestine** is a muscular tube about two and a half inches (6 cm) wide and five to six feet (2 m) long (see figure 4.23). Its primary job is to absorb and eliminate the remaining water, salts, and vitamins—in other words, waste. A small fingerlike projection called the appendix is at the start of the large intestine; its role is not fully understood. If this organ becomes swollen and infected by bacteria, it's important to seek medical attention right away. Treatment for this condition—appendicitis—requires a surgical procedure to remove the appendix.

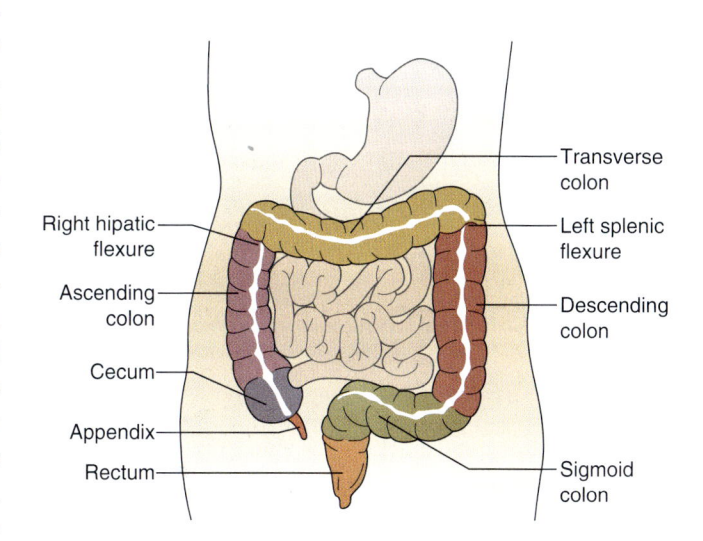

Figure 4.23 The large intestine.

175

LESSON 4.4 Food and Your Health

Your Gut Bacteria

Your digestive system is home to about 100 trillion (100,000,000,000,000) bacteria of which a majority are good. Good bacteria help break down the nutrients you eat and provide protection from infections. They also produce vitamin K and help make some important proteins. Research shows that gut bacteria can play an important role in overall health. Cancers, cardiovascular disease, and even your brain's health are linked to the balance of good and bad bacteria in your digestive system. The overall state of your digestive system, including the balance of your stomach acid and your good and bad intestinal bacteria, is called your **gut health**.

Prebiotics and Probiotics

Bacteria in your system are living organisms and, like you, need fuel to survive. Some foods, including bananas, garlic, onions, radishes, carrots, and tomatoes, can feed the bacteria in your gut. These foods are called **prebiotics**.

Probiotics, on the other hand, are the living bacteria found in food. Eating these live bacteria helps keep your gut healthy. Foods high in probiotics include fermented foods and drinks like some pickles and sauerkraut, tempeh, kefir, and kombucha, as well as Greek yogurt.

HEALTHY LIVING TIP
To get more probiotics in your diet, try eating yogurt on top of fresh fruit for a snack or dessert instead of choosing ice cream or other foods that are high in sugars and saturated fat.

Feed My Gut Grocery List

Prebiotics
- ☐ Bananas
- ☐ Berries
- ☐ Tomatoes
- ☐ Fresh vegetables
- ☐ Oatmeal
- ☐ Flaxseed
- ☐ Beans

Probiotics
- ☐ Greek yogurt
- ☐ Aged cheese
- ☐ Pickled beets
- ☐ Pickles
- ☐ Sauerkraut
- ☐ Miso
- ☐ Tempeh
- ☐ Sourdough bread
- ☐ Kombucha

Short-Term Challenges to Your Digestive Health

Upset digestion can result from a host of factors. You may experience short-term problems with how your system functions. You may also develop a problem in one of the organs of the digestive system. Some of these conditions include

- indigestion (a general feeling of stomach discomfort),
- constipation (when the movement of stool in the large intestine slows down),
- gas (air entering the intestines when certain foods are digested),
- vomiting (food exiting the body through the mouth),
- heartburn (pain occurring from acid in your stomach moving up into the esophagus),
- diarrhea (runny stool from not fully absorbing liquid in your large intestine),
- ulcers (small sores that occur inside your digestive tract), and
- hemorrhoids (swollen and painful veins in your anus and lower rectum).

Long-Term Challenges to Your Digestive Health

Other, more serious conditions that can harm the health of your digestive system are genetic or relate to eating habits, other diseases, or medications (see table 4.4). A doctor will diagnose and treat these conditions.

TABLE 4.4 Digestive System Conditions

Condition or disease	Description	Cause
Colitis and Crohn's disease	Swollen colon or small intestine	Unknown; could be partly genetic and made worse by stress or diet
Cirrhosis	Damage and scarring of the liver	Alcoholism or diseases that damage the liver
Colon cancer	Cancer in the large intestine; often begins as polyps, or noncancerous growths, in the colon	Genetics or unknown cause; diet and lifestyle play a role
Lactose intolerance	Inability to fully digest lactose (a form of sugar in milk)	Occurs when the small intestine does not make the enzyme needed to digest lactose
Irritable bowel syndrome (IBS)	Abnormality in colon function resulting in severe cramping, gas, diarrhea, and constipation	Could be caused by disruptions to muscle or nervous system in the colon or by infection

LESSON 4.4   Food and Your Health

The Urinary System

The urinary system removes liquid from the body. Two kidneys and two ureters, the bladder, and the urethra make up this system (see figure 4.24). The primary purpose of the urinary system is filtering and cleaning. You have two bean-shaped kidneys that are located in the lower back part of your torso. The kidneys' primary role is to filter waste from the blood. Excess fluid that needs to be removed from the body becomes urine and travels from the ureters to the bladder. The bladder stores urine until you can conveniently remove it from the body. A small donutlike muscle called a sphincter keeps urine in the bladder. When young children are trained to use the toilet, they are being trained to control this muscle.

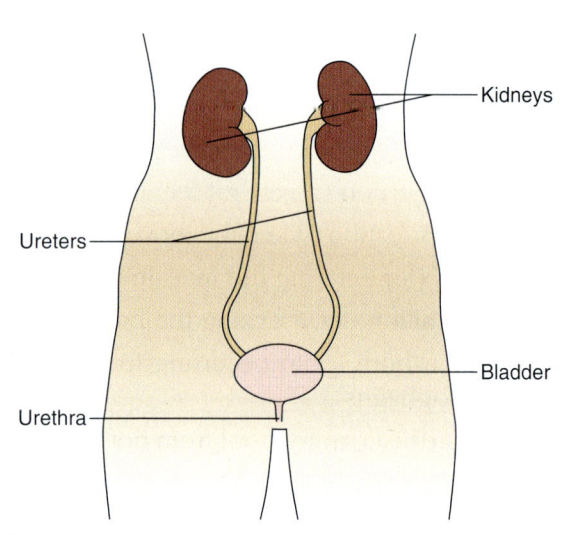

Figure 4.24   The urinary system.

When Things Go Wrong With Urinary Health

For the most part, urinary health is not a major issue. However, some serious conditions can occur. The next section discusses some of these issues.

Urinary Tract Infections

A urinary tract infection (UTI) is an infection to any part of the urinary system. UTIs are most common in the bladder or the urethra. Females are more likely than males to get these infections. Most people with UTIs experience a burning pain when urinating. They may also feel that they need to go to the bathroom often. It is important to see a doctor and to get antibiotics to treat the infection.

Kidney Stones

Some people develop small stonelike deposits in their urinary system that consist of minerals and salts that have been removed from the blood (see figure 4.25). In most cases, kidney stones will pass out of the body in the urine, but they are often very painful. Drinking plenty of water and taking over-the-counter pain medication helps. Sometimes, however, kidney stones are serious and require surgery.

Figure 4.25   Kidney stones look like small pieces of gravel.

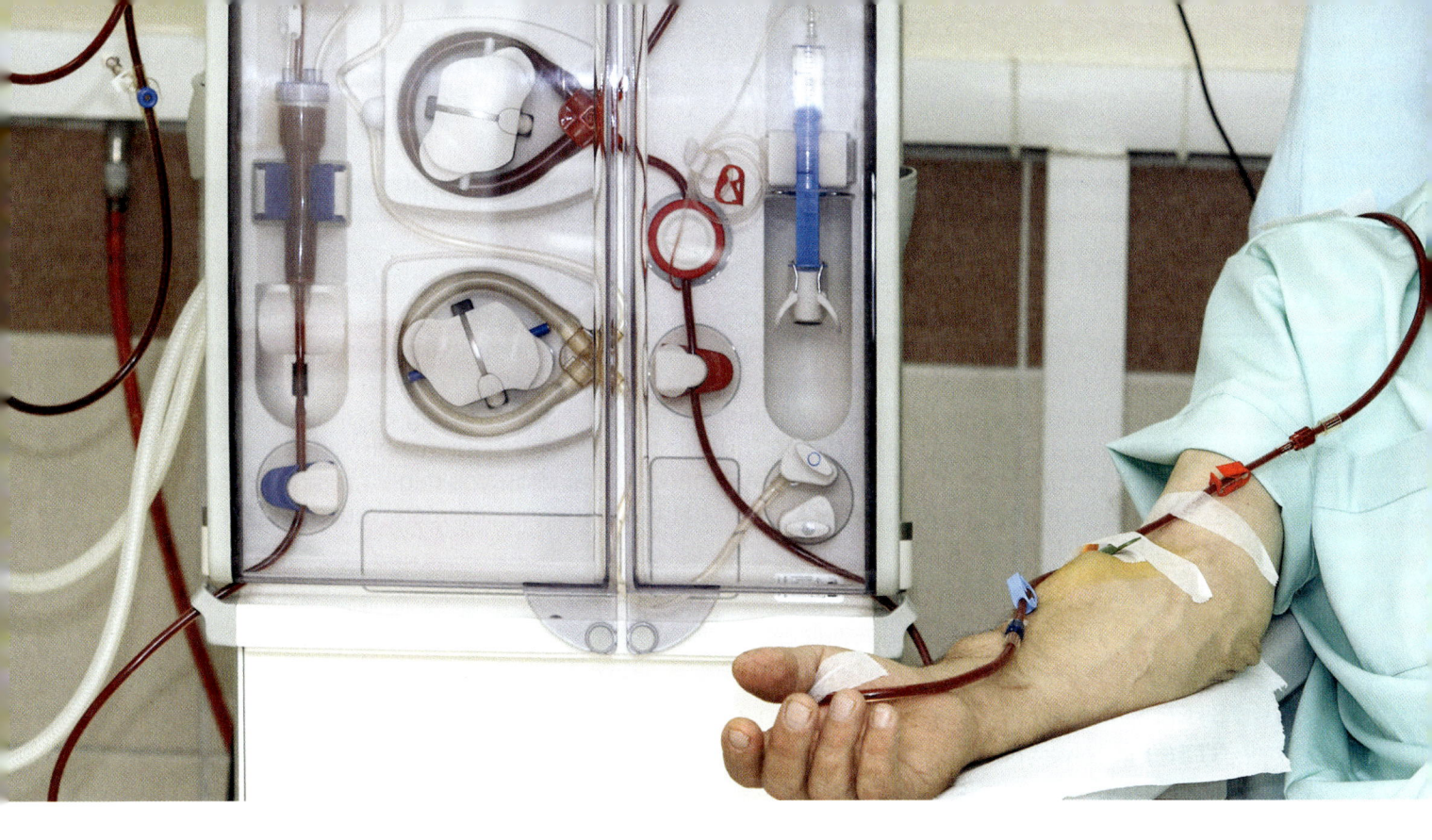

Kidney Disease

Kidney disease is when a person's kidneys gradually lose function. Often a person does not realize they have kidney disease until it has become serious. Kidney disease can't be cured, but treatment can prevent it from getting worse. People with advanced cases of kidney disease require **kidney dialysis**, a process in which artificial machines filter their blood for them. Without kidney function and dialysis, a person cannot survive long.

When a person's kidneys no longer function, kidney dialysis is needed.

Maintaining Good Digestive and Urinary Health

The following list presents ways to avoid experiencing digestive and urinary system problems.

- Eat foods higher in fiber like fruits, vegetables, beans, and whole grains.
- Stay hydrated by drinking plenty of water.
- Exercise regularly.
- Eat on a regular schedule.
- Eat prebiotic and probiotic foods regularly.
- Manage your stress.

Career Connection

GASTROENTEROLOGIST

A **gastroenterologist** is a medical doctor who either treats any part of the digestive tract or specializes in one area or on one disease. Gastroenterologists are trained to perform specialized procedures. To become a gastroenterologist, you must first earn a four-year college degree and then complete medical school. Postgraduate work requires an additional three years during which you learn this specialty at a teaching hospital.

LESSON 4.4   Food and Your Health

Skill-Building Challenge

Promoting Digestive Health

Most people don't enjoy discussing their digestive health with others, and many find the topic too embarrassing when terms like *vomiting*, *gas*, and *diarrhea* creep up in conversation. But understanding these bodily functions and realizing they are common can help you feel more comfortable and generally less afraid of them. More importantly, having a sense of whether it is normal can make it easier to ask informed questions and seek medical help when you need it.

Using the following five steps for health advocacy, explain how you might promote good digestive health to your peers. Choose any topic from this lesson that interests you in completing this challenge.

STEP 1: Identify the healthy behavior or outcome you want to address.
STEP 2: Support your message with facts.
STEP 3: Find a healthy, positive, or good reason to do the behavior or work toward the outcome.
STEP 4: Identify the specific group of people who would most benefit from your message.
STEP 5: Create your message using the format that works best for the group you want to help.

Healthy Living Skills

This lesson focused on promoting good digestive health. Here are some more ways you can develop healthy living skills related to this lesson.

ACCESSING INFORMATION

Conduct online research of kidney disease. Visit the website of the National Kidney Foundation when doing your research. Try to answer these questions: How common is kidney disease? Who is most likely to get kidney disease? How do you know whether you have kidney disease? How is it treated?

HEALTHY COMMUNICATION

Identify two digestive problems that you might experience in the next year. For each problem, write a short script on what you might say to a health professional about your symptoms. Practice your script with a partner until you feel comfortable talking about the problems you identified.

LESSON 4.4 Review: The Digestive and Urinary Systems

LESSON SUMMARY

- The digestive system includes the mouth, tongue, esophagus, stomach, pancreas, liver, small intestine, and large intestine. The digestive system is involved in the breakdown, transport, and absorption of food.
- The urinary system includes the kidneys, ureters, bladder, and urethra. The system extracts, holds, and eliminates unused fluid from the body.
- Having a good balance of healthy and unhealthy bacteria in your body can help prevent digestive and other health problems.
- The digestive system can experience problems like diarrhea, nausea, gas, constipation, and heartburn.
- Kidney disease can occur over time if the kidneys gradually begin to lose their function. When kidney disease is serious, people must have their blood cleaned through the process of kidney dialysis.
- To maintain good digestive health and urinary health, eat foods higher in fiber, drink plenty of water, exercise regularly, eat regularly, eat probiotic foods, and manage your stress.

REVIEWING CONCEPTS AND VOCABULARY

1. _____ is the mechanical and chemical breakdown of foods.
2. _____ is the movement of digested food from the digestive system into the cardiovascular system.
3. _____ is the process of getting rid of undigested food and body waste.
4. Food that you eat travels from the mouth to the _____ to the stomach.
5. The _____ secretes bile to help you digest fats.
6. The _____ intestine absorbs water before food is eliminated from the body.
7. The _____'s primary role is to filter waste from the body into the urine.
8. Kefir, yogurt, and tempeh are foods that have many _____ in them.

THINKING CRITICALLY

What happens to a bite of a hamburger as it travels through your digestive system? In one or two paragraphs, describe its journey by providing details of the bite's route and what it might experience or encounter along the way. Be sure to consider the nutrients in the hamburger and bun in your response.

TAKE IT HOME

Conduct a digestive health inventory of your home by surveying which over-the-counter medicines are stocked for common digestive problems as well as any foods that support good digestive health. Pay attention to prebiotics and fiber (from fresh fruits and vegetables, beans, and whole grains) and probiotics (from yogurt, kefir, and fermented foods like sauerkraut and pickles) in your inventory. Make a list of your findings and identify areas in need of improvement to better support digestive health. Share your ideas with an adult member of your household.

LESSON 4.5

Making Healthy Nutrition Decisions

Terms to Learn

antioxidant
food toxic environment
processed food
saturated fat
sodium
unsaturated fat

The Big Picture

We are faced with nutrition and food choices every day, whether at home, in school, or out with friends and family. Making healthy choices in challenging situations requires knowledge, self-awareness, and self-control. By making healthy eating decisions, you can develop other healthy habits.

Learning Targets

- Understand what processed foods are and explain how they contribute to a food toxic environment.
- Explain how type 2 diabetes is related to food choices.
- Using three examples, explain how different food choices contribute to overall health or disease.
- Compare and contrast healthy and unhealthy fats.
- Explain the benefits of eating a nutritious breakfast.
- Use the decision-making process to demonstrate how to choose a healthy breakfast.
- Compare and contrast grilling and broiling with frying and describe how each relates to health.

Write About It

Over the course of a typical week, what percentage of your diet comes from premade or prepackaged foods? Are the choices you make healthy? Why or why not?

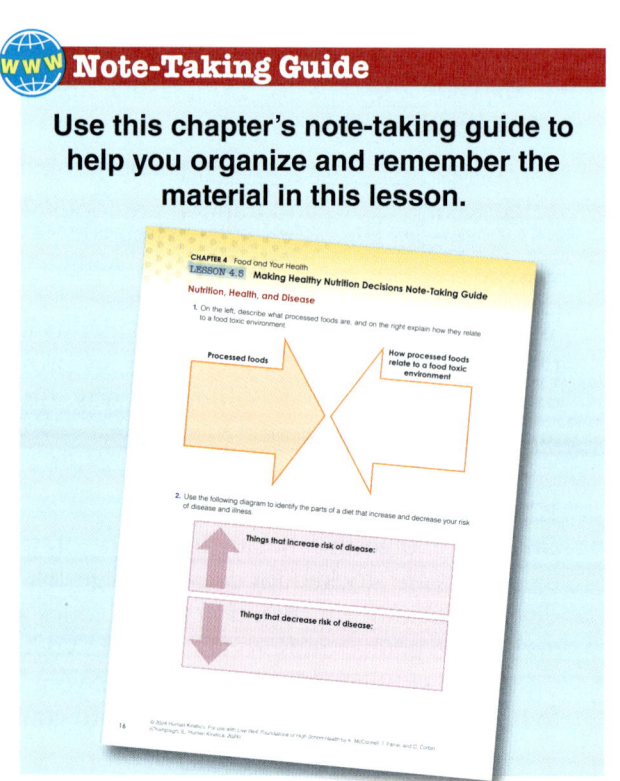

Note-Taking Guide

Use this chapter's note-taking guide to help you organize and remember the material in this lesson.

Making Healthy Nutrition Decisions **LESSON 4.5**

Natasha's dad is always talking about the importance of eating a clean, healthy diet. When her dad cooks dinner, he brags about how he is making medicine for the family, not food. He always uses an abundance of fresh vegetables, herbs, and spices and seems to know how each food affects the body. When Natasha picks out her lunch at school, she can hear her dad's voice in her head, and she thinks about how her choices might influence her health. Unfortunately, she often makes bad choices anyway because of what is available. Besides, her friends tease her—which she hates—for being such a picky eater, so it is easier to just go along with their choices. What could Natasha do to help her make the healthier decisions she wants to make? What are some specific ways her friends could be more supportive of her choices?

Nutrition, Health, and Disease

Making healthy choices every day can be hard. In the United States, we have access to a lot of cheap, convenient, and unhealthy foods. Oftentimes, healthier options like whole fruits and vegetables either aren't available or aren't fresh. Many of our convenient options are prepackaged and **processed foods**—raw foods that have been altered from their original form before they are sold or eaten (figure 4.26). During processing, these foods lose healthy vitamins and minerals and have unhealthy, high levels of salt, sugar, and chemicals added to them. Some examples of processed foods include boxed macaroni and cheese, cereal, chips, and canned soups.

Unprocessed or minimally processed foods like fruits, vegetables, and nuts are unaltered or have been slightly altered for the main purpose of preservation. The nutritional content of the food is not changed.

Processed culinary foods are food ingredients like flour and oil that are made from pressing, refining, grinding, or milling. They are used to prepare minimally processed foods and are typically not eaten on their own.

Processed foods are foods like breads, pastas, and canned fish that have added sugar, salt, or fat.

Processed foods, commonly referred to as "highly processed foods," are foods that contain salt, sweeteners, or fat and also include artificial colors and flavors and preservatives that help with shelf stability, preserve texture, and increase flavor.

Figure 4.26 Processed foods have more calories, chemicals, salt, and sugar than whole foods.

LESSON 4.5   Food and Your Health

Our society has unfortunately become known as a **food toxic environment**, where easy access to cheap, unhealthy convenience foods—most of which are highly processed—has become the predominant norm. Living in this type of environment makes it much more difficult to eat healthy, especially because fresh food options often are limited, more expensive, or both.

Added Sugars

Added sugars are a big concern when it comes to health. As you already learned, added sugars give you empty calories and often take the place of healthy food choices (see figure 4.27). Added sugars should be no more than 10 percent of your diet. This is harder for a lot of people to do than it sounds. For example, an average female should have no more than 160 calories of added sugars a day. That is about nine teaspoons of sugar per day. A single can of soda has about nine teaspoons of added sugars—a full day's worth. Sugars are also hidden in many processed foods, often serving as a preservative that helps to keep foods fresher for longer. Diets high in added sugars make it more likely that you may end up with type 2 diabetes, cancer, or heart disease.

Figure 4.27   Most soda drinks have a full day's worth of added sugars in them.

Diet and Diabetes

Nutrition and physical activity are important for people with either type 1 or 2 diabetes. Eating a healthy diet and being active helps maintain a safe blood sugar level. People with diabetes must eat high-fiber foods that contain some protein and avoid foods with added sugars to keep their blood sugar stable. They also must balance what they eat and drink with the physical activity they do. Making informed choices regarding what to eat, when to eat, and portion size plays a critical role in achieving a healthier lifestyle while living with diabetes.

Making Healthy Nutrition Decisions LESSON 4.5

Added Salt

Sodium, the main ingredient found in salt, is a mineral that the human body needs and is a common part of many people's diets. You can get your daily requirement of salt in various ways, from sprinkling it on your food for added flavor to eating canned and processed foods. Sodium assists your muscles—including your heart—with their ability to contract. It also helps keep blood pressure at normal levels. Most Americans consume much more sodium than the recommended daily allowance, and this often leads to serious and dangerous health conditions (see figure 4.28). Excessive amounts of sodium in your diet often lead to high blood pressure, or hypertension, a condition where pressure in your blood vessels is higher than normal. Hypertension is a dangerous disease that can cause damage to your blood vessels and lead to other diseases such as stroke.

Healthy and Unhealthy Fats

Certain types of fats we consume in our diets are also linked to diseases (see figure 4.29). Eating large amounts of **saturated fat**—most often derived from animal fat (e.g., butter, lard)—can lead to heart disease and heart attack and therefore is not recommended. On the other hand, **unsaturated fats** are good for you. These healthy fats are found in plant-based foods (e.g., nuts, seeds, vegetable oils) and in oily fish (e.g., salmon, tuna, sardines).

Figure 4.28 Diets excessive in sodium can lead to disease.

Antioxidants

Other foods help fight diseases. Fresh fruits and vegetables are good sources of **antioxidants**, which work to eliminate dangerous chemicals in your body. Antioxidants are substances, including some vitamins and minerals, that can prevent or slow damage to cells. Eating a diet rich in antioxidants reduces risk of cancers and other diseases. An added bonus is that foods high in antioxidants are also high in fiber, making them especially good at keeping you healthy. Table 4.5 presents a few of the most important ways diet can harm or help health.

Figure 4.29 Unsaturated fats (good) come from plant-based seeds, nuts, and oils and oily fish. Saturated fats (bad) come from baked goods and fried foods and should be avoided.

LESSON 4.5   Food and Your Health

HEALTHY LIVING TIP

To help you eat less sodium, avoid salting foods until after you have tasted them. Instead of using salt to add flavor to food, try different herbs and spices like garlic, pepper, and seasoning blends that you can find in the spice section of your local grocery store.

TABLE 4.5   Foods That Can Harm or Help Health

Food or category	Negative or beneficial effects	Example foods
Harmful foods		
Foods high in added sugars	Increases risk for type 2 diabetes, cancer, and cardiovascular diseases	Soda, candy, ice cream, flavored yogurt, peanut butter (some), canned fruits (some), juice drinks
Foods high in saturated fats	Increases risk for cardiovascular diseases	Fatty cuts of beef, pork, and other meats; cream, whole milk and whole milk cheeses, butter
Foods high in sodium	Increases risk of high blood pressure (hypertension) and cardiovascular diseases	Canned and packaged foods, chips, salted nuts and salted seeds, processed lunch meat
Beneficial foods		
Foods high in unsaturated fats	Reduces risk of cardiovascular diseases	Plant-based oils, nuts (especially avocados), seeds, salmon, tuna, dark chocolate
Foods high in antioxidants	Reduces risk of cancers and cardiovascular diseases	Colorful fresh fruits (especially berries), vegetables (especially dark leafy greens), nuts, beans, dark chocolate
Foods high in fiber	Reduces risk of cancers and cardiovascular diseases	Whole fruits and vegetables, whole grains including whole grain breads, beans

Making Healthy Breakfast Decisions

What is it about breakfast that makes it such an important meal? Breakfast helps to replenish the nutrients your body has lost during sleep and prepares you for the day ahead. Skipping it decreases your ability to focus and increases feelings of tiredness, restlessness, and crankiness as the hours of a school day tick away. Studies have correlated missed breakfasts to lower academic performance. You can strategize ways around skipping this important meal:

- Prepare grab-and-go breakfasts ahead of time.
- Avoid selecting unhealthy foods when you are at a grocery store.
- Plan ahead the night before for what you're going to eat the next day to avoid making an unhealthy choice in the moment.

HEALTHY LIVING TIP

Making healthy changes to your diet takes work. Remember to start small. If you don't usually eat breakfast, start by eating something simple like a banana or drinking a glass of milk. If you eat an unhealthy breakfast, try to add fresh fruit to your plate. You can keep adding small changes until you find yourself eating a healthy breakfast every day.

Ideas for a Healthy Breakfast

Making Healthy Decisions When Eating Out

Whether eating out is healthy or unhealthy depends on the decisions you make. It's important to consider the type of place you choose to eat at and the way in which food is prepared. This is just one way to help you determine how relatively healthy it is. Another option is to request the nutrition information about the foods on their menu, which restaurants should be able to easily provide to you. This is a great way to make better and more informed decisions. Figure 4.30 provides some basic decision-making tips that you can use to help you eat healthier in any restaurant.

LESSON 4.5 Food and Your Health

Tips for Eating Out

- *Start with a glass of water.* Drinking water will help you realize you aren't as hungry as you thought.
- *Pick your vegetables first.* Determine which vegetables from the menu you want and *then* select the rest of your meal. Ask for extra vegetables in place of items you don't like.
- *Finish your meal before ordering dessert.* It is okay to treat yourself to dessert occasionally. Wait until you are completely finished eating to decide whether to order dessert . . . you might find you don't want it.
- *Choose meats that are grilled or broiled.* If you eat meat, grilled or broiled meat is the way to go. It is cooked with direct heat, like a barbeque grill or oven. Grilled and broiled meats don't need any extra fat to cook, and some of the fat in the meat will melt off.
- *Avoid fried foods.* Fried foods are cooked in large amounts of hot oil and add excessive calories and amounts of fat to your diet. Eating fried foods over time increases your risk for cardiovascular diseases. So skip those greasy sides of French fries, potato chips, and breaded mozzarella sticks.
- *Avoid excessive amounts of salad dressing, gravy, or sauces.* A meal loaded with vegetables quickly turns unhealthy once it is submerged in gravy or coated with cheese sauce. Salads with creamy dressings also have more calories than some meals. If you can't swear off the sauce, ask for a reduced amount or get the dressing on the side.
- *Taste your food before salting it.* Many prepared foods already have too much salt in them. If after tasting it, you still think it could use some additional flavor, ask the waitstaff to season it with other complementary herbs and spices as an alternative.

Figure 4.30 Use these tips when you're eating out.

Making Healthy Nutrition Decisions **LESSON 4.5**

Steps to a Healthy Decision

Step 1: Understand the problem.
Example: You feel outrageously hungry, but the nearest food option at the moment is a fast food place that has a limited menu primarily consisting of hamburgers, fries, and the like. You know that you don't feel your best after eating meat and fries or drinking sugary soda, but you don't have enough time to go anywhere else.

Step 2: Gather information and know your options.
Example: Study the menu carefully to see whether healthier, lower-calorie alternatives are available. Perhaps you could order a salad in place of fries. Ask questions to find out if you can get your hamburger prepared a certain way. Consider leaving off cheese and mayonnaise and adding mustard, lettuce, and tomato. Find out whether they have water, sugar-free iced tea, or other nutritious beverages that don't have added sugars.

Step 3: Know the consequences.
Example: If you don't eat, you will probably get tired and that current strain behind the back of your eye will turn into an ugly, raging headache. If you eat a hamburger and fries, you know it's going to make you feel sluggish and your stomach will feel heavy. Add to that a soda, and that tops off your already unhealthy meal with a ton of sugar, which will raise your blood sugar level. The last thing you want to feel is jittery or anxious.

Step 4: Make a decision.
Example: You decide you really need to eat and that you can get the hamburger with lettuce and tomato and skip the fries. You also decide to have water instead of soda.

Step 5: Think about your choice.
Example: How do you feel about the decision you made? What, if anything, would you do differently next time? Think about your decision to help you be better prepared for the next choice you make.

Choosing Healthy Convenience Foods

During puberty, your body is developing and maturing at a near-constant rate and demands calories (fuel) for the amount of energy it is expending. It should come as no surprise that teens eat snacks throughout the day. Unfortunately, the calories you eat as snacks can add up quickly and can cause weight gain that you might not want. When choosing snacks, think about choosing fresh, unprocessed foods or foods low in fat, salt, and sugar like these following options.

Healthy Snack Options

- Carrots or celery; choose a low-fat ranch dressing if dipping and dip lightly
- Apple slices; add a small piece of cheese if preferred
- Bananas, oranges, blueberries, grapes, strawberries, and other easy-to-grab fruits
- Low-fat or fat-free yogurt with fresh fruit
- Whole grain crackers or toast
- A small handful of mixed nuts or seeds
- Air-popped popcorn
- Water, sugar-free beverages, low-fat milk, or 100% fruit juice

LESSON 4.5   Food and Your Health

STEM in Health

PHYTOCHEMICALS

Modern research has led to the discovery of small chemical compounds called phytochemicals that occur naturally in many unprocessed foods and give foods their bright colors. Science hasn't yet proven that phytochemicals are essential for human health. We do know, however, that eating them helps prevent a wide range of diseases including heart disease, diabetes, cancers, infections, eye diseases, and dementia. The best way to make sure you benefit from phytochemicals in your diet is to eat at least five to nine servings of colorful fruits and vegetables each day.

Eat Colorful Food

White	Yellow	Orange	Green	Purple	Red
Keeps your heart strong	Boosts immune system	Protects eye health	Powerful detoxes, fight free radicals	Helps memory, improved mineral absorption	Lowers blood pressure, fights against disease

Skill-Building Challenge

Making a Healthy Food Decision

You make nutrition decisions every day. Sometime today or tomorrow use the decision-making tips outlined in this lesson to help you choose a healthier snack, eat a healthier breakfast, or substitute an unhealthy option with a healthier one when eating out. Write down each step of your decision in the following list.

STEP 1: Understand the problem.

What is the nutrition issue you want to work on (like eating more fiber or less sugar)?

STEP 2: Gather information and know your options.

What information exists to help you make your decision (like labels or restaurant guides)?

What options are available?

STEP 3: Know the consequences.

Identify a consequence for each option that you have.

STEP 4: Make a decision.

What decision did you make?

STEP 5: Analyze your choice.

What did you learn from this decision process?

Healthy Living Skills

This lesson focused on making healthy decisions in a variety of settings. Here are some more ways you can develop healthy living skills related to this lesson.

ANALYZING INFLUENCES

What determines whether or not you eat breakfast? Brainstorm as many influences as you can and write them down. Next, think about how you are influenced by these factors. Do you skip breakfast because of how late you wake up? Do you avoid healthier choices because someone teases you? Do you avoid breakfast because you are afraid of gaining weight? What are two actions you can take to positively influence your breakfast decisions?

ACCESSING INFORMATION

Before you even go out, you can evaluate the nutritional value of many restaurant meals. To do this, conduct an online search for nutrition information by typing the name of the restaurant followed by the search term *nutrition information*. Select three restaurants you eat at regularly (or would like to eat at). Look up some of your favorite items from the website's linked menu. For each item, write the total calories and record the total fat, sodium, and added sugars. Then search for a healthier option from the menu. By using online nutrition information to identify healthy options before you get to a restaurant, you can learn to make and stick with healthy choices.

LESSON 4.5 Food and Your Health

HEALTHY COMMUNICATION
Practice being assertive the next time you feel someone pressuring you about your food choices. Be polite while defending your decision. Try saying, "I understand that you like eating this, but I want to make a different choice" or "It's important to me to try eating healthy, and I would appreciate your support." To help you, role-play the conversation with a trusted friend or adult first and then try it in real life when the situation arises.

PRACTICING HEALTHY BEHAVIORS
One way to get a varied diet is to eat foods that come in all different colors. Many of the healthiest foods are white, green, red, orange, yellow, and purple. Keep track of how many foods you eat from each color every day for a week. After the week is over, add up the foods for each color group. Did you get a good variety of foods in your diet based on the colors you ate?

ADVOCATING FOR GOOD HEALTH
Make a log of all the snack options that exist on your school campus. Use the information in this chapter to help you create a "Healthy Snack Attack" campaign for your school. Design posters, brochures, and flyers that promote the healthiest choices available on campus. Put together a snack-building kit that shows a variety of healthy snack options to bring to school. If you see someone making a healthy snack decision, be sure to reinforce to them that they have made a great choice.

LESSON 4.5 Review: Making Healthy Nutrition Decisions

LESSON SUMMARY

- Processed foods are foods that have been altered before being sold or eaten.
- The United States is considered a food toxic environment because of the easy access to cheap, unhealthy convenience foods.
- People with diabetes need to make sure they eat foods that keep their blood sugar stable. They also need to balance what they eat and drink with the physical activity they do.
- Diseases are related to your diet in many ways. Foods high in added sugars increase your risk for diabetes, cancer, and heart disease. Foods high in saturated fats increase your risk for cardiovascular disease. You may get high blood pressure by eating too much sodium.
- Eating foods high in unsaturated fats reduces your risk of cardiovascular disease. By eating foods rich in antioxidants (fruits and vegetables), you reduce your risk of cancer. High-fiber foods are beneficial in staving off colon cancer and cardiovascular diseases.
- Eating breakfast will help you focus and will keep you from being tired in school.
- Grilling and broiling involve cooking foods over direct heat. These cooking techniques are generally healthier than frying, which involves cooking food in large quantities of oil.

REVIEWING CONCEPTS AND VOCABULARY

1. _____ foods are altered from the original condition before being sold or eaten.
2. In a(n) _____ environment, unhealthy convenience foods are the predominant norm.
3. _____ is a mineral that your body needs and is the main ingredient found in salt.
4. _____ is a condition when the pressure in your blood vessels is higher than normal.
5. Derived from animal sources, _____ fat is usually a solid stored at room temperature.
6. Fruits and vegetables are good sources of _____, which help eliminate dangerous chemicals in your body.
7. Healthy fats, also known as _____ fats, are found in plant foods and oily fish.

THINKING CRITICALLY

Kateri, who is 15, typically skips breakfast. On mornings when she does eat, she enjoys a bowl of sugary cereal and an energy drink that gives her just the boost she needs. When there is fresh fruit juice in the house, she will drink that, but most of the time there isn't any. At school, she often hears her stomach growling before lunch. Coupled with the jittery feeling that outlasts the so-called boost from her energy drink, she has a hard time concentrating. How can you help Kateri learn to make healthier breakfast decisions? What advice would you give her? Write your response as a letter to Kateri.

TAKE IT HOME

Pick a meal that you and your family eat on a regular basis. Ask a parent or guardian for the recipe or look it up in a cookbook or online. Write down all the ingredients and then identify at least two ways to make the meal healthier. Share your modified recipe with a family member and encourage your family to try the healthier version together.

Chapter Review

ACTION PLAN: Eating for Good Health

Use the My Action Plan worksheet to set nutrition goals and practice good nutrition behaviors. Here is an example.

My Action Plan: Nutrition

STEP 1: Identify the health behavior you are going to work on.

> I am going to work on eating more fresh fruits and vegetables.

STEP 2: Write SMART goal(s).
Write one or two short-term goals (one day to one month long).

> I will eat two different fruits every day for one month.
>
> I will try one new vegetable this week.

Write a long-term goal (one to six months or more).

> I will eat five servings of fruits and vegetables every day.

STEP 3: Make a plan.
Identify two to five action steps (strategies) you could do to meet your goal.

> I will eat an apple or a banana every day at lunch.
>
> I will try every vegetable my dad serves at dinner.
>
> I will drink orange juice at breakfast.
>
> I will talk to my parents about making sure we have fresh fruit and vegetables to eat at home.
>
> I will go to the salad bar in the cafeteria at least two times each week.

STEP 4: Do your plan and track your progress.

Short-term goal 1
☒ Met   ☐ Not met   Date: April 12

Short-term goal 2
☒ Met   ☐ Not met   Date: May 30

Long-term goal
☐ Met   ☒ Not met   Date: _____

If you met your goal, what helped you to be successful?

> I kept track of which fruits and vegetables I ate every day for the first month. This helped to remind me of my goal and to stay on track.

If you did not meet your goal, what things made it harder for you to be successful?

> I didn't meet my long-term goal. I didn't eat at the salad bar, and sometimes I forgot about my goal.

Test Your Knowledge

Select the best answer for each question.

1. Which of the following nutrients provides your body with energy?
   a. vitamins
   b. minerals
   c. water
   d. carbohydrates

2. Which of the following is not a good source of vitamins?
   a. popcorn
   b. dark green vegetables
   c. beans
   d. citrus fruit

3. How much water should you drink each day?
   a. 2 cups
   b. 4 cups
   c. 6 cups
   d. 8 cups

4. The relationship between the calories you eat and the calories you burn off is your
   a. energy balance
   b. energy output
   c. energy intake
   d. energy reserve

5. A diet that gives you enough calories and nutrients to stay healthy is
   a. balanced
   b. varied
   c. moderate
   d. adequate

6. Which part of a food label shows you how much of the food is normally eaten?
   a. calories
   b. % DV
   c. serving size
   d. ingredients list

7. According to MyPlate, you should
   a. focus on fats
   b. make half your proteins meat
   c. make half your plate grains and vegetables
   d. make half your plate fruits and vegetables

8. The breakdown of food in your body is called
   a. digestion
   b. absorption
   c. elimination
   d. articulation

9. Hypertension, or high blood pressure, can be caused by eating too much
   a. sugar
   b. fat
   c. salt
   d. fiber

10. Which is most likely to happen if you skip breakfast?
    a. You will have more energy.
    b. You will feel less hunger.
    c. You will improve your concentration.
    d. You will gain weight.

PROJECT-BASED LEARNING: Posting Healthy Meals on Social Media

What to Remember

There are many things that make a healthy meal. A healthy meal should be balanced, varied, moderate, and adequate. It should also provide plenty of fiber and include foods that are prepared in healthy ways. A healthy meal provides carbohydrates, fats, and proteins in appropriate proportions and includes a healthy drink. A healthy meal can also reflect your food preferences and traditions.

Who It Is For

Your classmates

Why It Is Important

It will help your peers see healthy food options that may be accessible to them.

What to Do

As a team, use Twitter (or a similar social media application) to post photos of and share information about 10 healthy meals. Each meal should clearly demonstrate an important part of good nutrition. Make sure your tweet (maximum of 280 characters) explains what makes the meal healthy. If your team doesn't have access to Twitter or other social media, create a shareable Google document that features photos of healthy meals with your "post" typed underneath each photo. Your teacher may ask you to provide meals from different settings like home, school, and restaurants or from different mealtimes like breakfast, lunch, and dinner. Remember to include beverages with each meal.

How to Do It

- Use the information in this chapter to identify the 10 different features you want to highlight in your tweets. Remember, each post must display a photo of a healthy meal and should highlight a specific part of good nutrition.

- Work collaboratively to create a final script for each post. Then decide who among your teammates will be responsible for posting.

- Make sure you have the Twitter or social media handle for each team member (if you have them) and for your teacher (if the teacher provides this). As you tweet your meals and comments, make sure to send them to your team and your teacher. Ask your teacher whether other students in the class should receive your posts.

- If you don't have access to Twitter or other similar social media, work together to import photos into your Google document. Allow editing access and share the document with everyone in the class including your teacher. Use the Comments feature to post comments about the pictures and messages you developed.

CROSS-CURRICULAR CONNECTIONS: Math

Part of eating a healthy diet is knowing how many calories of each nutrient to eat each day. Answer the following math questions to help you practice mastering this concept.

Jaime needs 2,300 calories per day. He has eaten 1,495 calories in carbohydrates. If his protein intake should be 5 percent more than his fat intake, how many calories should come from protein? How many from fat?

Managing Good Nutrition

LESSON 5.1   Eating Well Across the Lifespan
LESSON 5.2   Food Access and Safety
LESSON 5.3   Maintaining a Healthy Weight
LESSON 5.4   Your Body Image
LESSON 5.5   Your Nutrition Plan

Understanding My Health

What Influences My Eating Behaviors?

Managing good nutrition involves numerous changing factors over your lifespan. Your age, stage in life, access to food, and efforts to manage your weight all have impacts on your diet. This self-assessment asks questions about how these factors influence your current choices. Answer each question in the following chart by selecting the response that is most accurate for you. When you are done, add up your points. The closer you are to 24 points, the healthier your diet is.

	Always	Sometimes	Never
I eat iron-rich foods like meat, shellfish, and dark green leafy vegetables daily.	3	2	1
I eat calcium-rich foods like milk, yogurt, cheese, and dark leafy vegetables daily.	3	2	1
I am able to eat food that is kept clean and cold and has been safely prepared.	3	2	1
I have access to enough food each day.	3	2	1
I haven't tried to lose or gain weight unless my doctor asked me to.	3	2	1
I like my body and am proud of what it can do.	3	2	1
I believe I am at a healthy weight.	3	2	1
I am willing to ask others to support me in eating healthy.	3	2	1

My score for What Influences My Eating Behaviors? = _____ (total number of points)

Good nutrition comes with many challenges. Teenagers experience rapid growth and development that require special attention. They often struggle with issues of weight gain, weight loss, and body image. Many teens lack access to healthy, affordable, and safe food. Proper goal setting and planning help reduce or manage these challenges.

LESSON 5.1
Eating Well Across the Lifespan

Terms to Learn
anemia
calcium
iron
longevity

The Big Picture
Nutrition is important at every stage of life, and our specific nutritional needs change over time. During the teenage years, certain nutrients like calcium and iron become especially important. Understanding the nutritional needs of people as they move from infancy to older age can help you make healthy choices for yourself and for others.

Learning Targets
- Compare and contrast the nutritional needs of people across the lifespan.
- Identify strategies that encourage children to eat healthy.
- Explain why calcium is important during the teen years.
- Use communication skills to make healthy nutrition decisions.

Write About It
In what ways have your eating habits changed since you were a young child? Do you ever think about how nutrition might affect the way you age?

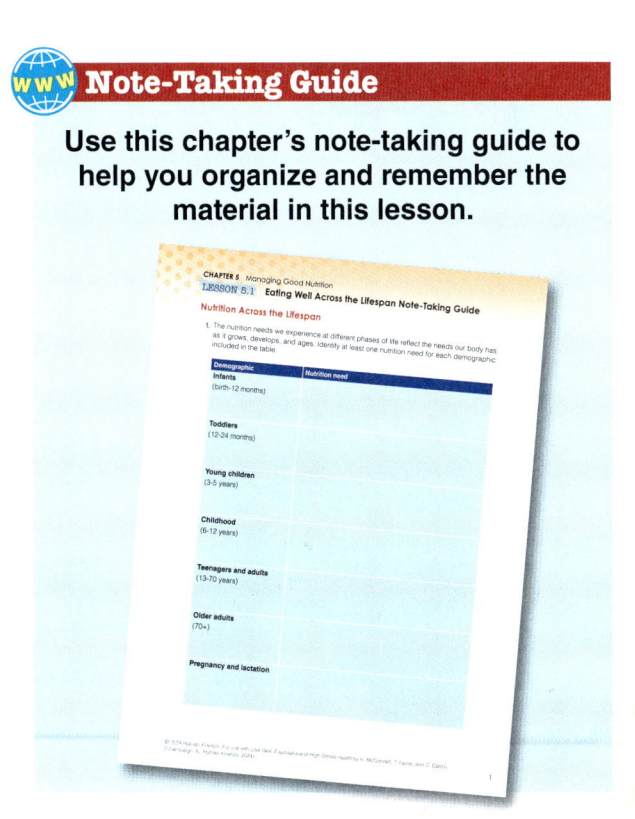

Note-Taking Guide
Use this chapter's note-taking guide to help you organize and remember the material in this lesson.

LESSON 5.1   Managing Good Nutrition

Quinn is a picky eater. She loves hamburgers and fries and pretty much avoids eating vegetables. Quinn's mom is vegetarian and her dad eats mostly seafood instead of other meat. Quinn is allowed to eat meat, but it sometimes makes her feel a little sick. Quinn generally eats a lot of junk food before and after dinner as well. Her favorite food options at school are bean and cheese burritos and French fries from the cafeteria. Quinn is a little heavy, but it doesn't bother her and even makes her feel tougher. Do you think Quinn should focus more on eating a healthy diet? Why or why not?

Nutrition Across the Lifespan

The nutrition needs we experience at different phases of life reflect the needs our body has as it grows, develops, and ages. As a growing teenager, you have specific nutrition needs, such as increased intake of iron and calcium, that differ from the unique nutrition needs for infants, toddlers, young children, and older adults. Some of the major nutritional considerations for these groups are provided in table 5.1. Life circumstances—for example, pregnancy, certain medical treatments or procedures, and disease—also may disrupt and change a person's specific nutrition needs. As you age and experience different life circumstances, it is important to revisit your nutrition needs and goals.

Nutrition and the Teenage Years

Most teenagers begin to make many of their own food and nutrition choices during middle school and high school. Although family still has an influence on nutrition decisions, peers gradually come into larger focus. During this time, many teens begin displaying their independence and establishing their own identity. They often are moving between school, activities, work, and family obligations. As a result, most adolescents don't consume enough fruits and vegetables. Easy, on-the-go beverages that are high in calories like soda, specialty coffees, and energy drinks and unhealthy convenience foods and snacks take the place of healthier options and become the more common nutrition choices. Yet, teens should be following the same nutrition advice for adults regarding adequacy, balance, variety, and moderation. There are specific minerals of special concern for adolescents as well. It is important for teenagers to realize that what they eat influences their **longevity**—the length or duration of one's life.

TABLE 5.1 **Lifespan Nutritional Needs**

Life stage	General nutrition requirements	Unique considerations and concerns
Infants (birth-12 months)	Diet should be 40-50% fat and no more than 20% protein. Infants rely on breast milk and formula for most nutrition.	Infants begin to consume solid food at around 6 months. Food allergies, choking, dehydration, and digestive issues are concerns.
Toddlers (12-24 months)	Total calorie needs rise to support increased movement and growth. Diets should be 30-40% fat and 45-65% carbohydrate. Toddlers need about 13 g of protein each day.	Toddlers are often given multivitamins and minerals as well as fluoride supplements. Toddlers can overdose quickly, so any supplement should be approved by a physician and should not have more than 100% of the RDA for any vitamin or mineral.
Young children (3-5 years)	Children grow about 2-4 in. (5-10 cm) per year until they reach adolescence. Calorie needs increase to meet this demand. Fat intake should be gradually reduced to reflect adult levels and the balance of macronutrients begins to look more like adolescents and adults.	Dental cavities, low calcium intake, body image concerns, and food insecurity are primary concerns at this age. Children's eating habits are strongly influenced by family eating patterns as well as food access at school.
Childhood (6-12 years)	Nutritional needs in childhood mirror adult needs but are proportionally less. Children need a diet with a variety of fruits and vegetables, whole grains, fat-free and low-fat dairy, protein, and oils (healthy fats). Solid fats and added sugar should be limited, as should sodium.	Prepackaged meals and foods and sugary drinks often mean that children are particularly vulnerable to diets high in solid fats and added sugar, which can contribute to the development of chronic diseases earlier in life.
Teenagers and adults (13-70 years)	Follow all standard nutrition guidelines for a diet that is moderate, balanced, adequate, and varied. Teens should ensure adequate calcium, vitamin D, and iron intake.	Avoid eating excess calories, especially empty calories from sugar and alcohol. A multivitamin and mineral supplement may be needed to help ensure adequate vitamin and mineral intake.
Older adults (70+)	Total energy needs decline with age, so older adults need less food. At the same time, they need more vitamin D, calcium, fiber, and B complex vitamins. This makes it important to get nutrient-dense foods.	Food preferences may change because aging reduces our sense of taste and smell and affects our gastrointestinal function. Many older adults also live on less money and are more isolated, so nutrition assistance and access to fresh, healthy foods are important.
Pregnancy and lactation (breast feeding)	Pregnancy places a heavy demand on the body, creating a need for more calories and an increase of nearly all nutrients. When a mother is breastfeeding, total calories, fat calories, and vitamins A, C, E, all B-vitamins, sodium, and magnesium are essential for healthy breast milk.	Folate and iron are two particularly critical minerals during pregnancy. Deficiencies in these important minerals can have negative impacts on the health of the fetus. If the mother's nutrition is inadequate, it can result in neural tube defects, spina bifida, low birth weight, anemia, and other health challenges for the infant.

LESSON 5.1   Managing Good Nutrition

Minerals for Healthy Development

Iron and calcium are two minerals that play critically important roles during the teenage years. **Iron** helps the hemoglobin in your blood carry oxygen to all of your cells, while **calcium** strengthens bones and assists in muscle contractions.

Iron and Teen Health

Eating a diet that is high in iron helps blood carry oxygen to the cells, which has a significant impact on your body's growth and development. Adequate amounts of iron are also essential to having sustained energy throughout the day. Without iron, your body can't produce enough red blood cells. Figure 5.1 shows iron-rich foods. Diets with iron deficiencies can lead to **anemia**, a condition resulting from low red blood cells. Figure 5.2 shows symptoms of anemia.

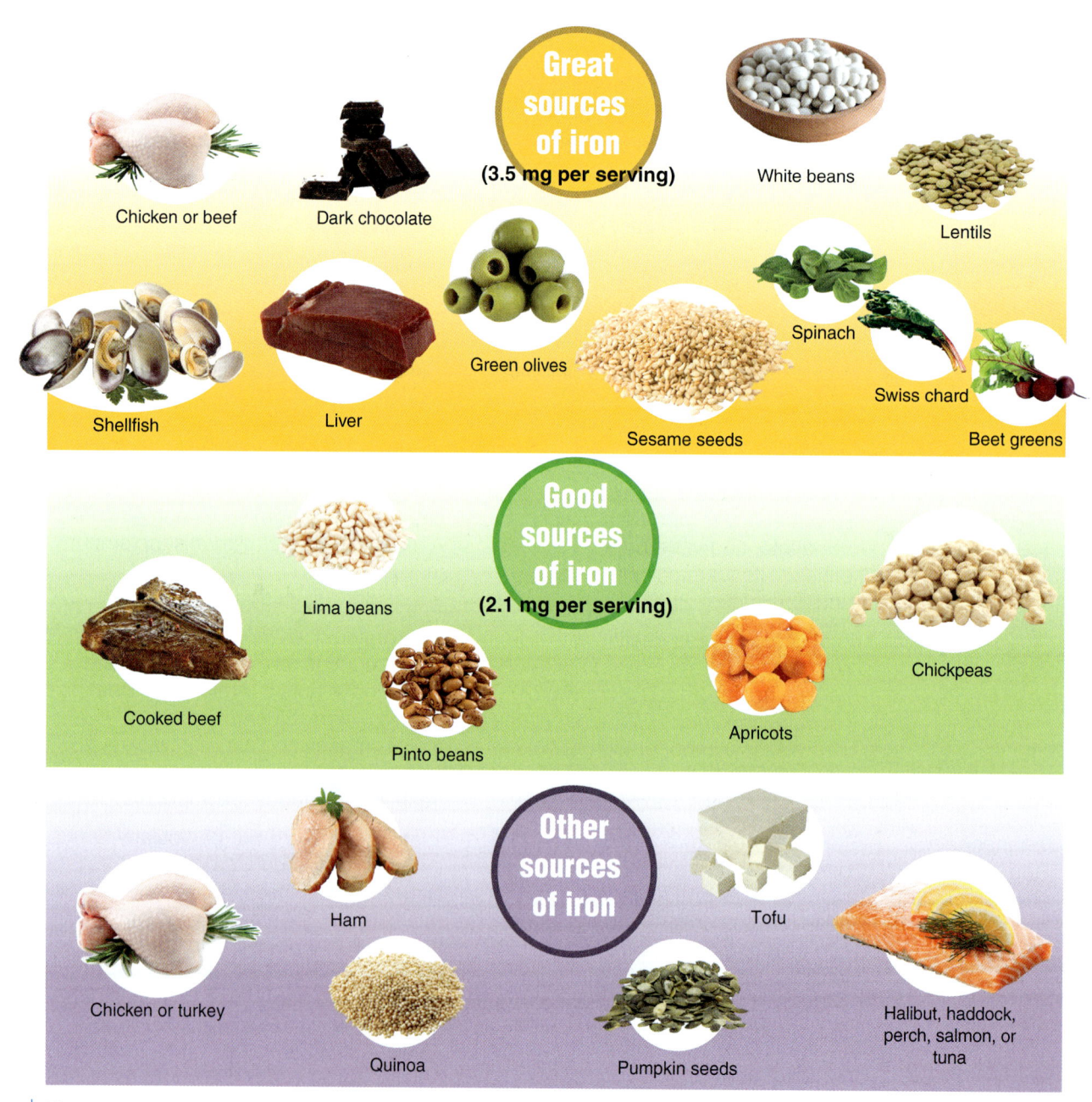

Great sources of iron (3.5 mg per serving): Chicken or beef, Dark chocolate, White beans, Lentils, Shellfish, Liver, Green olives, Sesame seeds, Spinach, Swiss chard, Beet greens

Good sources of iron (2.1 mg per serving): Cooked beef, Lima beans, Pinto beans, Apricots, Chickpeas

Other sources of iron: Chicken or turkey, Ham, Quinoa, Tofu, Pumpkin seeds, Halibut, haddock, perch, salmon, or tuna

Figure 5.1 Sources of iron in foods.

Eating Well Across the Lifespan **LESSON 5.1**

Sometimes teens don't get adequate B12, folate, or iron in their diets.

If one of these nutrients is low, their bodies cannot make enough oxygen-carrying red blood cells.

This condition is called anemia.

Be alert for these symptoms of anemia.

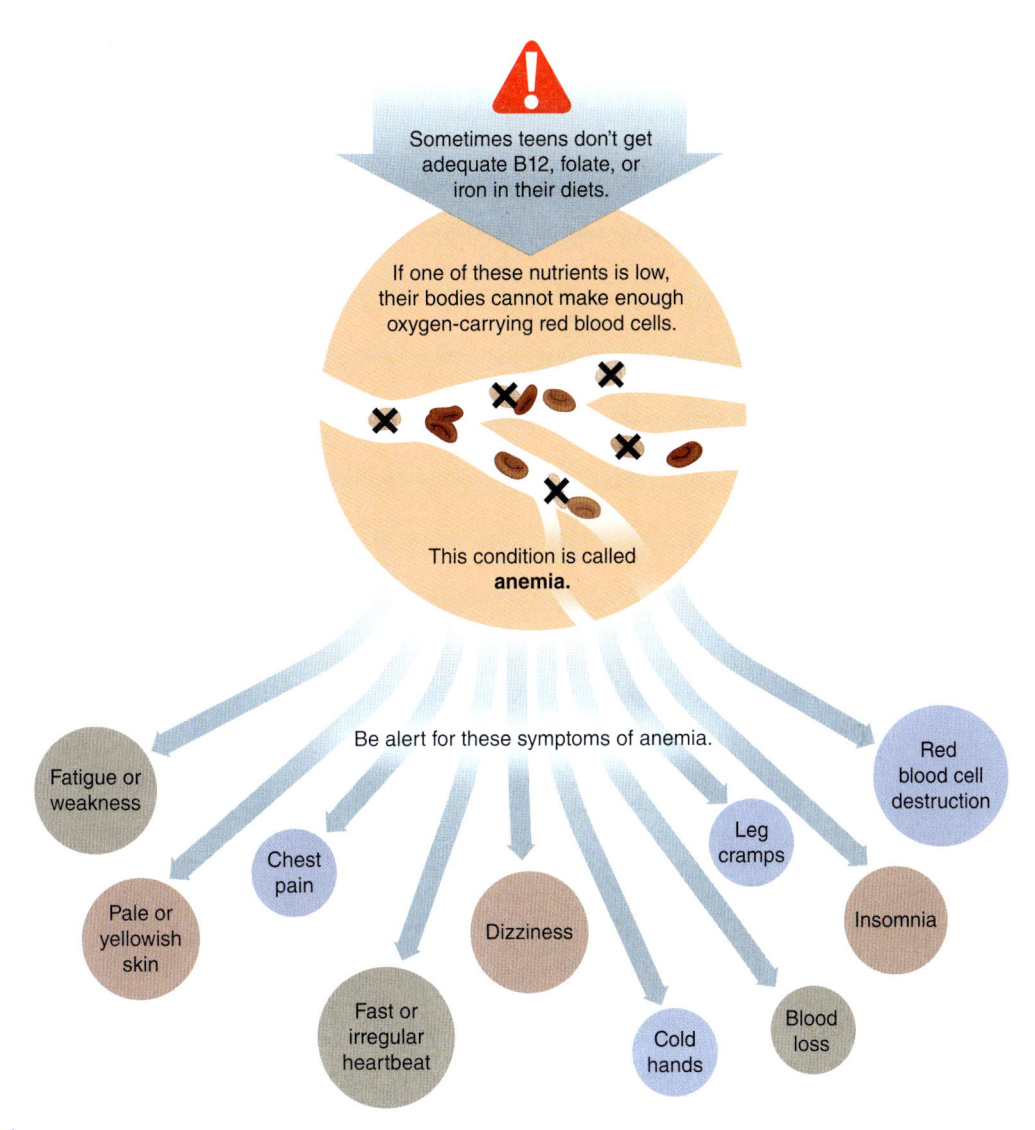

- Fatigue or weakness
- Pale or yellowish skin
- Chest pain
- Dizziness
- Fast or irregular heartbeat
- Cold hands
- Leg cramps
- Blood loss
- Insomnia
- Red blood cell destruction

Figure 5.2 Symptoms of anemia.

On average, teenage boys should get 11 milligrams of iron a day, and teenage girls should get 15 milligrams. Girls require more iron, especially during puberty, to supplement for the blood loss that occurs during menstruation. Athletes who participate in a lot of exercise tend to lose more iron as well. Teens who eat a vegetarian or vegan diet should take extra precautions. They should track how much iron they are getting from plant-based sources and take an iron supplement if they are under the recommended daily value.

HEALTHY LIVING TIP
Try eating dried apricots dipped in dark chocolate for an iron-rich treat.

Calcium, Vitamin D, and Teen Health

Your bones grow quickly during adolescence. If you don't get enough calcium and vitamin D during this time, your bones will not reach their peak bone density. This increases your risk for fractures and other serious issues, such as osteoporosis, later in life. Calcium is a primary mineral that helps your bones grow and your muscles function. Vitamin D helps regulate the calcium in your blood. In order to support bone growth, teens need 1,300 milligrams of calcium and 600 IU of vitamin D daily. Figure 5.3 provides examples of foods that are good sources of calcium and vitamin D.

LESSON 5.1 Managing Good Nutrition

Calcium and Vitamin D

Dairy products (calcium and vitamin D)
Low-fat milk, cheese, cottage cheese, and yogurt
Tip: Bring yogurt in your lunch or have cheese with an apple for a snack.

Vegetables (calcium)
Broccoli, dark green leafy vegetables like kale and collard greens, and mushrooms (also a good source of vitamin D)
Tip: Try a green smoothie that has one or more vegetable and mushrooms.

Soy foods (calcium)
Fortified tofu, soy milk, and soy yogurt
Tip: Try snacking on edamame (whole soybeans).

Beans (calcium)
Baked beans, navy beans, white beans, and others
Tip: Eat chili or tacos made with beans instead of meat.

Salmon (calcium and vitamin D)
Tip: Try adding canned salmon to pasta or a salad.

Foods with added calcium and vitamin D
Foods may also contain added calcium and vitamin D, such as orange juice, milk, breads, and cereals.
Tip: Eat a cereal with added calcium in milk for breakfast.

Figure 5.3 Foods high in calcium and vitamin D.

People begin to slowly lose bone mass after age 30. This means you have to pay attention to building strong bones before then. Many teens do not get the recommended amount of calcium in their diet. Teens and young adults who smoke or who drink caffeinated beverages like soda or coffee may get even less calcium. Caffeine can reduce how much calcium your body absorbs.

Teens, especially girls, who don't get enough calcium are at risk of developing the bone disease osteoporosis, a condition where you have weak bones. Osteoporosis increases the risk of bone fractures, which can cause serious disability and even death. Calcium also acts like a messenger to help muscles contract. In calcium-deficient diets, the body takes calcium from bones to make up for the loss in order to keep the heart and other muscles working. This causes further weakening of the bones. Combining a calcium-rich diet with physical activities like walking, jogging, and dancing can actually help you maximize bone growth during adolescence. The stronger your bones are now, the more likely they will remain strong throughout your life.

Communicating for Healthy Eating

It can be hard or uncomfortable to ask for what you want when it comes to nutrition. Learning to communicate your wants and needs is important so that you can make healthy choices. Sometimes you need to say "no" to someone who wants you to make an unhealthy eating choice; other times, you may need to ask for assistance in making a smart decision.

Saying "No" to Unhealthy Food Choices

It is common for people to offer food or to want you to eat something you would rather avoid. Oftentimes we don't want to turn down offers simply because we worry it would hurt the other person's feelings. The following section provides tips for saying "no" in unhurtful ways—an important skill for eating well.

The Power of "No"

Use the word *no*. There is no substitute. Everyone understands the meaning of the word *no*.

Strong *no*: "No, I do not want to eat that."

Weak *no*: "I don't know. I might eat one after I finish mine."

Communicate "no" nonverbally through body language.

For example:

Wave it off. Use a wave of your hand to help you say "no."

Stand up straight to project confidence. Slouching signals that you feel unsure.

Be serious. Say "no" without laughing and joking around, otherwise people won't think you are serious.

Use a strong voice to say "No, thank you." Often a "Thank you" or "Thanks for offering" helps the "no" be heard.

Repeat the "no" message as often as needed. If the person keeps asking, keep responding with "no." If you say "No, thank you," and a person asks "Are you sure?", respond by saying "Yes, I am sure, thank you."

LESSON 5.1 Managing Good Nutrition

Asking for Help

If the food options you have are confusing, don't be afraid to ask for help or suggestions. You can also ask for help in making a healthier choice by asking for the food to be made a certain way. Here are some examples of how you might ask for help with nutrition decisions.

- Use your research skills to look up nutrition information online before eating out. This can help you know which healthy choices the restaurant offers and make decisions easier once you arrive.
- Request more information from the wait staff by asking, "Can you give me the nutrition information about the food on the menu?"
- If the food you want appears to be sold out at a food stand or food counter, ask, "Do you know whether you have any more of these?"
- Get another opinion when choosing food at a fast-food restaurant by asking, "Which of these options has the fewest calories and fat?"
- Ask for a substitution on the menu. For example, "Can I get this sandwich with mustard and whole wheat bread instead of mayonnaise and white bread?"

Negotiating for Healthy Food Choices

Sometimes you need to negotiate with others. You and your friends might all want different things for lunch, and you have to decide what you will do. There may be tension or conflict between two or more people as you decide. Negotiation is a lot like decision making, except it involves working through a conflict with another person or other people. The following scenario is an example of how to successfully navigate a conflict.

Steps for Negotiating Healthy Food Choices

1. Identify the conflict. You and your friends want to go get lunch. However, Joaquin wants pizza, Emma wants tacos, and Jaylin wants a burger. No one seems willing to concede.
2. Brainstorm your options. You could (A) go to more than one place if there is time and the places are close enough together; (B) play rock, paper, scissors to decide where to go; or (C) agree that each person gets to take a turn choosing where to eat lunch and then decide who gets to choose today.
3. Evaluate solutions. There isn't enough time to go to all three places. It doesn't make sense to decide where to go by playing rock, paper, scissors because the same person could win each time you go out. You go to lunch every week, so it makes sense to take turns choosing.
4. Choose a solution. Since it makes the most sense and seems the fairest, you decide to take turns.
5. Do it. You decide the order, starting with Jaylin, then Joaquin, then you, and Emma.
6. Reflect on how it went. Once we got to lunch, there were lots of options to choose from, so I was happy, and it worked out fine. It makes sense to just keep rotating who gets to choose.

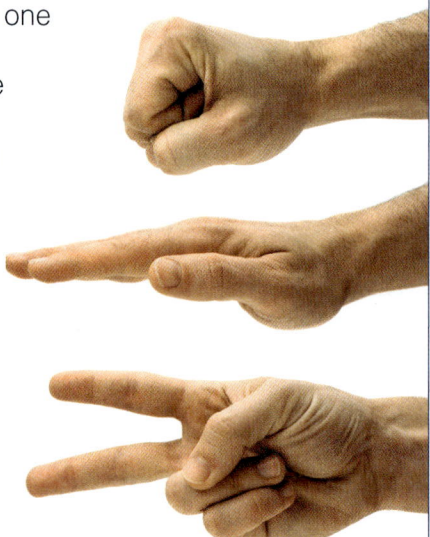

Skill-Building Challenge

Healthy Communication

Read each scenario and choose a communication strategy to use in the situation. Apply the strategy to the scenario and record what you think might happen as a result.

Scenario A: It is Jessep's birthday. Her friend Phoenix bought Jessep a fancy cupcake for her birthday and brought it to lunch for Jessep to eat. But Jessep is trying to cut back on sweets and added sugars and doesn't want to eat the cupcake.

1. What communication strategy or strategies could Jessep use to say "no" to the cupcake?
2. What is a potential outcome of using the strategy?

Scenario B: Mark is trying to get more nutrients in his diet, but he doesn't know what to pick for his lunch. The food truck he is at has a lot of options, but some are foods he doesn't recognize.

1. What communication strategy or strategies could Mark use to make the best choices to increase the nutrients in his diet?
2. What is a potential outcome of using the strategy?

Healthy Living Skills

This lesson focused on healthy communication. Here are some more ways you can develop healthy living skills related to this lesson.

PRACTICING HEALTHY BEHAVIORS

Eat a diet high in calcium, vitamin D, and iron. Identify three foods you like to eat that contain calcium or vitamin D. Then identify three other foods you enjoy eating that contain iron. Make a daily checklist that lists all six foods and track how many of each food you eat each day for a week. Reflect on your progress and adjust your list if needed.

ACCESSING INFORMATION

Select one of the populations discussed at the start of this lesson (infants, toddlers, younger children, older adults, pregnant women). Research more about the specific nutrition needs of this population. Use the Accessing Valid and Reliable Information skill cues as a guide and remember to find more than one source of information. Create a "How to Eat Healthy" handout based on the information you find for the group you selected.

LESSON 5.1 Managing Good Nutrition

LESSON 5.1 Review: Eating Well Across the Lifespan

LESSON SUMMARY

- Nutrition needs vary across the lifespan. Differences exist for infants, toddlers, young children, older adults, and pregnant women.
- Iron is important for growth and development. If you don't get enough iron, you could develop anemia.
- Your bones grow rapidly during your teenage years. Getting adequate calcium and vitamin D will help you grow strong bones now, which will also mean you will have strong bones later in life.
- Calcium and vitamin D are found in dairy products, fortified cereals and juices, and tofu.
- Learning to communicate your nutrition needs is important. Important skills to practice include saying "no," asking for help, and negotiating conflict.

REVIEWING CONCEPTS AND VOCABULARY

1. How long a person lives is their _____.
2. Meat, shellfish, and dark chocolate are examples of foods high in _____.
3. Headaches, dizziness, and fatigue are symptoms of _____.
4. Dairy products are an excellent source of vitamin D and _____.
5. People begin to slowly lose bone mass after the age of _____.
6. The first step in negotiating for healthy food choices is to _____ the conflict.

THINKING CRITICALLY

Reread the opening paragraph of this lesson. Which parts of Quinn's diet might be contributing to her calcium and iron intake? What recommendations would you make to Quinn to improve her intake of these minerals?

TAKE IT HOME

Make a list of snacks and lunch items you like that are high in calcium and iron. Share your list with your parent or guardian. Set a SMART goal together to help increase one or both of these minerals in your diet.

LESSON 5.2
Food Access and Safety

Terms to Learn
food additive
food chain
food insecurity
food preservative
food recall
foodborne illnesses
genetically modified foods
malnutrition
organic food
pesticides

The Big Picture
Not everyone has access to the same amount of food or to food that is healthy and safe to eat. Understanding issues like food insecurity and foodborne illnesses can help you advocate for accessible, healthy, and safe foods for yourself and your community.

Learning Targets
- Explain influences on food insecurity.
- Describe the food chain and identify ways that foods become contaminated.
- Explain the four steps to food safety.
- Practice advocating for food access and food safety.

Write About It
How does the location of where a person lives influence food supply? Which social and environmental factors make it more challenging to eat a healthy diet?

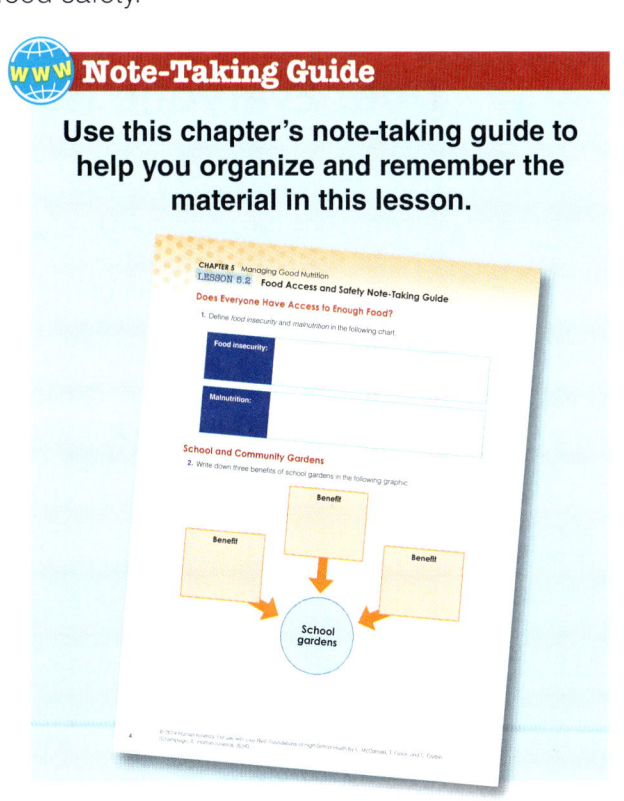

Note-Taking Guide
Use this chapter's note-taking guide to help you organize and remember the material in this lesson.

LESSON 5.2 Managing Good Nutrition

Zara and her family live in an immigrant community in an urban area. Her parents immigrated to the United States from Iran, and both work in unskilled jobs that pay minimum wage. They usually have enough money to buy some food each day. Sometimes their power is turned off because they've fallen behind on their monthly bills.

Zara's parents work hard to provide for their family. Zara's dad is a landscaper at a local business park, and her mom works as a night janitor at a downtown business office. Even though they are both working full time, they struggle to pay rent and buy food and other supplies. The apartment they live in is near a lot of restaurants and a couple of grocery stores, but they still often struggle to find food they can afford. It is common for the family to eat off of the dollar menu at one of the local fast food places for dinner. Zara qualifies for free breakfast and lunch at school, but the choices are often things she doesn't like or they aren't fresh or healthy choices. Whenever there is a good banana or apple in the cafeteria, she will try to bring it home to eat later. Most of her friends don't really know that Zara's family struggles to buy food and can't really afford healthier options. How might Zara's situation be affecting her health? What factors are influencing Zara's access to healthy food?

Does Everyone Have Access to Enough Food?

If you shop at a big grocery store or drive down a street crowded with fast-food restaurants, you might think that food is abundant and available to all people. The truth is, not everyone has regular access to affordable, healthy foods that are properly handled, stored, and cooked.

It is estimated that about one in every eight people in the United States experiences **food insecurity**—not having access to enough healthy food to support an active, healthy life. Some people may be food insecure because they don't have enough money to buy the food they need. Others may not be able to get to food supplies because they don't have access to transportation, or they are unable to move independently and must rely on friends, neighbors, or social services to bring them food. People who are food insecure are more likely to suffer from **malnutrition**, which means having inadequate (not enough) or unbalanced nutrition.

Having free breakfast and lunch programs in schools is a critical component for addressing food insecurity and malnutrition in many communities. Some high school campuses allow students to leave for lunch. In some cases, this creates a hostile environment in which students are stigmatized, or judged negatively, for staying on campus to eat. It is important to support others who need or want to eat a free meal on campus. For some, a meal at school may be the only balanced, hot meal they have in a day.

School and Community Gardens

Schools have begun incorporating gardens on their campuses that grow healthy, nutritious foods for students. Some gardens are traditional, whereas other grow fruits and vegetables in a nutrient-rich solution without any soil. School gardens help teach students about nutrition, agriculture, food safety, and cooking.

With community gardens, local communities set aside plots of land for shared use, where people can rent a portion of the garden to grow fresh produce. Community gardens are beneficial at both the individual and community levels. They provide healthy, outdoor, socially engaging recreational activity to members of a community who otherwise might not have access to their own yard or garden space.

Food Safety

There are several reasons why food may not always be safe to eat. Food can carry pathogens that cause **foodborne illnesses**, which people get from eating or drinking contaminated food.

How Foods Get Contaminated

Food goes through several steps, known as a **food chain**, before it gets to your plate (see figure 5.4). This food chain includes the production, processing, distribution, and preparation of food. Foods can become contaminated with pathogens at any point along this process. When people become ill from food in this scenario, a **food recall** is issued. This means that food from a particular supplier is pulled from store shelves and restaurants in order to keep more people from becoming sick. It is important not to eat any food that has been recalled.

PRODUCTION
- Growing plants and raising animals
- Contamination may come from irrigation water or illness in fish or animals

PROCESSING
- Preparing foods and food ingredients
- Contamination may come from water, dirty equipment, or infected fish and animals

DISTRIBUTION
- Transporting from the processing plant to the consumer
- Contamination may come from lack of refrigeration or dirty equipment

PREPARATION
- Preparing, cooking, and serving food
- Contamination may come from sick employees, dirty equipment and surfaces, cross contamination, and improper cooking

Figure 5.4 Food can become contaminated anywhere along the food chain.

LESSON 5.2   Managing Good Nutrition

Common Foodborne Illnesses and Symptoms

Viruses and bacteria are the most common pathogens that cause foodborne illnesses (see table 5.2). Other sources of contamination include parasites and fungi. Some foodborne illnesses make you sick soon after you eat, while others can take weeks to show symptoms. In general, foodborne illnesses cause nausea, stomach cramps, vomiting, and diarrhea that will last from one to three days. The most serious foodborne illnesses, like salmonella, can be deadly.

Foods most commonly infected include

- chicken, beef, pork, and turkey,
- fruits and vegetables,
- raw milk,
- eggs, and
- seafood and raw shellfish.

TABLE 5.2   **Common Foodborne Illnesses**

Pathogen	Symptoms	Source
Norovirus (the most common foodborne illness)	Diarrhea, vomiting, nausea, stomach pain	A contagious virus that can live on surfaces and foods
Salmonella	Diarrhea, stomach pain, chills, fever, vomiting, dehydration; requires medical care	Raw eggs, contaminated irrigation water, animal feces
E. coli	Diarrhea, stomach cramps, nausea; can cause kidney damage	Contaminated water, raw milk, cow manure
Listeria	Fever, muscle aches, diarrhea, headache, confusion; requires medical care	Animal feces, manure, raw milk
C. perfringens	Stomach cramps, diarrhea	Naturally occurring in the environment; killed with proper cooking
Campylobacter	Fever, headache, muscle pain	Contaminated water, animal feces, raw milk
Mold and fungus	Diarrhea	Moldy foods
C. botulinum	Weakness in muscles, including those used for breathing and swallowing; requires immediate medical care	Home-canned, preserved, or fermented foods as well as honey and corn syrup

Safe Food Handling and Preparation

How you handle and prepare your foods will affect how likely they are to become contaminated. This means that you need to pay attention to the foods you select and what happens to them once you leave the grocery store. It is important not to eat food that is moldy or has a foul odor. You should also check the best-by dates on food packages. Expired food is more likely to be contaminated and might be dangerous or unpleasant to eat. Once you have purchased food, the most important thing you can do when handling and preparing your food is to follow the four steps to food safety: clean, separate, cook, and chill (see figure 5.5).

HEALTHY LIVING TIP

Avoid eating at buffet restaurants that don't put fresh food out often. Trust your instinct if foods look old or are not kept at the proper temperature.

CLEAN: Always begin any food handling and preparation by washing your hands with warm, soapy water for at least 20 seconds. Make sure all utensils, cutting boards, and surfaces are clean. Wash all fruits and vegetables—even those you peel or cut—in order to keep bacteria from spreading. Once you are done preparing food, clean all surfaces and supplies thoroughly. Use a mild bleach-based cleaner on kitchen surfaces to kill any lingering bacteria.

CHILL: As soon as you are done eating, place all leftover food into the refrigerator. Use shallow dishes to allow foods to cool evenly. Foods that require refrigeration should not be left out at room temperature for more than two hours. When food is left out, colonies of bacteria can grow quickly. This is especially important at potluck parties and picnics, where food is often left out in warm environments for long periods of time.

SEPARATE: While shopping for food or when storing food in the refrigerator, separate produce from meats, eggs, and poultry. Use separate cutting boards, surfaces, and utensils to prepare meat, eggs, and poultry. Using the same surface or utensils can easily result in cross-contamination of bacteria and pathogens. For example, if raw chicken is placed on the cutting board and then the same board is used for making a salad, the bacteria from the uncooked chicken will get on the raw vegetables and could cause illness.

COOK: Cook foods to their proper temperature to kill known pathogens. Always serve food immediately or make sure to keep cooked foods above 140° F if they are not being eaten right away. If you are eating at a buffet restaurant or a party, make sure the food is being kept warm. If the food does not seem hot, avoid eating it.

Figure 5.5 Four steps to food safety.

Food Additives and Preservatives

Following the steps to food safety helps us keep our food safe. Another way we try to keep food safe is by using food additives and preservatives. A **food additive** is a substance added to food to add nutrition, or to improve freshness, taste, texture, or appearance.

When an additive is specifically designed to help a food last longer without spoiling, it is called a **food preservative**. While these substances might prevent food from spoiling too quickly, some may also bring their own risks. Antioxidant vitamins (like vitamin E) can act like a preservative in foods while also increasing the nutritional value of the food. Other preservatives include chemicals like nitrates, nitrites, and sulfites, which may be dangerous to your health. Food manufacturers today are offering more foods processed without dangerous additives. Check the ingredients list on foods you eat to make sure there are no dangerous additives listed.

Pesticides

Pesticides are chemicals used in the food production process in order to prevent damage to a crop from insects, weeds, and infections. Most pesticides are considered toxic on some level.

Some people choose to eat organic foods in order to avoid pesticides. **Organic food** is grown or produced without chemical pesticides on an organic-certified farm and contains no synthetic ingredients, bioengineering, or radiation. While they have not been proven to be more nutritious than traditionally farmed foods, organic foods have fewer dangerous chemicals. Some foods are more likely to absorb chemicals than others. The USDA maintains a list of fruits and vegetables that absorb the most chemicals and are best bought organic, called the *dirty dozen*, and those that absorb the least, called the *clean 15* (see figure 5.6).

The dirty dozen

1. strawberries
2. spinach
3. kale
4. nectarines
5. apples
6. grapes
7. peaches
8. cherries
9. pears
10. tomatoes
11. celery
12. potatoes

The clean 15

1. avocados
2. sweet corn
3. pineapples
4. frozen sweet peas
5. onions
6. papayas
7. eggplants
8. asparagus
9. kiwis
10. cabbages
11. cauliflower
12. cantaloupes
13. broccoli
14. mushrooms
15. honeydew melons

Figure 5.6 Produce that absorbs the most pesticides (the dirty dozen) and produce that has the fewest pesticides (the clean 15).

STEM in Health

GENETICALLY MODIFIED FOODS

The term *genetic engineering* refers to the use of biotechnology to modify plants or animals. The goal of genetically engineering food is to create plants with better flavor that grow better, have greater resistance to insect damage and plant diseases, or are able to last longer without spoiling or needing preservatives. In this process, scientists make targeted changes to a plant's genetic makeup to give the plant a new desirable trait. Most typically, genes from another plant or animal are added to the item being modified. Most of the soybeans and corn grown in the United States are genetically modified. Tomatoes, rice, and potatoes are also commonly modified. While **genetically modified foods** are generally considered safe to eat, controversy exists about their economic and environmental impacts.

Skill-Building Challenge

Advocating for Food Access

Part of the challenge people face in eating healthy on a regular basis has to do with their access to affordable, safe, and healthy foods and water. No matter where you live, you can advocate for improved access to one or more of the items in the following list. For this project, select one of the items from the list to help you practice your advocacy skills. Try to pick an item that affects you, your school, or your community.

- ☐ Access to affordable, healthy, and organic food options
- ☐ Access to safe drinking water
- ☐ Access to a school garden or community garden plots
- ☐ Access to safe food preparation

Use the steps to community advocacy to develop a campaign for your selected issue. Create a short speech and supporting materials to present to community or school leaders who might help change the situation you are addressing. These could include school officials, county or city council members, or business bureaus in your area.

Healthy Living Skills

This lesson focused on advocacy. Here is one more way you can develop healthy living skills related to this lesson.

ACCESSING INFORMATION

Conduct online research for bioengineered food, and make a list of three websites that provide accurate and valid information on your topic. Use the Accessing Valid and Reliable Websites Skill Cues to help you identify valid and reliable sources of information. Form an opinion based on your research about the safety and value of bioengineered foods in relation to food safety.

LESSON 5.2 Review: Food Access and Safety

LESSON SUMMARY

- Food insecurity refers to not having enough food to support an active, healthy life.
- The food chain includes the production, processing, distribution, and preparation of food. Foods can become contaminated with pathogens at any point along this process. Contaminated water supplies, dirty equipment, lack of proper refrigeration, and sick employees are common causes.
- Food safety involves keeping hands, surfaces, and cooking utensils clean. Raw meats and fish should always be stored and transported separately from other foods. Foods should also be cooked to the proper internal temperature; leftover foods should be refrigerated promptly after eating.

REVIEWING CONCEPTS AND VOCABULARY

1. Not having access to enough food to sustain an active, healthy life is called _____.
2. _____ is a term used to include any symptom or disorder that happens from eating or drinking contaminated food.
3. A _____ includes the production, processing, distribution, and preparation of food.
4. Food _____ are used to improve freshness, add nutrition, or improve the taste, texture, or appearance of food.
5. _____ foods are grown without normal pesticides and contain no synthetic ingredients, bioengineering, or radiation.

THINKING CRITICALLY

You have a budget of $40 to spend on food for you and one other person for a day. Determine how much food and the types of foods you can afford to buy in your neighborhood. Write down all of your selections and then compare your list with another student from your class.

TAKE IT HOME

Create a drawing or digital image that illustrates the four steps to food safety. Include words or phrases as needed to ensure that all key points in the steps are clear and easily understood.

LESSON 5.3

Maintaining a Healthy Weight

Terms to Learn

anabolic steroids
body composition
body mass index (BMI)
fat distribution
healthy weight
obese
overweight
weight cycling

The Big Picture

Weight is a complex concept that involves our genetics, environment, and behaviors. Weight can be related to health, although it alone cannot predict your overall health status. Sometimes we make good and bad decisions about food, exercise, and other health habits if we focus too much on our weight. It is important to explore weight and to understand how it affects our choices.

Learning Targets

- Explain influences on body weight.
- Describe what a healthy weight is.
- Explain healthy ways to lose and gain weight.
- Explain the risks of fad diets and supplements, including anabolic steroids.
- Access valid and reliable information about weight-loss supplements.

Write About It

Identify five influences on your weight. List them in order from most significant to least significant influence. Do you think others experience these same influences in the same way? Explain your response.

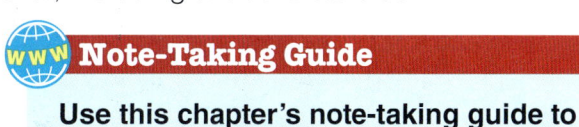

Note-Taking Guide

Use this chapter's note-taking guide to help you organize and remember the material in this lesson.

LESSON 5.3 Managing Good Nutrition

Elijah has been overweight most of his life. In elementary school, he was teased and bullied on the bus almost every day. His mom and grandpa are overweight, and the family doesn't usually eat very healthy. Elijah tries to make healthier choices at school, but his friends give him a hard time about it. The worst part is that he knows some people think he is lazy and stupid just because he is overweight. He just wishes people would get to know him before they judge him. Most people don't know that he walks almost three miles (5 km) every day with his dog and bikes with his dad on most weekends. Elijah likes who he is and knows he is a funny and smart guy who has big plans for the future. What are some of the influences on Elijah's weight? Do you think Elijah is healthy? Why or why not?

Why Is Weight Important?

Obesity is common in American society today. Forty percent of all adults and almost 19 percent of all youth aged 2 to 19 are considered to be overweight. Obesity is known to be linked to an increased risk of a variety of diseases including type 2 diabetes, coronary heart disease, and some cancers. It is also important to know that weight is only part of the story. For example, we know that people who are physically active are generally healthier than people who aren't, regardless of what either person weighs. We also know that genetics, the environment, and behaviors each plays a role in influencing weight, which makes the topic of weight and health complex.

Understanding Weight and Body Mass Index

Your body weight refers to how many pounds (or kilograms) you weigh. You can determine your body weight by stepping on a scale. Your **body mass index (BMI)** is a standard way of explaining weight as it relates to height. BMI is slightly better than weight as a predictor of the health effects of being overweight. To determine your BMI, you need to know your weight in pounds and your height in inches. Most research and most doctors consider a person with a BMI of 25 to 29.9 to be **overweight** and a person with a BMI of 30 or more to be **obese**. A BMI chart is included in the online resources.

What Is Body Composition?

Your body is made up of different tissues: muscles, bones, organs, and fat. When you weigh yourself or calculate your BMI, you aren't getting any information about the composition of your body. **Body composition** refers to the ratio of lean (muscle) tissue to fat tissue in your body. A person with more lean tissue and less fat tissue is generally at lower risk for most diseases. This is true even if the person's weight is above average.

The location of fat tissue on the body, or your **fat distribution**, can also play a role in your health (see figure 5.7). Abdominal fat, or fat located in and around the waist, is the most dangerous fat to have. Fat found around the hips and thighs is generally less dangerous to health. These are important factors to consider. For example, a strong, athletic female with a lot of muscle will weigh more than another person her size who has more body fat. If most of her body fat is around her hips and thighs, she may also be at lower risk for disease than a male of a similar size who has a fatter waist. In this example, physical activity levels, body composition, and body fat distribution tell us more about potential health risk than weight or BMI alone can.

Figure 5.7 Fat in the upper body is called an apple-shaped distribution; fat in the lower body is called a pear-shaped distribution.

How Do We Measure Body Composition?

There are several different ways to estimate body composition and fat distribution (see table 5.3). The most common method uses calipers to pinch the fat at different points on the body. If you have ever stepped on a scale that claims to tell you what your body fat is, then you are also familiar with bioelectrical impedance, or BIA. It uses electrical currents to determine how much water is the body. Water is found in muscle and not in fat. If you have more water in your tissues, you have more muscle.

LESSON 5.3 Managing Good Nutrition

TABLE 5.3 **Methods for Measuring Body Composition and Fat Distribution**

Technique	Description
Skinfold calipers	Fat just below the skin is pinched and measured.
Bioelectrical impedance (BIA)	A small current is sent through the body and the amount of water and lean tissue is estimated from the speed of the current. Handheld devices, body composition scales, and traditional electrode versions exist.
Underwater weighing	A person is weighed while under water. The volume of the body and the underwater weight of the body are used to estimate the amount of fat tissue in the body.
Waist-to-hip ratio	The waist is measured at the narrowest point and the hips are measured at the widest point. The waist measure is divided by the hip measure. A number under 0.80 for females and 0.95 for males is considered healthy.

What Is a Healthy Weight for Me?

Sometimes we hear mixed messages about weight and health. The reality is that we are all unique. Human beings come in all sorts of shapes and sizes, and we are all genetically different. The terms *underweight* and *overweight* are used as general descriptions that can help us think about things that might be influencing our health. Being underweight or overweight does not automatically mean you have a disease or have done something wrong. Your weight does not define who you are as a person, and it doesn't define your health.

What we do know is that each of us can work to be as healthy as possible. Finding the weight that is healthiest for you is important. A **healthy weight** is a weight that you are comfortable with and that can be maintained by following basic nutrition and physical activity guidelines. You and a friend could eat the exact same diet and do the exact same physical activity and still be two very different sizes and weights. It is important not to confuse weight with behaviors or to assume that someone behaves a certain way because of their weight. For example, an average-weight person who is sedentary and eats a poor diet is more likely to develop health problems than someone who is slightly overweight but gets daily physical activity and eats a healthy diet. What you do to take care of yourself is ultimately more important than what the scale says.

Losing and Gaining Weight

There are both safe and unsafe ways to gain and lose weight. Most of the safest ways also take the longest to work, which can lead people to turn to unhealthy choices instead. As a teenager, you should consult with your parents and your physician before making any decisions about losing or gaining weight. Since your teenage years are a critical time for your body's growth and maturation, you want to make sure you don't do anything that might cause long-term health challenges.

Gaining Muscle Mass

It is not uncommon for a person to want to gain muscle mass. Most people who are intentionally trying to gain weight want to gain muscle, not fat. The desire for increasing muscle mass is most common in males who are seeking to fit a perceived ideal appearance. Improving physical strength and athletic performance is another common reason given by both males and females who try to gain muscle. When you are trying to gain weight, it is important to focus on eating more nutrient-dense food. Eating foods high in sugar or fat may add weight more quickly, but the added weight is more likely to be body fat. Eating high amounts of protein is also not effective. The human body does not turn excess protein into muscle very easily. Eating a well-balanced, nutrient-dense diet higher in total calories and doing more resistance training is the most effective way to gain healthy lean body tissue. Even when diet and exercise are combined properly, some people simply are unable to become big and muscular.

Supplements designed to help with weight gain are generally not effective and can include dangerous ingredients. **Anabolic steroids** are a class of hormones that can stimulate muscle growth. Using any product containing steroids is very dangerous. Steroids can cause permanent damage to the cardiovascular system, liver, and kidneys. They can also cause severe acne, hair loss, and mood swings.

Healthy Weight Loss

There is no easy way to lose weight. In fact, a healthy rate of weight loss is between one and two pounds (0.5 to 1 kg) per week. This means that a person should decrease calories or increase physical activity by about 500 to 1000 calories per day. Most people would need to do 60 to 90 minutes of additional physical activity every day to burn 500 extra calories each day. Combining physical activity with eating less usually makes it easier to achieve weight-loss goals. Cutting back on sugary drinks and desserts, reducing portion sizes, and cutting back on snacking between meals or at night are strategies that can help. Eating the right amount of nutrient-dense foods while also increasing physical activity is the healthiest way to lose body fat and weight. It is also a good idea to have friends and family support your efforts and to keep a positive attitude.

HEALTHY LIVING TIP

If you are trying to gain or lose weight by eating healthy and doing more physical activity, try using an app like MyFitnessPal to track both your food intake and your energy expenditure.

LESSON 5.3   Managing Good Nutrition

Dangerous Dieting Habits

People often turn to fad diets and diet pills to try to lose weight (see figure 5.8). Oftentimes these products claim to offer quick and dramatic results. People who lose weight quickly on these diets and products often gain the weight back quickly as well. The process of repeatedly losing and regaining weight is called **weight cycling**. Weight cycling has been shown to slow down metabolism and increase body fat over time and can increase a person's risk for diseases. From a health perspective, it is often better to carry a few extra pounds than to repeatedly gain and lose weight.

It is important to consider the evidence behind any fad diet or supplement you might try. Many diet-related products rely on testimonials or personal stories that may not even be true. They also often include modified photos and false claims to sell their products. Pay special attention to the type of claims and promises these products make. Look for unbiased evidence and be sure to consider known or potential health risks when making a decision about using these products.

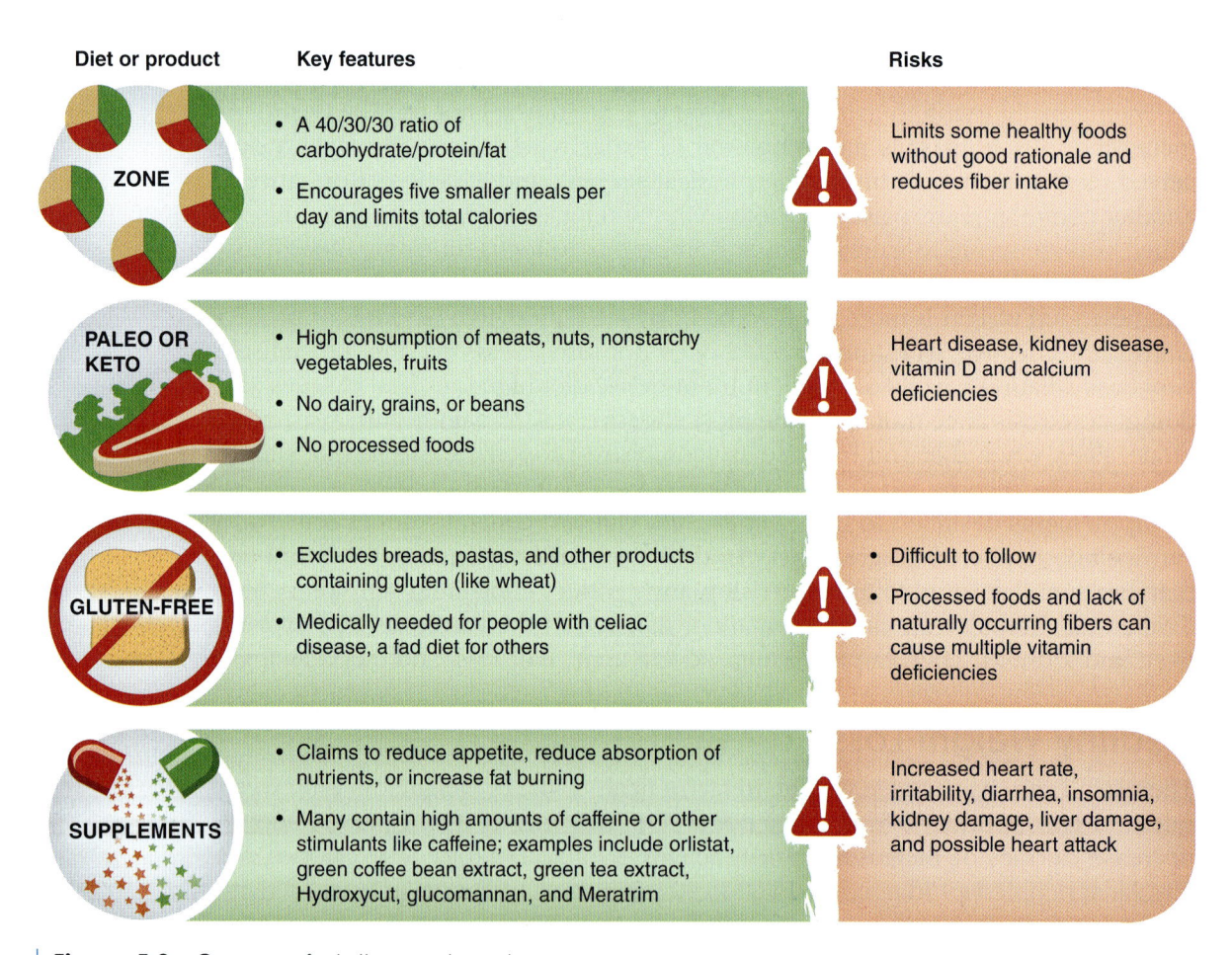

Diet or product	Key features	Risks
ZONE	• A 40/30/30 ratio of carbohydrate/protein/fat • Encourages five smaller meals per day and limits total calories	Limits some healthy foods without good rationale and reduces fiber intake
PALEO OR KETO	• High consumption of meats, nuts, nonstarchy vegetables, fruits • No dairy, grains, or beans • No processed foods	Heart disease, kidney disease, vitamin D and calcium deficiencies
GLUTEN-FREE	• Excludes breads, pastas, and other products containing gluten (like wheat) • Medically needed for people with celiac disease, a fad diet for others	• Difficult to follow • Processed foods and lack of naturally occurring fibers can cause multiple vitamin deficiencies
SUPPLEMENTS	• Claims to reduce appetite, reduce absorption of nutrients, or increase fat burning • Many contain high amounts of caffeine or other stimulants like caffeine; examples include orlistat, green coffee bean extract, green tea extract, Hydroxycut, glucomannan, and Meratrim	Increased heart rate, irritability, diarrhea, insomnia, kidney damage, liver damage, and possible heart attack

Figure 5.8 Common fad diets and products.

Maintaining a Healthy Weight **LESSON 5.3**

Skill Building Challenge

Accessing Weight Loss Information

There is no shortage of weight loss supplements and fad diets on the market. Conduct online research of a weight loss supplement or fad diet trend. You can begin by choosing something from figure 5.8, or you may find another option. Once you choose which supplement or diet to review, find at least three websites that provide information on the product. Analyze the information for validity and reliability and fill in the information in the following list. Pay particular attention to whether or not there is scientific and unbiased information available and the role that testimonials play in the marketing. Remember to use your Accessing Valid and Reliable Websites Skill Cues to help you.

1. Name of supplement: _____
2. How does it help with weight loss? _____
3. Is the information logical and does it make sense (validity)? Yes or no?
4. Is the information consistent across sites (reliable)? Yes or no?
5. Is it a safe product? What are the risks of using it? _____

Healthy Living Skills

This lesson focused on accessing valid and reliable information. Here are some more ways you can develop healthy living skills related to this lesson.

ANALYZING INFLUENCES

How does a person's cultural traditions and expectations influence their likelihood of being overweight? What cultural traditions and expectations exist in your community that might influence obesity rates?

HEALTHY COMMUNICATION

If your friend asked you to stop at the supplement store to help them pick out a diet pill, what would you say to them? Describe a realistic conversation you might have with someone you know in this situation.

LESSON 5.3 Review: Maintaining a Healthy Weight

LESSON SUMMARY

- Influences on body weight include genetics, the environment, and behaviors like diet and physical activity.
- A healthy weight is a weight that you are comfortable with and that can be maintained by following basic nutrition and physical activity guidelines.
- Healthy weight gain requires eating a highly nutrient-dense diet and engaging in resistance training exercises.
- Anabolic steroids can cause permanent damage to the cardiovascular system, liver, and kidneys. They can also cause severe acne, hair loss, and mood swings.
- Healthy weight loss occurs at a rate of one to two pounds (0.5 to 1 kg) per week and is best achieved by a reduction of total calories and an increase in physical activity.
- People often turn to dangerous fad diets or diet pills to try to lose weight. These diets can work in the short term but often don't work for the long term.

REVIEWING CONCEPTS AND VOCABULARY

1. BMI stands for _____.
2. A weight you can maintain by eating a well-balanced diet and doing regular physical activity is called your _____ weight.
3. Bioelectrical impedance is a method of measuring body _____.
4. An apple shape refers to a body type with more fat around the _____ than around the hips.
5. _____ are a class of hormones that can stimulate muscle growth.
6. A person who loses weight in a healthy way will lose _____ pounds per week.
7. When a person repeatedly gains and loses weight, it is called _____.

THINKING CRITICALLY

Read the following descriptions and decide which of the three you think is the healthiest person. Support your choice with facts.

Trayvon: 68 inches (173 cm) tall and 160 pounds (73 kg). Waist-to-hip ratio of 1.10. Eats an okay diet but never works out.

Mariah: 62 inches (157 cm) tall and 120 pounds (54 kg). Waist-to-hip ratio of 0.92. Loves to read and play video games while snacking on chips and cookies.

Keni: 64 inches (163 cm) tall and 160 pounds (73 kg). Waist-to-hip ratio of 0.76. Loves to jog and run 5k races. Eats a well-balanced diet.

TAKE IT HOME

Provide emotional support to a friend or family member who struggles with their body weight. Remind them that behaviors are more important than the numbers on a scale and encourage them to make healthy choices.

LESSON 5.4
Your Body Image

Terms to Learn
body image
body shaming
disordered eating
eating disorders
negative body image
positive body image
social comparison
weight prejudice

The Big Picture
How you feel about your body can influence the choices you make throughout the day. It is important to understand what influences your body image, how a negative body image can affect your health, and how to improve your body image.

Learning Targets
- Explain what body image is.
- Explain why having a positive body image is important.
- Compare and contrast common eating disorders.
- Describe how media, including social media, influence body image.
- Identify five ways to improve your body image.

Write About It
How often do you compare yourself to images you see in the media? How do you feel when you compare yourself to others?

Note-Taking Guide
Use this chapter's note-taking guide to help you organize and remember the material in this lesson.

LESSON 5.4 Managing Good Nutrition

Kelly just started her first year of high school. She has always been tall and thin. Her younger sister Dierdre is strong and more athletic, and Kelly wishes she looked more like her. Kelly tries to avoid showing more than her face on her social posts. Sometimes she'll post a full image if she's wearing baggy pants or a heavy sweater that makes her feel bigger and stronger. At school Kelly tries to eat as much as she can, but a lot of her friends are actually trying to lose weight so she ends up feeling uncomfortable eating in front of them. She often eats bite-size candies and chocolate during the day, just to get more calories. Sometimes she'll also sneak one of her mom's protein drinks from home to have at school. Kelly feels awkward being tall and is jealous of her sister and friends because they are more proportioned than she is. How does the way Kelly feels about her body influence her nutritional choices?

What Is Body Image?

HEALTHY LIVING TIP
Put Be Kind notes on the mirrors in your bathroom and your bedroom to remind yourself to say positive things about how you look whenever you look in the mirror.

It is very common for people to struggle with body image. Your **body image** includes your thoughts, feelings, and behaviors related to your body size, shape, and appearance. Body image is not what you project to others or how you actually look; it is how you feel about yourself and the way you look. Models and other people who are considered physically beautiful can suffer from **negative body image**. When someone has a distorted view of their appearance, or they think and feel negatively about how they look, they have a negative body image. In contrast, a person with a **positive body image** has a realistic sense of how they look and is less likely to believe their character, value, or worth is tied to their appearance.

BENEFITS OF A POSITIVE BODY IMAGE

- Good emotional health
- Improved self-confidence
- Improved self-esteem
- Healthier relationships
- Healthier habits (exercise, healthy eating)

Negative Body Image and Health

People may think that a negative body image doesn't really cause any other issues. The truth is that negative body image is associated with a lot of other unhealthy behaviors. When a person does not like their appearance, they are more likely to have low self-esteem and to engage in unhealthy dieting practices, take supplements, smoke or vape, drink alcohol, and develop eating disorders (see figure 5.9). People make the mistake of thinking that these behaviors will help them feel better about themselves, but they don't. A negative body image is also related to higher rates of depression and suicide in teenagers.

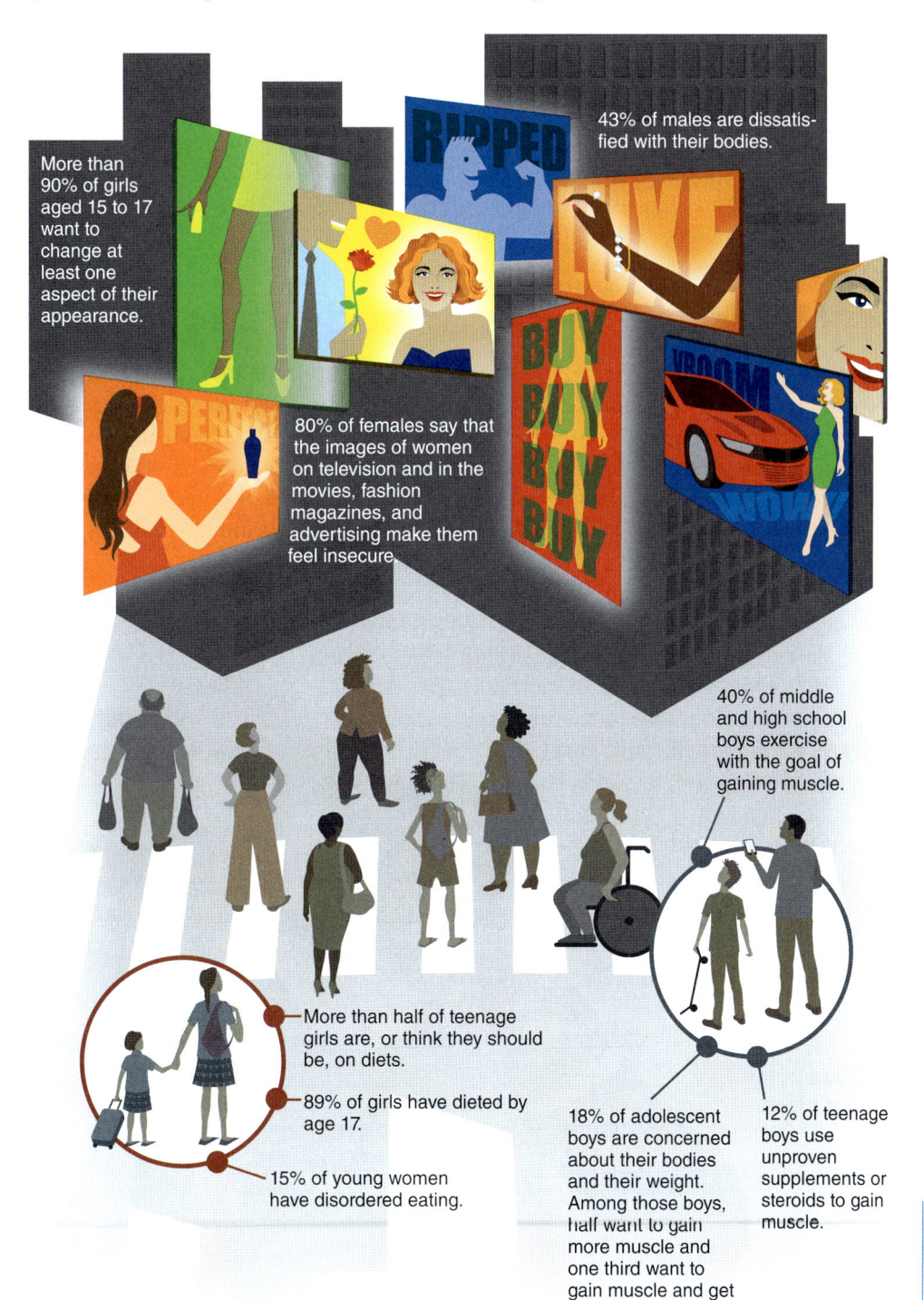

- More than 90% of girls aged 15 to 17 want to change at least one aspect of their appearance.
- 43% of males are dissatisfied with their bodies.
- 80% of females say that the images of women on television and in the movies, fashion magazines, and advertising make them feel insecure.
- 40% of middle and high school boys exercise with the goal of gaining muscle.
- More than half of teenage girls are, or think they should be, on diets.
- 89% of girls have dieted by age 17.
- 15% of young women have disordered eating.
- 18% of adolescent boys are concerned about their bodies and their weight. Among those boys, half want to gain more muscle and one third want to gain muscle and get thinner.
- 12% of teenage boys use unproven supplements or steroids to gain muscle.

Figure 5.9 People from all ages and walks of life can struggle with negative body image.

LESSON 5.4 Managing Good Nutrition

Weight Prejudice

One reason why people become focused on weight and body image is fear of how others will treat them if they are viewed as overweight or obese. **Weight prejudice** is the presence of negative beliefs, attitudes, and behaviors toward people who appear to be overweight or obese. Believing that all fat people are lazy or stupid is an example of weight prejudice.

Negative physical, social, and psychological consequences have been associated with weight prejudice just as with other forms of prejudice. Even though we see more diverse images in the media than we used to, weight prejudice against people has become more common in the United States over the past 10 years. Studies show that overweight and obese people are often stereotyped as lazy, unsuccessful, unintelligent, or lacking in self-discipline. These labels can result in prejudice and discrimination against obese people in the workplace, health care facilities, educational institutions, the mass media, and within close family and personal relationships. It is important to reflect on any bias you may have toward people who are overweight or obese and to remember that we are all different sizes and shapes. Everyone should be seen for their character and not judged on their appearance—including on their weight.

Media Influences on Body Image

We all see media images every day that portray ideal figures. Models and celebrities are paid to sell all sorts of products. Their beauty is equated with wealth, success, and power in most forms of entertainment including video games and social media. These ideal images are not realistic. The ideal woman in most media images is relatively thin, tall, and large-chested. She often has very narrow hips, large eyes and lips, and long hair. The ideal man is typically shown as extremely fit with cut abdominal muscles, broad shoulders, a tan, and a full head of hair.

It is common for people to compare themselves to these media images and to feel bad when they do. We call this behavior **social comparison**. The truth is that 95 percent of people lack the genetic traits to look like these models and celebrities. When we compare ourselves to these images, we become vulnerable to the messages the media are selling us. Beauty products, weight-loss products, fitness services, and all sorts of other products promote an ideal image as a way to manipulate us into wanting to buy what companies are selling.

Healthy bodies come in a variety of sizes.

Altering Images

The images we see in the media and on social media are not only unrealistic but also typically altered digitally to remove imperfections. The shape of a person's face or features or their body size and shape can be changed. Imperfections on the skin can be erased; hair can be made to look fuller and shinier. In fact, 100 percent of fashion images are digitally altered in some way (see figure 5.10), and 70 percent of women aged 18 to 35 admit to altering their own images on social media before posting them. This means that even the people in the photos usually don't look like their image.

Social Media

Altered images aren't the only way media can influence body image. When you post a picture on social media and others comment on how you look, it can affect your body image. Teenagers are particularly vulnerable to connecting likability on social media with body image. When a posted photo gets a lot of likes and positive comments, body image can temporarily go up. Teens admit to only posting photos that represent their best selves or those that are "thinspirational" (inspiring or celebrating thinness) so that they can get more likes. These types of behaviors further perpetuate expectations around beauty and size and are also a subtle form of weight prejudice.

Body shaming is a type of bullying behavior when making cruel comments about someone's body, and it is unfortunately common on social media. Body shaming someone is very hurtful and can have damaging effects on a person's self-esteem and well-being. If someone is body shaming you on a regular basis, consider avoiding that person on social media. You should also think about whether you make comments to others that could be considered body shaming. If you do, make a commitment to stop and to celebrate other people instead.

Figure 5.10 One hundred percent of fashion images are digitally altered in some way.

> Love your look today.
>
> Thx. At least I look better than Morgan.
>
> Yeah. Not a flattering look for her at all.
>
> Do you think she even looked in the mirror today?
>
> She wouldn't have come to school if she did.

Remember FACE When Using Social Media

Use the FACE acronym to limit how social media influences your body image.

F — Filter out sites that make you feel bad when you see them.

A — Avoid being social media friends with people who use social media to be mean or to cut others down.

C — Be careful of comparisons; remember, you are unique and don't need to compare yourself to others.

E — Evaluate the images you see, and recognize that most images are altered.

Other Influences on Body Image

The media are a powerful influence on body image, but they are not the only one. A parent or guardian who pressures you to look a certain way or to lose weight influences how you view your body image. This is especially common among mothers and their daughters. On the other hand, a parent or guardian who has a positive body image can help you have one too. How they talk about and treat their own bodies will influence how you feel about yourself.

Friends, teammates, coaches, and teachers can also influence how you feel about your body. For example, if you are teased by friends, your body image will be negatively influenced. If you play a sport, your teammates can also pressure you to take supplements or go on fad diets. These types of pressures make us feel inadequate or like we aren't good enough as we are. If a coach or teacher makes a comment to you about how you should lose weight, you are also likely to experience a negative body image. All of these groups and individuals can also influence you in a positive way if they support you and focus on complimenting your achievements instead.

> **HEALTHY LIVING TIP**
> Challenge yourself to post authentic photos that show you as you really are and like your friends' photos that do the same.

Disordered Eating and Eating Disorders

One of the major challenges associated with negative body image is **disordered eating**, a range of irregular eating behaviors like skipping meals, stress eating, periodic fasting or occasional bingeing, or eating only certain foods or avoiding certain categories of foods completely. People believe they can change their weight or appearance by engaging in these unhealthy eating habits. Disordered eating can result in a variety of health consequences such as a higher risk of obesity and eating disorders, bone loss, gastrointestinal issues, electrolyte and fluid imbalances, low heart rate and blood pressure, and increased anxiety, depression, and social isolation.

The signs and symptoms of disordered eating may include the following:

- Frequent dieting
- Having anxiety associated with eating specific foods or skipping meals
- Constantly gaining and losing weight
- Rigid rituals and routines surrounding food and exercise
- Feelings of shame and guilt associated with eating
- Preoccupation with food, weight, and body image that negatively affects quality of life
- A feeling of loss of control around food, including compulsive eating habits
- Trying to "make up for bad eating" by using exercise, fasting, restricting food, or purging

Disordered eating often leads to eating disorders. **Eating disorders** are serious, diagnosable mental illnesses that can develop at any time in a person's life but develop most commonly among teenagers. Depression and anxiety are common among those with eating disorders.

There are different types of eating disorders (see figure 5.11). In all eating disorders, people use food as a way to be in control of themselves and their lives. People of all sexes, races, ethnicities, shapes, and sizes can have an eating disorder.

Your Body Image **LESSON 5.4**

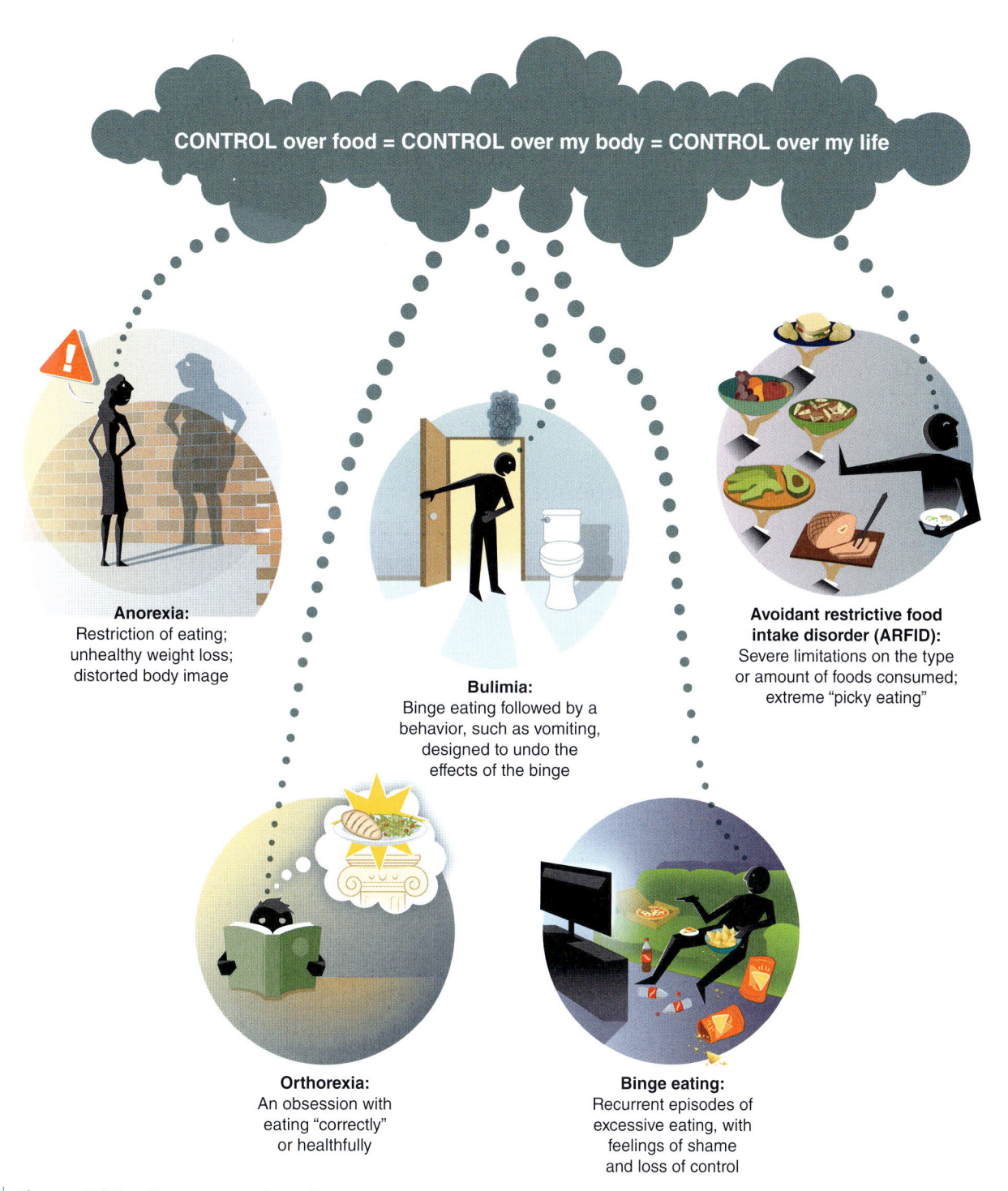

CONTROL over food = CONTROL over my body = CONTROL over my life

Anorexia:
Restriction of eating; unhealthy weight loss; distorted body image

Bulimia:
Binge eating followed by a behavior, such as vomiting, designed to undo the effects of the binge

Avoidant restrictive food intake disorder (ARFID):
Severe limitations on the type or amount of foods consumed; extreme "picky eating"

Orthorexia:
An obsession with eating "correctly" or healthfully

Binge eating:
Recurrent episodes of excessive eating, with feelings of shame and loss of control

Figure 5.11 Common eating disorders.

All forms of eating disorders are very dangerous and can be fatal. Having an eating disorder is a long-term challenge that can take years of intense professional help to learn to overcome or manage. It is critical for anyone with symptoms of an eating disorder to seek professional help. To find help via phone, text, or messaging, contact the National Eating Disorders Alliance at www.nationaleatingdisorders.org or the National Alliance for Eating Disorders at www.findEDhelp.com.

LESSON 5.4   Managing Good Nutrition

Improving Your Body Image

There are things we can all do to improve our own body image. It is important to remember that it can be hard to feel good about yourself all the time. The key is to always work to appreciate your own good qualities and celebrate the qualities and achievements of others that aren't related to how they look.

Tips for Improving Your Body Image

- Accept your body. Be less of a critic and more of a friend to yourself.
- Don't body shame yourself or others. Saying mean or negative things about how you or other people look is hurtful and can be harmful.
- Focus on the things you like about yourself. Give yourself permission to feel good about who you are.
- Focus on what your body can do, not just on how it looks.
- Be mindful by paying attention to how your body feels, moves, and plays.
- Take care of your body. Eat healthy foods and get plenty of physical activity and sleep.

CASE STUDY

Maria's Struggle

Your friend Maria has always been popular at school. From the cool clothes she wears and her beautiful, olive complexion to being a good student and a star athlete who also happens to volunteer a lot in the local community, it's hard not to be jealous of Maria. Not to mention, her parents are both successful lawyers and Maria's oldest brother just got accepted into a good college.

Lately you've noticed that Maria has become hypercritical of how she looks, calling herself fat and ugly multiple times every day on social media. Maria's posts are mostly complaints about how she hates herself in her clothes. Maria is very particular about how she poses for photos, too. It is hard for you to understand, because you think Maria is very attractive. You've also noticed how she only picks at her food lately and seems to be almost obsessive about burning off calories.

Think About It

1. How could you show support for Maria? What could you say to her that would express caring and affection?
2. How is Maria being influenced by social standards of beauty? How might Maria change the way she uses social media to help her feel better about herself and promote self-acceptance?

Your Body Image   **LESSON 5.4**

Skill-Building Challenge

Analyzing Influences on Body Image

Media play a big role in how we view ourselves and how we understand social expectations around appearance. Conduct a content analysis of your favorite television or social media shows. As you watch and consume your favorite media, keep track of how often people comment positively or negatively about their appearance or the appearance of others. Mark each positive and each negative comment using a tally mark (a line or check mark). In the notes and examples area, keep track of what types of things were said. For example, are the comments about weight, size, or fitness? Are they about hair, skin, makeup, or clothing? Are the comments different by gender, age, or ethnicity? When you are done, report the percentage of positive references and negative references. Summarize your observations and respond to the following question.

Type of comment	Tally	Notes and examples
Positive		
Negative		

Positive comments %: _____

Negative comments %: _____

Observations:

How might your body image be influenced by the types of comments you are exposed to?

Healthy Living Skills

This lesson focused on analyzing influences. Here are some more ways you can develop healthy living skills related to this lesson.

HEALTHY COMMUNICATION

Write a song, poem, or rap that explains what body image is and how it affects a person's health and well-being. Include factual information and make your creation easy for others to remember.

LESSON 5.4 Review: Your Body Image

LESSON SUMMARY

- Your body image includes your thoughts, feelings, and behaviors related to your body size, shape, and appearance.
- Positive body image is linked to good emotional health, improved self-confidence and self-esteem, healthier relationships, and healthier habits like exercising regularly.
- Media images represent a narrow view of beauty that 95 percent of people are genetically unable to meet.
- Body image can be improved. Accept yourself, don't body shame yourself or others, focus on characteristics you like about yourself, focus on what your body can do and not just how it looks, pay attention to how your body feels, and take care of your body.
- Eating disorders are serious, diagnosable mental illnesses that can develop in people of either gender at any age and require professional help to overcome.

REVIEWING CONCEPTS AND VOCABULARY

1. Your body image includes your thoughts, _____, and behaviors related to your body's size, shape, and appearance.
2. A person with a(n) _____ body image has a realistic sense of how they look and are less likely to believe their character, value, or worth is tied to their appearance.
3. _____ is a form of bullying on social media where people say mean things about how others look.
4. _____ comparison happens when people compare themselves to media images and feel bad when they do.
5. Irregular eating behaviors like skipping meals or eating only certain foods are symptoms of a condition called _____.

THINKING CRITICALLY

How would you talk to a younger person about their body image if they were unhappy with their appearance? What would you want them to know? What tips or suggestions could you provide to help them manage the pressures they may be feeling about looking a certain way?

TAKE IT HOME

Make your room a safe body image space. Take down images and posters that make you feel bad about yourself. Post positive messages to yourself on mirrors, doors, nightstands, and in drawers. Focus on what you like about yourself and what you can do well. Whenever you are in your safe space, don't allow yourself to say anything negative about your appearance. Finally, avoid body shaming yourself or anyone else.

LESSON 5.5

Your Nutrition Plan

Terms to Learn
food log

The Big Picture
Thoughtful planning can help you make healthy food choices even when circumstances are challenging. Developing the knowledge and skills you need to take responsibility for your eating behaviors is important.

Learning Targets
- Describe how to keep a food log.
- Describe two ways to analyze your diet.
- Practice setting SMART nutrition goals.
- Follow your nutrition plan and reflect on your progress.
- Demonstrate how to ask for help with meeting your nutrition goals.

Write About It
Do you ever make a choice about what to eat based on how well or how much you have been eating that day? How do you keep track of your diet and whether or not it is well balanced?

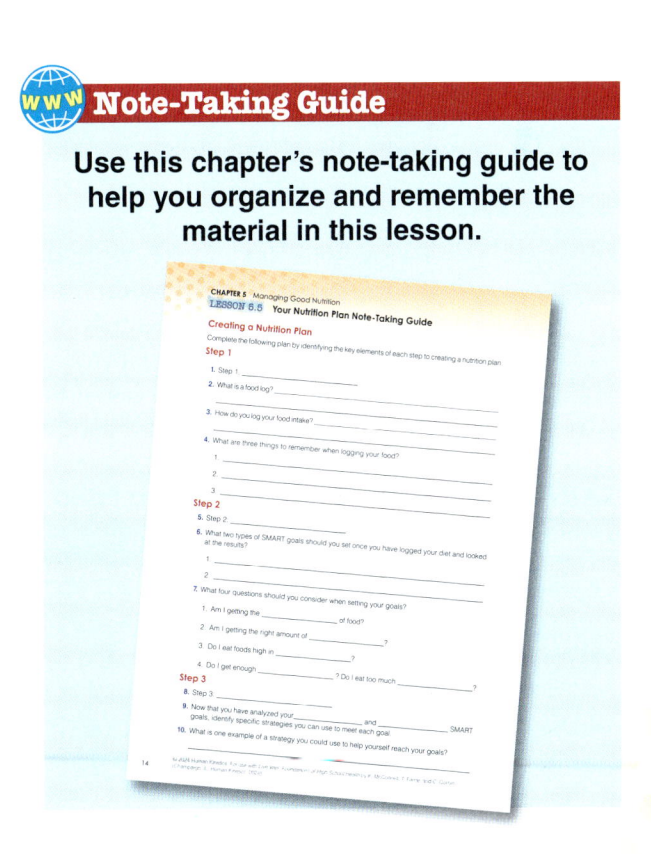

Note-Taking Guide

Use this chapter's note-taking guide to help you organize and remember the material in this lesson.

LESSON 5.5 Managing Good Nutrition

In health class, Delaney learned valuable principles about nutrition. First, a good diet requires getting adequate calories from a balance of healthy carbohydrates, fats, and proteins. Second, a person's diet should be colorful and full of vegetables and fruits. Last, when it comes to health, what you eat is more important than how you look.

Delaney has decided to make some changes to her diet, but she's not exactly sure what to do or what changes to make first. She knows she shouldn't eat so many prepackaged and premade foods. How might Delaney go about making healthy changes to her diet? How will she know what changes are the most important for her to make or if she has been successful?

Creating a Nutrition Plan

It is not realistic to think that you will keep track of what you eat every day for the rest of your life. In fact, it is not healthy to obsess over your food intake every day. When it comes to planning for good nutrition, you should focus on identifying the general weaknesses in your diet and develop goals and strategies to help you improve them. Monitoring your diet periodically over time can help you track how much progress you make on your goals. Over the long term, goals will become habits, and your dietary health will improve. Follow the steps in this lesson to help you set SMART nutrition goals and eat a healthier diet.

Step 1: Log Your Food Intake and Analyze Your Diet

When you want to make a serious effort to eat healthy, it is important to evaluate your diet first. By writing down what you eat and keeping track of your diet, you can learn about your habits and preferences. Sometimes you don't realize you aren't eating enough of a nutrient, or that you are eating too much, until you really pay attention. A **food log** is a list of all the foods you ate and the amount of each food you ate over a set period of time. The most common food logs record three days, but you can log food for one day or for a full week. To monitor your diet over a longer period of time, log three days once a month to check your habit development.

To log your food intake, write down or use an app to enter everything you eat and drink for one 24-hour period. You can recall everything you ate and drank in the last 24 hours, or you can keep track of what you eat for the next 24 hours. Be sure to keep track of the amount you eat for each food. There are different ways to record and analyze your food log. Choose a method from table 5.4 that works best for you or that your teacher instructs you to use. Two app options are MyPlate Plan and MyFitnessPal.

TABLE 5.4 **Methods for Keeping a Food Log**

Logging food groups and servings	Recording foods and amounts via app
• Using a blank sheet of paper, list the foods you ate for breakfast, lunch, dinner, and snacks.	• Enter the foods you ate into an app. Consider MyFitnessPal or MyPlate Calorie Counter.
• Write down the food group of each food and the equivalent serving you ate of each food.	• Be sure to use an app that counts calories and provides basic nutrition information.
• Use ChooseMyPlate.gov to generate your own MyPlate Plan that shows how many servings of each food you should have each day and compare your results to your list.	• Analyze your diet for total calories, fats, protein, and carbohydrates. If possible, also look at iron, calcium, sodium, and fiber.

Career Connection

FOOD SCIENTIST

Food science is a broad field that includes potential careers involving chemistry, biochemistry, nutrition, microbiology, and engineering. Food scientists use scientific knowledge to solve real-world problems associated with the food system. These include issues related to the processing and transportation, safety, preparation and storage, nutrient content, and nutritional value of food. Food scientists must have at minimum a bachelor's degree in food science. They typically work in laboratories and large and small food corporations. Salaries vary by position and experience.

No matter how you log your food, remember the following:

- Write down or enter everything you eat, even a handful of chips or a bite-size piece of candy.
- Include all drinks; many drinks contain calories.
- Don't forget condiments and sauces. The mayonnaise on a sandwich or the ketchup you had with fries count in your daily intake.
- Be honest. Your analysis will be accurate only if you keep track of everything you eat.
- Honor confidentiality; don't ask others to show you their food log and don't comment on anyone else's eating habits.

There are different ways to go about analyzing your diet. Consider each option and do what works best for you.

Step 2: Identify Your Goals

Once you have logged your diet and looked at the results, identify short- and long-term SMART goals. It is especially important that your nutrition goals are realistic. Think carefully about what you can and can't do. Keep in mind that small improvements in your diet will add up over time. Write down your goals so that you don't forget them.

To help you set your goals, look at your food log and consider these questions:

1. Am I getting the right amount of food? If not, set a goal to increase or decrease your daily calories by a specific amount. Remember, if you are trying to lose weight, you don't want to reduce your calories too low. Increasing physical activity is also important.
2. Am I getting the right amount of each food group? If not, identify specific foods you should eat more or less of.

LESSON 5.5 Managing Good Nutrition

3. Do I eat foods high in iron and calcium? If not, identify specific foods you should eat more or less of.
4. Do I get enough fiber? Do I eat too much sodium? Are there other problems with my diet? If you see a specific problem, identify specific foods you should eat more or less of.

Step 3: Develop Your Plan

Now that you have analyzed your diet and established SMART goals, identify specific strategies you can use to meet each goal. Remember, you have to take responsibility for reaching your own goals. Use a chart similar to the one in figure 5.12 as a guide for making your plan.

SMART goal	Strategy
I will eat more fiber by eating at least three servings of fruits and vegetables every day.	I will eat at least one fruit with my breakfast. I will take carrots, celery, or radishes in my lunch whenever I can. I will always eat vegetables with dinner.

Figure 5.12 Create your own chart to identify specific strategies to meet each of your goals.

Step 4: Log Your Progress

Now that you've developed a plan, create a behavior checklist to track your progress. It should include your goals and the specific strategies you want to use. You can track your progress daily over the short-term or periodically over the long-term (see figure 5.13).

Goal: Consume more fiber by eating at least three servings of fruits and vegetables every day.	Mon	Tues	Wed	Thu	Fri	Sat	Sun
Eat at least one fruit with my breakfast.	✓	✓	✓		✓		
Take carrots, celery, or radishes in my lunch whenever possible.		✓	✓	✓	✓		
Always eat vegetables with my dinner.	✓	✓	✓	✓	✓	✓	✓

Figure 5.13 Create a behavior checklist to track your progress.

Step 5: Reflect on Your Progress

After you have worked on meeting your goals for a couple of weeks, you will want to reflect on how well you are doing. If you aren't having much success in meeting your short-term goals, or your strategies don't seem to be working, you may need to adjust one or both. Remember, a SMART goal is a realistic goal. Sometimes we think a change will be easier to make than it actually is. If something isn't working, adjust your goal or your strategies to be more realistic.

Skill-Building Challenge

Asking for Support

If you want to stick with nutrition goals, chances are you will struggle to stick to your plan. Tempting foods are all around us, and it can be easy to make unhealthy food choices. Social support will help you stick to your plan. It is important to share your goals with people you trust who are most likely to be around you at mealtimes or in other situations where food is likely to be present.

When you are asking for support from others it is a good idea to take the following steps:

Explain what you are trying to do and why it is important to you.

> *I am trying not to drink soda at lunch because the caffeine makes me jittery and I know the sugar is bad for me.*

Identify the situations when you might need the most support.

> *It is hard when I am at school because my only choices are water, juice, or soda and I don't really like water or juice.*

Explain the type of support you need.

> *It would help me if my friends encouraged me to drink water and if some of them also did this with me.*

Write your own script that will help you ask for the support you need in order to stick to your nutrition plan.

Healthy Living Skills

This lesson focused on asking for support. Here are some more ways you can develop healthy living skills related to this lesson.

HEALTHY COMMUNICATION

Use social media to promote good nutrition habits you already have. For example, if you are consistent with drinking water instead of other beverages, include a bottle of water in as many of your social media posts as you can. Challenge yourself to use images to communicate as many of your healthy nutrition habits as you can.

PRACTICING HEALTHY BEHAVIORS

Select two different population groups that have specific dietary needs like athletes, pregnant women, diabetics, or those with allergies. Summarize the unique dietary needs of the population and then create an example of a one-day meal plan for each population you selected. Be sure that your plans provide an adequate number of calories and meet unique dietary needs.

LESSON 5.5 Review: Your Nutrition Plan

LESSON SUMMARY

- To keep a food log, write down everything you eat (including condiments) and drink, and the amounts you eat and drink, for a period of one to three days.
- To analyze your diet, compare what you eat to what you should eat based on MyPlate guidelines or enter your food log into a diet analysis app.
- Remember to use realistic SMART goals when it comes to nutrition.
- When you've set nutrition goals, be sure to identify strategies that will help you reach your goals and use a checklist to monitor your progress.
- Sticking to a nutrition plan can be hard. When asking support of others, explain what your goals are, when you need the most support, and what kind of support you need.

REVIEWING CONCEPTS AND VOCABULARY

1. It is most common for food logs to be kept for _____ days.
2. When logging your food intake, remember to include the serving _____ of everything you ate.
3. When making a SMART nutrition goal you should also include at least one specific _____ you can use to help you reach your goal.
4. It is important to ask for _____ to help you achieve your nutrition goals and to stick to your plan.
5. Step 5 in creating a nutrition plan is to _____ on your progress.
6. Chemistry, biochemistry, nutrition, microbiology, and engineering are all part of the study of _____.

THINKING CRITICALLY

Create a restaurant menu with meals that would align with your nutrition goals. Come up with two lunch items and two dinner items for your menu. Give each item a name and description of the ingredients.

TAKE IT HOME

Share your nutrition plan with a member of your family. Share with that person what they can do to help support you in reaching your goals.

Chapter Review

ACTION PLAN: Improving My Body Image

Use the My Action Plan worksheet to improve your body image or body weight. Here is an example.

My Action Plan: Improving My Body Image

STEP 1: Identify the health behavior you are going to work on.

I am going to celebrate my physical skills and worry less about my appearance.

STEP 2: Write a realistic SMART goal(s).

Write one or two short-term goals (one day to one month long).

I will avoid making negative comments about myself when I am working out or at practice.

I will share with a friend one thing I felt good about each day that is related to my body's ability to move, be fit, or be athletic.

Write a long-term goal (one to six months or more).

I will be a good positive body role model to my teammates and classmates.

STEP 3: Make a plan.

Identify two to five strategies (action steps) you could do to meet your goal.

I will wear a hairband on my wrist at practice as a reminder to avoid saying negative things.

I will ask my friends to call me out if I make a negative comment about my body.

I will pay extra attention to my achievements in sports and PE class and will write those things down on a list that I can look at every day. I'll put a check mark next to each item that I shared with someone else.

STEP 4: Do your plan and track your progress.

Short-term goal 1

☒ Met ☐ Not met Date: *September 7*

Short-term goal 2

☒ Met ☐ Not met Date: *September 14*

Long-term goal

☐ Met ☒ Not met Date: _____

If you met your goal, what helped you to be successful?

Taking pride in my athletic and fitness accomplishments made me feel differently about how I look.

If you did not meet your goal, what made it harder for you to be successful?

I am not yet fully proud of my appearance, but I am no longer mean to myself. Society makes it hard—everyone expects you to criticize yourself, and other people are always judging everyone else's looks.

Test Your Knowledge

Select the best answer for each question.

1. Which age group should have a diet of 40 to 50 percent fat?
   a. infants
   b. young children
   c. adolescents
   d. older adults

2. The mineral that helps your bones grow and your muscles function is called
   a. iron
   b. calcium
   c. folate
   d. vitamin C

3. Which is the best description of what food insecurity is?
   a. being anxious about how much food to eat
   b. eating most of your meals away from home
   c. not having access to enough healthy foods
   d. not knowing what kinds of foods are healthy

4. The four steps to food safety are
   a. separate, clean, cook, chill
   b. transport, cook, chill, dispose
   c. produce, process, distribute, prepare
   d. separate, clean, cook, dispose

5. Body image is
   a. the thoughts, feelings, and behaviors you have about your body and appearance
   b. how you look to others
   c. your BMI
   d. all of the above

6. Positive body image is related to
   a. lower self-esteem
   b. lower self-confidence
   c. BMI
   d. higher self-confidence

7. The process of repeatedly losing and regaining weight is called
   a. weight recycling
   b. weight cycling
   c. weight training
   d. weight rebound

8. Which BMI is associated with being overweight?
   a. under 20
   b. 20 to 24.9
   c. 25 to 29.9
   d. over 30

9. Which set of traits is least healthy for a person to have?
   a. active, fat around hips and thighs
   b. less active, fat around the waist
   c. very active, has a high BMI
   d. active on job, average weight

10. When you record what you eat for one to three days it is called a
    a. food log
    b. fitness log
    c. nutrition diary
    d. nutrition checklist

PROJECT-BASED LEARNING: Beautiful Body Week

What to Remember
Health is more than your appearance. It is important to teach all people to love who they are and to take the best care of themselves that they can. It is also important to avoid weight prejudice and to treat others with respect. When we focus only on how we look, we often feel like we are never good enough. We can also make unhealthy choices just trying to look a certain way.

Who It Is For
This is an advocacy campaign for the students in your school. The goal is to raise the awareness of these issues and to empower people to make healthier choices.

Why It Is Important
Providing positive messages about beauty and health promotes the acceptance of people of all shapes and sizes and encourages healthy nutrition choices for all people.

What to Do
Develop an advocacy campaign that will last one week. Each day you will focus on a specific part of body image and healthy nutrition. Select the topics from the following list or create your own topics with your teacher's approval.

- ☐ Positive body image
- ☐ Weight prejudice
- ☐ Healthy weight
- ☐ Unrealistic media images
- ☐ Social media and body shaming
- ☐ Healthy ways to lose and gain weight
- ☐ Other: _____

How to Do It
Develop a "Beautiful Body Week" campaign using social media platforms or posters, flyers, postcards, or other materials.

For your campaign, focus on providing factual information that is encouraging and supportive. When selecting information, remember to use valid and reliable sources. Each day of your campaign should include the following:

1. Important facts and figures
2. Important definitions and an explanation of the issue
3. Examples, images, and stories that will help people understand the issue
4. Specific action items that people can follow

Your campaign needs to work at your school. Make a list of the resources you have available to you and come up with a plan on what you will do. Consider making posters, flyers, postcards, or other materials to put up at school or to hand out. If you are using social media, make sure to have your teacher's permission and have all posts approved before making them public.

CROSS-CURRICULAR CONNECTIONS: Writing

Create a short story with a first-person point of view about being overweight. Make sure the story relates their experiences with body image, weight prejudice, and weight loss. Include vivid descriptions and an interesting and engaging narrative. The story can be positive and inspirational, or it can reflect challenges of being overweight. Be sure to use empathy in your story.

Staying Active and Healthy

LESSON 6.1 Being Physically Active and Physically Fit
LESSON 6.2 Health-Related and Skill-Related Fitness Components
LESSON 6.3 Preparing for Physical Activity
LESSON 6.4 Fitness Planning

Understanding My Health

How Physically Active Am I?

Being physically active is an important habit for overall good health and wellness. Answer each question in the following chart by selecting the response that is most accurate for you. When you are done, add up your points. The closer you are to 15 points, the healthier your physical activity habits are.

	Always	Sometimes	Never
Are you physically active for at least 60 minutes every day? (The 60 minutes can be broken up throughout the day.) Being physically active may include playing sports or games, exercising, riding a bike, walking, or lifting weights.	3	2	1
Are you able to perform your daily activities without feeling exhausted?	3	2	1
Do you participate in a physical activity that you could see yourself doing when you are 60 years old or older?	3	2	1
When you are being physically active, do you participate at a level that makes it a little hard to breathe? (For example, you have difficulty talking to someone at the same time as you are being physically active.)	3	2	1
Do you participate in physical activities that work muscular strength, muscular endurance, and flexibility?	3	2	1

My score for How Physically Active Am I? = _____ (total number of points)

Physical activity is a general term that covers all types of activities such as playing sports, dancing, walking, and biking. Just about anything you do that involves the large muscles of the body is classified as physical activity. The U.S. Department of Health and Human Services recommends that teens do 60 minutes or more of moderate-to-vigorous physical activity daily. A great guide to making sure you are getting the types of physical activity you need is to participate in health-related fitness activities on a regular basis with skill-related fitness components added in for specific sports and function.

LESSON 6.1
Being Physically Active and Physically Fit

Terms to Learn

aerobic
exercise
physical activity
physical fitness

The Big Picture

Physical activity is a broad term that covers most types of activities you do in your day. Being physically active has many benefits, including better sleep, reduced anxiety, and improved academic achievement. Being physically active improves your physical fitness, which helps you to be healthy and able to perform all the daily activities you need to.

Learning Targets

- Compare and contrast physical activity, exercise, and physical fitness.
- Evaluate the physical, mental, and social benefits of physical activity on your health.
- Predict how physical activity can affect your health status.
- Identify three activities you could do at home when taking an activity break.
- Design a schedule you could use daily to get your 60 minutes of exercise completed.
- Analyze the influence of your personal values and beliefs on inactivity in your life.

Write About It

We often associate *physical activity*, *exercise*, and *physical fitness* to being active. List two ways you think the three terms are similar and two ways the three terms are different from each other.

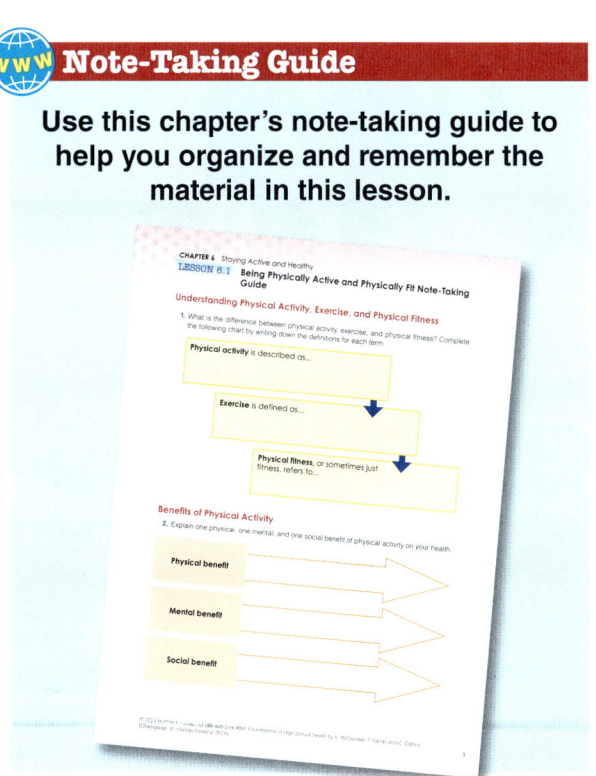

Note-Taking Guide

Use this chapter's note-taking guide to help you organize and remember the material in this lesson.

247

LESSON 6.1 Staying Active and Healthy

Sophia enjoys being physically active. She plays lacrosse and swims on her school teams and is in great cardiorespiratory shape. While both sports involve training her heart and lungs, she knows she needs to work more on her flexibility and muscular endurance. What are two activities she could do to get stronger arms and legs to help her in both sports? Since she does a lot of running and swimming for her sports, what are two stretches she could do for her legs to help her be more flexible?

Understanding Physical Activity, Exercise, and Physical Fitness

Physical activity is movement that uses the large muscles of your body and includes walking, running, dancing, swimming, biking, climbing stairs, and sports and games. Anything you can do that involves the large muscles of the body and gets you moving is a physical activity. You may be physically active for a specific purpose or just for fun. If you decide to be physically active for a specific purpose that is used to maintain or increase your physical fitness, you are doing **exercise**—the planned, structured, and repetitive physical activity for the purpose of improving or maintaining one or more components of fitness. You may exercise to feel healthier, to get in shape to play a sport, or just because it makes you feel better at the end of the day. **Physical fitness**, or fitness, refers to your body systems' ability to work together efficiently to allow you to be healthy and perform all the daily activities you need to. It means you are able to handle all the things you need to do in a day without getting easily tired. See figure 6.1 for the differences among physical activity, exercise, and physical fitness.

Figure 6.1 The differences among physical activity, exercise, and physical fitness.

Benefits of Physical Activity

Participating in physical activity on a regular basis produces multiple physical, mental, and social health benefits.

- Physical health benefits include building healthy bones and muscles, improving sleep, and decreasing the likelihood of obesity. Stronger bones and muscles will help decrease injuries and help prevent osteoporosis. People who are physically active have a more restful sleep, wake up less during the night, and stay asleep longer, which improves their ability to concentrate. Being physically active also helps to maintain or achieve a healthy weight. Physical activity and eating healthy can help people maintain and regulate their weight.

- Mental health benefits of physical activity include helping to reduce anxiety and depression, increasing concentration, and improving thinking and memory. These benefits will help you be more focused during your school day and on the other responsibilities you have.
- Social benefits include meeting new people, developing new friendships, and learning to work with others. Being part of a physically active team or group, recreationally and competitively alike, builds social connections with people.

Physical Activity and Disease Prevention

Being physically active on a regular basis can help reduce your risk of chronic diseases such as type 2 diabetes, heart disease, cancer, high blood pressure, and dementia. If you are physically active as a teen, you are more likely to be physically active throughout your life. Currently in the United States, about one in two adults have at least one chronic disease, and only half of the adult population get the physical activity they need to help reduce and prevent chronic diseases.

Physical Activity Guidelines for Teens

The U.S. Department of Health and Human Services recommends that all teens get 60 minutes or more of moderate-to-vigorous physical activity daily. Moderate physical activity is equal in intensity to brisk walking. It can also include some daily living activities such as walking to school or doing yardwork or housework. Vigorous physical activity increases your heart rate, makes you breathe faster, and is continuous; for example, jogging or aerobic dance. The recommended 60 minutes of activity each day can be a combination of moderate and vigorous physical activity. The Physical Activity Pyramid in figure 6.2 represents the division of these activities:

- Aerobic exercises: steps 1, 2, and 3
- Muscle-fitness exercises: step 4
- Flexibility exercises: step 5

As you can see in figure 6.2, the most time is given to **aerobic** activities (also known as cardiorespiratory endurance activities), which increases your body's ability to use oxygen over longer periods of time. When you do aerobic exercise, you'll notice that your heart beats faster and you breathe harder than normal.

LESSON 6.1 Staying Active and Healthy

The Physical Activity Pyramid

Energy Balance
Energy out (Activity) — Energy in (Diet)

STEP 5 — Flexibility exercises
- Stretching exercises
- Yoga
- Gymnastics

F = 3+ days per week
I = Stretch overload
T = 10-30 sec, 2-4 reps of major muscle groups*

STEP 4 — Muscle fitness exercises
- Resistance training
- Calisthenics
- Wall climbing
- Plyometrics

F = 2-3 days per week
I = Muscle overload
T = 8-12 reps, 2-4 sets of major muscle groups*

STEP 3 — Vigorous sports, Vigorous recreation, Anaerobic activities, Mixed fitness activities
- Tennis, soccer
- Skating, skiing
- Interval training, HIIT
- Circuit training

F = 3+ days per week
I = Reach target heart rate
T = At least 20 min/day*

STEP 2 — Vigorous aerobics
- Jog
- Aerobic dance
- Bike
- Swim
- Stair stepper

F = 3+ days per week
I = Reach target heart rate
T = At least 20 min/day*

STEP 1 — Moderate physical activity
- Walk
- Do yard work
- Go bowling
- Do active household chores

F = Daily
I = Equal to brisk walking
T = At least 30-60 min/day*

*For teens, at least 60 minutes of moderate to vigorous activity is recommended each day. Activities from the pyramid can be combined to meet this recommendation.

Avoid excessive sitting and excessive screen time

Figure 6.2 The Physical Activity Pyramid shows you how to include different types of physical activity in your life.
© C.B. Corbin

HEALTHY LIVING TIP
Create a list of activities you can do so that, on your activity break, you can pick three or four activities, do them, and then get back to work if you need to.

If 60 minutes of activity seems like a lot to do at once, consider dividing your 60 minutes into smaller amounts of time. You could divide your 60 minutes into four 15-minute physical activity breaks, three 20-minute breaks, or even six 10-minute breaks. Doing six 10-minute physical activity breaks might seem much less overwhelming than doing an hour of activity. Make your activity breaks energizing (e.g., go for a short walk or jog) or relaxing (e.g., do yoga or stretches)—whichever you need at that moment. Plan your physical activities around what you enjoy doing so that you can look forward to taking your break. The most important thing is that you are getting up and being active during your day.

You can get in a complete workout wherever you are with nothing more than your imagination (and motivation) to create a workout. For instance, you might decide to make this a family activity and play in your backyard, at your school, or in a nearby park. When watching TV, you could be physically active with your family during commercials. Have contests to see who can do the longest wall sit or the longest plank, for example. You don't need to spend hours at a gym or have special equipment to be physically active. You just need to take the opportunities you have throughout your day and be active. Think about how you could incorporate physical activity into your daily routine. Being physically active gives you more energy and makes you feel better, so remember to find activities you enjoy. Being physically active should be something you *want* to do, not *have* to do.

Avoiding Inactivity

The most important concept for you to remember about physical activity is to be physically active. You have previously read about how physical activity can help prevent diseases and that you can break your physical activity into smaller chunks if 60 minutes all at once is too much. Think of ways to avoid being inactive. Table 6.1 shows common reasons for inactivity and provides suggestions to overcome those reasons.

HEALTHY LIVING TIP

Think about a past excuse you may have made for not exercising and write it down. Now write how you would overcome the excuse.

TABLE 6.1 **How to Overcome Inactivity**

Reason for inactivity	Overcoming your reason
I don't have the time.	Plan 10-minute activity breaks throughout your day. These can include taking the stairs instead of the elevator and stretching while watching television.
None of my friends exercise.	Talk with your friends and see if you can find something everyone can do together. For example, go for a walk after school, join a team, or participate in an online group fitness activity together.
I'm not good at sports.	Being physically active doesn't have to be about sports at all. You can be physically active by walking, riding your bike, swimming, dancing, doing yoga, taking the stairs, kickboxing—doing anything that gets you moving. Sports is an option but definitely not the only option.
I'm too tired.	Many people find that once they get started in their workout, they have more energy. The hardest part about being active some days is being motivated to start. Begin slowly and gradually increase the amount of activity you are doing.
People will make fun of me.	Find activities you enjoy and that you can do by yourself. Wear clothing you are comfortable in and remember, your workout is for you, not anyone else.

LESSON 6.1   Staying Active and Healthy

Skill-Building Challenge

Advocating for Physical Activity

Being physically active throughout the school day not only is good for health but also improves your concentration in school. Work with a partner to advocate for brain boosts or activity breaks during the school day for all students. Review the Advocacy Skill Cues to help you think about how to best advocate for this change. If your school already participates in regular brain boosts or activity breaks, advocate for another school that doesn't already do this. Create a letter for your school administrators, using the following questions as a guide.

1. What do you want to see changed in your school?
2. What information will you use to help get your message across? (Use facts to support your message.)
3. Who is your audience? (Think about the information you gathered and whether it is appropriate for that audience.)
4. What is your message? (Keep it simple and clear.)
5. If you had the chance to share your letter, did your message work? (Did you get the outcome you wanted?)

Healthy Living Skills

This lesson focused on advocacy. Here are some more ways you can develop healthy living skills related to this lesson.

MAKING HEALTHY DECISIONS

You have decided you want to start working out. You asked three friends what they do for their workouts to get some ideas. One friend is training for a 5K and runs four days a week, another lifts weights three days a week, and the other does yoga five days a week. Using the decision-making steps, decide which of your friends' workouts is best for you.

ANALYZING INFLUENCES

Many people use smart watches to help them track their physical activity and to keep them motivated to stay active. You are looking for a new smart watch and want one that can track your heart rate, steps, activity, and calories burned; can play music; and has a stopwatch. Conduct online research for three different smart watch options. Create a chart showing each watch's features and cost. Compare the choices and rank the watches based on which one you would be most likely to want. Consider the most realistic option for you and try not to be influenced by what is a popular or trendy choice. Use the Analyzing Influences Skill Cues to help you work through the process of choosing a new watch.

LESSON 6.1 Review: Being Physically Active and Physically Fit

LESSON SUMMARY

- Physical activity is movement that uses the large muscles of the body.
- Exercise is planned, structured, and repetitive movement.
- Physical fitness is also about being active and focuses on your body systems working together so you can handle all the things that happen in a day without getting easily tired.
- Regular physical activity can improve physical, mental, and social health.
- Activities you can do at home could include jogging, dancing, planks, wall sits, and stretches.
- Avoid inactivity by finding activities you enjoy. Get your daily 60 minutes of exercise by doing it for a full session; if that is too daunting, you can divide the hour into four 15-minute physical activity breaks, three 20-minute breaks, or even six 10-minute breaks.
- To avoid inactivity, find activities you enjoy doing. Talk to friends or family members about activities they enjoy or search workout videos to find something you've never tried before and see if you like it.

REVIEWING CONCEPTS AND VOCABULARY

1. Movements such as running, swimming, and biking that use the large muscles of your body are known as _____.
2. _____ is the planned, structured, and repetitive movement for improving or maintaining components of fitness.
3. When you have _____, your body systems work together efficiently so you are able to perform all the daily activities you need to.
4. Aerobic activities help your body use more _____ over longer periods of time.
5. People often suggest they're inactive because they don't have time, but they could plan short _____ breaks throughout the day to overcome this issue.

THINKING CRITICALLY

Talk to an adult—a family member if possible—and ask them about any chronic diseases they or someone else in your family may have. You learned in this lesson that being physically active can help prevent many chronic diseases. Based on the chronic disease(s) the adult you spoke to may have or know about, does it influence you to be more physically active daily? Why or why not?

TAKE IT HOME

Take note of how inactive or active you, your friends, and your household members are. Observe for a weekend whether you and the people you surround yourself with are active or inactive. Talk with them about being more active or maintaining their activity level. See if you all can agree on some physical activities you'd be willing to do together. If no one is willing to participate, find others who will and get active!

LESSON 6.2

Health-Related and Skill-Related Fitness Components

Terms to Learn

cardiac muscles
cardiorespiratory endurance
cartilage
circulatory system
dynamic stretching
flexibility
health-related fitness
joints
ligaments
maximum heart rate
muscular endurance
muscular strength
muscular system
nervous system
rating of perceived exertion (RPE) scale
respiratory system
skeletal muscles
skeletal system
skill-related fitness
smooth muscles
static stretching
target heart rate zone
tendons

The Big Picture

Health-related and skill-related fitness components are important aspects of physical fitness that positively contribute to your overall health and wellness. Health-related fitness components include cardiorespiratory endurance, muscular strength and endurance, flexibility, and body composition. Skill-related fitness components include coordination, agility, balance, speed, power, and reaction time. Both sets of components are related to multiple systems at work throughout your body such as the circulatory, respiratory, muscular, and nervous systems when you are physically active.

Learning Targets

- Compare and contrast health-related fitness and skill-related fitness.
- Explain each of the five health-related fitness components.
- Use the target heart rate calculation to determine your cardiorespiratory endurance intensity.
- Summarize the benefits of regular muscular strength and muscular endurance exercise.
- Describe the benefits of regular flexibility exercises.
- Distinguish how at least four of the six skill-related fitness components can be used in sports and everyday life.

Note-Taking Guide

Use this chapter's note-taking guide to help you organize and remember the material in this lesson.

Write About It

This lesson discusses in detail the six skill-related fitness components: speed, balance, coordination, agility, power, and reaction time. List one way you think each skill could be used in a sport and one way it could also be used in everyday life.

Health-Related and Skill-Related Fitness Components **LESSON 6.2**

River enjoys his physical education class and being active overall. The class is currently doing fitness testing, which River usually does well at. This time, though, River doesn't pass the flexibility test and is surprised by that. Even though he hasn't excelled at the test, he has always passed it until now. As River is reflecting on his fitness testing results, he realizes he doesn't stretch much outside of class and decides he needs to include more flexibility types of exercises into his fitness routine. What types of flexibility exercises should River do to become more flexible overall?

Health-Related Fitness Components

Health-related fitness is the physical fitness components that help you to stay healthy. As previously mentioned, the components of health-related fitness are cardiorespiratory endurance, muscular strength and endurance, flexibility, and body composition.

Cardiorespiratory Endurance

Cardiorespiratory endurance is the ability to exercise for an extended period of time. Two systems that work with cardiorespiratory endurance activities are the circulatory system, which comprises your heart and blood vessels, and the respiratory system, which is primarily composed of your lungs, mouth, nose, trachea, and diaphragm. Some examples of cardiorespiratory endurance exercises are brisk walking, jogging, biking at a moderate pace, dancing, and swimming. These are aerobic exercises that are the foundation for being physically active. Your cardiorespiratory endurance improves as you become more physically active.

Aerobic physical activities increase your heart rate and benefit your heart by improving cardiorespiratory endurance. When physical activity is done at a moderate intensity, your heart beats faster and you breathe faster than normal. At a moderate intensity, you still are able to carry on a conversation while exercising. Vigorous-intensity activities increase your heart rate even more and make you breathe faster than moderate-intensity activities do. Talking while exercising becomes more difficult as well. Benefits of regular aerobic exercise include improvements in sleep, mood, and self-esteem; reduced risk of type 2 diabetes; and maintenance of or decreases in weight and body fat percentage.

Circulatory System

The **circulatory system** controls the blood flow in your body and consists of your heart, blood vessels, and blood (see figure 6.3). Your heart pumps blood to cells throughout your body through the four valves in your heart. These four valves open and close in perfect rhythm, pumping oxygen-rich blood through your arteries. The heart contracts, on average, 70 times per minute and pumps five quarts of blood each minute. The benefit of being physically active for your heart is that it becomes a stronger muscle, can pump more blood with fewer beats, and works more efficiently overall.

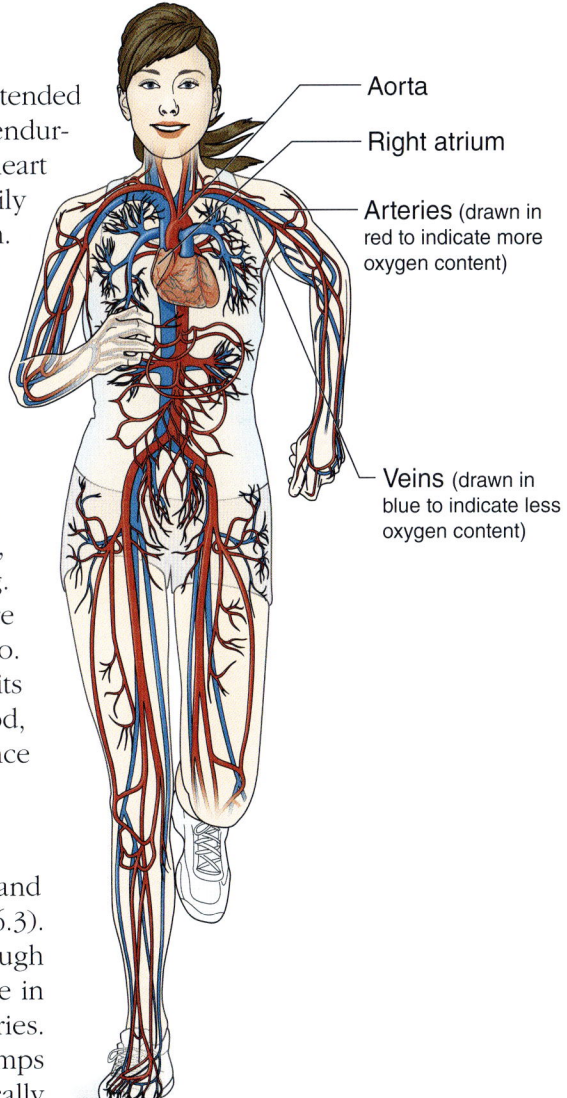

- Aorta
- Right atrium
- Arteries (drawn in red to indicate more oxygen content)
- Veins (drawn in blue to indicate less oxygen content)

Figure 6.3 The circulatory system controls the flow of blood in your body and consists of your heart, blood vessels, and blood.

LESSON 6.2 Staying Active and Healthy

Respiratory System

The **respiratory system** controls the flow of oxygen in your body. Its main components are your mouth, nose, trachea, diaphragm, and lungs (figure 6.4). The respiratory system primarily functions to supply your blood with oxygen and to get rid of carbon dioxide, the waste gas that is produced when carbon is combined with oxygen.

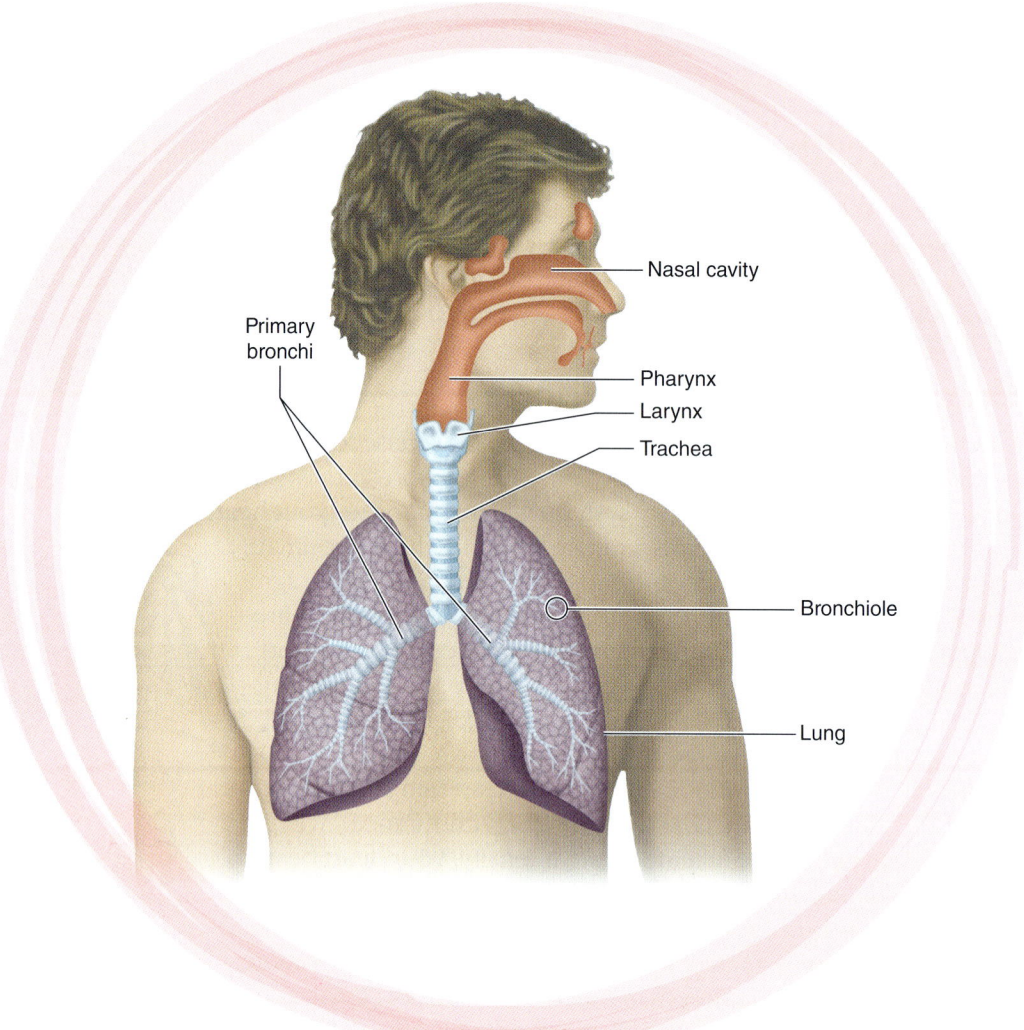

Figure 6.4 The respiratory system controls the flow of oxygen in your body and is made up of your mouth, nose, trachea, diaphragm, and lungs.

Determining Your Cardiorespiratory Endurance Intensity

To gain the most benefit from being physically active, you should make sure you are working at the proper intensity. An easy way to determine if you are working at a moderate- or vigorous-intensity level is to use the **rating of perceived exertion (RPE) scale** (see figure 6.5). The numbers on the RPE scale correlate with how easy or difficult you feel your aerobic activity is. For moderate-intensity activity, your aim should be levels 4 to 5; for a vigorous-intensity activity, you need to work at levels 6 to 7. Your perceived exertion level might be quite different from that of someone else who is doing the exact same workout, based on each person's fitness level.

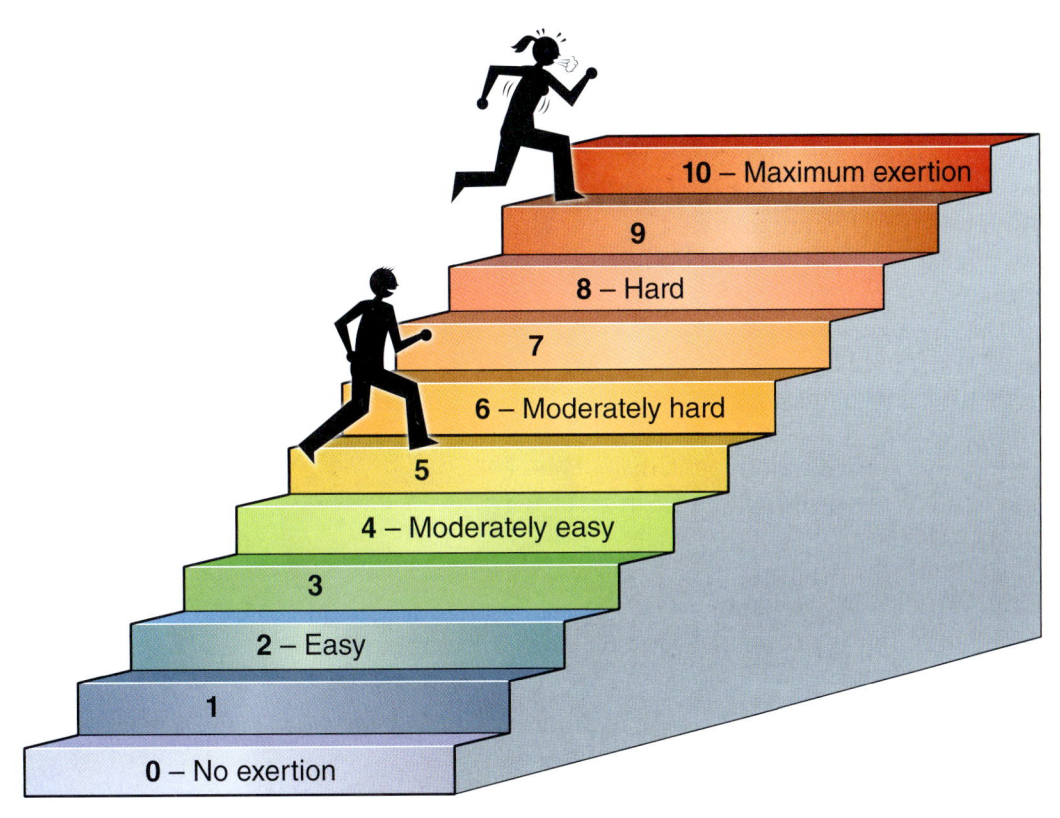

Health-Related and Skill-Related Fitness Components   LESSON 6.2

Figure 6.5 You can use the rating of perceived exertion (RPE) scale to determine the intensity level of your activity.

A second way to determine if you are working at a moderate- or vigorous-intensity level is to make sure you are working in your **target heart rate zone**—a range of two numbers that you stay in when exercising to get the most benefit from your workout. At a moderate-intensity level, your target heart rate should be at 60 to 75 percent of your maximum heart rate; for vigorous intensity, 75 to 90 percent. Your **maximum heart rate** is the highest your heart rate should be when exercising. To determine your maximum heart rate and moderate- and vigorous-intensity target heart rates, complete the following steps:

1. 220 − your age = maximum heart rate in beats per minute
2. Multiply your maximum heart rate by the low percentage (60 percent) and the high percentage (75 percent) for moderate intensity. Example:
    a. 220 − 16 = 204
    b. 204 × 0.6 = 122.4
    c. 204 × 0.75 = 153
    d. Moderate-intensity target heart rate zone: 122 to 153 beats per minute
3. Multiply your maximum heart rate by the low percentage (75 percentage) and the high percentage (90 percent) for vigorous intensity. Example:
    a. 220 − 16 = 204
    b. 204 × 0.75 = 153
    c. 204 × 0.9 = 183.6
    d. Vigorous intensity target heart rate zone: 153 to 184 beats per minute

LESSON 6.2 Staying Active and Healthy

Muscular System

The **muscular system** is responsible for all movement and consists of more than 650 muscles (see figure 6.6). There are three types of muscle tissue: skeletal, cardiac, and smooth (see figure 6.7). **Skeletal muscles** are attached to your bones and enable you to move your body. Skeletal muscles are voluntary muscles, meaning you control them. When you are developing muscular strength and muscular endurance, you are strengthening the skeletal muscles. **Cardiac muscles** are found only in the walls of the heart. They contract automatically and regularly so your heart can pump blood throughout your body. **Smooth muscles** are found in the walls of hollow organs such as your esophagus and stomach. Smooth muscles are involuntary, so they contract automatically in response to a command from your nervous system.

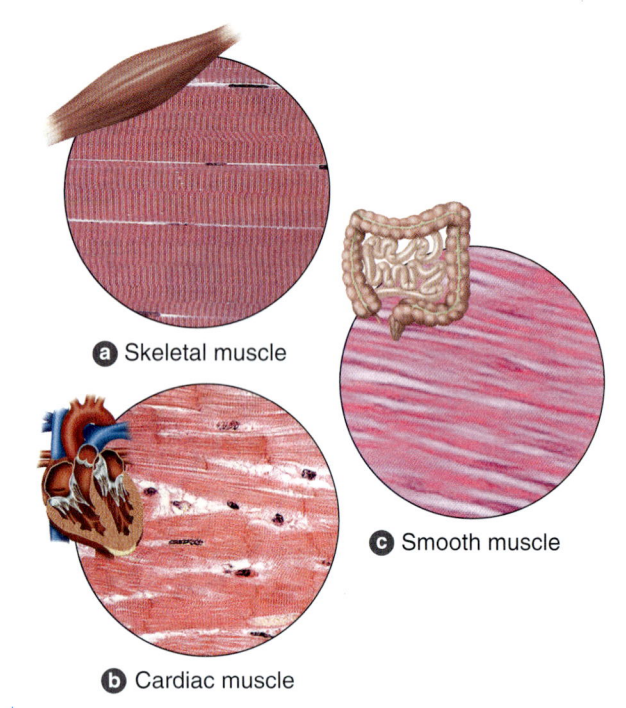

a Skeletal muscle
b Cardiac muscle
c Smooth muscle

Figure 6.7 The three types of muscle tissue.

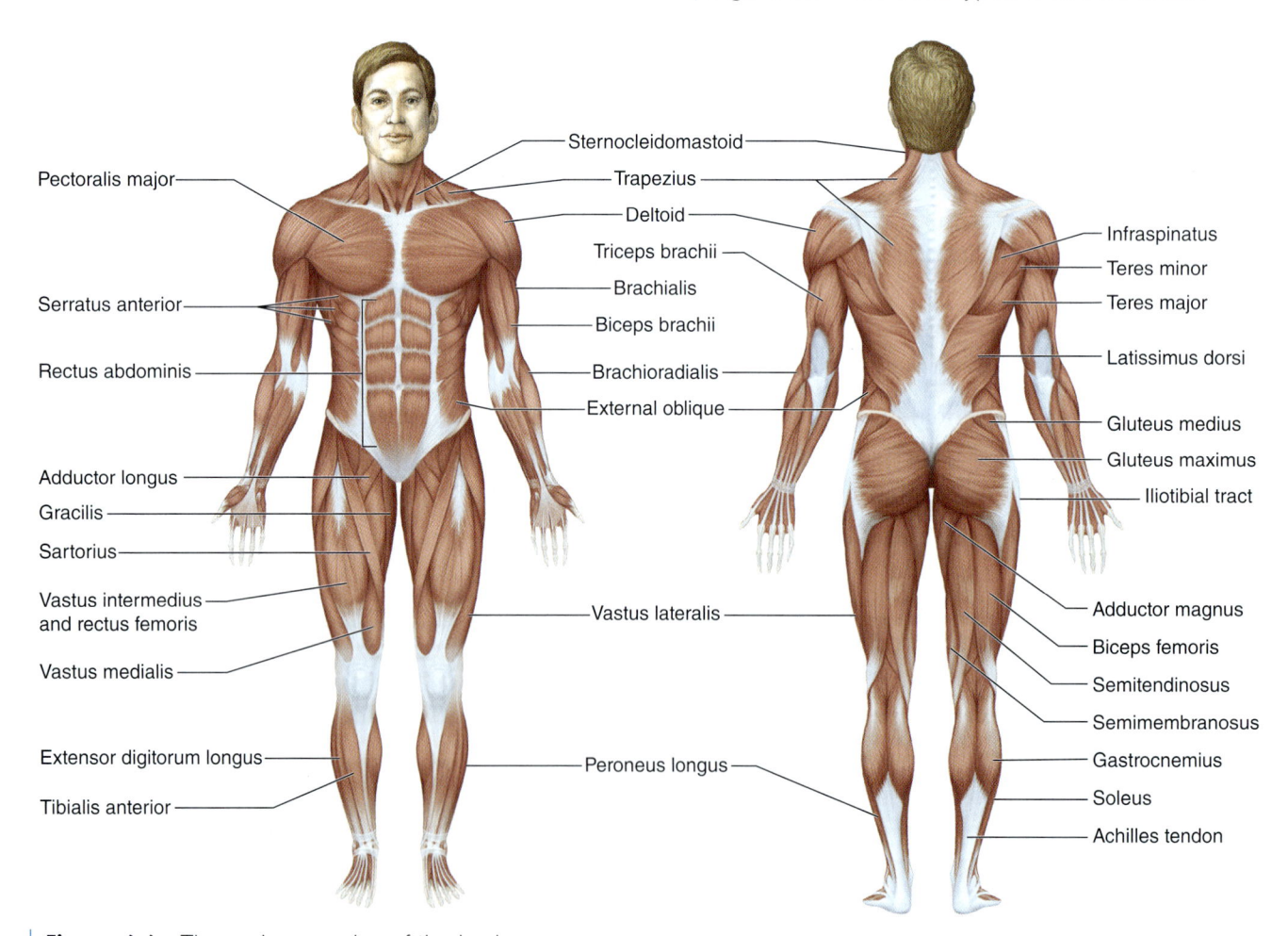

Pectoralis major
Serratus anterior
Rectus abdominis
Adductor longus
Gracilis
Sartorius
Vastus intermedius and rectus femoris
Vastus medialis
Extensor digitorum longus
Tibialis anterior
Sternocleidomastoid
Trapezius
Deltoid
Triceps brachii
Brachialis
Biceps brachii
Brachioradialis
External oblique
Vastus lateralis
Peroneus longus
Infraspinatus
Teres minor
Teres major
Latissimus dorsi
Gluteus medius
Gluteus maximus
Iliotibial tract
Adductor magnus
Biceps femoris
Semitendinosus
Semimembranosus
Gastrocnemius
Soleus
Achilles tendon

Figure 6.6 The major muscles of the body.

Muscular Strength and Endurance

Muscular strength and endurance exercises are activities that make your muscles work. Some examples are lifting weights, using resistance bands (which come in different strengths so you can find a resistance that is right for you), and using your own body weight when doing exercises like push-ups and sit-ups (see figure 6.8). **Muscular strength** is the amount of force a muscle can produce. **Muscular endurance** is the ability of the muscle to perform continuously without tiring. Benefits of regular muscular strength and muscular endurance exercise include keeping bones strong, increasing energy levels, helping maintain correct posture, increasing lean body mass, reducing the risk of injury, and helping perform everyday tasks such as climbing stairs more easily.

Nervous System

The **nervous system** provides all the electrical signals that control your movements. You can run, jump, throw, stretch, and move in general because of your nervous system. It is organized into two parts: the central nervous system (CNS) and the peripheral nervous system (PNS), as seen in figure 6.9. The central nervous system comprises your brain and spinal cord, whereas the peripheral nervous system is a network of nerves that connect your brain and spinal cord to the rest of your body. Your brain receives and processes all the information you take in and sends messages to the other parts of the body. The spinal cord relays information to and from the brain and all parts of the body, which allows you to move.

Figure 6.8 Push-ups can improve your muscular strength and endurance.

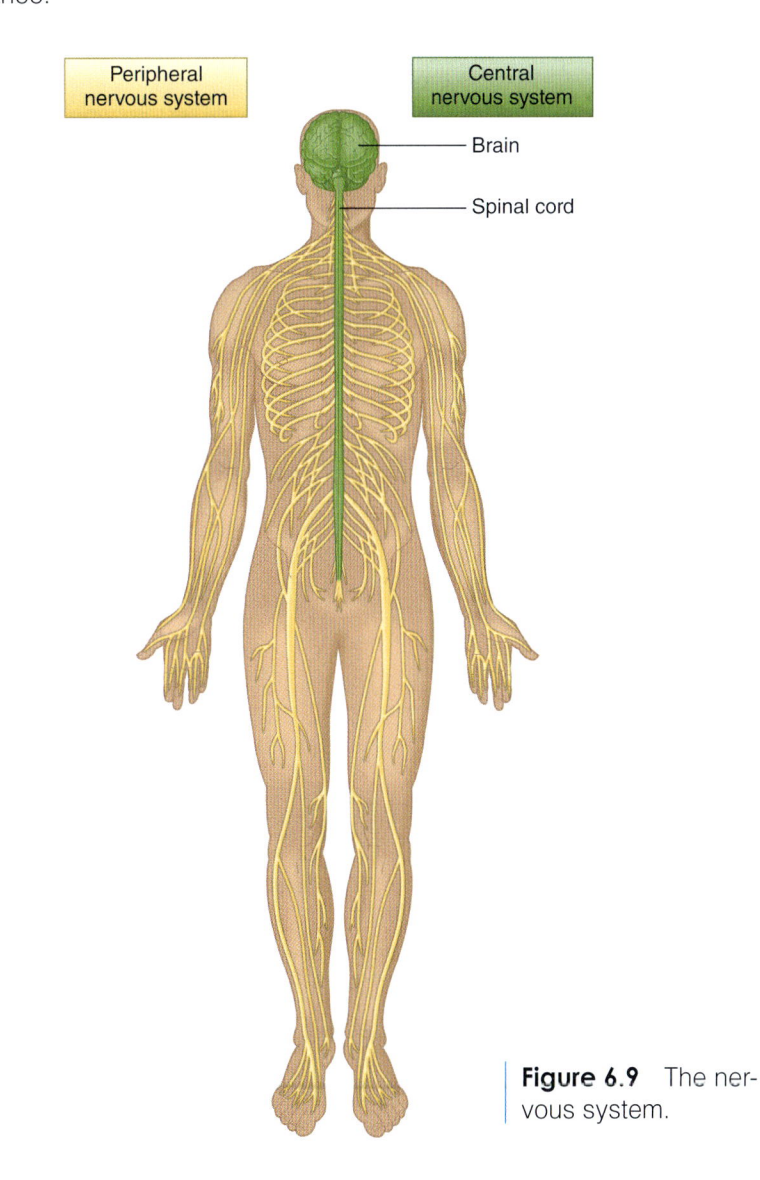

Figure 6.9 The nervous system.

LESSON 6.2 Staying Active and Healthy

Skeletal System

The **skeletal system** is made up of your bones and the tendons, ligaments, and cartilage that connect the bones together. The skeletal system gives your body support. It also protects other parts of your body—internal organs such as the brain, heart, and lungs—from injury and allows movement (see figure 6.10). **Tendons** are tough bands of tissue that connect bones to muscles and can shorten or lengthen just like muscles. **Ligaments** are strong bands of tissue that connect bones together. **Cartilage** is a connective tissue that cushions joints and helps them move smoothly and easily. The skeletal system can move due to **joints**, where two or more bones meet (see figure 6.11). There are four main types of joints based on the kind of movement they allow: hinge joints, gliding joints, pivot joints, and ball-and-socket joints (see table 6.2).

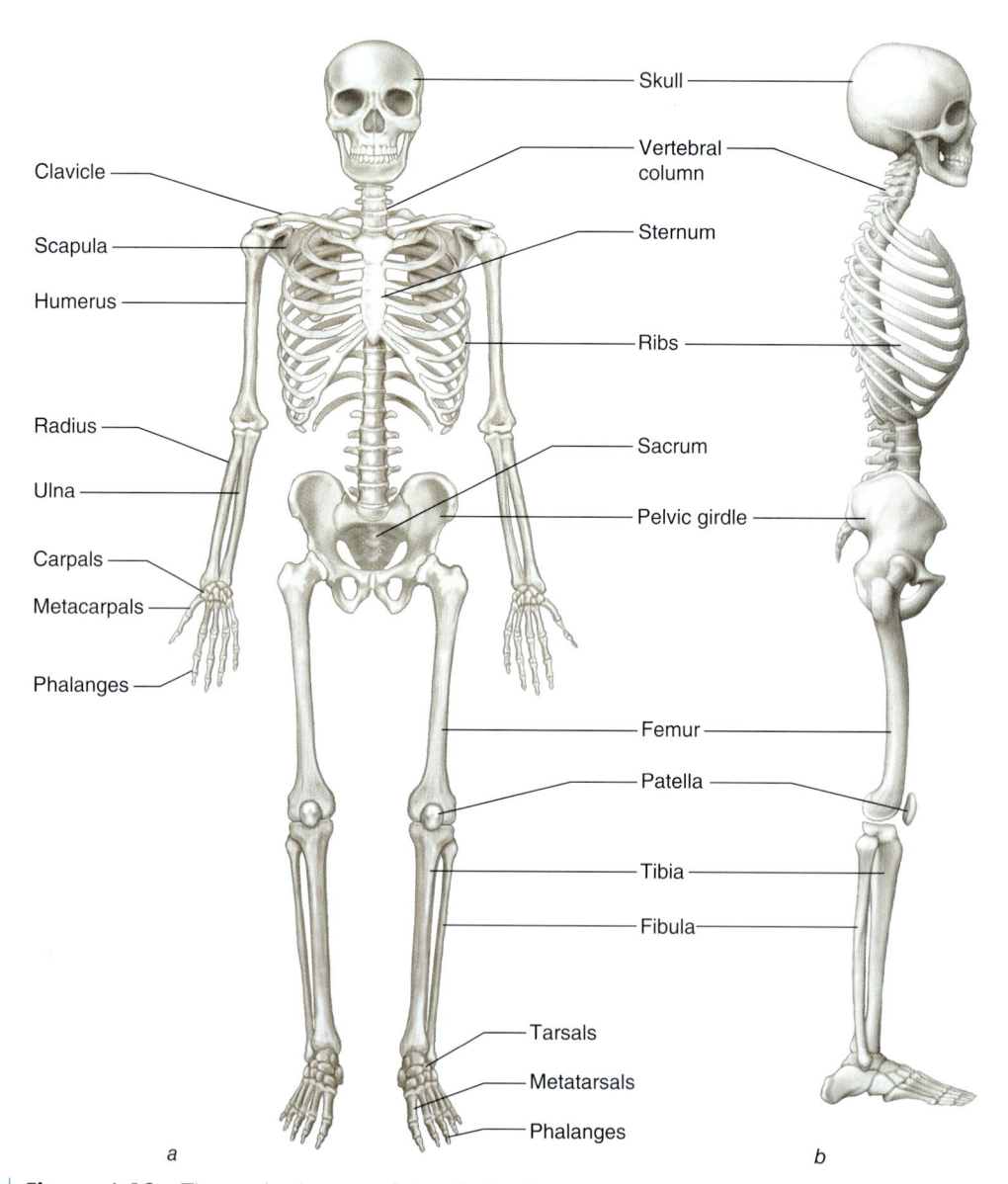

Figure 6.10 The major bones of the skeletal system.

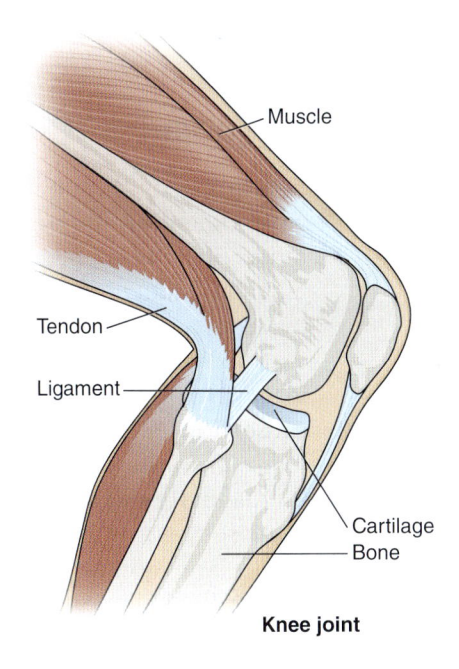

Figure 6.11 The knee joint showing tendons, ligaments, and cartilage.

TABLE 6.2 **Types of Joints**

Joint name and location	Joint function	Image of joint
Hinge joints: elbows and knees	To move in one direction only	
Gliding joints: wrists and ankles	To allow bones to slide over each other	
Pivot joint: between neck and head	To allow movement from side to side, up and down; allows for limited rotation	
Ball-and-socket joints: hips and shoulders	To move in all directions, allowing rotation	

LESSON 6.2   Staying Active and Healthy

Flexibility

Flexibility is the ability to use your joints fully through a wide range of motion. Your range of motion is influenced by the mobility of the muscles and tendons that surround the joint. Injury, inactivity, or a lack of stretching causes loss of normal joint flexibility. In order to maintain and increase flexibility, stretching exercises should be done daily. There are several benefits of regular flexibility exercise: better performance in sports and activities (see figure 6.12), increased physical and mental relaxation, greater freedom of movement, improved posture, and reduced risk of injury.

Figure 6.12 Flexibility can improve your performance in sports and other activities.

Dynamic and Static Stretching

To develop flexibility, you should participate in both dynamic and static stretching. **Dynamic stretching** requires dynamic movements of the muscles through the full range of motion in the joints. Butt kicks, high knees, and lunges are examples of dynamic stretching. **Static stretching** is maintaining an extended stretching position. Hamstring and quad stretches are examples of static stretching. Before you begin dynamic or static stretching, it is important you warm your muscles up to increase blood flow throughout your body. By doing this, you increase your muscles' range of motion and prevent muscle strain. Examples of other flexibility training activities besides stretching include yoga, Pilates, and tai chi.

HEALTHY LIVING TIP

Develop a stretching routine that includes all the major muscle groups in your body. When you are feeling stressed, take a few minutes and, after a short warm-up, stretch the major muscle groups to relax.

Body Composition

Body composition refers to the ratio of lean (muscle) tissue to fat tissue in your body (see figure 6.13). Different types of tissue that make up your body include fat, muscle, bone, and organs. Two people can weigh the same amount yet look quite different due to their body composition. A teen who regularly exercises may have more lean tissue, resulting in a lower body composition compared to the teen who doesn't regularly exercise and may have more fat tissue, resulting in a higher body composition. While all the other health-related fitness components have specific exercises and different ways to train, body composition is affected by your cardiorespiratory endurance, muscular strength and endurance, and flexibility.

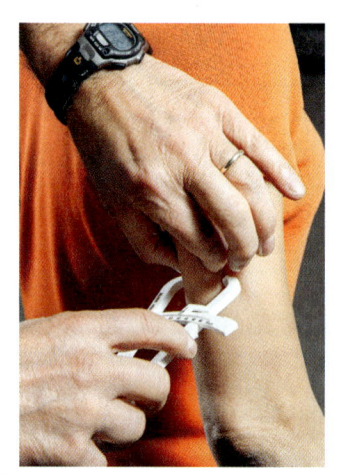

Figure 6.13 Body composition can be estimated by using skinfold calipers.

Skill-Related Fitness

Skill-related fitness helps you perform well in sports and other activities that require specific skills. The components of skill-related fitness are speed, agility, balance, power, coordination, and reaction time (see figure 6.14). Health- and skill-related fitness components are important to both your overall daily living activities and sports. Some of the skill-related fitness components you use in other parts of your life have nothing to do with sports—for example, driving a car, which uses

Health-Related and Skill-Related Fitness Components LESSON 6.2

Six Components of Skill-Related Fitness

Speed
Speed is the ability to perform a movement or cover a distance in a short period of time. Leg speed is used to run fast, and arm speed is used to throw fast.

Balance
Balance is the ability to keep an upright posture while standing still or moving. Skateboarding, ice-skating, and riding a surfboard are among several activities that require many quick movements and require balance for staying upright and changing direction quickly.

Coordination
Coordination is the ability to use your senses together with your body parts or to use two or more body parts together. Coordination is necessary for catching a football and kicking a soccer ball. Whenever you use your hands and eyes together in catching, you're using hand-eye coordination. Foot-eye coordination is when you use your feet and eyes together in kicking.

Agility
Agility is the ability to change the position of your body quickly and to control your body's movements. You need agility to play tennis and badminton so you can change direction to contact the implement. You also use agility in football and soccer to avoid people.

Power
Power is the ability to use strength quickly and involves both strength and speed. You need power for jumping.

Reaction Time
Reaction time is the amount of time it takes you to move once you realize you need to move. You need good reaction time when leaving the blocks in a 50-meter race or when leaving the blocks in a swimming race.

Figure 6.14 The six components of skill-related fitness.

coordination and reaction time; walking up and down stairs, which uses balance and coordination; and moving quickly to get out of the way of something, which uses agility and possibly speed. Just as you may not be great at all the health-related fitness components, you may find some of the skill-related fitness components to be more challenging than others.

> ### Career Connection
>
> **PERSONAL TRAINER**
>
> A personal trainer usually works with one person at a time and helps them to achieve their personal fitness goals. Personal trainers typically design an exercise program specific for their client. They demonstrate exercises, spot as needed, help with technique, and monitor the client's progress. There are no requirements for becoming a personal trainer, but certified personal trainers tend to make more money than those who are not certified, and reputable fitness centers and health clubs tend to hire certified trainers over individuals who lack certification. To become certified as a personal trainer, you should research the requirements through the professional organizations of the National Academy of Sports Medicine (NASM), American Council on Exercise (ACE), and the American College of Sports Medicine (ACSM).

Skill-Building Challenge

Using *I* Messages and Active Listening

Meghan's grandma Ruth is 65 and wants Meghan to help her work on getting in better shape. Ruth no longer jogs because of her bad knees but otherwise seems healthy. Ruth told Meghan she only wants to focus on cardiorespiratory endurance because that is most important. Meghan learned in her physical education class that cardiorespiratory endurance is important but so are muscular strength and endurance and flexibility.

Write an *I* message to Meghan stating how she could tell her grandma the benefits of incorporating flexibility and muscular strength and endurance exercises into her workout. Make sure to use facts from the lesson to write your *I* message. Then write a response to Meghan's *I* message from her grandma using the four parts of active listening.

Healthy Living Skills

This lesson focused on healthy communication. Here are some more ways you can develop healthy living skills related to this lesson.

ACCESSING INFORMATION

You have decided you are going to exercise more and want to focus on lifting weights. Your teacher has told you there are free exercise apps you can use as well as subscription-based exercise apps that fitness experts have created. Many of the apps are valid and reliable, but you have to do some research to make sure the "fitness expert" really is a fitness expert. Find an app that has the type of workout you want to do and list the name of the app. Answer the following questions using the Accessing Valid and Reliable Information Skill Cues.

- Is the information on the app research based and from either an expert in the field or a person with formal training? Or is it from someone who likes to work out, and so they created the app?
- Are step-by-step instructions that demonstrate how to do the exercises provided?
- Are there modifications to the exercises?
- Does the app include multiple exercises, or will you be doing the same thing day after day?

PRACTICING HEALTHY BEHAVIORS

You know the importance of cardiorespiratory endurance activities and you regularly bike, jog, and kickbox. You think you're getting a good workout, but you aren't entirely sure. You've decided it's time to be more intentional in your workouts, so you'll need to determine what your target heart rate zone is. That way you will know if you are getting the most out of your cardiorespiratory workouts. Use the information in this lesson to determine your target heart rate. Then use the Practicing Healthy Behaviors Skill Cues to work on monitoring your cardiorespiratory workouts to see if you are consistently working in your target heart rate zone.

LESSON 6.2 Review: Health-Related and Skill-Related Fitness Components

LESSON SUMMARY

- Health-related fitness refers to engaging regularly in physical activity to be healthy, whereas skill-related fitness develops your performance in sports that require specific skills. Each type of fitness is important to maintaining good health.
- The five health-related fitness components are: (1) cardiorespiratory endurance—being able to exercise for extended periods of time, (2) muscular strength—how much force a muscle can produce, (3) muscular endurance—continuous muscle performance without tiring, (4) flexibility—using your joints fully through their range of motion, and (5) body composition—your body's lean tissue to fat tissue ratio.
- Use the RPE scale and your target heart rate calculation to determine your cardiorespiratory endurance intensity.
- Regular muscular strength and endurance exercises help maintain correct posture and bone strength, increase energy levels and lean body mass, and reduce risk of injury.
- Regularly doing flexibility exercises will enhance your performance, increase physical and mental relaxation, provide greater freedom of movement, improve posture, and reduce injury risks.
- Skill-related fitness components that relate to everyday life or sports are balance and coordination (for walking up and down stairs), reaction time and coordination (for driving), and agility (for moving quickly to avoid getting hit by someone or something). The other skill-related fitness components are speed and power.

REVIEWING CONCEPTS AND VOCABULARY

1. _____ fitness components refer to fitness activities you need to do regularly to keep healthy.
2. The ability to exercise your entire body for a long time without stopping is known as _____.
3. The _____ is used to measure the intensity of your exercise based on a description of how you would be feeling at a certain level.
4. The _____ system is responsible for all movement.
5. _____ is the ability to use your joints fully through a wide range of motion.
6. _____ fitness components help you perform well in sports and other activities that require specific skills.

THINKING CRITICALLY

Discuss with a classmate how you know you are at a 4 to 5 level or at a 6 to 7 level when using the RPE scale. How do these two levels feel different to you?

TAKE IT HOME

Create either a health- or a skill-related fitness program for a family member or family friend that incorporates as many of the components as possible. Talk to the person so you can pick components they like and can successfully do.

LESSON 6.3
Preparing for Physical Activity

Terms to Learn
cool-down
dehydration
dual sports
individual sports
team sports
warm-up

The Big Picture
The first step in understanding how to get active is to know how to include physical activity in your daily life. Find an individual, dual, or team sport you can participate in over your lifetime. Being physically active should include a warm-up, the activity itself, and a cool-down. Once you get active, you will want to stay active. One way to do this is to keep from getting injured by using the proper protective equipment in those physical activities that require it.

Learning Targets
- Describe the three parts of a workout.
- Identify three benefits of being physically active throughout your life.
- Explain two things an individual, dual, or team sport can teach you.
- Analyze the importance of three pieces of protective equipment you should wear when being physically active.
- List three strategies you think are important for preventing an injury.

Write About It
What is your favorite physical activity and why? Is it something you can do throughout your life? Can you do it anywhere? Do you need special equipment for it?

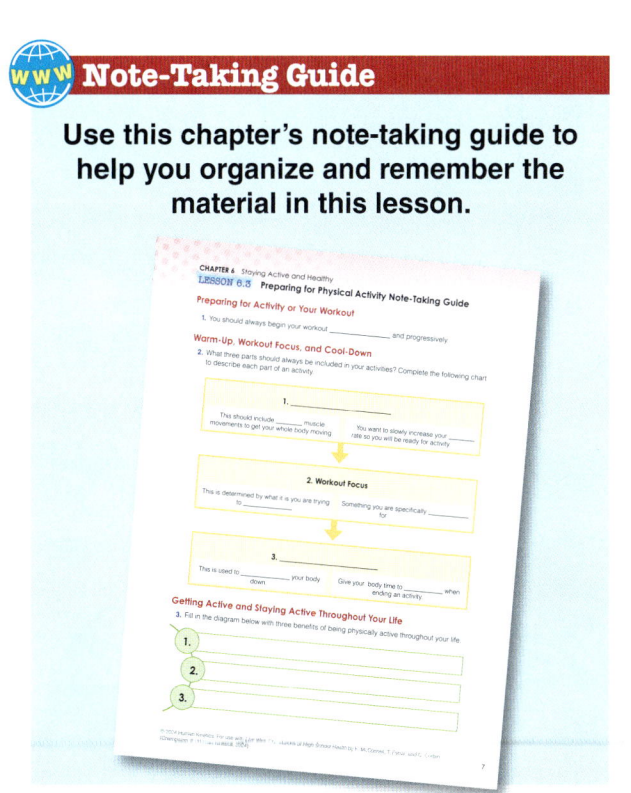

Note-Taking Guide
Use this chapter's note-taking guide to help you organize and remember the material in this lesson.

LESSON 6.3   Staying Active and Healthy

Joanna wants her family to be active together. Some of her family members have medical problems, and she has learned in her health class that daily exercise can help. No one in the family is very physically active. A gym membership is not an option because Joanna has four siblings, two of whom are much younger than she is. Her plan is to start the family out slowly so everyone can participate and no one gets injured. List five activities that Joanna and her family could begin doing.

Preparing for Activity or Your Workout

Whether you are just starting to be physically active or you already have a regular routine, you should always begin slowly and progressively work into your actual activity for the day. Regardless of what your workout will be, it should always include three parts: a warm-up activity, the focus of your workout (e.g., cardiorespiratory, muscular strength and endurance, or flexibility), and a cool-down activity. You could incorporate flexibility exercises into the warm-up, focus, or cool-down activity, or they could be a part of both the warm-up and cool-down, depending on the type of flexibility you are doing.

Warm-Up

Your **warm-up** should include large muscle movements that get your whole body moving. You want to slowly increase your heart rate so you will be ready for your activity. Many warm-ups last 5 to 10 minutes and often involve some form of dynamic stretching or a lighter version of the focal activity. As you may recall, dynamic stretching is performed through a range of motion in a controlled fashion; it is stretching with movement. Dynamic stretching examples are

- walking knee to chest,
- walking forward lunges,
- butt kicks, and
- high knees.

Workout Focus

The focus of your workout is determined by what you are trying to improve or training for. For example, if you are training for a 5K race, your workout's focus should be cardiorespiratory endurance activities such as jogging, biking, or swimming because they improve your circulatory and respiratory systems. On the other hand, if your goal is to increase arm strength, then your focus should be muscular strength and endurance activities such as bench presses, arm curls, push-ups, and triceps presses. No matter what you may be training for, it is important to focus your workout around that specific activity. There are many different types of exercises and activities to meet the focus of your workout, so try new things to keep your workouts challenging and fun.

Cool-Down

A **cool-down** slows your body down to give it time to adjust when ending an activity. A good way to cool down is to gradually reduce the intensity of your activity to get your heart rate back to normal. For your cool-down, you also may want to include static stretching to help improve flexibility and reduce pain and stiffness. Static stretching involves standing, sitting, or lying still and holding a stretch for 15 to 30 seconds. Static stretching examples are

- hamstring stretch,
- quadricep stretch,
- calf stretch, and
- cross-body shoulder stretch.

Getting Active and Staying Active Throughout Your Life

Being active can have different meanings for different people. Perhaps it is going for a run or going to the gym to lift weights or do a group fitness class. It could also mean going to practice because you are on a sports team or just being active with friends or family. The most important thing about being active is doing something you enjoy doing and getting your 60 minutes of exercise each day. Consistent

LESSON 6.3 Staying Active and Healthy

physical activity in all health-related fitness areas (cardiorespiratory endurance, muscular strength and endurance, and flexibility) is both good for you in the moment and has lifelong benefits. These include maintaining blood pressure and having a healthy heart, preventing diseases, maintaining appropriate weight and percentage of body fat, and reducing stress.

A goal of being physically active while you are young is to find something you enjoy doing so you will stay active as you grow older. There will always be days you don't feel like exercising, are sick, or are too busy to exercise. There could be times when it has been weeks, months, or even years since the last time you were physically active. Most important is making sure you start exercising again and that you find something you enjoy doing. Your interests may change as you go through high school, college, and into adulthood, yet you should always be able to find something you are interested in and want to do. You may be able to still do the same activities you are involved in right now when you are 50, 60, or even 80 years old. There are adult sports leagues you can join for softball, basketball, volleyball, track and field, bowling, disc golf, and many more. You can do many activities such as jogging and biking well into your 60s and beyond. Being physically active throughout your life helps to reduce the risk of falling and fracturing bones; improves balance, muscle strength, and joint mobility; lowers the risk of high blood pressure and strokes; improves sleep; and may help delay the onset of cognitive decline.

Individual, Dual, and Team Sports

Individual, dual, and team sports are ways to be active. **Individual sports** like swimming and golf are played by one person. In **dual sports** such as tennis doubles and pickleball, two people play. **Team sports** are played by groups of people; basketball and ultimate frisbee are just two examples among the wide range of team sports.

You have many opportunities to be involved with sports both at school and through recreation programs or select sports. There are several individual and dual sports you could play at school or in your community. Individual and dual sports include skating, bowling, disc golf, badminton, archery, biking, and skiing, among others. Individual and dual sports help promote self-resilience, self-motivation, and personal accomplishment. Track and field is a sport you compete in as an individual, but you are also part of a team as points are scored that add to team totals. This way you still get the benefits of being part of a team, but you are only competing with yourself for personal bests, and you don't necessarily have to rely on teammates to be successful for every event.

Perhaps team sports interest you more. A few examples include lacrosse, soccer, softball and baseball, football, rugby, team handball, ice and field hockey, volleyball, and crew. Being involved in any kind of sport, whether it's individual, dual, or team, helps to keep you healthy and can teach you about working with others. You can also learn about being a good sport (both on the field and off it), managing time, and staying persistent when things may not be going the way you want them to. All sports have benefits; you just need to decide whether you prefer working by yourself, with a partner, or on a team.

Dressing for Physical Activity

When being physically active, you should make sure you are dressed correctly and have the proper equipment to keep you safe. When dressing to be active, include wearing comfortable clothes so you can move freely, dressing in layers if you are exercising outside so you can take layers off if you get too warm and put them back on if you get cold, wearing proper socks to prevent blisters, and wearing proper shoes for the activity you are participating in.

Physical Activity and Using Protective Equipment

Many activities you are involved with may have protective equipment you should be using to stay safe and help prevent injuries. You need to make sure the protective equipment fits you properly and is in good shape. Common equipment you may need includes the following.

- Helmets for a variety of sports and activities are usually made of a hard material to resist impact. You should wear a helmet when you ride your bike, skateboard, snow ski, or snowboard and when playing football, softball or baseball, hockey, or lacrosse. Helmets help reduce the risks of concussion, brain damage, and death.
- Mouth guards are used in multiple sports such as football, basketball, lacrosse, rugby, and baseball or softball. They protect your teeth from being knocked out and your jaw from being broken.
- Protective padding such as knee pads, wrist pads, and elbow pads are important in activities like skateboarding, snowboarding, ice hockey, football, and lacrosse. They provide protection if you fall or are hit.
- Face masks should be worn by softball and baseball catchers and lacrosse players. Goggles are used in swimming to protect your eyes from the chlorine and to help you see underwater more easily.
- Reflective clothing should be worn when running or biking along the side of the road.

Shoes are also an important part of your equipment. If you are running on the road, make sure you have shoes that give you the support you need. If you are playing on grass, wear the proper cleats so you don't slip and hurt yourself. If you are playing on a court or doing a number of different types of activities, wear shoes that will give you support and cushion. One pair of shoes may be all you need for the activities you are involved in—just make sure they fit well and are comfortable.

Preventing Injuries While Being Active

Anytime you become physically active, there is a possibility of an injury. Some injuries are very minor and require little more than a bandage. A more severe injury may cause you to stop being active for a period of time, or you may have to see a doctor. Making good choices about your physical activity by following the guidelines shown here will help prevent injuries. Here are the best ways to prevent injuries when being active:

HEALTHY LIVING TIP

While being physically active, wearing comfortable clothes is a must. If you aren't comfortable, it may negatively affect how you feel about exercising; it also may restrict your movement or prevent you from completing your workout.

- Rest and take at least one day off from exercise each week.
- Take a day off between doing muscular strength and muscular endurance activities.
- Use proper technique when exercising.
- Vary your activity so you aren't using the same muscle groups each day.
- Don't play through pain because that often turns a minor injury into a major injury.
- Warm up and cool down properly.
- Wear the right protective equipment to keep from being injured.
- Stay hydrated by drinking water regularly before, during, and after your physical activity. This regulates your body temperature and blood pressure so you don't get overheated, which can interfere with your performance and recovery.

Exercising in Hot Weather

Being active in hot weather can lead to heat-related emergencies that are caused by overexposure to heat and by dehydration. **Dehydration** occurs when you lose more fluid than you take in. If you are exercising in hot weather and don't drink enough water, you may become dehydrated. This can lead to heat cramps, heat exhaustion, or heat stroke. You will learn about these conditions in chapter 14.

To prevent heat-related emergencies, do the following:

- Wear light-colored and lightweight clothing.
- Avoid exercising in high heat and humidity if possible.
- Drink water before, during, and after exercising to maintain proper hydration.
- Rest frequently in the shade and use cool towels to help keep cool.
- Know the signs and symptoms of heat-related emergencies—muscle spasms, nausea, headache, dizziness, and extremely high body temperature where sweating is absent.

Exercising in Cold and Wet Weather

Being active in cold and wet weather can lead to cold-related emergencies caused by overexposure to cold. This overexposure may lead to frostbite or hypothermia. You will learn about these conditions in chapter 14.

To prevent cold-related emergencies, do the following:

- Wear several layers of clothing rather than one heavy jacket.
- Wear clothing to protect your head, hands, face, ears, and feet from the cold to prevent frostbite.
- Drink water before, during, and after exercising to maintain proper hydration.
- Avoid exercising in cold and wet weather if possible. Make sure to check the wind chill factor so that you know how cold it really is.
- Know the signs and symptoms of cold-related emergencies—a body part becoming numb, skin becoming cold to the touch, shivering intensely, feeling confused, and losing consciousness.

Preparing for Physical Activity **LESSON 6.3**

Skill-Building Challenge

Analyzing Influences

Think about who influences your decision on whether or not to wear protective gear like helmets, mouth guards, face masks, reflective gear, and different protective pads. List four influences. Mark a star for positive influences that encourage you to wear protective gear and an X for negative influences that discourage or belittle you for wearing protective gear. Explain briefly how each influence affects you using the Analyzing Influences Skill Cues. Then determine whether or not you will wear the appropriate protective gear for your activity.

Healthy Living Skills

This lesson focused on analyzing influences. Here are some more ways you can develop healthy living skills related to this lesson.

ADVOCATING FOR GOOD HEALTH

You and a few of your classmates want to start a recreation program at your school. You enjoy playing different sports, but you just want to have fun, don't want to practice a lot, or be very competitive. You would like to have two days a week when students can get together and play different sports. You've even thought about having different seasons—for example, two weeks dedicated to each of these sports: badminton, volleyball, spikeball, and disc golf. That way some students could put teams together and other students could just show up and play. Your teacher has told you this would be a great advocacy project and you should put together a presentation you could show to your principal and school board.

ACCESSING INFORMATION

Put together a list of different people in your community who know about physical activity and healthy eating to interview for a podcast. The podcast will allow everyone to have access to it. To ensure you have qualified people presenting the information, ask them the following questions:

- What makes you qualified to present on your topic? Do you have a degree or certification in the area you will be talking about?
- Is your information up-to-date and accurate? Where do you get your information from?
- What type of information will you share with high school students and families?

LESSON 6.3 Review: Preparing for Physical Activity

LESSON SUMMARY

- A proper workout starts with a warm-up, or moving your whole body; then it shifts to the focus, or what you are trying to improve in or training for; and ends with a cool-down, which gives your body time to slowly adjust when ending an activity.
- Some benefits of being physically active throughout your life include maintaining the ability to live alone and reducing the risk of falling and fracturing bones; improving balance, muscle strength, and joint mobility; and lowering the risk of high blood pressure and strokes.
- Individual, dual, and team sports can teach you about self-resilience and self-motivation as well as working with others, being a good sport, managing time, and persisting.
- When being physically active, it is important to wear the proper protective equipment specific to the activity to prevent injury. Protective equipment includes helmets, mouth guards, protective padding, face masks, reflective clothing, and shoes.
- To prevent an injury while being physically active, use proper technique, vary your activity, and stay hydrated by drinking water regularly.

REVIEWING CONCEPTS AND VOCABULARY

1. Your _____ should include large muscle movements that get your whole body moving.
2. Stretching with movement is also known as _____ stretching.
3. _____ sports are played by two people.
4. Slowing your body down and giving it time to adjust when ending a workout is called a _____.
5. _____ stretching involves standing, sitting, or lying still and holding a stretch.
6. A(n) _____ sport is played by one person.
7. Groups of people play a(n) _____ sport.
8. _____ occurs when you lose more fluid than you take in.

THINKING CRITICALLY

List different places you could go in your community to be physically active. Include places like local parks, fields, and facilities. Next to each item, identify the groups of people who are most likely to benefit from that facility (for example, school kids, parents, older adults, individuals with differing abilities, professionals, athletes, etc.). When identifying groups, think about who has access and what the facility offers.

TAKE IT HOME

Interview three family members or friends about an injury they have had. Ask them how they got the injury and if they could have done anything to prevent it. Create a list of their injuries and possible ways you think the people you interviewed could have prevented their injury.

LESSON 6.4
Fitness Planning

Terms to Learn
fitness plan
FITT formula
frequency
intensity
overload
progression
specificity
time
type

The Big Picture
Fitness planning gives you the opportunity to develop a program to help you reach your fitness goals. Your fitness test results or examining an area you know needs improvement gives you crucial information for developing a personal fitness plan. By using your fitness plan, the FITT formula, and SMART goals, you have the ability to determine what you specifically need to do to reach your fitness goals.

Learning Targets
- Complete your fitness plan using the FITT formula correctly.
- Explain why it is important to set SMART goals.
- Apply the training principles of specificity, overload, and progression to your fitness plan.
- Analyze why it is important to monitor your fitness plan.
- Examine your use of technology when being physically active.

Write About It
Explain why you think it might be important to develop a weekly fitness plan to keep track of the physical activity you are doing. How would a fitness plan help you keep track of whether you are making progress toward your physical activity goals?

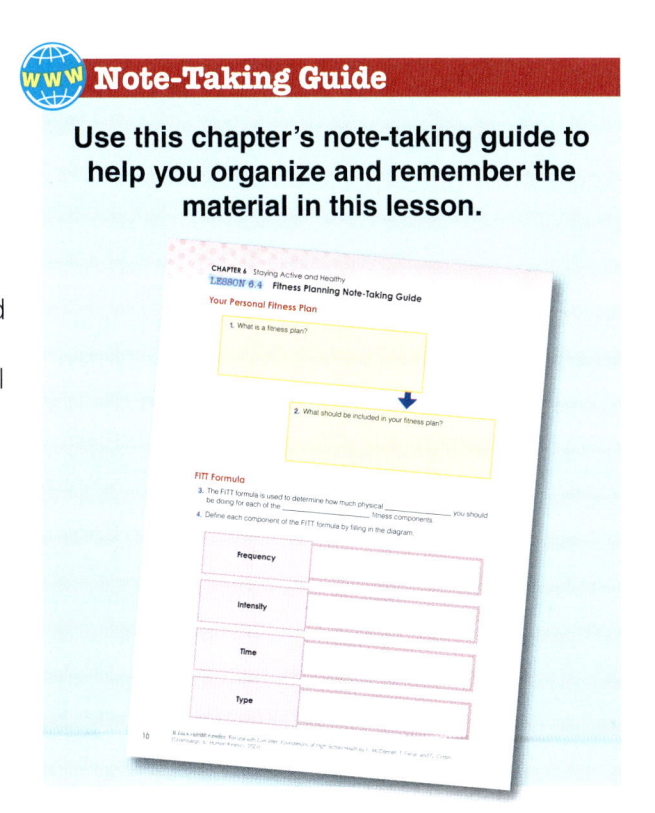

Note-Taking Guide

Use this chapter's note-taking guide to help you organize and remember the material in this lesson.

LESSON 6.4   Staying Active and Healthy

Anna just finished her fitness test, and based on the results, she now wants to do better on the sit-up retest at the end of the semester. Anna currently can do eight sit-ups, so she sets a SMART goal of 15 sit-ups. List three exercises Anna could do at home to help increase her sit-up score.

Your Personal Fitness Plan

Now is the time to put what you have learned about physical activity into designing your own fitness plan. A **fitness plan** is a detailed plan you design to help you meet your fitness and activity goals. The fitness plan should include cardiorespiratory endurance, muscular strength and endurance, and flexibility activities. To achieve success with this, it is recommended that you start by first determining your fitness levels for each component. The next section discusses this in further detail.

Fitness Tests for Health-Related Fitness Components

Fitness testing is something your health teacher or physical education teacher may have you do. Completing the fitness tests would give you an idea about specific areas you may want to improve. The following list include the most common fitness tests for each of the health-related fitness components.

- Cardiorespiratory endurance. One-mile (1.6 km) run, 20-meter PACER test, three-minute step test
- Muscular strength. Push-ups at a predetermined pace you need to keep up with
- Muscular endurance. One-minute sit-up test
- Flexibility. Sit-and-reach test

FITT Formula

Using the **FITT formula** (frequency, intensity, time, type) determines the amount of physical activity you should be doing for each of the health-related fitness components. **Frequency** is how often you exercise and depends on whether you are doing a cardiorespiratory endurance, muscular strength, muscular endurance, or flexibility activity. **Intensity** is how hard you exercise. If your activity is too easy, you won't gain any benefits from it; likewise, if it is too difficult, you might not continue with it. Intensity is different for each health-related fitness component you are working on. **Time** is how long you exercise and also depends on the activity you are doing. For cardiorespiratory endurance, your time is in minutes or hours. For muscular strength and endurance, it is the number of sets and reps you perform. For flexibility, it is how long you hold a stretch. **Type** refers to the actual exercise you choose to do based on the fitness component you've selected.

Cardiorespiratory Endurance and FITT Formula

To benefit from cardiorespiratory endurance exercise, you should do moderate-intensity aerobic exercise a minimum of five days a week, at an RPE level of four to five or 60 to 75 percent in your target heart rate zone. You could also do vigorous-intensity aerobic exercise at least three days a week for 20 to 25 minutes at an RPE level of six to seven or 75 to 90 percent in your target heart rate zone. See table 6.3 for guidelines for using the FITT formula.

TABLE 6.3 Cardiorespiratory FITT Formula Intensity Guidelines

	Moderate intensity	Vigorous intensity
Frequency	5 days a week	3 days a week
Intensity	RPE levels 4-5 or 60%-75% in your target training zone	RPE levels 6-7 or 75%-90% in your target training zone
Time	60 min	20-25 min
Type	Aerobic activity	Aerobic activity

Muscular Strength and Endurance and FITT Formula

To develop muscular strength, you will usually do fewer repetitions than for muscular endurance, and you will lift heavier weights. To develop muscular endurance, you will usually do more repetitions than for muscular strength, and you will lift lighter weights (see table 6.4).

TABLE 6.4 Muscular Strength and Endurance FITT Formula Guidelines

Muscular Strength	
Frequency	3 days a week
Intensity	Moderate-heavy weights
Time	1-3 sets of 8-12 reps
Type	Muscular training activities
Muscular Endurance	
Frequency	3 days a week
Intensity	Light-moderate weights
Time	1-3 sets of 15-20 reps
Type	Muscular training activities

Flexibility and FITT Formula

To develop flexibility, you should do both dynamic and static stretching daily. Dynamic stretches are great for your warm-up as you slowly begin moving the muscles through their full range of motion and increase your heart rate. Static stretching should be done after the muscles are completely warmed up. This is often after your workout (i.e., during cool-down), and each stretch should be held from 15 to 30 seconds to a point of discomfort. It is important when holding a stretch that you do not experience pain of any kind. See table 6.5 for flexibility guidelines using the FITT formula.

TABLE 6.5 Flexibility FITT Formula Guidelines

Frequency	Daily
Intensity	To the point of discomfort
Time	Hold each static stretch for 15 to 30 seconds
Type	Static and dynamic stretching

As you begin thinking about planning your fitness or activity program, consider responding to the following statements:

- List activities you currently do that you enjoy and want to continue doing.
- List activities you have tried before that you might want to try again.
- List activities you have only seen but would like to try.
- List activities you know you don't like and will not do.

After listing your activities, assign each activity to a health-related fitness component: cardiorespiratory endurance, muscular strength, muscular endurance, or flexibility. You want to design a fitness plan that is comprehensive. Creating lists like these provides insights on whether your activities cover all the health-related fitness components or if additional activities are needed.

Training Principles

As you think about the activities you will be doing as a part of your fitness plan and how they fit into the FITT formula, you will also want to consider the training principles of fitness. The training principles of fitness help you get as much out of your fitness plan as possible. They consist of **specificity**, **progression**, and **overload**.

- *Specificity.* The exercises you do must be specific to improving certain muscles or particular types of fitness. For example, do push-ups and upper body exercises to improve on your push-ups. If you want to improve your running times, you need to run and do other cardiorespiratory endurance exercises.
- *Progression.* As your workouts become easier, they need to be fine-tuned. To do this, gradually increase the amount or the intensity of the exercise to continue to see progress. Without fine-tuning, you will not meet your SMART goal.
- *Overload.* You must work your way to doing more physical activity than in previous workouts. This can happen by exercising more often, increasing the intensity of your exercise, exercising longer, or doing extra sets and reps. As with the progression principle, you need to challenge yourself to get new results.

Setting SMART Goals

Once you determine the health-related fitness components you want to work on, either through your fitness test results or by your own determination, it is time to set a SMART goal (see figure 6.15). If you are unsure about a specific goal to set, have a general goal to increase daily physical activity, and then be specific about what you are going to do each day to achieve your goal. Setting goals is important because they clarify what it is you want to achieve, help keep you accountable, and sustain your motivation.

HEALTHY LIVING TIP
When setting a SMART fitness goal, make sure you enjoy doing the exercises and activities you've chosen. Your workout should be something you look forward to rather than something you *have* to do. If you focus on exercises and activities you like to do along with some that may challenge you, you are more likely to exercise on a regular basis and reach your fitness goal.

SMART Goal Reminder

- **S** = Specific. What exactly will you do? (Is it a cardiorespiratory activity? Muscular strength or endurance? Flexibility?)
- **M** = Measurable. How much or how often will you do this? (What is your new mile time? How many push-ups or curl-ups will you be able to do? How far will you be able to stretch?)
- **A** = Achievable. Is the goal something you can actually do with some effort? (You need to think about what you will be able to do in the amount of time you give yourself to achieve your goal.)
- **R** = Realistic. Does the goal make sense, and will it help you achieve what you want? (Is the goal associated with one of your fitness testing components or a physical activity you want to improve in?)
- **T** = Timely. When will the goal be met? How long will it take? (Find out when your next fitness test will be or what the timeline is for an activity goal you may have set for yourself.)

Figure 6.15 A summary of how to set a SMART goal.

Use the FITT formula as a guideline for setting your SMART goal.

Frequency—How often will you work on your goal?

Intensity—How hard will you work? Remember, this depends on your goal.

Time—How long do you need to do the activity for, or how many sets and reps?

Type—Will you work on a cardiorespiratory, muscular strength, muscular endurance, or flexibility activity?

After setting your SMART goal, you should decide on action steps to make sure you work toward achieving it. Your action steps for achieving your SMART goal will be your fitness plan based on the FITT formula and the training principles. Each week, you should create a fitness plan to help you stay on track to meet your SMART goal. Creating a fitness plan can be a great reminder to be physically active each day and can help you make it a part of your daily routine. It is important to schedule your physical activity into your day just as you schedule school or chores you have to do. If you don't plan for or set aside time for your exercise, often it won't happen. See figure 6.16 for a fitness plan. Monday has been completed for you.

LESSON 6.4   Staying Active and Healthy

Day/date	Activity	Type	Time	Comments
	The activity or activities you did each day	Cardiorespiratory Muscular strength Muscular endurance Flexibility	Track how long you did the activity or keep track of your sets and reps.	Include any comments you have about the intensity of your workout or changes you want to make to it.
Monday	Elliptical machine **Lifting:** bench press, arm curls, triceps press	Cardiorespiratory Muscular strength Muscular endurance	20 min 3 sets of 8	Today's workout was great. I had a lot of energy going into it and even more when I was done.
	Stretching: front arm cross body, arm stretch on wall, triceps stretch	Flexibility	30-sec hold for each stretch	
Tuesday				
Wednesday				
Thursday				
Friday				
Saturday				
Sunday				

Figure 6.16 Using a fitness plan will allow you to keep track of what you are doing on a daily and weekly basis, which will help you stay on track and motivated to meet your SMART goal.

Monitoring Your Fitness Plan

When you begin your fitness plan, determine how many weeks you have until you want to meet your goal. Each week, you should try to improve from the week before. Using the training principles allows you to make sure you are continuing to see improvement and challenging yourself each week as is safe and appropriate for your fitness level. At the halfway point toward your goal, reevaluate the goal you set to see whether it really is achievable or if you will exceed it. Make adjustments to your goal at this time if needed. There is nothing wrong with having to set a new goal—there can be many reasons why the goal you originally set was either too difficult or too easy. Monitoring your fitness plan to see whether it is working as you need it to is important for the following reasons:

- You will be more likely to reach your goals.
- You will be able to see what you have already done and know what you still need to do for the week.
- It keeps you accountable to the goal you set.
- It gives you an opportunity to modify your goal.

- It can be motivating for you to see the progress you have made, or it can motivate you to keep working and to work harder if necessary.
- It helps keep you committed to your plan.

Planning Your Fitness With Technology

Many apps such as MyFitness Pal, Nike Training Club, and 30 Day Fitness are available for use if you want to bypass having to write or type in a fitness plan. Each app has ideas for exercises you could do to help you meet your SMART goal. With so many choices, you should be able to easily find exercises that are different and will keep you interested in working out.

STEM in Health

WEARABLE TECHNOLOGY

Wearable fitness technology helps you regularly track your health. It also makes you more aware of how many steps you took and your heart rate. Students involved with STEM programs are now getting opportunities to work with and help create wearable technology. At the prototype stage, they are putting together designs and custom-coded circuits that would be sewn on fabric, gloves, and tennis shoes. Initial designs focus on basic circuit boards. However, in time, as they continue to move forward, students will be shaping the future with a variety of more advanced wearable technology.

LESSON 6.4 Staying Active and Healthy

Skill-Building Challenge

Setting SMART Fitness Goals

Using your fitness test scores or a specific area of fitness you have chosen to work on, decide on one or two areas you want to improve on between now and the end of the semester. Once you have decided what you want to work on, set a SMART goal to improve your specific area of fitness.

Healthy Living Skills

This lesson focused on setting healthy goals. Here are some more ways you can develop healthy living skills related to this lesson.

PRACTICING HEALTHY BEHAVIORS

Identify one fitness and one nutrition concept you want to work on. They can be as simple or complex as you would like. An example might be doing 20 jumping jacks each day and drinking two glasses of water each day. Create a simple Monday through Sunday checklist where you can mark off whether you did your fitness and nutrition concept each day. At the end of the week, see how you did. If you were successful with achieving your concepts all seven days, reflect on why you think you were successful; for days missed, think about what prevented you from meeting your goals. Use simple checklists to be more consistent for your fitness and nutrition behaviors.

ANALYZING INFLUENCES

Do you use any type of technology or media when you are physically active? Do you have a smart watch or a fitness tracker that helps you keep track of your heart rate or how far you have run? Do you like to listen to music when you exercise? If you exercise indoors, do you watch TV or stream shows on your phone or tablet? Or is your physical activity time when you completely unplug and don't use technology at all? Think about your answers to the previous questions as you answer the following questions:

- If you do use technology or media, what do you use and how does it influence your activity?
- If you don't use technology or media, who or what has influenced your decision not to use it?

LESSON 6.4 Review: Fitness Planning

LESSON SUMMARY

- A fitness plan is a detailed plan you design to help you meet your fitness and activity goals. An important component of a fitness plan is the FITT formula.
- The acronym FITT stands for frequency (how often you exercise), intensity (how hard you exercise), time (how long you exercise), and type (the actual exercise you choose to do).
- Setting SMART goals is important for clarifying what it is you want to achieve, keeping you accountable, and helping you stay motivated.
- By applying the training principles of specificity, progression, and overload, you can adjust your exercises over time to get the most benefits from each workout.
- Monitoring your fitness plan gives you the opportunity to reach and surpass your goals, be more efficient in your workouts, and be motivated and committed to your plan.
- With technology being so prevalent, many students now use apps and smart watches when monitoring their workouts and streaming videos to enhance their workouts.

REVIEWING CONCEPTS AND VOCABULARY

1. A guide for meeting your fitness goals is a _____.
2. The FITT formula is used to determine the _____, intensity, time, and type of physical activity you should be doing for each health-related fitness component.
3. In the FITT formula, how often you exercise is defined as _____.
4. _____ is the actual exercise you choose to do based on the fitness component you are working on.
5. The training principle of _____ states you must do certain kinds of exercise to improve particular muscles or types of fitness.
6. The training principles include _____, _____, and _____.

THINKING CRITICALLY

Show a classmate your fitness plan and explain to them how you are progressing toward your fitness goal. Discuss how you are monitoring your progress and whether you are on track to meet your fitness goal.

TAKE IT HOME

Teach a family member or friend how to set a SMART goal for incorporating physical activity into their daily life. Make sure to explain why it is important to set SMART goals.

Chapter Review

ACTION PLAN: Develop a Fitness Plan

Use the My Action Plan worksheet to develop a fitness plan. Here is an example.

My Action Plan: Develop a Fitness Plan

STEP 1: Identify the health behavior you are going to work on.

I want to improve my push-up score.

STEP 2: Write SMART goal(s).
Write one or two short-term goals (one day to one month long).

I will do 10 push-ups three times a week for the next three weeks.

Write a long-term goal (one to six months or more).

I will be able to do at least five full push-ups in three months when we do our next fitness test.

STEP 3: Make a plan.
Identify two to five action steps (strategies) you could do to meet your goal.

I will set a reminder on my phone for Monday, Wednesday, and Friday at 8:00 p.m. to do my 10 push-ups.

STEP 4: Do your plan and track your progress.

Short-term goal
☐ Met   ☒ Not met   Date: _____

Long-term goal
☒ Met   ☐ Not met   Date: *May 15*

If you met your goal, what helped you to be successful?

I met my long-term goal of doing five full push-ups in May because, even though I didn't always do my 10 push-ups three times a week, I did do 10 push-ups at least once a week every week for three months, which made a difference.

If you did not meet your goal, what made it harder for you to be successful?

Despite having set a reminder in my phone to do my push-ups three times a week, I sometimes was too busy to do them.

Test Your Knowledge

Select the best answer for each question.

1. _____ is a general term that includes sports, dance, and various activities that involves movement of the body's large muscles.
    a. Exercise
    b. Physical activity
    c. Aerobic
    d. Fitness

2. When using the RPE scale, which level should you be working at for a moderate-intensity activity?
    a. three to four
    b. four to five
    c. five to six
    d. six to seven

3. What are the words in the correct order for the FITT formula?
    a. frequency, intensity, time, type
    b. frequency, interval, type, time
    c. frequency, intensity, target, training
    d. frequency, interval, target, train

4. Which system is responsible for controlling blood flow?
    a. respiratory
    b. cardiorespiratory
    c. muscular
    d. circulatory

5. Which set of components refers to parts of fitness you need to exercise regularly to keep healthy?
    a. skill-related
    b. fitness-related
    c. health-related
    d. activity-related

6. Which list includes three training principles?
    a. overload, progression, recover
    b. warm-up, workout, cool-down
    c. stretch, lift, breathe
    d. overload, progression, specificity

7. Which activity should include large muscle movements that get your body moving to increase your heart rate?
    a. warm-up
    b. cool-down
    c. team sport
    d. individual sport

8. Which piece of safety equipment when worn properly can reduce the chance of concussions and death?
    a. knee pads
    b. mouth guard
    c. helmet
    d. neck roll

9. Improving or maintaining one or more components of fitness through planned, structured, and repetitive movements is
    a. exercise
    b. physical activity
    c. aerobic
    d. fitness

10. Which of the following is a designed plan that uses the FITT formula to help you meet your fitness and activity goals?
    a. exercise
    b. activity
    c. physical
    d. fitness

PROJECT-BASED LEARNING: Fitness Instagram

What to Remember

Everyone will have different fitness goals, access to different types of equipment, and varying time frames to exercise in. It is important for teens to have options in their workout so they can make the exercise work for them.

Who It Is For

Students in your class

Why It Is Important

Your classmates will see a variety of different exercises they may not have thought of and can learn how to do them.

What to Do

Create Instagram stories or TikTok videos about different exercises that other people can use to help them be more physically active.

If you can't post on Instagram or TikTok, see if there is another app you could use such as Snapchat or see if you could record yourself and post it as a video on your school website.

How to Do It

With a group, discuss which social media platform you will use. Make sure you know your group's and teacher's social media names. Next, you should decide which exercises to assign to each group member, keeping in mind that you'll be posting one exercise for each day of the week. For their assigned exercise, that person is responsible for creating an outline of the FITT formula; the rest of the group works as a quality assurance team to ensure the exercise's name, FITT formula components, and video are done correctly. Post and share a new exercise each day and ask your teacher if the whole class should be a part of the post also.

When creating your social media ideas be sure to do the following:

- Use your own fitness plans and SMART goals as ideas for your Instagram, TikTok, or other social media posts.
- Include the exercise name, the FITT formula components, and a video of the exercise being performed properly.

CROSS-CURRICULAR CONNECTIONS: Science

Use a clothespin, small ball, or another object that you can squeeze for this experiment. Squeeze the object as many times as you can for two minutes. Record the number of times you squeezed the object. Rest for one minute and repeat the experiment again. Record your results on the second attempt. Describe what happened and explain why you think the results came out the way they did.

UNIT III

Your Emotional, Mental, and Social Well-Being

CHAPTER 7   Emotional Wellness

CHAPTER 8   Mental Health

CHAPTER 9   Relationships and Social Health

Emotional Wellness

LESSON 7.1 Your Emotional Health
LESSON 7.2 Building Self-Awareness
LESSON 7.3 Developing Emotional Health and Mental Toughness
LESSON 7.4 Recognizing and Managing Stress
LESSON 7.5 Understanding Grief and Loss

Understanding My Health

My Emotional Health

This self-assessment will help you understand your emotional health. The following statements reflect different parts of good emotional health. Select the answer that is most accurate for you. Be honest in your responses so that you can have an accurate understanding of where you are. Add up your points. The closer you are to 30 points, the better your emotional health is.

	Always	Sometimes	Never
I know my own strengths and weaknesses.	3	2	1
I feel like I am a good person.	3	2	1
I believe that I deserve to be treated with respect.	3	2	1
I like who I am.	3	2	1
When something goes wrong, I am able to bounce back.	3	2	1
I am able to keep going and reach my goals even when things are hard.	3	2	1
I recognize when others are hurting, and I understand how they feel.	3	2	1
I can learn from my mistakes, and I always try to improve.	3	2	1
I feel in control of my emotions.	3	2	1
I am able to empathize with others who are grieving.	3	2	1

My score for My Emotional Health = _____ (total number of points)

Your emotional health plays a major part in defining who you are and how you experience life. If you can't manage your emotions, you are more likely to make dangerous or impulsive decisions. Poor emotional control and lack of empathy make it very difficult to develop and maintain healthy and meaningful relationships with others. It is also important to know how to manage stress and cope with grief and loss in order to maintain long-term emotional well-being.

LESSON 7.1
Your Emotional Health

Terms to Learn
emotional health
emotional intelligence
impulsiveness
mental health

The Big Picture
Your emotions are a big part of your experience as a person. The feelings we experience color our daily lives and motivate our behaviors. How well you identify and manage the emotions you have will influence all the other parts of your health and well-being. This lesson explains what emotional health is and focuses on fundamental emotional skills like communicating emotion, showing empathy, and developing impulse control.

Learning Targets
- Explain how emotional health relates to overall health and wellness.
- Describe influences on emotional health.
- Explain each of the four parts of emotional intelligence.
- Explain why empathy is important to relationships.
- Describe the risks of not having good impulse control.

Write About It
When is the last time you felt empathy from someone else? Describe the situation and explain how their response affected how you felt in the situation.

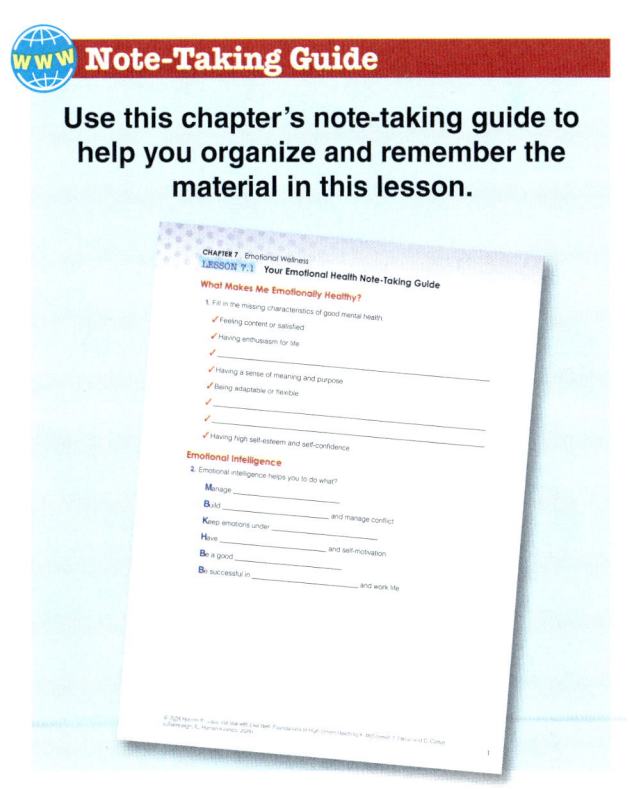

Note-Taking Guide
Use this chapter's note-taking guide to help you organize and remember the material in this lesson.

LESSON 7.1   Emotional Wellness

Alexis felt really angry toward her younger sister Emilia after Emilia used her makeup and didn't put it back. Alexis had an important event after school, and she couldn't afford to look anything but her best. Without her makeup, Alexis felt vulnerable and insecure. She was so angry that she stormed into Emilia's room and knocked over her dresser. It fell on the nightstand nearby and broke Emilia's new phone.

After hearing the noise, their parents ran up the stairs, saw what happened, and told Alexis she was grounded. She also would have to pay to replace her sister's phone. Alexis missed her event, and her sister wouldn't speak to her for weeks. Have you ever felt angry enough to do something reckless like Alexis did? How did you manage your emotions? What did you learn from the experience?

What Is Emotional Health?

Having good **emotional health** means that you have a positive state of well-being that allows you to function in society and meet the demands of your daily life. Emotional health is focused on maximizing your potential and living your best life. It is an important part of overall wellness and includes self-esteem, body image, resilience, empathy, and impulse control.

The terms *emotional health* and *mental health* are often designated as meaning the same thing, but they are slightly different. **Mental health** involves successful thinking and mental processing. It includes your ability to stay focused, process information, store and retrieve information, understand what you see and hear, and reason and make decisions. Mental health exists on a spectrum from optimal functioning to serious mental illness.

What Are Emotions?

Emotions are physiological; in other words, emotions are electrochemical signals that flow through the body in an unending cycle. The purpose of emotions is to help us focus our attention and motivate our behavior. In this way, emotions themselves are neither positive nor negative. How we choose to respond to emotions is what affects our emotional health. Emotions can help us survive and thrive just as easily as they can interfere with our decision making and cause us to make bad choices. Emotions are also contagious in that how we experience and express our emotions can directly affect others around us.

What Makes Me Emotionally Healthy?

Several factors are at play in having good emotional health. Emotional health deals with optimum functioning, so it should come as no surprise that people with good emotional health share many strong and positive characteristics (see figure 7.1). Good emotional health is also connected to the other parts of wellness. When you are functioning at your best emotionally, you are also more likely to have better physical, spiritual, intellectual, and social wellness.

Learning to identify and use emotions in productive ways is at the center of having good emotional health and emotional intelligence. **Emotional intelligence** refers to your ability to perceive, manage, and regulate emotions and includes self-awareness, self-management, social awareness, and social skills (see figure 7.2).

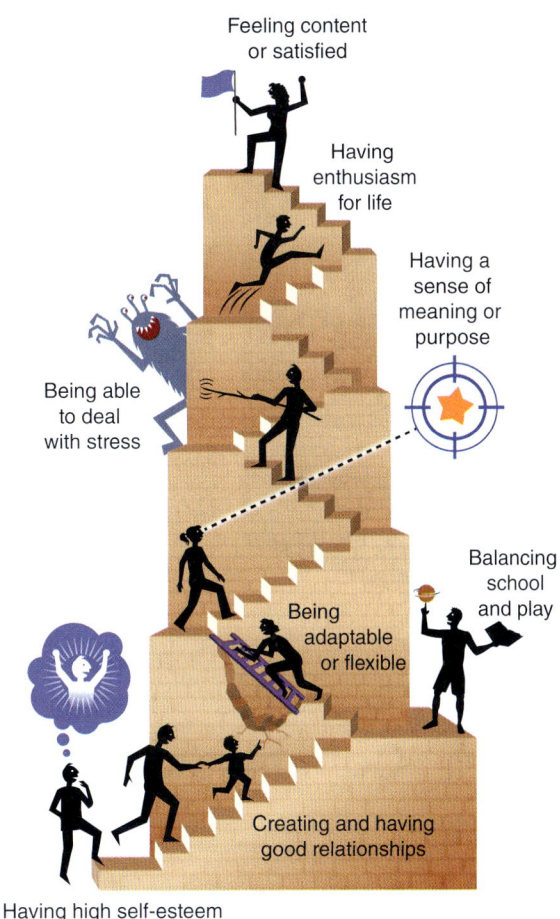

Figure 7.1 Characteristics of positive emotional health.

Having good emotional health and being emotionally intelligent affects things like

- your ability to manage stress,
- your ability to build relationships and manage conflict,
- your ability to keep emotions under control,
- your self-confidence and self-motivation,
- your leadership abilities, and
- your success in academics and work life.

LESSON 7.1   Emotional Wellness

RECOGNITION

Self-awareness
Knowing your own strengths, weaknesses, thoughts, beliefs, motivations, and emotions

Social awareness
How well you recognize and understand the emotions of others

Social skills
How you handle relationships and build connections with others

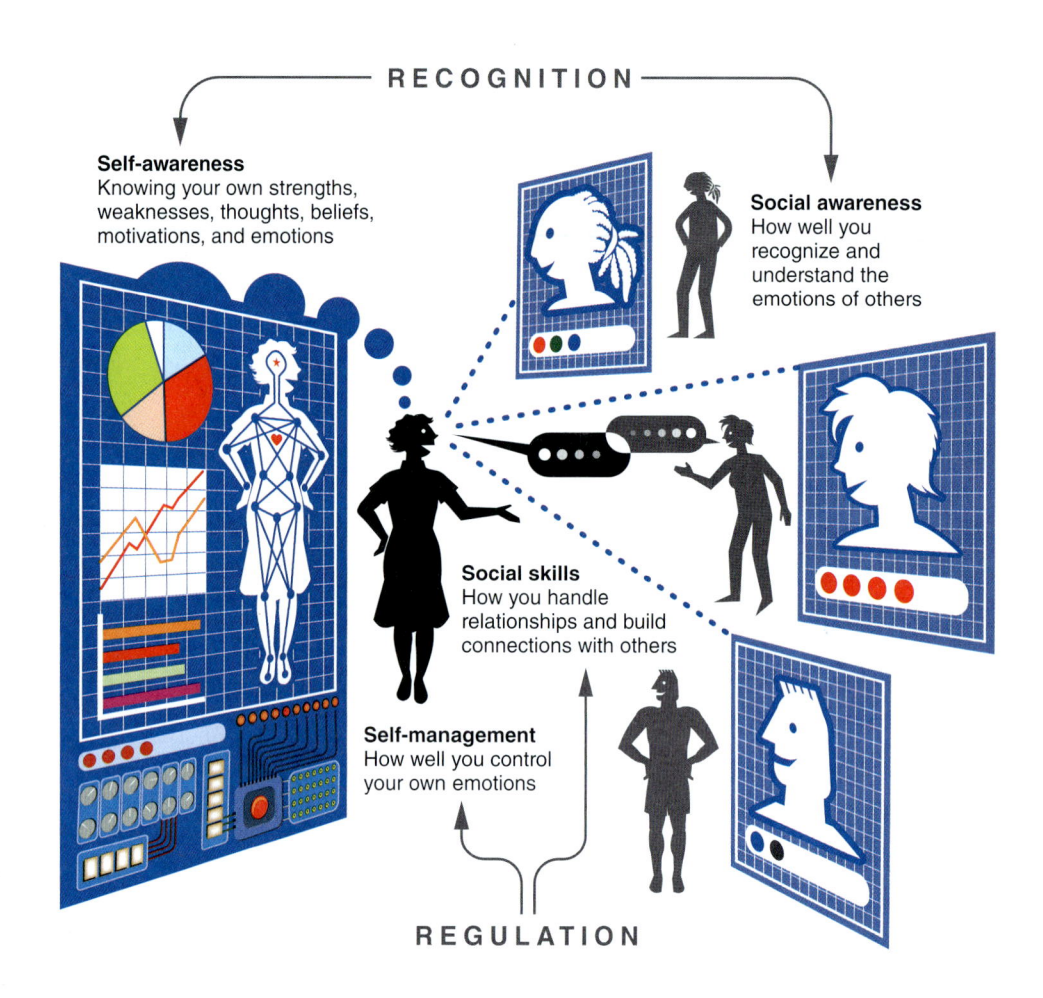

Self-management
How well you control your own emotions

REGULATION

Figure 7.2 Emotional intelligence requires the ability to accurately recognize and effectively regulate emotions.

Communicating Your Emotions

People are social beings, and emotions drive much of our connection with others. When we share an emotional experience with others, it can strengthen and bond the relationship. When we are struggling with our emotions, talking to other people can have beneficial effects. Both positive and negative emotions should be shared and expressed with others (see figure 7.3). It can be especially hard to express emotions like pain and sadness. Sometimes people are afraid that others will judge them as being weak or unable to control their emotions. The truth is, expressing pain and sadness is the best way to make the feelings stop, and it is how others come to understand how you are feeling. When others understand what you are going through, they can provide the support and encouragement you need to manage your emotions successfully.

Developing Empathy

Empathy is your awareness of the feelings and emotions of other people. It involves feeling the way and understanding how someone else feels. Empathy is at the center of every relationship you have in life and is essential for good emotional health. If you are unable to relate to the emotions of others, it is challenging to develop meaningful relationships or to function fully in society.

Your Emotional Health **LESSON 7.1**

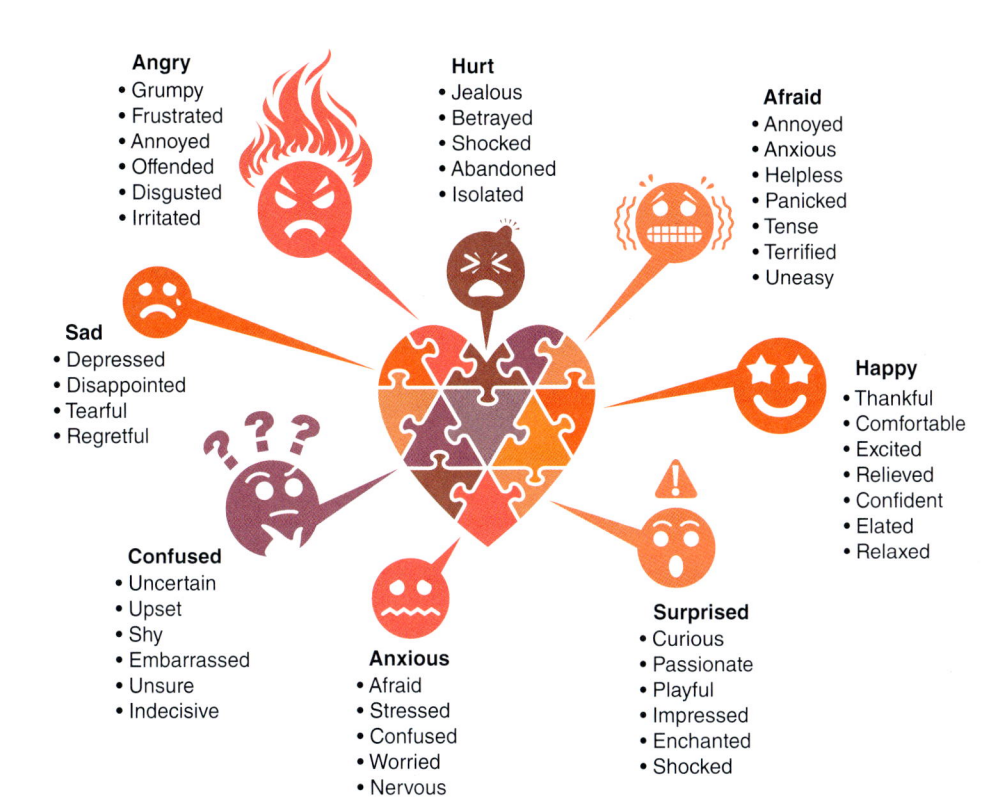

Angry
- Grumpy
- Frustrated
- Annoyed
- Offended
- Disgusted
- Irritated

Hurt
- Jealous
- Betrayed
- Shocked
- Abandoned
- Isolated

Afraid
- Annoyed
- Anxious
- Helpless
- Panicked
- Tense
- Terrified
- Uneasy

Sad
- Depressed
- Disappointed
- Tearful
- Regretful

Happy
- Thankful
- Comfortable
- Excited
- Relieved
- Confident
- Elated
- Relaxed

Confused
- Uncertain
- Upset
- Shy
- Embarrassed
- Unsure
- Indecisive

Anxious
- Afraid
- Stressed
- Confused
- Worried
- Nervous

Surprised
- Curious
- Passionate
- Playful
- Impressed
- Enchanted
- Shocked

Figure 7.3 Building a varied and robust emotional vocabulary helps us communicate emotions more effectively.

Here are some ways we can develop empathy.

- *Share in the life stories of others.* Seeing how another person experiences life causes us to imagine and wonder what it feels like.
- *Make an effort to understand differences in social cultures, values, and traditions.* The more you reach out and get to know other people who are different from yourself, the more empathy you can develop.
- *Ask questions and learn about situations different from your own.* Understand what it is like to have a particular disability, live in a different neighborhood, be adopted, or be of a different economic status. The more you learn about different circumstances, the more empathy you can develop for others in those circumstances.

Sometimes we don't value others who are different from us because we assume they don't feel or behave like we do. We also are less likely to feel empathy if we blame someone for their circumstances. For example, if someone is robbed at night and we blame them for being out late, we are less likely to feel empathy toward them or their situation. It is important to keep circumstances from getting in the way of having empathy toward others.

HEALTHY LIVING TIP

Read books about the lives of others. Being exposed to differences in culture, lifestyle, and experience can help you expand your capacity for empathy.

Influences on Emotions

There are several influences on the emotions we experience. As a teen, emotions are most influenced by physical changes associated with maturation and through interactions with peers, especially on social media.

295

LESSON 7.1 | Emotional Wellness

Physical Influences

The physical changes you go through during puberty can change how you experience emotions. Your emotions can change for any of the following reasons.

- *Your hormone levels are changing.* These changes can make emotions feel more intense. You may notice that you have bigger mood swings (moving from one extreme emotion to another). You may also experience more irritability or anxiety.
- *Your sleeping is disrupted.* Physical changes occur that can disrupt your sleeping patterns. Not sleeping well generally leads to more moodiness and irritability.
- *Your brain is not fully developed.* The human brain does not reach maturity until the early 20s. As a result, kids and teenagers have a more difficult time managing, or regulating, emotions.
- *You are going through social changes.* During adolescence, you also go through a lot of social changes. Friendships can shift when you change schools, sport teams, or groups; popularity can shift as people develop and grow at different rates; and social media use can increase and trigger more frequent and more intense emotional reactions. All of these changes can make your emotions feel scary and out of control.

Peer and Technology Influences

Social media affect the way we express our emotions and influence how we feel. Research shows that we use emotion as a way to get the attention of others on social media. Strong emotional reactions increasingly are used to draw attention to sociopolitical issues too. This is particularly true of anger and frustration. In addition, how your peers and social groups react on social media has a bigger influence on your emotions than the reactions of strangers do. If you find yourself feeling more negative emotions than you once did, consider cutting back on social media use.

Taking Control of Your Emotions

It is important to learn how to control your emotions, especially when you feel angry or frustrated. We all feel urges and extreme emotions now and then. It is okay to feel—in fact, feeling things deeply probably means that you care. The challenge is not in trying to avoid emotions; it is in learning to apply the brakes before you respond recklessly to what you feel. Our thoughts, emotions, and behaviors are all connected. Reacting to emotions without stopping to think, evaluate, and respond appropriately can result in behaviors that have negative and unintended consequences (see figure 7.4).

Situation
You think a friend ignored you in the hallway.

Thoughts
You think she doesn't like you, but she just didn't see you.

Emotions
You feel angry, confused, and sad.

Physiology
Your heartbeat is faster, your mouth is dry, and your hands are shaky.

Behaviors
You make a mean social media post, and your other friends get mad at you.

Figure 7.4 There can be unintended and negative consequences when you don't control your emotions.

No single strategy for controlling emotions works for everyone. In fact, no single strategy works in every situation. Developing a box of tools will help you to find the right tool for the right situation. Controlling intense emotions like anger, frustration, and anxiety is hard work. Read through the Healthy Ways to Manage Emotions on the following pages and think about which approaches might work best for you.

Managing Impulses

Being impulsive is one consequence of not being able to manage emotions well. **Impulsiveness** refers to acting suddenly while ignoring the consequences of the decision or behavior. It is important to recognize that impulsive behaviors are usually dangerous or risky (see figure 7.5). In recent years, studies have linked impulsiveness to higher risks of smoking, drinking, drug abuse, compulsive gambling, aggressive behaviors, and eating disorders. Being a teenager, experiencing intense emotions, and being influenced by peers are not excuses for being impulsive. You are always responsible for your own actions, even when you don't take time to really think them through.

Examples of Impulsive Behavior

- Being dishonest
- Breaking the rules
- Having tantrums (slamming doors, throwing things, hitting walls)
- Destroying property when angry
- Being mean or putting others down
- Cyberbullying
- Punching something or someone
- Being verbally aggressive
- Stealing
- Borrowing without asking
- Running away
- Overeating
- Smoking cigarettes or vaping
- Using drugs
- Drinking alcohol
- Gambling
- Cutting yourself or doing other self-harming behaviors

Figure 7.5 Impulsive behaviors are usually dangerous.

Healthy Ways to Manage Emotions

Breathe and Pause
When a situation makes you feel angry or frustrated, pause immediately to take a deep breath. As you inhale, count to yourself until you get to the count of four. Exhale fully before reacting. If you need a little bit more, try saying *relax* or *stay calm* to yourself as you exhale. Taking a slow, deep breath is especially effective if you feel angry and are likely to be physically aggressive.

Collect Your Thoughts
When you want to make a quick response to a situation, take a moment to collect your thoughts. Making sure you know what to say and how you want to say it will help keep you from saying something impulsive that worsens the situation. Try saying, "Just give me a second here," so that those around you know you are collecting your thoughts.

Express Your Anger Calmly
Once you are thinking clearly, express what you are feeling in a way that is assertive and not aggressive. Use *I* messages; redirect your focus away from placing blame on others to how you feel. Remind yourself that anger won't fix anything and is likely to make the situation worse.

Take a Time-Out
If you find yourself in a situation that has you feeling tense or on edge, take time to get out of the situation briefly. Step away and go outside or into another room. If social media is the source of your emotions, unplug for a few hours. A short break from a stressful environment allows you to collect yourself and will help you keep things in perspective.

Stop Your Thoughts
If you feel your emotions rising up, silently tell yourself to *stop* as soon as you feel yourself beginning to react. Repeat the word *stop* as often as you need to as a way to collect your thoughts and refocus your energy.

Distract Yourself
When you are in an ongoing situation that creates anger or frustration, find something that will distract you from that situation. Listen to music, repeat a favorite poem or song lyric, focus on something in your environment, or use all of your senses to imagine being in a peaceful place.

Listen Actively and Carefully
Poor listening skills are at the root of most miscommunications. When others are speaking, listen to what they are saying and try not to focus on your own response. If you are thinking about yourself when someone else is talking, you are probably missing out on what it is they are really trying to say.

Practice Empathy
If another person is the source of your anger or frustration, try your best to imagine the situation from their perspective. Oftentimes there is no clear right or wrong in a stressful situation. Simply acknowledging that the other person genuinely does feel a certain way and then trying to understand why they do can often calm the situation down.

Do Regular Physical Activity
Exercise is one of the best ways to keep your stress levels down. When you feel less stress in general, you are less likely to feel frustrated or angry when things intensify. The body is built to move when situations are stressful or dangerous (fight or flight). Take advantage of that natural reality.

Focus on Solving the Problem
People often get stuck focusing on what happened rather than thinking about how to resolve a situation calmly. If you feel angry with someone or something, don't keep reliving the trigger over and over. Instead, focus on what you can do to resolve the situation and calm your emotions.

Forgive and Let It Go
If you feel angry because of something someone did to you, try your best to understand what happened and then work to forgive the other person. Everyone makes mistakes. When we hold a grudge against another person, we let our anger grow until it eventually explodes again.

Try to Laugh About It
Sometimes we realize we reacted to a situation in a way that was unnecessary. If you've let your emotions get the best of you, try to laugh at yourself. Acknowledging your own shortcoming and laughing about it will help others feel calmer and can quickly help angry feelings go away. When using humor to calm your anger, direct it only at yourself and avoid sarcasm.

Keep a Journal
If you feel angry often, try keeping a journal. Writing down what you are feeling will help you understand what is making you angry, frustrated, anxious, or scared. Journaling is a way of processing emotions. When you make sense of your emotions, you allow your brain to let things go.

Seek Help If You Need It
One of the most important things you can do if you aren't feeling in control of your emotions is to seek help. Talking to a trusted adult is an important first step. Or you may need to see a professional therapist to help you get full control over your emotions.

LESSON 7.1 Emotional Wellness

Skill-Building Challenge

Practicing Emotional Control

Look over the three scenarios shown in the following chart. For each scenario, identify a strategy that the person could use to help control their emotions and then explain how that strategy might affect the outcome. An example is provided for you. Once you have completed the scenarios, describe a situation you have been in where you did not use good emotional control. Identify a strategy you could try next time you are faced with a similar situation.

Scenario	Strategy	Possible outcome
Julia was so mad at her friend she could feel her body get tense, and she just wanted to hit or break something.	Julia could take a deep breath and count to four before she responds.	Julia might feel her body relax, and she might be able to avoid doing something impulsive.
Mario can tell he is mad at his friend, but he is trying to keep it hidden so that their friendship won't be hurt. His anger is making him impatient with others.		
David's home life is hard. His brothers fight all the time, and he feels angry when he hears the way they talk to each other.		
Kwan accidentally typed the wrong word in a post, and her friends are all making fun of her. She feels stupid and is mad at herself for looking foolish.		

Healthy Living Skills

This lesson focused on practicing emotional control. Here are some more ways you can develop healthy living skills related to this lesson.

ACCESSING INFORMATION

Conduct online research on how the brain develops over the lifespan, with special attention focused on the adolescent and early adult years. Search for articles, images, and graphics that summarize (1) the major changes to the brain's structure over time and (2) how brain function changes as a result. Create a visual time line (graphic) that runs from infancy through age 25 and highlights your findings. Make sure your graphic includes information about how cognitive, social, and emotional health may be affected.

PRACTICING HEALTHY BEHAVIORS

Pick one of the emotional control strategies in this lesson and practice it for at least two weeks. Record in a journal how you felt each day and how often or when you used your chosen strategy. Identify any changes or trends you notice in yourself over this period of time.

LESSON 7.1 Review: Your Emotional Health

LESSON SUMMARY

- An emotionally healthy person meets the demands of daily life and shows characteristics like enthusiasm, the ability to deal with stress, flexibility, high self-esteem, and a sense of purpose in life.
- Teenagers often struggle with managing emotions and can be negatively affected by sharing their emotions on social media.
- Emotional intelligence involves self-awareness of emotions, self-management of emotions, awareness of others' emotions, and the social skills necessary to develop and maintain relationships.
- Empathy is your awareness of the feelings and emotions of other people. It involves feeling the way and understanding how someone else feels and it is at the center of every relationship you have in life.
- When you act suddenly while ignoring the consequences of the decision or behavior, you are displaying impulsiveness.
- Impulsive behaviors include being dishonest, breaking the rules, being a hater on social media, and drinking alcohol. Being impulsive can result in risky decisions that can cause harm to your health and relationships. Substance use, dangerous or aggressive activities, conflict, and violence can all result from a lack of impulse control.
- Ways to manage emotions include taking a deep breath and counting to four before reacting, engaging in regular exercise, distracting yourself from an emotional environment, and keeping a journal.

REVIEWING CONCEPTS AND VOCABULARY

1. _____ health focuses on maximizing your potential and living your best life; it is an important part of overall wellness.
2. Your ability to stay focused, reason, and make decisions are part of your _____ health.
3. A person with good _____ is aware of and manages their own emotions and can understand and respond appropriately to the emotions of others.
4. _____ is when you do something without thinking about the consequences of the decision or behavior.
5. Being dishonest and breaking rules are examples of _____ behaviors.

THINKING CRITICALLY

Select one characteristic of emotional intelligence. Conduct some research on how or why that element might affect someone's emotional health. Write a one- or two-paragraph summary of your findings.

TAKE IT HOME

Share the strategies for managing emotions with someone in your home or family. Find out which strategy or strategies they use to help them regulate emotion and why.

LESSON 7.2
Building Self-Awareness

Terms to Learn
self-awareness
self-confidence
self-esteem
self-image

The Big Picture
You are unique and unlike any other person on the planet. Your experiences in life and the successes you have depend on how accurately and well you know yourself and how you feel about who you are. Developing self-awareness and self-esteem will help you be the best version of yourself that you can be.

Learning Targets
- Compare and contrast self-image and self-esteem.
- Explain how self-esteem can influence health.
- Demonstrate how self-esteem can influence decision making.

Write About It
What makes you unique and different from other people?

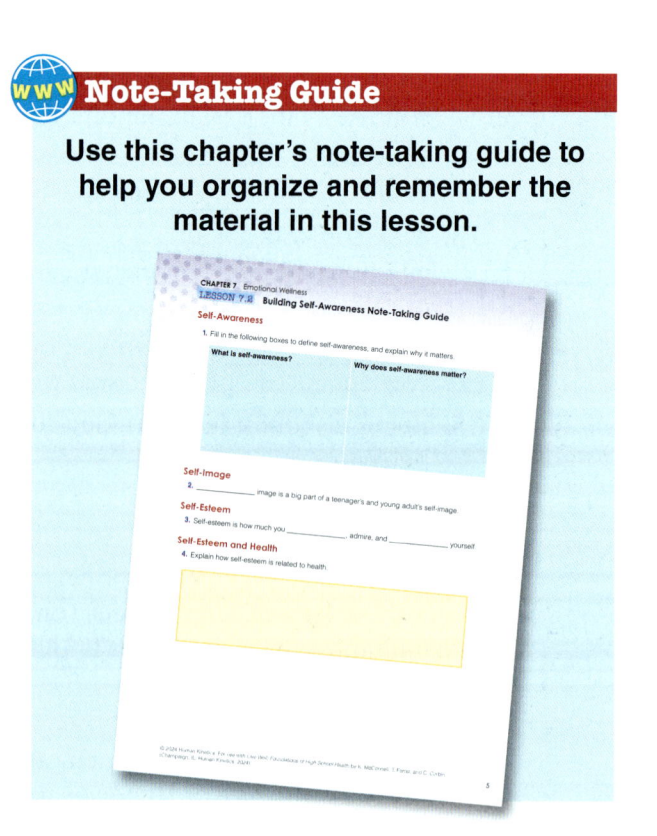

Note-Taking Guide
Use this chapter's note-taking guide to help you organize and remember the material in this lesson.

LESSON 7.2 Building Self-Awareness

Marianna didn't feel like she was good at much, especially math and science. Every time she had a math assignment or had to do a science lab, she didn't do very well. Marianna started to think about what she was good at—softball and running. She also knew she was comfortable being in front of a group. As Marianna focused on her strengths, she began thinking of herself as an athlete and leader. Knowing who she was and what she was good at boosted her confidence. She stopped worrying about the fact that she wasn't good at some subjects in school. What makes Marianna a good role model for others?

Self-Awareness

Do you know what makes you special and different from other people? Can you identify your strengths and weaknesses? Do you know what things make you uncomfortable? What things motivate and inspire you? All of these questions relate to your **self-awareness**—having a clear sense of your personality, including your strengths, weaknesses, thoughts, beliefs, motivations, and emotions. Having self-awareness allows you to understand how other people see you, and that understanding enables you to respond to others effectively and appropriately.

Who Am I?

- What are my strengths?
- What are my weaknesses?
- What gives me energy?
- What causes me to feel stressed? Angry? Happy? Anxious?
- What motivates me to do better?
- What do I love doing with my free time?
- What kind of friend am I?
- How do I respond to feedback or criticism?
- What do I do when I fail at or fall short of something?
- When do I feel disappointed in myself?
- When do I feel proud of myself?

Self-Image

In modern society, we use a lot of different words that start with *self* to describe how people think or feel about who they are and contribute to self-awareness (see figure 7.6). **Self-image** is what you think about yourself and is influenced by what you think others think of you. You may think you are smart, or nerdy, or funny, in part because you think others think these things.

Body image is a big part of a teenager's and young adult's self-image. Your body image comes from the thoughts, feelings, and behaviors you have about your body weight, shape, size, and appearance. Unfortunately, it is common for people of all ages and appearances to struggle with their own body image. American society places high value on appearance, and we often compare ourselves to unrealistic images in the media. The teenage years are particularly challenging to your body image because of how your body is growing and changing and the pressures you feel to fit in.

Self-esteem
How much you like, admire, and value yourself

Self-image
What you think about yourself

Self-confidence
The trust you have in yourself to manage challenges, opportunities, and difficult situations

Figure 7.6 Words that start with *self* describe how we feel about ourselves.

Building Self-Awareness LESSON 7.2

Self-Esteem

Different from self-image, **self-esteem** is a measure of how much you like, admire, and value yourself without regard of other people's opinions (see figure 7.7). It is possible to value and like yourself even if you think others don't like you, but it is hard. Most people want to be liked and respected by others, and changes to our social standing, relationships, and sense of belonging can result in positively or adversely affecting our self-esteem. Some people try so hard to be liked by others that they actually behave in ways that are inauthentic to who they really are. When this happens, the person could have a strong self-image because they think others like who they are pretending to be. At the same time, however, the person has low self-esteem because they no longer like themselves. This is also why well-liked and popular people can still suffer from low self-esteem.

Figure 7.7 Self-esteem comes from being yourself and believing in yourself.

305

LESSON 7.2   Emotional Wellness

Self-Esteem and Health

Self-esteem and physical health have a strong relationship (see figure 7.8). People with high self-esteem tend to take care of themselves by eating well, exercising, and being good to themselves and others. The bottom line is this: When you think you matter and have value, you are more likely to want to stay healthy. On the other hand, low self-esteem can lead to a variety of negative health outcomes.

High self-esteem
- Maintaining healthy relationships
- Setting and achieving goals
- Positive attitude and resilience
- Healthy eating habits
- Exercise

- High blood pressure
- Sleep problems like insomnia
- Eating disorders
- Self-harm behaviors like cutting
- Depression and suicide risk

Low self-esteem

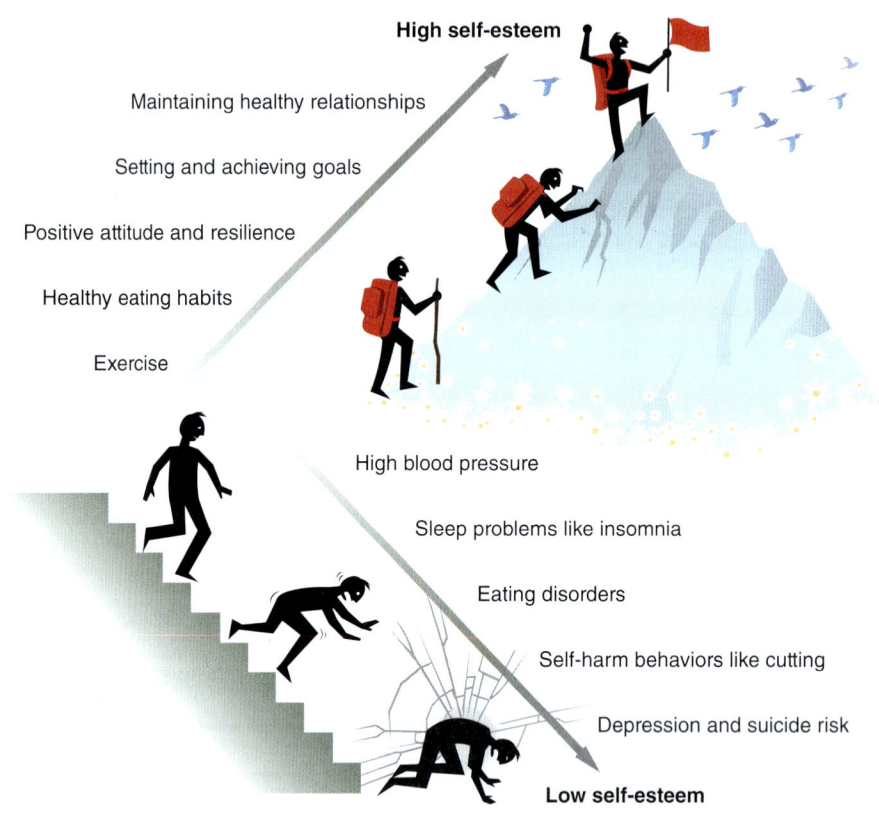

Figure 7.8 High self-esteem is associated with healthy behaviors, and low self-esteem negatively affects health and wellness.

Self-Confidence

Having **self-confidence** does not mean that you think you are better than anyone else. It means that you trust yourself to manage challenges, seize opportunities, and deal with difficult situations. If you successfully complete a project at school, your confidence around academic work will probably go up. If you overcome a fear of talking in front of others when you give a presentation in class, your confidence in public speaking will be boosted. Being successful at tasks helps us improve our confidence. Confidence also helps us tackle more challenging tasks. In this way, we learn to trust our ability to overcome challenges—we become more confident. Confidence is also specific to each task. A person can have a lot of confidence in some area of life, like science class, soccer, and artistic expression, but they also can have low confidence in other areas, like social skills, writing, and swimming.

You can improve both your self-esteem and your self-confidence. Many of the same strategies work for both. Use the following strategies to help boost your self-esteem and self-confidence.

Boosting Your Self-Esteem and Your Self-Confidence

Learn your strengths and weaknesses. Keep a list of the things you do well and the things you struggle with. Ask someone you trust to make a list of your strengths and weaknesses too. Compare the list to see how similar they are. Having accurate self-awareness will help you challenge yourself in meaningful ways that help you grow.

Be kind to yourself. We often treat ourselves much worse than we would ever imagine treating someone else. If you are being critical of yourself, ask yourself how you would talk to a friend in the same situation. Chances are you say more hurtful criticisms to yourself than you do to your friends. Treat yourself like you are your own best friend.

Grow from your mistakes. Mistakes can result from taking risks and challenging ourselves to do something for the first time or to do something better than ever before. You grow from making positive mistakes—they are worth making.

Know when to ask for help. Asking for help is not a sign of weakness; instead, it shows you have self-awareness. When we aren't able to handle something on our own and we don't get help from others, we are more likely to fail or experience a negative outcome. Self-confident people are quick to get help when they need it.

HEALTHY LIVING TIP

The next time you feel like you aren't able to do something, or you failed at something, try adding the word *yet* to your self-talk. For example, say, "I am not a good soccer player *yet*" or "I can't play this song *yet*." Doing this provides a sense of hope and future accomplishment that can boost confidence.

LESSON 7.2 — Emotional Wellness

Skill-Building Challenge

Self-Esteem and Decision Making

Pair up or get into groups according to your teacher's instructions. Read the following story. Ask yourself: How would this story end if Bharat had low self-esteem or high self-esteem? Write two alternate endings, one in which Bharat has low self-esteem and the other high self-esteem. As you write the two endings, consider ways in which self-esteem could influence Bharat's decisions. Use the Decision-Making Skill Cues as a reminder of which decision-making steps should be included in the story.

BHARAT'S DECISION

Bharat was hanging out with friends after school. His friend Rachit told everyone he wanted to skip school the next day to play in an esport competition. Dillan responded that he might be able to sneak some food out of his house after his mom left for work. Then Joseph added that he could probably bring his brother's expensive controllers for the games. Everyone was exuberant about the plan they just hatched except for Bharat, who felt anxious about the whole situation. He had a paper due in history class tomorrow, and he knew his friends sometimes did stupid things.

Healthy Living Skills

This lesson focused on self-esteem and decision making. Here is another way you can develop healthy living skills related to this lesson.

ADVOCATING FOR GOOD HEALTH

Organize a "brag day" for your class. Using posters, classroom whiteboards, a class website, or a word cloud generator, have everyone in class contribute three words that represent three things they do well or are good at. Fill the board or space with the words you collect. Look over the words and reflect on how many different types of strengths your class has. Think about how it feels to focus on individual and collective strengths.

LESSON 7.2 Review: Building Self-Awareness

LESSON SUMMARY

- Self-image is what you think about yourself, and self-esteem is how much you like, value, and appreciate who you are.
- Self-confidence, or the trust you have in yourself to overcome challenges, is important because it allows you to manage challenges, seize opportunities, and deal with difficult situations.
- Learning your own strengths and weaknesses, being kind to yourself and using positive self-talk, accepting and growing from your mistakes, and knowing when to ask for help are all ways to improve your self-esteem.
- People with strong self-esteem are better able to resist pressures from others and can make decisions that are best for them and that align with who they are and what they value.

REVIEWING CONCEPTS AND VOCABULARY

1. Self-_____ is when you know your own personality, including strengths and weaknesses.
2. The way you think of yourself is your _____.
3. _____ is especially challenging during the teen years when our bodies are changing and there is constant societal pressure about appearance.
4. A person with strong _____ values and appreciates who they are.
5. If you trust in yourself and your ability to overcome challenges, you have strong self-_____.

THINKING CRITICALLY

Many positive and negative health behaviors are associated with high and low self-esteem. Choose a health behavior (such as eating healthy, exercising, managing stress, or not vaping or drinking alcohol) and research how self-esteem might influence it. Make a bullet point list of what you learn.

TAKE IT HOME

Write down as many traits and characteristics as you can about what makes you who you are. Once you are done, identify which characteristics you share in common with your immediate family members and ones that are unique to you alone.

LESSON 7.3

Developing Emotional Health and Mental Toughness

Terms to Learn

fixed mindset
grit
growth mindset
mental toughness
optimistic
pessimistic
resilience
self-talk
skill
trait

The Big Picture

Emotional health and mental toughness develop when we take control of our emotional responses and learn skills that help us manage our emotions and our thoughts. People with better emotional health and stronger mental toughness are generally healthier and happier.

Learning Targets

- Explain the concept of mental toughness.
- Compare and contrast resilience and grit.
- Contrast a growth mindset with a fixed mindset.
- Provide three examples of negative self-talk.

Write About It

Describe someone in your life who can keep going even when things aren't going the way they want them to. What do you think gives them this type of strength or ability?

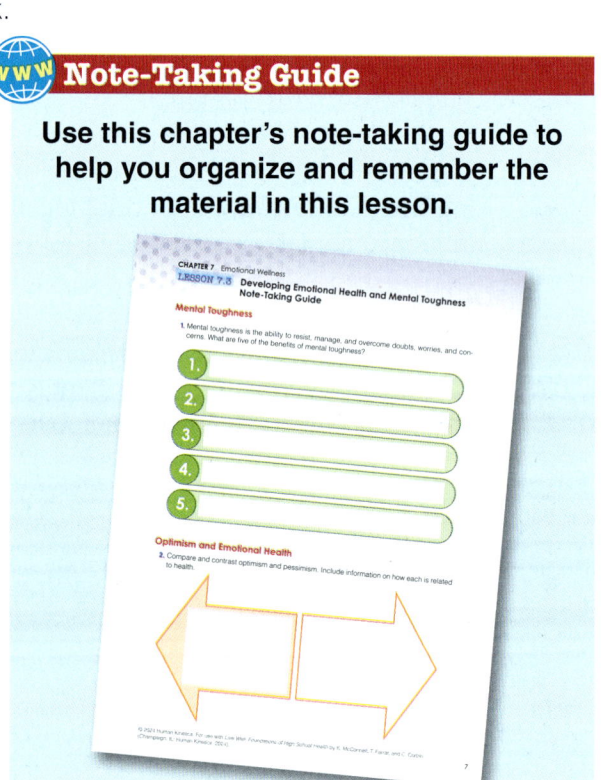

Note-Taking Guide

Use this chapter's note-taking guide to help you organize and remember the material in this lesson.

Addison doesn't have the easiest life, but she is pretty tough and always seems to have a positive attitude. Her mantra is "Never give up on your dreams, or you are giving up on yourself." Last week, her mom lost her job, so they spent the last few days scrambling to pack up because they had to move back in with Addison's grandma. Addison is back to not having a room of her own. Plus her grandma's neighborhood is pretty run down—Addison is certain it has seen better days. Despite her disappointment, she knows she will still do well in school, and besides, her dream of going to college isn't dependent on whose house she is living in.

Between the stress and upheaval from last week, Addison ended up not doing as well on the math test as she usually does. She was upset for a day, and her friend Kayla could tell she was a little down—but typical of Addison, she brushed herself off and just studied harder for this week's test. Kayla respects her friend and admires her mental toughness. Do you know anyone like Addison? What do you think makes that person mentally tough?

Mental Toughness

Mental toughness is the ability to resist, manage, and overcome doubts, worries, concerns, and circumstances that prevent you from succeeding, or excelling. Mental toughness can be developed just like physical toughness can. Research has shown a lot of benefits to being mentally tough.

- Performing at higher levels in school and work
- Experiencing greater well-being and better health
- Being more engaged and having stronger social ties
- Having greater contentment and openness to learning and new ideas
- Managing stress and change more effectively
- Having higher ambitions and life goals

Mental toughness is a concept that originated in sports, about athletes who compete at high levels. However, this concept also applies to non-athletes and to everyday life. People who are mentally tough tend to do the following:

- View challenges as opportunities rather than obstacles
- Believe that they are in control of their life and their destiny
- Have the ability to stick to tasks and see them through to completion
- Possess strong self-belief in their ability to succeed

LESSON 7.3   Emotional Wellness

Optimism and Emotional Health

Developing mental toughness and improving your emotional health requires some degree of optimism. A person who has a generally positive outlook and positive emotions is considered to be **optimistic** (see figure 7.9). The more positively you can approach your emotions, the better off you will be. This does not mean that you must be happy all of the time—it signifies that you look for the positive in situations and work to have a positive response. You can be sad when something bad happens and still believe that things will eventually get better.

Optimistic people tend to have better emotional health. Optimism is also related to lower blood pressure, reduced risk for heart disease, better blood sugar levels, and a longer life. In contrast, being **pessimistic**—tending to see the worst aspect of situations or expecting the worst will happen—can increase your risk for these same health conditions and shorten your lifespan.

Figure 7.9 Optimism versus pessimism.

Growth Mindset

Fostering emotional health and mental toughness requires you to have a **growth mindset**—belief in yourself that you can develop your talents and skills and learn from and grow through any situation. For example, when you don't do well on a math test, do you tell yourself, "I'm not smart enough to figure out math", or do you say, "If I keep studying and learning, I will eventually be better at math"? With a growth mindset, you believe you can become better at math if you study more. Conversely, with a **fixed mindset**, you immediately give up because you assume you are just never going to be smart enough to learn math. Or you may believe some people are inherently good at math while others, including yourself, are inherently bad at it. Fixed mindsets cause people to give up and to lose confidence in situations. We will all experience both growth and fixed mindsets in our lifetime depending on circumstances and situations we encounter. It is important to be persistent in your efforts to develop and maintain a growth mindset as much as possible. Students who have a growth mindset excel in academics and develop more resilience than students with fixed mindsets (see figure 7.10).

Developing Emotional Health and Mental Toughness **LESSON 7.3**

Growth mindset

- Challenges help me to grow
- I am inspired by the success of others
- Failure is an opportunity to grow
- Feedback is constructive
- My effort and attitude determine my abilities
- I like to try new things
- I can learn to do anything I want

Fixed mindset

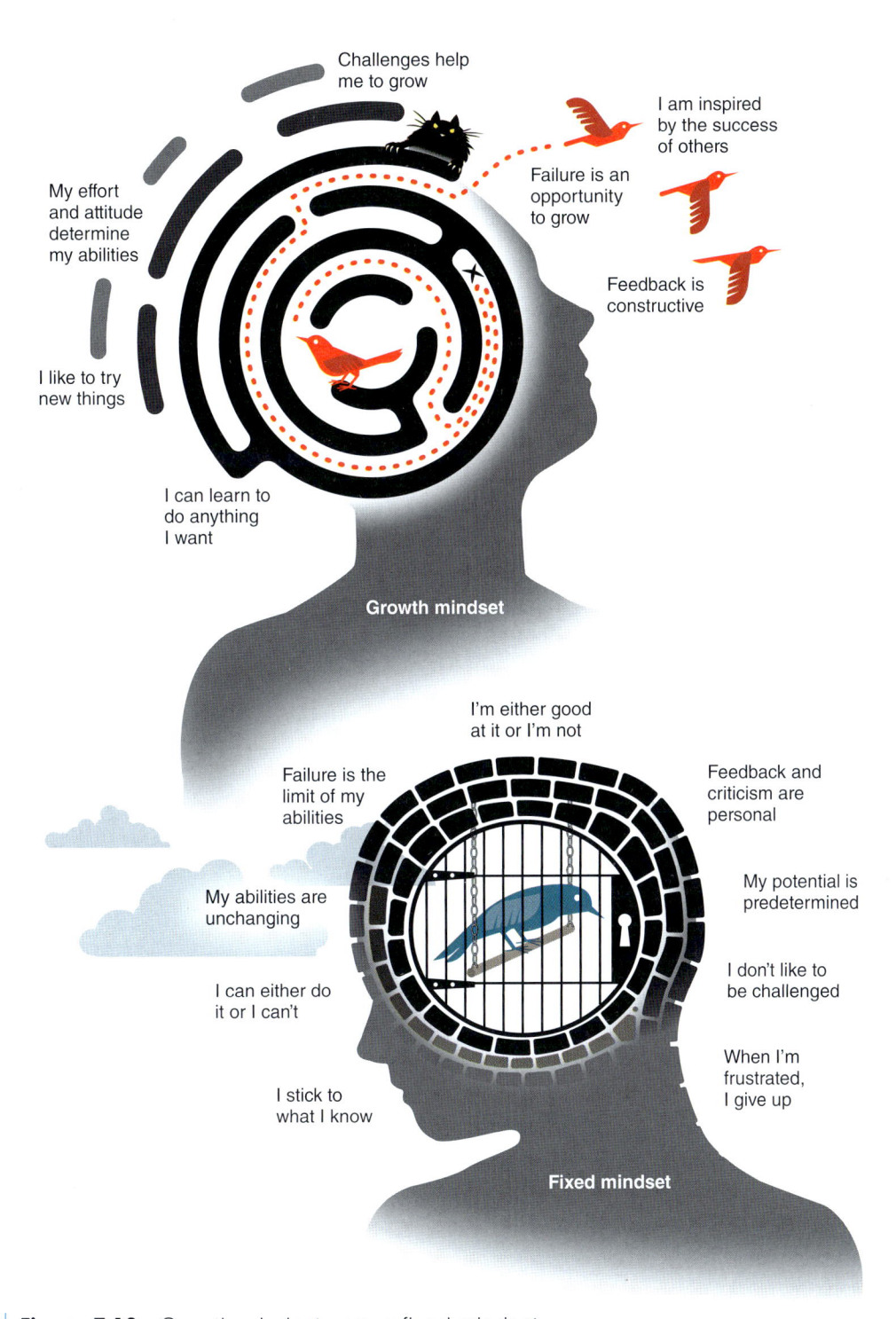

- I'm either good at it or I'm not
- Feedback and criticism are personal
- Failure is the limit of my abilities
- My potential is predetermined
- My abilities are unchanging
- I don't like to be challenged
- I can either do it or I can't
- When I'm frustrated, I give up
- I stick to what I know

Figure 7.10 Growth mindset versus fixed mindset.

Becoming Resilient

Being mentally tough requires **resilience**—the ability to bounce back from a difficult or stressful situation. Resilience is like a bouncing ball: When the ball hits the ground, it comes back up, sometimes higher than before. If you have resilience, you are able to do the same thing. Resilience is not a trait; it is a set of skills. A **trait** is something you are born with, like your hair or eye color. A **skill** is something you

313

LESSON 7.3   Emotional Wellness

can develop and improve with effort. People with resilience have better emotional health and higher satisfaction with their lives. This means that they are happier and are more optimistic about their present and future. To become more resilient, work on each of the following skills:

Develop Your Competence
Competence is your ability of knowing how to handle a situation because you have done it successfully before. Develop competence by making good decisions and learning from your mistakes. Learning from mistakes is a critical part of building your resilience.

Believe in Yourself
Confidence is the belief you have in your own abilities. You develop confidence by knowing your strengths and weaknesses, using positive self-talk, learning from your mistakes, and asking for help when you need it. Having confidence helps you to believe you can get through something challenging. Confidence helps fuel resilience.

Create Connections
Nobody can get through the challenges of life alone. Having friends and others you can trust and reach out to is important. Spend time with the people who provide support and who challenge you to grow and be better. Connections give you the support you need to be brave and take chances in life and to keep pushing forward when things are tough.

Show Your Character
A person with strong character has a clear sense of right and wrong. Character is reflected in how you treat yourself and others. When a situation is tough, your character can act as a lighthouse to guide you forward.

Make a Contribution
Give something back to the world by volunteering to help others. Volunteering strengthens the other resilience skills by connecting you to others and by building your confidence, competence, and character. Making meaningful contributions also helps build self-worth. If you see the ways you can contribute to society, you are also more likely to push yourself forward in tough times.

Learn to Cope
Everyone, regardless of wealth, popularity, beauty, or success, has to learn to cope with stressful circumstances. Part of coping is paying close attention to how you respond to stress and what you do to gain control and to feel better. Managing emotions and actions during stressful times is at the heart of building resilience.

Take Control of Your Actions
Being in control of yourself means that you learn to make your own decisions and take responsibility for your actions. You gain control when you can set and honor boundaries, make smart decisions, and delay gratification. Sometimes things are out of our control. When you have resilience, you can bounce back, partly because you can regain your self-control.

Developing Emotional Health and Mental Toughness   LESSON 7.3

Grit

Another important aspect of mental toughness and good emotional health is **grit**—the dedication and passion to achieve long-term goals. Grit and resilience are related. Like resilience, grit is a skill that can be developed and improved. If you are resilient and can bounce back from difficult situations, you will probably also be able to continue making progress toward a long-term goal. Imagine you are riding your bike in a race over a very long distance. You would need resilience if you hit some loose gravel and fell off your bike. Resilience would help you to get back on the bike and keep pedaling. You need grit when you are exhausted and the road ahead of you is still long. Grit is what keeps you going toward the end even if you feel completely exhausted. To help you develop grit, do the following:

Be Courageous
Stand up for what you believe in, take a chance on something or someone when others won't, show patience when others show panic, or reach out to help someone in need.

Be Conscientious
Do the right thing in the right way. Cutting corners, cheating, or giving up are not conscientious behaviors.

Stick With It
Push forward on the path toward any goal you set, regardless of the challenges you face. Follow through on large and small commitments that you make to yourself and to others.

Seek Mastery
When you pursue excellence, you seek to master what is in front of you. You want to do it to the best of your ability, and you keep working in order to keep making improvements.

Self-Talk for Mental Toughness

Everyone engages in **self-talk**—the messages we send to ourselves. Think of it as an inner conversation with yourself. Self-talk can be negative or positive. The type of self-talk you use will have a significant impact on your emotional wellness and your mental toughness. By learning to recognize negative self-talk—the unhelpful and harsh things we say to ourselves—we can challenge and change these messages and the feelings they create (see table 7.1). Negative self-talk has some well-known patterns that we tend to fall victim to. Can you think of examples of your own negative self-talk?

HEALTHY LIVING TIP

Reward yourself when you have demonstrated resilience or grit in your life. For example, buy yourself something small that you have been wanting, take some time to yourself, or spend some social time with people who make you laugh. It is important to reward ourselves and acknowledge when we have done something hard.

315

LESSON 7.3 Emotional Wellness

TABLE 7.1 Some Ways We Engage in Negative Self-Talk

Pattern	Description	Example
Jumping to conclusions	Failing to think things through and jumping to a quick, negative conclusion	My friend didn't text me, so she must hate me.
Making things your own fault	Making everything about you or your fault (personalizing)	My friend did poorly on his exam because I wasn't able to study with him the night before the test.
Making things worse	Making something far more significant or dramatic than it is (catastrophizing)	I got a B on my quiz. I'm totally going to fail now.
Making things smaller	Making accomplishments smaller than they really are	Even though I got an A on the test, I missed the easiest question. I'm so dumb!
Making things bigger	Applying something specific to a bigger thing	I forgot my permission slip. I can't remember anything.
Giving it a name	Calling yourself names (labeling)	I'm so fat and stupid.

Skill-Building Challenge

Goal-Setting for Mental Toughness

Mental toughness is something that you can develop. Set short- and long-term SMART goals to help you build the skills you need to be mentally tough. Revisit your goals to evaluate your progress and reflect on what helped or hurt you in achieving your goals.

Short-term goal: _____

Short-term goal: _____

Long-term goal: _____

Healthy Living Skills

This lesson focused on goal-setting for mental toughness. Here are some other ways you can develop healthy living skills related to this lesson.

HEALTHY COMMUNICATION

Research a successful athlete or performer in a sport or activity you like. Read about that person's life and try to find out what challenges they had to overcome to be successful. Challenges could be things like moving away from home at a young age, overcoming injuries, or traveling hours every week to practice. Summarize the challenges this person faced and how they overcame them. Focus on their resilience and grit.

ACCESSING INFORMATION

Conduct online research on the concept of *performance psychology*. Focus your research on what it means to be a mental skills coach, or sport psychologist, for an athlete or a team. Visit at least two different websites that you think are reliable and make a list of the types of work mental skills coaches do. Summarize how the work helps to build mental toughness in athletes or other performers.

LESSON 7.3 Review: Developing Emotional Health and Mental Toughness

LESSON SUMMARY

- Mental toughness refers to the idea of being able to push past failures or disappointments and to remain positive, focused, and driven.
- A person who has a generally positive outlook and positive emotions is said to be optimistic.
- If you have a growth mindset, you believe that you can learn and grow all the time. If you have a fixed mindset, you believe that certain things just are the way they are and can't be changed.
- Resilience is your ability to recover quickly from a difficult or stressful situation.
- Grit is the dedication and passion you have to achieve long-term goals.
- To have good emotional health and mental toughness, you must avoid negative self-talk such as calling yourself names (labeling), making things worse than they are (catastrophizing), and making everything your own fault (personalizing).

REVIEWING CONCEPTS AND VOCABULARY

1. If you have a generally positive outlook on life, you are said to be _____.
2. Your ability to bounce back when things are hard is called _____.
3. A(n) _____ is something you are born with, like your hair or eye color.
4. A(n) _____ is something you can learn, like writing or playing an instrument.
5. If you have _____, you are able to continue to move forward even when you face obstacles on your path.
6. If you learn from your mistakes and believe you can get better at something, you have a _____ mindset.
7. The inner conversation you have with yourself is called _____.

THINKING CRITICALLY

Compare and contrast optimism and pessimism and the impact each has on physical, social, and emotional health and well-being. Create a table or other graphic representation that demonstrates your thinking.

TAKE IT HOME

Make yourself an inspiration board at home. It could be a poster, a single sheet of paper, or something you draw on your tablet or phone. Use photos of people who inspire you and identify words and phrases that encourage you. Reflect on your board anytime you need inspiration or motivation.

LESSON 7.4

Recognizing and Managing Stress

Terms to Learn

distress
fight-or-flight response
optimal stress
relaxation technique
stress
stress management technique
stressor

The Big Picture

Stress is a part of life. It can be positive if you can manage it and use it as a motivation to do your best. However, negative stress can lead to poor health. Learning how to use stress management techniques and relaxation techniques can help reduce the unfavorable effects of stress.

Learning Targets

- Explain what stress is.
- Identify four examples of common stressors.
- Describe how negative stress can affect you.
- Identify three ways to manage stress.

Write About It

When was the last time you felt stressed? What caused you to feel that way? How did you handle the situation?

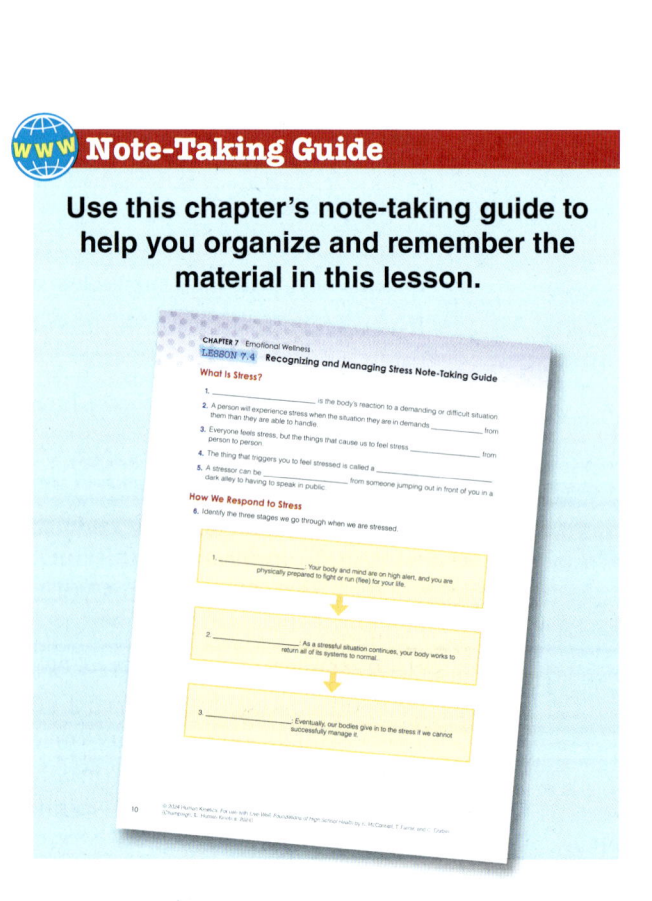

Note-Taking Guide

Use this chapter's note-taking guide to help you organize and remember the material in this lesson.

Recognizing and Managing Stress   **LESSON 7.4**

Luna is feeling stressed. She has a paper to finish, which is due tomorrow, but she has to work after school until 9:00 p.m. Even when things are slow, her boss won't allow her to do school work during her shift. Luna loves her job, but she knows that it is having an effect on her school work. She's been under a lot of pressure to do well on her other papers and projects so that she can keep her grade-point average high. Whenever she gets anything lower than an A, she feels disappointed in herself. She constantly worries that without a 4.0 GPA, she won't have the opportunity to attend college on a badly needed scholarship. Of all nights, her shift at work tonight was unexpectedly busy, adding to Luna's anxiousness and irritability. By the time she got home, she was exhausted and didn't want to work on the paper. Even if she tried, she knew she didn't have the mental capacity to do well on it. What signs of stress is Luna having?

What Is Stress?

Stress is the body's reaction to demanding or difficult situations. When a situation demands more from you than you are able to handle, you experience stress. Sometimes the stress we feel is positive because it motivates us to work harder or be at our best, like when we are competing in a sport or music competition. We all feel stress, but the things that cause us to feel stress differ from person to person. A **stressor** is what triggers you to feel stressed; it can be anything from someone jumping out in front of you in a dark alley to meeting your teacher for the first time.

The famous researcher Hans Selye helped us understand how the body responds to stress. In his work, he identified three stages that we go through when we become stressed (see figure 7.11). First, we react to the stressor. This is called the alarm stage, or the **fight-or-flight response** (see figure 7.12). Our muscles tense up, our pupils dilate, and our hearts seem to skip a beat. When you are in the fight-or-flight response, your body and mind are on high alert, and you are physically prepared either to fight or to flee for your life. As the stressful situation continues, your body works to return all of its systems to normal. This is called the resistance stage. If we cannot successfully manage it, our bodies eventually give in to the stress. This is called exhaustion; it's what happens when we become ill or diseased because of chronic exposure to stress.

Stage 1:
The alarm reaction

The body reacts to the stressor

Stage 2:
Resistance

The body resists the stressor

Stage 3:
Exhaustion

The body succumbs to the stressor

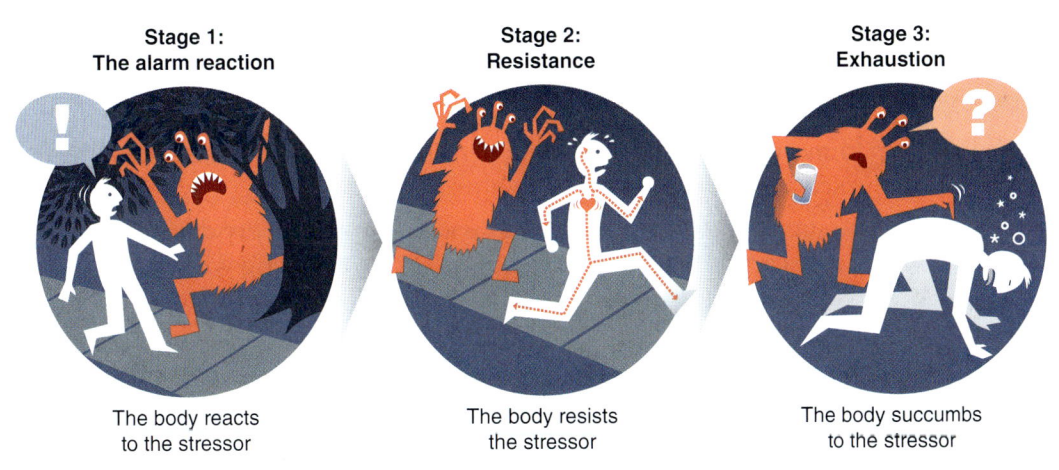

Figure 7.11 The three stages we go through when we become stressed.

LESSON 7.4 Emotional Wellness

Fight or Flight Response

Eyes
Pupils dilate allowing more light in to enhance vision

Heart
Heart rate increases and the strength of the contraction gets stronger to deliver more blood per beat and per minute; coronary arteries dilate to increase blood supply to the heart muscle

Stomach
In a major emergency, digestion is nearly completely halted

Liver
Glucose is released to be delivered to the muscles

Intestines
Contractions in the intestines are reduced greatly because digestion has been reduced

Buttock or abdomen
Fat, triglycerides are broke down and released from storage into the blood stream to supply energy

Blood vessels
Blood redistribution occurs so more blood is directed to the working muscles and less to the gut and skin; blood pressure increases

Ears
Hearing becomes more acute and able to detect a greater range of sounds

Mouth
Saliva and mucus decreases because digestion has halted

Lungs
Bronchi within the lungs dilate to allow more air flow into and out of the lungs

Adrenal glands
Release epinephrine and cortisol which further stimulate heart rate and contraction strength and increase energy release into the blood stream (glucose and fatty acids)

Pancreas
Decreases insulin secretion which reduces energy storage

Kidneys and bladder
Kidneys reduce output (urine production slows down); bladder relaxes and the urge to urinate often occurs (emptying bladder decreases body weight making it easier to move)

Muscles
Vessels dilate in the working muscle groups to deliver more blood and oxygen

Armpit and feet
Perspiration increases especially in the armpits, groin, hands, and feet before sweating for thermoregulation purposes begins

Figure 7.12 The fight-or-flight response.

Types of Stressors

HEALTHY LIVING TIP
Keep a notebook in your room and write down all the sources of your stress each day when you come home from school. Then use drawings, poems, song lyrics, or any other form of expression that helps you recognize and release your stress. Reflect on which practice helped you release the most stress.

Lots of different things can cause you to experience stress. Your ability to cope with the stress and manage it effectively may depend on what type of stressor you experience.

- Acute, or short-term, stressors last from minutes to a couple of hours. Examples include taking a test, giving a presentation in class, and trying out for a sport team.
- Chronic, or long-term, stressors keep recurring or happen over a period of days to months or longer. Examples include feeling nervous and scared in a new school and worrying about a relative who is sick.
- Routine stressors are the small things you experience every day that you find annoying, scary, or frustrating. Examples include dealing with a demanding boss, getting homework done, and deciding what to wear each day.
- Major life events can trigger stress. Examples include having to move to another neighborhood or state, losing a loved one, and dealing with the divorce of parents. Some major life stressors are positive experiences that still cause large amounts of stress because they often come with a lot of unknowns. Getting married, graduating from high school, and getting your first job are examples of these types of stressors.

- Trauma causes enormous stress. Terrorist attacks, major accidents, and assault are examples of traumas that can result in high levels of stress.

Stress and the Body

The human body is built to deal with physical stressors like a bear on your path or someone chasing you. Our bodies respond in a way that prepares us to react physically by running or fighting. In modern society, most of the stressors we encounter are psychological or emotional stressors and not direct physical threats.

Imagine sitting at a desk working on your computer. You suddenly realize that you have a big project due the next day that you haven't started. This will probably cause you stress. Your body will go into the fight-or-flight response even though your computer is not actually attacking you. You don't need to physically fight with your computer, and it won't do you much good to get up and sprint away. This mismatch between the type of stressors we tend to experience and how our body responds is why stress can be so dangerous to health. If you did run away from your computer, your body would use the physiological changes it is going through to help you. But when you have to sit there and solve the problem by working harder, all of the physiological changes you are experiencing have nowhere to go and nothing productive to do. We call this negative form of stress **distress**. Figure 7.13 shows some of the common signs of distress.

HEALTHY LIVING TIP

If you are experiencing stress or know that a situation you are facing will cause stress, avoid drinking caffeine for several hours. Energy drinks, sodas, and coffee drinks can make your stress response worse.

Common Stressors Teens Experience

- Taking tests and doing homework
- Interacting with friends
- Maintaining positive relationships with siblings
- Having a significant other
- Moving to a new home and school
- Starting college
- Dating
- Having expectations that are too high
- Engaging in sports and other extracurricular activities
- Getting or losing a job
- Feeling socially excluded
- Having too much to do
- Developing (physically) either too quickly or too slowly
- Having family crises including alcohol and substance abuse
- Failing to achieve something that you really wanted
- Being concerned about finances
- Experiencing or witnessing violence at school or in the neighborhood

LESSON 7.4　Emotional Wellness

Figure 7.13 Common signs of distress.

Stress and Performance

The good news is, because your body is physiologically alert during stress, the right amount of stress can help you perform at your best. When your stress levels are neither too high nor too low, your performance in athletics, acting, school, and music will benefit. This happens because you hit an ideal level of alertness, and your senses, like hearing and vision, are at their best. Feeling a few butterflies before practice or a performance is a good thing as long as the butterflies don't turn into dragons. This level of stress is called **optimal stress** (see figure 7.14). Having optimal levels of stress means you are invested in what you are doing. If you are invested in something, it means that you care and are devoted to doing well.

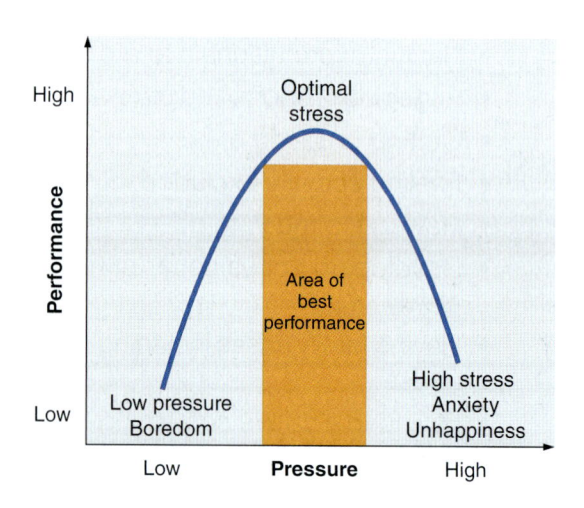

Figure 7.14 Optimal stress is stress that allows you to perform your best.

Recognizing and Managing Stress **LESSON 7.4**

Stress and Health

Chronic stress can also contribute to a wide range of health problems, including

- type 2 diabetes,
- high blood pressure,
- heart disease,
- obesity,
- ulcers,
- irritable bowel syndrome,
- insomnia,
- skin conditions, and
- infections.

Managing Stress

Managing your stress is similar to managing your emotions. People who are good at managing their stress are able to cope with stressful situations quickly and return to normal functioning without too much disruption to their daily lives. People who can't manage stress well are often emotional, volatile, and aggressive because they are overwhelmed.

Stress management technique refers to the use of any strategy to control how much stress affects you (see figure 7.15). Stress management can include things

Breathe deeply
Take slow, deep breaths. Deep breathing signals your brain to relax.

Use positive self-talk
Say: I CAN
I WILL
I AM
Try not to criticize yourself.

Reframe the situation
Look for a positive reason that a stressful event is happening.
Focus on a positive outcome.

Remove yourself
If you can, leave the stressful situation.

Tend to yourself
Get plenty of sleep and eat well. You will be able to manage stress better if your body is healthy.

Be mindful
Don't worry about what has already happened in the past.

Figure 7.15 Approaches to stress management.

323

like time management and positive self-talk. Stress management can also include **relaxation techniques**, or specific stress management strategies that reduce the intensity of the fight-or-flight response. People who are good at relaxation techniques are generally more able to keep themselves from overreacting to stressors. Many relaxation techniques are focused on reducing muscle tension in the body. It is important to remember that approaches to stress management and relaxation work differently for different people, and many take time to master.

Skill-Building Challenge

Goal-Setting for Stress Management

You can't learn to manage your stress if you are always waiting for stress to happen. To effectively manage stress, you need to learn and practice stress management techniques before you need them. Use your Goal-Setting Skill Cues and your SMART goal skill steps to help you write one short-term and one long-term goal and set action steps that will help you manage your stress. Consider the techniques provided in this lesson as well as other strategies you may know.

My short-term SMART goal for stress management is:

_____

_____

My long-term SMART goal for stress management is:

_____

_____

List three to five action steps you can take to help you reach your goals:

_____

_____

Healthy Living Skills

This lesson focused on goal-setting. Here are some more ways you can develop healthy living skills related to this lesson.

ANALYZING INFLUENCES

How much do social issues influence your stress levels? Do you spend a lot of time or energy worrying about what is happening in society? Make a list of the ways social issues influence you and put a plus sign (+) next to the positive influences and a minus sign (-) next to the negative influences.

ACCESSING INFORMATION

Conduct online research on diseases related to stress that might affect a person's long-term health. Collect your information from at least three websites and remember to focus on finding valid and reliable information. Consider the information you found and use it to develop a Health Risks of Stress flyer.

LESSON 7.4 Review: Recognizing and Managing Stress

LESSON SUMMARY

- Stress is the body's reaction to a demanding or difficult situation.
- Common stressors among teens include taking tests and doing homework, dating, moving to a new school or home, and having expectations that are too high for yourself.
- Negative stress is called distress. It can affect your body, mood, behavior, and long-term health.
- Using techniques such as deep breathing, time management, and positive self-talk are ways to manage stress.

REVIEWING CONCEPTS AND VOCABULARY

1. _____ is the body's reaction to a demanding or difficult situation.
2. Something that causes you to feel stress is called a(n) _____.
3. When you experience stress, your heart and breathing rates increase as part of the _____ response.
4. _____ is negative stress that can cause health problems.
5. Athletes and other performers can benefit from a(n) _____ level of stress because it helps them be alert and in tune with their surroundings.
6. Time management and exercise are examples of stress _____ techniques.
7. Meditation and yoga are examples of _____ techniques.

THINKING CRITICALLY

Research how technology might be linked to higher rates of stress in people. Use your findings to write a short public service announcement that helps warn people of the dangers of technology when it comes to their stress and health.

TAKE IT HOME

Search for free apps that claim to help reduce stress or provide stress management. Make a list of five different apps, describe what each app does, and then try at least one out. Show the list to other members of your family and also have them try one. Identify the strengths and weaknesses of each app and then share your recommendations with others.

LESSON 7.5

Understanding Grief and Loss

Terms to Learn

bereavement
customs
grief
mourning
rituals

The Big Picture

Death and dying are normal parts of the human experience. How different people experience and deal with death can differ based on things like their age, religious beliefs, and culture. Understanding how people experience grief and mourn losses can help you better cope with death and dying in your life.

Learning Targets

- Describe how children understand the concept of death.
- Explain how and why people might experience grief differently.
- Compare and contrast grief and mourning.
- Describe how cultural influences can affect our understanding or experience of grief and mourning.
- Describe ways that customs and rituals may be part of the mourning.

Write About It

What experiences do you have with losing someone or something you loved and cared about? Reflect on your experience and the different emotions you felt during that time.

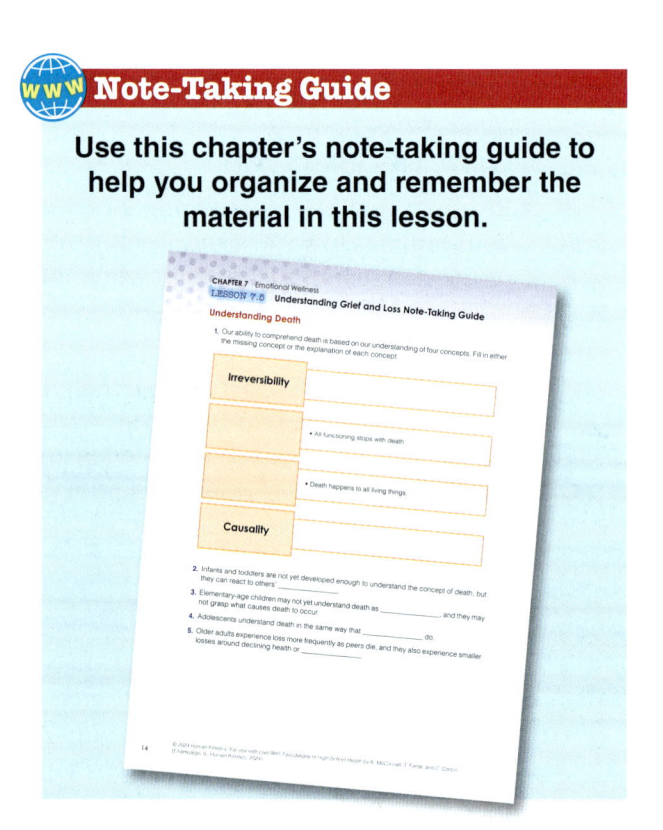

Note-Taking Guide

Use this chapter's note-taking guide to help you organize and remember the material in this lesson.

Sloane was doing well in school and enjoying her social life when her mom was killed in a car accident. Her mom's death was sudden and shocking, and Sloane didn't know what to do or how to cope. Sloane's younger sister, Amber, had a hard time understanding that her mom wasn't coming home. Amber kept asking, "When will mommy get home?" Sloane never knew what to say and she would just start crying. She took some time off of school and she and Amber went to their church to talk to the pastor a few times. She appreciated the comfort he provided and she liked thinking about her mom being in a better place. Their dad also had a friend come over who lost a parent when he was young. Listening to his story, Sloane realized that she was coping with the loss of her mom in pretty healthy ways. She started to understand that grieving was going to take a long time and that she and Amber needed to accept the different emotions they experienced as normal and as part of the healing process. Have you ever thought about grief as something people might experience in really different ways?

Understanding Death

Death is a natural and an unavoidable part of life. We will all experience the death of loved ones, and, eventually, we ourselves will die. Our understanding of death develops as we grow and age, and we process and react to death differently across the lifespan. How we understand death depends on our ability to comprehend four concepts:

1. Irreversibility (death as permanent)
2. Finality (all functioning ceases)
3. Inevitability (certainty that all living things die)
4. Causality (the general causes of death)

Young Children and Death

Infants and toddlers are not yet developed enough to understand the concept of *death*, but they can react to others' emotions. By the time a child reaches preschool, they view death as temporary. Children at this age only understand concrete and clear concepts, so when talking with a young child about death, be direct and avoid saying "They have gone to sleep". A child understands this to mean the person has gone to bed and will be getting up again. Young children will often ask when the person is coming back again. Therefore, communication about the death may need to be repeated over a period of time.

LESSON 7.5   Emotional Wellness

School-Age Children and Death

Elementary-age children may not yet understand death as irreversible, and they may not grasp what causes death to occur. Children of this age will often think they did something to make the deceased person go away and may need to be comforted and reassured. Children will also take cues from adults—if they see adults coping with the loss in productive ways, they will process their grief better as well.

Teens and Death

Adolescents understand death just as adults do. Many adolescents have not experienced a significant loss, however, and may not feel comfortable talking about death or sharing how they are feeling when someone dies. Experiencing a loss during these years can also trigger questions about the meaning of life. Patience and opportunities to talk openly and in safe spaces are important for processing grief at this age.

Older Adults and Death

Older adults experience loss more frequently as peers die, and they also experience smaller losses around declining health or independence. It is important for older adults to have social support and connections so that they can process losses while also engaging fully in life.

Experiencing Grief

Everyone eventually experiences losses in their lives. **Grief** refers to the internal emotions a person experiences when coping with loss. You can experience grief for anything that you have an emotional connection to—loss of a loved one, loss of a family pet, loss of a job, loss of independence—to name a few. When the loss is significant, like the death of a loved one, grief can be experienced for a long time. It is common to experience grief related to a death for several years around holidays, birthdays, and special events when reminders and memories of the loved one are elevated. It is important to experience grief and to talk about feelings of loss. People generally experience a range of emotions with grief, and everyone experiences grief differently (see table 7.2). There is no single way to grieve a loss. Most people experience several stages of emotions as they move through the grieving process (see figure 7.16). People may experience these emotions in different ways and in different orders. It is important to allow the feelings to happen and to understand that they are a normal part of managing the emotional pain of losing someone or something you care about. The process of grieving is natural, and it is not the same thing as depression or mental illness.

Understanding Grief and Loss **LESSON 7.5**

TABLE 7.2 **Types of Grief**

Anticipatory	This type of grief can happen before the loss occurs. For example, you can feel grief if someone is terminally ill before the death happens.
Normal or common	Some people are able to continue on with their normal routine or activities despite their feelings of grief. To others, they may not appear to be grieving.
Delayed	Grief does not hit everyone on the same time frame. For some, grief intensifies months after the loss when the initial aftermath has passed.
Inhibited	This type of grief involves staying busy and trying to avoid feeling the emotions of grief. Oftentimes it can lead to physical symptoms like migraines and digestive issues. It can also evolve into complicated grief.
Complicated	This type of grief is less common, but it can lead to self-harm or mental illness. It involves irrational thoughts and behaviors that keep the person from acknowledging the loss.
Disenfranchised	This type of grief happens when the person experiencing the loss does not get support or acceptance for their grief. This can happen with the loss of a pet, a non-family member, or with our own loss of a limb, hearing, vision, etc.
Absent	Absent grief happens if a person refuses to believe that the person has died or the loss has occurred. This type of grief is rare and may accompany unsolved crimes, disappearances, and other complicating factors.
Exaggerated	Exaggerated grief extends over a long period of time, and a person's ability to function does not improve. Exaggerated grief can happen when multiple losses occur close together and lead to depression.

Denial
This isn't happening to me!

Anger
Why is this happening to me?

Bargaining
I promise I'll be a better person if...

Depression
I don't care anymore.

Acceptance
I'm ready for whatever comes.

Figure 7.16 Stages of grief and loss.

Mourning and Bereavement

In comparison to grief, **mourning** refers to the external process and behaviors associated with grieving the loss of a loved one. Mourning is what others see when we experience grief. There are many ways to mourn a loss, and mourning can be influenced by family, religious, cultural, spiritual, and community-based traditions. Some examples of how we mourn include:

- Crying or wailing
- Wearing a certain color or type of clothing
- Attending a funeral even if you yourself are not experiencing grief

LESSON 7.5 Emotional Wellness

- Visiting a gravesite on a loved one's birthday or holiday
- Celebrating their life each year to remember someone important to you
- Lighting a candle on the anniversary of a loved one's loss

Our cultural and religious traditions can also influence our **bereavement**, which refers to the amount of time you experience grief and express mourning.

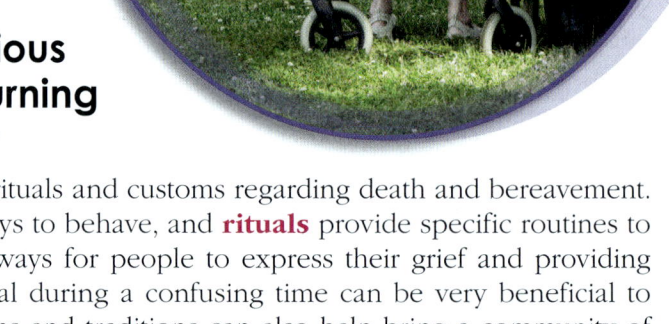

Cultural and Religious Influences on Mourning and Bereavement

Every culture on earth has rituals and customs regarding death and bereavement. **Customs** are traditional ways to behave, and **rituals** provide specific routines to follow. Having acceptable ways for people to express their grief and providing a sense of routine and ritual during a confusing time can be very beneficial to the healing process. Customs and traditions can also help bring a community of bereaved people together and provide opportunities for social support.

These same customs and rituals can also feel burdensome if they do not match the experience of grief a person is feeling. It is important to recognize personal differences in how we feel and what makes us comfortable and uncomfortable. Allowing people to grieve in their own way as much as possible is important as well. The following are examples of different ways customs and rituals may be experienced when dealing with death:

- The way in which a body is handled after death, including who can handle the deceased and whether the body is buried or cremated
- Prayers, sacraments, and ceremonies performed on the deceased after death
- Type of funeral service and the specifics of those services
- Whether or not grief is expressed privately or publicly, including whether or not wailing or crying is appropriate or expected
- The way in which people of different genders and ages are expected to experience loss
- Whether people are expected to grieve alone or in groups
- Expectations about the acceptable length of times loved ones should grieve and when people are allowed to return to activities such as dating, celebrating holidays, or re-marrying
- Roles and responsibilities children and others are expected to take on after a parent or family member dies

HEALTHY LIVING TIP
Spend some time learning about how your own culture and religion respond to death and dying. Reflect on the traditions and rituals that mean the most to you and share your thoughts with someone you trust.

Social Support During Mourning and Bereavement

How we interact with and support others during their grief can affect how they manage their experience and move on with their life. Social support during grief is important and it comes in many forms. Ways to offer support include the following:

- Ensuring the person feels cared for and loved, has worth and value, and feels that they matter to others
- Helping to alleviate the complexities of a death, from assisting with funeral arrangements to helping manage financial and estate matters
- Assisting with connecting the person with community resources like grief support groups
- Encouraging the person to establish or re-establish networks and friendships

Communicating Support for Those in Grief

Communicating in a helpful way is one of the most challenging things to do when supporting others through their grief. While there is no single correct way to support those who are grieving, the following is a list of some general suggestions:

Suggestions for Communicating Support

Express your condolences.
In other words, simply share that you are sorry for their loss.

Do small yet helpful things.
Show support by bringing them a hot meal, washing the dishes, or taking care of a pet.

Be available and present.
Sometimes you don't have to do or say anything. Just be there and let the person know you are available.

Listen and share.
If the person is telling stories about their loved one, listen even if you've heard the story before. Talking about the deceased person is natural and normal and can help the person feel comforted and cope.

Stay connected.
Many people may show up for a funeral or be present for the person initially. Understand that grief can take time and stay with the person even when it seems hard to do. Your effort of support does not need to be a big thing; small things over a period of time can matter more.

LESSON 7.5　Emotional Wellness

Avoid making the following comments:

- "It will all be fine." While this may seem okay, if often makes the person feel like their pain and sorrow are unnecessary.
- "They are in a better place now." While some religious traditions believe this, for many people in mourning, this sentiment neither acknowledges how they are feeling nor helps the person process their sorrow or loss.
- "I know how you feel." Even if you have experienced a similar loss, no one knows exactly how someone else is feeling; a person in grief needs time and space to process their own experience.

Career Connection

MORTICIAN

Morticians, also known as funeral directors, play a vital role in helping grieving families manage the ins and outs of a funeral service. Some of the responsibilities of the job include scheduling the burial, coordinating funeral arrangements, preparing the body for the service, submitting paperwork to certify the death, and providing emotional support for family members and loved ones. Being a mortician requires at minimum a two-year associates degree from an approved program, and a bachelor's degree is often preferred. An apprenticeship and licensing exam are also required.

Skill-Building Challenge

Healthy Communication

Talking to people who are grieving a loss can be uncomfortable and challenging. Write out an example of something you could say in each of the following scenarios. When you are done, compare your responses with another person or group. Collectively, identify what you think are the two best examples you came up with and role-play those scenarios.

SCENARIO 1: KRYSIA

Krysia's 15-year-old cat Max died recently. Her family adopted him when she was just a toddler, and Max was a constant presence throughout her life. To Krysia and her family, Max was considered more than a pet—he was family.
- What could you say to Krysia to show support?
- What challenge might Krysia be facing as she grieves this loss?

SCENARIO 2: MIKAILA

Mikaila's mom passed away after a three-year battle against cancer. Mikaila is a first-year high school student. Her parents got a divorce when she was 11 years old, and she spent most of the time with her mom.
- What could you say to Mikaila to show support?
- What could you do to help Mikaila?

SCENARIO 3: JOHN

John's wife Colleen passed away suddenly after 45 years of marriage. John and Colleen were inseparable and did everything together. John feels lost and alone.
- What could you say to John?
- What are some ways you could show support for John?

Healthy Living Skills

This lesson focused on healthy communication. Here is one more way you can develop healthy living skills related to this lesson.

ACCESSING INFORMATION
Research the resources in your community that deal with death, dying, and grief support. Create a list of morticians, funeral homes and graveyards, grief counselors, and other services that help people cope with and manage the loss of a loved one.

LESSON 7.5 Review: Understanding Grief and Loss

LESSON SUMMARY

- Understanding death requires a person to be able to understand the concepts of irreversibility, finality, inevitability, and causality.
- Young children cannot fully understand death and may continue to ask about when the person is returning.
- Grief is a normal emotion that occurs when someone experiences a loss. Types of grief include anticipatory, normal, delayed, inhibited, complicated, disenfranchised, absent, and exaggerated.
- Common stages people experience during grief include denial, anger, bargaining, depression, and acceptance.
- Mourning refers to the external process and behaviors associated with grieving the loss of a loved one; bereavement refers to the amount of time a person experiences grief or expresses mourning.
- Cultural and religious traditions can have significant impacts on mourning and bereavement, including expectations around customs and rituals.

REVIEWING CONCEPTS AND VOCABULARY

1. To understand death, children must comprehend irreversibility, _____, inevitability, and causality.
2. _____ is a normal emotion that is caused by the loss of a loved one or a pet.
3. If someone doesn't experience grief until months after a death, they have _____ grief.
4. The stages of grief include denial, _____, bargaining, depression, and acceptance.
5. _____ refers to how a person expresses their grief.
6. The period of time that a person expresses grief is known as _____.

THINKING CRITICALLY

Identify two religious traditions and research their customs and rituals surrounding death and dying. Identify what the two customs have in common and what makes each unique.

TAKE IT HOME

Ask your parent or guardian if they have any special wishes for when they die. Find out what cultural or religious traditions they hope others will honor.

Chapter Review

ACTION PLAN: Emotional Wellness

Use the My Action Plan worksheet to set goals for your emotional health. Here is an example.

My Action Plan: Improving My Emotional Health

STEP 1: Identify the health behavior you are going to work on.

I am going to work on daily stress management.

STEP 2: Write SMART goal(s).
Write one or two short-term goals (one day to one month).

I will use positive self-talk at least 50 percent of the time.

I will practice using deep breathing every time I begin to feel stress.

Write a long-term goal (one to six months or more).

By feeling less stress in my daily life, I will sleep better and have more energy.

STEP 3: Make a plan.
Identify two to five action steps (strategies) you could do to meet your goal.

I will keep a stress management journal to track my self-talk and identify my negative self-talk.

I will pay attention to how I am feeling and will take long, deep breaths when I feel anxious or stressed. When something challenging happens or I don't do well at something, I will reframe how I think and look for something positive.

STEP 4: Do your plan and track your progress.

Short-term goal 1

☒ Met ☐ Not met Date: *October 4*

Short-term goal 2

☒ Met ☐ Not met Date: *October 6*

Long-term goal

☒ Met ☐ Not met Date: *November 10*

If you met your goal, what helped you to be successful?

Keeping my journal helped me the most. I was able to see how I used self-talk, how I felt each day and how often I was doubting myself.

If you did not meet your goal, what obstacles made it harder for you to be successful?

I met my goals.

Test Your Knowledge

Select the best answer for each question.

1. Your emotional health includes
    a. your focus
    b. your self-image
    c. your ability to process information
    d. your ability to remember information

2. Emotional intelligence refers to your ability to perceive, manage, and _____ your emotions.
    a. talk about
    b. ignore
    c. regulate
    d. understand

3. Low self-esteem tends to lead to all the following *except*
    a. eating disorders
    b. sleep problems
    c. setting ambitious goals
    d. depression

4. Your awareness of the feelings and emotions of others is called
    a. self-esteem
    b. self-confidence
    c. empathy
    d. optimism

5. When we experience stress, our body physically responds by
    a. increasing heart rate
    b. carrying more blood to the organs
    c. reducing sweating
    d. relaxing muscles

6. When a person can bounce back after a difficult situation, they are showing
    a. a trait
    b. their resilience
    c. their grit
    d. a fixed mindset

7. When you make something much worse than it actually is, you are using which type of negative self-talk?
    a. personalization
    b. labeling
    c. assumption
    d. catastrophizing

8. When you act suddenly while ignoring the consequences of your decision or action, you are being
    a. resilient
    b. gritty
    c. impulsive
    d. none of the above

9. Healthy ways to manage your stress include
    a. engaging in positive self-talk
    b. using deep breathing
    c. being mindful
    d. all of the above

10. Impulsive behaviors include
    a. breaking the rules
    b. destroying property
    c. running away
    d. all of the above

PROJECT-BASED LEARNING: Stress Management Tool Kit

What to Remember

High school is a challenging time for a lot of students, especially when it comes to managing the stresses of moving into adult life. Learning strategies for how to manage stress is an important part of developing good emotional health.

Who It Is For

Your tool kit is for you and your classmates to use whenever you need to be reminded of how to manage feelings about daily stressors.

Why It Is Important

It is important to learn how to gather resources and make them accessible so that they can be easily used. It is also important for you and your classmates to have tools available that can help promote good emotional health.

What to Do

Work together as a class to develop a stress management tool kit that students can use to help improve their emotional health and well-being.

Using the information from this chapter, create as many simple tools as possible that someone could use to understand and manage stress. Then do additional research on stress management and coping strategies. Add at least three more strategies to your toolbox. Make sure your tools cover all the following categories:

- Deep breathing
- Positive self-talk
- Reframing
- Removing yourself from situations
- Tending to yourself
- Mindfulness

How to Do It

Work in a small group or team. Think about different strategies or approaches you can use to help manage stress. The different strategies and approaches you develop are the tools that will go in your tool kit. Make at least one tool for each category listed in the What to Do section plus at least three others in areas of your own research. Your tools should provide descriptions about what something is and why it is important to work on improving the skill or strategy. They should also be specific, accurate, and useful. Consider color-coding note cards so that everything related to mindfulness (for example) is the same color. Use images and drawings to help make the tips engaging.

See if you can find an old toolbox that you can use to hold your stress management tools. A lunch box, shoebox, or similar item will also work. You will also need a stack of index cards and access to images from magazines, papers, or online (if you can print them).

CROSS-CURRICULAR CONNECTIONS: Language Arts

Write the story of your life (your biography). Write in the first person and explain how you have experienced your life so far. Include detailed descriptions of places, people, or experiences that help the reader understand and be interested in what you are writing. Focus on the organization of your story and use sensory language to convey a vivid picture of the experiences, events, and settings you share.

8

Mental Health

LESSON 8.1 Understanding and Treating Mental Disorders
LESSON 8.2 Anxiety and Anxiety Disorders
LESSON 8.3 Depression and Mood Disorders
LESSON 8.4 Self-Harm and Suicide

Understanding My Health

My Anxiety and Emotions

This self-assessment will help you understand how you experience anxiety and sadness. The following statements reflect different ways these emotions can be experienced. Select the answer that is most accurate for you. Be honest in your responses so that you can have a full understanding of how you experience these emotions. When you are done, add up your points. The closer you are to 27 points, the better able you are to recognize and manage your emotions.

	Always	Sometimes	Never
I recognize when I am feeling anxious.	3	2	1
I know what things normally cause me to feel anxious.	3	2	1
I know what to do if I start to feel anxious.	3	2	1
I practice relaxing when I am anxious.	3	2	1
I feel in control of my fears and anxieties.	3	2	1
When I feel anxious or fearful, I can still concentrate and stay focused.	3	2	1
I recognize when I am feeling sad.	3	2	1
I can motivate myself to do daily activities even if I am feeling sad or depressed.	3	2	1
I feel hopeful about the future even when I am feeling sad.	3	2	1

My score for My Anxiety and Emotions = _____ (total number of points)

Many factors can challenge our mental health. Anxiety and depression are two of the most common mental disorders we face. Learning how to recognize, manage, and seek help for these conditions is important to maintain your overall health and wellness.

LESSON 8.1
Understanding and Treating Mental Disorders

Terms to Learn
mental disorder

psychotherapy

stigma

The Big Picture
Mental disorders are common and can affect anyone. In fact, it is estimated that 1 in 25 adults in the United States is living with some sort of mental disorder. Fortunately, people can learn to be productive members of society with proper care and treatment. Learning about the signs of common mental disorders is an important first step to recognizing a mental disorder in yourself or others.

Learning Targets
- Explain what a mental disorder is and provide two examples.
- Describe what a stigma is and explain how it can affect someone with a mental disorder.
- Explain different ways that mental disorders may be treated.

Write About It
What do you know about mental disorders? What factors do you think influence a person's risk of developing a mental disorder?

Note-Taking Guide
Use this chapter's note-taking guide to help you organize and remember the material in this lesson.

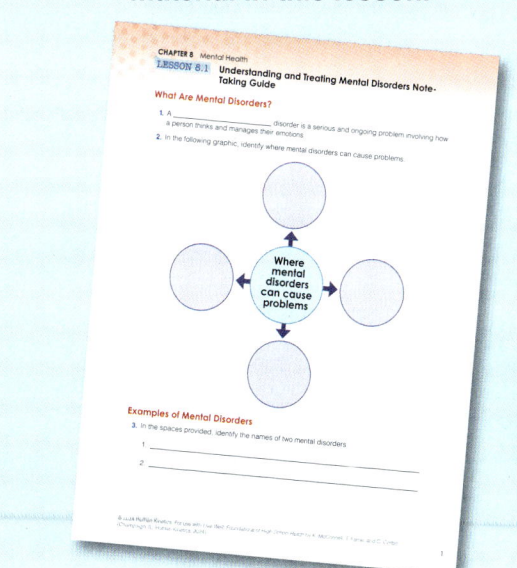

LESSON 8.1 Mental Health

Riley is like a lot of kids she knows. She has a cousin who has post-traumatic stress disorder after being in a bad accident, and her dad struggles with depression. It seems like everyone Riley knows has some sort of mental challenge, but most people don't really talk about it. Lately Riley has noticed that her sister is showing signs of being depressed too, and Riley doesn't really know the right things to say or do to help. It's as if everything she tries makes things worse. What types of challenges do you think Riley faces in her daily life? What could she do to help herself and her family?

What Are Mental Disorders?

A **mental disorder** is a serious and ongoing condition involving how a person thinks and manages their emotions. Mental disorders can also cause issues in relationships, school or work, or other important activities. There is a wide range of mental disorders, and only a mental health professional can diagnose them (see figure 8.1).

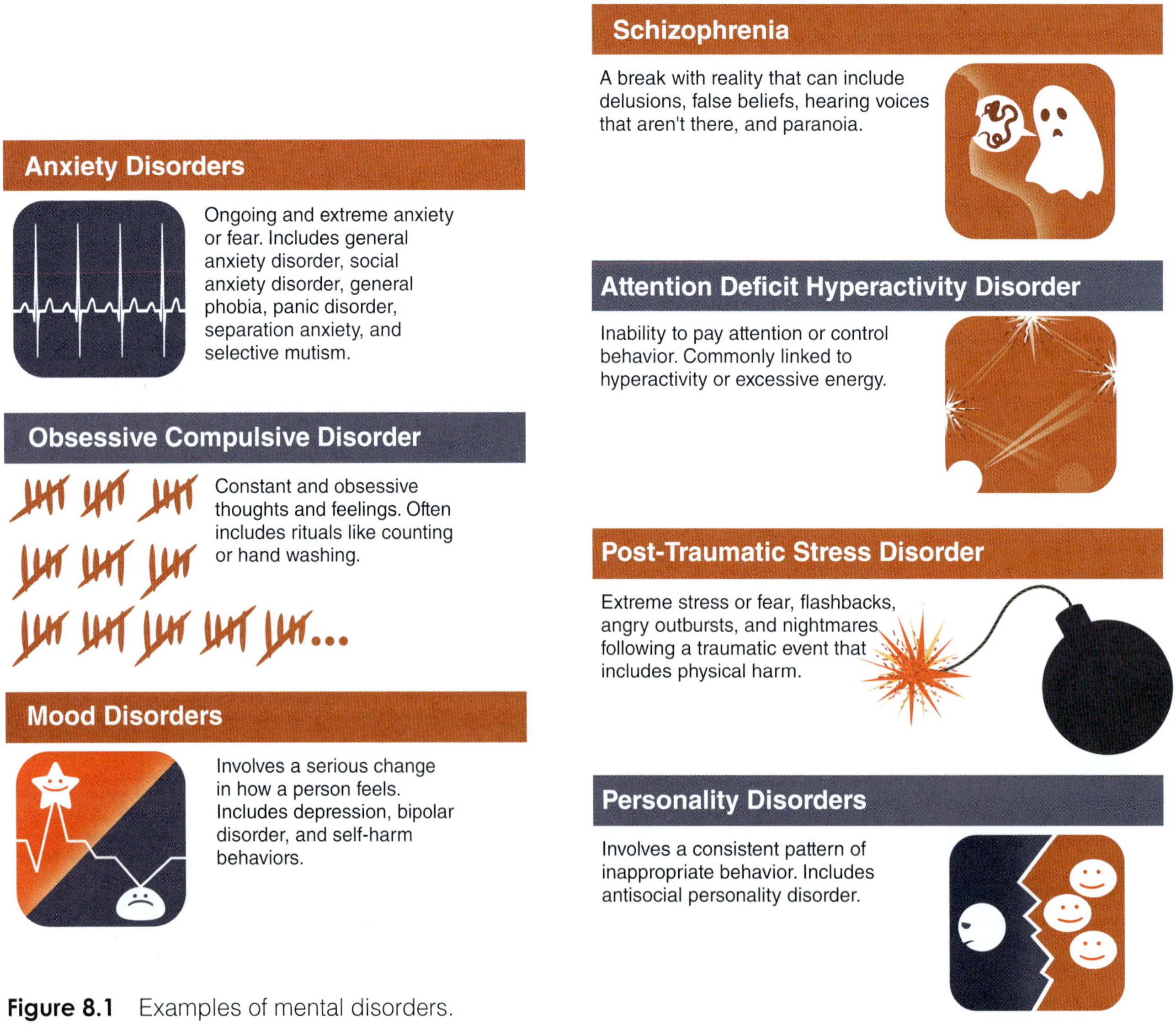

Anxiety Disorders
Ongoing and extreme anxiety or fear. Includes general anxiety disorder, social anxiety disorder, general phobia, panic disorder, separation anxiety, and selective mutism.

Obsessive Compulsive Disorder
Constant and obsessive thoughts and feelings. Often includes rituals like counting or hand washing.

Mood Disorders
Involves a serious change in how a person feels. Includes depression, bipolar disorder, and self-harm behaviors.

Schizophrenia
A break with reality that can include delusions, false beliefs, hearing voices that aren't there, and paranoia.

Attention Deficit Hyperactivity Disorder
Inability to pay attention or control behavior. Commonly linked to hyperactivity or excessive energy.

Post-Traumatic Stress Disorder
Extreme stress or fear, flashbacks, angry outbursts, and nightmares following a traumatic event that includes physical harm.

Personality Disorders
Involves a consistent pattern of inappropriate behavior. Includes antisocial personality disorder.

Figure 8.1 Examples of mental disorders.

Understanding and Treating Mental Disorders LESSON 8.1

Mental Disorders and Youth by the Numbers

- More than 1 in 3 high school students had experienced persistent feelings of sadness or hopelessness in 2019, a 40 percent increase since 2009.
- In 2019, approximately 1 in 6 youth reported making a suicide plan in the past year, a 44 percent increase since 2009.
- During the COVID-19 pandemic in 2021, 37 percent of high school students reported they experienced poor mental health, and 44 percent reported they persistently felt sad or hopeless.
- Cases of anxiety, depression, and self-harm among U.S. teens aged 13 to 18 all increased between 2019 and 2022.

Causes of Mental Disorders

Most of the time, we don't know what causes a mental disorder. A variety of factors come together to affect a person's likelihood of developing a mental disorder.

Genetics and Family History

Mental health conditions can be genetic. This doesn't mean you will develop a mental disorder if your parents or grandparents have one. Pay special attention to your emotional and mental health if your family has a history of disorders, and seek help from a mental health professional if needed.

Environment and Experiences

The type of home life and experiences you have can affect your risk for mental disorders. A stable, loving environment might reduce your risk for mental disorders. Traumatic events like a death in the family or financial hardships might increase your risk. Alcohol and substance abuse are contributing factors as well.

Brain Injury

A traumatic brain injury (TBI) increases your risk for a mental disorder. Blows or jolts to the head can cause temporary or permanent damage to brain tissue and function.

Prenatal History

How your birth mother cared for herself during her pregnancy with you affects your risk. Substance use, poor nutrition, trauma, and exposure to certain chemicals or viruses all have an effect.

LESSON 8.1   Mental Health

How the Brain Functions

How your brain thinks and processes information and emotions can contribute to mental disorders. Anxiety, anger, and low self-esteem or feelings of worthlessness can make you more susceptible to certain types of mental disorders like mood and anxiety disorders.

Care and Treatment of Mental Disorders

Many treatment options are available for mental disorders. The exact treatment or combination of treatments depends on the disorder and the person. Treatment may be provided by a health care team, which can include a physician, a pharmacist, and a mental health professional (e.g., psychologist, psychiatrist, or social worker). Common treatment options include psychotherapy, counseling, medication, and substance abuse counseling. Additional treatments, such as hospitalization, may be used in more severe situations. In some cases, a mental disorder is so severe that a doctor, loved one, or guardian oversees the care until the affected person is well enough to participate in decision making.

Counseling and Psychotherapy

Psychotherapy and counseling are methods of treating mental disorders that involve talking about the condition and related issues with a mental health care provider. During psychotherapy or counseling sessions, a person learns about their condition and their moods, feelings, thoughts, and behaviors. The person uses insights and knowledge gained from the treatment to learn coping and stress-management skills.

> **HEALTHY LIVING TIP**
>
> Many schools have counseling services, and insurance plans often cover counseling or psychotherapy sessions as well. Find out if you have access to mental health services at school or through your family's insurance plan. Knowing what mental health services you have access to can make it easier to seek help if and when you need it.

Psychotherapy helps to treat mental disorders.

Understanding and Treating Mental Disorders   **LESSON 8.1**

STEM in Health

VIRTUAL REALITY

Research shows that virtual reality can be used as a distraction tool to reduce pain and anxiety, and it can help people with emotional control such as with anger management. Virtual reality is also proven to be an effective technology for helping people deal with anxiety-related conditions and disorders.

Virtual reality is a technology interface that allows users to experience a real-life situation in a controlled setting. For example, a person dealing with claustrophobia (a fear of enclosed spaces) can experience a simulated elevator ride without having to physically go and ride an actual elevator. The technology can be used to help the person move from a short ride in a larger elevator to a longer ride in a smaller virtual space. The virtual experience is responsive to the user's movement, making it fully immersive and realistic. This results in the person having similar physiological reactions as the real experience. By carefully exposing the person to the environmental conditions that cause their anxiety, the person can practice using coping mechanisms like deep breathing during the experience, which can help them gradually overcome their anxiety.

There are many types of psychotherapy, each with its own approach to improving a person's emotional wellness. Psychotherapy often can be successfully completed in a few months, but in some cases, long-term treatment is helpful. It can be done one-on-one, in a group, or with family members.

Medication

Medication does not cure a mental disorder, but it can provide significant relief from symptoms and help the person function more fully. Psychiatric medication can also help other treatments, such as psychotherapy, to be more effective. The selection of medication depends on the particular situation and how the person's body responds. Here are some of the most commonly used classes of prescription psychiatric medication.

- *Antidepressant medications.* Antidepressants are used to treat various types of depression and sometimes other conditions. They can help improve such symptoms as sadness, hopelessness, lack of energy, difficulty concentrating, and lack of interest in activities. Antidepressants are grouped into more specific categories determined by how they affect brain chemistry.

Medication can be used to treat some of the symptoms associated with mental illness.

- *Mood-stabilizing medications.* Mood stabilizers are most commonly used to treat bipolar disorder, which is characterized by alternating episodes of mania and depression. Sometimes they are used with antidepressants to treat depression.
- *Anti-anxiety medications.* These medications are used to treat anxiety disorders, such as generalized anxiety disorder and panic disorder. They may also help reduce agitation and insomnia. They are typically fast acting, helping to relieve symptoms in as little as 30 to 60 minutes. One major drawback, however, is their potential for addiction.
- *Antipsychotic medications.* Also called neuroleptics, these medications are typically used to treat psychotic disorders such as schizophrenia. Psychotic disorders involve a loss of contact with reality.

Substance Abuse Counseling

Substance abuse commonly occurs along with mental illness; in such cases, it often interferes with treatment and worsens the problem. Specialized treatment is needed if a person is unable to stop using drugs or alcohol on their own. For children and adolescents, treatment for substance abuse and mental health issues should include parental and physician involvement. All types of treatment are proven to be more effective when parents or guardians are informed and are actively involved. Substance abuse treatments are discussed in later chapters and include the following:

- Psychotherapy
- Medication
- Hospitalization to address withdrawal (detox)
- Support groups, such as 12-step programs

Social Stigma and Mental Disorders

A **stigma** is a distinguishing characteristic or personal trait that is thought to be, or actually is, a disadvantage. Unfortunately, many people stigmatize mental disorders, which often leads to prejudice against and negative impact on people with the disorders.

Harmful effects of prejudice on people with mental disorders include

- fear of seeking treatment;
- lack of understanding by family, friends, coworkers, or others;
- fewer opportunities for school, work, or social activities or trouble with bullying, physical violence, or harassment, and;
- believing they will never succeed.

Learning about mental disorders and developing empathy for the challenges mental disorders present will help to reduce any prejudice you may have. Use the STOP tool in figure 8.2 to help you recognize your own negative feelings toward people with mental disorders.

Understanding and Treating Mental Disorders **LESSON 8.1**

Stereotype
Assuming a general truth about someone because of their mental disorder.

Trivialize
Trivializing a person's mental disorder and treating them like it doesn't matter.

Offend
Saying mean, cruel, or offensive things to, or about, a person with a mental disorder.

Patronize
Treating people with a mental disorder like they aren't as good as you or other people.

Figure 8.2 Use STOP to help you recognize stigma and avoid applying it.

Communication and Mental Disorders

Whether you or anyone you know develops a mental disorder, you should consider how your responses to situations might be inappropriate and hurtful if someone is dealing with a mental disorder. Try an appropriate response that fits one or more of the following guidelines.

- Begin with concern for the other person. "I noticed _____. Are you okay?"
- Offer assistance. "Is there anything I can do to help you with what you are experiencing right now?"
- Provide an open space for listening. "I can see you are dealing with something. I'm here if you want to talk."
- Share your own concerns with *I* statements. "I am worried about you. Are you okay?"

345

LESSON 8.1   Mental Health

Skill-Building Challenge

Communicating About Mental Health

Work with a partner or a small group based on your teacher's instruction. Read each of the following scenarios. Each situation includes an inappropriate response from a friend. Discuss appropriate responses that the friend could use. Revisit the Communication and Mental Disorders section to help you identify appropriate strategies. Decide which response you think works best for the situation and practice it with your partner or in your group.

> Levi is stressing out over school and is overeating to deal with all the anxiety he feels. Tia says, "Ew, you are grossing me out. Aren't you worried you'll get fat?"

What would a helpful response from Tia be?

> Stella has anxiety to the point that she feels like she can't breathe. When this happens, she stops, sits down, and stares straight ahead. When Violet sees this, she says "You are such a drama queen. Everyone knows you're just wanting attention."

What would a helpful response from Violet be?

> Piper has been sad and depressed the last week for no apparent reason. Her friend Coco says, "You are being way too much of a downer. I don't want to hang out with you anymore."

What would a helpful response from Coco be?

> Reagan has been counting to 10 before walking into any room. Her friend Sawyer says, "Stop being so weird. You're freaking me out!"

What would a helpful response from Sawyer be?

Healthy Living Skills

This lesson focused on healthy communication. Here are some more ways you can develop healthy living skills related to this lesson.

ANALYZING INFLUENCES
How does social media influence your perception of mental illness? Do you see posts, reactions, or interactions that portray stereotypes or make fun of people who are suffering? Do you see examples of positive support? Write a description of one negative and one positive influence.

MAKING HEALTHY DECISIONS
If someone has a mental disorder, do you think they are able to make decisions about their care and treatment on their own? Identify two reasons why someone might need help in decision making if they have a mental disorder.

ADVOCATING FOR GOOD HEALTH
Working in a small group, research one of the mental disorders discussed in this lesson. Gather information about the disorder's causes, risk factors, major symptoms, and treatment options. As a class, decide the best way to share the information you gathered with others in your school or community. Consider making flyers, posters, or a website to share your information. Finally, as a class, share your collective work by organizing a mental health awareness advocacy campaign or day on your campus.

LESSON 8.1 Review: Understanding and Treating Mental Disorders

LESSON SUMMARY

- Mental disorders, such as anxiety and mood disorders, are serious and ongoing conditions involving how a person thinks and manages their emotions.
- A stigma is a distinguishing characteristic or personal trait that is thought to be, or actually is, a disadvantage.
- Mental disorders can be treated in a variety of ways including medication, counseling and psychotherapy, and hospitalization.

REVIEWING CONCEPTS AND VOCABULARY

1. A mental disorder affects how a person _____ and manages their emotions.
2. Genetics, environment and experiences, brain _____, and pre-natal history can cause mental disorders.
3. A(n) _____ is a distinguishing characteristic or personal trait that is thought to be, or actually is, a disadvantage.
4. _____ and counseling are methods of treating mental disorders that involve talking about the condition and related issues with a mental health care provider.
5. An antidepressant is an example of a(n) _____ that can be used to treat mental disorders.
6. _____ commonly occurs alongside mental illness; in such cases, it often interferes with treatment and worsens the problem.

THINKING CRITICALLY

Research a common mental disorder that interests you. Use the information you find to write a short story about what it might be like to have the disorder. Write from the point of view of the person with the disorder and be sure to demonstrate empathy in your writing.

TAKE IT HOME

Create a list of emergency and crisis numbers and hotlines for different mental disorders or mental health crises. Put the list somewhere you will remember.

LESSON 8.2
Anxiety and Anxiety Disorders

Terms to Learn
- anxiety
- anxiety disorders
- gratitude
- phobia

Learning Targets
- Compare and contrast anxiety and anxiety disorders.
- Identify five symptoms of anxiety disorder.
- Explain three common influences on teen anxiety.
- Describe the value of gratitude and explain two ways to practice it.

The Big Picture
Anxiety is a common emotion that all people feel from time to time. When anxiety becomes severe and begins to interfere with a person's ability to carry out daily tasks, it might be a sign that the person has an anxiety disorder. Recognizing the symptoms of anxiety and understanding the different ways anxiety can appear are essential to managing and treating anxiety disorders.

Write About It
What does it feel like to be anxious? Identify a time when you were feeling anxiety and try to describe what it felt like and what you noticed about how you felt.

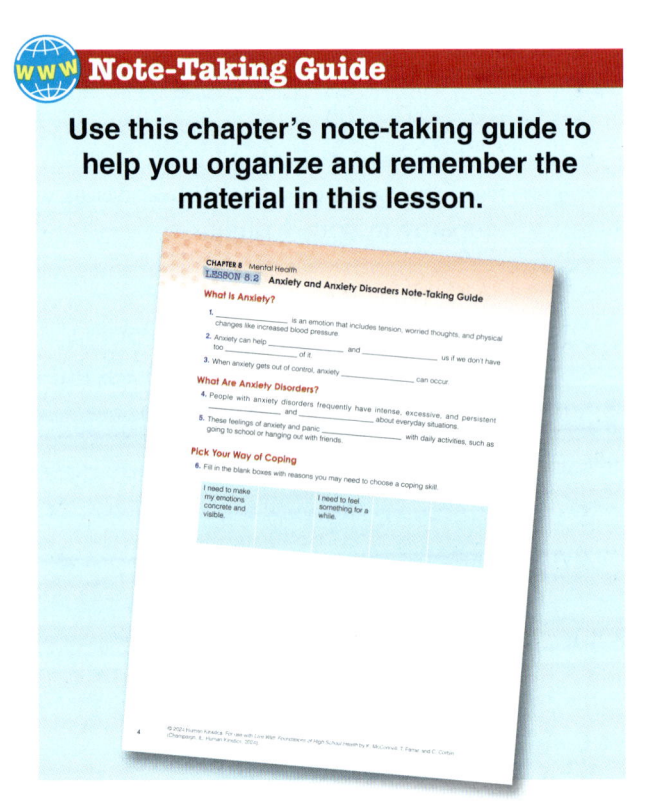

Note-Taking Guide
Use this chapter's note-taking guide to help you organize and remember the material in this lesson.

Anxiety and Anxiety Disorders **LESSON 8.2**

Leah is a good student and has a few close friends. Leah also has a secret. Most people don't know that she has anxiety and sometimes has panic attacks that make her feel like she is going to die. Leah is in therapy and takes medication to help her manage her condition. When she does feel a panic attack coming, she knows to find a quiet, private space where she can do deep breathing and refocus. She's had a few attacks at school, but usually they happen during lunch or passing periods, and she is able to duck away without being noticed. Her panic attacks can be scary because her heart beats hard and fast and she feels like she can't breathe. Leah worries a lot about her grades—most of her panic attacks relate to her fear of failing in school. Do you relate to any of Leah's story? Are there things that cause you to feel anxious?

What Is Anxiety?

Anxiety disorders are some of the most common mental disorders among children and teens. It is important to understand that there is a difference between feeling anxious and having an anxiety disorder. **Anxiety** is an emotion that includes tension, worried thoughts, and physical changes like increased blood pressure. It is normal to feel anxiety sometimes. Just as with stress, anxiety can help motivate and engage us if we don't have too much of it. Stress and anxiety are similar. Stress occurs as a response to our environment. When stress is long-term, it can have a negative impact on our health. Anxiety is a feeling of fear and almost always includes a sense that something really bad is going to happen. A person can experience anxiety simply by thinking about something that they fear or worry about. The source of the anxiety is not always known or recognized, which can make things worse. When anxiety gets out of control, anxiety disorders can occur.

What Are Anxiety Disorders?

We all experience anxiety; it is a normal part of life. However, people with **anxiety disorders** frequently have intense, excessive, and persistent worry and fear about everyday situations. A **phobia**, or a persistent, excessive, or unrealistic fear of an

A simple phobia, such as the fear of flying, is a type of anxiety disorder.

LESSON 8.2 — Mental Health

I'm Feeling Anxious, Now What?

Managing normal feelings of anxiety can be challenging. Coping skills are used to help manage anxiety. Some of the same techniques used to manage stress also work with anxiety.

Pick Your Way of Coping

When choosing a coping skill, start by asking yourself, "What do I need right now?" The following are some common answers to that question.

- *I need to release emotions.* When you feel the need to release emotions, your response can be either physical or non-physical. For a physical release, try exercising or punching a pillow (on a soft surface). For a non-physical release, consider talking to a friend, journaling, or creating music or poetry.
- *I need to make my emotions concrete and visible.* Writing, painting, and drawing are great outlets to make something seem more concrete and real. It doesn't matter if what you create is good—it only matters that it reflects what you feel.
- *I need to stop feeling for a while.* Soothing and relaxing activities can be good for drowning out emotions that feel overwhelming. Try deep breathing; taking a short nap; or using a distraction like a movie, game, book, or music.
- *I need to feel something for a while.* Oftentimes we cope by shutting down and going numb. When this happens, we sometimes have a need to feel something. Choose an action that focuses on sensation like holding an ice cube in your hands, splashing cold water on your face, tensing and then relaxing your muscles, or watching or reading something that will make you laugh.
- *I need to get a sense of control.* When things feel out of control, try doing things that focus on organization. Make lists of what you want or need to do or clean and organize your closet or room.

Manage Your Expectations

Coping skills don't usually work immediately, and it will take time to learn what works best for you. Be patient and give each skill you try a fair chance. Use the following guidelines to help you cope successfully.

- Try each a few times. Sometimes a skill has to grow on you for it to start to work.
- It is okay to jump from one skill to another if something doesn't work after you've given it a fair chance.
- Recognize that nothing will work 100 percent of the time. Even if you find a skill or two that usually work, don't be hard on yourself if things don't go the way you want. If you get down on yourself, it might make things worse, not better.
- Don't give up and focus on being resilient.

object, person, animal, activity, or situation, is an example of an anxiety disorder. See table 8.1 for more examples of common anxiety disorders. These feelings of anxiety and panic interfere with daily activities like going to school or hanging out with friends. The feelings are difficult to control, are out of proportion to the actual danger, and can last a long time. Symptoms may start during childhood or the teen years and continue into adulthood (see figure 8.3).

TABLE 8.1 **Common Anxiety Disorders**

Disorder	Description
General anxiety disorder	People with this disorder experience ongoing and excessive anxiety and worry about activities or events, even ordinary routines. The worry is disproportionate to the actual circumstance, is difficult to control, and affects how you feel physically. It often occurs along with other anxiety disorders or depression.
Panic attacks (i.e., panic disorder)	Panic attacks involve repeated episodes of sudden feelings of intense anxiety and fear or terror that reach a peak within minutes. You may have feelings of impending doom, shortness of breath, chest pain, or heart palpitations (rapid, fluttering, or pounding heart). Having panic attacks may lead to worrying about them happening again or avoiding situations in which they've occurred.
Social anxiety disorder	Fear and avoidance of social situations stem from feelings of embarrassment, self-consciousness, and concern about being judged or viewed negatively by others. Social anxiety disorder leads to high levels of anxiety in most social environments.
Simple phobia	A simple phobia is when you're exposed to a specific object or situation and have a desire to avoid it. Phobias cause panic attacks in some people. Common simple phobias include fears of flying, public speaking, spiders, and heights.
Separation anxiety	Separation anxiety is a childhood disorder where the anxiety a child feels when being separated from parents is excessive for the child's developmental level.
Selective mutism	This is a childhood disorder where a child consistently fails to speak in certain situations, such as in school, even when they can speak in other situations, such as at home with close family members. This can interfere with school, work, and social functioning.

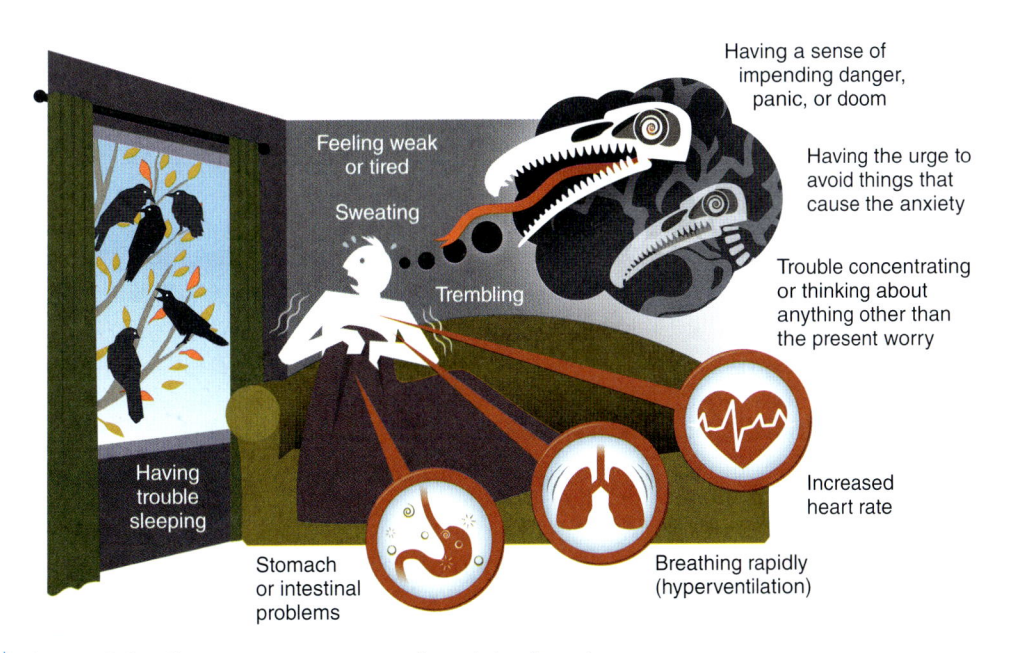

Figure 8.3 Common symptoms of anxiety disorders.

Influences on Anxiety Disorders in Teens

According to the National Institutes of Health, almost one-third of all U.S. adolescents between ages 13 to 18 will experience an anxiety disorder. The number of teens with anxiety disorders has been steadily rising since 2007. Anxiety during the COVID-19 pandemic has also increased, especially in relation to social anxiety. There are several social influences that have contributed to the rise in anxiety-related disorders among teens.

High Expectations and Pressure to Succeed

The pressure to perform well academically and the desire to get into top-ranked colleges have contributed to the increase in teen anxiety. Research on incoming first-year, U.S. college students shows that the number of students feeling overwhelmed has increased from 18 percent in 1985 to 80 percent in 2021.

Social Threats and Violence

An increase in school shootings, mass shootings, and other violent attacks in the United States has contributed to anxiety levels. Anxiety can be triggered from watching or reading news reports that detail these situations.

Social Media

Teens today are bombarded with social media and are almost constantly connected to a source of potential judgment and criticism. Teens often compare themselves and their lives to others, and they do so unfavorably. This can affect self-esteem and contribute to feelings of anxiety.

Getting Help for Anxiety Disorders

Anxiety disorders can be difficult to manage. You can apply the same techniques for managing stress levels and controlling emotions to the management of your anxiety. The

---

Diversity Matters

Asher's Challenge

My name is Asher. I have a lot of anxiety when I am around other people or in public. I prefer to keep to myself, and I don't really like talking to others. I am afraid of what others will think of me, and I am always worried that I will say the wrong thing. Some people think that I am stupid just because I don't talk much, but I'm not. I just can't seem to feel safe when others are around, and I can't shake the feeling that everyone is thinking negatively about me. I get sick to my stomach, and sometimes I shake a little, and I struggle to make eye contact. I have been diagnosed with general anxiety disorder, and I am working to manage my condition, but it is hard. When things are bad, my heart races, and I can even feel dizzy or faint or like I can't breathe. It's really hard to make friends, and it can be really lonely too.

Question: Can you relate to how Asher feels? Explain your answer. What are some ways you can show respect and compassion for someone with an anxiety-related disorder?

severity of anxiety disorders and their interference with ordinary life often lead people to seek professional help to manage their condition. Without treatment, anxiety disorders can lead to self-medicating behaviors like alcohol and substance abuse.

HEALTHY LIVING TIP
Next time you find yourself feeling anxious, do a cardiorespiratory exercise that will make you breathe deeper and harder for a few minutes. Jumping jacks, running in place, ski jumps, and similar exercises can help distract you and use some of the excess energy you are feeling.

Common techniques for managing anxiety-related disorders include therapy, medication, support groups, and self-care

- **Therapy** can help people deal with anxiety by providing them with an understanding of how to behave, think, and react to stressful situations and objects.
- **Medication** does not cure an anxiety disorder, but it can help manage the symptoms.
- **Support groups** provide a therapeutic setting for people with similar issues to meet each other and share their experiences together. Always take precautions when joining an online support group because these environments encourage sharing of personal information and may encourage predators. If you are seeking a support group, consult a therapist first for suggestions.
- **Self-care.** Getting plenty of exercise changes important hormone levels that can help with anxiety. Good quality sleep and a healthy diet are also important parts of self-care for anxiety.

Practicing Gratitude

Gratitude refers to being appreciative for the large and small things you have and experience in life. Gratitude is both an attitude and an action that can become a habit. When we express our gratitude, it tends to overshadow other feelings we might have and can help us refocus in a positive and calming way. Some strategies for practicing gratitude include the following:

- *Daily three.* Identify three things each day that you are grateful for and say them out loud.
- *Counting your blessings.* On the first day of each month, brainstorm what makes you grateful. Start out with small blessings, working your way up to the larger ones and then write them down.
- *Gratitude alphabet.* Name what you are grateful for each corresponding letter of the alphabet. For example, A: Aunt Kathy, B: batting practice, and so on.
- *Journal.* Write about what you were most grateful for each day in a journal before you go to bed. Occasionally read through your entries to be reminded of all the positive things you have to hold on to.

353

LESSON 8.2   Mental Health

Skill Building Challenge

Practicing Healthy Behaviors: Gratitude

Having gratitude doesn't necessarily just happen. We have to practice it and make it a choice if we want to experience it. Many people find that being increasingly grateful provides them with optimism as well as eases the burden of managing their own anxieties. Review the strategies in the Practicing Gratitude section and also think about other ways that you might practice having gratitude. Identify two options that might work for you. Try out each strategy for at least one week and then reflect on the following questions.

1. Which strategies did you choose and why? Would you make a different choice now? Explain your response.

2. What were the short-term benefits of doing the behaviors you chose? How did being grateful make you feel, and did it change the way others respond to you?

3. What are some potential long-term benefits of gratitude? Identify as many as you can.

Healthy Living Skills

This lesson focused on practicing healthy behaviors. Here are some more ways you can develop healthy living skills related to this lesson.

ANALYZING INFLUENCES

This lesson identified some common reasons why anxiety levels are rising in teens. What are some influences that affect your level of anxiety? Include social, personal, environmental, and lifestyle factors in your list and be sure to identify each influence as positive, negative, or both.

MAKING HEALTHY DECISIONS

What should you do if you think you might be developing an anxiety disorder? When should you reach out to others? Use the Decision-Making Skill Cues to outline the steps you would take in deciding when, how, and from whom to ask for help.

LESSON 8.2 Review: Anxiety and Anxiety Disorders

LESSON SUMMARY

- Anxiety is an emotion that includes tension, worried thoughts, and physical changes like increased blood pressure. It is normal to feel anxiety sometimes.
- It is important to identify what you need if you feel anxious and to use the most appropriate coping strategy you can.
- Anxiety disorders exist when there is intense, excessive, and persistent worry and fear about everyday situations. These feelings of anxiety and panic interfere with daily activities like going to school or hanging out with friends.
- Anxiety disorders can cause increased heart rate and breathing, trembling muscles, difficulty with concentration and sleeping, and a desire to avoid situations (or people) that increase your symptoms.
- Common anxiety disorders include panic disorder, general anxiety disorder, social anxiety disorder, and phobias.

REVIEWING CONCEPTS AND VOCABULARY

1. If you have intense feelings of worry and panic that interfere with your daily life, you may have a(n) _____ disorder.
2. Exercise is a coping strategy that might be used to help you _____ your emotions.
3. Treatments for anxiety disorders include therapy, _____, support groups, and self-care.
4. Major anxiety that happens when someone is exposed to a specific object or situation is called a simple _____.
5. Common anxiety disorders include panic, general, _____, and phobia.
6. _____ refers to being appreciative for the large and small things you have and experience in life.

THINKING CRITICALLY

Research a common anxiety disorder that interests you. Use the information you find to create a social media thread about the disorder from the point of view of the person with the disorder. Try to convey what it would be like to have that disorder.

TAKE IT HOME

Write down comparisons and contrasts of anxiety and anxiety disorders. Include common ways each is managed or treated and provide at least one resource for each (e.g., an app that provides coping skills instruction, the name of a nearby mental health professional or office, etc.). Share your work with a parent or guardian and ask them if they have ever thought about what makes everyday anxiety different from an anxiety disorder.

LESSON 8.3

Depression and Mood Disorders

Terms to Learn

depression
mood disorders
sadness

The Big Picture

Depression is the most common mental disorder in the United States. More than 7 percent of the population suffers from depression each year, and depression is most common among young adults ages 18 to 25. When depression is not treated, it can affect a person's overall health and interfere with daily life.

Learning Targets

- Explain what mood disorders are and describe their characteristics using three examples.
- Describe risk factors associated with mood disorders.
- Compare and contrast sadness and depression.
- Identify five signs of depression.

Write About It

When was the last time you felt really sad? How long did your sadness last, and what impacts did it have on your daily activities and relationships?

Note-Taking Guide

Use this chapter's note-taking guide to help you organize and remember the material in this lesson.

Ellie knows that she is struggling with how sad she feels. Her only real friend moved to a new city, and her favorite aunt died last month. Ellie feels like everything is going wrong and nobody really cares about how she is feeling. Both her parents are always at work, and she is home alone a lot. Lately she's been keeping to herself, alone in her room even when they are home. She stopped using her social media altogether. Ellie likes to sleep because when she is awake, she just starts crying out of nowhere. Everything feels hopeless and like there is no real way out. She misses hanging out with her friend, and she and her parents fight more without her aunt being around. Ellie is experiencing depression. Where could she go for help? What might happen to her if she doesn't get the help she needs?

What Are Mood Disorders?

Mood disorders affect a person's emotional state in ways that make the person experience long periods of extreme happiness, extreme sadness, or both. Figure 8.4 lists common types of depression and mood disorders. Major depression, persistent depressive disorder, and bipolar disorder are the most common mood disorders.

Causes of Mood Disorders

There are many factors that might contribute to the development of mood disorders.

- *Imbalances in brain chemicals.* Imbalances in some brain chemicals like neurotransmitters may be one part of a person's mood disorder. However, chemical imbalances alone are not believed to cause a major mood disorder.
- *Life events and psychosocial factors.* Major life events like divorce, a move to another city or location, or the death of a loved one or pet can result in loneliness, grief, and sadness and can be significant factors in the development of mood disorders. Other serious medical diagnoses like cancer can also contribute to mood disorders, as can alcohol and substance abuse.
- *Genetics and family history.* When a family member is diagnosed with a mood disorder, the risk of mood disorders in other family members increases. Mood disorders are more frequently reported and diagnosed in women; however, women are more willing to seek help for mental disorders in general. Therefore, our understanding of how common such disorders are in men is likely distorted.

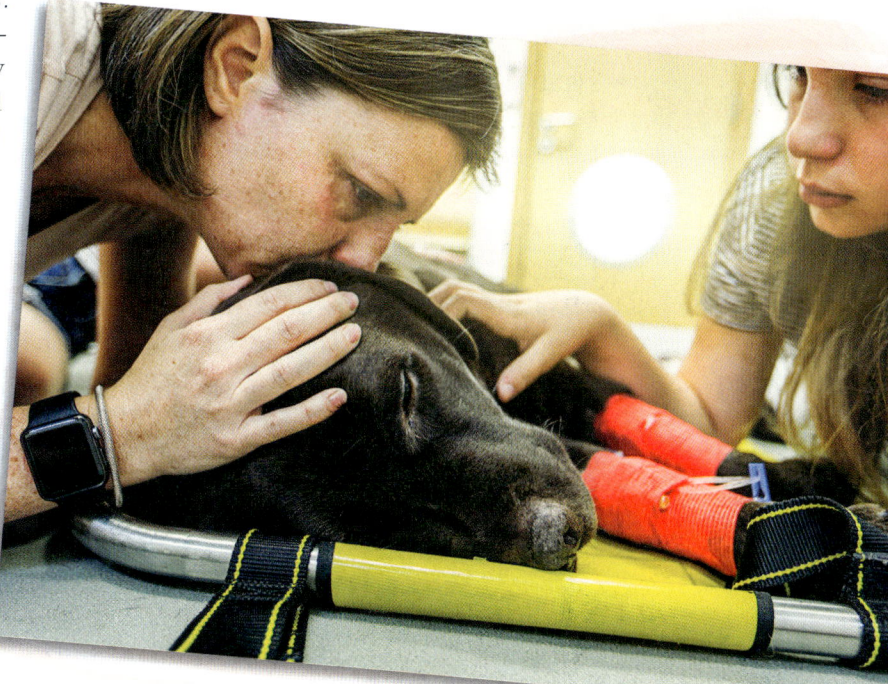

The death of a pet can be a factor in the development of a mood disorder.

Specific Types of Depression

Persistent depressive disorder
- Ongoing major depression that lasts for two years or longer

Postpartum depression
- Feelings of extreme sadness, anxiety, and exhaustion during pregnancy or after birth
- Can severely affect the mother's ability to complete daily caretaking of herself and the child

Psychotic depression
- Severe depression with false beliefs (delusions) or hearing or seeing things that don't exist (hallucinations)

Seasonal affective disorder
- Depression during the winter months or in areas where there is less natural sunlight
- Typically leads to social withdrawal, increased sleep, and weight gain
- Typically returns every year

Bipolar disorder
- Episodes of extremely low moods that meet the criteria for depression (called "bipolar depression") mixed with extremely high moods

Disruptive mood dysregulation disorder
- Diagnosed between ages 6 and 18, usually beginning by age 10; symptoms must be present for 12 months
- Irritable or angry mood most of the day, nearly every day
- Severe temper outbursts (verbal or behavioral) at least three times per week
- Trouble functioning in multiple settings (school, home, etc.) because of irritability

Figure 8.4 Specific types of depression and related mood disorders.

Understanding Depression

There are several types of depression. Major, or clinical, **depression** is a common but serious mood disorder that affects the way you feel, think, and handle daily activities like doing schoolwork, sleeping, having relationships, and eating. Anyone can become depressed, but females are slightly more likely than males to become depressed. In 2018, prior to the COVID-19 pandemic, 8 percent of teenagers suffered from major depression. That number increased to 10 percent in 2021. Depression is the most common mental health disorder among teens. Risk factors for teen depression include the following:

- Personal or family history of depression
- Major life changes
- Trauma
- Stress
- Certain physical illnesses and medications

Depression can look different in different people. To be diagnosed with depression, a person must have symptoms for longer than two weeks. Symptoms of depression include the following:

- Feeling depressed throughout each day on most or all days
- Lack of interest and enjoyment in activities you used to find pleasurable
- Trouble sleeping, sleeping too much
- Trouble eating or eating too much, coupled with weight gain or weight loss
- Irritability, restlessness, agitation
- Extreme fatigue, loss of energy
- Relationship problems
- Rebellious or high-risk behavior
- Unnecessary or excessive feelings of guilt or worthlessness
- Frequent physical complaints (headaches, stomach aches, etc.)
- Difficulty with achieving in school or work
- Inability to concentrate or make decisions
- Suicidal thoughts or actions, thinking a lot about death and dying

Depression and Health Conditions

People who are dealing with a major depression often struggle to take care of their health. Preparing food and eating healthy, attending to personal hygiene, engaging in physical activity, and getting adequate sleep are all challenges that depression causes. As a result, people who are suffering from depression can also develop other chronic illnesses, like high blood pressure, or they can be more susceptible to common illnesses, such as colds and the flu.

Depression may occur in people who are dealing with a serious medical illness, such as diabetes, cancer, heart disease, or Parkinson's disease. The chronic pain, social isolation, and medications associated with these conditions increase a person's risk for depression. Once the person becomes depressed, the symptoms of their disease can get worse. In this way, depression and chronic illnesses become a cycle, each making the other worse. Getting proper treatment for both the medical condition and the associated depression is needed in these cases.

Sadness Versus Depression

Sadness is different from depression. **Sadness** is a typical human emotion that we feel as a result of a situation or event, but it does not impede us from going about our daily tasks. When we are sad, we generally are able to recognize that things will get better. It is okay to feel sad when a situation is difficult, for example, when you are lonely or have an argument with a friend or a sibling. Sadness can last for several days or even up to two weeks. Depression is different from sadness because it is a state of being that limits a person's ability to engage in routine activities. Depression causes a feeling of hopelessness, and often people suffering from it don't see a way out. Depression interferes with a person's life and usually requires professional help to cure.

HEALTHY LIVING TIP

Practice random acts of kindness by doing or saying something nice to three different people. Try to make at least one act anonymous so that the person doesn't know it was you who did it. Being kind and supportive to others will help you feel not only good about but also more confident about reaching out to others when you need support.

Managing and Treating Depression

When mood disorders like depression are correctly diagnosed and treated, people with the disorders can lead stable, productive, and healthy lives. Common approaches to treatment include the following:

- Antidepressants and mood-stabilizing medications
- Psychotherapy
- Family therapy or counseling
- Brain stimulation therapies

Depression and other mood disorders are complex mental illnesses that require professional guidance and help. It is important to recognize that you alone cannot help yourself or others with these problems. Counseling by a mental health professional, medications, and appropriate support services can make a difference.

Career Connection

SCHOOL COUNSELOR

School counselors work in all grade levels to help ensure academic success and to support the mental and emotional health of students. School counselors advise students to determine their path forward and work to match students' skills, abilities, and interests with careers and educational opportunities. School counselors also work with parents, teachers, and community organizers to bring people together in support of the whole child. At younger grade levels, school counselors can play a critical role in evaluating and supporting the mental and emotional development of kids. School counselors must earn a master's degree in school counseling, complete clinical training hours, and pass a national licensing exam. The job forecast for school counselors is strong.

Depression and Mood Disorders — LESSON 8.3

Self-Care and Depression

In addition to medical treatment options, self-care is an important element to managing a mood disorder. The following lists self-care strategies:

- Stay physically active and get regular exercise.
- Set realistic goals for yourself.
- Spend time with other people, especially those you trust and can talk to.
- Avoid isolating yourself and reach out to others for support.
- Respect that improving your condition will take time, even with medication.
- Avoid making sudden or rash decisions like quitting a job or school.
- Continue to learn about depression to help you understand your condition.

Skill-Building Challenge

Making Healthy Decisions

Making healthy decisions will affect all parts of your life, including your mental well-being. Use a decision tree described in the following paragraph to map the choices you have when you are dealing with a situation that could, or does, make you feel sad. Think of a situation you are or have been in and use it for your tree. If you are struggling to identify your own situation, try to create a realistic scenario based on someone you know or a character you know from a book, movie, or TV show.

A decision tree is a way to visually show the options you have when making a decision. It can help you move through all the important steps that are part of the Decision-Making Skill Cues. Here is an example of a decision tree.

Once you have completed your tree, decide which decision you think has the best outcome, and explain your decision.

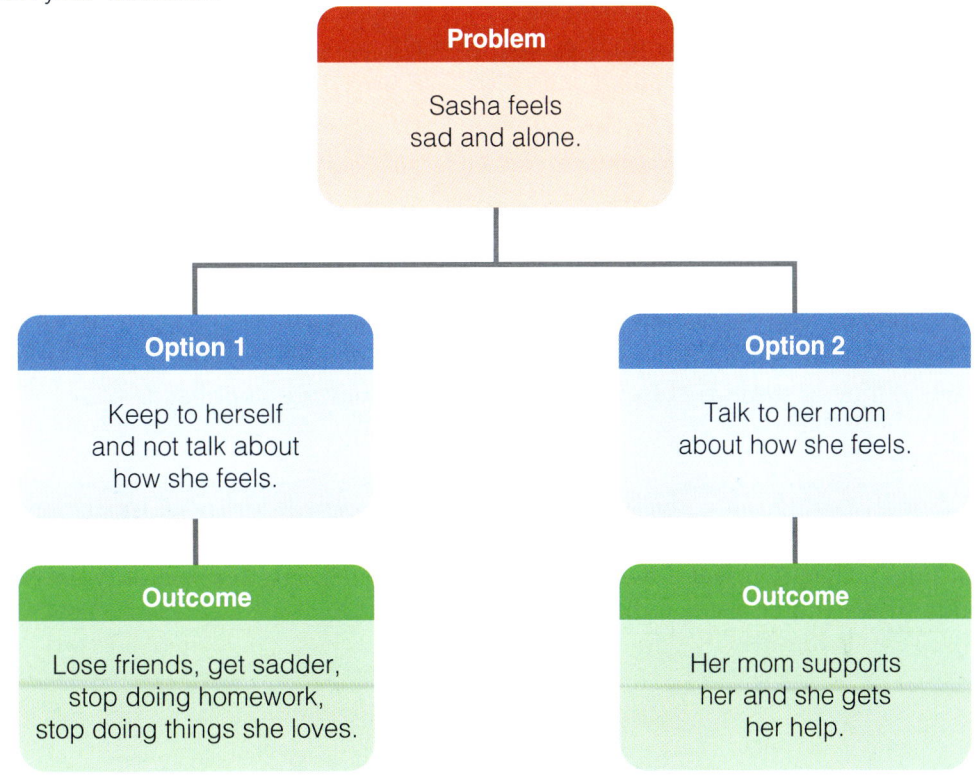

Problem
Sasha feels sad and alone.

Option 1
Keep to herself and not talk about how she feels.

Option 2
Talk to her mom about how she feels.

Outcome
Lose friends, get sadder, stop doing homework, stop doing things she loves.

Outcome
Her mom supports her and she gets her help.

LESSON 8.3 Mental Health

Healthy Living Skills

This lesson focused on decision making. Here is one more way you can develop healthy living skills related to this lesson.

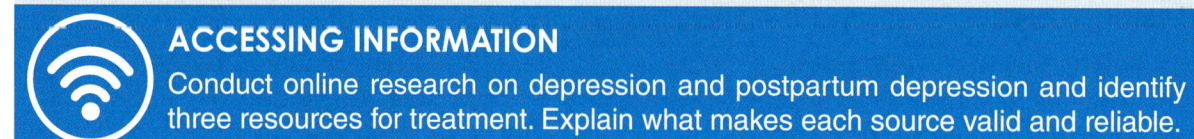

ACCESSING INFORMATION

Conduct online research on depression and postpartum depression and identify three resources for treatment. Explain what makes each source valid and reliable.

LESSON 8.3 Review: Depression and Mood Disorders

LESSON SUMMARY

- Mood disorders affect a person's emotional state by causing the person to experience long periods of extreme happiness, extreme sadness, or both.
- Common mood disorders include major depression and bipolar disorder. Mood disorders can also occur as a result of another medical condition or alongside substance abuse.
- Sadness is a normal human emotion that may last from minutes to a couple of weeks. Depression, on the other hand, is a common but serious mood disorder that negatively affects how you feel, think, and handle daily activities.
- Signs of depression include loss of interest and enjoyment in activities, changes to sleep and eating patterns, fatigue, difficulty concentrating, and suicidal thoughts or actions.

REVIEWING CONCEPTS AND VOCABULARY

1. Mood disorders can involve long periods of both extreme _____ and _____.
2. Mood disorders may be influenced by chemical imbalances, life events, and _____.
3. _____ is a normal human emotion that may last from minutes to two weeks.
4. _____ is the most common mental disorder among teenagers.
5. Changes to sleep and eating patterns are potential signs of _____.

THINKING CRITICALLY

How could you help a younger student understand the difference between sadness and depression? Create a story, checklist, or tool that you could use with elementary students to teach them how to recognize when they or someone else is sad versus when they are depressed.

TAKE IT HOME

Spend some time seeking out comic relief. Consider video clips from social media, favorite songs and movies, or funny people who make you laugh. Write out your list and place it in a convenient location for times when you feel down or sad and need something that will lift your mood. Share your list with others and encourage them to do the same.

LESSON 8.4
Self-Harm and Suicide

Terms to Learn
self-harm
suicide
suicide attempt
suicide cluster
suicide contagion
trigger

Learning Targets
- Describe what is meant by the term *trigger* in the context of mental health.
- Explain how self-harm is related to emotional health.
- Describe the warning signs of suicide.
- Describe three suicide prevention strategies.
- Identify resources for suicide prevention.

The Big Picture
Suicide is the 10th leading cause of death in the United States, resulting in more than 47,500 deaths in 2019, which is about one death every 11 minutes. Suicide affects all ages and is the second leading cause of death for people ages 10 to 34. Understanding the warning signs of suicide and knowing what to do when you encounter them are critical parts of good emotional health.

Write About It
How do you think social media influences your (or your peers') perceptions of self-harm and suicide? Explain your response.

Note-Taking Guide
Use this chapter's note-taking guide to help you organize and remember the material in this lesson.

LESSON 8.4   Mental Health

Alex started self-harming a month ago. He cut his forearm with a razor once every few days. The cuts are not very deep, but they bleed and hurt. Alex has been wearing long sleeves every day to keep others from noticing. When Alex's mom noticed a bloody tissue in the trash, Alex just shrugged and said indifferently, "I had a bloody nose." He has been feeling depressed and doesn't see much of a future ahead. All of his emotions are dull, but self-harming gives him the sense that he is alive and can feel again—despite the pain. Alex knows the behavior isn't helping him cope with the depression and hopelessness he feels, but he just doesn't know what else to do. If you saw the scars on Alex's arm, would you know what to say or do?

Understanding Self-Harm

Self-harm is the act of purposely causing injury to yourself. A common form of self-harm is cutting yourself with any sharp object; other examples include an impulse to burn yourself, to pull out hair, or to pick at wounds to prevent healing. This can be an issue for young people of either sex; in fact, it is estimated that 10 percent of U.S. teenagers engage in some form of self-harm.

Self-harm is a sign of emotional distress. People who self-harm often do so as a way of distracting themselves from overwhelming emotions that they are unable to cope with. Self-harm often results from a **trigger**—an external event or circumstance that affects your emotional state, often significantly, by causing extreme distress. Self-harm may release feelings of anxiety temporarily, but the emotions will come back. Engaging in self-harm also brings feelings of guilt and shame. These feelings will continue until the root of the problem is addressed and healthier coping skills are learned.

Self-harm is sometimes misunderstood as attention-seeking behavior. Most people who engage in self-harming behaviors are not trying to get attention. Many people hide their behavior from others for long periods of time. Self-harm is most often a misguided coping strategy, not a call for popularity or attention.

Factors That Contribute to Self-Harm

There are several contributing factors to why someone might self-harm. Among the most common are the following reasons:

- Pressures at school or work
- Bullying
- Financial challenges
- Sexual, physical, or emotional abuse
- Grieving
- Experiencing stigma or bias
- Breakdown of a relationship
- Loss of a job
- Illness or health problem
- Low self-esteem
- Increased stress
- Inability to manage or express emotions and feelings

Supporting Others Who Self-Harm

Finding out that someone you care about is self-harming can be emotionally challenging. It is common to feel upset, confused, responsible, and any number of other difficult emotions. It is important to be calm and not overreact. How you choose to respond to your friend or family member will have an impact on how much they open up to you and others about their self-harm in the future. Remember, self-harm is a way of managing and coping with emotions and experiences, and in the majority of cases, it is different than suicidal feelings.

Keep the following suggestions in mind if you discover a friend is self-harming:

- Try your best to be empathetic and nonjudgmental.
- Let the person know that you are there to support them.
- Engage with them as a whole person; in other words, don't make everything about the self-harm.
- Remember that they are in control of their decisions.
- Be supportive by offering to go with them if they want to tell a parent or other adult.
- Offer to help them find a mental health professional in the community.
- Focus on their positive qualities and things they do well.
- Be honest and share your own fears or anxieties about the situation.

Suicide and Suicide Prevention

Suicide is a deliberate act of violence against oneself as a means of death, whereas a **suicide attempt** is the act of trying to kill oneself but surviving the attempt despite one's actions. Suicide is a public health problem and the second leading cause of death among people ages 10 to 34 in the United States.

Sometimes people are influenced by other people's suicides. They become more likely to attempt suicide themselves, which is a phenomenon known as **suicide contagion**. A spate of suicide attempts or suicides within a community in a relatively short period of time is known as a **suicide cluster**.

Facts About Suicide in the United States

- The rate of suicide increased by 35 percent from 1999 to 2018.
- In 2020, there were 45,979 deaths by suicide.
- Suicide is the third leading cause of death for 15- to 24-year-old Americans.
- There is one suicide death in the United States every 11.5 minutes.
- The rate of suicide is highest among middle-aged white men.

Recognizing and Responding to Warning Signs of Suicide

The first step in preventing suicide is to recognize the warning signs. Most people show warning signs before attempting suicide. They may even hint at, or even share, their plans. It is very important to take any mention of suicide seriously and to talk to a trusted adult right away.

Warning Signs of Suicide

- Talking about committing suicide
- Writing poems or stories about suicide
- Giving away valued possessions
- Engaging in reckless or dangerous behavior
- Glamorizing or romanticizing death
- Saying, posting, or writing goodbyes to friends and family
- Referencing death or the end on social media

Suicide Prevention Strategies

Suicide prevention is complex. People who are suicidal are in need of immediate mental health services and support. Anxiety, depression, and other mental health conditions often underlie the issue. In order to prevent a person from becoming suicidal, these underlying health conditions must be managed and treated by mental health professionals.

While suicide is ultimately an individual action, communities and society can help prevent or reduce the risk of suicides using the following strategies:

- Institute policies and practices that strengthen economic supports in a community (access to low-income housing).
- Provide reliable and affordable access to mental health care.
- Establish protective environments that reduce access to contributing factors like firearms and alcohol.
- Invest in opportunities for interpersonal connections (clubs, organizations, community events).
- Educate students and adults about effective coping skills.
- Create public awareness about recognizing and responding to the warning signs of suicide.

Reaching Out for Help

Even among people who have risk factors for suicide, most never attempt suicide. It is hard to predict who will act on suicidal thoughts. If you have any of these warning signs or suspect that a friend is suicidal, take action right away. Call 1-800-273-TALK for 24-hour suicide prevention and help through the National Suicide Prevention Lifeline. You can also text the Crisis Text Line at 741741. Major social media outlets including Facebook, Instagram, Twitter, Snapchat, and Tumblr provide

HEALTHY LIVING TIP

Create a Help card to keep in your backpack or bag. Put the Suicide Prevention Lifeline phone number on the card. If you are under the care of a counselor, add their name and number too. Identify other trusted adults you could talk to and list their names and contact information on the card. Having a Help card makes it easier to reach out for help when you need it.

guidance on how to respond if you see suicidal posts on their sites. If you are not sure where to go, talk to a trusted adult like a school nurse or counselor, a teacher, or a parent or relative.

Supporting Loss Survivors

When someone commits suicide, it has a challenging effect on loved ones who are left behind. Loss survivors may feel a sense of guilt if they think they could have done something to prevent the suicide from occurring. Thinking that their love for the victim was not enough to stop them from wanting to commit suicide produces feelings of anger, confusion, and anguish. Suicide can be very difficult to talk about as a result, and many loss survivors are too embarrassed or ashamed to seek help. Support groups for loss survivors can be extremely beneficial since most experience similar emotions and challenges.

For Help:
Call or *text* 24 hours:
9-8-8
or *chat*
988lifeline.org

CASE STUDY

Leo's Story

When you had to move to a new state in the fifth grade, Leo was the first to befriend you, and the two of you have been friends ever since. You've always admired Leo's positive outlook on life. He's patient and always kind to everyone, including total strangers. He's a high achiever and isn't embarrassed to admit he's a good student. In a lot of ways, you wish you could be more like him.

As first-year high school students, neither of you had much difficulty transitioning to this new world, and making new friends was fairly easy. The following year, you both earned spots on the basketball team and celebrated the achievement by watching movies and playing video games practically all night.

Over the past month, you've seen a dramatic shift in Leo's behavior. The first indication was when he suddenly stopped eating lunch with your mutual group of friends. It was strange seeing him by himself at a different table. You asked him why he wasn't eating with everyone, and he responded, "What's the point really?"

Soon after this, Leo stopped meeting up with you at your locker after school. He now just walks straight home by himself. He said he has chores to do and can't waste time. You've tried inviting him to come over after school to play video games, but Leo repeatedly says he's too tired or that he has chores to do. This past week, he missed two basketball practices, which is totally unlike him. Worse yet, last night you saw a couple of worrisome posts Leo made to his social media account that read "I want out of this life" and "Callin' it quits."

Think About It

1. What do you think is wrong with Leo?
2. Are you worried about him? Why or why not?
3. How could you show support for Leo?
4. What resources exist in your school or community that might help or support Leo?
5. Should you tell anyone else about your concerns? If so, who would that be?

LESSON 8.4 Mental Health

Skill-Building Challenge

Healthy Communication

Finding out that someone is self-harming or suspecting that someone might be suicidal is a stressful experience. Oftentimes friends and loved ones feel paralyzed with not knowing what to say or do. It is helpful to consider how you would respond before such a situation occurs. By practicing your communication now, you will be better able to support someone in the future. Remember to use *I* messages when talking to a person about a potentially sensitive topic. Start by expressing your own emotions and how you are feeling.

Scenario 1: You noticed what appeared to be recent scars on a friend's arm that could be from self-harming behavior. During his parents' divorce, the friend has been going through a hard time and doesn't seem like himself.

1. How would you share your concerns, and what would you say to your friend?
2. How else might you support your friend?

Scenario 2: You noticed a friend was posting statements like "I just want to die," "Time to check out," "I want to kill myself," and "I've had enough of this stupid existence" on her social media. It isn't like her, and you've also noticed that she seems quieter and more withdrawn.

1. How would you respond on social media?
2. What would you say to the friend in person?
3. How would you communicate your concerns with a trusted adult?

Healthy Living Skills

This lesson focused on healthy communication. Here are some more ways you can develop healthy living skills related to this lesson.

ANALYZING INFLUENCES
How do you think access to online sites such as YouTube influences young people's understanding of self-harm and suicide? Identify the positive and negative impacts of this technology on self-harm and suicide risk.

ADVOCATING FOR GOOD HEALTH
How could you advocate for better suicide prevention services in your community? Use the Advocacy Skill Cues to help you write a brief speech that you could deliver to your local city council, mayor, or other leaders and officials.

LESSON 8.4 Review: Self-Harm and Suicide

LESSON SUMMARY

- Self-harm is the act of hurting yourself on purpose. People use self-harm as a way of distracting themselves from overwhelming emotions.
- Suicide is when someone directs violence at themselves with the intent to end their life, and they die as a result of their actions. A suicide attempt is when someone harms themselves in an attempt to end their life, but they do not die because of their actions.
- An external event or circumstance that affects your emotional state, often significantly, by causing extreme distress is called a trigger. Triggers can result in self-harming behaviors.
- Warning signs of suicide include talking about committing suicide, giving away possessions, saying goodbye to family and friends, and making social media posts that reference death or the end.

REVIEWING CONCEPTS AND VOCABULARY

1. _____ is the second leading cause of death among people ages 10 to 34 in the United States.
2. _____ is sometimes misunderstood as an attention-seeking behavior rather than as an attempt to create distraction from disturbing emotions.
3. When talking to someone about their self-harming behavior, it is important to be _____ and nonjudgmental.
4. When someone tries to end their own life, it is called a(n) _____.
5. The first step in preventing suicide is to recognize the _____ signs.

THINKING CRITICALLY

Medically assisted suicide is legal in some states. Research what medically assisted suicide is and determine what laws exist in different states. Write a paragraph supporting people's right to medically assisted suicide and another paragraph that opposes it.

TAKE IT HOME

Use the number for the National Suicide Prevention Hotline and other community resources you may find to create a graphic design, drawing, painting, or other creative art. Share your creation with a friend or family member.

Chapter Review

ACTION PLAN: Coping Skills

Use the My Action Plan worksheet to set goals to learn and improve coping skills. Here is an example.

My Action Plan: My Coping Skills

STEP 1: Identify the health behavior you are going to work on.

I am going to work on learning to cope with difficult emotions.

STEP 2: Write SMART goal(s).

Write one or two short-term goals (one day to one month long).

I will identify specific causes that make me feel anxious or sad every day and understand why they make me feel that way.

I will identify and practice one coping skill that might work for me.

Write a long-term goal (one to six months or more).

I will be able to identify when I feel anxious or sad and will use my coping strategy.

STEP 3: Make a plan.

Identify two to five action steps (strategies) you could do to meet your goal.

I will monitor my emotions to better understand what causes me to feel anxious or sad.

I will engage in vigorous physical activity when I am feeling anxious.

I will reach out to my best friend whenever I feel sad.

STEP 4: Execute your plan and track your progress.

Short-term goal 1

☒ Met   ☐ Not met   Date: *March 1*

Short-term goal 2

☒ Met   ☐ Not met   Date: *March 20*

Long-term goal

☒ Met   ☐ Not met   Date: *May 21*

If you met your goal, what helped you to be successful?

I kept a journal about how I felt each day. I made stars on the pages whenever I felt either anxious or sad. I usually felt most anxious in social situations with my peers and I felt sad when I didn't do well in school or when my family was not getting along.

If you did not meet your goal, what things made it harder for you to be successful?

I did better doing physical activity than I did reaching out to my friend. I learned that I didn't always feel confident telling my friend how I was feeling.

Test Your Knowledge

Select the best answer for each question.

1. A mental _____ is an ongoing condition involving how a person thinks and manages their emotions.
   a. situation
   b. health
   c. disease
   d. disorder

2. A person's mental health might be influenced by
   a. a traumatic brain injury
   b. family history or genetics
   c. environment and experiences
   d. all of the above

3. A negative view of someone because of a characteristic or trait they have is called a
   a. stigma
   b. trauma
   c. crime
   d. none of the above

4. Examples of anxiety disorders include
   a. panic attack
   b. depression
   c. schizophrenia
   d. personality disorders

5. Anxiety is an emotion that commonly includes
   a. sadness and hopelessness
   b. tension and worried thoughts
   c. confusion and loss of memory
   d. debilitating fear that interferes with daily life
   e. all of the above

6. Having feelings of embarrassment, self-consciousness, and concern about being judged or viewed negatively by others is a common sign of
   a. phobias
   b. manic depressive disorder
   c. social anxiety disorder
   d. panic disorder

7. _____ is the sadness we feel when we lose someone we love.
   a. Depression
   b. Anxiety
   c. Grief
   d. Suicide

8. Being appreciative for large and small things in life is known as
   a. self-harm
   b. self-esteem
   c. gratitude
   d. empathy

9. Causes of mood disorders include all but which of the following?
   a. major life events like divorce or relocation
   b. genetics and family history
   c. high blood pressure
   d. imbalances in brain chemicals

10. Self-harm is
    a. a call for attention and fame
    b. a sign of being abused by others
    c. a way of distracting oneself and trying to cope
    d. none of the above

PROJECT-BASED LEARNING: Building Support Systems

What to Remember

Everyone needs help at some point in their life, especially when dealing with mental disorders like depression.

Who It Is For

The students in your school

Why It Is Important

Mental health is a serious issue that affects many people. Helping people recognize the signs of mental disorders and giving them the information and confidence they need to seek help could save lives. Ensuring that resources exist in a community and that people within that community are aware of them is critical to this process.

What to Do

Create an advocacy campaign to raise awareness of mental health resources at your school and propose additional resources as needed.

How to Do It

Step 1: Get into small groups according to your teacher's instructions. Research either a mental disorder featured in this chapter or another disorder that has been approved by your teacher. Your research should include a description of the disorder, the risk factors, the signs and symptoms, who is most likely to suffer from it, and how it is treated. Create a brochure about your assigned mental disorder. Make sure to include all of your research in the brochure as well as a contact (phone, text, or other) for where to get help.

Step 2: Interview teachers, counselors, and administrators at your school to find out what they know about the mental health disorder you researched. Find out what resources exist at your school that provide help and support to people with the condition. Focus on identifying gaps in services and strategizing ways those gaps might be closed.

Step 3: Hold an event during Mental Health Awareness Month (May) to share your research and resources. As part of your efforts, schedule a meeting with school personnel to share your vision for how both mental health awareness and services could be improved at your school.

CROSS-CURRICULAR CONNECTIONS: Social Studies

Research the history of either depression or anxiety in the United States. Write a report that indicates important dates and describes changes in how we understand and treat the disorder you selected.

Relationships and Social Health

LESSON 9.1   Relationships and Communication Skills
LESSON 9.2   Family Relationships
LESSON 9.3   Friendships
LESSON 9.4   Dating Relationships

Understanding My Health

Is My Relationship Healthy or Unhealthy?

Think about a family member, a friend, or a dating partner. Answer *yes* or *no* to each of the following statements. If you have more *yes* answers than *no*, you seem to have a healthy relationship with that person—keep it up!

If you have more *no* answers than *yes* or you have an even number of *no* and *yes* answers, you may have an unhealthy relationship with the person you chose. Keep this self-assessment in mind as you read the chapter and think about some changes you may need to make.

	Yes	No
I can be honest with this person.		
I can easily talk to this person about things I need to.		
I like the fact that decisions in our relationship are made by both of us.		
I rarely (less than half of the time we are together) fight or argue with this person.		
I respect their personal boundaries, and they respect mine.		
I rarely (less than half of the time we are together) feel pressured to do things I don't want to do.		
I think it is important to hang out with friends without this person sometimes.		
I like to do many of the same things they like to do.		
I have not changed who I am, what my goals are, or what I believe in for this person.		
Most (over half) of my close friends like this person.		

My score for Is My Relationship Healthy or Unhealthy? = _____ (total number of *yes* answers)

Healthy relationships are positive connections you have with people every day. You have different kinds of relationships with the different people in your life, and each of those relationships is different in what you talk about and do together. The key to all your relationships is communication. For your communication to be effective, you must be able to both talk and listen well. In this chapter, you will learn more about family, friendship, and romantic partners, including how texting and social media may be a part of your relationships and how they can have both a positive and a negative impact.

LESSON 9.1
Relationships and Communication Skills

Terms to Learn
active listening
aggressive communication
assertive communication
communication
healthy relationships
nonverbal communication
passive communication
passive-aggressive communication
relationships
social health
unhealthy relationship
verbal communication

The Big Picture
You have many different types of relationships and connections with the different people in your life. Some of your relationships are healthy and others are unhealthy. Knowing which relationships are unhealthy will help you to be assertive and stand up for yourself and for others who need your support. Being able to communicate in person and through text messages and social media your needs from the healthy relationships in your life will help you continue to lead a positive, happy life.

Learning Targets
- Evaluate similarities and differences between verbal and nonverbal communication.
- Compare and contrast characteristics of healthy and unhealthy relationships.
- Evaluate your communication style using the four communication styles described.
- Demonstrate how to use an *I* message and active listening properly.
- Analyze how a text message or a message on social media could be interpreted in two different ways.

Write About It
Describe a text message, social media post, or conversation that was taken out of context from how you intended.

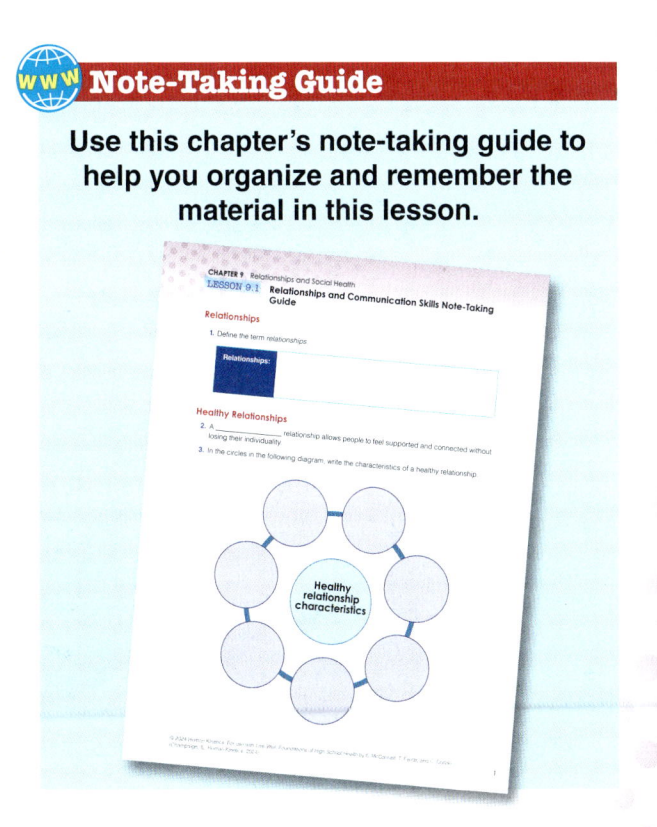

Note-Taking Guide

Use this chapter's note-taking guide to help you organize and remember the material in this lesson.

LESSON 9.1   Relationships and Social Health

Olivia and Tatum enjoy spending time together and often go out for coffee together on Saturdays. Each Saturday, they tend to have the same conversation about where to go for coffee. Olivia and Tatum have three spots they both like, but neither of them is good at making a decision. Their reasoning for this is they want the other person to choose in an attempt to make them happy. What Olivia and Tatum don't realize is that neither of them are happy, and their Saturday time together is beginning to be something they both want to avoid rather than do. Tatum just sent a text message to Olivia asking where she wants to meet for coffee tomorrow. What should Olivia text back to Tatum?

Relationships

Relationships are connections between people. You can have different relationships with each person in your family. For instance, you might be very close to one sibling and are able to talk with them about anything, or you might have a sibling who you think is too irritating. At school, you might be very close to a few of your friends and do a lot together, or you might sit by a certain person in your math class and talk to them during math, yet never hang out together outside of class. You also have relationships with different adults in your life, such as your teachers, coaches, grandparents, family friends, and neighbors. You might really be able to talk with some of them while you never talk with others. Romantic relationships will differ depending on how old you are and how long you have been dating.

Healthy Relationships

Healthy relationships, regardless of whom they are with or how close or distant they are, allow people to feel supported and connected without losing their individuality. In addition to support, individuality, and connection, healthy relationships have other certain characteristics including mutual respect, trust, honesty, good communication, and empathy (see figure 9.1).

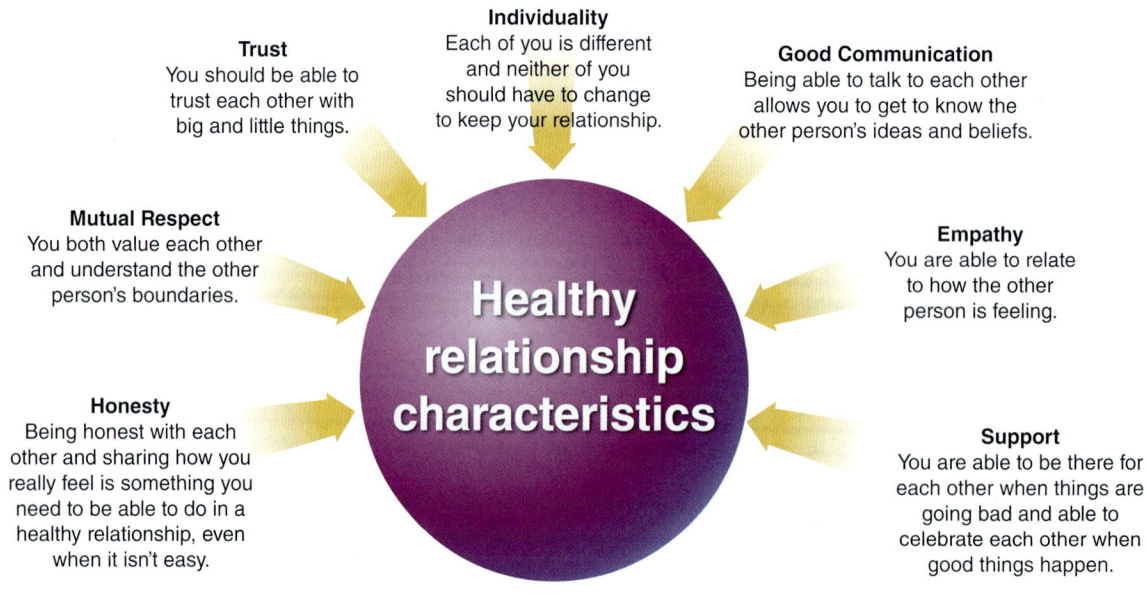

Healthy relationship characteristics

- **Trust**: You should be able to trust each other with big and little things.
- **Individuality**: Each of you is different and neither of you should have to change to keep your relationship.
- **Good Communication**: Being able to talk to each other allows you to get to know the other person's ideas and beliefs.
- **Mutual Respect**: You both value each other and understand the other person's boundaries.
- **Empathy**: You are able to relate to how the other person is feeling.
- **Honesty**: Being honest with each other and sharing how you really feel is something you need to be able to do in a healthy relationship, even when it isn't easy.
- **Support**: You are able to be there for each other when things are going bad and able to celebrate each other when good things happen.

Figure 9.1   Healthy relationship characteristics.

Social health is your ability to interact and form meaningful relationships with others. The better you can get along with someone, the healthier your relationship with that person will be. Sometimes you must take risks to get to know people by stepping outside your comfort zone and taking a chance that the people you want to get to know and create a relationship with will reciprocate. Humans are social beings and therefore require interactions with others to be healthy. We enjoy relationships with people who are fun to be around, make us happy and laugh, and are supportive of who we are individually. In relationships, we learn more about ourselves—for example, what makes us happy, sad, angry, or bored. We also learn how to communicate better, listen better, and work through conflict. Knowing how interactions with others affect us emotionally is important for helping us to discover and cultivate the many relationships in our lives.

Healthy relationships are also good for our physical health. They help you have less stress, have a healthier immune system, and help you heal faster from injuries or surgeries. Mental and emotional benefits of having healthy relationships include being happier, having less anxiety and depression, and sleeping better. The healthy relationships you have as a teen can influence lifelong friendships. Friends you have today may be kept throughout your life and you may also learn what qualities you want from a lifelong friend based on friendships you currently have.

Unhealthy Relationships

An **unhealthy relationship** leaves you feeling uncomfortable, sad, or afraid. It's hard to think that someone important in your life may not be treating you well, but it does happen. Everyone has arguments and gets mad at their friends and family members from time to time. This isn't an automatic sign of an unhealthy relationship; these happen in healthy relationships also. Arguments in healthy relationships happen occasionally, and the people involved are mutually respectful and work to resolve the conflict. Arguments in unhealthy relationships occur frequently, and resolution is rarely a possibility because at least one of the people involved does not care to come to an agreement.

Relationships should never include disrespect, controlling behavior, dishonesty, lack of communication, and constant fighting (see figure 9.2). Sometimes it is difficult to recognize the signs of an unhealthy relationship, especially if you are in one. Making excuses for the other person is often the most telling sign of an unhealthy relationship. There is never a reason or an excuse for hurting someone you supposedly care about regardless of whether it is mentally, physically, or emotionally hurtful. Unhealthy relationships have negative effects on a person's health including increased stress levels, difficulty sleeping, loss of confidence, and anxiety or depression.

LESSON 9.1   Relationships and Social Health

Dishonesty
Keep information from each other.

Disrespect
Can include name calling and constant criticism of your ideas and decisions.

Lacking Communication
Not being able to talk about important things with the person or there may be a lot of misunderstandings that never get worked out.

Unhealthy relationship characteristics

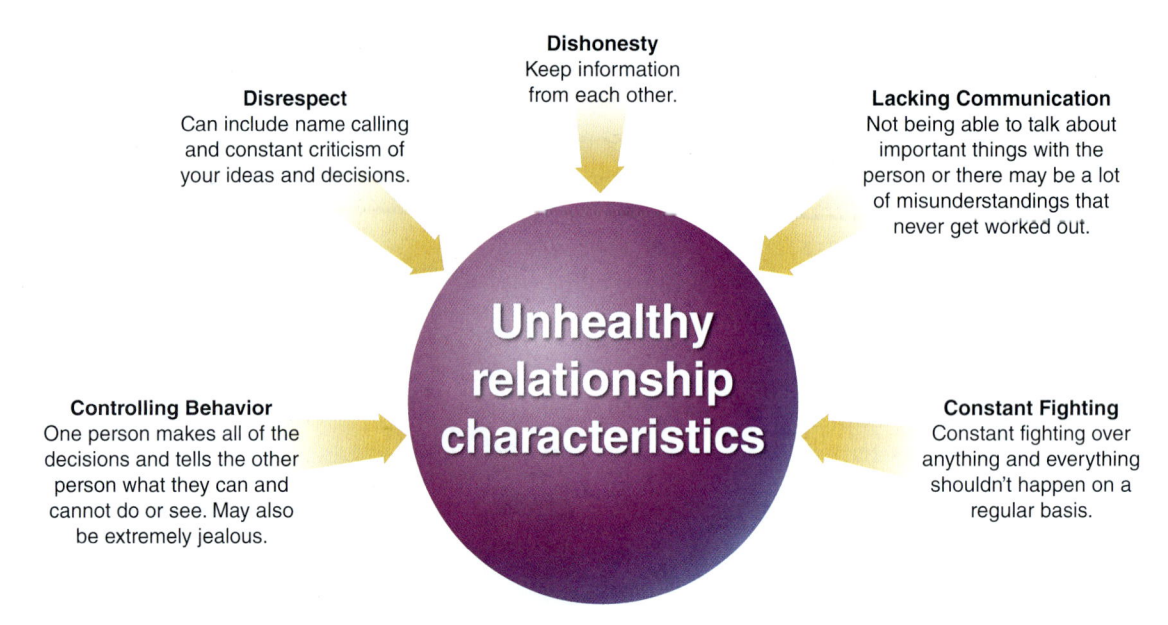

Controlling Behavior
One person makes all of the decisions and tells the other person what they can and cannot do or see. May also be extremely jealous.

Constant Fighting
Constant fighting over anything and everything shouldn't happen on a regular basis.

Figure 9.2 Unhealthy relationship characteristics.

Communication Is a Two-Way Street

Whether you are hanging out with your family, friends, or dating partner, being able to communicate and share your feelings with them is the key to any relationship. **Communication** involves the exchange of information (thoughts, feelings, beliefs, etc.) between two or more people. In healthy relationships, effective communication is two-fold: You must be able to both talk and listen. Good communication involves verbal and nonverbal communication and active listening.

Verbal and Nonverbal Communication

Verbal communication is the spoken or written use of words to express the information you are sharing. In **nonverbal communication**, your body language expresses the information. Body language includes facial expressions, hand gestures, tone of voice, and how loud or soft your voice is. A person's facial expression or hand gesture can sometimes be more expressive than words alone. Sometimes verbal and nonverbal communication are used together. It is important to pay attention to your nonverbal communication because it may be giving a different message than you intend. If you tell someone you are really interested in what they are saying yet you are looking at your phone and not at them, you are sending a mixed message. In that situation, most people will stop talking or cut their story short because it is clear you aren't interested even though you said you were.

Active Listening

Active listening involves giving your full attention to the speaker and actively showing verbal and nonverbal signs you are listening. You can show your interest verbally by making comments such as "yes, mmm hmm, go on" or by asking questions or paraphrasing what you have heard. You can show your interest nonverbally with such actions as making eye contact, having good posture, nodding your head, and smiling. Your nonverbal communication will make it clear whether you are really listening or not.

I Messages

I messages help express how you are feeling and what you need. They don't point blame at anyone, unlike *you* statements, which often result in a defensive or argumentative response. *I* messages are an excellent way to show empathy because they let you express your understanding of how someone else is feeling.

An *I* message has four parts:

1. "I feel . . ." (taking responsibility for your own feelings)
2. "when you . . ." (stating the behavior that is a problem)
3. "because . . ." (what it is about the behavior or its consequences that you don't like)
4. "I would really like it if . . ." (offering a preferred alternative or a compromise)

An *I* message might sound like this:

- *I feel* like you don't really care about my day *when you* don't let me finish my story *because* you start telling me what I should do. *I would really like it if* you let me finish because sometimes, I don't need you to tell me what to do; I just want to vent about my day.

A response to an *I* message uses active listening, which also has four parts:

1. "You sound . . ."
2. "that / because . . ."
3. "Next time I will . . ."
4. "and I . . ."

For example, a response to an *I* message could be as follows:

- *You sound* frustrated *that* I don't let you finish your story about your day. *Next time I will* wait until you are done with your story before talking, *and I* am sorry for doing that.

Communicating and listening effectively, both verbally and nonverbally, has an impact on the person you are speaking and listening to. How you communicate and listen to your friends, family, teachers, and others shows whether your relationship is healthy or unhealthy. Paying attention to others and caring about what they have to share are important characteristics of a healthy relationship.

Communication Styles

Communication styles are how you interact and exchange information with others. The four communication styles people use are passive, aggressive, passive-aggressive, and assertive (see figure 9.3).

- *Passive communication.* People who tend to avoid expressing their opinions or feelings use **passive communication**. They rarely refuse when asked to do something and often don't make eye contact when speaking or being spoken to. They are easy to get along with because they try to avoid confrontation and just follow what others are doing. They often have their feelings hurt and don't speak up for themselves when they really need to.

- *Aggressive communication.* People who express their feelings and opinions in an intimidating manner without regard to how it makes others feel use **aggressive communication**. These types of communicators usually speak loudly, issue commands rather than ask people to do things, ask questions rudely, and often fail to listen to others.

- *Passive-aggressive communication.* People who appear to be passive yet will act out in indirect ways such as spreading rumors or giving people the silent treatment rather than confronting the person use **passive-aggressive communication**. These types of communicators tend to build up resentment that leads to negative attitudes, causing others to give in to them rather than confront them often due to fear of retaliation.

- *Assertive communication.* People who express their own needs, feelings, and goals while being respectful of others use **assertive communication**. These types of communicators often use *I* messages and take responsibility for their feelings without blaming anyone else. They are able to stay calm, use active listening skills, and ask questions to get the other person's input and to hear their feelings and needs. Assertive communication is the most effective form of communication.

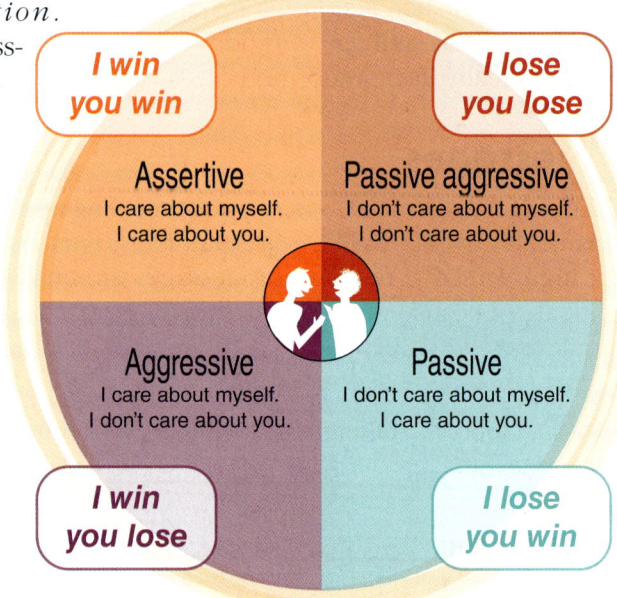

Figure 9.3 The four communication styles.

HEALTHY LIVING TIP

When posting on any type of social media, consider asking yourself two questions: *If I read this post about myself, how would I feel?* If you would be upset or embarrassed by it, then don't post it. *What would an adult I care about think about my post?* If you think they would be disappointed or angry at you, then don't post it.

Communicating Through Text Messages and Social Media

Today's technology is great for short messages and posting things you want to share with everyone, but it doesn't always convey your message the way you intended it. When you text someone or post something on social media, much of the information is shared through emojis, GIFs, and texting language such as LOL, IDK, and IMO. This mixture of nonverbal emojis and verbal texting language can be misinterpreted. Pictures posted on social media can also tell a different story than what really happened or what you told others you were doing. Snapchat posts might seem perfectly harmless since they only appear for a short amount of time before disappearing, but all it takes is one person's screenshot, and that picture or post you wrote lives on forever. People on the receiving end of your social media and texts aren't privy to seeing all of your nonverbal language or hearing your tone of voice or the communication style you are using. To make sure there's no room for misinterpretation, which can be hurtful not only to others but also yourself down the road, make sure to write clearly and think carefully how your writing will be perceived before you post and send messages.

Skill-Building Challenge

Communicating Using *I* Messages and Active Listening Skills

Isla and Kay have been best friends since grade school. Isla decided to get a job after school to earn money for a car. Kay's guardian says Kay needs to focus on her schoolwork more, so Kay can't get a job. Kay is happy Isla is making money to buy a car, but it also means they don't get to hang out much anymore. Isla works so much that she often has to finish her homework before school or at lunch, so Kay can't even talk with her then either. Kay is having some problems at home and really wants to talk with Isla, but every time she has tried, Isla tells her she doesn't have time.

1. Write an *I* message explaining how Kay feels, making sure to use the four parts:
    a. "I feel . . ." (taking responsibility for your own feelings)
    b. "when you . . ." (stating the behavior that is a problem)
    c. "because . . ." (what it is about the behavior or its consequences that you don't like)
    d. "I would really like it if . . ." (offering a preferred alternative or compromise)

2. Write a response Isla could make to Kay's *I* message, using active listening and making sure to include the four parts:
    a. "You sound . . ."
    b. "that / because . . ."
    c. "Next time I will . . ."
    d. "and I . . ."

Act out your *I* message and active listening response with a partner from class. Make sure you effectively use verbal and nonverbal communication.

LESSON 9.1   Relationships and Social Health

Healthy Living Skills

This lesson focused on healthy communication. Here are some more ways you can develop healthy living skills related to this lesson.

ADVOCATING FOR GOOD HEALTH

A healthy school environment requires that the students have healthy relationships with each other. Create a flyer, web page, poster, or other resource that advocates for healthy relationships in your school. Be sure to use your advocacy to educate people about healthy relationships and to give them tips on strategies for making and keeping healthy relationships. Use the Advocacy Skill Cues to put your plan into action using the following questions.

- What do you want to change?
- Are there other schools that have done something similar? What do healthy relationships in a school look like?
- Whom are you trying to reach with your advocacy?
- What is your message?
- If you were able to distribute your materials, do you think your advocacy campaign worked? Why or why not?

PRACTICING HEALTHY BEHAVIORS

Lately you have started using more abbreviations in your text messages and emails. In the last three days, you've managed to get into three fights—one with your guardian and two with friends—because your abbreviations autocorrected to something different from what you were actually saying. You also realized that in an email you sent to your teacher, you used texting abbreviations *and* spelled some words wrong because you were in a hurry to send it and didn't read over it. You know you really need to pay more attention to what you are doing when you're texting and emailing so you don't offend people. You have already identified the behavior you need to change, now make a simple checklist for the next seven days to monitor your progress. At the end of each day, take three minutes and think about the texts and emails you sent that day and give yourself a checkmark for each time you used texting language, abbreviations, or misspelled words. Your goal by the end of the seven days is to have fewer checkmarks. If you don't text or email or if you do but don't use abbreviations, texting language, or misspell words, pay attention to messages and emails you get from people and see if you can help them to be more aware of what they are doing.

LESSON 9.1   Review: Relationships and Communication Skills

LESSON SUMMARY

- Characteristics of a healthy relationship include honesty, mutual respect, trust, individuality, good communication, empathy, and support.
- Physical benefits of healthy relationships include having less stress and having a healthier immune system; emotional benefits include being happier and having less anxiety and depression.
- Healthy relationships should consist of good communication and active listening skills.
- Characteristics of an unhealthy relationship include controlling behavior, disrespect, dishonesty, lack of communication, and constant fighting.

- Verbal communication uses words to express information, whereas nonverbal communication uses body language including facial expressions, hand gestures, tone of voice, and how loud or soft your voice is.
- People use four communication styles for how they interact and exchange information with others: passive, aggressive, passive-aggressive, and assertive communication.
- *I* messages consist of four parts and are used to express how you are feeling and what it is you need.
- The texting abbreviations and emojis you use may not mean the same to someone else as they do to you. If people don't understand your message, they may interpret it differently than you intended; such miscommunication can cause confusion and hurt feelings.

REVIEWING CONCEPTS AND VOCABULARY

1. _____ are connections between people.
2. Your ability to get along with people is an example of your _____ health.
3. When two people feel supported and connected with each other without losing their individuality, they are in a(n) _____.
4. When someone you care about leaves you feeling uncomfortable, sad, or afraid, you are in a(n) _____ relationship.
5. _____ involves the exchange of information (thoughts, feelings, beliefs, etc.) between two or more people.
6. _____ communication uses words to express information.
7. _____ communication uses your facial expressions, body language, hand gestures, tone of voice, and how loud or soft your voice is.
8. When you are giving your full attention to the speaker and actively giving verbal and nonverbal signs, you are practicing _____ listening.
9. People who don't like to express their feelings, who don't like to tell others no, and who don't make eye contact when speaking or being spoken to use _____ communication.
10. People who don't really care about other people's feelings are using _____ communication.
11. _____ communicators may act as if they agree with the person but then give the person the silent treatment or spread rumors behind the person's back.
12. _____ communicators often use *I* messages, taking responsibility for their feelings without blaming anyone else.

THINKING CRITICALLY

A friend wants to copy your homework but you don't want her to. Write a conversation between the two of you that is aggressive and then rewrite it in an assertive way.

TAKE IT HOME

Ask an adult family member or family friend how they communicated with their friends before there were cell phones and social media. Ask them how technology has affected their communication with their friends. Think about how you communicate with your friends compared to how your family member or friend did at your same age. Do you think communication with your friends would be better without smartphones and social media? Why or why not?

LESSON 9.2
Family Relationships

Terms to Learn
cultural norms
emotional awareness
emotional needs
family
mental needs
physical needs
sibling rivalry
social needs
social norm

The Big Picture
The word *family* has many different meanings because of the different types of family we have in our society. As you grow up, you realize each family member is expected to live by certain family, social, and cultural norms, and that some of them are easier to adhere to than others. You have a unique relationship with each member of your family that influences the interactions and conflicts within your relationships.

Learning Targets
- Describe five types of families in today's society.
- Distinguish three benefits of a healthy relationship with your parent or guardian.
- Examine your relationship with your siblings.
- Analyze two changes that occur within families and ways to adjust to them.

Write About It
If you have a sibling, do you think you have a healthy or an unhealthy relationship with them? Explain why. If you don't have a sibling, do you wish you did? Explain why you do or do not.

Note-Taking Guide
Use this chapter's note-taking guide to help you organize and remember the material in this lesson.

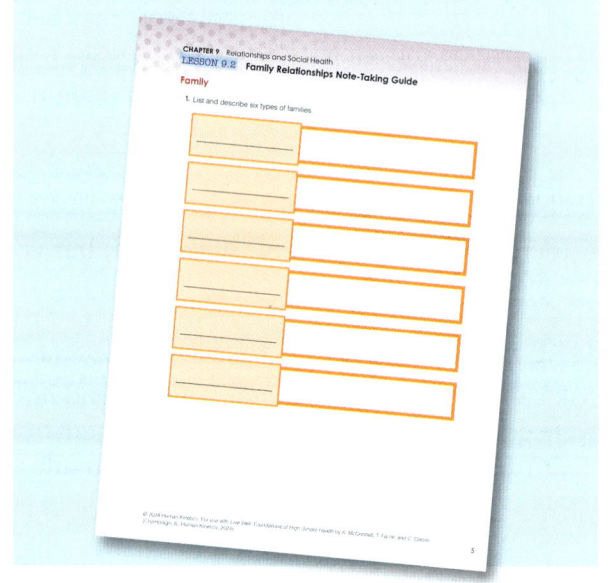

384

Family Relationships   LESSON 9.2

Gracie and Latisha are twins and come from a tight-knit family. Now in their senior year of high school, Gracie is an accomplished athlete, and Latisha is a talented actor. Two universities have offered them scholarships, but neither school seems the best fit. Gracie is set on attending a university in the Pacific Northwest, while Latisha wants to go to New York to further her studies in drama. To add to their dilemma, their parents are pushing for them to go to the same university to help make paying multiple tuitions and being able to visit easier and more affordable. The constant tension has turned what should be an exciting time for Gracie and Latisha into a really stressful situation, and it's begun to affect their relationships with not only their parents but also each other. What compromises could Gracie and Latisha make that would both alleviate their parents' concerns and also fulfill their own needs without too much sacrifice?

Family

Family comprises the people you are related to by blood, marriage, adoption, or other emotional and social ties. However, the term *family* is not limited to those with whom you live; it can also be used to describe a group of people you feel very connected to, such as a team you play on or a group you are a part of.

There are many different types of families.

- A nuclear family consists of two parents and their biological children.
- A single-parent family consists of one adult and at least one child.
- A multigenerational family consists of three or more generations living together.
- An extended family includes near relatives such as grandparents, aunts, or uncles in addition to the parents and children.
- An adoptive family includes adults and at least one child who was adopted.
- A foster family includes adults and at least one child who is living with the adults on a temporary basis.
- A never-married family consists of two adults who are not married but who live together and have at least one child.
- A blended family includes the children from a previous marriage of one or both spouses.
- A grandparents-as-parents family is one in which grandparents take over the primary role of raising a child or children.
- A childless family consists of two adults who do not have children.

Family Needs

Families work together to try to meet the physical, emotional, mental, and social needs of everyone in the family. **Physical needs** are met when families have shelter, food, clothing, and medical care. These are the basic things that every person needs to survive. Parents or guardians are usually the ones responsible for providing these basic needs. Children may help contribute by doing chores and possibly even getting a job if they are in high school or college. **Emotional needs** are met when family members have emotional security so they feel accepted, supported, and loved by their family. Attending events, spending time with you, helping to work through disappointments, encouraging you to be yourself, and just letting you know you are loved and valued are just some of the many ways emotional needs are met. **Mental needs** are supported when family members help you develop self-esteem and confidence in your abilities. Finally, **social needs** are met when family members can communicate with each other, get along, accept responsibility, and respect each other's rights and individuality.

You began learning about physical, emotional, mental, and social needs when you were a baby. As you grew up, some responsibilities were shifted from family members to you; for example, helping with chores to meet not only your own physical needs but those of other family members as well. Your emotional, mental, and social needs have all been nurtured and developed by family members and other significant people helping you to be more confident and resilient as you try new activities, challenge yourself in different classes and projects, and open yourself up to meeting new people and making new friends. Self-esteem and confidence can be difficult at any age, but you have been nurtured to challenge yourself and are mentally prepared for whatever happens.

Social Norms

A **social norm** is a rule that guides your behavior as a member of society or of a specific group. Your family provided you with your first set of norms when you were learning the difference between acceptable and unacceptable behaviors in your family. Your family may also have cultural norms that influence how you live and act. **Cultural norms** are the standards you live by; they are the shared expectations and rules that guide the behavior of people within a specific culture.

When you started school, you had to learn new norms. In elementary school, you learned to follow directions and be respectful to your teacher, who was a new authority figure; you may also have learned how to share, work together, and wait your turn. In middle school, you also learned new norms, such as getting to class before the bell rings. You had different teachers for multiple classes; these teachers each had their own set of norms they expected you to follow in their class. Now in high school there may be new clubs, groups, and teams to be a part of with possibly new leadership roles. You may also be working at a job that may have its own set of social and cultural norms you will have to adapt to in order to meet the expectations of employment.

Social norms dictate people's behavior—most people do what's expected of them to avoid potential embarrassment or being labeled an outcast. It's important, however, to be aware of problems that stem from norms and to understand that following precedent, or what others have done before you, can be limiting and potentially oppressive.

Family Roles

The traditional nuclear family model, where one parent (typically male) is the single provider while the other parent (typically female) is the nurturer who rears the children and organizes the family has evolved. In many present-day families, both parents share these responsibilities. Often the father stays at home when children get sick, while the mother goes to work. In single-parent or multigenerational households, all the adults in the family may be out in the workforce.

Regardless of gender, guardians in all types of families now share the family responsibilities and work together to clean the house, mow the lawn, and care for the children. Family roles are changing alongside the changing norms of society.

Guardian Relationships

Your relationship with the guardian in your life is one of the most important relationships you can have and often lasts well into adulthood. At your current age, you may notice changes occurring in your relationship with your guardian. Right now, you're at that in-between stage—no longer a child, you are more self-sufficient, yet you aren't quite ready to make all of your own decisions without guidance from your family.

This is a time when conflicts between you and your guardian may arise, primarily because you want more independence from your family to make your own decisions. Independence can be difficult for your guardian to give; they want you to make your own choices, but they also want to make sure those choices are safe. Your guardian may allow you to make some choices on your own, while other choices will be up for debate. You will both need to compromise. See table 9.1 for common problems, solutions, and benefits of guardian relationships.

TABLE 9.1 Common Problems, Solutions, and Benefits of Relationships Between Teens and Guardians

Problems	Solutions	Benefits
Arguing more than usual	Talk to your guardian on a daily basis, even if it's just about random things that happened at school. Your guardian really does want to know what you are doing.	You feel open and comfortable talking about difficult subjects.
Feeling like your guardian isn't listening to you	Spend time with your family because they still want to be part of your life.	You develop independence, confidence, optimism, and identity from having the support of your family.
Having friends your guardian may think are negative influences	Let your guardian know the truth about what you will be doing, even if you think they might tell you that you can't go. Being honest up front is better than lying to them at any time.	You are overall happier and healthier because your healthy relationship acts as a buffer against negative influences. It reduces risky teen behavior such as alcohol and other drug use.
Thinking certain restrictions are unfair, such as curfew or cell phone use	If you are going to disagree with your guardian about something, do so calmly and explain why you disagree. Know what you want from the conversation before you start it.	You will have a sense of consistency and predictability knowing the rules and expectations of your behavior.

Sibling Relationships

A healthy and positive relationship with a sibling increases your ability to make and maintain friendships, to get along with people from different backgrounds, and to comfort and help others. It also increases your **emotional awareness**, which is the ability to recognize and make sense of both your own and others' emotions. Being emotionally aware and having empathy for your sibling are similar; both are about the ability to understand the emotions of someone else. Siblings provide emotional, social, and psychological support to each other.

The quality of your sibling relationships is one of the most important predictors of mental health in older adults. People who have healthy sibling relationships are known to have higher life satisfaction and lower rates of depression later in life. Your relationship with your sibling is often one of the longest relationships you will ever have. Your experience with your sibling is completely authentic because you usually grow up in the same environment, have the same parents, and have common memories and similar experiences. Your sibling is a part of who you are with a shared history that makes your relationship unique and very valuable.

Sibling relationships can also be difficult, and you may not always get along, which is actually quite normal. Just as in any relationship, you have to work on having a healthy relationship with your sibling because there will be bad times as well as good times. Some reasons you may not get along with your sibling include the following:

- You have different personalities.
- There may be an age difference.
- You enjoy different activities.
- You might be competing against each other. The competition between siblings is known as **sibling rivalry**, which can lead to anger or jealousy between siblings.

You might not get along with your sibling at this point in your life, but keep working on your relationship with them because they may turn out to be one of your very closest friends.

HEALTHY LIVING TIP
Be kind to or compliment a family member with whom you have had conflict. Apologize by explaining how you want to work on building a healthy relationship.

Changes to the Family

Just as you have changed over the years, your family structure may undergo periodic transitions, and such changes affect everyone in the family in some way. If guardians decide to get a divorce, a restructuring may occur in which children may need to live primarily with one parent. A single guardian may decide to get married or remarry, so you become part of a blended family. A blended family consists of a parent, a step-parent, and the child or children of one or both parents. Regardless of their nature, these changes will affect you—some more positively than negatively and vice versa.

Family situations may also change. At times, this may be more challenging to work through than changes to the family structure. Here are some situations that families may encounter.

- *Moving*. This can be stressful regardless of the distance you move. Sometimes you may also have to change schools and will need to make new friends, which can be both sad and exciting. Moving can be part of something positive, such as a promotion for your guardian. Even though it's a positive situation, it can still be difficult if you have to physically leave friends.
- *Financial problems*. Unexpected bills can make other financial problems even worse. Sometimes a guardian may lose a job, and the whole family must cut back their spending; in some instances, others in the family may need to get jobs if they are able.
- *Illness and disability*. A family member may be diagnosed with a serious illness or

LESSON 9.2   Relationships and Social Health

disability. Other family members may need to take on a new role as caregiver and other, new household responsibilities.

• *Death of a family member.* A family member may pass away suddenly and unexpectedly or due to an ongoing or terminal illness. Family members may need to take on new responsibilities due to the death. A family member who had been serving as a caregiver may experience their diminished role and responsibility equally as stressful as a family member with sudden new responsibilities.

• *Substance use disorder.* A family member may have a substance use problem involving alcohol or other drugs. The other family members may feel added stress of taking care of the person.

Remember that families can be difficult at times and not everyone will always get along. Keep working on communicating how you feel and what you need from your family members. While your relationship will change with everyone in your family at different times, it is important to keep working on getting along with your family to get through the challenging times.

Career Connection

MARRIAGE AND FAMILY THERAPIST

A licensed marriage and family therapist (LMFT) counsels people who are young, old, dating, engaged, or married or who want to improve their relationship. A couple seeking counseling may have a specific problem they want to work on or may be experiencing a time of increased stress or transition; perhaps they have financial problems, health issues, or parenting conflicts. The LMFT helps them find solutions and make changes.

This career can be emotionally difficult and stressful because of the personal investment in the clients' lives. To become an LMFT, you will need to earn a master's degree, complete a set amount of experience hours, as established by each state, working as a therapist intern, take and pass a licensing exam, and continue with education as part of the licensure renewal process.

Skill-Building Challenge

Influences on Your Perceptions of Family Roles

Family roles are the positions each family member holds in the household. It involves how we are expected to conduct ourselves within the family. Spend some time thinking about the following questions and write a brief response to each. When you have finished, share your answers with a partner. Remember to be respectful of your partner's opinions.

1. How does your culture influence your perceptions of family roles?
    a. Who or what is the greatest influence from your culture?
    b. Is the influence valid, or is it time for change? (With culture, different generations may not change with the times, so generational cultural influence is challenged with regard to whether it is still a valid response in today's society.)
    c. Do you agree with the influence your culture has on people's perceptions of family roles?

2. How does media influence your perceptions of family roles?
    a. Who or what is the greatest influence from the media on your perception of family roles?
    b. Is the media influence valid? Does it represent the current society you live in, or is it time for change?
    c. Do you agree with the influence media have on people's perceptions of family roles?

3. How do important people in your life influence your perceptions of family roles?
    a. Of the important people in your life, who has the greatest influence?
    b. Do you agree with the influence this person has on people's perceptions of family roles?

Healthy Living Skills

This lesson focused on analyzing influences. Here are some more ways you can develop healthy living skills related to this lesson.

ACCESSING INFORMATION

Many cultures have different traditions, customs, and expectations when it comes to family roles. Using the Accessing Valid and Reliable Information Skill Cues, find information about family roles for two other cultures different from your own.

HEALTHY COMMUNICATION

Getting along with family can be difficult, and conflict is inevitable, especially with siblings. Think of a situation in which you and a sibling had an argument. If you don't have siblings or you do not argue with your sibling, choose a family member or close friend with whom you have had an argument. Use the Communication Skill Cues to write about how you could resolve your conflict if that same argument happened again. Make sure to include I messages and active listening as a part of your communication skill cues.

LESSON 9.2   Relationships and Social Health

LESSON 9.2 Review: Family Relationships

LESSON SUMMARY

- There are many different types of families: nuclear, blended, never married, grandparents as parents, childless, single parent, multigenerational, extended, adoptive, and foster. All have similarities and differences that make each family type unique.
- Having a healthy relationship with your guardian results in many benefits such as being able to talk to your guardian openly and honestly about difficult subjects, having a buffer against negative influences, and having a sense of consistency and predictability because you know the rules and expectations of your behavior.
- Having a positive relationship with your siblings increases your ability to make and maintain friendships and also increases your emotional awareness.
- Several changes can occur within a family that everyone must learn to adjust to. Families may have to move because a guardian's job changes, or an illness in the family may require family members to help take care of the person or take on other household responsibilities.

REVIEWING CONCEPTS AND VOCABULARY

1. _____ is less about who you are related to or live with and more about the people whom you include and consider significant to you.
2. Shelter, food, clothing, and medical care are basic needs everyone needs to survive and are known as _____ needs.
3. _____ needs are met when family members feel accepted, supported, and loved by their family.
4. _____ needs are supported when family members help you develop self-esteem and confidence in your abilities.
5. When families have good communication, get along, and respect each other's rights and individuality, a person's _____ needs are met.
6. A(n) _____ is a rule that guides your behavior as a member of society or of a specific group.
7. Competition between siblings is referred to as _____.
8. Emotional _____ is the ability to recognize and make sense of your own emotions and those of others.

THINKING CRITICALLY

Write a paragraph that explains your family structure. Identify how each family member is connected to you (what relationship you have) and how family roles influence your daily life.

TAKE IT HOME

Talk to an adult family member about how when they were growing up, their family may have encountered some of the changes discussed in this lesson or other changes not discussed here. Ask how they adjusted to the changes and what they would do differently if they went through them again. If you have experienced any of the changes to the family in this lesson, discuss with the family member what your experience was like and what you would do differently, if anything.

LESSON 9.3
Friendships

Terms to Learn
acquaintance
drama
emotional connection
gossip
jealousy
virtual friend

The Big Picture
Your friends play an important part in your life during your high school years. Your close friends are the ones who influence you the most, although you may also be influenced by your acquaintances, casual friends, and even your virtual friends. Friendships are just like your family in that there will be times when you don't get along. Three causes of problems in friendships are social media, jealousy, and drama.

Learning Targets
- Differentiate your friends into the four types of friends discussed in the lesson.
- Explain the four qualities a close friend needs to have.
- Analyze how social media, jealousy, and drama can cause problems in a friendship.
- Create a plan to work on a quality you need to improve on to be a better friend.
- Use healthy ways to express love in a friendship.

Write About It
High school is a time when your friends may be changing depending on the classes you are in and the activities you are involved in. Think about the qualities you want in a friend and write those down. Do your current friends have the qualities you want them to?

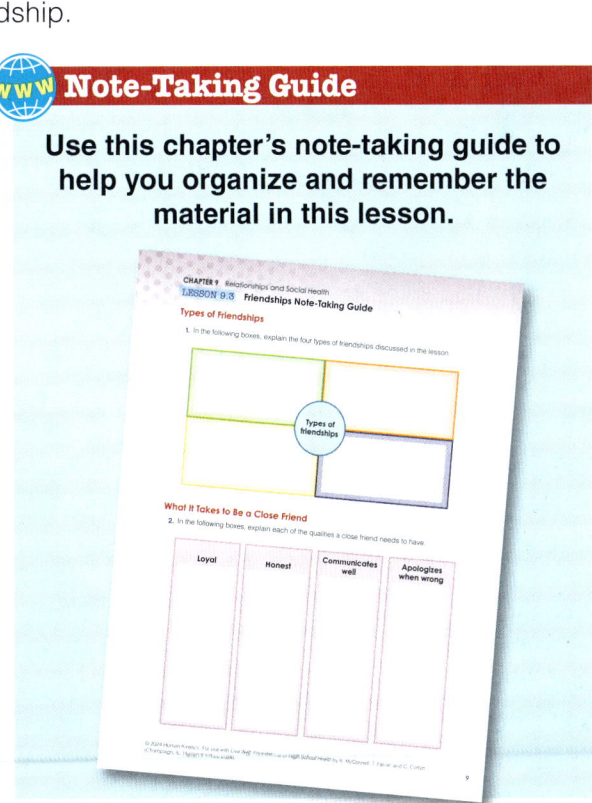

Note-Taking Guide
Use this chapter's note-taking guide to help you organize and remember the material in this lesson.

393

LESSON 9.3 Relationships and Social Health

Malia and Jerome are virtual friends and only know each other through Snapchat and TikTok. They snap each other multiple times during the day to share how their day is going and often share TikTok videos with each other. One day, Malia shares a TikTok video Jerome made for her on her social media. Many people are commenting and making fun of Jerome for his video. He's embarrassed—it was just supposed to be viewed by Malia. What should Jerome do?

Types of Friendships

Your relationships with friends become very important during adolescence. Your friends may begin to influence the choices you make. Your friendships can be a support for you and can help you feel like you belong and are part of something special. An important part of any friendship is the **emotional connection** it brings for you to be able to trust and respect the person and share anything with them. The stronger an emotional connection, the closer you and your friend will be.

Positive friendships can help you learn to cooperate with others, communicate well, and resolve conflicts. With positive friendships, you learn more about being caring and honest with your friends and whom you can talk with about problems. Having friends you can talk to when things are difficult and feeling close to your friends can help you recover more quickly from problems and challenges. By now, you have probably realized you have different types of friends (see figure 9.4).

Acquaintances

Some people in your life are more like acquaintances than true friends. An **acquaintance** is a person you barely know—for example, it may be someone you talk to only in health class. You and your acquaintances don't usually have the same friends, don't participate in the same activities, and don't spend any time outside of class together unless you need to work on a project together.

Casual Friends

A casual friend is someone you have spent time with and with whom you have activities or interests in common. You may hang out together at different times and even have some friends in common, yet you stay casual friends because you don't have an emotional connection. You don't mind hanging out with them especially when you are in a group with other friends, but that's as far as it goes.

Close friends
These are the people you spend your time with and share everything with—good and bad.

Casual friends
You have activities or friends in common but don't have an emotional connection.

Virtual friends
You only know these people virtually through social media or gaming.

Acquaintances
You don't know them well and only talk to them in the class you have together.

Figure 9.4 The four types of friendships.

Close Friends

Close friends are the people with whom you have an emotional connection and will share anything. You spend time with each other, are supportive of each other, have a history of shared experiences together, and see each other on your best and worst days and are there for each other no matter what.

Virtual Friends

A **virtual friend** is someone you know only online because you met them virtually, through social media or gaming. You've probably acquired quite a number of virtual friends, so there is always someone to chat with; play games with and against; or like your pictures, videos, comments, and so on.

What It Takes to Be a Close Friend

Developing a healthy friendship and being a close friend take a lot of work. To develop a close friendship, you need to make time for each other and spend time together in person. Texting each other is a great way to communicate when you're not together, but when you *are* together, you should be talking to each other, not texting other people or checking your social media. A close friend is there for you when you need them, in good times and in bad. They are also there for little things such as helping with homework. Don't take friends for granted—to keep your friendships strong, it takes ongoing effort. Figure 9.5 shows four of the qualities close friends should have.

LESSON 9.3 Relationships and Social Health

Loyal
They will be your friend even when you aren't being a very good friend back.

Apologetic
While it isn't always easy to apologize when you have done something wrong, it is very important.

Honest
They will tell you what you need to hear, even if you don't really want to hear it.

Qualities of close friends

You never want to hurt your friend's feelings, so realizing when you do hurt their feelings and being able to say you are sorry and mean it by making changes to your actions will mean a lot to them.

Your close friends are the people who can tell you the truth about something you did or how you acted. While you may not like what they have to say, you know they are being honest with you and trying to help you see what you did.

Communicates well
Being able to communicate easily with your close friend is also very important. As you have learned already about relationships, communication is the key. If you can talk to your close friend honestly and be a great listener, that will really help to keep your friendship strong.

Figure 9.5 The four qualities close friends should have.

When Friendships Have Problems

It is natural for close friends to experience problems with each other from time to time. This doesn't mean you are no longer close friends, but if you want to stay close friends, you need to be proactive in working through issues that crop up. Friendships change over time as people change. Many factors, such as no longer being involved in the same activities, attending different schools, and moving away, may change or even end friendships.

Sometimes, it is simply a matter of no longer wanting to be friends with someone from your past due to incompatibility. Perhaps your interests and activities have diverged, or one or both of you have become close friends with other people. There is often no instance that definitively pinpoints when friendships drift apart. However, when specific reasons cause people to stop being friends, the problems often arise from social media, jealousy, and drama.

Social Media

Social media offers plenty of opportunities for problems to arise in friendships. When your friends post pictures of a party or social gathering you weren't invited to, it can be hurtful especially if you didn't know about it prior to the posts. Someone who publicly airs out a disagreement or fight they had with you without getting your consent is not being a good friend. Genuine friends call or have an in-person conversation with you to work out the issue; they don't post it online for everyone to see and be able to give their opinion of what should happen. Don't resort to texting your friend as an attempt to fix problems; you never know when your text will be taken the wrong way and make things even worse.

Jealousy

Jealousy can happen with different types of friends you have, including your best friends. **Jealousy** is a strong negative emotion that usually occurs when a person perceives a threat to a valued relationship from a third person. Jealousy can happen between friends, siblings, coworkers, and dating partners. When people experience jealousy, a common yet unhelpful reaction they have is to compare themselves to the person they feel jealous toward. There is nothing wrong with feeling a little jealousy from time to time—it's a natural human emotion. Just make sure your behavior isn't intentionally hurtful to the person you are jealous of, especially if they are a close friend. Think back to what you just read about what it takes to be a close friend: One of the qualities is honesty. Be honest with your friend and let them know you are jealous; it's important you share your feelings with them.

Drama

Drama involves gossiping about another person, and often the gossip is untruthful. When teens **gossip** or spread rumors, they share deeply personal details of someone's life without the person's permission. Gossip usually causes pain and embarrassment for the person being gossiped about. People tend to gossip or spread rumors to make themselves feel superior, feel accepted by their group of friends, get attention, gain power in the group, or to get revenge on someone they may be jealous of.

Healthy Ways to Express Love in a Friendship

High school friendships tend to have more emotional attachment because you are relying more on your friends for advice and emotional support than in previous years. Your friends are the people you want to spend time with and share experiences with. Having close friends or best friends is a special kind of love. The word *love* can mean many different things, and in a friendship, it means you really care about the person. You can show a friend how much you love them in simple ways.

HEALTHY LIVING TIP

If you hear someone gossiping about another person, stop them and tell them you don't want to hear it or walk away. Gossip just spreads information that usually isn't completely true and can end up ruining people's reputations.

LESSON 9.3   Relationships and Social Health

- Be there for them when they need you.
- Tell them how much they mean to you.
- Show them social media love by posting a picture or a memory the two of you have.
- Celebrate their accomplishments by sending a handwritten card or a gift.
- Do something you've always talked about doing but never have.
- Be a loyal and caring friend every day. Make sure they know they can count on you through good times and bad.

Skill-Building Challenge

Deciding to End a Friendship

Aliya and Rahmi have been friends their entire lives. Now that they are in high school, they don't see each other as much and have both made some new friends. Aliya likes to play sports and hang out with her other friends. Rahmi is more of a risk taker and rule breaker. Last week, Rahmi asked Aliya if she wanted to hang out with her. When Aliya met up with Rahmi after school, there were other people around that Aliya knew were often in trouble at school. Aliya was uncomfortable with their behavior, especially when a couple of them began vaping. Later that night, Aliya realized that she and Rahmi no longer have anything in common and that their values are completely different. Aliya isn't sure she wants to be friends with Rahmi anymore. What do you think Aliya should do? Answer the following questions as you work through your decision.

1. What is the problem with this relationship?
2. What are Aliya's options?
3. What are the consequences of each option Aliya has?
4. What decision do you think Aliya should make?
5. Why is this the best decision?

Healthy Living Skills

This lesson focused on decision making. Here are some more ways you can develop healthy living skills related to this lesson.

PRACTICING HEALTHY BEHAVIORS

To be a close friend, you need to be loyal, honest, able to communicate well, and able to apologize when you are wrong. Choose one of those four qualities you think you need to work on to be a better friend. Use the Practicing Healthy Behaviors Skill Cues to write out what you will do to be a better friend and then keep track of it to make sure you are making the change.

ANALYZING INFLUENCES

What do you think influences the social media posts you make? Make a list of everything that might influence what you and others put out on social media. For each influence, decide if you think it is positive, negative, or both. For each negative influence you list, explain how you might turn it into a positive influence or how you might eliminate that influence altogether.

LESSON 9.3 Review: Friendships

LESSON SUMMARY

- There are four specific types of friends you may have throughout your life: acquaintances, casual friends, close friends, and virtual friends.
- Social media can cause friends to feel left out of fun activities or betrayed if a friend posts something bad about them or something that was meant to be private.
- Jealousy is a strong emotion that can cause friends to say and do hurtful things.
- Gossiping about someone causes drama, which can lead to friends being embarrassed and left out.
- Qualities of a close friend include being loyal and honest, having great communication skills, and being able to know when they need to apologize and make changes.
- Healthy ways to express love in a friendship can include being there for your friend, telling them how much they mean to you, posting fun pictures and special memories on your social media, celebrating their accomplishments, and being a loyal and caring friend every day.

REVIEWING CONCEPTS AND VOCABULARY

1. Having a(n) _____ connection means you trust and respect the person and can share anything with them.
2. A(n) _____ is a person you don't know very well.
3. A(n) _____ friend is someone you know primarily online.
4. A strong emotion that people naturally experience when they are unhappy about what someone else has is _____.
5. When you gossip about another person, you are causing _____.
6. _____ is the act of sharing a personal detail about someone who didn't want it to be shared.

THINKING CRITICALLY

Think about two or three of your friends. For each friend, write down at least two qualities about them that make them a good friend. Make sure not to mention any quality or characteristic more than once. When you have your list, reflect on which qualities you have. Then write a response to the statement: I am a good friend because _____.

TAKE IT HOME

In this lesson you learned about four types of friends: acquaintances, casual friends, close friends, and virtual friends. Ask a family member who is out of high school if they have friends who fit into these four categories. Ask the family member if their relationships with their friends are different now than when they were in high school and how the relationship has changed. If they are no longer friends with people from high school, ask them why they think that is.

LESSON 9.4
Dating Relationships

Terms to Learn
abstinence
boundaries
dating
emotional attraction
emotional intimacy
intimacy
love
physical intimacy
refusal skills
sexting
sexually transmitted diseases

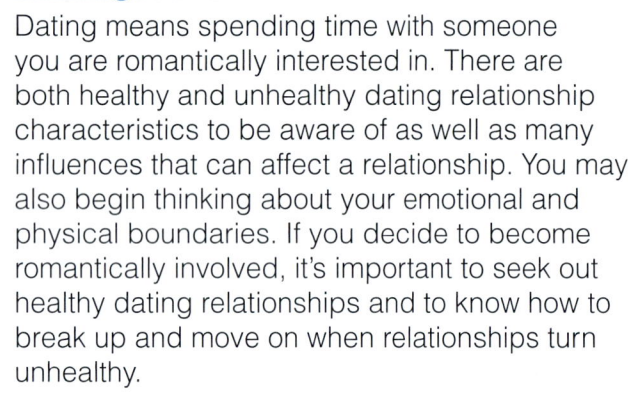

The Big Picture
Dating means spending time with someone you are romantically interested in. There are both healthy and unhealthy dating relationship characteristics to be aware of as well as many influences that can affect a relationship. You may also begin thinking about your emotional and physical boundaries. If you decide to become romantically involved, it's important to seek out healthy dating relationships and to know how to break up and move on when relationships turn unhealthy.

Learning Targets
- Examine the characteristics of a healthy dating relationship.
- Explain three advantages to choosing abstinence.
- Practice your refusal skills for a potential physically intimate situation.
- Summarize the consequences of early and unprotected sexual behaviors.

Write About It
List three qualities the person you date must have and explain why you need them to have those qualities.

Note-Taking Guide
Use this chapter's note-taking guide to help you organize and remember the material in this lesson.

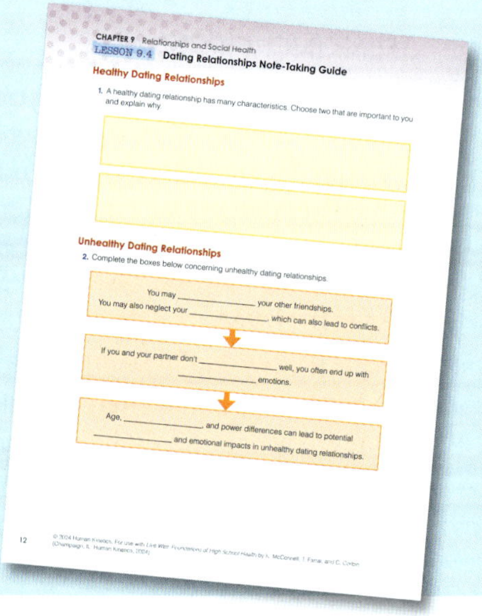

400

Jubl and Rama have been dating, and they both want to be abstinent until they are married. They understand the complications of having a baby while they're too young and do not want to take the risk. Lately, they have found themselves in situations where they are alone together and it would be really easy to do more than just kiss. What are some things Jubl and Rama could do together that would be fun and let each other know how much they care but would help keep them from being sexually active?

Teen Dating Relationships

Dating is spending time with someone you are interested in romantically. Dating can be much different in real life than how it's depicted in advertisements. Couples are shown having a great time together, they may be on the beach or biking or traveling, and there aren't any problems. They get along and have fun, and the good times seem endless, which is often how the beginning stage of dating seems. However, dating can be (or become) difficult, especially if your or your partner's time is limited due to other responsibilities like chores, homework, after-school practice, a job, or having to babysit a sibling.

Healthy Dating Relationships

A healthy relationship, regardless of its type, has certain characteristics such as trust, honesty, good communication, and mutual respect. A healthy dating relationship has those characteristics as well as the following.

- *The people dating like each other.* Sometimes people are interested in each other for a particular quality. For instance, an athlete may like someone who is also athletic, and so it seems like a perfect match because they can spend time playing basketball together. As time goes on and the couple spends more time together, one person might realize they don't actually like their partner's personality: for example, their partner doesn't have a good sense of humor or isn't kind toward others. For a relationship to last, you have to like the person you're with and enjoy spending time together.

- *The people dating are attracted to each other.* Initially, people may be attracted to one another due to their physical traits, but to sustain a relationship, a deeper kind of attraction is needed. An **emotional attraction** is a connection people feel based on traits such as personality, sense of humor, ways in which they share and care for things, and loyalty to their family and friends. The people dating genuinely like being together even if they are doing nothing; it's like dating your best friend.

LESSON 9.4 Relationships and Social Health

- *The people dating keep their individuality.* People don't change who they are to be with their partner, nor do they ask their partner to change who they are to be with them. Each person's values and beliefs, likes and dislikes, and friends and family comprise who they are and shouldn't be compromised for their romantic partner. Each person in a relationship needs space at times to take care of themselves as well, knowing the other person will still be there for them.

- *The people dating know the relationship is stable.* While the people dating love spending time together, they also like spending time with their other friends. It is important people keep a balance in their life and not shut out their other friends. Your friends need to spend time with you, and you need to spend time with them.

- *The people dating need to feel safe with each other.* Couples should always respect each other's personal boundaries and always feel safe with their partner. Feeling safe should include physical, emotional, and mental safety.

- *The people dating are equals.* Both partners in the relationship should have an equal say in everything they do, and they should both put equal effort into their relationship. At times in any relationship, one person may have to do more than the other person, but one person should never feel they put in all the effort to keep the relationship going.

As you begin dating, you will begin to have different feelings for the person you are with, and these dating relationship characteristics will be especially important as you begin to decide on the type of person you want to be in a relationship with.

Unhealthy Dating Relationships

Dating can be challenging, difficult, and emotional, which can lead to anxiety and depression. You and your partner may not be very good at communicating with each other, so you often find yourselves angry with each other and may not even really know why. If you and your partner don't communicate well and don't share what you are actually thinking and feeling, you often end up with conflicting emotions. In one moment, you are happy with each other and in the next moment, you are both mad about something and then happy again. This back and forth of emotions is unhealthy for both of you and your relationship.

Sometimes in unhealthy dating relationships, people may find they have neglected their other friendships. You may be spending more time with your partner and less time with your friends. You may be missing out on some really fun things your friends are doing. You may even end up losing friends if you don't spend time with them. Sometimes the conflict lies between your friends and the person you are dating. If your friends don't like the person you are dating, it makes it even more difficult because you don't have the opportunity to be with everyone at once, so doing something together is never an option. It's not always easy to listen to your friends, but you should get their thoughts on the person you want to date before you do so. Even after you are dating someone, listen to what your friends have to say if they don't like the person. They might have some important insights you may not be able to see because you are in the relationship. You may also be neglecting your family because you want to spend more time with your partner; this can lead to conflicts as well. As you read in the healthy dating section, keeping your friends and being true to yourself are important qualities to have in a relationship; if these qualities are missing, you may want to rethink who you are dating.

Age, status, and power differences can lead to potential legal and emotional impacts in unhealthy dating relationships. Age differences are a common occurrence in relationships. When one person is in high school and the other person is away at college or working full time, this can often result in a power difference. The older person may speak for the younger person, make the majority of the decisions in the relationship, or disregard their partner's opinion or feelings. In addition, the older person may view their partner as inexperienced in comparison to their own new responsibilities and experiences.

When partners have different status in society, families, or relationships, it is often difficult for the person with lower status to feel comfortable speaking up for themselves or to feel respected in the relationship. Relationships may also begin in settings where there is a power difference due to positions in the setting such as at work or school. Depending on the policies of the workplace, being in a relationship with someone who is in a position of authority over you can result in favoritism, sexual harassment, and termination from their job.

Dating Emotions

You will experience several different emotions when you are dating someone. Two strong emotions people tend to have are infatuation and love. Infatuation may be a step in the process of getting to love, but it is very different than love. Infatuation is often characterized as an intense but short-lived passion or admiration for someone, so there is a sense of excitement, newness, and often rapid development in the relationship in a very short amount of time. **Love** is a complex emotion that involves intense feelings of affection and is often explained as involving chemistry, closeness, and commitment with your partner:

Chemistry is the electricity or magic you feel when you meet someone and are instantly attracted to them. It's that nervous, anxious, awkward way you behave when you're around someone you're attracted to.

Closeness happens after you are dating for a while. You share secrets, develop trust, and really feel like you know each other. This is when you may begin to think you love the person you are with.

Commitment is about staying together even if you are having a difficult time. Maybe you had a big fight and things were said that were hurtful, but even though it was difficult, you were able to talk through it and stay together.

Teen relationships may not make it past chemistry, the easy and fun part of dating. Closeness and commitment take time and work, but that's not a bad thing. You're a teen, and you don't necessarily need to be thinking about having a serious, close, and committed relationship. Adults who may have a lot of life experience and relationship skills will also tell you that the commitment part can be hard and often takes a lot of work.

Family Influences on Dating Relationships

Before you even begin thinking about dating, your guardian may make some decisions for you. It is not unusual, even for high school students, for your guardian to decide at what age you can begin dating, what your curfew will be when you are dating, where you can or can't go on a date, who is going to drive, as well as a requirement that the guardians meet before you can go out on a date at all. Your family will also influence how you view being in a dating relationship. If your guardians have a happy, mutually respectful relationship, that may be what you expect dating to be like. Conversely, if your guardians argue all the time, that may be your expectation of what a relationship is supposed to be like.

Online Relationship Communication

While technology can make you feel close to someone, it can also cause problems if your partner doesn't respond either fast enough or how you wanted them to, and this can cause hurt feelings and unnecessary fights. If your partner doesn't respond quickly to a text, you may start wondering if they are mad at you, what they are really doing (they said they were going to be doing homework), what could be wrong, and on and on. Such thoughts cause people to be jealous and mad at their partner for no reason other than they didn't respond quickly enough.

Inherent Risks of Online Dating Websites and Apps for Teens

Teens do so much online with social media and texting that they might also begin relationships online. While teens may use websites and apps to date, the bigger problem may be not having the resilience to deal with issues that develop from having an online relationship. While many online dating sites have been developed just for teens and dating sites have people enter their date of birth to verify age, people are not always honest. The person on the other end of the dating conversation really could be 16 and looking for a friend, but they just as easily could be 39 and looking for an inappropriate relationship with a minor. Regardless of the platform being used, it is important to remember you may not really know who you are texting or messaging and what you say or the pictures you share can be shared worldwide whether you want them to be or not. This is why you must be careful about the kind of information you give out because you don't really know who it is you're talking to or what they may actually do with it. Figure 9.6 lists the Dos and Don'ts of online dating.

Don'ts of Online Dating

- Don't give out your real name, address, date of birth, the school you go to, or where you work to anyone you are meeting online. The person you are talking with may not really be who they say they are, so you don't want them to know personal details about you.

- Don't give out information that can identify who you really are, because someone could steal your identity.

- Don't meet online friends offline alone. Take a friend or two with you and be sure to meet in a crowded public place like a shopping mall. You should also tell an adult and have them go with you.

- Don't engage in sex talk or send sexual pictures. Remember that what you post online can always be traced back to you and can be shared and spread to other websites. Guard your reputation and your dignity by not posting anything offensive.

Dos of Online Dating

- Many of the online dating sites now have apps that can be downloaded to your phone. Turn off your phone's built-in GPS locator when using a dating website so that your location can't be tracked through your phone.

- Report any offensive or negative online conversations or pictures someone sends you to the website's administrator and to your guardian. This is a form of bullying and needs to be reported.

- Keep private information private.

- Be yourself online. If you are really serious about finding a friend or a date online, you need to be yourself.

- Assume the person you are chatting with on the Internet may not be who they claim to be. This will help to keep you from giving out information about yourself.

Figure 9.6 Keep these tips in mind if you are considering online dating.

LESSON 9.4   Relationships and Social Health

Sexting

Sexting means sending photos or videos containing nudity or seminudity or that show or simulate sex acts; it also refers to text messages that discuss or propose sex acts. While sexting usually occurs through text messages, it can be done via any electronic means: email; messaging apps via Instagram, Snapchat, Facebook Messenger; and social media sites. See figure 9.7 for reasons why some teens sext and for reasons why teens should not sext.

Anything shared electronically may not stay with the person it was intended for and may be shared worldwide. Consequences of sharing any type of sexting image or message may include arrests, jail time, and fines. There also is the possibility of being charged with the distribution or possession of child pornography, which can carry the designation of sex offender. This is a very serious offense; each state has different laws around sexting.

Reasons Why Teens Should Not Sext

- Once you hit send or post the photos, your message is out on the Internet, and you can't get it back. Even if you delete it, there's no guarantee someone else hasn't already downloaded it or taken a screenshot of it to share publicly.

- You should always ask yourself, "If everyone at school saw this, what would they think of me?" If you don't like the answer, don't hit the send button.

- Whether you are the person who sent the sext (even if it is of you) or the person receiving the sext (whether you asked for it or not), both you and the receiver may be charged with child pornography, depending on your state laws. Even if you aren't charged with child pornography, you can be charged with some other offense because each of you is in possession of nude or seminude photos of a minor or sex messages from a minor.

- People may use the sext to sexually bully you—known as slut shaming—because people assume you are willing to engage in sexual activity. It is also called cyberbullying if the sext is used to embarrass or humiliate you.

Reasons Why Teens Might Sext

- Teen girls say they are pressured by guys to send explicit pictures or messages.

- Teens might send photos of themselves as a way to flirt or to get compliments, or they might send them as a joke or because someone dared them.

- Teens who are dating might exchange photos as proof of their commitment to each other.

- Teens might also sext photos of other teens after a relationship ends, as revenge, or they might send photos they took in the bathroom or the locker room without the other person knowing, in order to bully or humiliate them.

Figure 9.7 Teens should not sext, but there are reasons why some teens do.

Another consequence of sexting is that you may have to deal with the embarrassment and humiliation of the picture being seen by many people if the picture didn't remain with the person it was sent to. You may even lose friends if they distance themselves from you for fear they will also be bullied for being your friend. Sexting never seems to only be between two people, and the consequences of the sext will affect many people whether they even knew about it or not.

Dating Relationships: Intimacy and Boundaries

In a healthy dating relationship, you will eventually experience some type of intimacy with your partner. **Intimacy** is a one-on-one closeness and connectedness with another person that includes trust, acceptance, honesty, safety, compassion, affection, and communication. Developing intimacy takes time; it's the ability to be vulnerable with another person and share anything with them. Intimacy isn't only found in dating relationships; people can have levels of intimacy with family members and friends as well. **Emotional intimacy** is a sense of closeness with your partner through empathy, respect, and communication. It includes characteristics such as being able to tell your partner your deepest fears, dreams, and disappointments while feeling safe and understood. You can share the very best of you and the very worst of you, and they will still be there for you. Emotional intimacy may also include saying *I love you*. You and your partner may not get to that point at the same time. Never feel pressured to say it back if you aren't ready. Tell your partner how you feel when they say it to you and let them know how you feel about them and what your relationship means to you. Don't feel bad if you aren't ready to tell your partner you love them. You may just not be ready yet. If your partner doesn't respect your feelings, you need to think about whether this is really the relationship you thought it was.

Physical intimacy is something you will eventually experience in a healthy dating relationship. **Physical intimacy** is physical sharing, giving, and getting through touch. It may be as simple as holding hands, hugging, and kissing or it could mean

HEALTHY LIVING TIP
Write out what your boundaries are for physical intimacy. That way you will have thought about what you are and are not comfortable doing and will already know rather than trying to figure it out when you're under pressure to make a decision.

LESSON 9.4   Relationships and Social Health

you or your partner may consider engaging in sexual activity. It's important to know that people can have physical intimacy without being in a sexual relationship.

As your dating relationship becomes more serious, it is important that you think about how you feel about physical intimacy and what you may or may not be comfortable with. This will determine your **boundaries**, which define what behavior you will and will not accept from others. Once you've determined your boundaries, it's important to share them with your partner and to enforce them throughout your relationship. If your partner is pushing to be more physical than holding hands and kissing, you need to reevaluate how you feel about your relationship and what you may or may not be ready for. Your boundaries might even change, and if they do, you need to let your partner know what the new boundaries are. There is no rush to be sexually active, and being abstinent often shows the relationship is based on mutual trust and respect, rather than physical needs alone. Being physically intimate should be an ongoing conversation with your partner so that you have a firm understanding of each other's boundaries.

Abstinence

One of the physical boundaries you may decide on in a dating relationship is to practice abstinence. **Abstinence** is the practice of refraining from any type of sexual activity. Being in a steady dating relationship in high school can lead to conversations and decisions on whether to be sexually active or not. You may be with a partner who wants to pressure you into doing something you're not ready for. Other risky behaviors associated with teen dating include using alcohol and other drugs and lying to your friends and family in order to keep your partner happy. Any time you are feeling pressured by your partner to do something you don't want to do, you need to reassess whether this is really the right person for you. Abstinence has no medical side effects, is free, can be used at any time, and is 100 percent effective in protecting against pregnancy and **sexually transmitted diseases** (STDs). Sexually transmitted diseases are infections passed from one person to another during vaginal, anal, or oral sex. There are advantages and challenges in choosing abstinence (figure 9.8).

Advantages to Being Abstinent

- There are no health risks, you will not get pregnant or get your partner pregnant, and you will not contract a sexually transmitted disease (STD).
- You can choose to be abstinent whenever you want to be.
- Being abstinent is free and readily available.
- You can honor your personal, moral, or religious beliefs.
- Abstinence reduces emotional problems because you have nothing to feel guilty about.
- Abstinence reduces social problems because you have nothing to hide from anyone.
- You should wait until you know you are ready for a sexual relationship.

Challenges to Being Abstinent

- It can be hard to abstain from having sex.
- There may be pressure from your partner or friends to have sex.

Figure 9.8 The advantages to being abstinent far outweigh any challenges.

Refusal Skills

Being able to communicate effectively is very important when you are expressing your desire to be abstinent. You must be able to get your point across in such a way that it is direct and clearly stated so that it leaves no vague areas for interpretation by your partner. **Refusal skills** are techniques you use to say no to something you don't want to do. If you are in a situation where your partner is suggesting or pressuring you to kiss, hug, touch each other, or be sexually active and you want to refuse, it is important to use a combination of verbal and nonverbal communication to emphasize your point. Make sure your nonverbal response matches your firm and confident verbal response. For example, if your verbal response is "I don't want to kiss you," your nonverbal response could be shaking your head no or putting your hand up like you are stopping someone from getting close to you. No matter how difficult it is to say no in a situation where someone is pressuring you to be physically intimate, the most important thing is that you do what is right for you.

Breaking Up

Relationships end for many reasons. Sometimes you change your mind or your feelings change for the person you are with. Breaking up is not an easy decision, and it may take time for you to completely decide that breaking up is what you want to do. Make sure you completely understand why you want to break up, and then have a face-to-face conversation. Never break up by text message, social media, or email, or have someone else do it for you. When breaking up, think about the concepts shown in figure 9.9.

LESSON 9.4 Relationships and Social Health

Breaking Up

- Make sure you know what you want to say and how the other person might react. Will they be surprised or sad or mad or relieved, or will they have all of those feelings? Think about how you will deal with their reaction.

- Be honest, but not mean. Tell the person why you want to break up, but don't point out all the qualities you don't like about them. Keep the focus on what you need and why you have made this decision.

- Stick to your decision even if the other person promises to change. Change should have been part of a conversation long before you break up.

- Don't just avoid the person and hope they will get the hint you don't want to date any longer. That isn't fair to them, and you wouldn't like it if someone did it to you. Make time to have the breakup conversation.

- After the breakup, don't gossip about or be mean to the person. Even if you have to see them every day because they are in a class with you, you can still be respectful and say hi. If they don't respond, it's probably because they are hurt and maybe even embarrassed, so give them time.

- There is no reason to untag, delete, unfriend, or block your former partner after a breakup.

Figure 9.9 Breaking up with someone can be difficult, but following these concepts can make it easier.

Developing and Maintaining Reproductive and Sexual Health

Abstinence is the preferred choice for teens. One reason to choose abstinence is that there are potential dangers and responsibilities that come with being sexually active. Sexual activity is much more complicated than just the physical act. Responsibilities of sexual activity include contraceptive decisions and the prevention of unwanted pregnancies and sexually transmitted diseases (STDs).

There are physical, social, mental health, and emotional risks and consequences to being sexually active as a teen:

- *Physical risks* can include becoming pregnant or contracting a sexually transmitted disease (STD). Sexually transmitted diseases (STDs) are also referred to as sexually transmitted infections or STIs and are passed from one person to another through unprotected sexual activity.

- *Social risks* may involve feelings of not belonging or not being "normal" if teens are comparing their own sexual activity or lack of sexual activity to what their peers may say they are doing or what they see in social media. Teens may have unrealistic expectations of how their relationship might be after having sex. The relationship may change or end, resulting in possible depression.

- *Mental health risks* include possible anxiety about the consequences or about being pressured to be sexually active. Depression may also be a factor if an individual feels guilty about being sexually active.
- *Emotional risks and consequences* can include not having the emotional maturity to manage a sexual relationship, which can be damaging to teens' self-esteem.

Abstinence is the most effective way to avoid unintended pregnancy or getting an STD. See the appendix for more information about other ways to reduce the risk of infection and for information about testing and treatment methods.

Skill-Building Challenge

Healthy Communication

Chris and Harper have been dating for quite some time. Harper is ready to be sexually active, but Chris is not. One night Chris is at Harper's house, and Harper's guardians decide to go out with friends, leaving Chris and Harper alone. Harper begins pressuring Chris to have sex. Using the following refusal skills, write what you would say to Harper if you were Chris.

1. Say no.
2. Use an *I* message to state your reason for not wanting to have sex.
3. Use an assertive voice and have your nonverbal body language match your verbal language.
4. Stick with your position—state your reason in a different way to continue to get your point across.
5. If this does not work, remove yourself immediately from the situation.

Healthy Living Skills

This lesson focused on healthy communication. You can improve health skills by completing the following skill activity.

ANALYZING INFLUENCES

You learned in this lesson that abstinence is the only way to completely prevent pregnancy and STDs. You also realize that it may not always be easy to choose abstinence. Using the Analyzing Influences Skill Cues, identify the people or situations that would influence you to be abstinent and think about both ways you may be influenced to be or not to be abstinent.

LESSON 9.4 Review: Dating Relationships

LESSON SUMMARY

- A healthy dating relationship should consist of liking each other, being emotionally attracted to your partner, being able to keep your individuality, having a stable relationship, feeling safe with each other, and being equals in the relationship.
- Some advantages of abstinence are you have no medical side effects, it is free, you can use it at any time, and it is 100 percent effective in protecting against pregnancy and sexually transmitted diseases (STDs).
- It is important to know what your individual boundaries are if you are thinking about being physically intimate. Knowing what you will and will not do ahead of time will make it easier to use your refusal skills and set appropriate boundaries in your relationship.
- There are physical, social, mental, and emotional risks and consequences to being sexually active as a teen. Physical risks can include contracting a sexually transmitted disease (STD) and becoming pregnant. Social risks may involve feelings of not belonging or not being "normal" if they compare themselves to social media. Mental risks may include anxiety or depression about being sexually active. Emotional risks may include lower self-esteem.
- STDs are most commonly transmitted through unprotected sexual activity.

REVIEWING CONCEPTS AND VOCABULARY

1. _____ is spending time with someone you are interested in romantically.
2. Emotional _____ is a physical and emotional connection you feel with your partner.
3. A complex emotion that involves intense feelings of affection and is often explained as involving chemistry, closeness, and commitment with your partner is known as _____
4. Sending seminude or nude photos or videos electronically is called _____.
5. _____ involves feelings of emotional closeness and connectedness with another person.
6. Being able to tell your partner your deepest fears, dreams, and disappointments while feeling safe and understood is _____ intimacy.
7. _____ intimacy is intimacy through physical touch.
8. Determining what behavior you will and will not accept from others is known as having _____.

THINKING CRITICALLY

Why do you think it would be important in a relationship to establish boundaries around physical intimacy?

TAKE IT HOME

Talk to a family member or trusted adult about expectations of dating. Are your expectations about dating and what rules apply to dating the same as those of your family member or trusted adult? Write a paragraph explaining your response.

Chapter Review

ACTION PLAN: Open Communication With a Guardian

Use the My Action Plan worksheet to keep communication open with your guardian. Here is an example.

My Action Plan: Communicating With My Guardian

STEP 1: Identify the health behavior you are going to work on.

I want to be able to communicate better with my guardian.

STEP 2: Write SMART goal(s).

Write one or two short-term goals (one day to one month long).

I will tell my guardian at least one thing about my day when they ask. Before I say things that are mean, I will count to 10 and think about my response when I am angry with my guardian 50 percent of the time.

Write a long-term goal (one to six months or more).

I will use I messages 50 percent of the time when I get into a disagreement with my guardian.

STEP 3: Make a plan.

Identify two or three action steps (strategies) you could take to meet your goal.

On my way home from school, I will think of one thing I can share with my guardian if they ask.

I will practice counting to 10 before I react in a mean way to my friends. This may make it easier for me to react in a nonconfrontational way when my guardian and I disagree.

I will practice using I messages in other parts of my life so that it will be easier when I try to use them when I'm in a disagreement with my guardian.

STEP 4: Execute your plan and track your progress.

Short-term goal 1

☒ Met   ☐ Not met   Date: *April 15*

Short-term goal 2

☒ Met   ☐ Not met   Date: *April 25*

Long-term goal

☐ Met   ☒ Not met   Date: _____

If you met your goal, what helped you to be successful?

On the way home from school, I thought about what I wanted to share with my guardian. I practiced counting and pausing before I said anything, which helped me make better comments instead of being mean.

If you did not meet your goal, what things made it harder for you to be successful?

Sometimes when I'm in a disagreement, I don't want to think about using I messages, I just want to say what's on my mind, which isn't always helpful. I will continue to work on this because when I have used I messages, the disagreement has gone better for both of us.

Test Your Knowledge

Select the best answer for each question.

1. The four specific types of friends you have throughout your life are
   a. casual friends, good friends, acquaintances, virtual friends
   b. acquaintances, close friends, virtual friends, good friends
   c. acquaintances, casual friends, close friends, virtual friends
   d. casual friends, good friends, acquaintances, close friends

2. Avoiding all forms of sexual activity is known as
   a. contraceptives
   b. abstinence
   c. emotional intimacy
   d. casual sex

3. Using facial expressions and body language is what kind of communication?
   a. nonverbal
   b. interpersonal
   c. verbal
   d. written

4. Which of the following is not a typical characteristic of an unhealthy dating relationship?
   a. poor communication
   b. power differences
   c. feeling safe with each other
   d. neglecting other friends

5. Drama in a friendship is most often caused by _____.
   a. missed connections
   b. hurtful comments
   c. sharing secrets
   d. spreading false rumors

6. Your ability to get along with people is known as
   a. social health
   b. physical health
   c. emotional health
   d. mental health

7. What is an example of a close friendship?
   a. You share some information, but not your most personal feelings.
   b. You let go of the friendship if your friend gets angry with you.
   c. Your friend tells you when something you're doing isn't right.
   d. You don't need to apologize, because your friend understands you.

8. Having a higher overall life satisfaction and lower rates of depression later in life are two characteristics of which kind of relationship?
   a. guardian
   b. sibling
   c. healthy
   d. unhealthy

9. The last part of an effective *I* message offers _____.
   a. an urgent demand or requirement
   b. an alternative or compromise
   c. an ultimatum
   d. a subtle apology

10. Having feelings of emotional closeness and connectedness with another person is known as
    a. emotional intimacy
    b. social intimacy
    c. mental intimacy
    d. physical intimacy

PROJECT-BASED LEARNING: Keeping Healthy Friendships

What to Remember
Healthy relationships are an important part of overall wellness. Healthy relationships provide us with the support we need in order to make healthy choices.

Who It Is For
You and your friends

Why It Is Important
It is important to understand the benefits of healthy relationships with friends. This is a time in your life when you often start spending more time with your friends and relying on them more. It is also a time when teens begin dating, getting jobs, and having more responsibilities, so it is hard to find time to be with friends outside of school. This can lead to friends sometimes turning on each other, spreading rumors, ignoring each other, and creating drama in their lives. Learning to communicate and listen effectively is important to maintaining healthy relationships.

What to Do
Practice using active listening skills and *I* messages in order to become a better friend.

How to Do It
Work with a partner or a group of three. Begin by creating three realistic scenarios that you and your friends might face and might want to talk about. Describe each scenario by writing it out in a paragraph. Take turns acting out each scenario and practice using active listening and *I* messages. Give each other feedback on how the conversation went using *I* messages and Active Listening Skill Cues as guides. Be willing to use your listening skills with friends and others in your school and keep track of how many times you were able to help others by using these skills.

CROSS-CURRICULAR CONNECTIONS: Speaking and Listening

Engage in one-on-one and group discussions about the benefits of healthy friendships and relationships. Develop scenarios of negative conversations that friends might have so you can practice your *I* messages and active listening. By practicing with different scenarios, you will be better prepared when the real situation arises.

UNIT IV

Destructive and Damaging Behaviors

CHAPTER 10   **Violence and Conflict**

CHAPTER 11   **Alcohol**

CHAPTER 12   **Tobacco and E-Cigarettes**

CHAPTER 13   **Legal and Illicit Drugs**

Violence and Conflict

10

LESSON 10.1 Understanding Violent Behavior
LESSON 10.2 Anger, Aggression, and Conflict
LESSON 10.3 Bullying and Hazing
LESSON 10.4 Violence, Weapons, and Gangs
LESSON 10.5 Relationships and Violence

Understanding My Health

My Knowledge of Anger and Conflict

This self-assessment is designed to examine your behaviors related to anger and conflict. Understanding how to recognize and deal with anger and conflict will help you be more successful in relationships, school, and eventually your career. When you are done, add up your points. The closer your score is to 24, the more you seem able to deal with anger and conflict in productive ways.

	Always	Sometimes	Never
When I feel angry, I am able to control my emotions.	3	2	1
When I feel angry, I know how to calm myself down without being violent to myself or others.	3	2	1
I understand that conflict is a normal part of life.	3	2	1
I refuse to stand by and do nothing if I see bullying or other aggressive behavior.	3	2	1
I know an adult I could talk to if I felt threatened or unsafe.	3	2	1
I appreciate diversity and celebrate differences in others.	3	2	1
I avoid saying things online that I wouldn't be willing to say in person.	3	2	1
I am clear on what my personal boundaries are, and I don't allow others to change them.	3	2	1

My score for My Knowledge of Anger and Conflict = _____ (total number of points)

Conflict, anger, and violence can be uncomfortable or even frightening to deal with. Good health doesn't require people never to feel angry or never to experience conflict. Staying healthy and safe does require us to understand how to avoid risk, manage conflict, and get out of violent situations.

LESSON 10.1
Understanding Violent Behavior

Terms to Learn
- bias
- emotional violence
- intolerance
- offender
- physical violence
- prejudice
- sexual violence
- victim
- violent behavior
- witness

The Big Picture
Violence comes in many forms and can happen between strangers, couples, family, friends, and acquaintances. Understanding what leads to violent behavior and the consequences of violence can help you keep yourself away from violence and encourage others to do the same.

Learning Targets
- Compare and contrast physical and emotional violence.
- Explain how personal, social, family, and community influences affect violent behavior.
- Explain how prejudice, bias, and intolerance are related to violent behavior.
- Compare and contrast the consequences of violent behavior to the victim, bystander, and offender.
- Communicate respect for others.

Write About It
How might your opinion of someone else influence the way you treat that person? How might opinions lead to violent behavior?

Note-Taking Guide
Use this chapter's note-taking guide to help you organize and remember the material in this lesson.

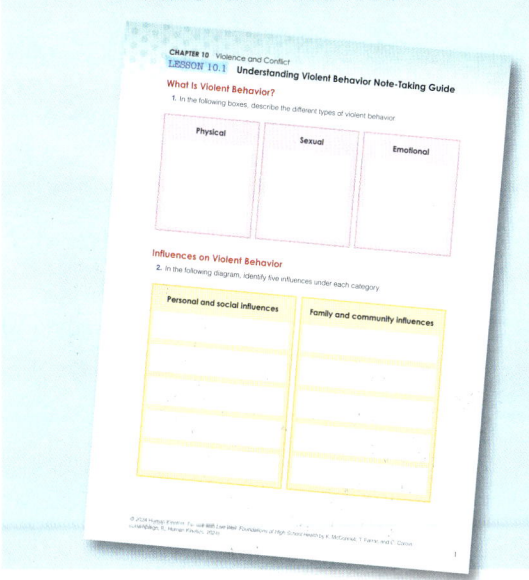

LESSON 10.1 Violence and Conflict

Abdul noticed that his friend Rasheed was wearing long-sleeved shirts to school even though it was pretty hot outside. He also saw a bruise on Rasheed's face. When Abdul asked what the bruise was from, Rasheed said that he got hit in the face with a baseball when he was playing with his brother. Rasheed was also quieter than usual and seemed nervous and anxious. Abdul worried that his friend had been beaten up by someone, but he couldn't get Rasheed to say anything, and Abdul didn't want to make him uncomfortable. Rasheed is showing signs that he might have been a victim of violence. What should Abdul do to best support his friend?

What Is Violent Behavior?

Violent behavior is the intentional use of words or actions that cause or threaten to cause injury (see figure 10.1). Violent behavior often starts with words and quickly escalates into a physical act. **Physical violence** is the use of bodily force; some examples are hitting or kicking someone, forcing someone to do something against their will, and destroying property. **Sexual violence**, or any sexual activity against another person's will or without their consent, is a specific form of physical violence.

While we often think of violence as being a physical act, it is also possible to be violent in other ways. Threatening others, destroying another person's reputation, or causing damage to another person's relationships are also forms of violent behavior. This type of violence—**emotional violence**—can result in psychological injury or injury to another person's emotional and social well-being. Emotional violence often goes unseen and can be difficult to talk about.

Bullying
Repeated aggressive behavior toward someone that causes the person injury or discomfort

Hazing
The use of pressure by a group to make someone do something embarrassing or even dangerous in order to be accepted by the group

Cyberbullying
A form of bullying that occurs electronically or through social media

Neglect
An adult's or caretaker's failure to meet the basic physical, emotional, medical, or educational needs of a child or other dependent

Physical abuse
An intentional act that causes physical harm to someone else

Emotional abuse
Attitudes or controlling behaviors that harm a person's mental health

Sexual abuse
Any sexual activity that is done without the other person's consent or when a person cannot consent (e.g., because of age or condition)

Child abuse
Any intentional act done to a child that threatens or causes harm to the child

Sibling abuse
Physical, emotional, or sexual violence between siblings

Elder abuse
Physical, emotional, or sexual violence against an elder person; also includes financial abuse and neglect

Animal abuse
Torture, abuse, or neglect of an animal

Hate crimes
Threats or attacks against someone because of their race, ethnic origin, disability, sexual orientation, gender, or religion

Homicide
Taking the life of another person

Terrorism
The use of violence or threats to frighten and control groups of people

Human trafficking
The use of force, fraud, or coercion to lure someone and force them into labor or sexual exploitation

School violence
Violent behavior that occurs on school property, at school-sponsored events, or on the way to or from school

Gang violence
Violent behavior carried out in a group as part of membership and inclusion in the group

Figure 10.1 Categories of violent behaviors.

LESSON 10.1 Violence and Conflict

Influences on Violent Behavior

A person who commits a violent act is referred to as the perpetrator or **offender**. Offenders are different in different situations. A person who acts out in violent ways in one situation (e.g., at home) may not act out in another situation (e.g., at work or school). The person on the receiving end of the violent behavior, known as the **victim**, may also be different in different situations. Children, underrepresented groups, women, and older adults are more commonly the victims of violence, but anyone can be a victim. Some forms of violence leave physical evidence—bruises, scratches, or broken bones. Other forms of violence may be impossible for others to see. In these ways, violent behaviors are very different.

Despite the differences in perpetrators and victims, there are some common risk factors for violent behavior (see figure 10.2). Risk factors only suggest that a person might be more likely to commit violence. It is possible to be surrounded by risk factors and not experience violence or become violent yourself. How risk factors ultimately influence a person's behavior is a complex process that will vary from person to person.

Figure 10.2 Risk factors for violent behavior.

Prejudice, Bias, and Intolerance

Unfortunately, violent behaviors are often associated with prejudice and bias. **Prejudice** is having an unreasonable opinion or assumption about someone or something that is not based on actual experience. People most often have prejudice toward others they think are different from themselves. **Bias** occurs when we treat a person, thing, or group differently based on how we think about them. Biased behavior is also called *discrimination*, especially when the bias affects the legal rights of a person or group.

People have a lot of different prejudices. We learn prejudice through socialization—adapting our behaviors, values, and beliefs in order to fit in with a particular culture or social group. If you have a negative opinion about women, or about a particular race or religious group, you have a prejudice against them. If you treat the people in that group differently because of what you assume about them, you are being biased. **Intolerance** is an unwillingness to examine personal prejudices and biases and accept the beliefs, values, or behaviors of others. Intolerance can lead to hate. When this happens, violent acts can follow.

Consequences of Violent Behavior

Violent behavior always comes with consequences for victims, offenders, and bystanders (see figure 10.3). A bystander, or **witness**, is someone who sees the violent act but does not participate in the act. Violent acts themselves may only last a short amount of time, but their consequences can last a lifetime for those affected.

HEALTHY LIVING TIP

Join a club, an organization, or an activity in your school or community that provides you and your family the opportunity to interact with people who are different from yourself. Engaging in common activities with others can help you appreciate differences and similarities in cultures, values, and traditions. It can provide safe alternatives to violent behaviors such as in gangs.

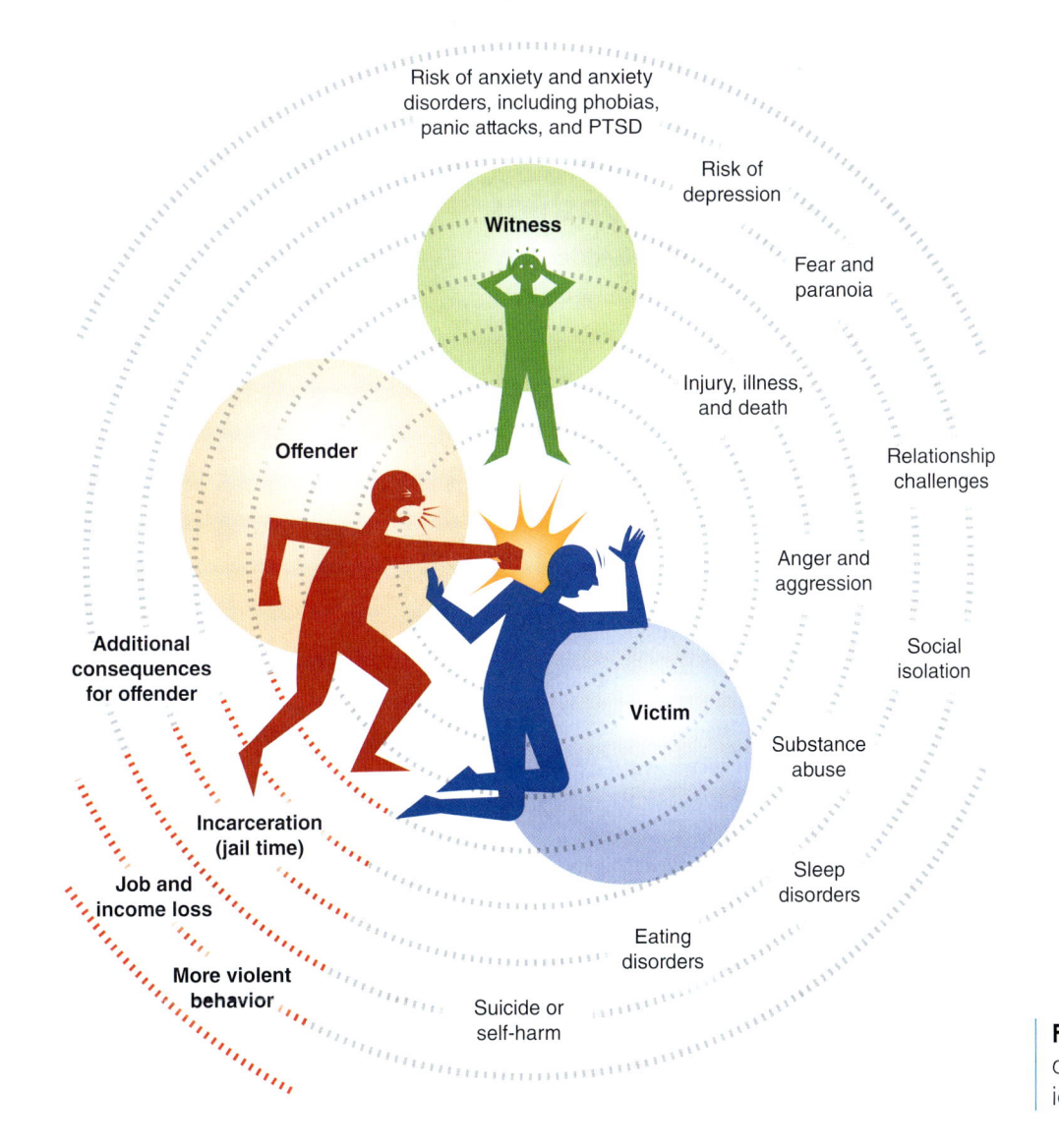

Figure 10.3 Consequences of violent behavior.

LESSON 10.1 Violence and Conflict

Violence can affect a person's physical health directly (broken bones, internal injuries, head injuries, etc.) as well as their emotional health. Anxiety and related disorders are particularly common following a violent encounter. Violence can also lead to a wide range of other longer-term effects on health and well-being. For example, victims of child abuse may run away from home. This can cause the person to drop out of school, become a victim of street crimes, go hungry, lose sleep, and experience extreme stress. All of these outcomes can increase the risk of other diseases and disorders. In fact, the violence a child or young person experiences can affect them for a lifetime.

Reporting Violence

People who witness a violent act can help by calling 911 to report the crime or by telling a trusted adult about the situation. Quickly responding to a violent act can help the victim get the medical assistance they need and can also help the authorities find the offender. Reporting violence is the right thing to do, even when it feels unsafe.

Preventing Violence

Violence is complicated, which makes its prevention challenging. There are ways we can help as individuals, in our relationships with others, as a community, and as a society.

Individuals and Relationships

Individuals can help prevent violence by examining the attitudes, beliefs, and behaviors they have toward others. Recognizing that it is okay to be different from others and understanding that all people deserve to be treated with respect is a good start. Individuals can also pay attention to risk factors that might make them more likely to be a victim of violence in order to recognize and avoid potentially risky situations. This includes examining our closest social circle of friends, family, and peers and working hard to surround ourselves with people who are supportive, respectful, and accepting.

R — Recognize how others respond to what you are saying. Pay attention and watch for signs that you are aggravating or upsetting the other person. Watch your tone and use good nonverbal skills.

E — Eliminate negative words and phrases from your vocabulary. Don't use slang or other words that can be hurtful, offensive, or misinterpreted.

S — Speak with people, not at them or about them. Engage in a conversation, not a debate, or a lecture.

P — Practice appreciation. If a conversation is challenging, pause to notice something you appreciate about what the other person said or did.

E — Earn respect from others by modeling respectful behaviors. Don't expect respect from others if you are being mean or dismissive yourself.

C — Consider others' feelings and point of view before speaking and acting.

T — Take time to listen. Don't interrupt. Always listen first.

Figure 10.4 Talk with RESPECT to help reduce violence.

Community and Society

Communities and societies can help reduce violence by working to improve access to public transportation and affordable housing and by supporting employment and education opportunities for all. Working to develop processes, policies, procedures, and laws that ensure equity for all members in a society also helps to reduce violence.

Communicating Respect for Others

One of the very best ways to help prevent violence is to learn to communicate effectively and respectfully with people who are different from yourself. Effective communication can reduce or eliminate misunderstandings, conflict, hurt feelings, and anger and decrease the chances that a situation may become violent. The RESPECT acronym can help you communicate respectfully with others (see figure 10.4).

LESSON 10.1 Violence and Conflict

Skill-Building Challenge

Communicating Respect for Others

Select one of the following topics that reflects something about your own identity, or use a topic your teacher assigns. Write a short response to the prompt you selected and then share it with a classmate or in a small group. As you discuss your topic, use the RESPECT acronym to guide how you engage in conversation with others. When someone else is speaking, do your best to ask questions that will help you better understand their experience and perspective. At the end of the conversation, or when your teacher tells you to stop, reflect on how you did. Evaluate yourself on each part of the RESPECT acronym.

- What your family is like and how it feels to be you in your family
- What your race is and what it is like to be that race
- What your hobbies and interests are and how they influence what others think of you

Element of RESPECT	How I did
Recognized how others respond to what you are saying	
Eliminated negative words or phrases	
Spoke with people, not at them	
Showed appreciation for something they said	
Modeled respect by making eye contact and being kind	
Considered others' feelings and perspectives before talking	
Listened without interrupting	

Healthy Living Skills

This lesson focused on healthy communication. Here are some more ways you can develop healthy living skills related to this lesson.

ANALYZING INFLUENCES

Look through the influences and risk factors for violent behavior identified in this lesson. Create a list of the risk factors that apply to you. Determine whether you can make changes to reduce each risk factor. If you can, identify what those changes may be.

ACCESSING INFORMATION

Select one of the types of violence defined in the chapter. Using valid and reliable information from online searches, write a one-page summary about that type of violence. Include a description, risk factors, statistics, and consequences in your report.

PRACTICING HEALTHY BEHAVIORS
If you observe someone being bullied or teased, speak up and tell the bully that what they are doing is not okay. Show respect and kindness to the victim and then reflect on your actions.

ADVOCATING FOR GOOD HEALTH
Work with other students in your class to design a campaign that promotes respect for individual differences in your school.

LESSON 10.1 Review: Understanding Violent Behavior

LESSON SUMMARY
- Physical violence uses bodily force to inflict harm.
- Sexual violence involves any sexual activity done against a person's will or without their consent.
- Emotional violence causes psychological, emotional, or social injury to another person.
- There is a wide range of influences on violence, including personal, social, family, and community influences.
- A prejudice is an unreasonable opinion or assumption about someone or something that is not based on experience.
- A person who is biased treats a person differently because of what they assume about the person.
- Violence has a wide range of consequences for the victim, the offender, and the witness.

REVIEWING CONCEPTS AND VOCABULARY
1. Violent _____ includes the intentional use of words or actions that cause or threaten to cause injury to someone or something.
2. Threatening someone or destroying their reputation are examples of _____ violence.
3. A person who commits a violent act is known as a perpetrator or _____.
4. Having an opinion about someone or something that is not based on experience is called a(n) _____.
5. An unwillingness to accept the beliefs or behaviors of others is called _____.
6. A(n) _____ is someone who sees a violent act but does not participate in it.
7. It is important to communicate with _____ when talking to people, especially when they have different beliefs, thoughts, or opinions than you.

THINKING CRITICALLY
Research one form of violent behavior and gather information about that particular behavior. Focus on statistics, data, and facts. Write down at least eight pieces of information that you learned. Put the information that you think is most important for people to know at the top of the list in descending order.

TAKE IT HOME
Ask a sibling, friend, teammate, or other peer in your community about their cultural, ethnic, or religious background and use the RESPECT acronym to help you listen and understand their perspective.

LESSON 10.2

Anger, Aggression, and Conflict

Terms to Learn
aggression
assertiveness
conflict
conflict resolution
escalate

The Big Picture
Anger and aggression are not the same as violence, and aggression is not the same as assertiveness. It is important to know how to manage anger and be assertive without being violent.

Learning Targets
- Compare and contrast aggression and assertiveness.
- Illustrate each common cause of conflict using a realistic example.
- Compare and contrast two styles of managing conflict.
- Practice the steps of conflict resolution.

Write About It
When you experience a conflict, how does it make you feel? How do you usually handle conflict?

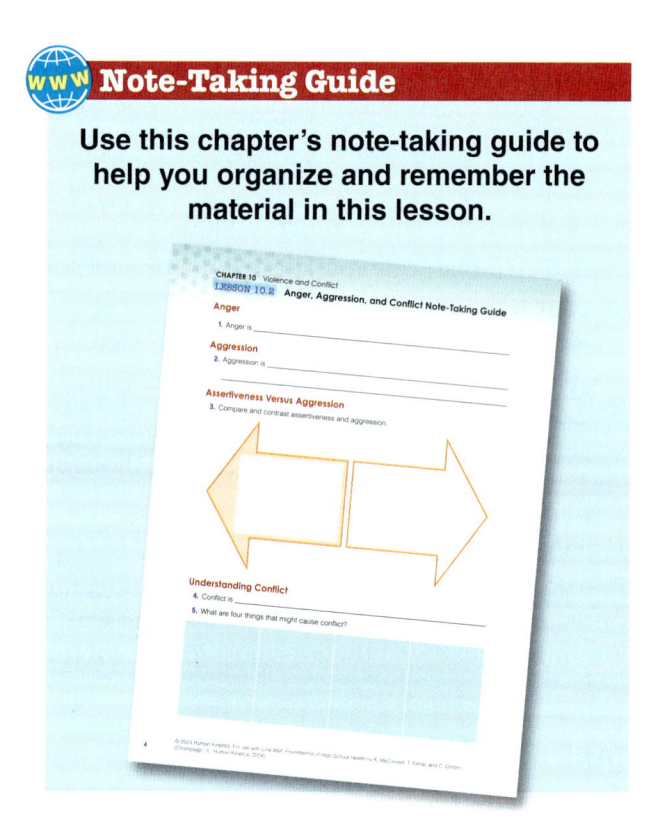

Note-Taking Guide
Use this chapter's note-taking guide to help you organize and remember the material in this lesson.

Anger, Aggression, and Conflict **LESSON 10.2**

Jordyn was feeling really angry because his parents told him he couldn't attend a chaperoned party at a friend's house over the weekend. They worried that the party might attract an aggressive or a violent crowd and put Jordyn in danger. His best friend Devon tried to encourage him to brush it off. Jordyn kept to himself most of the week so that no one would ask him if he was going to the party. On the night of the party, Jordyn went up to his room and slammed the door. Jordyn's dad came up and yelled at him for slamming the door and told Jordyn that he was grounded for a week. Jordyn refused to talk to his dad the rest of the night. How could Jordyn have handled this situation differently? If he did handle it differently, how might the outcome change?

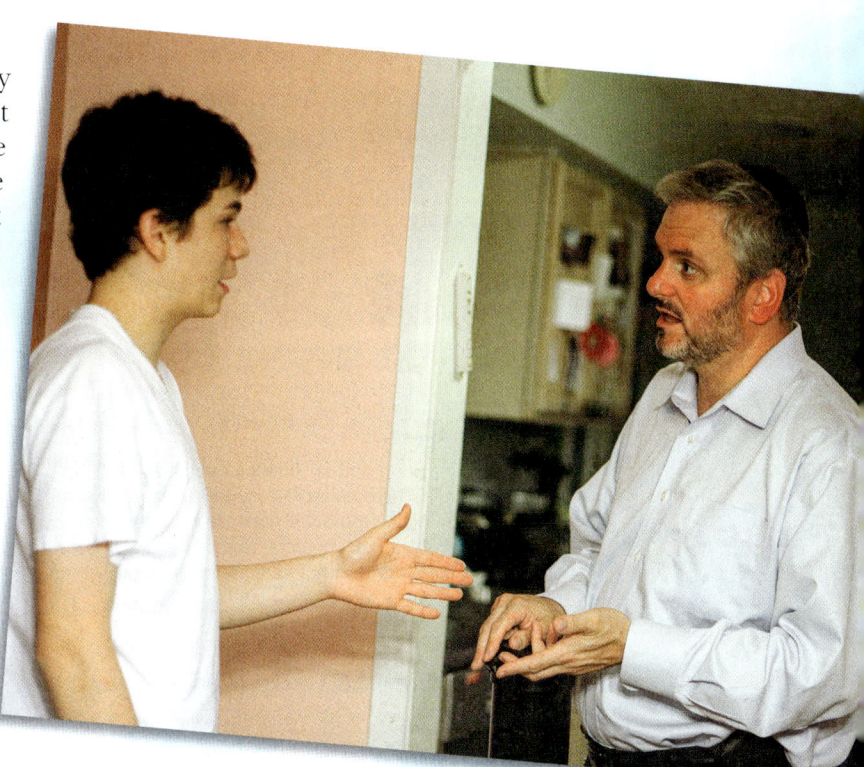

Anger

Anger is a normal emotion all people feel. When we express our anger appropriately, others are able to understand that we are frustrated, fearful, or hurt, and we are better able to control our anger. It is okay to feel angry, but it is not okay to direct anger toward other people in aggressive and violent ways.

Aggression

Aggression occurs when someone engages in a forceful action with the intent to dominate or control another person or situation. Aggression is a behavior, not an emotion. Sometimes people act aggressively in nonviolent ways. For example, a person may cut in front of another person in a lunch line or change lanes often and quickly while driving. In certain situations, like in competitive sports, we may refer to someone as being aggressive in the way they play the game. Usually this means they are giving a full, hard effort in an attempt to win the competition or dominate their opponent's play. On the other hand, aggressive behavior can also be violent. Using force to push someone out of line is aggressive behavior that is violent, as is shoving someone out of your way when walking.

Assertiveness Versus Aggression

Sometimes people confuse assertiveness with aggression even though they are not the same thing. Aggression is forceful or violent, while **assertiveness** is a nonviolent and confident way of expressing your needs and point of view (see figure 10.5). There are significant differences between the two behaviors. Being assertive is usually viewed as a positive thing, while being aggressive is viewed more negatively.

HEALTHY LIVING TIP

If you find yourself feeling angry, take a deep breath and calm yourself down before taking any action. When you are ready to communicate your feelings, remember to focus on using *I* messages to express how you feel. Even if someone did something to make you feel angry, try not to start out with *You* statements. For example, instead of "You messed up, and now I lost my turn," try "I am frustrated that I didn't get a chance to play."

431

LESSON 10.2 Violence and Conflict

Assertiveness
- Show self-confidence and strength
- State opinion in a respectful way
- Help others feel comfortable and safe
- Make eye contact, remain calm and open
- Value yourself as equal to others
- Seek to express yourself without hurting others

Aggression
- Use forcefulness or violence
- Attack others and force your opinions on others
- Not in tune with others or focused on what they want
- Stare and appear irritated with others
- Value yourself as more important or better than others
- Seek to hurt others

Figure 10.5 Assertiveness versus aggression.

Understanding Conflict

Conflict is an unavoidable reality of life. We all experience conflict with others and within groups and organizations. Conflict is not always necessarily bad. In fact, conflict can motivate us to grow and appreciate others, solve problems, and find solutions to challenges.

Conflict occurs when two or more people disagree on an issue. Conflict itself usually does not lead to aggression or violence. Sometimes conflict can make people feel angry. When a person feels angry and is threatened by a situation, they can have a difficult time managing their emotions. This can lead to difficulties in listening, empathizing, and remaining neutral and open in the situation, often creating further conflict and making the situation worse. Values, relationships, interests, and resources can cause conflict in the following ways:

Values. Differing principles and standards of behavior can lead people to disagree on important decisions.

Relationships. Different personalities, styles, and personal boundaries between people can lead to disagreements about what to do, how to handle a situation, or what is acceptable in the relationship.

Interests. People do not always share the same concerns or find the same things appealing, and this can hinder their ability to reach a consensus (i.e., agreement).

Resources. If there isn't enough of something to go around (including time), people may disagree with each other on how to manage the resource.

Managing Conflict

When we don't manage conflict effectively, the situation can **escalate**, or intensify. Unresolved conflicts can lead to increased feelings of stress and anxiety, which can harm one's health and well-being. Without proper management, conflicts can cause relationships to fall apart, which can lead to violent confrontations. It's important to deal with conflicts, no matter how difficult they may be.

People have different approaches, or styles, when it comes to managing conflicts in nonviolent ways. As individuals, each of us has characteristics and traits that will affect how we tend to solve conflicts with others. Having self-awareness about how you handle conflict will help you improve your conflict resolution skills. The styles for managing conflict can also be viewed as strategies, or options (see figure 10.6). Each has pros and cons.

HEALTHY LIVING TIP
One way to appreciate other people is to share in their interests. Do something with a friend or family member that they love to do, even if you think you won't like it. Being open to new experiences will help you understand and appreciate others.

Styles for Managing Conflict

Accommodating approach
This is when you cooperate to a high degree, even letting go of your own goals, objectives, and desired outcomes, in order to reach a solution. This approach works best when the other party is the expert or has a better solution. Sometimes we use this approach when the situation is not serious and we want to avoid hurting a friendship or relationship.

Avoiding approach
This is when you simply avoid the cause of the conflict. People choose avoidance when the issue is not important or they have no chance of making things go their way. Sometimes people avoid conflict if the situation is very emotional or if serious consequences, like violence, are likely to occur. Generally speaking, avoidance is not a healthy long-term solution for resolving conflict, but it may be necessary in the short term.

Collaborating approach
This is when you work together to try to achieve everyone's goals. Some people refer to this as trying to find the win-win solution because there is no loser. When a conflict is really complex, this approach is useful. Collaboration does require a lot of trust, time, and effort to make sure everyone is truly satisfied with the outcome.

Competing approach
This is the win-lose approach in which the goal is to achieve your own goals without concern for the other party. Generally speaking, this approach results in people feeling hurt or left out. However, it may be necessary in an emergency or when a quick decision is called for.

Compromising approach
In this approach, neither party really achieves all of what they want. Compromising is good for short-term solutions to conflict, but it can leave people feeling dissatisfied. It is often easier to compromise than to collaborate, but collaboration generally has better long-term results.

Figure 10.6 There are different styles, or approaches, for avoiding conflict.

LESSON 10.2 Violence and Conflict

Conflict Resolution

Conflict resolution is the informal or formal process that two or more individuals or groups use to find a peaceful solution to their disagreement. When you are working to resolve a conflict, follow the steps to conflict resolution shown in figure 10.7 to help you find a solution.

Figure 10.7 Steps to conflict resolution.

- Take a deep breath and calm yourself. Conflicts are best resolved when emotions are under control.
- Listen to the perspective of others. Use active listening skills and work to find what you agree on and have in common.
- Brainstorm your options. Consider all possibilities and evaluate the potential consequences of each option.
- Identify your best option or strategy. Look for the win-win solution when possible.
- Make a decision. Come to a decision and make sure everyone knows what it is.

Career Connection

SOCIAL WORKER

Social work is a large field that includes a variety of professionals who serve people in need. Social workers can serve children and families, work in medical and public health, and focus on mental health and substance abuse. Social workers often provide counseling and education, and they connect people in need with appropriate public and private resources. Social workers often deal with victims of violence—especially children and victims of domestic violence. Most states require at least a bachelor's degree from a university offering an accredited program for someone to practice as a social worker.

Skill-Building Challenge

Resolving Conflicts

Read through each of the following scenarios. Discuss which conflict management approach is illustrated in each and describe why the approach is harmful or unsuccessful. Decide how best to resolve the conflict in order to provide a helpful and successful solution. Remember to brainstorm your options and identify the best strategy or strategies to use. Once you have made your decision, explain how your choice supports a helpful and successful resolution to the conflict and identify the possible short- and long-term consequences of your choice.

SCENARIO 1

Emily and Zoe are both friends with Mateo, and they both have a crush on him. Emily has more classes with him and gets to see him often, but Zoe lives next door to Mateo's family. Lately Zoe has been hanging out with Mateo between classes and after school, and it's made Emily jealous. She's also angry because it feels like Zoe is trying to keep her away from Mateo. Emily and Zoe had a fight yesterday, and now they just don't seem to be getting along at all anymore.

SCENARIO 2

Thomas and Dylan have been friends a long time. Last week, Dylan was giving Thomas a hard time about a picture he posted of himself on Instagram. Thomas texted Dylan and told him to lay off. Instead, Dylan made a sarcastic comment back to Thomas on Instagram. Thomas is really mad at Dylan, and Dylan thinks Thomas is blowing everything out of proportion.

Healthy Living Skills

This lesson focused on making healthy decisions. Here are some more ways you can develop healthy living skills related to this lesson.

ACCESSING INFORMATION

Many schools offer opportunities to learn about conflict resolution, community building, or peace and justice. Determine if your school offers any related trainings or opportunities for students and create a list of them. If you can't identify any, make a list of the type of opportunities you think the school should offer and give it to your teacher.

HEALTHY COMMUNICATION

Demonstrate the difference between assertive and aggressive communication. Think of a common conflict you or your peers experience. Write a story about the situation and give it two different endings: one that represents what would happen if the characters were aggressive in dealing with their situation, and one that demonstrates how the situation might look if the characters used assertive communication instead.

LESSON 10.2 Violence and Conflict

LESSON 10.2 Review: Anger, Aggression, and Conflict

LESSON SUMMARY

- Anger, aggression, and assertiveness are all different. Anger is an emotion. Aggression is a forceful behavior with the intent to control another person or situation. Assertiveness is a nonviolent way to express your needs and point of view.
- Conflict occurs when people disagree on an issue. Common sources of conflict include differences in values, relationship expectations, and interests and an insufficiency of resources.
- Approaches to conflict management include accommodation, avoidance, compromise, and competition.
- If you are in a conflict, try to take a deep breath or do something safe and appropriate that will calm you down. Then listen to the perspective of the other person. Brainstorm all of your options for a solution and identify your best strategy. Then make the decision.

REVIEWING CONCEPTS AND VOCABULARY

1. Aggression is a(n) _____, not an emotion.
2. Stating your opinion in a respectful way and valuing others as equal to yourself are important parts of being _____.
3. _____ occurs when two or more people disagree on an issue and feel threatened in some way.
4. A situation can _____ when we don't manage conflict effectively.
5. _____ occurs when people are able to find a peaceful solution to their disagreement.

THINKING CRITICALLY

Conflict can lead to positive outcomes. Write a paragraph about a situation in which a conflict, if handled well, might lead to a positive outcome for the people involved. Explain the situation and why the outcome might be positive.

TAKE IT HOME

Share the conflict management strategies with someone in your family or community and ask them which approach they think they use the most. Ask questions and try to get an example of a time they used the approach and what happened as a result.

LESSON 10.3
Bullying and Hazing

Terms to Learn
bully
bullying
cyberbullying
hazing

The Big Picture
Bullying and hazing can affect people of all ages and walks of life. Young people are particularly vulnerable to being both perpetrators and victims of these behaviors. Understanding risk factors and how to prevent and respond to both bullying and hazing behaviors can help keep individuals and communities safer.

Learning Targets
- Compare and contrast traditional bullying and cyberbullying.
- Identify strategies for preventing all forms of bullying.
- Describe how victims of bullying can seek help.
- Explain how violating laws against cyberbullying may affect one's future.
- Compare and contrast bullying and hazing.
- Identify long- and short-term consequences of participating in hazing.

Write About It
Do you think teasing someone is the same as bullying? Explain your answer.

Note-Taking Guide
Use this chapter's note-taking guide to help you organize and remember the material in this lesson.

LESSON 10.3 Violence and Conflict

Steven is a pretty small guy. In fact, he is the shortest guy in his class. He also wears glasses and describes himself as a nerd. Steven is a first-year high school student. When he gets to campus, some of the older guys tease him. Sometimes they will crowd around him and trip him up or push him hard enough that he starts to stumble. Steven tries to ignore them and doesn't want to do anything to escalate the situation or make it more violent. The worst part is that all the other kids in the hallway watch and sometimes laugh—no one seems to care. Steven is a friendly kid, but it seems as if no one wants to hang out with him at school. Why do you think the older students choose to be mean to Steven? Why do you think the other students just watch and don't choose to help?

Bullying

Bullying is a common occurrence in schools across the United States. One in five high school students reports being bullied on school property, and one in seven high school students is a victor of cyberbullying (texting, Instagram, Facebook, or other social media). **Bullying** refers to any unwanted aggressive behavior by one person or group of people who are not siblings or dating partners. Bullying involves a real or perceived difference in power and is repeated multiple times. In other words, the person doing the bullying, or **bully**, thinks they are more important or powerful than the person they are bullying. Figure 10.8 highlights the four types of bullying and examples of each: physical, emotional, social, and cyber. **Cyberbullying**, also referred to as *electronic bullying*, is a type of bullying through the use of technology.

Influences on Bullying Behavior

People often become bullies when they have been bullied themselves, or when they have been the victim of other forms of abuse or violence. A person who is both the victim of bullying and the offender is called a *bully victim*. There are common characteristics among many bullies, and among many victims of bullying as well (see figure 10.9).

Physical bullying
hitting, kicking, punching, spitting, tripping, pushing

Emotional bullying
teasing, name calling, inappropriate sexual comments, verbal or written threats

Social bullying
excluding someone, spreading rumors, making embarassing comments

Cyberbullying
hurtful rumors, sharing private content without permission, posting lies about others, posting hateful or embarrassing comments about others

Figure 10.8 Types of bullying.

438

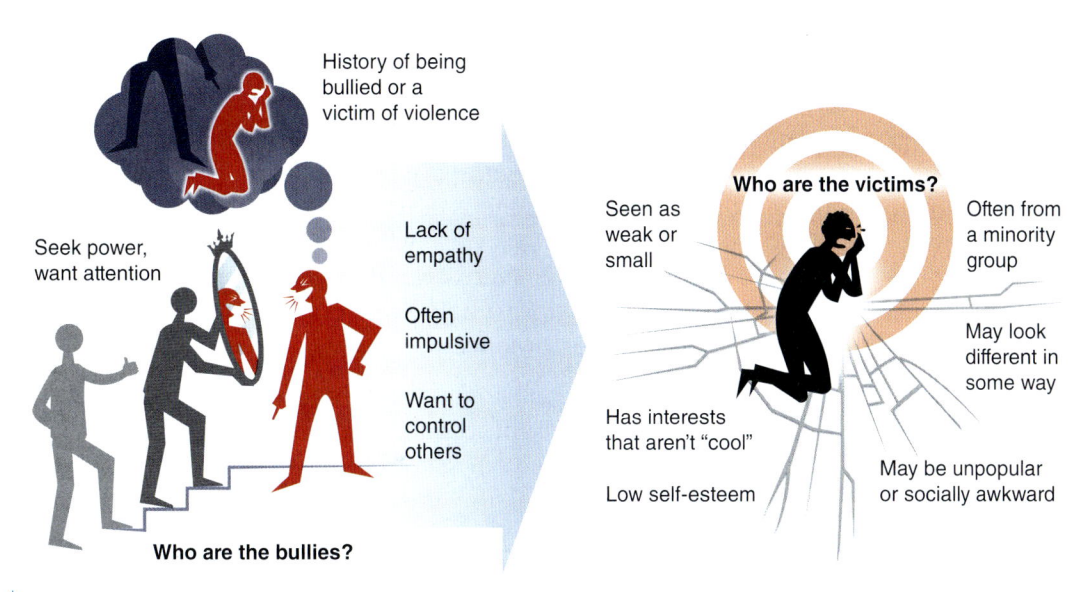

Figure 10.9 Characteristics of bullies and victims of bullying.

Consequences of Bullying

Bullying is an unacceptable social behavior that can have short- and long-term consequences and even lead to the suicide of the victim. Young people who experience bullying may be afraid to go to school and may have difficulty concentrating. This can lead to poorer academic performance or dropping out of school. Bullying leads to a number of issues including depression, anxiety, and sleep difficulties, and can make a person fearful or distrusting of others. This can negatively affect relationships and social support.

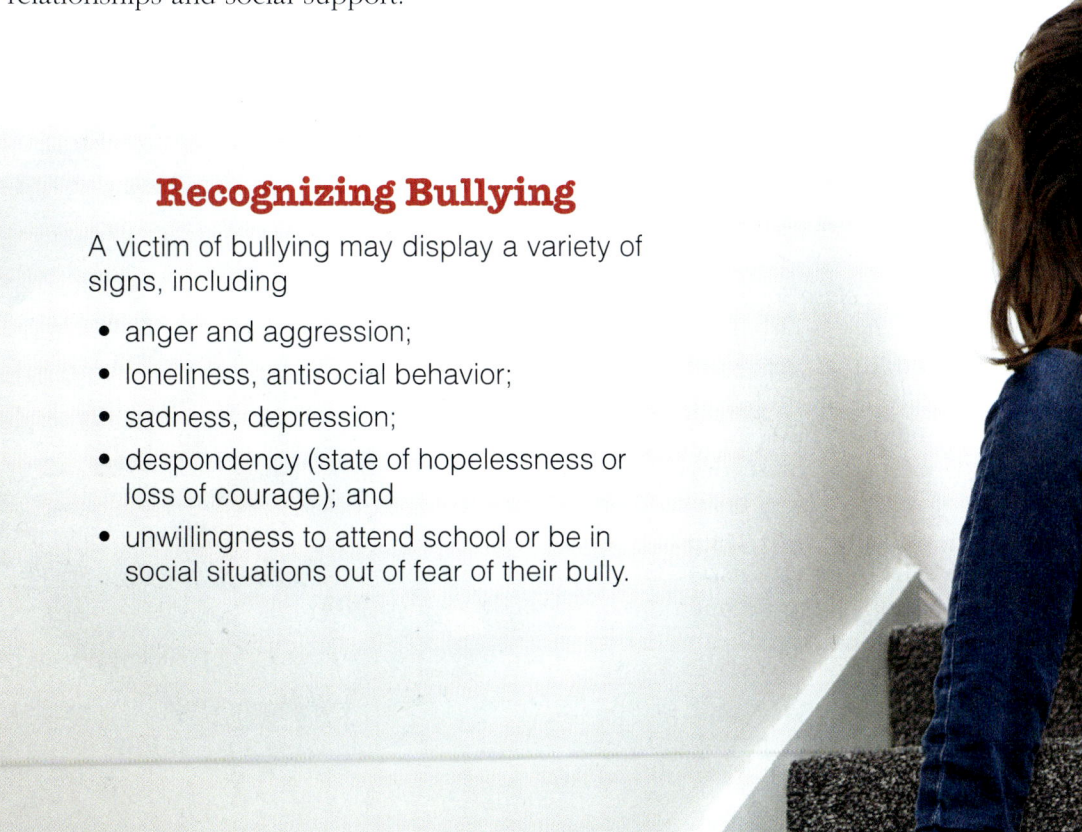

Recognizing Bullying

A victim of bullying may display a variety of signs, including

- anger and aggression;
- loneliness, antisocial behavior;
- sadness, depression;
- despondency (state of hopelessness or loss of courage); and
- unwillingness to attend school or be in social situations out of fear of their bully.

Responding to Bullying

If you are being bullied, it is important to do something to try to stop the behavior. Remember, you want to work toward an assertive, not aggressive, communication style in these situations. If you respond to aggressive behavior with more aggression, the situation will get worse. When someone is assertive, they express themselves effectively and stand up for their point of view while also respecting the rights and beliefs of others. When someone is aggressive, they don't consider the rights and beliefs of others. Here are some tips to help you be assertive when standing up to bullying or other forms of peer violence.

- *Speak up and tell someone.* The most important thing you can do if you are being bullied is to tell someone. A parent, coach, teacher, school counselor, or other trusted adult is a good choice. Use your school reporting system if you have one. Remember that you are valued and no one deserves to be bullied. Advocating for strong school policies that prevent bullying can also be a good way to turn a negative experience into a positive outcome.

- *Ask the bully to stop.* Use assertive communication to firmly and confidently ask the bully to stop. Use a calm, even tone of voice, make eye contact, and be honest and direct. Being assertive with a bully works best when it is done early, before the bullying becomes aggressive or excessive. It is also helpful to tell an adult about the situation and to be assertive with others around you who will support you.

- *Don't respond; instead walk away.* If it is possible, avoid the bully and walk away from verbal comments. Bullies want to get a response, especially fear. If you remain emotionless in your expression and walk away from the situation, you are preventing them from getting what they want.

- *Avoid a physical confrontation.* Whenever possible, avoid fighting back if a bully shoves or pushes you. If a situation turns violent, self-defense may be necessary. Otherwise, don't stoop to the bully's level; instead be stronger and better than they are.

- *Stay close to friends and adults.* Avoid being isolated or alone when the bully is around. Staying near teachers, other staff members, or security employees during breaks and walking with friends between classes can help. You are more likely to be bullied if you are alone.

Don't Be a Bystander

If you are a bystander to bullying, it is also important that you do something. It is not okay to know someone is being bullied and not speak up. Consider these options:

- *Say something to the bully.* People who bully may think they're being funny or cool. If you feel safe, tell the person to stop the bullying behavior. Tell them that you don't like it and it isn't funny.
- *Don't bully back.* It won't help if you use derogatory names or actions. This will likely only make things worse.
- *Be a friend to the victim.* Be kind to the person being bullied, offering sentiments of support like, "I'm sorry about what happened." Help them see that it isn't their fault. Be a friend and invite the student to do something with you, like walking to class together, or working together on a project. Tell the student being bullied to talk to someone about what happened, and offer to go along.
- *Say something to other bystanders.* Speak up if there are other bystanders and tell them that it isn't okay to just watch and not help.
- *Tell an adult.* Think about whom you could tell in your school—a teacher, counselor, nurse, principal, bus driver, or coach.

Cyberbullying

Cyberbullying is similar to traditional bullying in a lot of ways. It shares most of the same influences and consequences. In other ways, it is quite different and can even be worse. Electronic media is not only fast but instant, so rumors, lies, and hurtful posts spread quickly and widely. People are often more aggressive online because they can hide behind the screen and remain anonymous, sometimes making cyberbullying even more aggressive and cruel than traditional bullying. See figure 10.10 for examples of what cyberbullying looks like. Hurtful rumors, sharing another person's private photos and messages, and other behaviors can spread especially fast among students at school as they check their phones throughout the day and chat in person about the messages.

LESSON 10.3 Violence and Conflict

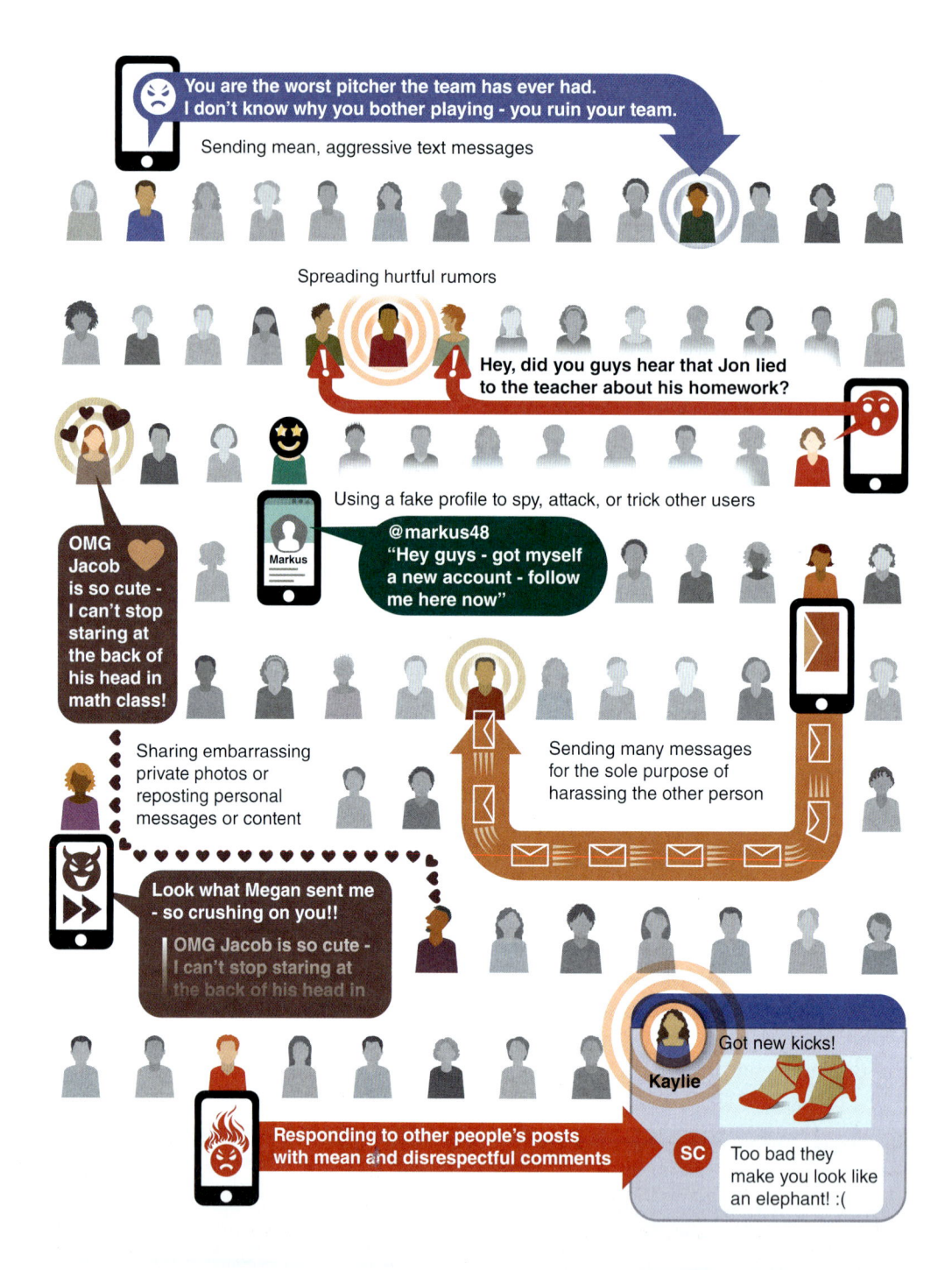

Figure 10.10 What cyberbullying looks like.

Sometimes people are trying to be funny and to get attention on social media, and they hurt someone else in the process. If this happens rarely, it is not cyberbullying. True cyberbullying happens repeatedly over time and is intentional. If you hurt someone online by accident, it is important to apologize to the person. Removing a hurtful post and apologizing publicly online shows maturity.

Digital Communication and Cyberbullying

We live in a world of rapid communication that happens mainly in digital forms like texting, social media, and email. How you communicate in a digital environment can have serious consequences for yourself and others now and far into the future. Cyberbullying is a common example of how digital communication can be misused when we don't exercise good digital citizenship (see figure 10.11). To be a better digital citizen and help prevent cyberbullying you should do the following:

- Learn how to share your emotions and point of view while respecting others.
- Understand how to balance rights to free speech with rights that others have to be free of harassment.
- Understand legal consequences for some forms of digital communication.

Figure 10.11 Being a good digital citizen—things to ask yourself when using digital forms of communication.

Responding to Cyberbullying

Whether cyberbullying occurs at school or elsewhere, you can respond in ways that are similar to responding to traditional bullying. It can be hard to talk to others about cyberbullying, especially if it means sharing an embarrassing photo or post in the process. It is important to tell a trusted adult about what is happening. The sooner you let someone know, the sooner the situation can be addressed. Also remember the following:

- Don't join in on cyberbullying.
- Pay attention to group chats you join or are added to.
- Avoid adding or supporting mean comments and becoming part of the problem.
- Reach out to the person being cyberbullied and offer support.
- Block anyone who cyberbullies you.
- Do not respond to a cyberbully because it only reinforces the bully and will make them do more.
- Screenshot an image and keep it as proof that you have been cyberbullied by the person. That way if the post is removed from a site, you still have evidence of what happened.
- Consult the social media site you are using for guidelines and policies about how to handle bullying on their site.

LESSON 10.3 Violence and Conflict

> **HEALTHY LIVING TIP**
> Take the time to learn about privacy settings on the social media platforms you use and be cautious about sharing too many details about your life. Criminals and other people who might want to harm you can use that information to gain your trust or to attack your character.

When Is Bullying and Cyberbullying Illegal?

Certain forms of bullying and cyberbullying that include harassment can be considered crimes. People engaged in bullying can face a range of potential legal charges and consequences. The seriousness of both the charge and the consequences varies depending on the state you live in, the type of bullying, the circumstances surrounding the bullying, and the extent to which the victim was affected. Bullying someone because of their race, national origin, gender, sexual orientation, disability, or religion may overlap with discriminatory harassment and civil rights laws. Many of these cases get prosecuted as harassment and result in fines, community service, or jail time. Some cases of bullying are considered hate crimes. Committing online hate crimes can result in federal criminal charges under the Computer Fraud and Abuse Act.

State Laws and Cyberbullying

Each state enforces different rules that relate to bullying. All fifty states have some sort of bullying legislation in place, but not all states recognize bullying as a crime. For example, North Carolina law (§ 115C-407.16) requires each local school administrative unit to adopt a policy prohibiting bullying or harassing behavior, including cyberbullying, on school property, at school-sanctioned events, or outside of school. North Carolina and many other states also allow cyberbullying to be reported anonymously and provide injunctions (for example, a restraining order that requires the bully to stop). Anyone who violates an order to stop cyberbullying can face criminal charges that can result in jail time and financial penalties. Schools can also impose separate consequences including school suspensions or expulsions.

Sexting, Child Pornography, and Cyberbullying

In some cases, cyberbullying can become a much more serious federal crime. Sexting is one example of how cyberbullying can result in very serious charges and consequences. A person who sends sexual or explicit images online or through social media can be charged with distributing pornography. If the victim(s) in the shared photo is a minor, the charge becomes distributing child pornography. This is true even if a minor takes the photo and sends the photo themselves and does so willingly. Being found guilty of the distribution of child pornography is a serious federal offense that will result in a prison sentence and being registered as a lifelong sex offender.

Hazing

Hazing is any activity expected of someone joining or participating in a group that humiliates, degrades, abuses, or endangers them. Hazing is similar to bullying, but it has one major difference. Bullying involves a power imbalance and is done specifically to cause harm to others. Hazing, on the other hand, is a ritual done as a way of trying to include others as part of a group. People who engage in hazing often fail to see their behavior as harmful. Hazing may involve mental or physical discomfort, embarrassment, humiliation, or ridicule. Hazing is often thought of as something that happens only in colleges, especially in fraternities and sororities. In reality, as many as 47 percent of U.S. high school students have experienced hazing when joining clubs, groups, or teams. The most common types of hazing that students experience involve binge drinking, verbal abuse, humiliation, isolation, and sleep deprivation. Specific examples include the following:

- Assigning embarrassing tasks to victims as a form of public humiliation
- Banning victims from associating with certain people
- Depriving victims of necessities such as sleep or food
- Forcing victims to binge drink or participate in drinking games
- Making victims act as a personal servant to older group members

As with bullying, if you experience hazing, talking to a trusted adult and getting the support and help you need are important. Healthy groups, clubs, and teams do not need to engage in dangerous or risky rituals in order to help new members feel welcomed and included. If you are in a position of leadership, it is also important to critically evaluate the traditions that may be in place to ensure that hazing is not occurring.

Consequences of Hazing

In the United States, hazing rituals account for at least one death and cause injury or illness to many others annually. Alcohol poisoning from forced drinking is the number one cause of death and serious illness related to hazing. People who instigate hazing are likely to face suspension or expulsion from school and criminal charges—especially when the hazing event involves underage drinking or excessive drinking by adults. Victims of hazing may experience anxiety, depression, or other emotional and mental health consequences.

Skill-Building Challenge

Analyzing Influences

Reflect on yourself and your own circumstances. Think about your risk for engaging in bullying or cyberbullying and your risk of being a victim of bullying or cyberbullying. Write down as many positive and negative influences that you can think of that relate to your risk. Then identify which category each influence represents: individual, peer, family, media, technology, societal. Positive influences protect you from becoming a bully or a bully victim. Negative influences make you more likely of becoming a bully or bully victim. Label each positive influence with a plus sign and each negative influence with a minus sign to determine which risk is higher for you.

Healthy Living Skills

This lesson focused on analyzing influences. Here are some more ways you can develop healthy living skills related to this lesson.

ACCESSING INFORMATION

Research and identify both your state's law(s) and school's rules and policies that are specific to bullying and cyberbullying. Summarize them in your own words and then use a realistic example to illustrate a cyberbullying behavior that could result in either legal charges or serious school penalties.

MAKING HEALTHY DECISIONS

Jesse wanted to be a part of a club at his school. It is a tradition for new members to steal a beer from a grocery store in order to be admitted into the club and he wasn't so sure if it was worth taking the risk just to be in the club. What are two potential short- and long-term impacts for Jesse if he participated in the tradition, and if he refused to participate in the ritual?

LESSON 10.3 Violence and Conflict

LESSON 10.3 Review: Bullying and Hazing

LESSON SUMMARY

- Traditional bullying consists of aggressive acts that are physical (e.g., hitting), social (e.g., spreading rumors), or emotional (e.g., name-calling).
- Cyberbullying is a form of bullying done through technology and can include starting rumors, saying cruel things, and harming someone's reputation online or via text.
- Bullies, who themselves may have been victims of bullying or violence, often want to exert power over someone else or seek attention.
- Victims of bullying can speak up and tell an adult, ask the bully to stop, walk away, avoid a confrontation, and stay close to friends and adults.
- Both bullying and cyberbullying can be against the law and can result in criminal charges. This is especially true of cyberbullying that involves sexually inappropriate messages or images.
- Hazing is similar to bullying except that hazing is done as a ritual way to include others in a group, while bullying is done as a way to harm and exclude others.

REVIEWING CONCEPTS AND VOCABULARY

1. Bullying can occur through physical, emotional, electronic, or _____ actions.
2. Sending mean, aggressive text messages is an example of _____.
3. If someone is bullied because of race, national origin, gender, sexual orientation, disability, or religion, the bullying may overlap with discriminatory harassment and _____ laws.
4. Forcing someone to drink alcohol in order to join a club is an example of _____.

THINKING CRITICALLY

What are some ways that a group or team could build cohesion and honor rituals for new members without engaging in hazing? Provide specific examples and explain how they might help a group bond in a healthy and supportive way.

TAKE IT HOME

Reach out to a younger kid in your neighborhood or community and teach them about strategies for preventing all forms of bullying and cyberbullying. Teach them what they should do if they are ever bullied.

LESSON 10.4

Violence, Weapons, and Gangs

Terms to Learn
gang
suspicious activity
youth violence

The Big Picture
Youth violence, including school violence and gang activity, is a serious problem in many U.S. schools and communities. If we are to reduce or stop youth violence, we need to understand what causes it and how it affects us individually and as a community. This includes understanding the risks associated with owning and carrying weapons.

Learning Targets
- Compare the risks associated with various types of weapons.
- Describe the risks and consequences of gang involvement.
- Explain how to avoid and report gang violence.
- Analyze how public policies regarding weapons influence the health and safety of communities.

Write About It
How do you feel about gun ownership? Do you think guns help prevent or contribute to violent behaviors?

Note-Taking Guide
Use this chapter's note-taking guide to help you organize and remember the material in this lesson.

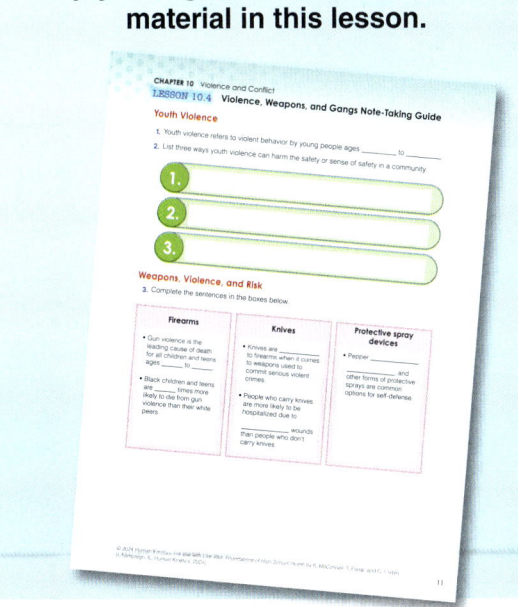

LESSON 10.4   Violence and Conflict

Sierra's boyfriend Max has been hanging around a pretty rough crowd lately. She is worried that Max's new friends are part of a local gang. Sierra has tried to hang out with the group hoping that Max would behave differently if she was around, but that hasn't happened. Last night the group shoplifted from a local convenience store, and Max took one item to make sure he impressed his new friends. One of the guys had a concealed gun in his pocket, but fortunately, he never took it out. Max had never stolen anything before. Sierra is worried about the way Max is changing, and she doesn't know what to do or who to talk to. She is also worried for her own safety—she doesn't want to be pressured to join the group, but she also doesn't want to lose Max. What can Sierra do in this situation?

Youth Violence

Youth violence refers to violent behavior by young people ages 10 to 24. Most often, it is peer-to-peer violence involving fights, threats with weapons, and gang activity. Bullying is also a form of youth violence, especially when the bullying involves physical aggression. Perpetrators of youth violence often show aggressive behavior at a very young age and lack impulse control, emotional control, and social and problem-solving skills.

Youth violence is a common occurrence in the United States. Consider some of these statistics:

- In 2020, firearm-related injuries increased by 30 percent and became the leading cause of death among children and youth under 18.
- Among young people ages 15 to 24, 56.6 percent of firearm deaths were homicides (murder).
- An estimated 16,644 children and teens were injured with guns in 2018—one every 32 minutes.
- In 2019, nine children and teens were killed with guns each day in America—one every 2 hours and 36 minutes.

Violence, Weapons, and Gangs **LESSON 10.4**

Youth violence doesn't just affect the young people involved—it can also harm the safety or sense of safety in a community. Violence increases the need of young people needing emergency medical care. It causes people to avoid living in certain neighborhoods, making these neighborhoods less desirable for other businesses and services. Violence also prevents social services from social workers, police, and public defenders from providing adequate assistances to victims of other crimes.

Weapons, Violence, and Risk

Weapons are an unfortunate part of violent actions and behaviors. While a majority of weapons are intended to be used for legal activities like hunting, or for self-protection, all weapons pose their own risks and can cause harm to the user. The presence of weapons in a house, on school grounds, or in public settings increases the likelihood of both accidents and violent events. The following sections highlight the dangers associated with a variety of commonly owned weapons.

Firearms

Firearms like pistols, rifles, and shotguns are dangerous weapons that have deadly consequences. In fact, 76.7 percent of all homicides in 2020 in the United States were gun related. Gun violence is the leading cause of death for all children and teens ages 1 to 19; Black children and teens are four times more likely to die from gun violence than their white peers.

Understanding and following all gun safety rules and having good gun handling skills are important parts of being a responsible gun owner. Even when gun safety is followed, the presence of a gun in the home, at school, or in public increases the risk of accidental shootings, suicide, and homicide (see figure 10.12).

Knives

Knives are second to firearms when it comes to weapons used to commit serious violent crimes. Not all people who carry a knife have criminal intent. Some people will choose to carry a knife because it makes them feel safer. Some-

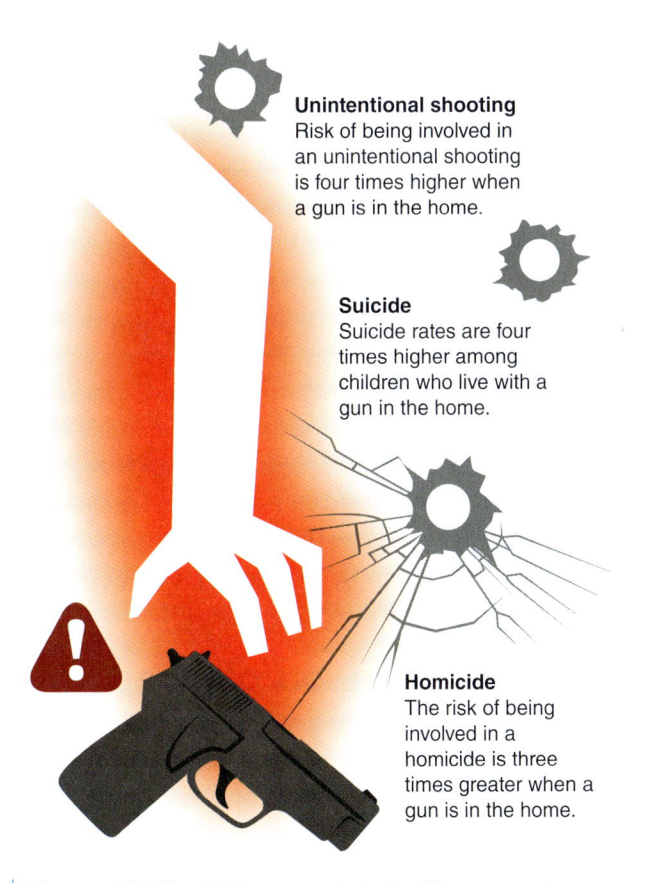

Unintentional shooting
Risk of being involved in an unintentional shooting is four times higher when a gun is in the home.

Suicide
Suicide rates are four times higher among children who live with a gun in the home.

Homicide
The risk of being involved in a homicide is three times greater when a gun is in the home.

Figure 10.12 Risks associated with access to firearms.

times people choose to carry a knife because they think it is less dangerous than carrying a gun. The reality is that carrying a knife also means carrying risk. If you carry a knife, you are carrying a dangerous weapon—it can result in a prison sentence even if you never use the knife to hurt anyone. Knives can also be taken from you and used against you. In fact, people who carry knives are more likely to be hospitalized due to stab wounds than people who don't carry knives. Knife wounds can cause serious injury and can be fatal—even when a person is not trying to kill someone.

Protective Spray Devices

Mace, pepper spray, and other forms of protective sprays are common options for self-defense. The most common of these products is pepper spray, which is legal for anyone over age 18 to carry in all states. It's an economical and relatively safe choice for self-defense: It can help hold off an attacker long enough for a potential victim to escape to safety.

Pepper spray is designed to temporarily disrupt breathing and vision. An accidental discharge that gets into a victim's lungs or eyes could make it harder to escape a dangerous situation. When carrying pepper spray, it is critical to know how to safely discharge the device in order to help avoid this risk. Other available self-defense sprays may be made from chemicals that are more potent than pepper spray.

Gang Violence

A **gang** is a group of people who commit violent and illegal acts. There are many reasons why youth actively join or find themselves pressured into joining a gang. Gangs often promise economic benefits (often from illegal activity like theft or drug sales), and they claim to offer protection, friendships, and status. While gangs can provide a feeling of safety and protection from other violent youth, gangs are actually unsafe and dangerous because they involve violent, often illegal, behaviors. Although no single, universal feature definitively makes a group into a gang, some common characteristics exist:

- Gangs have three or more members.
- Members share an identity, often linked to a name and other symbols.
- Members view themselves as a gang; likewise, others recognize them as a gang.
- Gangs have some permanence and a degree of organization.
- Gangs are involved in an elevated level of delinquent or criminal activity.

Risk Factors of Gang Violence

The factors that put a young person at risk for gang involvement are similar to the risks seen in other forms of youth violence. These factors are influenced at the individual, peer, school, family, and community levels (see figure 10.13).

Consequences of Gang Violence

Even if a young person is only a member of a gang for a short time, the consequences can last a lifetime. Gang members who are not killed or seriously injured often abuse alcohol or drugs or both. They develop extensive police records that can limit education and employment opportunities in the future. Gang members are also more likely to be incarcerated and to become victims of violent crime themselves.

INDIVIDUAL
Illegal gun ownership
Drug trafficking
Aggression
Alcohol or drug use
Previous delinquency
Previous victim of violence

PEER
Affiliation with gang members
Friends who use drugs
Strong friendships with delinquent peers

SCHOOL
Poor performance
Low motivation
Negative labeling by teachers
Lack of role models
Low connection to school

FAMILY
Parent or guardian drug or alcohol abuse
Family members who are gang members
Lack of role models
Family violence or neglect

COMMUNITY
High poverty
High crime
Drug availability
Firearm availability
Cultural norms around gangs

Figure 10.13 Risk factors of gang violence.

Avoiding Gang Violence

Young people can help reduce gang violence by not joining gangs in the first place. Joining clubs, sport teams, and student organizations or participating in available after-school or community programs is a better way to find a place where you belong that is healthy and safe. It is also important to avoid gangs and areas frequented by gangs whenever you can. Even if you aren't part of a gang, you can become a victim of gang violence. Gangs are well skilled at using pressure to coerce young people into participating. If someone is pressuring you to get involved in a gang, use the following refusal skills and talk to someone you trust who will support you in your decision:

- Use a strong voice, stand up tall, and be clear that your answer is "no."
- Give a reason why you are saying "no."
- Walk away and go to a safe place like your classroom, home, or a community center.

Reporting Gang Violence

It is important to talk to adults you trust if you feel pressured by gang members or are a victim of gang violence. Others can help you make decisions that will keep you safer in dangerous situations. It is also possible to get help in safely leaving a gang. If you are a victim of gang violence and you don't know where to turn for help, you can call the National Center for Victims of Crime (855-484-2846) or text or call the HopeLine (919-231-4525 or 877-235-4525).

School Violence

School violence is any violent act committed on school grounds or at school functions. It occurs in hallways, on buses, in classrooms, in bathrooms, and at concerts or events. Fights, the use of weapons at school, and bullying are examples of school violence. Schools should be a safe place for all students, faculty, and staff.

Violence in school can have consequences for an offender's education and can result in criminal charges. Most schools maintain violence-prevention programs and have school policies and procedures in place in the event of a violent act. The best way to prevent violence at school is to follow the rules designed to keep you safe and to report violent or suspicious activity. A **suspicious activity** is anything that causes a feeling that something is wrong or that someone is doing something wrong.

Suspicious behavior at school might include the following:

- Something that looks out of place like an unattended backpack in the hallway
- Someone hanging out where they don't belong or usually don't hang out
- A strange adult lingering near the parking lot or athletic fields
- A group of people trying to be secretive about their actions, potentially buying and selling drugs

Violence, Weapons, and Gangs   **LESSON 10.4**

It is also important not to allow your own biases to influence how you view the behaviors of people who are different from yourself. Being different is not the same thing as acting suspicious.

Skill-Building Challenge

Analyzing Influences

Research federal and local laws related to owning and carrying weapons. Describe these laws and analyze how they might influence individual behaviors and choices and the health and safety of communities. Develop a two-minute speech that either supports the value of the existing laws or supports changing the laws. Share your speech with a classmate and discuss your respective positions.

Healthy Living Skills

This lesson focused on analyzing influences. Here are some more ways you can develop healthy living skills related to this lesson.

ACCESSING INFORMATION
Research the unique dangers associated with handguns, knives, shotguns, and rifles. Consider issues of storage, safety, and common accidents in addition to criminal activity. Create a chart that compares and contrasts the risks each type of weapon poses.

HEALTHY COMMUNICATION
Write about how you would talk to an adult if you were in a threatening situation. Remember to explain the situation, describe the threat, and identify the risks to you and others. Be sure to also ask for help.

MAKING HEALTHY DECISIONS
What are the short- and long-term consequences of becoming involved in a gang? Develop a decision tree or write a short story that illustrates what might happen to someone who chooses to join a gang versus someone who does not.

PRACTICING HEALTHY BEHAVIORS
Identify the individuals and places in your life that might make you more likely to engage in violent behaviors or be the victim of violence. Consider ways to avoid or limit your exposure to the people and places on your list and follow through with some of your ideas.

LESSON 10.4 Review: Violence, Weapons, and Gangs

LESSON SUMMARY

- Youth violence is violence committed by and against individuals ages 10 to 24 and includes fights, threats with weapons, gang violence, and bullying.
- Firearms, knives, and protective spray devices are weapons that can provide both protection and dangers for the owner.
- Unintentional shooting, suicide, and homicide are all consequences of having access to firearms.
- Knives are second to firearms when it comes to weapons that are used to commit violent crimes.
- A gang is a group of people who commit violent and illegal acts.
- School violence can happen anywhere on campus or at a school event. Hallways, restrooms, isolated areas, and buses are common places for school violence to occur.
- Gang violence can be avoided by joining safe and healthy clubs or organizations like sports teams, band, or other student organizations.
- It is critical to report gang violence to a trusted adult or to the National Center for Victims of Crime (855-484-2846).

REVIEWING CONCEPTS AND VOCABULARY

1. Bullying committed by people ages 10 to 24 is an example of _____.
2. Access to firearms increases the likelihood of unintentional shootings, _____, and homicide.
3. _____ are used in more violent crimes than any other weapon.
4. There is no single defining feature of a _____, but it shares some common characteristics.
5. Someone hanging out where they don't belong or usually don't hang out is an example of _____.

THINKING CRITICALLY

What could be done in your community to help prevent kids and young people from joining gangs? Come up with at least one idea and explain why you think it would work.

TAKE IT HOME

Talk to a parent or guardian to understand their views on owning weapons like mace, knives, and guns. Try to understand what influences their perspectives and choices. In a paragraph, reflect on how your family's views might influence your personal views about owning weapons.

LESSON 10.5
Relationships and Violence

Terms to Learn
abuse
coercion
domestic violence
elder abuse
human trafficking
neglect
personal boundaries
sex trafficking
sexual assault
sexual coercion
sibling abuse

The Big Picture
Humans are social creatures. We benefit from being in healthy relationships with others. Healthy relationships are free from coercion, violence, and intimidation. If relationships are unhealthy, they can become violent. Understanding the ways in which relationships can be violent can help you make smarter choices and stay safe.

Learning Targets
- Compare and contrast abuse and neglect.
- Identify signs and symptoms of child abuse.
- Explain how domestic violence usually begins and identify the consequences of domestic violence for the victim.
- Provide examples of how coercion and sexual coercion may be used in a relationship.
- Explain how to recognize and protect yourself from human trafficking.

Note-Taking Guide
Use this chapter's note-taking guide to help you organize and remember the material in this lesson.

Write About It
How often does the media you use portray violence in romantic relationships? Do you think these portrayals reflect what happens in real life? Why or why not?

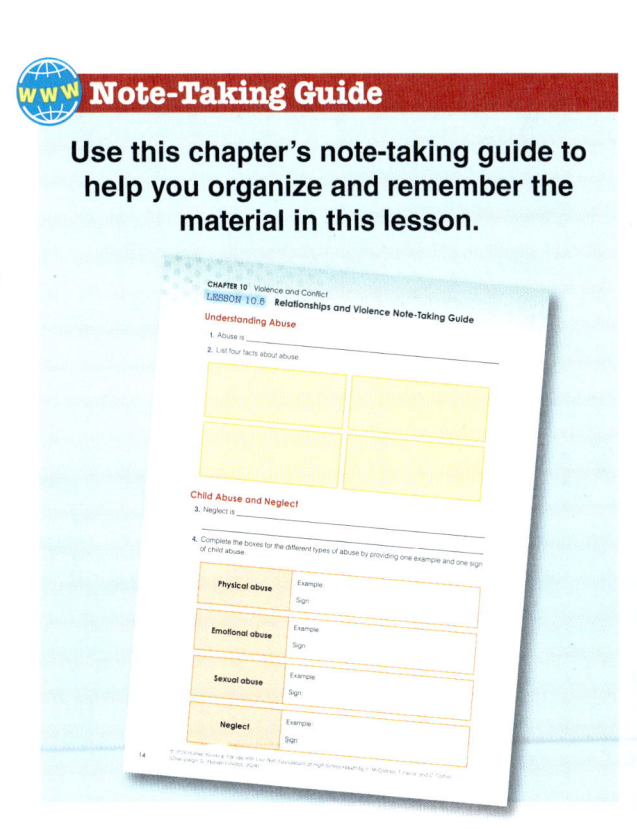

455

LESSON 10.5 Violence and Conflict

Sara really liked dating Noah. They spent time at sporting events and liked going to see movies together in the summer. After a couple of months, Noah started to call Sara almost every hour of the day to see what she was doing. One day at a baseball game, Sara and another guy were talking about a popular movie. When Noah saw them, he came over and abruptly told Sara it was time to go. As soon as she said she didn't want to leave yet, Noah grabbed her by the arm and pulled her behind him as he walked away. When they were alone, Noah accused Sara of flirting and told her that if she talked to him or anyone else again, she'd be sorry. Do you think Sara and Noah have a healthy relationship? Do you think these events should concern Sara? What would you advise Sara to do in this situation?

Understanding Abuse

Healthy relationships are not abusive relationships, meaning you should not experience violence or be afraid that violence could happen to you by your partner. **Abuse** is the consistent and violent mistreatment of a person and can occur in all types of relationships. A parent who hits their child, a brother who locks his sister in her room, and someone who shoves their partner into the wall are all being abusive in their relationships.

Being a form of violence, abuse can be physical, emotional, and sexual in nature. Abuse that occurs in relationships where people love and care for one another can be especially confusing and hard to understand. Oftentimes the abuser tries to blame the victim for the abuse. A spouse might say, "I wouldn't have to treat you like this if you didn't dress the way you do," or a sibling might say, "I'm doing it for your own good." No matter what the relationship or the situation, abuse is never the victim's fault. The abuser is always the one responsible for the abuse.

There are several reasons abuse may go unreported. Victims may be afraid to speak up or defend themselves because they don't want things to get worse; they don't have the financial ability to leave the relationship; or they are afraid of losing the relationship completely. These complexities and challenges can be difficult and frustrating for others to understand. That being said, abuse is never okay, and it should be reported to the police.

Child Abuse and Neglect

A report of child abuse is made every 10 seconds in the United States. Child abuse is when a parent or caregiver causes injury, death, emotional harm, or risk of serious harm to a child. Child abuse can occur through a violent action or from **neglect**—a caretaker's failure to meet the basic physical, emotional, medical, or educational needs of a child. Child abuse and neglect cause multiple short- and long-term consequences for the victim (see figure 10.14).

- **Physical** harm like broken bones, brain damage, burns, and bruises
- **Psychological** harm like anxiety, depression, PTSD, eating disorders, anger, and emotional outbursts
- **Relationship** harm like inability to trust others, be vulnerable, and make meaningful connections
- Links to smoking, alcohol, and drug abuse, criminal activity, and difficulty in school

Figure 10.14 Consequences of child abuse and neglect.

Risk Factors for Child Abuse and Neglect

Child abuse and neglect are forms of violent behavior, so naturally, they share many of the same risk factors as other forms of violence. Stress, substance abuse, and poverty are just a few examples of such risk factors. In addition, child abuse and neglect are associated with teen pregnancy, marriage difficulties, and lack of parenting knowledge (e.g., difficulties with a child, such as disobedience, frequent crying, or challenging medical conditions).

Recognizing and Reporting Child Abuse and Neglect

A person who suspects that a child is the victim of abuse or neglect should report it to authorities. See table 10.1 for signs and symptoms of child abuse. States often maintain specific hotlines for reporting the abuse of a child, and a national hotline is available at 800-4-a-Child (800-422-4453). The Childhelp website (www.childhelp.org) also maintains a searchable database of local child protective services numbers.

People in certain professions are considered mandatory reporters. A mandatory reporter is a person who, because of their profession, is legally required to report any suspicion of child abuse or neglect to the relevant authorities. Laws about mandatory reporting vary by state. Professions typically included in these laws are social workers, teachers, health care workers, childcare providers, law enforcement, mental health professionals, and other educators and medical professionals. In some states, all citizens are required to report suspected cases of child abuse.

LESSON 10.5 Violence and Conflict

TABLE 10.1   Signs and Symptoms of Child Abuse

Type of abuse	Examples of abuse	Signs of abuse
Physical abuse	Burns the child Hits, kicks, or bites the child Holds the child under water Shakes or throws the child Throws objects at the child Ties up the child	Bruising Severe injuries (e.g., broken bones) Several injuries spread over the body Injuries over a period of time
Emotional abuse	Abuses others when the child is around Fails to show love and affection Ignores the child and doesn't give emotional support and guidance Shames, belittles, criticizes, or embarrasses the child Teases, threatens, bullies, or yells at the child	Withdrawn Anxiety Difficulty sleeping Difficulty concentrating Aggressive or inappropriate behavior
Sexual abuse	Forces the child to take part in sexual images Has any sexual contact with the child, including kissing Talks to child in sexually inappropriate ways Sends the child sexually explicit emails, texts, or other messages Exposes (abuser's) genitals to the child Shows pornography to the child Tells dirty jokes or stories	Fear of being touched Pain when walking or sitting Torn clothing Bruising around genitals Sexual knowledge not typical for child's age Inappropriate touching
Neglect	Fails to provide clothing Fails to provide food Fails to provide heat in cold weather Forces the child to live in unclean or unsanitary conditions Does not provide needed medical care	Missing school Poor hygiene Underweight Lack of development

Sibling Abuse

Sibling abuse is the mistreatment of one sibling by another. It is estimated that about 80 percent of people with siblings experience some degree of sibling abuse at some point in their childhood. Sibling abuse is most common between an older brother and a younger sibling, especially a sister, but it can occur in any sibling relationship. It is common for siblings to verbally fight on occasion, or to have a healthy rivalry, but aggressive or violent interactions should not occur. When injury occurs between siblings, it can be hard for parents to accept, and the victim can feel embarrassed or ashamed to come forward. In a healthy family environment, any act of violence is discussed and appropriate actions are taken to stop the behavior.

Elder Abuse and Neglect

Elder abuse is the mistreatment of older adults that occurs in their home, in nursing homes, in hospitals, or in other settings. Caregivers and family members are the most likely people to commit elder abuse. As with child abuse, the abuse of older people can be physical, emotional, and sexual, and it can involve neglect. Older adults, particularly those in nursing homes, who are dependent on the care and kindness of others, are especially vulnerable to elder abuse.

Domestic Violence

Violence between people in a romantic relationship, or between a married couple, is called **domestic violence**. In the United States, 20 people are victims of domestic violence every minute. Most often, this type of violence is used by one person in the relationship to try to control the other person. It can also occur between former partners and ex-spouses. Domestic violence among teenagers is called teen dating violence, or TDV. Nearly 1 in 11 female and 1 in 15 male high school students report having experienced TDV in the last year.

Domestic violence can begin at any point in a relationship. Most typically, it begins with verbal insults and controlling behavior. Examples of controlling behavior might include a partner monitoring what the other person is doing all the time (including stalking the other person), a partner who limits whom the other person can talk to or spend time with, or a partner who controls how the other person spends their own money. Over time, these behaviors become more common and can lead to violent confrontations. Assaults, batteries, rapes, and murders occur in domestic violence situations.

Domestic violence is never okay, and abuse has no place in a healthy romantic relationship. When someone is the victim of domestic violence, they should leave and seek help right away. Violence in a romantic relationship rarely happens just once, and the longer a person stays in a violent relationship, the harder it often becomes to break free of that relationship. Domestic violence leads to physical and emotional injuries. Anxiety and depression are common among abuse victims. Fear of coming forward, combined with a controlling partner, can also lead to social isolation and hopelessness.

Sexual Assault

Sexual assault is any forced or unwanted sexual contact. Both sexes and people of all ages can be the victims of sexual assault. It is most common for a sexual assault victim to know their offender, and teenagers are more likely than other age groups to be victims of a sexual assault. It is important to understand the truth about sexual assault in order to protect yourself and others. Table 10.2 features common myths about sexual assault.

TABLE 10.2   **Common Myths and Facts About Sexual Assault**

Myth	Fact
Sexual assault is often the result of miscommunication or a mistake.	Sexual assault is any unwanted sexual contact. It is obtained without consent through the use of force, threat of force, intimidation, or coercion. Sexual assault is a crime, not a mistake or result of miscommunication.
Victims cause the violence that has happened to them.	It doesn't matter what someone is wearing or how they are acting—no one asks to be raped or sexually assaulted. Rape and sexual assault are crimes of violence and control that stem from a person's determination to exercise power over another. Forcing someone to engage in nonconsensual sexual activity is sexual assault, regardless of the way that person dresses or acts.
There is no reason for a victim not to report being raped to law enforcement.	Rape is the least reported and convicted violence crime in the United States. There are many reasons related to fear, shame, pressure, and distrust that may keep a victim from reporting the crime to law enforcement.
If a person goes to someone's room or house, or if they go to a bar, they should know that sex is expected of them. They know what they are doing.	This myth wrongfully places the responsibility of the offender's actions on the victim. Even if a person goes voluntarily to someone's residence or room and consents to engage in some sexual activity, it does not serve as a blanket consent for all sexual activity.
It's not sexual assault if it happens after drinking or taking drugs.	A person who is under the influence of alcohol or drugs cannot legally give consent. Having sex with someone who is legally unable to give consent is sexual assault.
It's only rape if the victim puts up a fight and resists.	There are many reasons why a victim of sexual assault would not fight or resist their attacker. They may feel that fighting or resisting will make their attacker angry, resulting in more severe injury or death.

Impacts of Sexual Assault

People who have been sexually assaulted may show a range of emotional and behavioral reactions that can have wide-reaching and long-lasting impacts. Teenage victims of sexual abuse may be more likely to abuse substances or engage in high-risk behaviors, including risky sexual behaviors (unprotected sex, multiple sexual partners). A teenager who seeks to avoid reminders of their abuse may withdraw socially. Self-harming and suicidal behaviors are also more common among adolescent victims.

Sexual assault is not part of a healthy relationship. Victims of sexual assault often experience emotional trauma, fear, guilt, self-blame, victim-blaming, and shame when they tell others about what happened. It can also be extremely difficult to report a sexual assault for these same reasons. The experience of having evidence collected and moving through the criminal justice system can result in additional emotional trauma as well. If you are the victim of a sexual assault it is critically important to report the assault as soon as possible so that evidence can be collected and you can be provided with the resources and support you need in order to recover. You can also reach out to the National Sexual Assault Hotline at https://www.rainn.org/.

Coercive Relationships

Relationships can also be abusive when they involve **coercion**—the act or process of persuading someone to do something they don't want to do. It can exist in any type of relationship, including friendships and family relationships. Coercion is not healthy and can result in risky behaviors, violence, and abuse.

In romantic relationships, or in dating situations, **sexual coercion** may occur. This is when someone uses pressure, alcohol, drugs, or coercion to have sexual contact with the other person against their will. You have control over your body and your choices in a relationship, and a person who loves and respects you should never use sexual coercion.

> **The following are some example tactics of coercion:**
> - The person tries to make you feel like you owe them something.
> - The person uses extreme compliments to get you to agree to do something.
> - The person uses the fact that you are in a relationship to get you to do something to prove you love them.
> - The person pressures you after you say "no."

Human and Sex Trafficking

Perpetrators of human trafficking and sex trafficking use coercion. **Human trafficking** happens when people are forced to perform a service or job against their will or in exchange for a basic human right like food or water. When the victim is required to perform sexual acts, it is called **sex trafficking**. It is estimated that about 80 percent of human trafficking cases involve sex trafficking.

Human trafficking and sex trafficking are inhumane. Victims are taken or coerced from their lives and placed in exceptionally painful situations where they are separated from family members, confined to small spaces, and regularly abused and mistreated. Human trafficking and sex trafficking are global issues and are major crimes that should be reported first to a parent or other trusted adult, and then to local authorities.

Victims of Sex Trafficking

Young children and young teenagers are especially vulnerable to sex trafficking predators. The average age of a sex trafficking victim is 12, and either gender can be victimized. Predators will use coercion to make a young person feel desired, wanted, appreciated, and loved. Older individuals may use online chat rooms and apps to deceive others into thinking they are innocent, younger peers, who just want to meet up for fun. They may also use flattery and seduction and establish a dating relationship with a younger victim before forcing them into the sex trafficking world. Predators may pose as modeling agents, photographers, or others who promise to help you improve your image or help you become a successful model or online influencer. Be cautious of such promises and always talk to an adult before engaging with others in this way.

Protect Yourself From Human Trafficking

Protecting yourself and others from human trafficking involves paying close attention to your personal safety. Avoid walking alone or going to public places alone. Do not give out personal information online or talk to strangers. Always take an adult or a group of at least three friends with you if you are meeting up with someone you met online. If the person really is someone worth being friends with, they will respect that you are protecting your safety. Finally, no older person should pursue a romantic relationship or friendship with you and tell you not to tell anyone about it. This is a very dangerous sign that the relationship is not healthy and may be coercive. If this occurs, always talk to a trusted adult about the situation. Figure 10.15 provides a list of potential signs that someone may be a victim of human trafficking.

Signs of Human Trafficking
- Appearing underweight
- Showing signs of physical injuries and abuse
- Avoiding eye contact
- Missing school
- Lying or not answering questions
- Spending time with older individuals
- Appearing to be in poor physical or mental health
- Being anxious or depressed

Figure 10.15 Someone who is a victim of human trafficking may show some of these signs.

Social and Emotional Consequences of Abuse

All forms of abuse can harm the health of the victim—especially their social and emotional well-being. Some of these consequences are common across all types of abuse. For example, victims of harassment, sexual abuse, sexual assault, and sex trafficking are all at a higher risk for anxiety and depression. Oftentimes a victim of abuse may not realize the impact of what has happened to them until sometime after the abuse or assault has stopped. The impact of abuse on someone's social and emotional well-being can be short- and long-term, lasting days, weeks, or even years. Sometimes future relationships, especially romantic relationships, can cause the victim to realize that they are carrying emotional trauma that they have not yet dealt with. Victims of all sorts of abuse are more likely to engage in high-risk behaviors like drinking, taking drugs, or engaging in illegal or dangerous activities.

Breaking the Cycle of Abuse

In all cases of abuse, the most important first steps are getting the victim necessary medical help for their injuries and reporting the abuse. Keep in mind that abuse is not a one-time situation—it will repeat. Even when it appears that the abuse has stopped, chances are the change is only temporary.

For abuse to stop, it is important to do the following:

- Acknowledge the abuse. Don't make excuses for others or for the abuser.
- Avoid trying to be the hero. Abusive situations need professional help. Victims need support and resources, and abusers need professional help if they are to stop their behavior.
- Be brave and help an abuse victim leave the situation. Help the victim by identifying crisis shelters and providing them with contact information.

Setting Personal Boundaries

Personal boundaries are the limits we set with other people (see figure 10.16). Personal boundaries can vary from person to person and be intellectual, emotional, physical, social, or spiritual. Establishing personal boundaries will help you know when a situation isn't good for you or is potentially dangerous or abusive. Personal boundaries are like other types of boundaries in that they help you know which lines you should not cross or should not let others cross. Honoring your boundaries will help keep you safe and can help prevent sexual coercion and sexual assault. The ability to know and honor your boundaries generally comes from valuing and respecting yourself.

HEALTHY LIVING TIP
Other people, especially romantic partners, need to know what your personal boundaries are. Being open and honest with what is and is not acceptable to you will help your partner to understand and respect your wishes.

LESSON 10.5 Violence and Conflict

Intellectual Boundaries
You are entitled to your own thoughts and opinions.
Others should not silence your perspective or disrespect your thoughts.

Emotional Boundaries
You are entitled to your own feelings.
Others should not tell you how you should feel or dismiss how you feel.

Physical Boundaries
You are entitled to your own space.
Others should never touch you without permission or try to coerce you into sexual acts.

Social Boundaries
You are entitled to your own friends and your own social activities.
When someone tries to isolate you from others, they may be crossing this boundary.

Spiritual Boundaries
You are entitled to your own spiritual beliefs.
When someone disrespects your religion or beliefs, they may be crossing this boundary.

Figure 10.16 Types of personal boundaries.

Skill-Building Challenge

Making Healthy Decisions

Read through the following scenarios and use the decision-making process to decide what the person should do. After you have made your decisions, identify one short-term and one long-term consequence of the decision.

SCENARIO 1: COLBY AND JOEL

Colby is three years older than his brother Joel. Both are athletes, and Joel is also a musician. He practices guitar with some of his friends in their family's garage. Colby is at his wit's end with their so-called garage band that plays what he calls "the bad music." Colby and his friends just want to play video games without all the background noise. Colby doesn't want his friends to stop coming over because of his little brother. One night, Colby decided he'd had enough. He forced Joel's hand in their bedroom's doorway and then slammed the door shut. Joel couldn't play guitar for a couple of weeks because of the injury.

What should Colby do in this situation?

_____

_____

Potential short-term consequence of decision:

_____

_____

Potential long-term consequence of decision:

_____

_____

SCENARIO 2: JADEN AND MORGAN

Jaden and Morgan are friends, but Jaden's feelings for Morgan have developed into romantic feelings for some time now. Jaden even bought Morgan an expensive gift last week. Today Jaden said, "Come on Morgan, just give me a kiss. I bought you that expensive gift last week. I think you kind of owe me something."

What should Morgan do in this situation?

_____
_____

Potential short-term consequence of decision:

_____
_____

Potential long-term consequence of decision:

_____
_____

Healthy Living Skills

This lesson focused on making healthy decisions. Here are some more ways you can develop healthy living skills related to this lesson.

ACCESSING INFORMATION
Use valid and reliable Internet sites to conduct research on teen dating violence. Use at least two sources and make sure your information is accurate. Use what you learn to create a webpage or handout on the issue. Include important statistics and facts and be sure to provide a list of resources for teenagers to use if they need help dealing with an abusive partner.

PRACTICING HEALTHY BEHAVIORS
Think about your personal boundaries and what is and is not acceptable to you in your relationships. Make a list of your boundaries and practice maintaining those boundaries in your relationships with others. For example, "It is not okay for people to call me names because of my race, and I won't be friends with anyone who does that" or "I don't like it when people put their arms around me without my permission, and I will ask people not to if they do." Keep track of how well you do in honoring your personal boundaries.

LESSON 10.5 Review: Relationships and Violence

LESSON SUMMARY

- Abuse is a type of violence that can be physical, emotional, or sexual in nature. Neglect is a type of abuse that occurs when a person's basic human needs like food or medical care are not being met.
- Child abuse can involve physical abuse that results in broken bones, bruises, or burns. Emotional abuse of a child happens if the child is not shown love or affection or is shamed, teased, or bullied. Sexual abuse of a child happens if a child is forced to engage in any sexual contact or activity.
- Domestic violence occurs in romantic relationships or marriages.
- Coercion can be used in any relationship for one person to control another or to get what they want from the other person.
- Human trafficking is a crime that involves the exploitation of individuals through threat or use of force, coercion, abduction, fraud, and deception. Sex trafficking is a specific type of human trafficking where people are forced to perform sexual acts in exchange for basic human needs like food and shelter.

REVIEWING CONCEPTS AND VOCABULARY

1. Abuse is a type of _____.
2. When a person's basic needs are not being met by their parent or caregiver, it is called _____.
3. The abuse of an older person in a nursing home or other setting is called _____.
4. Violence between a married couple or people in a romantic relationship is called _____ abuse.
5. _____ is any forced or unwanted sexual contact.
6. _____ is an inhumane crime.
7. Establishing _____ will help you know when a situation isn't good for you or is potentially dangerous or abusive.

THINKING CRITICALLY

Research human trafficking and write a paragraph analyzing strategies to avoid becoming a victim of human trafficking. Consider which strategies would be most effective.

TAKE IT HOME

Research your community's available resources including hotlines for victims of child abuse and sexual exploitation. Provide a brief explanation of each service and how it can be contacted. Show your list to someone in your family to see if they know of any other resources you should add.

Chapter Review

ACTION PLAN: Preventing Violence

Use the My Action Plan worksheet to set goals and practice preventing violence. An example follows.

My Action Plan: Preventing Violence

STEP 1: Identify the health behavior you are going to work on.

I am going to respect others and help prevent cyberbullying on social media.

STEP 2: Write SMART goal(s).

Write one or two short-term goals (one day to one month long).

I will post only positive and encouraging content on my social media this week.

I will not like any posts on social media this week that could be hurtful or harmful to another person.

Write a long-term goal (one to six months or more).

I will friend and genuinely support new people on social media who are usually bullied or left out.

STEP 3: Make a plan.

Identify two to five action steps (strategies) you could do to meet your goal.

I will focus on making positive comments on social media.

I won't participate in any group chats that include cyberbullying comments.

If I see cyberbullying, I will reach out to the victim and tell them it isn't their fault and that they did nothing wrong.

I will not only tell my friends about my plan to friend and support victims of cyberbullying but also ask them to join me.

STEP 4: Execute your plan and track your progress.

Short-term goal 1
☒ Met   ☐ Not met   Date: *February 25*

Short-term goal 2
☒ Met   ☐ Not met   Date: *February 25*

Long-term goal
☐ Met   ☒ Not met   Date: _____

If you met your goal, what helped you to be successful?

I paid extra attention to my social media posts and posted only positive content.

I told my friends I wasn't going to like any post that I thought was mean to others. This helped them know why I might not respond to something they post.

If you did not meet your goal, what made it harder for you to be successful?

I didn't friend someone I should have because I was afraid that my best friend would cancel me if I did.

Test Your Knowledge

Select the best answer for each question.

1. Threatening others, destroying another person's reputation, or causing damage to another person's relationships is
   a. physical violence
   b. sexual violence
   c. emotional violence
   d. neglect

2. The person who commits a violent act is called the
   a. victim
   b. offender
   c. bystander
   d. witness

3. Having an opinion about someone or something that is not based on reason or actual experience is
   a. bias
   b. prejudice
   c. violence
   d. victimization

4. A nonviolent and confident way of expressing your needs and point of view is called
   a. anger
   b. aggression
   c. assertiveness
   d. conflict

5. When you work together to achieve everyone's goals and resolve a conflict you are using the _____ approach to conflict management.
   a. accommodating
   b. avoiding
   c. competing
   d. collaborating

6. Teasing someone, calling someone names, or using verbal or written threats is _____ bullying.
   a. physical
   b. emotional
   c. social
   d. spiritual

7. To help protect yourself from becoming a victim of human trafficking, you should
   a. avoid walking alone or being alone in public places
   b. never give out your personal information online
   c. always go with a group when meeting up with someone you met online
   d. all of the above

8. If someone has several bruises and injuries over a period of time, they might be the victim of
   a. physical abuse
   b. neglect
   c. cyberbullying
   d. isolation

9. Violence between people in a romantic relationship or a married couple is called
   a. elder abuse
   b. sibling abuse
   c. sexual assault
   d. domestic violence

10. When someone tries to isolate you from friends and family, they are potentially crossing which type of personal boundary?
    a. emotional
    b. social
    c. spiritual
    d. physical

PROJECT-BASED LEARNING: Creating Resources for Violence Prevention

What to Remember
It is important to know which community resources exist to help with violence prevention.

Who It Is For
Other students in the school and their families

Why It Is Important

If people do not know which resources exist to them, they are unable to get help. It is important to know the resources available to you in the community.

What to Do

Create resources focused on different types of violence.

How to Do It

1. Work in a small group or team for the focus area your teacher assigns you from the following list:
   a. Conflict
   b. Cyberbullying
   c. Child abuse and neglect
   d. Domestic violence
   e. Elder abuse and neglect

2. Using this book and the Internet to conduct research, gather as much information as you can about the focus area your group is assigned. Use the information you find to create a pamphlet, poster, website, or social media page that highlights what you learned. Decide as a class what format you are going to use so that you can combine the information when everyone is done. As part of your information, you must also include the following.

   a. Write a story about a victim of the type of violence you are assigned. The story must be realistic and accurate and should reflect the risk factors, patterns, and consequences of the type of violence being highlighted. Pay special attention to issues of bias, prejudice, and intolerance in your work.

   b. Create a list of community resources or services related to your assigned focus area. Consider shelters, counseling services, law enforcement services, hotlines, and social services. Make sure your class agrees on what you consider to be your community. You might look for services and products within a certain number of miles of your school, or within a neighborhood or town limit. Make sure you also consider services at school. Think about asking other teachers, parents, and adults for recommendations on what to include in your resource list.

3. Share your creation with the other groups in your class. Create a Violence Prevention campaign that pulls together your resources and makes them available to other students in your school.

CROSS-CURRICULAR CONNECTION: Math

Research the rates of homicide, suicide, and accidental deaths by firearms for a recent year in the United States. Create a bar graph that shows the rates according to age groups. Determine the best age groups to use based on the statistics you find. Be sure to label the axis and provide a legend for your graph.

Alcohol

LESSON 11.1 Alcohol Use, Effects, and Consequences
LESSON 11.2 Influences and Alcohol
LESSON 11.3 Treating Alcohol Use Disorders

Understanding My Health

What Do I Know About Alcohol?

Consuming any amount of alcohol can have long-term consequences on a person's physical, mental, emotional, and social well-being. Complete the following self-assessment by putting an X in the box below the word *true* or *false* for each question to help you understand your knowledge about alcohol. After completing the self-assessment, check your answers with the answer key at the bottom of the assessment.

	True	False
1. Alcohol is a stimulant.		
2. Alcohol is legal for people 20 years of age and older.		
3. A long-term effect of drinking alcohol could be brain damage and cirrhosis of the liver.		
4. Binge drinking is when females drink eight or more drinks in a week and males drink 15 or more drinks in a week.		
5. Blood alcohol content is the amount of alcohol found in a person's bloodstream to determine how intoxicated they are.		
6. Two main reasons people drink are to fit in with their friends and to decrease their risky behavior decisions.		
7. Teens who use social media are three times more likely to drink alcohol.		
8. Alcohol is banned from all schools, meaning you cannot have any type of alcohol on school grounds.		
9. A designated driver is the person who agrees to have only one drink at the party, so they can still safely drive home.		
10. Alcohol use disorder means a person depends on alcohol to get through their day.		

Answers: 1. false, 2. false, 3. true, 4. false, 5. true, 6. false, 7. true, 8. true, 9. false, 10. true

My score for What Do I Know About Alcohol? = _____ (total number of correct answers)

Alcohol is a drug that can have short- and long-term consequences for you. On a daily basis, your family and friends, media, and technology have some degree of influence on you. These influences may be positive or negative and may affect the choices you make about whether to drink alcohol. Being alcohol free and avoiding situations that include alcohol are positive choices you can make to be safer and healthier. They will also help keep you out of trouble with your family, your school, and the law. If you do end up in a situation in which you need help avoiding alcohol, there are many prevention and treatment options available.

LESSON 11.1
Alcohol Use, Effects, and Consequences

Terms to Learn

alcohol overdose
binge drinking
blood alcohol content (BAC)
cirrhosis of the liver
depressant
designated driver
fetal alcohol spectrum disorder (FASD)
fetal alcohol syndrome (FAS)
intoxicated
minor in possession (MIP)
moderate drinking
underage drinking

The Big Picture

Alcohol is a depressant that slows the functions of the central nervous system, making brain function slower than normal. A number of factors influence a person's reaction to alcohol: body size, food intake, medications, and the amount of and rate at which alcohol has been consumed. Understanding the health effects of alcohol use as well as the legal implications of underage drinking can help you avoid life-altering consequences.

Learning Targets

- Describe standard drink sizes of alcoholic beverages.
- Analyze specific components of the fetal alcohol spectrum disorders.
- Illustrate how teen alcohol use has an impact on risk-taking behaviors.
- Compare how alcohol consumption can affect school and job performance.
- Examine the potential impacts drinking and driving has on a person's life.

Write About It

What do you know about the different types of alcoholic drinks? Do they all contain the same amount of alcohol? Is there a standard drink size?

Note-Taking Guide

Use this chapter's note-taking guide to help you organize and remember the material in this lesson.

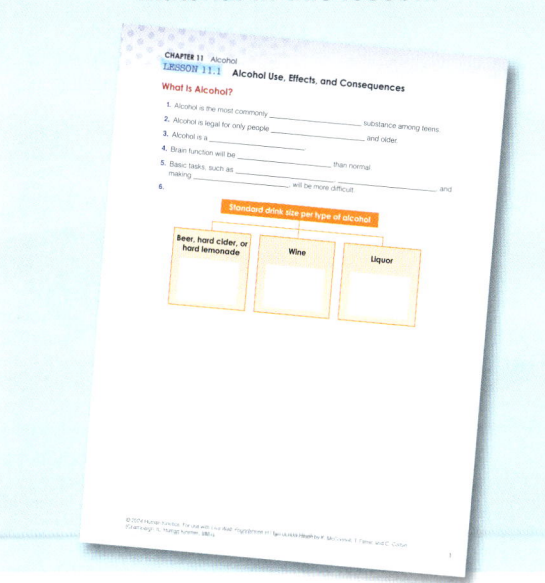

LESSON 11.1 Alcohol

After the basketball game on Saturday night, Sean went to Eduardo's house to celebrate the win. Eduardo's guardians were out of town and had told him it was alright to have a few friends over. Most of the team and some other students from school showed up. Some of the students brought beer, and Sean and some of the other players decided having one or two beers wasn't a big deal. It wasn't long before a couple of beers turned into four, then five, then a couple more.

Sean had to be home by 1:00 a.m. Eduardo told him he would drive him home since he hadn't been drinking, but Sean was adamant he could drive without any problems: It was only eight blocks away, he argued, and not only that, but it was late, and no one would be out. No big deal. Shortly after Sean left, Eduardo heard sirens close by and looked out the door. Sean's car had smashed into a telephone pole and was badly damaged. How do you think driving under the influence of alcohol contributed to Sean's accident? What kind of impact do you think this will have on Sean?

What Is Alcohol?

Alcohol is the most commonly used substance among teens in the United States despite the legal minimum drinking age of 21. **Underage drinking**—consuming alcohol under the age of 21—has many repercussions. It can lead to lifelong alcohol use, physical and sexual violence, failure in school and work, social problems, changes in brain development, and even death. Alcohol slows down the functions of the central nervous system and is therefore a **depressant**. This means your brain function will be slower than normal, and it will be more difficult to do basic tasks such as walking, talking, and making simple decisions (see figure 11.1).

The most common types of alcoholic beverages are beer, wine, and liquor such as vodka, rum, and whiskey. Each type of alcohol has a standard amount of pure alcohol or ethanol in it. The following are the standard drinks for each kind (see figure 11.2):

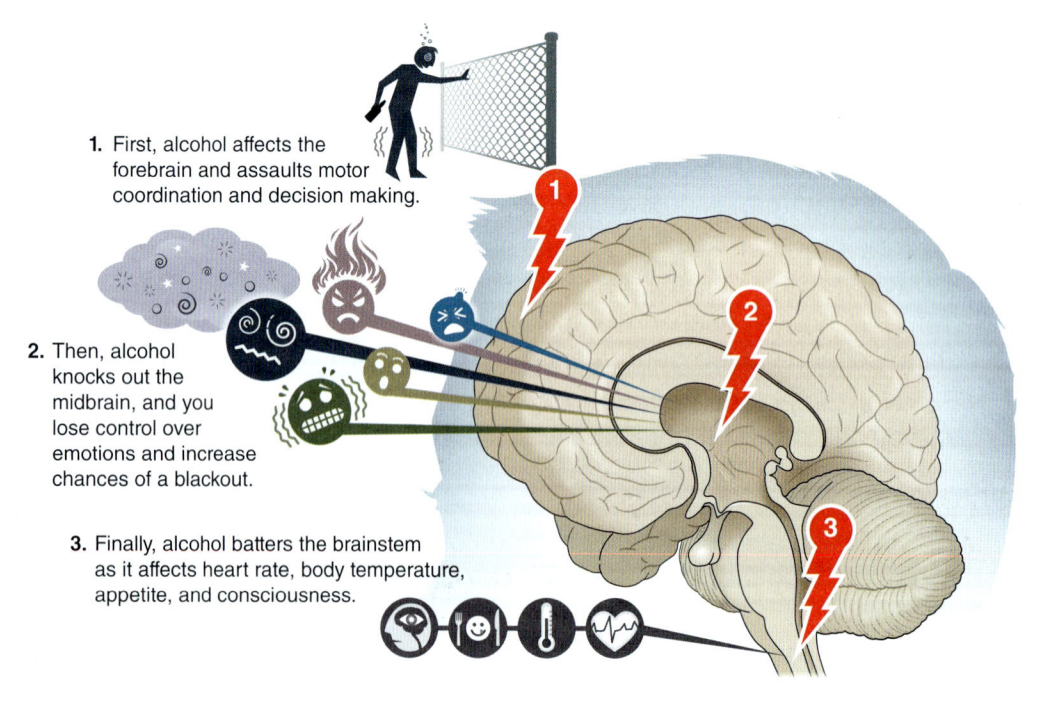

1. First, alcohol affects the forebrain and assaults motor coordination and decision making.

2. Then, alcohol knocks out the midbrain, and you lose control over emotions and increase chances of a blackout.

3. Finally, alcohol batters the brainstem as it affects heart rate, body temperature, appetite, and consciousness.

Figure 11.1 How alcohol affects the different parts of the brain.

Alcohol Use, Effects, and Consequences **LESSON 11.1**

12 fl. oz. regular beer	=	8-9 fl. oz. malt liquor (shown in a 12 oz. glass)	=	5 fl. oz. table wine	=	1.5 fl. oz. shot of 80-proof distilled spirits (bourbon, gin, rum, tequila, vodka, whiskey, etc.)	=	<2/3 of a 3 fl. oz. margarita	=	6.3 fl. oz. gin and tonic
about 5% alcohol		about 7% alcohol		about 12% alcohol		40% alcohol		about 30% alcohol		about 10% alcohol

Figure 11.2 Standard sizes of alcoholic drinks.

- Beer, hard cider, or hard lemonade: 12 ounces
- Wine: five ounces
- Liquor (e.g., tequila, vodka, whiskey): one and a half ounces

Alcohol Consumption

In the United States, people who are 21 years of age and older are able to drink alcohol but should do so in moderation. **Moderate drinking** is typically considered as having up to one drink per day for females and up to two drinks per day for males. People who drink moderately usually do not drink every day. This type of drinking is also associated with social drinking, meaning a person drinks only occasionally, such as with friends or for a special occasion.

Binge drinking is consuming many drinks in a short amount of time, on a regular basis. This typically means five or more drinks for males and four or more drinks for females during a two-hour period. Males are twice as likely as females to engage in this dangerous behavior. One of the largest risks of binge drinking is the possibility of **alcohol overdose**, because it can be fatal.

Alcohol overdose occurs when the body is unable to process the amount of alcohol consumed in such a short amount of time. Signs of alcohol overdose include confusion, seizures, extremely slow breathing, irregular breathing, bluish or pale skin, and unconsciousness. If you ever suspect alcohol overdose, you should immediately call 911. Here are some strategies for avoiding binge drinking:

- Change your environment so you are not with people or in places that may lead to binge drinking.
- Know your reasons for drinking excessively and ask friends or family members for help.
- Set a limit to the amount of drinks you will have and stick to it.
- Get an accountability buddy who will help to hold you accountable to the changes you want to make.

Heavy drinking is having more than four drinks a day or 15 drinks or more per week for males and more than three drinks a day or eight drinks or more per week for females. The more drinks a person has in a day or a week, the more likely they are to have health and personal problems related to their drinking problem. While drinking is legal for people 21 years of age and older, drinking should only be done occasionally and in moderation or not at all.

Teen Alcohol Use and Risk-Taking

There are several downsides to teen alcohol use. When drinking, teens are more likely than those who have not been drinking to take certain risks. This is in part due to their need to explore their own limits, express themselves, and create their own identities. It is also in part due to their pre-frontal cortex, which is the part of the brain that is responsible for decision making and judgment, not being fully developed. The pre-frontal cortex does not completely develop until approximately the age of 25.

The risks teens take may be unintentional and seem inconsequential at the time, but drinking can cause accidents like falls, drownings, burns, firearm injuries, and even death. Teens who drink are more likely to become violent either to themselves (cutting, suicide) or to others (getting into physical fights with friends and family members). Drinking often gives teens a false sense of courage, which can lead them to impulsive acts, such as driving at high speeds or deciding to use drugs without thinking about the possible consequences.

Being under the influence of alcohol obscures, or impairs, your ability to make responsible decisions. You become much less cautious, making yourself vulnerable to being in situations or doing things that the sober version of you would not do. For example, you might try an illicit drug, you might be coerced into having sex, or you might think it's okay if, just this one time, you have unprotected sex. These are not healthy decisions and can result in illicit drug use, sexually transmitted diseases (STDs), and unwanted pregnancies. The more often teens use alcohol the higher the incidence of risk-taking activities.

Emotional Reasons for Alcohol Use

People may choose to drink alcohol because it can initially change their mood and how they feel. There are four main reasons people drink: (1) to increase a positive mood, (2) to gain approval of others or membership in a group, (3) to reduce the pain of negative feelings, and (4) to fit in.

- *Increase positive mood.* The effects of alcohol can happen quickly, making people feel happy, relaxed, and excited. We know these feelings don't last long and can lead to more alcohol consumption, which is just a short-term fix for emotions a person may not want to face.

- *Gain approval.* When people drink alcohol, they may do and say things they wouldn't normally do. People may be able to open up and show more of their personality, which can lead to gaining approval of those around them and fitting in with a group of people they may want to be friends with. Yet oftentimes a person says or does inappropriate things that hurt others' feelings. Another unfortunate situation is the person may embarrass themselves and actually make them less connected to the group when they are sober again. This isn't a healthy way to make friends or gain approval from anyone. If friends only approve of a person when they are drinking, they aren't very good friends.

- *Reduce painful, negative feelings.* Sometimes people drink alcohol to forget about their problems or negative feelings for a while. When the alcohol wears off, the problems or negative feelings will still be there. Everyone has problems or feelings they may not want to deal with, but drinking won't make anything better. Talking to someone and working through difficult feelings can help people feel less alone. Knowing that others are feeling the same way can make a positive difference, and it is much better than creating another problem by drinking.

- *Fit in.* If a person can only fit in when they have been drinking, they need to think about whether these are really people they want to be friends with. Drinking to fit in also comes with the mentality that if a person says or does anything that's unintelligent, everyone simply can blame the alcohol. Friendships you do have can be lost and reputations ruined because of what is said and done while drinking.

Reducing Teen Alcohol Consumption

Teens are naturally inclined to assert their independence, seek new challenges, and engage in risky behavior. It is easy to view alcohol as a means to eliminate any fears they may have of these perceived challenges. Having easy access to alcohol through family members or finding it in their homes makes teens more likely to experiment with alcohol. According to the Centers for Disease Control and Prevention (CDC), 29 percent of U.S. teens drink alcohol regularly, 14 percent binge drink, 5 percent drink and drive, and 17 percent have ridden with a drunk driver.

Due to the multiple factors that influence teen substance use, there are no easy courses of action to prevent teens from using alcohol. Yet there are possible ways to reduce the amount of alcohol teens are consuming if they do choose to drink. If you or your friends are likely to use alcohol, think about alternative ways to either celebrate or work through something that doesn't involve drinking. Reward yourself by binge-watching a favorite show, going to a movie with a friend, or trying a new video game or coffee shop. Find something you view as meaningful to do instead of drinking, such as volunteering somewhere, being a tutor, or finding a new hobby. If you do choose to drink, do it safely:

- Make sure to eat before and while drinking to protect your liver and stomach lining, and to avoid blackouts.
- Set a limit to the amount you will drink and tell a friend to help keep you accountable.
- Never mix medication with alcohol—the result can be fatal.
- Drink slowly and drink a water or soda in between drinks to help pace yourself and help prevent binge drinking.
- Most importantly, avoid drinking alcohol altogether.

LESSON 11.1 Alcohol

Signs of Alcohol Use

We know there are many different reasons why teens drink, such as fitting in with their current group of friends and hiding their feelings. Some simply do so out of curiosity—perhaps it seems everyone has tried drinking except for them (which is never the case). If you or someone you know used one of these reasons to drink, it does not necessarily mean there is a drinking problem. It can, however, indicate some other underlying problem. Signs of underage drinking are shown in figure 11.3.

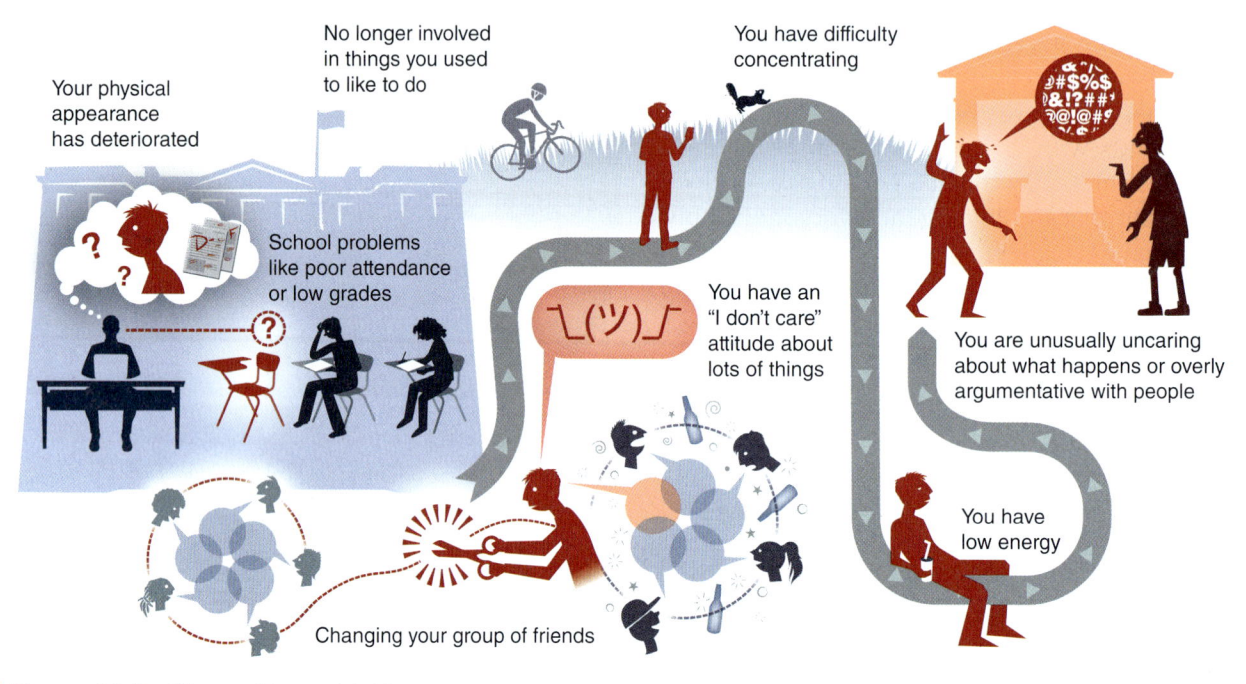

Figure 11.3 Signs of teen drinking.

STEM in Health

THE BREATHALYZER

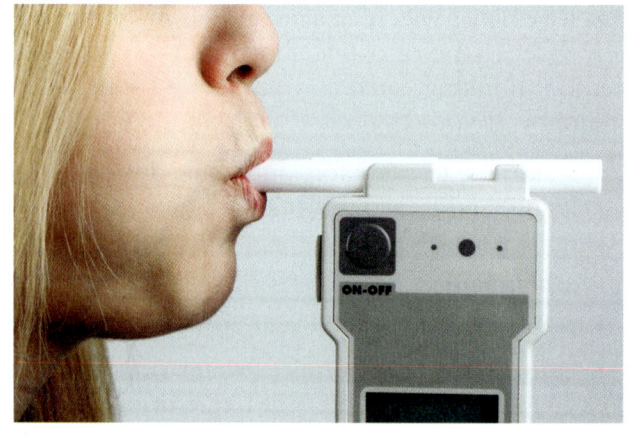

Law enforcement uses a breathalyzer to determine if you have been drinking alcohol. The breathalyzer has two chambers. One chamber contains a liquid that, after you've blown into the mouthpiece, changes from reddish-orange to green if you have been drinking. The other chamber contains the same liquid, but it isn't affected when you blow into the mouthpiece. The photocell sensor compares the color of the two chambers and produces an electrical current that is converted into a blood alcohol content (BAC) number. The degree of the color change is directly related to the level of alcohol in your system.

478

Factors That Influence the Effects of Alcohol

Each person reacts differently to the amount of alcohol they drink. Even a small amount of alcohol can affect a person in a negative way. The following are examples of factors that will influence how alcohol affects a person.

- *Body size.* The larger a person is, the more drinks it will take for them to become intoxicated, when even the simplest of tasks, like walking, can be difficult to do. If two people drink the same amount of alcohol, it will have a faster effect on the smaller person than on the larger person, regardless of their sex.
- *Rate at which alcohol is consumed.* The faster a person drinks alcohol, the faster they will become intoxicated.
- *Food.* Food that has already been eaten and digested helps to slow down how fast alcohol gets into the bloodstream. If people drink on an empty stomach, their alcohol level will be higher at a faster rate than if they ate before they started drinking or are eating while they are drinking.
- *Medications.* Taking medicine and alcohol at the same time can be dangerous and even deadly. Sometimes alcohol will make medicines work differently in the body than they should. The medicine can also make the effect of alcohol stronger.
- *Amount consumed.* The level of alcohol in a person's bloodstream rises as they drink more. If it becomes too high, an alcohol overdose will occur. An alcohol overdose can be deadly, so it is important to get medical attention right away. Figure 11.4 shows what to do if you think someone has overdosed on alcohol.

If you think someone has an alcohol overdose, do not leave them alone. **Take the following actions:**

Breathing
Slow (less than 8 breaths per minute) or irregular (10 seconds or more between breaths). Monitor the person's breathing. If they stop breathing you will need to perform CPR.

Unconsciousness
Lay the person on their side with their ear to the floor so if they do vomit, it can come out their mouth and they won't choke on it.

Vomiting

Mental confusion
Person may not know where they are or what is happening. Do not leave them alone.

Figure 11.4 Follow these guidelines if you think someone has overdosed on alcohol.

LESSON 11.1 Alcohol

Physical Effects of Alcohol on the Body

When a person drinks alcohol, it is quickly absorbed into their bloodstream. The blood then carries the alcohol throughout the body, affecting multiple organs (see figure 11.5).

Neurological
- Vision is blurred
- Speech is slurred
- Sensations and perception are less clear
- Inhibitions are reduced
- Coordination is impaired
- Reflexes become sluggish

Cardiovascular
- Increased heart rate
- Increased blood pressure
- Blood flow to the skin increases, causing more rapid loss of body heat

Liver
The liver breaks down between 0.5 and 1 ounces of alcohol per hour

Digestive
- Alcohol is absorbed in the stomach and small intestine
- Too much alcohol in the stomach causes vomiting

Kidneys
The kidneys produce more urine, drinker loses more water than usual

Figure 11.5 Effects of alcohol on the body.

The following are some short- and long-term effects of alcohol use on your body.

Short-term effects

- Blurred or double vision occurs.
- Sweating increases and skin becomes flushed.
- The liver breaks down alcohol at an average rate of one standard drink per hour. The more you drink, the longer it takes for your liver to process the alcohol, so you become drunk faster.
- Dehydration occurs.
- Nausea, vomiting, diarrhea, and indigestion may occur.

Long-term effects

- Risks of brain damage, memory loss, and stroke are higher.
- You may develop cardiovascular disease and high blood pressure.
- **Cirrhosis of the liver**—an irreversible scarring of the liver—may occur. The scar tissue blocks the blood flow through the liver and eventually keeps the liver from working properly.
- The immune system has less ability to fight off infections.
- The stomach lining may become inflamed and bleed.
- You have a higher risk of cancer of the esophagus.

Effects of Alcohol Use During Pregnancy

There is no safe time or amount of alcohol that a person who is pregnant should be drinking. Drinking during pregnancy causes the fetus to absorb the alcohol. Alcohol in the blood passes to the fetus through the umbilical cord. Drinking alcohol during pregnancy can cause miscarriages, stillbirths, and **fetal alcohol spectrum disorder (FASD)**. FASD refers to a group of conditions that can cause physical, behavior, and learning problems. These include **fetal alcohol syndrome (FAS)**, alcohol-related neurodevelopmental disorder (ARND), alcohol-related birth defects (ARBD), and neurobehavioral disorder associated with prenatal alcohol exposure (ND-PAE). These disorders can be determined based on the child's symptoms (see figure 11.6).

Fetal Alcohol Syndrome (FAS)
- Most severe FASD
- FAS symptoms:
  - Poor coordination, delayed development, heart defects, distinctive facial features, behavior problems, and poor social skills.

Alcohol-Related Neurodevelopmental Disorder (ARND):
- ARND symptoms:
  - Difficulty learning and communicating, behavior problems, lack of impulse control, and problems taking care of themselves.

Alcohol-Related Birth Defects (ARBD)
- May have problems with how some organs are formed and how they function including:
  - Heart
  - Kidneys
  - Spine
  - Ears
  - Eyes
- May also have one of the other FASDs.

Neurobehavioral Disorder Associated With Prenatal Alcohol Exposure (ND-PAE)
- ND-PAE symptoms:
  - Thinking and memory problems, behavior problems such as tantrums and irritability, difficulty getting along with others, and problems taking care of themselves.

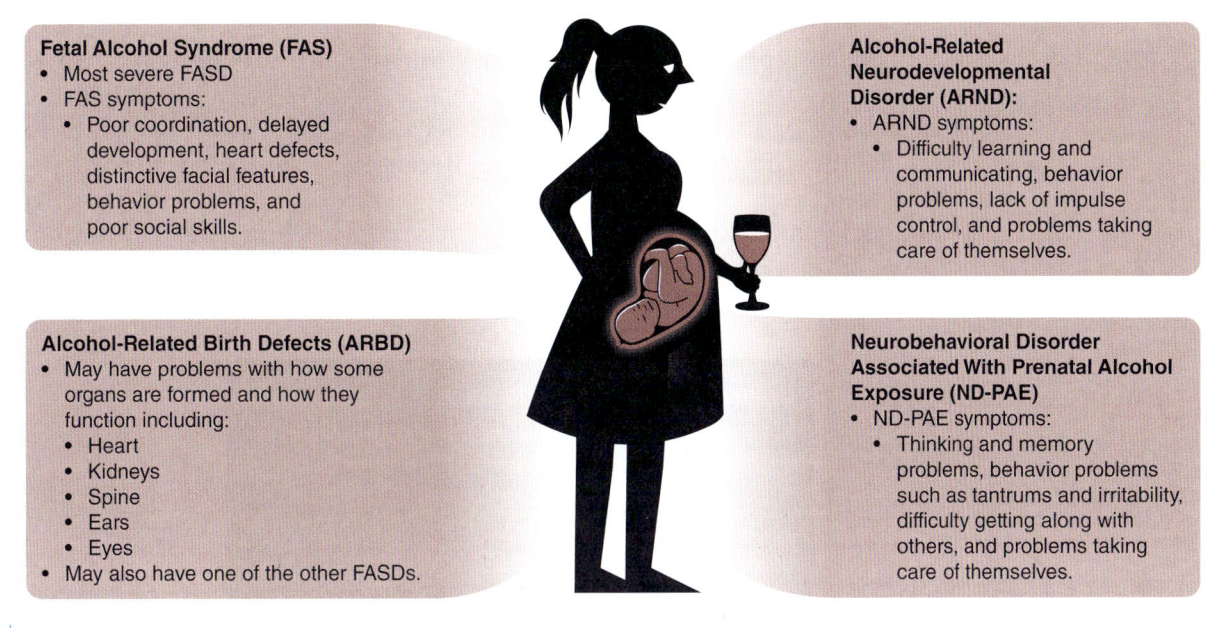

Figure 11.6 Types of fetal alcohol spectrum disorders.

Consequences of Alcohol Use

There are several reasons why teens may drink. Some teens will drink only when their friends are drinking at parties. Others will use alcohol as a way to cope with circumstances in their life. Yet some teens may never use alcohol. The range of consequences of underage drinking varies from simple things like making someone mad to life-altering changes like killing someone as a result of drinking and driving.

Mental Consequences of Alcohol Use

Alcohol affects the brain and a person's ability to do simple, routine tasks. Even one or two drinks can affect a person's ability to walk, see, speak, react, and think clearly. Short-term effects of drinking alcohol may last a few hours depending on how much the person drank. People may think alcohol affects them only while they are drinking, yet repeated drinking can cause long-term effects on a teen's brain as they continue to grow and develop.

LESSON 11.1   Alcohol

Long-term effects of drinking alcohol may last a lifetime.

Short-term consequences may include:
- Having difficulty in decision making
- Engaging in inappropriate or risky behavior
- Being less likely to recognize potential dangers
- Displaying aggressive or violent behavior

Long-term consequences may include:
- Having difficulty understanding information
- Experiencing difficulty learning new information
- Developing an increased risk of alcohol use disorder later in life

Alcohol affects a person's brain, and if they drink regularly, there will be long-term effects that they may never be able to change. Alcohol has a more dramatic effect on a brain of a teen than on an adult because a teen's brain continues to develop until they are about 25 years of age. Because of how the brain develops, teens who have been drinking tend to be more prone to taking risks than teens who have not been drinking. A developing brain is more easily damaged by alcohol than a fully developed brain. Figure 11.7 shows the differences in brain activity between a 15-year-old non-drinker and a 15-year-old heavy drinker.

Brain activity while performing a memory task. Heavy drinker is sober during this test.

Brain activity 15-year-old non-drinker

Brain activity 15-year-old heavy drinker

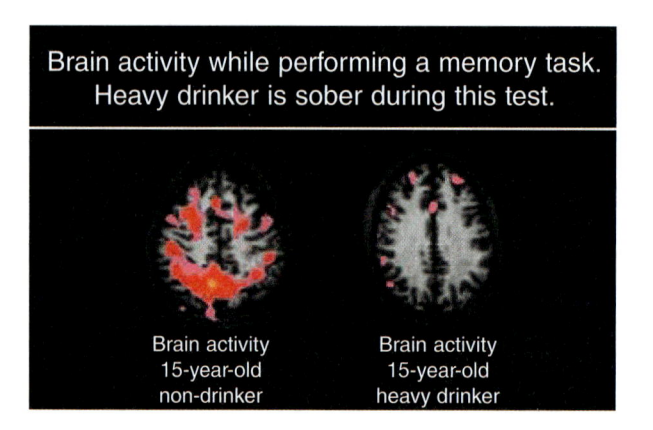

Figure 11.7 Brain activity in a teen who drinks alcohol versus one who doesn't.

HEALTHY LIVING TIP

There are many reasons for you not to drink, but if nothing else has convinced you, think about the damage you may be doing to your brain by drinking as a teen. There are long-term effects to your developing brain that may be happening to you if you are drinking that you don't even know about yet. Why take the risk? Don't drink!

Social Consequences of Alcohol Use

Using alcohol will affect the relationships people have. Friends may be lost because they don't want to be around someone when they are drinking or the person has prioritized drinking rather than their friends. While in the moment, teens may think they will make other friends, but oftentimes, these so-called friendships, especially when based around drinking, are fleeting.

Teens may experience feelings of guilt because they engage in behaviors they otherwise would not. For example, they may begin sneaking out of their homes or skipping school to drink. They may steal money from friends and family members to buy alcohol, or they may lie to go to a party instead of being with their friends. As a result, their friends, family members, teachers, coaches, and employers lose trust because of the frequent lying, absences, and lack of accountability.

How Alcohol Consumption Affects School Performance

CDC studies have shown a significant association between alcohol consumption and school grades of U.S. high school students. It is clear that students who binge drink are more likely to miss classes and fall behind in their schoolwork and they spend less time studying overall.

- Of those who drank alcohol for the first time before the age of 13, 34 percent had mostly Ds and Fs.
- Of those who drink at least one alcoholic drink in a 30-day period of time, 52 percent had mostly Ds and Fs.
- Of those who drink five or more alcoholic drinks in a row on at least one day in a 30-day period, 34 percent had mostly Ds and Fs.

How Alcohol Consumption Affects Job Performance

Alcohol consumption can cause employees to be late to work or call in sick on a regular basis. Employees may struggle to focus; making poor decisions can cost the employee opportunities or cause on-the-job accidents. Alcohol use may also cause employees to be confrontational with their supervisors, coworkers, and customers.

Legal Consequences of Alcohol Use

A **minor in possession (MIP)** charge occurs when anyone under the age of 21 is apprehended for consuming, being in possession of, or being in the same area as alcohol. Laws vary from state to state. In some states, an MIP also carries a misdemeanor charge, which is a criminal offense that can result in up to a year in jail. Most states require teens to pay a fine, take an alcohol education class, meet with a substance abuse counselor, and do community service. If a teen is charged with an MIP at school or at a school-sponsored event, they may be suspended from school for a specific amount of time. If they are an athlete, they will usually face suspension from their team. While these are just some immediate consequences, there are also potential consequences that could affect their future and career goals, depending on their state laws.

Drinking and Driving

The United States has zero tolerance for underage drinking and driving. This policy, otherwise known as the *not-a-drop* law, means it is illegal to have any detectable amount of alcohol in your body while driving if you are under 21 years old. Charges vary state to state and include DWI (driving while intoxicated) or DUI (driving under the influence), which are essentially the same charge with the same consequences. A teenage driver convicted of a DUI or DWI either has their license suspended or permanently revoked; they also are fined and may serve jail time.

Drinking and driving increases the risks of vehicle accidents. Alcohol slows reaction time, reduces concentration, impairs judgment, and decreases coordination. Consider the following:

- In the United States, two out of three people will be involved in a drunk driving accident within their lifetime.
- Car crashes are the leading cause of death for U.S. teens. Nearly one out four crashes involve an underage person who had been drinking.

Choosing to drive while under the influence of alcohol can have long-term consequences for the person driving, passengers in the car, family members, innocent people, and even the community. Aside from damage you incur to your vehicle as well as the other driver's vehicle, everyone involved can sustain serious injuries, and worse yet, die. People often blame and stigmatize drivers who made the choice to drink and drive, especially when the outcome is permanent injury or death of loved ones. If you choose to drink and drive, remember that you may live the rest of your life with debilitating regret. If you are charged with a DUI or DWI, it can be on your permanent record, and this can prevent you from getting jobs.

If you are in a situation where your friends have been drinking and you can drive, volunteer to be the designated driver. As the **designated driver**, you agree not to drink any amount of alcohol so you can safely drive your friends home or pick them up, no questions asked. Ideally underage drinking would never happen, but when it does, being prepared by having a designated driver is critical.

Blood Alcohol Content

Blood alcohol content (BAC) is the amount of alcohol in the bloodstream. When a person drinks an alcoholic beverage, the alcohol moves from the stomach to the small intestine where it is absorbed into the bloodstream and distributed throughout the body. The amount of alcohol in the bloodstream indicates how intoxicated a person is. **Intoxicated** means affected by alcohol to a point that doing simple tasks and controlling emotions become difficult.

In the United States, a person is considered legally intoxicated if they have a BAC of 0.08 percent or higher. There is no average amount of drinks a person can

Alcohol Use, Effects, and Consequences **LESSON 11.1**

have before they reach this BAC simply because so many factors influence BAC: body size, biological sex, food consumption, the rate at which a person drinks, and current medications. Even one drink can cause a person to feel the effects of the alcohol. The effects alcohol has on a person depends on their BAC level (see figure 11.8).

- BAC levels under 0.05 percent may make a person light-headed and relaxed.
- A 0.08 percent BAC level may have an impact on balance, speech, reaction time, and self-control.
- A BAC over 0.20 percent may cause disorientation, blackouts, and severe impairment of mental and physical functions.
- BAC levels over 0.30 percent may result in alcohol overdose, coma, or death.

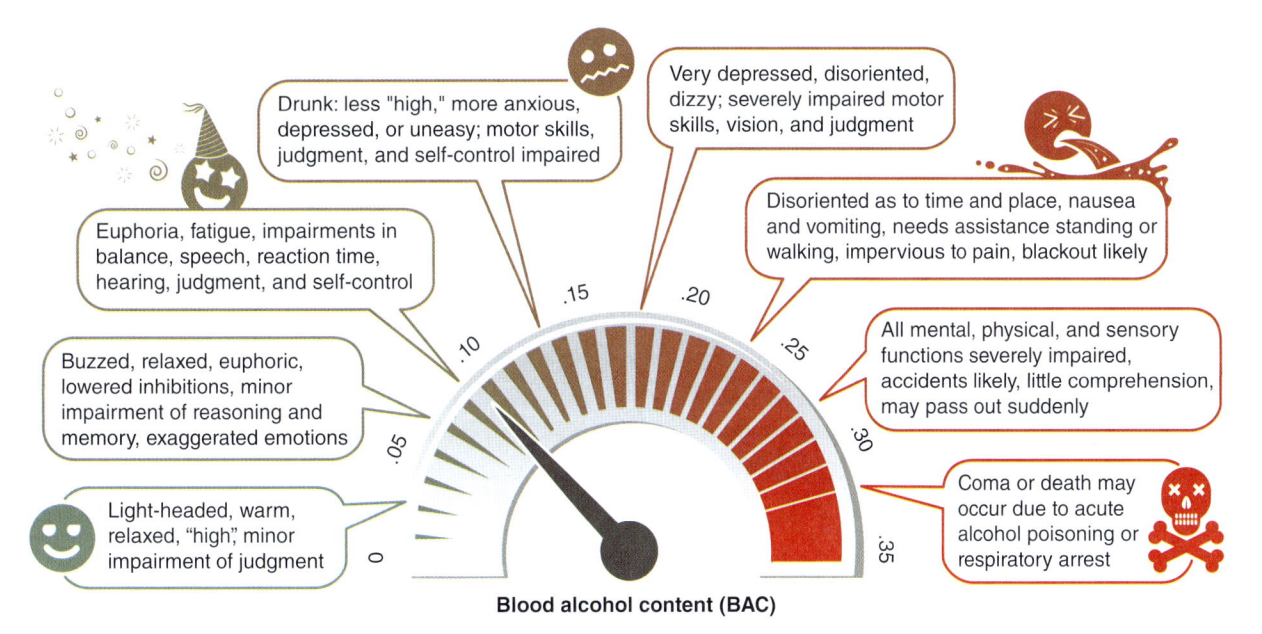

Figure 11.8 Blood alcohol content and its effects.

Skill-Building Challenge

Promoting an Alcohol-Free Lifestyle

Advocate for your school to set up their own chapter of Students Against Destructive Decisions (SADD) if you don't already have one. Conduct online research of the national chapter of SADD organization. From the website's Resources tab, click on the Initiatives and Programming and choose a topic you are interested in. Once you have decided on a topic, determine how you can get your school involved.

Using the information you gained from the SADD website, explain how you would use the health skill of advocacy to advocate for having a chapter of SADD at your school. Use the questions below to help get started.

1. What is the issue you need to advocate for?
2. What solutions can you brainstorm to help create answers for the issue?
3. Who will help you create and support your solutions?
4. How will you put your plan into action? Who will help you put your plan into action?

LESSON 11.1   Alcohol

Healthy Living Skills

This lesson focused on advocating for good health. Here are some more ways you can develop healthy living skills related to this lesson.

ACCESSING INFORMATION

Search online for information on fetal alcohol spectrum disorders (FASD). The websites should have information from a person or an organization in the medical field or from a nationally recognized agency like the CDC or the World Health Organization (WHO). Choose one of the disorders and answer the following questions.
- What are the specific causes of the disorder?
- To get a proper diagnosis of the disorder, what are the specific symptoms that a baby must display at the time of birth?
- What problems will the baby have as they become toddlers, children, teens, and adults?
- What are the names of the websites from where you obtained your information?
- How do you know the websites you used are valid resources you can trust?

MAKING HEALTHY DECISIONS

You have read about the different physical, mental, and social effects of drinking alcohol as well as the impact of alcohol use and risk-taking. Using the health skill of decision-making, you will decide whether it is a good decision to drink as well as the potential consequences of risky decision making if you do choose to drink. Remember, the more a person drinks, the more likely they are to make risky, unsafe decisions that can have short- and long-term impacts.

LESSON 11.1   Review: Alcohol Use, Effects, and Consequences

LESSON SUMMARY

- Standard drink sizes of alcoholic beverages are: 12 ounces of beer, hard cider, or hard lemonade; 5 ounces of wine; and 1.5 ounces of liquor such as tequila, vodka, or whiskey.
- Fetal alcohol syndrome (FAS), alcohol-related neurodevelopmental disorder (ARND), alcohol-related birth defects (ARBD), and neurobehavioral disorder associated with prenatal alcohol exposure (ND-PAE) comprise the range of fetal alcohol spectrum disorders (FASD).
- Teens are more likely to take risks when drinking because their pre-frontal cortex, which is responsible for decision making and judgment, is not fully developed. Some reasons teens might have for drinking include fitting in, gaining approval, and reducing the pain of negative thoughts and feelings.
- Alcohol consumption can result in absences from school or work, poor grades or work performance, and a tendency to be confrontational with teachers, bosses, friends, and coworkers.
- Potential impacts of drinking and driving are short- and long-term and can lead to a permanent injury or death, a permanent criminal record, and a life-long regret.

Alcohol Use, Effects, and Consequences **LESSON 11.1**

REVIEWING CONCEPTS AND VOCABULARY

1. Alcohol is a(n) _____ because it slows down the functions of the central nervous system.
2. _____ drinking is described as a female having up to one drink a day and males up to two drinks a day.
3. If a person drinks enough alcohol that it impairs their ability to walk, they are _____.
4. _____ drinking is when males consume five or more drinks and females consume four or more drinks in a short period of time.
5. The amount of alcohol in the bloodstream is the _____.
6. A(n) _____ causes blackouts or even death when the part of the brain that controls basic life-support functions begins shutting down.
7. _____ of the liver is irreversible scarring of the liver.
8. Drinking alcohol during pregnancy can cause _____ alcohol _____ disorders that cause physical, behavioral, and learning problems.
9. The most severe of the FASDs is _____.
10. A _____ charge occurs when anyone under the age of 21 is apprehended for consuming, being in possession of, or being in the same area as alcohol.
11. A(n) _____ agrees to pick their friends up who have been drinking, no questions asked.
12. _____ drinking is when someone under the age of 21 consumes alcohol.

THINKING CRITICALLY

How are school-related work and employment similarly affected by alcohol consumption?

TAKE IT HOME

Imagine you find yourself at a party where there is alcohol. Talk to a trusted adult about how you should get out of the situation without getting in trouble, regardless of your reason for being there. Have a conversation with the trusted adult about giving you a get-out-of-trouble-free card if you make the choice to call them and do the right thing by leaving.

LESSON 11.2
Influences and Alcohol

Terms to Learn
influence
social media
values

The Big Picture
Friends, peers, family, and media are all capable of influencing, whether positively or negatively, the choices we make daily. It is also important to know that not all teens drink alcohol. In fact, many find exceedingly better alternatives for activities that are much more enjoyable than drinking alcohol. Learning who influences you positively as opposed to negatively is key in knowing which people you can count on to help you make the best choices in your life.

Learning Targets
- Identify who and what influences your decisions about drinking.
- Evaluate how media (e.g., movies and streaming shows) may affect your decisions about drinking.
- Discuss how social media may influence your drinking decisions especially in regard to advertising and what your friends post.
- Analyze how your values influence your decisions about whether or not to drink alcohol.
- Plan for an alcohol-free lifestyle.

Write About It
Everyone has people in their lives who influence them. Who in your life has the most influence over you? Is their influence on you positive or negative?

Note-Taking Guide
Use this chapter's note-taking guide to help you organize and remember the material in this lesson.

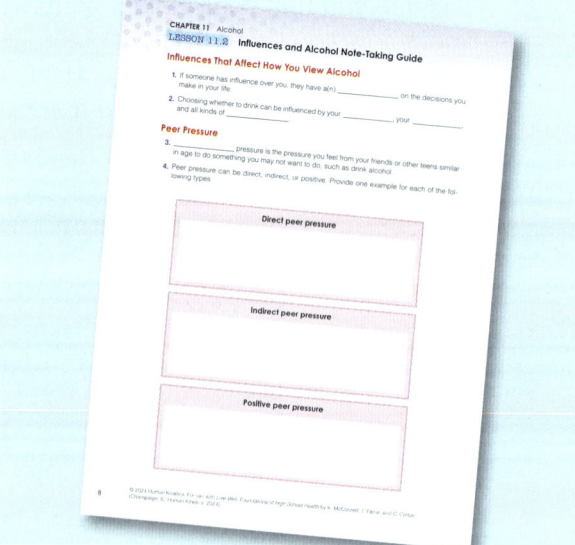

Juan and Blakely are on their first date. They decided to double up with Ang and Elena, who are also dating, and go to a movie. After getting their seats, Elena shows them four small bottles of vodka—one for each of them—and hands them out. Blakely, Ang, and Elena excitedly pour the vodka into their cups and mix it with their soda. Juan, who doesn't drink but really likes Blakely and is trying to make a good impression, reluctantly goes along. Once the lights dim and the movie begins, they start drinking their soda and vodka. Juan doesn't like how it tastes and doesn't want to keep drinking it, but everyone else seems to be quickly finishing theirs. Juan knows there can be negative consequences at school and with family and other friends if they find out he has been drinking. While Juan really likes Blakely, he doesn't want to disappoint his family and other friends. What should Juan do in this situation? What are some of the potential consequences of Juan's choices?

Influences That Affect How You View Alcohol

If someone has **influence** over you, they have an effect on the decisions you make in your life. Deciding not to drink may be an easy or a hard decision depending on various circumstances. Choosing whether to drink can be influenced by your friends, your family members, and all kinds of media. To navigate your way through situations, and especially those where you encounter alcohol, weigh the pros and cons of each choice you make every day. Turn to the people you trust in your life for help in making decisions both big and small.

Peer Pressure

Your friends and peers likely have an influence over many of the decisions you make. Peer pressure is the pressure you feel to do something you may or may not want to do. Even if you know you should or shouldn't do something, peer pressure can be hard to ignore.

Wanting to fit in with your friends is typical. If you are at a party where your friends are drinking, it may be difficult for you to choose not to drink. Peer pressure can be direct; for example, someone may hand you a drink or give you a hard time if you aren't drinking. If you say "no," you may feel like an outsider and your friends may ghost you. Peer pressure can also be indirect; for example, at that same party, no one pressures you to drink. In fact, no one says anything to you about it. If you are the only person not drinking, you may feel left out or as if you not fully participating like everyone else is.

Peer pressure can have an upside, however. In the same scenario, you may have friends at the party who *aren't* drinking, and in that situation, it could be just as difficult to choose to drink. If drinking isn't something you feel pressured to do, then you probably won't. In fact,

LESSON 11.2 Alcohol

> **HEALTHY LIVING TIP**
> Create a list of your friends and label them as a positive or negative influence when it comes to their influence on your use of alcohol.

you might feel pressure *not* to drink if you are thinking about drinking. Think about the friends you hang out with and how they influence you. Friends have a large influence on the decisions you make about consuming or not consuming alcohol. Make sure you surround yourself with friends who will help you make healthy decisions about alcohol.

Family Influence

Everyone's family is different, and alcohol affects everyone differently. The choices family members make influence other family members, especially those who are closest in proximity to them. The way in which you perceive and experience your family's rules of and habits with drinking can have both positive and negative impacts on your decision making.

If you have a family member who drinks often or a lot at one time, consider asking yourself whether you think they drink *too* often or *too* much and what they are like when they are drinking. Your answers may affect your decisions about when, if ever, you decide to start drinking. Seeing family members drink after a tough day at work may make you think it seems like a good way to relax and cope with difficulties. On the other hand, you may view it as using alcohol as a means to avoid dealing with problems or that it could easily turn into an unhealthy habit.

What if your family members drink to celebrate special occasions? What are the pros and cons of this? Are they happy and still able to function, or do they get intoxicated and become confrontational or violent? If they drink moderately and responsibly, maybe you won't view drinking as a problem and will wait until you are of legal age to drink. Some families are absolutely against drinking, view it negatively, and enforce rules against drinking. Depending on how you experience this, you may choose to avoid alcohol because you don't want to bear the consequences, or you may deliberately rebel against those rules as a way to assert your independence or fulfill your curiosity.

Media Influence

Alcohol advertising uses various forms of media and celebrities to communicate how society should view and feel about alcohol. Many streaming shows and

---

Diversity Matters

Influence of Culture

Culture also plays a part in your decision to drink or not. Your culture is the different customs that identify you and where you come from and includes ethnicity, religion, country or city, and language. Some religions may use wine as part of a religious service. In this situation, it is sometimes acceptable for children to drink the wine. Alcohol is also legal at a younger age in some countries. For example, in Antigua and Barbuda, the minimum age to drink alcohol is 10. In countries like Germany, Spain, and Denmark, the drinking age varies from 16 to 18. Iceland and Japan have a minimum drinking age of 20, while the United States, Oman, and Samoa have a drinking age of 21. In Iran, Qatar, and Sudan, it is illegal to drink alcohol at any age.

Social Media Statistics to Think About

- Teens who are regular users of social media are three times more likely to drink alcohol.
- Teens who encounter web-based alcohol marketing are 98 percent more likely to drink.

movies make references to alcohol by showing people drinking or talking about it. Advertising's goal is to get consumers to think the product makes the occasion better and the individual more likeable. It is important to understand that alcohol advertising is trying to sell their product, and they will promote it any way they can. The cold reality is that many celebrities are cycling in and out of rehabilitation centers, breaking the law, and engaging in other risky behaviors.

Social media are any form of electronic communication in which people share information, ideas, personal messages, and many other types of content. This particular medium is yet another means for companies to advertise their brands of alcohol or restaurants and bars to drink at. Additionally, individual people post pictures and videos of themselves drinking. If you see your friends and peers drinking and having a good time, you are more likely to want to mimic that good time. Teens also post videos and pictures of others who are drunk, passed out, and being inappropriate on various social media sites with and without the permission of the person in the video or picture.

Influence of Your Values

Your family, friends, and role models influence your personal **values**, which are the principles that describe what is most important to you as a person. These internal thoughts and feelings inform you about what is right and what is wrong. If you know something is the right thing to do and that it will make you and the people who are important to you proud, then you are more positively influenced to do it. If, on the other hand, you know something is a bad choice and that the people who are important to you will be disappointed in you, and ultimately, you will be disappointed in yourself, this is also your value system at work.

The values you have about using alcohol will influence your decision about whether to drink. You must decide if drinking is something you think is okay to do or is something you want to avoid. Your decisions about alcohol directly correlate to your choices about who your friends are and the kinds of social situations you may find yourself in.

Deciding Not to Use Alcohol

We live in a world where we are bombarded with mixed messages about drinking alcohol. Your family and other important adults may tell you not to drink. Your friends may or may not tell you to drink. The media you watch and the advertising you see send different messages as well. Some shows and movies make drinking alcohol appear enjoyable and harmless while others focus on negative aspects of drinking alcohol and its harmful effects. With so many angles from which to view drinking alcohol, it is difficult to decide which messages are the right ones to listen to.

LESSON 11.2   Alcohol

Contrary to popular belief, not all teens drink. That may seem unlikely if you have surrounded yourself with friends who do drink. Teens with non-drinking friends find it difficult to understand why anyone would want to drink when it seems to cause so many problems. Understanding the situations you may put yourself in and the people you are with will make a difference on the decision of whether or not to consume alcohol (see table 11.1).

TABLE 11.1   Situations Make a Difference in Alcohol Use

Situations that may encourage you to drink	Situations that may encourage you not to drink
You have access to alcohol at your house, or you have friends who can get alcohol for you.	You don't have access to alcohol, you don't know how you would go about getting alcohol, or you don't want to drink alcohol.
You have a job, and your family may not know what you are spending your money on.	Your parents or guardians have hard and fast rules about alcohol use. If you decide to drink, you might lose your freedom to do things and the trust of your family.
You spend a lot of time alone and don't have a curfew or expectations of when to be home.	You are involved in school activities, and you don't think it's worth the risk being suspended from the activity if you were caught drinking.
You are around siblings, friends, or family members who began drinking at an early age.	Your family members don't drink, or they only drink on special occasions.
You may feel pressured to drink by the friends you hang out with.	The friends you hang out with don't drink, and you wouldn't fit in if you did drink.

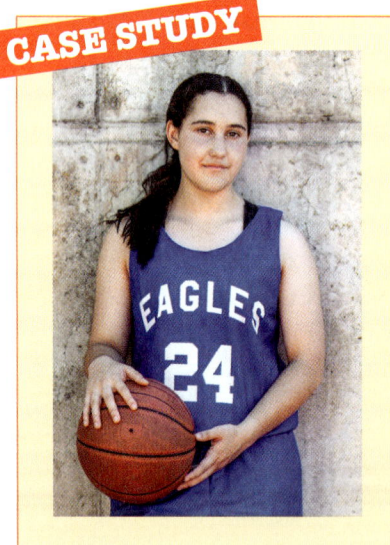

CASE STUDY

Faiza's Solution

Faiza began drinking about a year ago when her family moved to a new town and she started going to a new school. Faiza didn't have any friends, so she spent a lot of time alone. The alcohol was easy to get because her family always had alcohol in the house. There was a cupboard where a lot of alcohol was stashed, yet the adults in her family rarely drank. Most of the alcohol had been in the cupboard for a long time. Having a few hours after school alone made it easy for Faiza to have some alcohol without anyone noticing. Although Faiza wouldn't have much at a time, she began to enjoy the taste of it more and more.

One day at school there was an announcement about tryouts for the basketball team. Faiza had always enjoyed playing basketball and had been told she was good at it. Trying out for the basketball team would be something to get Faiza more involved in school. Maybe Faiza would make some friends, and basketball was something she knew she was good at.

Think About It

1. What are two current circumstances that may be enabling Faiza to drink at home?
2. Describe at least two ways in which Faiza would be encouraged to stop drinking if she made the basketball team.

Using Effective Communication Skills to Avoid Alcohol Use

Being able to communicate effectively is an important skill to help you not to consume alcohol. You can respond quickly and firmly with a solid "no," using verbal and nonverbal cues. The following refusal skills will help you make positive choices.

Refusal Skills

In situations where you are offered alcohol and you want to refuse, you need to use verbal and nonverbal communication to get your point across. Make sure your verbal response is firm and confident and that your nonverbal response matches it. For example, if your verbal response is "I don't drink," your nonverbal response could be shaking your head no or putting your hand up like you are stopping someone from getting close to you. This is an example of an *I* message and a refusal skill you learned about in chapter 1. Although it may be difficult in certain situations, it's important not to let your friends' and peers' negative influence stand in the way of what is right for you.

When refusing to drink, it is okay to be honest with the person, make up an excuse, or leave the situation. Use verbal communication such as the following:

- No, I don't drink.
- My family would disown me if they found out.
- I'd be kicked off the team.
- I need to go; I have to help a friend.
- Drinking makes me sick.

In addition, use nonverbal communication such as the following:

- Appearing busy to keep people from offering you an alcoholic beverage
- Already drinking a bottle of water or other non-alcoholic drink so they are less likely to offer you something to drink

It's best to be prepared for situations that may arise where alcohol is involved. Using your refusal skills and having thought ahead about different scenarios can provide you with potential plans of action. Think about what you would do in the following situations.

- Your friend offers you a drink at a party or at their house when no one else is home.
- You need to get home, but the person you rode with has been drinking.
- Your friend asks you to go to a party, but you know there will be alcohol.

These situations involve decisions you might have to make on your own. Share these situations and your decisions about them with a friend, family member, or supportive adult and ask if they have other suggestions for you. Being able to see different perspectives on a situation is often helpful for decision making.

Keep the following suggestions in mind to be better prepared for situations in which you must make a challenging decision or have a difficult conversation.

- Talk openly to your family members and supportive adults about what you should do if you are in a situation where alcohol is being used.

LESSON 11.2   Alcohol

- If you and a friend are trying to decide whether you should go to a party, think through the pros and cons of going and make a decision together. If you decide to go to the party, make sure you stick together and keep each other safe, especially if there is alcohol involved. If you decide not to go to the party, do something fun together. You don't need alcohol to have a good time.
- Imagine if a friend might have a drinking problem, but you aren't sure. You want to talk to them about your concerns, but you are afraid they will get mad at you. Talk to a trusted adult about what you should do.

Benefits of Being Alcohol-Free

Alcohol is one of the most commonly used drugs of high school students, but not every high school teen is drinking. Unfortunately, underage drinking is still a significant problem in the United States. Figure 11.9 highlights the many positive benefits of being alcohol-free.

Benefits to Not Drinking
- You have more energy.
- You have higher self-esteem.
- You have better relationships with your friends and family.
- You are better able to manage stressful situations.
- You eat healthier, because alcohol has a lot of empty calories and you may also tend to eat junk food when you drink.
- You have no hangovers, so you are healthier and feel better.
- You have higher grades than students who drink. Drinking may cause memory loss, which can affect your ability to do well in school.

Figure 11.9 Benefits of being alcohol-free.

Alternatives to Drinking Alcohol

Sometimes teens make a choice to drink alcohol because they don't realize they have alternative options. While it may not always seem obvious, you can always opt out of drinking by choosing to do the following instead:

- Go to a movie.
- Play video games, card games, or board games.
- Go to the mall.
- Volunteer to help at a hospital, your local Boys and Girls Club, or at a community center.
- Exercise.
- Find a new hobby or try something you've never done before.
- Spend time with a sibling or family member.
- Advocate for something you believe in.
- Try out for a sports team.
- Join a club at school or in your community.

Influences and Alcohol   **LESSON 11.2**

Skill-Building Challenge

Who Influences Me?

Based on the information you have just read, think about who and what influences the decisions you may make about drinking. List three to five names of people or concepts like the media that may influence your decision.

STEP 1

List three to five people or concepts of influence:

_____

STEP 2

In the following chart, place the names or concepts from step 1 in the appropriate column.

Positive influence: encourages you not to drink	Negative influence: encourages you to drink

STEP 3 Examine the people and concepts you listed in step 2: Are you making good choices about who your friends are and what you are paying attention to? If you answer "no," think about how you could encourage your friends to change their way of thinking. Would you consider finding new friends? How can you make better choices overall? Explain why you are or why you aren't making good choices.

Healthy Living Skills

This lesson focused on analyzing influences. Here are some more ways you can develop healthy living skills related to this lesson.

PRACTICING HEALTHY BEHAVIORS

Create a list of as many activities you can think of that you can do with your friends other than drink alcohol. Find a classmate and compare lists. Add any of their ideas to your list that you don't have. Use this list to do other things than drink. Every time you do something on your list, put a star next to the item. If you do find yourself in a situation where you chose to drink, put a check mark on your paper. At the end of the month, reflect on the progress you made. If this was easy for you, list two reasons why it was easy for you to have an alcohol-free lifestyle. If this was challenging for you, list two reasons why it was challenging for you to have an alcohol-free lifestyle. What might you do to make choosing alcohol-free alternatives easier?

LESSON 11.2 Alcohol

> **HEALTHY COMMUNICATION**
> Create a public service announcement (PSA) using I messages and refusal skills that tries to convince your classmates that alcohol advertising makes false claims about what drinking is really like. Keep in mind that the alcohol industry's initiative is to convince consumers that certain brands of alcohol will make them as interesting as the celebrities who endorse their products. Your PSA's initiative is to convince your peers about the falsehood of such marketing.

LESSON 11.2 Review: Influences and Alcohol

LESSON SUMMARY

- Your peers, friends, and immediate family influence your decisions about alcohol and whether you view it as a negative or positive experience.
- Media broadcast messages about alcohol use through advertisements, streaming shows, and movies, depicting both positive and negative experiences that can affect your perspective on alcohol.
- Social media is filled with marketing ploys that suggest you can only have a good time if you're drinking alcohol. Friends' posts of pictures of themselves at parties having a good time or of people passed out, drunk, and acting inappropriate also contribute to social media's influence on your decision making.
- Your internal thoughts and feelings are your personal values that influence whether drinking alcohol is right or wrong for you.
- Some alternatives to drinking are going to a movie, finding a new hobby, and joining a club or sports team.

REVIEWING CONCEPTS AND VOCABULARY

1. Important people in your life who affect the decisions you make are said to have a(n) _____ in your life.
2. _____ are the principles that describe what is most important to you as a person.
3. _____ consist of streaming shows, movies, TV, and the Internet.
4. Forms of electronic communication in which people share information, ideas, personal messages, and many other types of content are known as _____.
5. Teens who regularly use social media are _____ times more likely to drink alcohol.

THINKING CRITICALLY

Find a show or movie that depicts people drinking alcohol. As you watch it, make a list of which types of influences from this lesson (friends, peers, family, media, social media, values) are included in the show or movie. Then evaluate how movies, TV, or shows you stream may affect your decisions about drinking.

TAKE IT HOME

Discuss with a family member or other significant adult about how your values will influence your decisions about alcohol. Ask the person how their values over their lifetime have influenced their own decisions about drinking.

LESSON 11.3
Treating Alcohol Use Disorders

Terms to Learn
alcohol treatment program
alcohol use disorder (AUD)
mental health therapist
outpatient treatment
residential treatment center
student assistance program
substance abuse counselor

The Big Picture
Understanding whether a person has an alcohol use disorder is important in determining if the person needs professional help. Asking for help for a drinking problem is an important first step in recognizing there is a problem they can't fix by themselves.

Learning Targets
- Define what an alcohol use disorder is and how it is diagnosed.
- Describe three of the most common reasons for teen alcohol use disorders.
- Explain what outpatient treatment is.
- Summarize what a residential treatment center is.
- Identify what a student assistance program does.
- Discuss how family members can be involved in a teen's treatment program.

Write About It
List everything you know about treatment for an alcohol use disorder. Then write questions related to treatment that you would like to have answered.

Note-Taking Guide
Use this chapter's note-taking guide to help you organize and remember the material in this lesson.

LESSON 11.3   Alcohol

Cruz started drinking when his grandpa died a year ago. They were very close, and Cruz has never really gotten over him being gone. Cruz used to drink after school and on the weekends when his family members were at work. Lately, though, he's been drinking more often during the day, including a few mornings before going to school.

Cruz used to hang out with a couple of friends, but after showing up intoxicated at school, they stopped wanting to be around him. He has started skipping school so he can drink. On a day when Cruz happened to make it to school, his academic counselor Mr. Taylor asked Cruz to come into his office. Mr. Taylor is concerned about how Cruz's grades have plummeted from As and Bs last quarter to mostly Cs and a couple of Ds. He also has noticed Cruz spends most of his time by himself at school, and that he has been absent a lot. Mr. Taylor wants to talk to him about his concerns and to see if he can help him in any way. What do you think Mr. Taylor is most concerned about with Cruz? What kind of help do you think Cruz needs?

Alcohol Use Disorder

Alcohol use disorder (AUD) is a medical condition when a person's drinking causes distress or harm. The condition has three categories—mild, moderate, and severe. A person responds to 11 questions about their drinking experience in the past year. The diagnosis and severity of AUD are based on how many "yes" responses a person gives to the following questions:

1. Have there been times when you ended up drinking more or longer than you thought you would?
2. Have you wanted to try to stop drinking but couldn't?
3. Have you spent a lot of time drinking or being sick from drinking?
4. Have you experienced alcohol cravings where you had a strong need to have a drink?
5. Have you found that drinking or being sick from drinking interfered with your daily routine?
6. Have you continued to drink even though it was causing trouble with your friends or family?
7. Have you cut back on or stopped doing activities that were important to you in order to drink?
8. Have you more than once gotten into a situation while or after drinking that increased your chances of getting hurt (e.g., getting into a fight or having unsafe sex)?
9. Have you continued to drink even though it was making you feel depressed or anxious, or after having had a memory blackout?
10. Have you had to drink much more than you once did to get the effect you want?
11. Have you found that when the effects of alcohol were wearing off, you had withdrawal symptoms?

A "yes" response to any of the 11 questions is cause for concern. The severity of the AUD is defined as

- mild if a person answers yes to two or three questions,
- moderate if a person answers yes to four or five questions, and
- severe if a person answers yes to six or more questions.

Figure 11.10 highlights indications that a person may need help.

Figure 11.10 Indications that help may be needed for an AUD.

Possible Causes of Alcohol Use Disorder in Teens

There is no one specific reason anyone can point to for a possible cause of AUD. Yet it is known that genetics and psychological and social factors play a role in AUD in teens. We know that genetics has a significant role when a teen has a close relative who has an alcohol problem. They may be predisposed to alcohol being pleasurable regardless of the side effects the person may experience. Psychological factors may include people with mental health disorders such as anxiety and depression as well as people who are impulsive and take risks. Social factors also play a role in AUDs; for example, having friends who drink regularly; media portrayals of alcohol being used to have fun; and the influence of peers, family members, and other role models all are potential causes of AUD in teens.

LESSON 11.3   Alcohol

Getting Help for an Alcohol Use Disorder

You should get help for an alcohol use disorder when you begin to realize you lack energy and no longer want to do things you once liked to do. At this same time, you may also begin breaking promises you have made about when you will use alcohol. For example, you may promise to drink only on the weekends and then you find yourself drinking during the week as well. Other indications that you should seek help include having problems in school, at home, with other people, and with law enforcement.

- *School.* You may be having problems in school such as not turning in assignments, doing poorly on tests, skipping classes or school, and not being involved in activities you used to enjoy doing.
- *Home.* You may be fighting more with guardians and siblings at home than normal. You may also be distancing yourself from family members by staying in your room more often.
- *Other people.* You may be having more disagreements with friends, or you no longer want to hang out with your friends.
- *Law enforcement.* New or ongoing problems with law enforcement may be a sign of an AUD, but it's also a sign of a personal crisis.

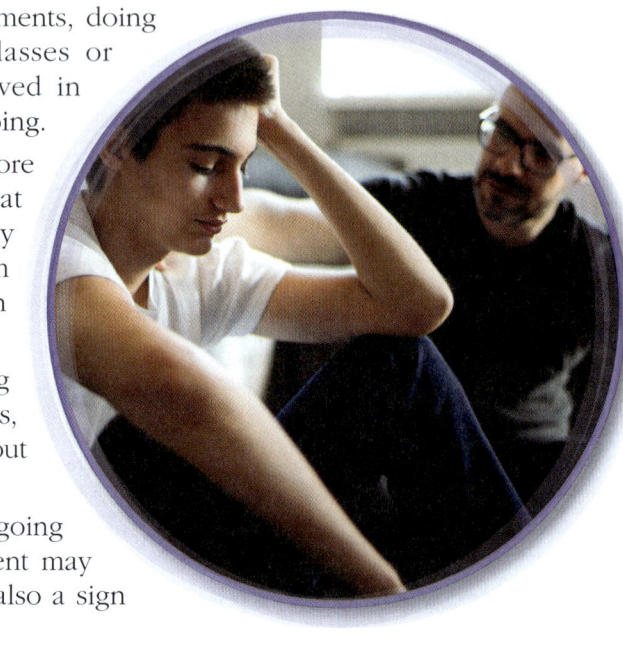

If you are having any of these problems or are seeing them in a friend, it is important you talk with a guardian or trusted adult and get help as soon as possible.

Helping Friends and Family Who Have an Alcohol Use Disorder

If a friend or family member suffers from an alcohol use disorder, they need help. It is important you talk with someone concerning your friend or family member. Talking to someone isn't being disloyal to them—it's seeking out information so you know how to talk with and help them. If you decide to talk with your friend or family member, here are some guidelines to help you.

- Talk with them when they are sober and use *I* messages.
- Express your concern about them and how much you care for them rather than accuse them of drinking too much or too often.
- Talk about your feelings by telling them you're worried and how you feel about their drinking.
- Tell them how you have felt when you have been around them when they were drinking. Tell them things they have said or done to you when they have been drinking.

HEALTHY LIVING TIP
Find out whether your school has a student assistance program. If it does, learn how to get involved. If your school doesn't have a program, talk to a school counselor about how a program could be started in your school to help students with alcohol, tobacco, or drug problems.

- Offer to go with them to get help for their alcohol use disorder.
- Be prepared for them to deny they have a problem or to be angry with you for talking to them.

Alcohol Treatment Programs

An **alcohol treatment program** is where people go to get professional help for an alcohol use disorder. Based on the severity of the alcohol use disorder and individual needs, there are multiple programs to help people stop drinking. It is just a matter of finding the treatment program or combination of treatment programs that work best for them.

Outpatient Treatment

Outpatient treatment centers allow students to go to school and live at home, but they have to attend counseling on a predetermined basis. A substance abuse counselor or mental health therapist determines the specific type of outpatient treatment and how many times a week a person has to attend sessions. A **substance abuse counselor** works with people who are dealing with an alcohol use disorder and other substance abuse disorders. A **mental health therapist** is a medical professional who helps people achieve emotional wellness.

- *Individual counseling.* One type of outpatient treatment is individual counseling with a substance abuse counselor or a mental health therapist. This type of treatment might focus on changing individual behavior that makes people want to drink, teaches people how to manage their stress and other factors that may cause them to drink, and helps people build a strong support system.
- *Group therapy.* In the group therapy setting, a person has the support of other members in the group who also have an alcohol use disorder and are experiencing similar problems.

Career Connection

SUBSTANCE ABUSE COUNSELOR

A substance abuse counselor works with several kinds of clients ranging from teens to older adults and military to corporate office professionals. On a daily basis, these professionals listen to clients explain their problems and what causes them to drink. Counselors help clients learn how to modify their behavior, teach coping mechanisms, create treatment plans, lead individual and group therapy sessions, set up aftercare plans, and meet with family members to provide guidance and support. In order to become a substance abuse counselor, most agencies require a master's degree in counseling or social work and appropriate certification.

- *Mutual support groups.* People who have the same problems or concerns comprise these groups. The best-known alcohol mutual support group is Alcoholics Anonymous (AA). The experience is very similar to group therapy; however the main difference is support groups help members *cope* while group therapy helps members *change*. The people in the mutual support group can offer understanding and advice and help keep people on track to recovery.
- *Student assistance programs.* Many schools have some type of **student assistance program**, in which substance abuse counselors are brought into the school and meet with students individually or as a group on a weekly basis. A student assistance program is designed to help students, families, and schools build a safe school environment for everyone to be successful in. These programs provide the following services:
  - Early alcohol, tobacco, and drug prevention and intervention services to students and families
  - Referrals to community services, including treatment providers
  - Assistance in getting students back into school if they have had problems with alcohol, tobacco, or other drugs
  - Informational workshops for guardians, school staff, and community members about how to assist students in need

Medications

Sometimes medications are prescribed to help stop or reduce drinking or to prevent a relapse. A relapse occurs when a person begins drinking again after they have attempted to stop. The following are the two most commonly used medications to make drinking less enjoyable:

- *Disulfiram (Antabuse).* This makes the person feel sick or causes them to throw up when they drink. Knowing the drug will produce these side effects may help the person avoid drinking.
- *Naltrexone (Revia).* This reduces a person's urge to drink.

Residential Treatment Centers

A **residential treatment center** requires the person to live full time for the length of their treatment. The length of treatment depends on the person's progress in the program, with the average treatment time being one to three months. People at residential treatment centers participate in individual and group counseling sessions as well as other therapeutic and educational activities. Residential treatment centers have very structured programs that focus on each person's individual recovery.

Family Involvement in Residential Treatment Programs

Residential treatment centers also want the family involved in the alcohol user's treatment. The programs teach family members about the alcohol use disorder and examine how family dynamics may help or hurt the alcohol user once they return home. Many teens who have an alcohol use disorder come from families where alcohol is a problem. Getting the family involved in the treatment program can be helpful for everyone. It is also important for family members to be able to talk with other people who have faced similar situations. There are two main support groups for families.

1. Al-Anon helps family members and friends learn how to help themselves as well as the person with the AUD.
2. Alateen is specifically for teens who have a family member or friend who has an AUD.

Skill-Building Challenge

Where Can I Go for Help?

Search online for the location of at least one alcohol treatment program for each of the following categories in your community:

- Individual counseling for teens with a substance abuse counselor
- Group therapy for teens who use alcohol
- Support group for teens who use alcohol
- Inpatient treatment center for teens who use alcohol

Provide the agency name, address, telephone number, and approximate distance from your home or school. If there isn't a treatment program available in your community, expand your search to a neighboring community or state. Focus on finding the treatment program closest to where you live.

Do the agencies you found appear to be valid and reliable (.gov, .org, or .edu)? Use the Accessing Valid and Reliable Information Skill Cues to explain your answer.

Healthy Living Skills

This lesson focused on accessing valid and reliable information. Here are some more ways you can develop healthy living skills related to this lesson.

ANALYZING INFLUENCES

Think about a sport star, celebrity, or friend who has sought help for their alcohol use disorder by seeing a substance abuse counselor or mental health therapist. Identify how you feel about the sport star, celebrity, or friend seeing a substance abuse counselor or mental health therapist. Are you more likely to seek help for an alcohol use disorder or other mental health problem because the sport star, celebrity, or friend did? Why are you more (or less) likely to seek help based on the decision of the sport star, celebrity, or friend?

HEALTHY COMMUNICATION

Using I messages, write a script you could use to talk with a friend whom you're concerned may have an alcohol use disorder. Use the guidelines in this lesson to help you determine what you would want to say to your friend. Once you have your script written, practice reading it to a classmate and get their feedback on what you wrote.

LESSON 11.3 Alcohol

LESSON 11.3 Review: Treating Alcohol Use Disorders

LESSON SUMMARY

- An alcohol use disorder (AUD) is a medical condition in which a person's drinking causes distress or harm. A person answers 11 questions about their drinking habits over the past year, and the number of "yes" responses determines if their diagnosis is mild, moderate, or severe.
- An alcohol treatment program provides professional help for an alcohol use disorder. There are multiple programs designed to help a person's individual need to stop drinking.
- *I* messages are useful for helping a friend who has an alcohol use disorder because you can express your concern and care for them, express your feelings about their drinking, and offer your support by going with them to get help.
- Alcohol, tobacco, and drug prevention and intervention services, referrals to community services, and assistance getting students back in school are just a few ways a student assistance program serves students and their families.

REVIEWING CONCEPTS AND VOCABULARY

1. _____ is a medical condition that is diagnosed when a person's drinking causes distress or harm.
2. In _____ treatment, you can still go to school and live at home, but you have to attend counseling.
3. A(n) _____ counselor works with people who are dealing with an alcohol use disorder and other substance abuse disorders.
4. A(n) _____ therapist is a medical professional who helps their patients achieve emotional wellness.
5. At a(n) _____, you participate in individual and group counseling sessions as well as other therapeutic and educational activities.
6. A(n) _____ program is designed to help students, families, and schools build a safe school environment where everyone can be successful.

THINKING CRITICALLY

Create a flyer announcing a student assistance program for teens who drink alcohol and for teens who want to support their friends who drink. Include statistics and other facts to signal the dangers of drinking and the benefits of a student assistance program. Include concepts that would make a student assistance program a safe space for students.

TAKE IT HOME

If someone in your family has an alcohol use disorder, talk to your family about how everyone can be involved in the person's treatment program. Create a list of ways each family member can support the person with the alcohol use disorder.

Chapter Review

ACTION PLAN: Be Alcohol-Free

Use the My Action Plan worksheet to set goals for being alcohol-free. Here is an example.

My Action Plan: Be Alcohol-Free

STEP 1: Identify the health behavior you are going to work on.

I want to focus on doing things with my friends without drinking alcohol.

STEP 2: Write SMART goal(s).
Write one or two short-term goals (one day to one month or more).

I will have fun with my friends without drinking alcohol.

Write a long-term goal (one to six months or more).

I will work on having friends who don't drink alcohol.

STEP 3: Make a plan.
Identify two to five action steps (strategies) you could do to meet your goal.

I will make a list of five activities my friends and I can participate in that don't involve alcohol.

I will focus on my friends who support my idea of not drinking.

STEP 4: Execute your plan and track your progress.

Short-term goal
[X] Met   [ ] Not met   Date: *May 15*

Long-term goal
[X] Met   [ ] Not met   Date: *August 23*

If you met your goal, what helped you to be successful?

I met my short-term goal because we found things we could do that were fun without drinking alcohol.

I met my long-term goal because I found out in my short-term goal who my friends were that didn't want to drink alcohol anymore, and I focused on them.

If you did not meet your goal, what things made it harder for you to be successful?

I met both my goals.

Test Your Knowledge

Select the best answer for each question.

1. Of the four fetal alcohol spectrum disorders, which is the most severe?
   a. ARBD
   b. ND-PAE
   c. FAS
   d. ARND

2. Alcohol is a
   a. stimulant
   b. depressant
   c. hallucinogen
   d. pain reliever

3. If a friend is talking to you about alcohol and gesturing with their hands a lot, they are using
   a. verbal communication and nonverbal communication
   b. refusal skills and *I* messages
   c. *I* messages and nonverbal communication
   d. nonverbal communication and refusal skills

4. A form of electronic communication in which people can share personal messages and videos of themselves drinking is known as
   a. streaming shows
   b. social media
   c. magazines
   d. television

5. The type of disorder that is diagnosed when a person's drinking causes distress or harm is
   a. abuse disorder
   b. drinking disorder
   c. alcohol use disorder
   d. depressant disorder

6. The program that has substance abuse counselors in the school meeting with students individually or in a group setting is a
   a. student assistance program
   b. group therapy program
   c. mutual support group program
   d. residential treatment program

7. The term used to describe pressure you feel from your friends when they want you to drink alcohol is
   a. friend
   b. student
   c. sibling
   d. peer

8. A common reason for teen alcohol use disorders is
   a. lack of family support
   b. withdrawal symptoms
   c. psychological factors
   d. use of other drugs

9. Zero tolerance laws may also be known as
   a. DWI laws
   b. DUI laws
   c. just-one-sip laws
   d. not-a-drop laws

10. A teen consuming five or more drinks in a short period of time describes
    a. heavy drinking
    b. hangover drinking
    c. moderate drinking
    d. binge drinking

PROJECT-BASED LEARNING: Alcohol Effects on Social Media

What to Remember

Teens often don't really understand the short- and long-term effects alcohol can have on them physically, mentally, emotionally, and socially. Physical effects of alcohol use can cause damage to major organs. Mental and emotional effects can make it difficult for a teen to concentrate, hindering their ability to cope with the daily demands of their life. Social effects can make it difficult for teens to have and keep friends. Alcohol use really can make their lives worse than they ever imagined.

Who It Is For

Students in your class

Why It Is Important

This exercise will help your peers understand the consequences of drinking alcohol, which can affect them well into their future.

What to Do

Get into groups of three and work together to develop a Facebook page or some other type of social media for other teens. On this social media platform, you will review the information on the short- and long-term effects of alcohol on a person physically, mentally, emotionally, and socially. You will need to write out a script of the information you are going to present so that you remember to include all the details.

See whether your school has some type of social media you might be able to link to. If not, you will need to create a social media page for this assignment. Regardless of the social media you use, it will be important for you to keep the page *private* in order to have control over who may access it. Starting out, it should be just your classmates and teacher; with teacher approval, you can expand your followers. If you don't have access to social media of any kind, create a poster or brochure of the information to share with several people.

How to Do It

Step 1: Use the information in this chapter to identify the physical, mental, emotional, and social effects of drinking alcohol. Make sure you include both short- and long-term effects.

Step 2: Decide which person in the group will be responsible for which components: physical, mental, emotional, and social. You should also include an introduction paragraph that explains what alcohol is and the different ways it can affect a person.

Step 3: Make sure each person in your group and your teacher have access to the social media platform you are using and that you have set the page to private.

Step 4: If you can't use social media, create a poster or brochure so your group can share the information with the class.

CROSS-CURRICULAR CONNECTION: Math

Create a graph that clearly displays the following information.

If a person has a BAC of 0.03 percent, they feel lightheaded. A BAC of 0.06 percent causes a person to have difficulty with their memory. With a BAC of 0.17 percent, a person is considered very drunk and will have blurred vision. With a BAC of 0.27 percent, a person experiences their physical functions to be severely impaired. With a BAC of 0.08 percent, a person is considered legally drunk and their reaction time is impaired. With a BAC of 0.14 percent, a person has gross motor impairment. With a BAC of 0.23 percent, a person will experience vomiting. Finally, a BAC of 0.31 percent could result in a coma or death.

Tobacco and E-Cigarettes

LESSON 12.1 Tobacco Products and Vaping
LESSON 12.2 Regulations and Influences on Tobacco Product Use
LESSON 12.3 Avoiding and Quitting Tobacco Product Use

Understanding My Health

What Do I Know About Tobacco Products?

Tobacco, regardless of how it is consumed, can cause short- and long-term consequences. People who are exposed to second- and thirdhand smoke can also suffer tobacco related illnesses. An interesting concept about tobacco is once you quit using, your body can begin to heal itself; however, it may not be able to recover completely depending on the severity of damage. Complete the following self-assessment by putting an X in the box below the word *true* or *false* for each question to help you understand your knowledge about tobacco products. After completing the self-assessment, check your answers with the answer key at the bottom of the assessment.

	True	False
1. Tobacco use is the number one cause of preventable deaths in the United States.		
2. E-cigarettes are a safe alternative to smoking regular cigarettes.		
3. Nicotine is the main addictive chemical in tobacco.		
4. Vaping is the act of inhaling and exhaling aerosol produced by e-cigarettes.		
5. A person cannot become addicted to e-cigarettes.		
6. Using e-cigarettes is the best way to stop smoking regular cigarettes.		
7. A person has to be 18 years old to purchase any type of tobacco product in the United States.		
8. There are multiple apps and text message programs you can download to help you quit using tobacco products.		
9. All 50 states have comprehensive smoke-free laws covering workplaces, restaurants, and bars, which means they are 100 percent smoke-free.		
10. Secondhand smoke is the tobacco residue that can remain on surfaces for months after someone smokes.		

Answers: 1. true, 2. false, 3. true, 4. true, 5. false, 6. false, 7. false, 8. true, 9. false, 10. false

My score for What Do I Know About Tobacco Products? = _____ (total number of correct answers)

Tobacco products come in many different forms: cigarettes, pipes, cigars, smokeless tobacco, and e-cigarettes. While tobacco is the main ingredient in most of the products, nicotine is the addictive chemical that hooks a person to continue using. There are multiple negative health effects that can affect a person who uses tobacco products. Second- and thirdhand smoke can affect nonsmokers. Being aware of who and what influences you will affect the decisions you make about using tobacco products. Tobacco product use is on the rise in teens due primarily to the use of e-cigarettes.

LESSON 12.1
Tobacco Products and Vaping

Terms to Learn

carcinogens
e-cigarettes
e-liquid
nicotine
secondhand aerosol
secondhand smoke
thirdhand smoke
tobacco
vaping

The Big Picture

E-cigarettes are heavily marketed toward teens, which has increased their popularity among teens who use them and think they are safer than other tobacco products. The addictive ingredient in tobacco is nicotine, which in combination with tobacco causes several short- and long-term health effects. Vaping (using an e-cigarette) gets its name from the clouds of vapor that are produced when using an e-cigarette device. Using e-cigarettes is a dangerous alternative to conventional smoking, primarily because of the much higher nicotine content found in many e-cigarettes. E-cigarettes entered the U.S. marketplace around 2007 and since 2014 have been the most commonly used tobacco product with U.S. youth. Due to e-cigarettes being relatively new there isn't enough information yet for health officials to determine all the potential health risks of vaping. Smoking or vaping also affects nonsmokers because of second- and thirdhand smoke.

Note-Taking Guide

Use this chapter's note-taking guide to help you organize and remember the material in this lesson.

Learning Targets

- Describe what tobacco is and name its main ingredient.
- Explain short- and long-term health effects of tobacco products on a person.
- Evaluate how vaping is as dangerous as smoking.
- Examine the impact of secondhand smoke, thirdhand smoke, and secondhand aerosol.

Write About It

Can you name four types of tobacco products? Can you list the common ingredient found in all forms of tobacco?

LESSON 12.1   Tobacco and E-Cigarettes

Amir vaped only a couple of times each day with his friends at first and didn't think it was a big deal. As time progressed, he began vaping several times a day. Amir thinks he is more focused after he has been vaping. Amir sings in the school choir and was recently asked to be a lead singer in a band his brother is in. Amir has begun noticing that he can't hold notes as long as he used to, and after only a few songs, he feels out of breath and needs a break. Why do you think Amir is having trouble holding notes or singing for an extended period of time?

Tobacco and Its Ingredients

Tobacco is a plant grown for its leaves, which are dried and put into tobacco products. Tobacco plants contain **nicotine**, the highly addictive chemical and main ingredient in tobacco. Nicotine stimulates the release of dopamine in the brain, which is the chemical responsible for feelings of excitement, relaxation, and stress relief. The release of dopamine and the feelings associated with it hook people into using tobacco products throughout the day in order to experience those feelings over and over again. Cigarettes and other forms of tobacco contain not only nicotine but also hundreds of other chemicals and substances (see figure 12.1).

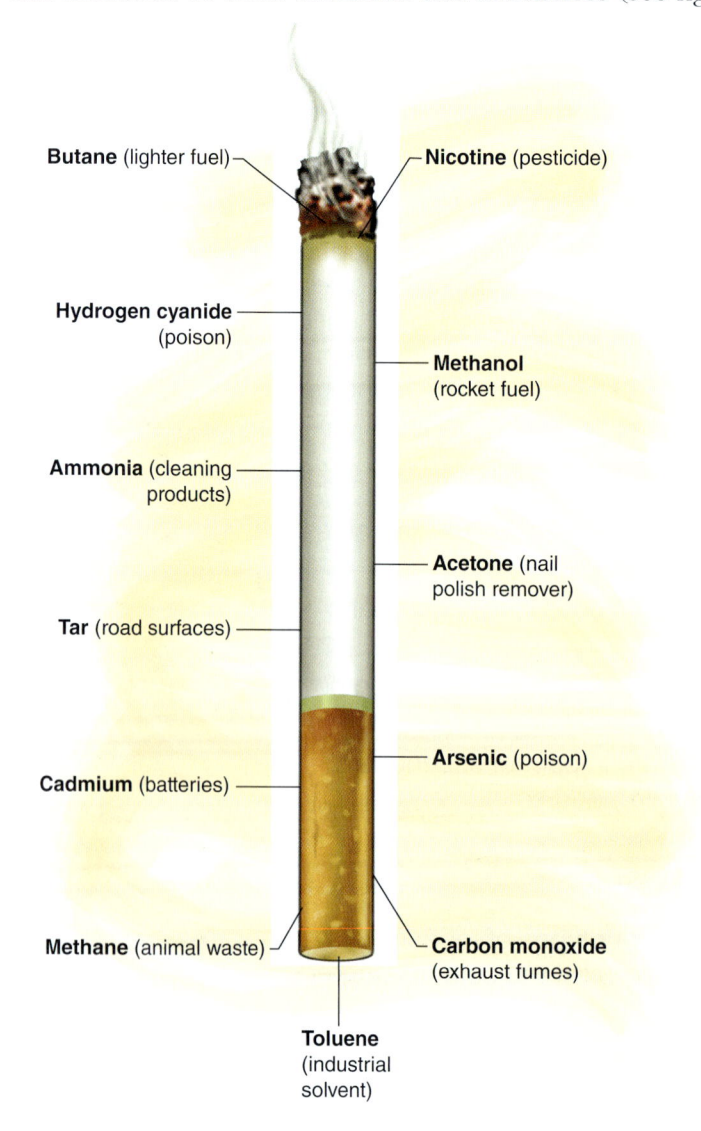

Figure 12.1 Common cigarette components and what else they can be found in.

- Butane (lighter fuel)
- Nicotine (pesticide)
- Hydrogen cyanide (poison)
- Methanol (rocket fuel)
- Ammonia (cleaning products)
- Acetone (nail polish remover)
- Tar (road surfaces)
- Arsenic (poison)
- Cadmium (batteries)
- Methane (animal waste)
- Carbon monoxide (exhaust fumes)
- Toluene (industrial solvent)

512

Tobacco Products and Vaping **LESSON 12.1**

Types of Tobacco Products

Tobacco is found in different types of products. Some you may be familiar with and others may be new to you.

Cigarette
A thin cylinder of ground or shredded tobacco that is wrapped in paper, lit, and smoked; the most conventional form of tobacco products

Cigar
A tube of tobacco that is thicker than a cigarette, is wrapped in a tobacco leaf, lit, and smoked; includes regular cigars, cigarillos, and little filtered cigars

Snuff and Snus
Finely ground tobacco that can be moist, dry, or packaged in pouches that look like tea bags; all kept in the mouth between the lower lip or cheek and gums

Electronic Cigarettes (E-Cigarettes)
Also known as vape pens, electronic nicotine delivery systems (ENDS), and e-pipes; use e-liquid, which may contain nicotine (derived from tobacco) and different flavors, but do not contain tobacco itself; liquid is heated to create an aerosol the user inhales (vaping)

Dissolvables
Finely ground tobacco pressed into shapes such as tablets, sticks, or strips that slowly dissolve in the mouth

Pipe
A tube with a small bowl at one end that is filled with tobacco, lit, and smoked

Chewing Tobacco
Loose-leaf, plug, twist, or roll; all kept in the mouth between the cheek and gums

Tobacco Facts

Tobacco product use in the United States is increasing in youth. According to the CDC, approximately one in five high school students has used a tobacco product in the last 30 days. Increased usage of e-cigarettes is primarily the reason for this uptick in tobacco use among teens. Tobacco use overall is the number one cause of preventable deaths in the United States (see figure 12.2).

LESSON 12.1   Tobacco and E-Cigarettes

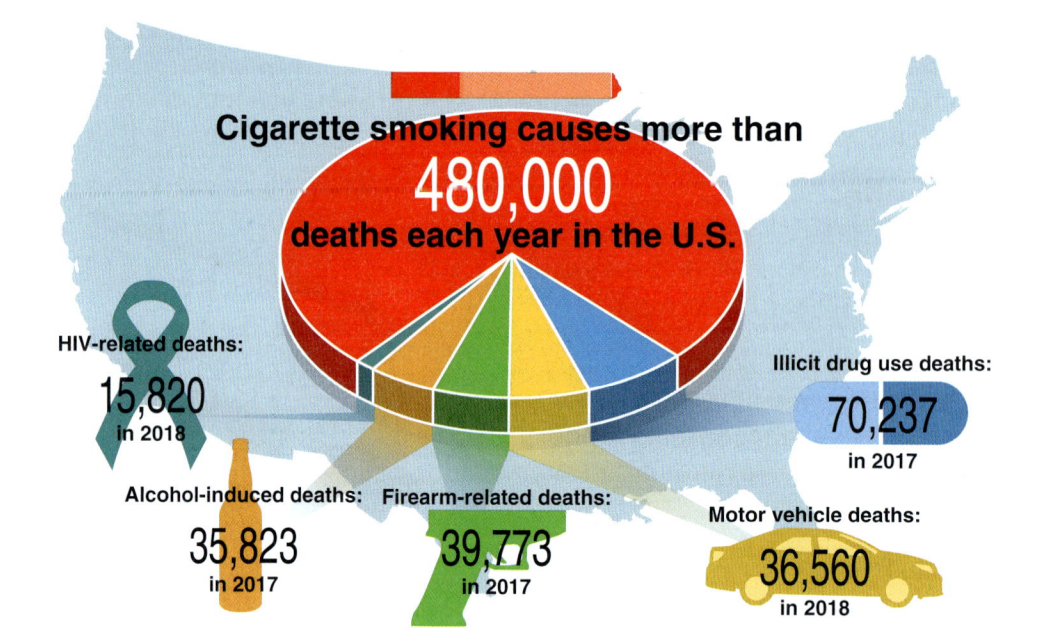

Cigarette smoking causes more than 480,000 deaths each year in the U.S.

HIV-related deaths: 15,820 in 2018

Alcohol-induced deaths: 35,823 in 2017

Firearm-related deaths: 39,773 in 2017

Illicit drug use deaths: 70,237 in 2017

Motor vehicle deaths: 36,560 in 2018

Figure 12.2 Common preventable deaths in the United States.

Tobacco's Effects

No matter what type of tobacco you use, it will have a consequence on how you feel and look (see figure 12.3). Tobacco and nicotine will also affect your mental health regarding dopamine levels in your brain.

Physical Effects of Tobacco Use

Teens who smoke may be more likely to develop asthma, bronchitis, and pneumonia. Asthma causes swelling and narrowing inside the lungs and restricts air supply. Bronchitis is an inflammation of the lining of the bronchial tubes, which carry air to and from the lungs. Pneumonia is an infection that inflames the air sacs in one or both lungs. All three of these conditions can cause coughing and difficulty breathing.

Cardiovascular diseases
- Heart attacks
- Stroke
- Heart disease
- Atherosclerosis
- High blood pressure
- Angina (chest pain)

Respiratory diseases
- Emphysema
- Chronic bronchitis
- Asthma

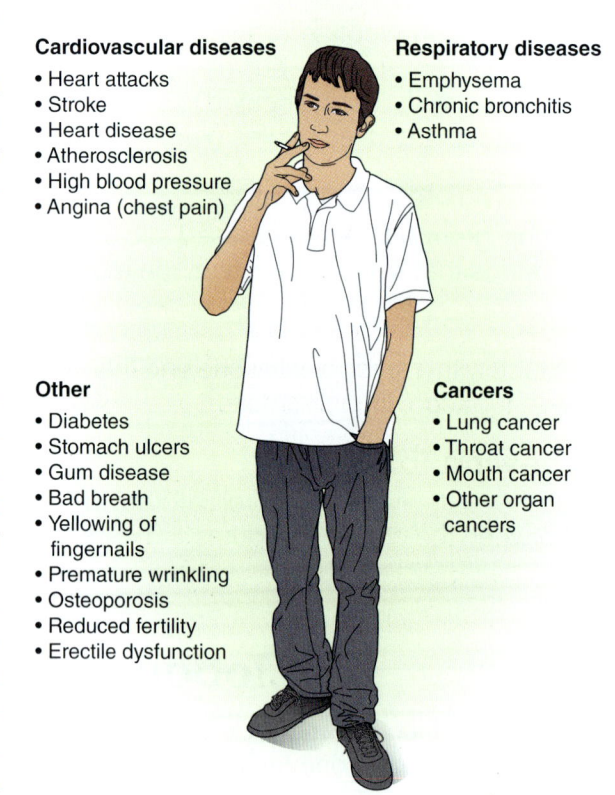

Other
- Diabetes
- Stomach ulcers
- Gum disease
- Bad breath
- Yellowing of fingernails
- Premature wrinkling
- Osteoporosis
- Reduced fertility
- Erectile dysfunction

Cancers
- Lung cancer
- Throat cancer
- Mouth cancer
- Other organ cancers

Figure 12.3 Effects of tobacco on the body.

514

When smoke is inhaled, chemicals from the smoke are absorbed into the lungs. This can result in progressive lung diseases including emphysema and chronic obstructive pulmonary disease (COPD), for which there are no cures. Emphysema causes shortness of breath because the air sacs in the lungs have been damaged. COPD is due to the airflow from the lungs being clogged, so it is hard to get enough oxygen. Eight out of 10 cases of COPD are caused by smoking.

Nicotine is the main ingredient in tobacco and is very addictive. As table 12.1 shows, tobacco has multiple short- and long-term effects on our bodies.

TABLE 12.1 Health Effects of Teen Tobacco Use

Short-term health effects	Long-term health effects
Less endurance due to decreased lung function, overall poorer physical performance, increased sports-related injuries due to decreased oxygen in blood, and poorer overall health	More likely to continue smoking throughout adult life
Constant irritation of the mouth, pharynx, and larynx from inhaling hot gases and small particles while smoking; may develop into hoarseness and coughing	Reduced life expectancy of seven years if smoking a pack or more of cigarettes each day
Resting heart rates that are two to three beats per minute faster than nonsmokers	Increased risk of heart disease and stroke
Increased blood pressure	Twenty times more likely to get lung cancer than a nonsmoker
More likely to see health professional for emotional or psychological problem, possibly due to nicotine addiction and continued use of tobacco to feel better	Lung development impeded due to inhalation of chemicals, which prevents lungs from performing at full capacity; may lead to lung diseases including emphysema and COPD
Three times more likely to use alcohol, eight times more likely to use marijuana, and 22 times more likely to use cocaine due to nicotine-induced changes to brain's structure, making it more likely to become addicted to other drugs	Anxiety, depression, and negative effects on learning, memory, and cognition caused by tobacco acting as a central nervous system stimulant
Yellowing of the teeth and fingertips along with development of leathery, dry skin	Increased risk of getting tobacco-related cancers

Effects of Nicotine on Your Mental Health

As you read earlier, nicotine in tobacco stimulates the release of dopamine in the brain, which temporarily improves mood. Within the first 10 seconds of inhaling, a dose of nicotine reaches the brain. Regular use of nicotine can lead to nicotine addiction, trapping the smoker in a perpetual cycle of using nicotine to increase dopamine. With every increase comes a decrease in dopamine as the nicotine supply drops, causing the smoker to use nicotine again to replicate the good feeling.

People may also use tobacco because they think it helps to reduce their stress, yet it is actually shown to increase tension and anxiety. As dopamine decreases, smokers often become anxious, which increases their desire for more nicotine. People with depression may have lower levels of dopamine than those without depression, and they may use tobacco as a means to increase deficient levels of dopamine in order to experience more positive feelings. One of the long-term effects of tobacco use is that it will actually slow the brain's ability to produce dopamine on its own—making users that much more reliant on highly addictive nicotine.

Social Consequences of Tobacco Use

Studies show teens are more likely to smoke or vape in social situations where other teens are smoking or vaping as well. Even teens who may not normally use tobacco are more likely to use it in a social situation with others as a way of blending in. People view themselves as being friendlier, extroverted, and less socially anxious when using tobacco, which we have learned is in large part due to the increased dopamine that nicotine causes. Teens may view smoking or vaping in social settings only as an acceptable use, and doing it now and then won't have an impact on them. Yet due to the strong effect that dopamine release has, the occasional social settings may become more frequent and could lead to using on a regular basis to experience the same feelings found in those social settings. Humans in general tend to be influenced by the people they associate with. The social settings we put ourselves into can influence our physical and mental health as well.

Financial Consequences Associated With Tobacco Use

In general, smoking is expensive. A pack of cigarettes can cost between $6.50 and $13.00 depending on the state a person lives in. In comparison, a vape pen or e-cigarette can cost anywhere between $10.00 and $500.00 depending on the type and quality purchased. On average, people tend to spend about $80.00 on a vape pen or e-cigarette and about $60.00 per month on refill cartridges, e-liquid, or other related vaping products.

In recent years, insurance companies have classified vaping the same as smoking when it comes to insurance policies, which means vapers and smokers alike are charged higher rates than nonsmokers. People who smoke or vape pay more for health and life insurance because they are considered at a higher risk for serious chronic illnesses. People who smoke or vape also tend to work fewer years, which results in a reduction in lifetime earnings, personal savings, and contributions to retirement plans. Overall, smoking-related illnesses in the United States costs more than $300 billion each year between direct medical care and lost productivity.

Pregnancy and Tobacco Product Use

Female smokers have more difficulty becoming pregnant than nonsmoking females. Male smokers can have damaged sperm and have difficulty getting their partner pregnant. Smoking while pregnant can cause many health problems to the mother and her baby (see figure 12.4).

Mother
- Smoking doubles the risk of abnormal bleeding during pregnancy and delivery.
- Ectopic pregnancy may occur. This is when a fertilized egg implants itself outside the uterus and begins to grow. An ectopic pregnancy always ends in a pregnancy loss.
- Miscarriage may happen, which is when a baby dies in the womb.
- E-cigarettes can contain nicotine, which is not safe to use during pregnancy.

Baby
- One in five babies has low birth weight.
- Babies are born prematurely (earlier than they should be).
- Babies have weaker lungs, which makes it more difficult for them to breathe.
- Sudden infant death syndrome (SIDS) may happen; this is when an infant dies unexpectedly in their sleep. Babies whose mothers smoke are three times more likely to die from SIDS.
- E-cigarettes containing nicotine can damage a developing baby's brain and lungs.
- Flavors used in e-cigarettes may be harmful to the developing baby.

Figure 12.4 Effects of smoking on the mother's and baby's health.

Health Effects of Smokeless Tobacco

Smokeless tobacco is also a serious risk to your mouth and overall health. Smokeless tobacco contains twice as much nicotine as conventional cigarettes, making it even more addictive than cigarettes. A single can of chewing tobacco has as much nicotine as four packs of cigarettes. Smokeless tobacco also contains carcinogens, just like cigarettes. There are a number of health consequences of smokeless tobacco that teens need to be aware of:

- Can lead to nicotine addiction
- Can cause cancer of the mouth, esophagus, or pancreas (a gland that helps with digestion and maintaining proper blood sugar levels)
- Destroys gum tissue and causes cavities, tooth decay, and bone loss around the teeth
- Causes tooth discoloration and bad breath
- Can cause leukoplakia, which can occur on the gums, inside of the cheek, and beneath the tongue (Leukoplakia is usually a white or grayish patch that tends to harden and have an irregular shape to it. It usually appears in an area near where the smokeless tobacco is held against the cheek.)

LESSON 12.1 Tobacco and E-Cigarettes

E-Cigarettes

E-cigarettes have many different names, such as e-cigs, vape pens, vapes, mods, tank systems, and ENDS, which stands for electronic nicotine delivery systems. E-cigarettes are battery-operated devices that heat a liquid and produce an aerosol that e-cigarette users inhale and exhale (see figure 12.5). The aerosol can contain the following: nicotine; flavorings; ultrafine chemical particles that can be inhaled into the lungs (from the e-liquid and from the metal in the heating coil of the e-cigarette); cancer-causing chemicals; and heavy metals such as nickel, tin, and lead. Using an e-cigarette is often known as vaping. **Vaping** is the act of inhaling and exhaling aerosol produced by an e-cigarette.

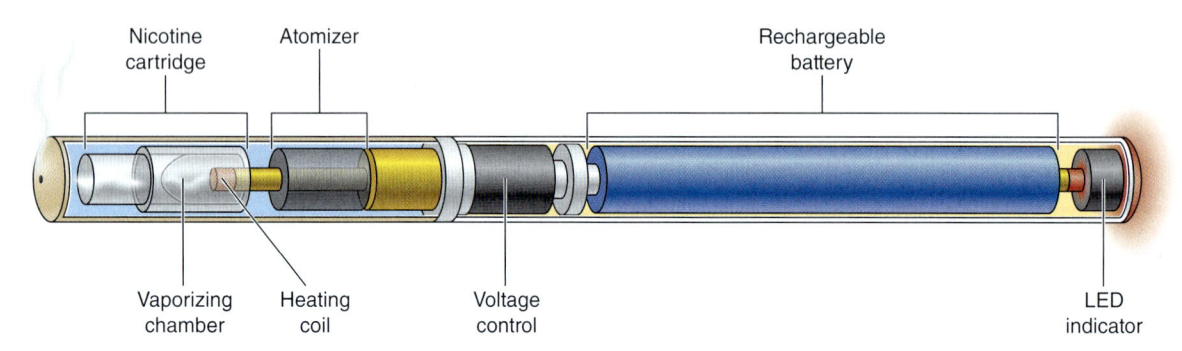

Figure 12.5 The internal part of an e-cigarette.

E-cigarettes come in many shapes and sizes. Some look like regular cigarettes and are usually disposable. Others look like USB flash drives or pens while others use tank systems, which are larger devices known as mods. The e-cigarettes that are in the form of USB drives, pens, and mods all have internal batteries and are all rechargeable. One appeal of e-cigarettes for teens is their close resemblance to commonly used items such as markers, USB flash drives, and highlighters, making them easy to hide in plain sight.

Most types of e-cigarettes have a battery, a heating element, and a place to hold liquid. The liquid, often referred to as **e-liquid**, usually contains nicotine, flavoring, and other chemicals. The amount of aerosol produced by the e-cigarette affects how much nicotine is consumed.

E-liquid comes in a number of flavors, including strawberry, bubblegum, orange, peppermint, coffee, cola, and pie flavors. The use of flavors is also part of the appeal to teens—it doesn't smell like traditional cigarettes, so it seems safer and more appealing. Teens cite the flavors as the leading reason for using e-cigarettes. For this reason, e-cigarettes using nicotine or synthetic nicotine in fruit flavors, as well as cartridges and flavored pods, are now regulated by the FDA. The sale of prefilled cartridge e-cigarettes in any flavor other than tobacco or menthol, unless authorized by the FDA, is prohibited.

Who Uses E-Cigarettes?

According to the CDC, more than three million teens in middle school and high school use e-cigarettes. The CDC has found that teens and young adults who are using e-cigarettes are at an increased risk to smoke cigarettes later in their lives, due in part to the addictive nature of nicotine. Some cigarette smokers, both young and older, are using e-cigarettes in places where cigarette smoking isn't allowed. By using two or more tobacco products, people are increasing their total exposure to nicotine and its harmful effects. Overall, the use of e-cigarettes seems to be more socially acceptable than smoking cigarettes. The aerosol doesn't smell bad like cigarette smoke does, nor does it make your breath and clothes smell bad. This is one of the more popular reasons people are using to justify their e-cigarette use.

E-Cigarettes Are a Dangerous Alternative to Smoking

E-cigarettes have been advertised as a safe alternative to smoking and as a method to help people try to quit smoking. A study by Harvard Health found that while some participants in their study stopped smoking, many began using e-cigarettes instead.

Whether a person smokes a conventional cigarette or an e-cigarette, nicotine usually becomes the main reason for doing so. Nicotine is the highly addictive component of tobacco, and although tobacco is not used in e-cigarettes, nicotine often is. There are approximately 10 milligrams of nicotine in a conventional cigarette, yet the average smoker inhales only some of the smoke from the cigarette and not all of each puff of the cigarette is absorbed in the lungs. On average, a person gets about 1 to 2 milligrams of nicotine in one cigarette. In contrast, a person vaping will use all the e-liquid, which usually contains a mixture of nicotine and flavoring. That means they are consuming a greater amount of nicotine through vaping than smoking a cigarette. For example, someone who uses a 2-milliliter e-liquid tank would get roughly the same amount of nicotine as if they had smoked 20 cigarettes. In general, 2 milliliters of e-liquid would last a low to moderate user approximately one day. E-liquids also come in a variety of nicotine strengths, which typically vary from 0 milligrams to 24 milligrams of nicotine, that also affect the amount of nicotine a user gets. It is possible to buy e-liquid that does not contain any nicotine, but users don't necessarily do that. Using e-liquid that does not contain nicotine is a better alternative when vaping, but again, the long-term, overall health risks of vaping in general are still unknown.

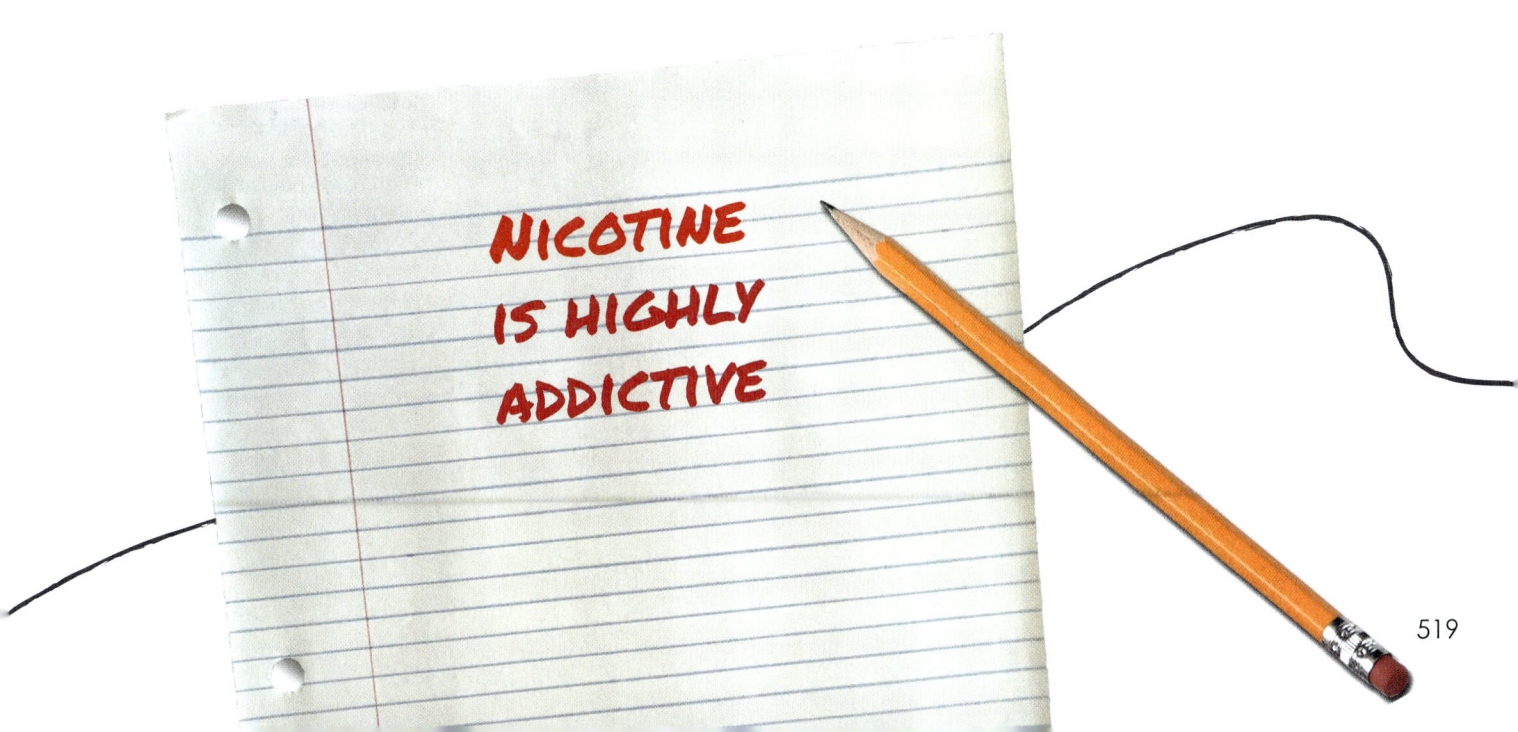

LESSON 12.1 Tobacco and E-Cigarettes

Health Risks and E-Cigarettes

Since e-cigarettes have only been popular in the mainstream since around 2017, the amount of research that has been done is fairly small in comparison to tobacco use. We know we still have a lot to learn about the long-term health effects e-cigarettes may have. Many of the health risks we currently are aware of are similar to those of smoking tobacco, but some are specific to vaping (see figure 12.6).

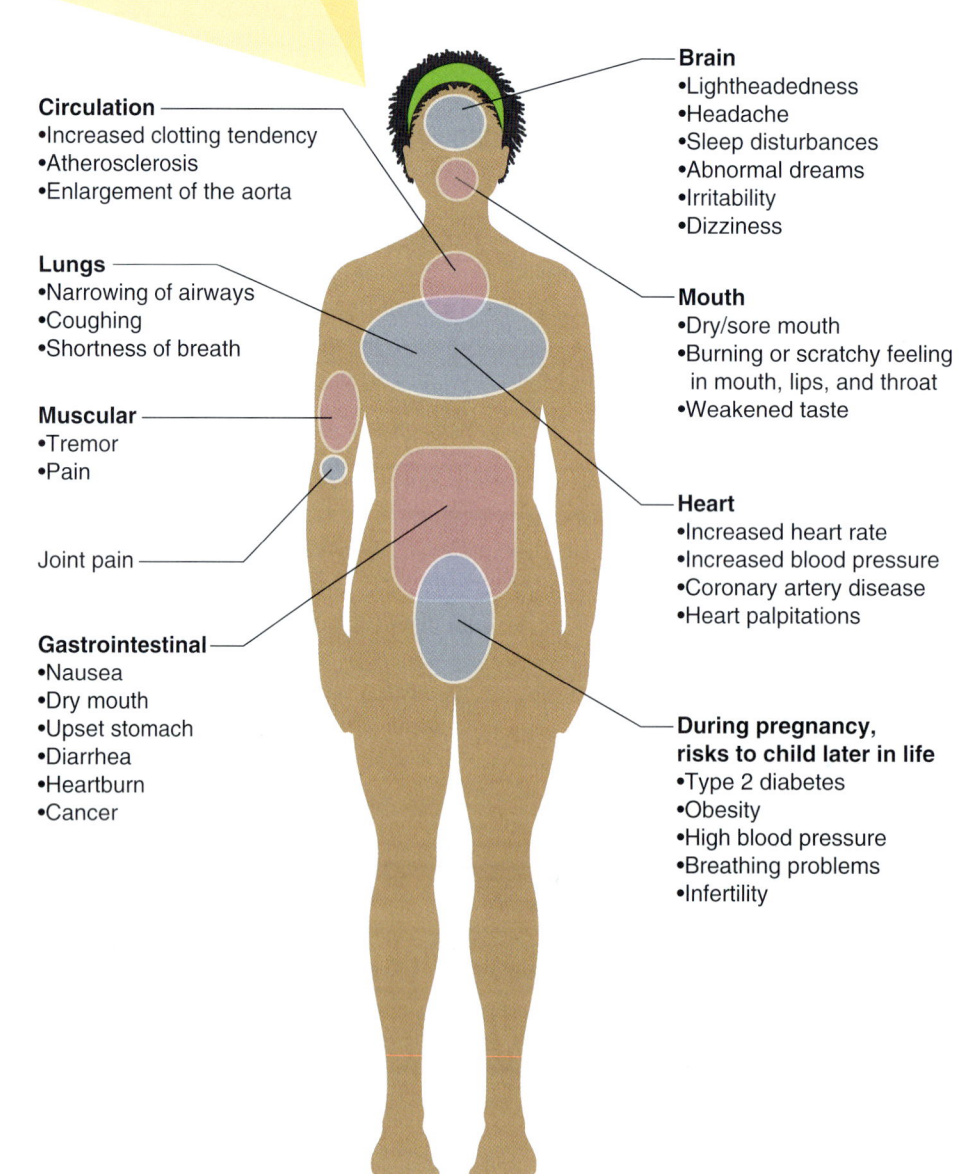

Circulation
- Increased clotting tendency
- Atherosclerosis
- Enlargement of the aorta

Lungs
- Narrowing of airways
- Coughing
- Shortness of breath

Muscular
- Tremor
- Pain

Joint pain

Gastrointestinal
- Nausea
- Dry mouth
- Upset stomach
- Diarrhea
- Heartburn
- Cancer

Brain
- Lightheadedness
- Headache
- Sleep disturbances
- Abnormal dreams
- Irritability
- Dizziness

Mouth
- Dry/sore mouth
- Burning or scratchy feeling in mouth, lips, and throat
- Weakened taste

Heart
- Increased heart rate
- Increased blood pressure
- Coronary artery disease
- Heart palpitations

During pregnancy, risks to child later in life
- Type 2 diabetes
- Obesity
- High blood pressure
- Breathing problems
- Infertility

Figure 12.6 Side effects of vaping.

Known and potential ongoing health risks of e-cigarettes are the following:

- Most e-cigarettes contain nicotine, which is highly addictive and can harm the parts of the brain that control attention, learning, mood, and impulse control.
- Some e-cigarette batteries have been defective and have caused fires and explosions, resulting in serious injuries.
- It is unclear what all the ingredients are that comprise e-liquid flavors, therefore, the side effects of e-liquid are unknown at this time.
- Some youth and adults have been poisoned by swallowing, breathing, or absorbing e-liquid through their skin and eyes.
- The aerosol from e-cigarettes contains cancer-causing chemicals, metals such as lead and tin, and ultrafine particles that can be inhaled into the lungs.
- Vaping can cause lung and cardiovascular diseases, recurrent coughing, heart palpitations, asthma, lung cancer, high blood pressure, headaches, and dizziness, among other health conditions. It also can reduce how well your immune system works.

Career Connection

CANCER RESEARCHER

Cancer researchers work to prevent and treat cancer. They spend much of their time in a laboratory conducting lab procedures and research as well as reading charts and graphs from lab data. Other cancer researchers conduct clinical trials on humans to learn whether new treatments are more effective and to see whether there are fewer side effects than with the standard treatment. In a clinical trial, researchers test new options with cancer patients who have not responded to prior treatment, closely observing the patients to determine the effectiveness of a new drug. They test drugs for toxicity (how poisonous it is to the patients), side effects, and dosages. Cancer researchers also may write grant proposals for funding their projects. Large health organizations give money so that researchers can fund their projects that could be potentially helpful in treating cancer. Once their research project is complete, researchers publish their information in journals for other researchers to see the results of their studies. Cancer researchers employed by universities might also teach classes on subjects related to their cancer interest. Cancer researchers usually have at least one graduate degree, and many attend medical school or work toward a PhD in a science field.

LESSON 12.1   Tobacco and E-Cigarettes

Secondhand Smoke, Secondhand Aerosol, and Thirdhand Smoke

Even if a person never smokes, they can be affected by being around people who do. Smoke from burning tobacco products, such as cigarettes, cigars, and pipes, and the smoke breathed out by a smoker are known as **secondhand smoke**. There are more than 7,000 known chemicals in tobacco smoke, and at least 250 of them are harmful. More than 60 of the chemicals, or **carcinogens**, are known to cause cancer. Anytime you breathe in tobacco smoke, you are being exposed to its harmful effects.

E-cigarettes, on the other hand, produce an aerosol, or vapor. The vapor that originates from the e-cigarette along with the vapor exhaled by the user are referred to as **secondhand aerosol**. Secondhand aerosol from vaping contains nicotine, ultrafine particles, and low levels of toxins that are known to cause cancer.

> **Both secondhand smoke and secondhand aerosol can cause health problems in children.**
>
> - Youth who breathe secondhand smoke and secondhand aerosol regularly get sick more often, specifically with bronchitis and pneumonia.
> - Secondhand smoke and secondhand aerosol can trigger asthma attacks in youth. The asthma attacks are more severe and frequent if youth are around secondhand smoke on a regular basis.
> - The level of secondhand smoke and secondhand aerosol youth are exposed to directly links to the likelihood of those youth using tobacco products as teens and adults.
> - Secondhand smoke and secondhand aerosol can also impair a youth's ability to learn. While there isn't much research on the long-term effects of secondhand aerosol on youth, it can be reasonably argued that secondhand aerosol and secondhand smoke have similar effects.

HEALTHY LIVING TIP

If you are around someone who is smoking or vaping, do your best to get as far away from the person as you can or open a nearby window to try to get fresh air.

Thirdhand smoke, which has been studied only in the last few years, is the nicotine and chemical residue that can remain on furniture, walls, clothing, carpets, and all other surfaces for months after someone smokes. People are exposed to thirdhand smoke through skin contact. When a surface is touched that has smoke residue on it, that residue ends up on a person's hands. While common cleaning such as dusting, repainting, vacuuming, and airing out a room may help, it will not entirely eliminate this residue.

Tobacco Products and Vaping **LESSON 12.1**

Skill-Building Challenge

Making Healthy Decisions

Zakai vapes and wants Oaklynn to try it. They spend a lot of time together, and Zakai feels Oaklynn is being judgmental about vaping without ever having tried it. Zakai is certain that Oaklynn would like it if only she gave it a chance. Oaklynn is learning about the effects of vaping and nicotine in her health class and doesn't think it's a good idea, but Zakai has been vaping for a while and doesn't seem to have any of the effects they are learning about.

Using the information in this lesson and your decision making steps, fill out the following chart to come to your decision as to whether Oaklynn should try vaping.

Decision-making steps	Possible decisions or outcomes
STEP 1: Understand the problem. What decision must be made?	
STEP 2: Gather information and know your options. What are the positive and negative choices Oaklynn could make?	
STEP 3: Know the consequences. Based on the positive and negative choices Oaklynn made in step 2, what are possible consequences for each choice?	
STEP 4: Make a decision. Of the choices you provided in step 2, which is the healthiest option for Oaklynn?	
STEP 5: Think about Oaklynn's choice. Evaluate and reflect on the outcome and explain why Oaklynn's decision was the right choice or why Oaklynn should make a different decision if given the opportunity.	

Healthy Living Skills

This lesson focused on decision making. Here are some more ways you can develop healthy living skills related to this lesson.

ADVOCATING FOR GOOD HEALTH

Create an anonymous survey to find out the types of tobacco products being used in your school and how frequently they are used. Make sure to include at least some of the examples listed in this lesson (e.g., cigarettes, cigars, pipes, smokeless tobacco, e-cigarettes) on your survey. Draw a blank line and label it "Other" to provide students the option to name a different type of tobacco product that may not have been included in your survey. You should also include a question about grade level so the information you collect can be more specific.

Once you have collected all the data, create a bar graph or pie chart to show the types of tobacco products used in your school and how often they are being used. Use the Advocacy Skill Cues to create a message centered on the most popular tobacco products used to advocate for your school to assist students in being tobacco-free. Create your advocacy message using the format you think would work best—posters around your school, social media messages, daily announcements, or a combination of all three formats.

LESSON 12.1 Tobacco and E-Cigarettes

> **ACCESSING INFORMATION**
> Using the Accessing Information Skill Cues, find information on the similarities and differences between smoking and vaping. Create a poster or flyer that explains the information you found.

LESSON 12.1 Review: Tobacco Products and Vaping

LESSON SUMMARY

- Nicotine is a highly addictive chemical and also the main ingredient in tobacco, a plant grown for its leaves, which are dried and put into commercial tobacco products.
- Some common short-term effects of tobacco products include decreased lung function, overall poor physical performance, and increased sports-related injuries; teens who smoke are three times more likely to use alcohol.
- Some common long-term effects for users of tobacco products include being more likely to continue smoking as adults if they smoke regularly as a teen, having lungs that may never perform at full capacity, and experiencing higher rates of anxiety compared to nonsmokers.
- Vaping is as, if not more, dangerous as smoking tobacco. The aerosol produced from the e-liquid contains extremely high levels of nicotine, ultrafine cancer-causing chemical particles, and heavy metals.
- Secondhand smoke and secondhand aerosol can cause adolescents to be sick more frequently, can trigger asthma attacks, and can impair adolescents' ability to learn.
- Chemical residue from thirdhand smoke remains on all surfaces and cannot be entirely eliminated, even with regular cleaning; therefore, anyone who touches these surfaces gets this residue on their skin.

REVIEWING CONCEPTS AND VOCABULARY

1. _____ use is the number one cause of preventable deaths in the United States.
2. _____ triggers the brain to release dopamine and is the main ingredient in conventional cigarettes.
3. A(n) electronic cigarette or _____ is an electronic device that heats a liquid and produces an aerosol.
4. The act of inhaling and exhaling aerosol produced by an e-cigarette is known as _____.
5. The liquid that heats into an aerosol and usually contains nicotine, flavoring, and other chemicals is known as _____.
6. _____ is what is exhaled by someone who uses a tobacco product.
7. More than 60 _____, or cancer-causing chemicals, are in tobacco smoke.
8. Thirdhand smoke leaves a chemical _____ on surfaces that can transfer to your skin when you touch surfaces that are contaminated with it.

THINKING CRITICALLY

Substantial health risks were discussed in this lesson concerning vaping and overall tobacco use. Based on the information provided in the lesson, why do you think teens continue to vape despite knowing its short- and long-term health risks?

TAKE IT HOME

Talk to an adult family member or close friend who has smoked or vaped before and discuss with them the effects of second- and thirdhand smoke or second- and thirdhand aerosol. If someone has smoked or vaped in your home or family car, examine the impact the residue in the home or car may still have on you, family, and friends.

LESSON 12.2
Regulations and Influences on Tobacco Product Use

Terms to Learn
external influence
Food and Drug Administration
internal influence
marketing

The Big Picture

We are surrounded by a constant presence of internal and external influences. Knowing how you might respond to influences ahead of time will help you make better decisions when faced with situations that involve tobacco products and their usage. Teens in particular experience a constant barrage of messaging from the advertising and marketing industry—a major type of external influence—through social media, television, magazines, and much more.

As previously discussed teen e-cigarette use has had a tremendous increase. Multiple federal, state, and local agencies are now working on ways to regulate the overall marketing and selling of tobacco products, requiring companies to provide warning labels on all products that contain nicotine, and holding companies accountable whenever they fail to meet these new standards. Setting higher restrictions aims to limit teen access to and prevent and reduce teen use of tobacco products.

Learning Targets

- Analyze why teens vape.
- Interpret the effectiveness of online vaping advertising.
- Analyze how the bans and restrictions on e-cigarettes by the FDA can reduce their use by minors.
- Describe how school policies can have an impact on teen use of tobacco.
- Formulate a plan to advocate for community vaping laws.

Write About It

Vaping has become popular with high school students. What do you think influences teens to vape? Try to brainstorm three to five influences.

Note-Taking Guide
Use this chapter's note-taking guide to help you organize and remember the material in this lesson.

LESSON 12.2 Tobacco and E-Cigarettes

Tommy and Brandon are friends and have two classes together. As Tommy is riding the bus home, he sees Brandon walking down the street vaping with a couple of other guys from school. Tommy is really surprised to see Brandon vaping because he always seemed against it when it was talked about at school. The next day, Tommy asks him about it, and Brandon says he only vapes once in a while. He goes on to tell Tommy that he should try it because there really isn't anything wrong with it. Tommy is supposed to go to Brandon's house tomorrow after school to work on a school project, but now he is a little worried about going there. Tommy wonders if Brandon is going to try to pressure him into trying vaping. What refusal skills could Tommy practice before going to Brandon's house?

Factors That Influence Tobacco Use

Vaping is the most common method of tobacco product use among U.S. high school students. E-cigarettes are discreet, they look high tech, and teens commonly think they are safer than other tobacco products, especially cigarettes. Many teens may think the e-cigarettes they vape don't contain nicotine, but they often are mistaken—many e-cigarettes do in fact contain this highly addictive chemical. Teens whose first e-cigarette had flavoring and teens who vape with flavored liquids vape longer than teens who do not use flavored e-liquid. A CDC study showed the most common reasons for trying e-cigarettes:

- Curiosity.
- Use by friends or family members.
- Availability of flavors.
- Tricks like creating big clouds and cloud shapes.

Regulations and Influences on Tobacco Product Use **LESSON 12.2**

General Factors That May Determine Whether Teens Use Tobacco Products

- *Age.* Teens are more willing to take risks and are more influenced by what others are doing than adults are. The age teens start vaping tends to be eighth or ninth grade but may even be younger. In the United States, a person must be 21 years of age in order to buy tobacco products.
- *Sex.* Females tend to smoke fewer cigarettes or vape fewer e-cigarettes overall than males. Males are more likely to use e-cigarettes than cigarettes.
- *Stressful events.* The more a teen experiences stressful events, the greater risk they are at of smoking cigarettes or vaping e-cigarettes.
- *Perception of risk.* Teens who see smoking as a great risk are less likely to smoke traditional cigarettes.
- *Media.* Movies, social media, magazines, and streaming content may portray tobacco products, especially e-cigarettes, as cool and sophisticated.

Teens are at a critical age in which they have more freedom to make choices independently and they begin to establish their own identity. It's a time to figure out who and what influences them. Everyone is influenced by someone or something. Your friends and family may influence you because they are usually a part of the decisions you make in your life. Celebrities or athletes may influence you to buy certain brands of clothing or spend money at a certain store because they tell you it's the brand they endorse or the store they shop at. The ways tobacco products are marketed and advertised can also influence decisions you may make about using tobacco products.

The two types of influences that will affect the decisions you make are internal and external. **Internal influences** come from within; they are your own thoughts and opinions that guide, persuade, or motivate your decision making. **External influences**, on the other hand, are from the outside and include the environment you live in, your family, your friends, clubs and organizations you belong to, and all types of media. Internal and external influences are guided by your values—the beliefs you have about what is important to you. The values you have about tobacco products will influence your decision to use or not. Using or not using tobacco products will also influence your friends and the social situations you find yourself in. Table 12.2 features some internal and external influences on use of tobacco products.

HEALTHY LIVING TIP
Practice saying "no" to tobacco products before you are offered them.

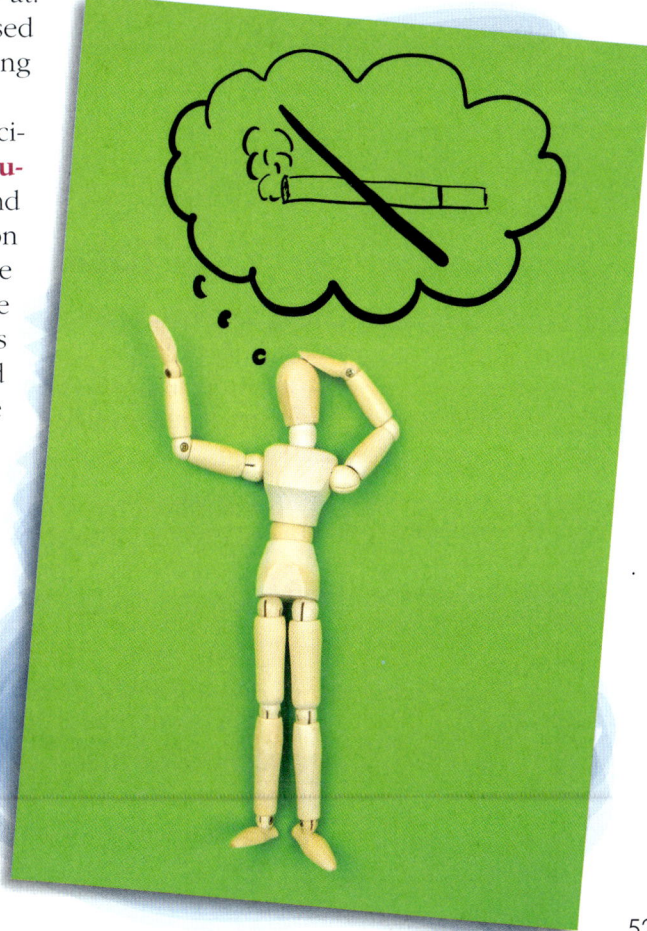

TABLE 12.2 **Internal and External Influences on Using Tobacco Products**

Internal influences	External influences
Your knowledge. Your knowledge about tobacco products can influence your decision.	*Your friends.* Research shows tobacco product use is strongly linked to a person's peer influence. Peer pressure from your friends can definitely influence the choices you make: If your friends don't use tobacco products, you will be less likely to use them as well; however, if they do use tobacco products, you may be influenced to use them also.
Your values. Do you think using tobacco products is a good or a bad idea for you? Your answer to this question is about your value system.	*Your environment.* If the adults in your life use tobacco products, you will be more likely to use them; if they don't use them, then you are less likely to use them as well.
Your self-esteem. How confident you feel can influence the way you may react to external influences—lower self-esteem may cause you to experience pressure to use tobacco products.	*Accessibility of tobacco products.* If tobacco products are easy for you to get, you may be more likely to use them.
Your view of social norms. Social norms are how a group of people function together based on what they think is normal for their group.	*Your media choices.* Media may influence your decision whether to use tobacco products, primarily e-cigarettes. Much of the media portray the use of e-cigarettes as being fashionable and carefree rather than emphasizing the negative health problems that come with using or even being around e-cigarettes.

Tobacco Norming in Society

In the entertainment industry, tobacco use continues to be portrayed as positive, socially acceptable, and rebellious and edgy. The entertainment industry contributes to the normalization of tobacco use through various forms of pop culture and entertainment. The five ways tobacco use is normalized and idealized are the following:

1. *TV streaming.* Tobacco use is prevalent and more prominent on streaming shows compared to broadcast TV shows. In popular Netflix shows, there were 319 depictions of tobacco compared to 139 depictions in seven broadcast shows, with 79 percent of the shows depicting smoking prominently.
2. *Video games.* Video game players reported that 94 percent of video games show tobacco use portrayed in a positive or neutral light. Many gamers say the use of tobacco by a character made them seem cooler, tougher, or grittier.
3. *Celebrities.* Celebrities who pose with cigarettes or are vaping and then post on social media are giving the tobacco industry free advertising and helping to normalize tobacco use.

4. *Movies.* Youth and young adults who are heavily exposed to tobacco imagery in movies are twice as likely to begin smoking as those with less exposure. More than one-third of movies rated PG-13 continue to include tobacco imagery.
5. *Sports.* Smokeless tobacco continues to have a cultural association with sports, especially baseball. Tobacco in general is banned in 16 stadiums across the United States. The collective bargaining agreement in the MLB prohibits new players from using smokeless tobacco, and it has been banned in the minor leagues of the MLB since 1993.

Advertising and Marketing Techniques on Tobacco Use

E-cigarette advertising continues to increase and takes many different forms—store signs, television ads, movies, Internet sites, social media, and magazines—all to get teens to notice their brand. Advertising is used to promote a particular company and its products. Two highly effective conduits for advertising e-cigarettes to teens have been brick-and-mortar stores and online (see figure 12.7). The U.S. tobacco industry spends billions on **marketing** each year to promote, sell, and distribute tobacco products in retail stores and online. E-cigarette ads purposely target teens through themes of independence, rebellion, celebrity figures, kid-friendly flavors, and convenience. Appealing to teen independence and rebellion is one of the most commonly used types of marketing because of its emotional influence on teens.

- 24% Newspaper/magazine ads
- 52.8% Retail ads
- 34.1% TV/movie ads
- 35.8% Internet ads

Figure 12.7 E-cigarette advertising targets teens in many different forms.

Using social media with celebrity endorsements and animation is also a highly effective marketing strategy. Teens who see pro-tobacco advertising on social media tend to think more positively about using tobacco products. Tobacco companies have used colorful packaging of their products for years, and the vaping industry has mimicked this with its packaging, colorful products, and flavored e-liquid. In addition, flavors specifically designed for youth increase the popularity of vaping and its acceptance among teens. Marketing by the tobacco industry is intentional in how its products are promoted, where they are placed in stores, and how they are priced.

- *Promotion.* In one year, the tobacco industry spent over $270 million to promote its products through branded signs, displays, and shelving units. Convenience stores have more tobacco marketing and sell more tobacco products than any other type of retail store. Seventy percent of youth tend to shop in a convenience store at least once a week.
- *Placement.* The checkout counter is the best strategical place for tobacco products and marketing materials to maximize exposure and to increase sales. When people stand in line, they are more likely to pick something up they may have otherwise avoided when shopping throughout the store.

- *Price.* Higher tobacco prices resulting from tax increases benefit public health, not the tobacco companies. The industry is very well aware of this, and to keep prices affordable, companies drop the wholesale prices, offer coupons, or have multipack discounts.

Tobacco companies also market e-cigarettes on social media sites, portraying vaping as a stylish and cool thing to do. Many ads for e-cigarettes feature young models in trendy clothes, which attract teens and young adults who want to emulate what they see. To gain more customers, e-cigarette companies have also sponsored music festivals with device charging stations, interactive social media photo booths, and samples of e-cigarettes.

While gains are being made to decrease e-cigarette advertising and marketing, teens are still gaining access to tobacco products. Convenience stores often sell to minors, and older friends and siblings often buy for younger friends and siblings. These are two of the most well-known examples of how teens and young adults under the age of 21 are getting tobacco products.

Preventing the Use of Tobacco Products

You will read about the different federal and local government regulations as well as school bans aimed at preventing the use of tobacco products in the following section. Yet we also know that peers and influential adults who do not use tobacco products significantly reduce the temptation teens would otherwise experience. Preventing tobacco use among teens must begin with their decisions of with whom they surround themselves and with the environments they occupy.

Food and Drug Administration's Role

The **Food and Drug Administration** (FDA) is responsible for regulating the manufacturing, marketing, and distribution of tobacco products to protect public health and to reduce tobacco use by minors. The FDA has banned the sale of e-cigarettes to minors, free samples of e-cigarettes, and vending machine sales of e-cigarettes except in adult-only facilities. It has also restricted sales of flavored e-cigarettes without prior authorization. Companies must submit an application for approval of flavored products before the products are placed on the market.

Regarding advertisements for all tobacco products, including e-cigarettes, the FDA has announced that companies must include the following addictiveness warning statement: "WARNING: This product contains nicotine. Nicotine is an addictive chemical." Companies are now required to place this warning label on packaging, billboards, and magazines and at online retailers.

Regulations and Influences on Tobacco Product Use **LESSON 12.2**

Government and Communities Role in Decreasing Tobacco Use

The CDC's Office on Smoking and Health (OSH) helps states and communities implement tobacco control programs through various campaigns and events (see figure 12.8). The OSH created the National Tobacco Control Program (NTCP) to coordinate national efforts to reduce tobacco-related diseases and deaths. The NTCP provides funding and support to state and territorial health departments. Each state has access to the CDC's OSH and NTCP resources to help inform and implement effective tobacco prevention and cessation best practices.

State Smoking Bans

Twenty-eight U.S. states and the District of Columbia currently have comprehensive smoke-free laws covering workplaces, restaurants, and bars, which means those

Federal Government:

- Tracks e-cigarette use and supports research on the health effects and factors contributing to youth e-cigarette use.
- Provides information to the public, including health care providers, on the health effects of e-cigarette use by teens.
- Develops regulations for e-cigarettes to reduce/prevent teen tobacco use.
- Funds and promotes campaigns that inform people about the dangers of tobacco product use including e-cigarettes.

States, Local Governments, and Communities:

- Fund tobacco prevention and control programs to prevent youth e-cigarette use.
- Work to limit where and how all tobacco products, including e-cigarettes, are sold to reduce youth e-cigarette use and ad exposure.
- Require age verification to enter e-cigarette vendor websites, make purchases, and accept delivery of e-cigarettes.
- Restrict the number of stores that sell tobacco products and regulate how close they can be to schools.
- Support efforts to implement and continue proven youth tobacco prevention approaches, including tobacco price increases, comprehensive smoke-free laws, and high-impact mass media campaigns.

Health Care Providers, School Personnel, and Family Members:

- Help teens understand the dangers of nicotine, e-cigarettes, and other tobacco products.
- Ask teens whether they use tobacco products, and encourage those who do to quit and provide help with quitting.
- Teach teens how to analyze media and Internet use to be able to tell what is truthful and what is not.
- Set a good example by not using tobacco products.

Figure 12.8 The roles of federal, state, and local governments; communities; health care providers; school personnel; and family members for decreasing e-cigarette use.

locations are 100 percent smoke-free. Three states have 100 percent smoke-free restaurants and bars and five states have either smoke-free workplaces or smoke-free workplaces and restaurants. Only 14 states do not have any smoke-free indoor areas; by taking no action to implement smoking ban requirements on indoor establishments, these states are choosing not to protect the general population from secondhand or thirdhand smoke or secondhand aerosol and subsequent illnesses

Tobacco Products and School Policies

School policies should positively influence students to continue to abstain from using tobacco products and also help students who are current users to quit. School policies prohibit the use of tobacco on school property by students and adults. Schools need to send a clear message that tobacco use of any kind by any person is not permitted on school grounds and then enforce that message when necessary.

Many state education departments and local school districts are adopting comprehensive tobacco-free policies that ban all tobacco products on school property in both indoor and outdoor areas. While states are adopting these policies, the local school enforcement of the policy varies when it comes to adult community members who are on school grounds to watch a football game or band concert for example. Schools are in a unique position to set a standard for students when it comes to tobacco use. Yet for students to understand the complete ramifications of their actions—from using to breaking the law—they must see adults being held

Regulations and Influences on Tobacco Product Use **LESSON 12.2**

accountable for their actions as well if they are found smoking, chewing, or vaping on school grounds, indoors or outdoors. Schools that effectively educate their students and staff about the dangers of all types of tobacco products and enforce the rules and laws of their community on the students as well as the community members find a decrease in the overall use of tobacco products.

Skill-Building Challenge

Advocating for Vape-Free Community Parks

Advocate for your community to create a law that prohibits vaping in community parks. Search online for other communities that already have vaping laws in place that you can get information from.

Once you have your information, explain how you would advocate for this new law in your community. Present your advocacy project to your class and take it to the next town council meeting to begin the process.

Use the following steps to community advocacy to complete this challenge.

1. Research your community parks so you understand what the issues are in your community around vaping.
2. Identify solutions to the problem of vaping in community parks. Brainstorm ideas, research, and know the laws.
3. Find students and community members who support your cause and can help you.
4. Implement your plan by taking it to the town council meeting and presenting your proposal.

Healthy Living Skills

This lesson focused on advocacy. Here are some more ways you can develop healthy living skills related to this lesson.

ANALYZING INFLUENCES

Find an online vaping ad to answer the following questions.
- What product is being advertised?
- Who appears to be the target audience of this advertisement?
- What is the message this ad is sending?
- Why do you think the message would or would not have an influence on its target audience?

MAKING HEALTHY DECISIONS

Using the information from your school handbook, help a friend make a healthy decision not to vape during lunch. Help your friend to understand other options they have besides vaping and the consequences they will face if they do vape at school. Based on the information in your school handbook, use the Decision-Making Skill Cues to help your friend make a healthy decision. Write out your answers to each of the decision-making steps and share your decision with a classmate.

LESSON 12.2 Tobacco and E-Cigarettes

LESSON 12.2 Review: Regulations and Influences on Tobacco Product Use

LESSON SUMMARY

- Friends, family, peers, celebrities, and advertising are all examples of who and what influences teens to vape.
- The FDA has banned sales of e-cigarettes to minors, free samples of e-cigarettes, and vending machine sales of e-cigarettes except in adult-only facilities and restricted the sale of flavored e-cigarettes in an attempt to reduce the use of tobacco products by minors.
- Tobacco companies advertise through store signs, in television commercials and shows, in movies, the Internet, social media, and in magazines. The advertisements are then intentionally marketed in how the products are promoted, where they are placed in stores, and how they are priced.
- Some states have comprehensive smoke-free laws in workplaces, restaurants, and bars and other states have only smoke-free workplaces or combinations of smoke-free workplaces and restaurants. Fourteen states currently have no laws requiring smoke-free indoor areas.
- School policies that positively reinforce continued abstinence from tobacco product use and help users quit, along with equally enforcing these policies for teens and adults alike, lead to a decrease in teen vaping.

REVIEWING CONCEPTS AND VOCABULARY

1. _____ influences come from your values and what you believe in.
2. _____ influences are learned by the environment you live in, such as your family and friends.
3. Five general factors that determine whether teens use tobacco products include age, _____, stressful events, perception of _____, and _____.
4. The promotion, selling, and distribution of tobacco products in retail stores and online is known as _____.
5. The FDA is responsible for regulating the manufacturing, _____, and _____ of tobacco products.
6. Marketing by the tobacco industry is intentional in how products are _____, where they are in stores, and how they are _____.

THINKING CRITICALLY

Write five examples of possible social media posts that you could use to discourage your friends from using tobacco products. Think about the dangers and consequences of tobacco products as you create your posts. Include an appropriate hashtag with each example.

TAKE IT HOME

Find out whether your state has a comprehensive smoke-free law and if it does, what exactly it covers. Talk to a family member about what you found and decide if you agree or disagree with the law in your state. Explain why.

LESSON 12.3
Avoiding and Quitting Tobacco Product Use

Terms to Learn

epinephrine
nicotine replacement therapy

The Big Picture

There are multiple ways to stay tobacco-free and to quit using tobacco if needed. Important concepts to be aware of include understanding that using tobacco causes health problems and learning methods to stop using tobacco. It is difficult to find treatment for teens who use tobacco products because nicotine addiction has primarily been an adult problem. In fact, due to how new vaping is, nobody really knows how to treat people of any age who are addicted to vaping. At this time, the best methods for treating a vaping addiction seem to be the same as those that are used to treat nicotine addictions.

Learning Targets

- Express three ways to stay tobacco-free.
- Recognize four signs of nicotine addiction.
- Analyze three benefits to being tobacco-free and quitting tobacco products.
- Assess different methods for quitting tobacco products and their effectiveness.

Write About It

Why do you think it is so hard for teens to quit using tobacco products once they start?

Note-Taking Guide

Use this chapter's note-taking guide to help you organize and remember the material in this lesson.

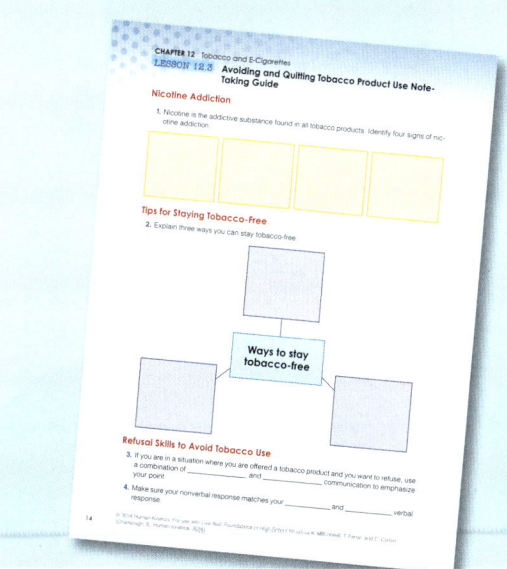

535

LESSON 12.3   Tobacco and E-Cigarettes

Maurice has been using smokeless tobacco for about a year. He used to chew only on the weekends but has found himself really wanting to chew more often. Today at lunch he went into the bathroom and put in a small dip because he was angry and upset for no reason and couldn't concentrate on anything that was happening in his class. He noticed throughout the afternoon that he was back to feeling normal and could pay attention in class. Maurice has begun to realize that in order to feel normal, he has to be using his chewing tobacco. Maurice knows it isn't a good idea to chew at school and that if he gets caught, he will be suspended. He also thinks if he only has a small dip he won't need to spit and he won't get caught. Do you think Maurice may be addicted to nicotine? What are some potential signs of nicotine addiction?

Nicotine Addiction

As you have previously read, nicotine is the addictive substance found in all tobacco products. It also is poisonous if used in its pure form. When nicotine is inhaled through smoking or vaping, the nicotine is distributed throughout the brain in about 10 seconds. The happy feelings from the **epinephrine**, or adrenaline, which causes blood pressure and heart rate to increase, and dopamine happen very quickly and also end very quickly, causing the person to need more nicotine in order to maintain the good feelings. This is the cycle of the smoking, chewing, and vaping habit: To continue feeling good, you must continue to use more tobacco products, and more frequently. A person doesn't get addicted to the tobacco products; they get addicted to the nicotine. Recognizing the signs of nicotine addiction is important because many people think that because they smoke only occasionally with their friends, or believe they can quit at any time, they aren't really becoming addicted, but often they are only fooling themselves. Figure 12.9 lists physical signs of nicotine addiction that are caused by the withdrawal of nicotine, which can occur in as little as two hours after not using tobacco.

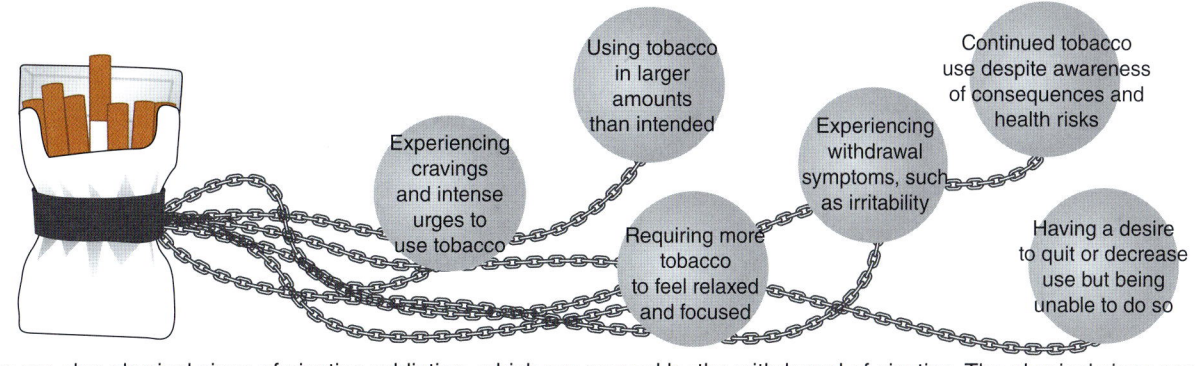

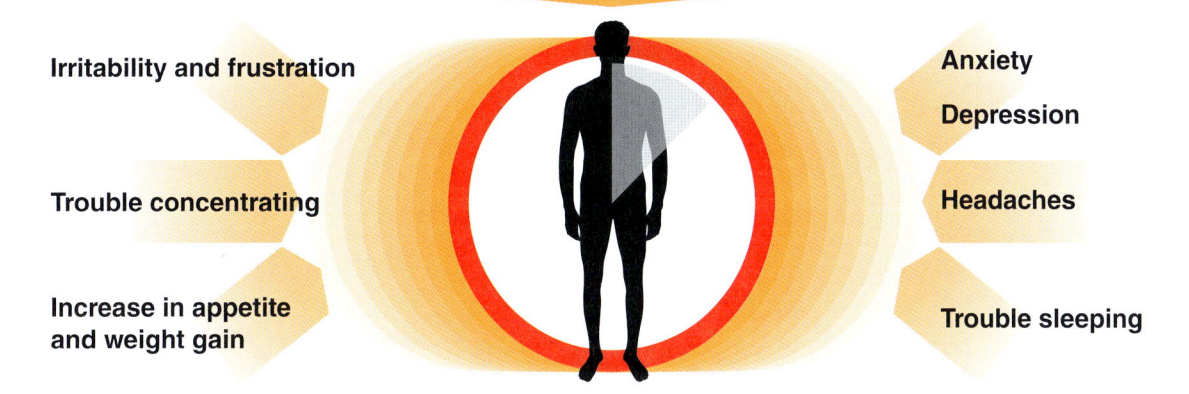

Avoiding and Quitting Tobacco Product Use **LESSON 12.3**

Figure 12.9 Signs of nicotine addiction.

Tips for Staying Tobacco-Free

Ideally, you shouldn't use any type of tobacco product, yet each teen has different life situations that may lead them toward using tobacco products or away from using. Here are some guidelines to stay tobacco-free:

- Stay away from situations where tobacco products may be used.
- Spend time with friends who don't use tobacco products.
- Create a plan or even specific things to say to help get you out of the situation; for example, "I have asthma and my doctor says I could become very ill if I try this," or, "I just don't think it's a good idea."

If you have used a tobacco product before and you have quit using, use the aforementioned guidelines, as well as these:

- Celebrate those moments you convince yourself not to give into your cravings and celebrate all the days you don't use.
- Recognize the situations, people, or places that may trigger you to want to use and try not to put yourself in those situations or places or with those people as much as possible.
- Replace using tobacco products with a new hobby or activity so that you have something to do when you want to use.
- Write down your reasons for quitting and look over them when you think about using again.

LESSON 12.3 Tobacco and E-Cigarettes

Refusal Skills to Avoid Tobacco Use

Being able to communicate effectively is very important when you are communicating your refusal to use tobacco products. You must be able to get your point across in such a way that the person you are communicating with can understand what you are saying. Refusal skills are techniques you use to say "no" to something you don't want to do. If you are in a situation where you are offered a tobacco product and you want to refuse, use a combination of verbal and nonverbal communication to emphasize your point. Make sure your nonverbal response matches your firm and confident verbal response. For example, if your verbal response is "I don't smoke," your nonverbal response could be shaking your head "no" or putting your hand up like you are stopping someone from getting close to you. No matter how difficult it is to say "no" in a situation where someone is pressuring you to smoke, chew, or vape—especially if everyone else seems to be using—the most important thing is that you do what is right for you.

Benefits of Being Tobacco-Free

Despite the many ways to quit using tobacco, the actual process of quitting is arduous due to the addictive nature of nicotine. One benefit of quitting is that your body can transform itself (or nearly transform itself, depending on the person) back to what a healthy body should be. Figure 12.10 shows several important benefits of quitting. The relative sizes of the circles represent the rate of improvement. For example, heart attack risk gradually decreases over the next 15 years, while lung function improves.

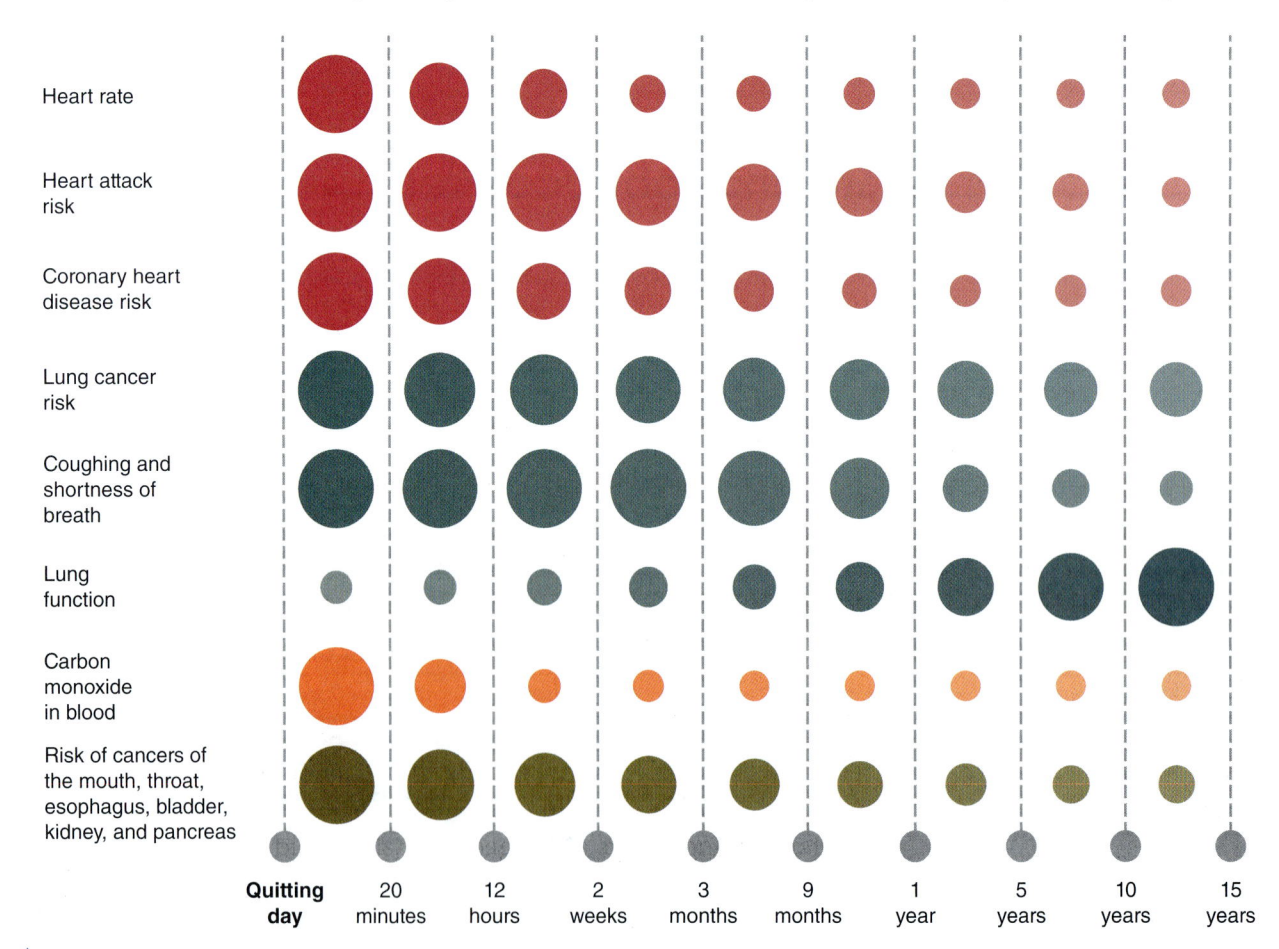

Figure 12.10 Quitting smoking and the effects on the body.

Avoiding and Quitting Tobacco Product Use   **LESSON 12.3**

Living in a tobacco-free environment and not using tobacco have no drawbacks, only benefits. The most important benefit is the prevention of diseases and early death. Other benefits include the following:

- You no longer will have to find specific places and times to smoke.
- You will have more money.
- Your skin and nails will look healthier, your teeth will look whiter, and your breath will be fresher.
- You will have more energy.
- You'll be able to do normal activities without losing your breath.
- You won't have to worry about exposing your family members and friends to your secondhand or thirdhand smoke.

Getting Help for a Nicotine Use Disorder

Once you realize you lack energy and no longer want to do things you previously enjoyed doing, it is time to seek help for your nicotine disorder. Other signs that indicate you're in need of help is if you begin having problems in school, at home, with other people, or with law enforcement. At this stage, it's possible that you will break the promises you've made about limiting your nicotine use. For example, you may pledge to vape, smoke, or chew on the weekends only and yet find yourself using during the week.

If you are experiencing any of these problems or are seeing them in a friend, it is important you talk with a guardian or trusted adult and get help as soon as possible.

- **SCHOOL:** having problems such as not turning in assignments, doing poorly on tests, skipping classes or school, and not being involved in activities you or your friends used to enjoy doing
- **HOME:** fighting more than normal with guardians or siblings; distancing yourself from family members by staying in your room more than usual
- **OTHER PEOPLE:** having more disagreements with friends or no longer wanting to hang out with them
- **LAW ENFORCEMENT:** having new or ongoing problems with law enforcement that could indicate nicotine use disorder as well as a personal crisis

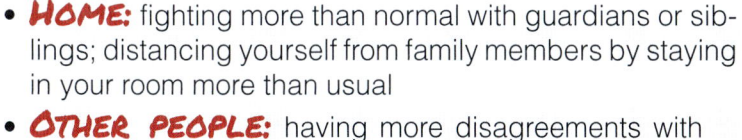

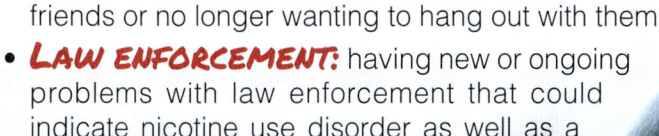

Quitting Methods

When deciding you are ready to quit using a tobacco product, the most important thing you need to do is prepare yourself to quit. Quitting isn't easy—there may be times when you aren't completely successful, but having a plan and the tools to help you stay on track is the most effective thing you can do. Being prepared to quit increases your chances of quitting successfully. In order to be successful, do the following:

- Set a quit date.
- Make a list of reasons why you want to quit.
- List everything that triggers you to use a tobacco product.
- Have a plan to fight the cravings and get rid of all smoking reminders.
- Work on sticking to your plan and keep trying to quit until you meet your goal.

Quitting a tobacco product is about your physical, emotional, and mental dependence on the product. Whatever method you choose to help you quit, it's important that you think about how it will help to support you with the physical, emotional, and mental aspects of quitting.

Quitting Methods via Apps and Text Messages

Several apps have been developed to help people with quitting tobacco product use. Many feature tracking systems for people to input what they are doing or feeling when they want to use a tobacco product. This helps them to identify potential triggers and potential moods they experience when using. Many apps notify users with positive reminders to help provide extra support throughout the day, which may be especially helpful to teens. The following is a partial list of apps that are free to use:

- Smokefree TXT is from the website www.smokefree.gov/smokefreetxt. Developed specifically for teens, this text messaging program provides them with three to five daily texts regarding tips, advice, and encouragement to help teens stay motivated to stop using tobacco products.
- Dipfree TXT is from the website www.smokefree.gov. It also is for teens who use smokeless tobacco.
- This Is Quitting, from the Truth Initiative website www.truthinitiative.org/thisisquitting, is another text messaging program specifically for quitting e-cigarettes.
- The quitSTART app is from the Smokefree website www.smokefree.gov and helps teens quit smoking with personalized tips, inspiration, and challenges.

Other Quitting Methods

Nicotine replacement therapy (NRT) is one of the most common ways to quit smoking. There are many different forms of NRT, including the patch, gum, inhalers, lozenges, and nasal sprays, that help to reduce the withdrawal feelings by giving a small, controlled amount of nicotine. Many can be purchased over the counter or by prescription. This small dosage of nicotine helps satisfy cravings and reduces the urge to smoke. Before using nicotine replacement therapy, people should check with their doctor to see which product might be right for them. NRTs can be used on their own or combined with the following methods as well:

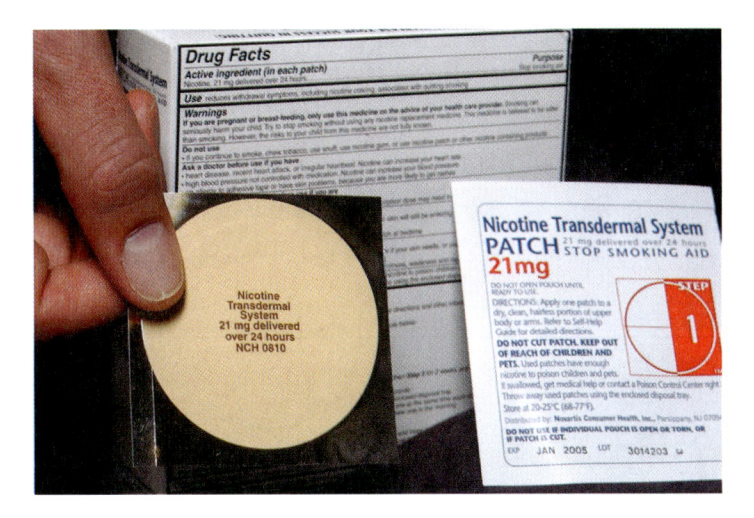

- *Counseling*. Depending on preference, individual, group, and telehealth counseling are available options. Seeking help is not a sign of weakness—it's a smart choice. If you feel comfortable, you can also talk to your friends and trusted adults.
- *Exercise*. Even a short walk can increase endorphins and help you feel good.
- *Decompression*. Find stress solutions, such as deep breathing and meditation, to relieve tension.

Support of Family and Friends

Having the support of family and friends while trying to quit is important. Inform your friends and family about your plans to quit and then try to surround yourself with people who don't use tobacco and who support their efforts to quit. Tell friends and family what is needed from them—for example, you may wish to have phone calls, text messages, or more time together. Having something to look forward to is always helpful and important to staying on track with quitting.

Using E-Cigarettes to Stop Cigarette Smoking

Information that supports the use of e-cigarettes to replace the use of cigarettes as a safer method of smoking is very limited. While it is too soon to know the long-term effects of e-cigarettes, we can only conjecture that vaping is a beneficial alternative when used in conjunction with one of the previously mentioned quitting methods. This is especially true for long-term smokers who have repeatedly, though unsuccessfully, tried quitting.

HEALTHY LIVING TIP

Choose an app you could use if you need help quitting a tobacco product or share it with a friend who may need help.

LESSON 12.3 Tobacco and E-Cigarettes

Skill-Building Challenge

Demonstrating Interpersonal Refusal Skills

Your friend has just offered you an e-cigarette. You do not want to offend your friend by refusing, but you definitely do not want to vape. Write a script between you and your friend that includes at least three health reasons why you would not want to vape. Include in your script *I* messages and refusal skills to reinforce your use of the word *no*:

1. Say "no."
2. Use an *I* message to state your reason for not wanting to vape.
3. Use an assertive voice and have your nonverbal body language match your verbal language (stand tall, look the person in the eye, and shake your head "no").
4. Be consistent with and stick to your position.
5. If none of the strategies works, remove yourself immediately from the situation.

Practicing ahead of time what you will say in a situation like this will make it easier for you if the situation actually happens.

Healthy Living Skills

This lesson focused on interpersonal communication skills. Here are some more ways you can develop healthy living skills related to this lesson.

ACCESSING INFORMATION
Determine which resources for quitting tobacco are available within your school and in your community and how you can access them. Find information on nicotine replacement therapy, individual counseling, group counseling, or telehealth counseling. List the organizations' names and include their corresponding phone numbers and web addresses so they will be easy to contact.

MAKING HEALTHY DECISIONS
Using the quitting tobacco apps located in the lesson, make a decision on which app you would use if you needed to quit vaping. Use the decision-making steps to choose the one that would work best for you.

LESSON 12.3 Review: Avoiding and Quitting Tobacco Product Use

LESSON SUMMARY

- Three ways to stay tobacco-free include avoiding situations where tobacco products may be used, having a well-practiced reason for saying "no" when someone pressures you, and hanging out with friends who don't use tobacco products.
- People with nicotine addiction may become irritable or anxious, have trouble sleeping or concentrating, and require more tobacco to get the same feeling they did when they began using.
- Teens vape due to curiosity, friends or family members who vape, the availability of flavors, and the appeal of doing vaping tricks.
- Some benefits of being tobacco-free are having more money, healthier-looking skin and nails, cleaner teeth and fresher breath, and more energy.
- Methods for quitting tobacco products include starting with a plan to quit, using specifically designed phone apps for motivational reminders, seeking nicotine replacement therapy, and getting counseling.

REVIEWING CONCEPT AND VOCABULARY

1. _____, or adrenaline, is a hormone released when a person inhales nicotine that causes blood pressure and heart rate to increase.
2. A common sign of nicotine addiction is requiring more _____ to get the same feeling you did when you began using.
3. A benefit of quitting tobacco products is that your _____ rate drops within 20 minutes of quitting and your _____ function begins to improve within 3 months.
4. One of the most common ways to quit smoking is using a _____ therapy.
5. Many of the apps used for quitting have people track potential _____ that cause them to want to use tobacco products.

THINKING CRITICALLY

Quitting tobacco products, particularly smoking, improves your mental health, not just your physical health. Research the mental health benefits of quitting smoking. Write a paragraph explaining why these benefits are just as important as the physical benefits.

TAKE IT HOME

If you have a friend or family member who smokes or chews or vapes, suggest to them one of the quitting apps or text messaging programs from this lesson. Have them use it for a few days or hopefully longer and have them review it for you. What were the pros and cons of the app or text messaging service? Write that information down and share it with the class.

Chapter Review

ACTION PLAN: How to Avoid Tobacco Use

Use the My Action Plan worksheet to avoid using a tobacco product. An example is provided for you.

My Action Plan: Avoiding Vaping

STEP 1: Identify the health behavior you are going to work on.

I will go home when my friends start vaping.

STEP 2: Write SMART goal(s).

Write one or two short-term goals (one day to one month long).

I will tell my friends as soon as they start vaping that I will see them tomorrow and leave.

Write a long-term goal (one to six months or more).

I will feel good about my decision to leave because I know it is the right thing to do for me.

STEP 3: Make a plan.

Identify two to five action steps (strategies) you could do to meet your goal.

I will talk to my friends ahead of time so they know that I'm leaving because I don't want to vape. It is not about them.

I will write in my journal each day I leave to remind myself of my achievement of doing the right thing.

After I have left three times in a row, I will play my video game for an hour as a reward.

STEP 4: Execute your plan and track your progress.

Short-term goal

☒ Met ☐ Not met Date: *April 29*

Long-term goal

☐ Met ☒ Not met Date: _____

If you met your goal, what helped you to be successful?

Writing in my journal every time I left helped remind me of how many times I had made the right choice for me.

If you did not meet your goal, what things made it harder for you to be successful?

My friends asked me to stay, and I worried that if I didn't, they may not want to be friends with me anymore.

Test Your Knowledge

Select the best answer for each question.

1. Secondhand smoke can cause health problems in children, including
   a. birth defects
   b. bronchitis
   c. learning deficiencies
   d. stroke

2. The act of inhaling aerosol is known as
   a. smoking
   b. chewing
   c. vaping
   d. inhaling

3. A product used in nicotine replacement therapy is
   a. pills
   b. apps
   c. programs
   d. gum

4. Tobacco companies focus their marketing on
   a. promotion, placement, and price
   b. placement, position, and price
   c. position, promotion, and placement
   d. price, publicity, and placement

5. Comprehensive smoke-free laws cover
   a. restaurants, bars, and workplaces
   b. hospitals, schools, and parks
   c. bars, schools, and workplaces
   d. restaurants, hospitals, and parks

6. The addictive chemical in tobacco is
   a. arsenic
   b. methanol
   c. nicotine
   d. butane

7. The organization responsible for regulating the manufacturing, marketing, and distribution of tobacco products is the
   a. FAA
   b. FDA
   c. FCA
   d. FIA

8. This uses a liquid that often contains nicotine as well as different flavors.
   a. cigarette
   b. cigar
   c. dissolvable
   d. e-cigarette

9. This lung disease causes shortness of breath due to the air sacs in the lungs being damaged.
   a. bronchitis
   b. COPD
   c. emphysema
   d. asthma

10. This causes swelling and narrowing inside the lung and restricts the air supply.
    a. asthma
    b. pneumonia
    c. emphysema
    d. bronchitis

PROJECT-BASED LEARNING: Quitting Tobacco Brochure

What to Remember

Once you have started using a tobacco product, it can be really hard to stop. While there are several different methods for quitting, you need to find one that works for you.

Who It Is For

Students at your high school

Why It Is Important

Having accurate information is critical to making a good choice when it comes to quitting a tobacco habit.

What to Do

In groups of three to five students, work together to find the pros and cons of a method for quitting tobacco use. Your teacher will assign you one of the following methods:

1. Apps
2. Websites
3. Social media sites (Facebook, Twitter, Instagram)
4. Nicotine replacement therapy
5. Counseling (individual, group, telehealth)

How to Do It

Step 1: Search online for the pros and cons of the method you were assigned.

Step 2: Make a list of pros to explain why students would want to use this method, how you think it could help them, how easy or difficult it might be, how effective it is, and at least one other question you decide to ask based on the information you find. You should have between three and seven reasons that explain why this method would be useful.

Step 3: Now make a list of cons to explain why students might find this method difficult to implement. Think about the amount of time it might take to use this method and the amount of money the student may need to spend on it. Add at least one other question you decide to ask based on the information you find. You should have between three and seven reasons that explain why this method would be challenging.

Step 4: Create a factual, well-organized brochure that features the pros and cons of your method. Distribute copies of your brochure to the other groups in your class.

Step 5: Assemble your brochure with the other groups' brochures to make one comprehensive informational packet about methods for quitting tobacco product use.

CROSS-CURRICULAR CONNECTION: Language Arts

Create an advertisement for your assigned method for quitting tobacco product use from your Project-Based Learning assignment. If you didn't do the Project-Based Learning assignment, choose one of the quitting methods from it to write about.

Your advertisement should include a photograph or illustration of your method, an original slogan you came up with, and at least two facts that state why people should use this particular method.

13

Legal and Illicit Drugs

LESSON 13.1 Over-the-Counter and Prescription Drugs
LESSON 13.2 Illicit Drugs
LESSON 13.3 Influences on the Use of Drugs
LESSON 13.4 Prevention, Treatment, and Being Drug-Free

Understanding My Health

What Do I Know About Legal and Illicit Drugs?

Using over-the-counter or prescription drugs can be dangerous if not used as directed. Illicit drugs come with their own set of complications and danger that lead to potentially life-altering problems including legal issues and death. Complete the following self-assessment by marking X for *true* or *false* next to each corresponding question to help you understand your knowledge about legal and illicit drugs. After completing the self-assessment, check your answers with the answer key that is provided directly after the assessment.

	True	False
1. Medicines are divided into two categories: over-the-counter (OTC) and prescription.		
2. The general purpose of an OTC label or a prescription label is to tell you what the drug is used for and how to use it safely.		
3. Teens misusing prescription medicines is not a problem in the United States.		
4. Drug use increases your ability to complete tasks and retain information.		
5. Hallucinogens alter your awareness of your surroundings as well as your thoughts and feelings.		
6. The main ingredient in methamphetamine is THC.		
7. Opioids are used as medicines because they contain chemicals that relax the body and relieve pain.		
8. Social media does not influence teens and the choices they make.		
9. A substance use disorder will not affect your day-to-day life.		
10. Behavioral therapy and medicines are effective types of treatment for substance use disorders.		

Answers: 1. true, 2. true, 3. false, 4. false, 5. true, 6. false, 7. true, 8. false, 9. false, 10. true

My score for What Do I Know About Legal and Illicit Drugs? _____ (total number of correct answers)

Over-the-counter and prescription drugs are legal for teens to use, but they often are misused. Some of the drugs discussed in this chapter are considered illicit, meaning illegal, while others can be prescribed and purchased at a pharmacy or drugstore or are obtained at most grocery stores. Analyzing what influences your choice about drug use is an important concept to understand at this age because you may get into situations where you feel pressured to use drugs. The goal is to use them correctly and be free of illicit drugs and of those not prescribed to you.

LESSON 13.1
Over-the-Counter and Prescription Drugs

Terms to Learn
addiction

creatine

drug facts label

medicine

nonprescription or over-the-counter (OTC) drugs

prescription drugs

side effects

The Big Picture
Medicines are drugs used to maintain health or treat health issues. Medicines are classified as either over-the-counter (OTC) or prescription. OTC means you can buy the medicine at a store, directly off the shelf, without a prescription. A prescription medicine is one for which a doctor writes a prescription, and which you must purchase at a pharmacy. It is important to use any type of medicine correctly by following the directions on the label.

Learning Targets
- Compare and contrast the similarities and differences between over-the-counter and prescription medications.
- Explain the general purpose of a drug facts label.
- Describe why teen use of prescription drugs is one of the major drug problems in the United States.
- Analyze why teens might continue using OTC and prescription drugs other than the way they should be used.

Write About It
Explain why teens might use a friend's prescription medicine.

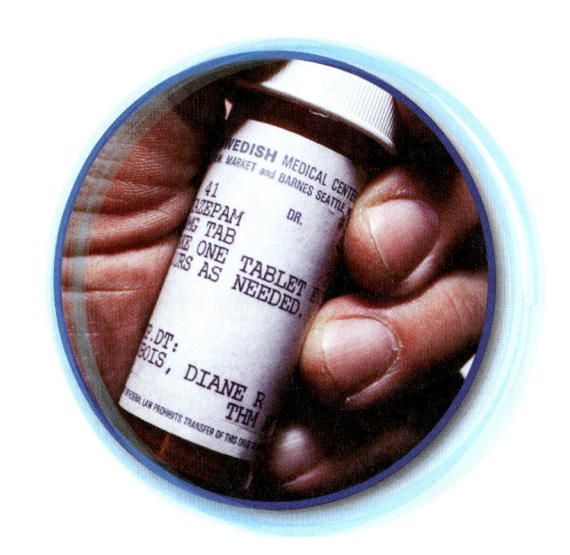

Note-Taking Guide
Use this chapter's note-taking guide to help you organize and remember the material in this lesson.

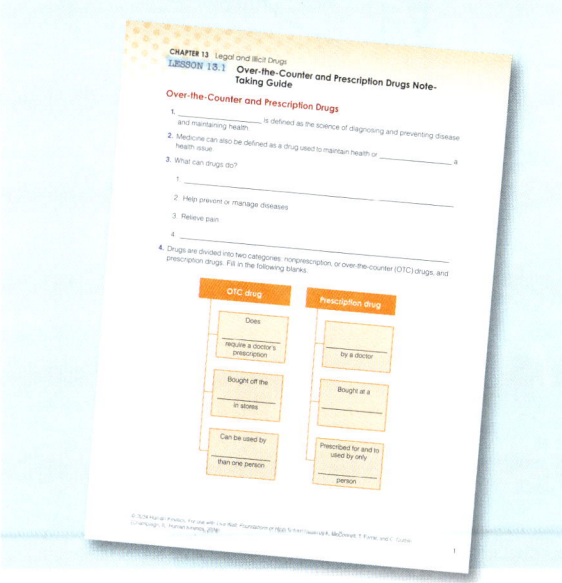

549

LESSON 13.1 Legal and Illicit Drugs

Fernando hurt his arm pitching in the game on Friday. He didn't want to tell anyone about it because state is next weekend and he wants to play. Fernando's friend Jamie has some prescription pain medicine left over from her surgery a month ago and offers it to Fernando to help with the pain in his pitching arm. Fernando knows if he starts using the pills, it will help his arm. Plus, it will only be for the week, so it's not a big deal. What could happen to Fernando and his arm if he decides to take the pills?

Over-the-Counter and Prescription Drugs

Medicine is not only the science of diagnosing and preventing disease and maintaining health but also a drug used to maintain health or treat a health issue. In this chapter, you will focus on the definition of medicine as a drug. Drugs can ease symptoms, help prevent or manage diseases, relieve pain, and treat multiple conditions. When used as a medicine, they are divided into two categories: **nonprescription or over-the-counter (OTC) drugs** and **prescription drugs** (see table 13.1). Prescription drugs are categorized as stimulants, opioids, or depressants.

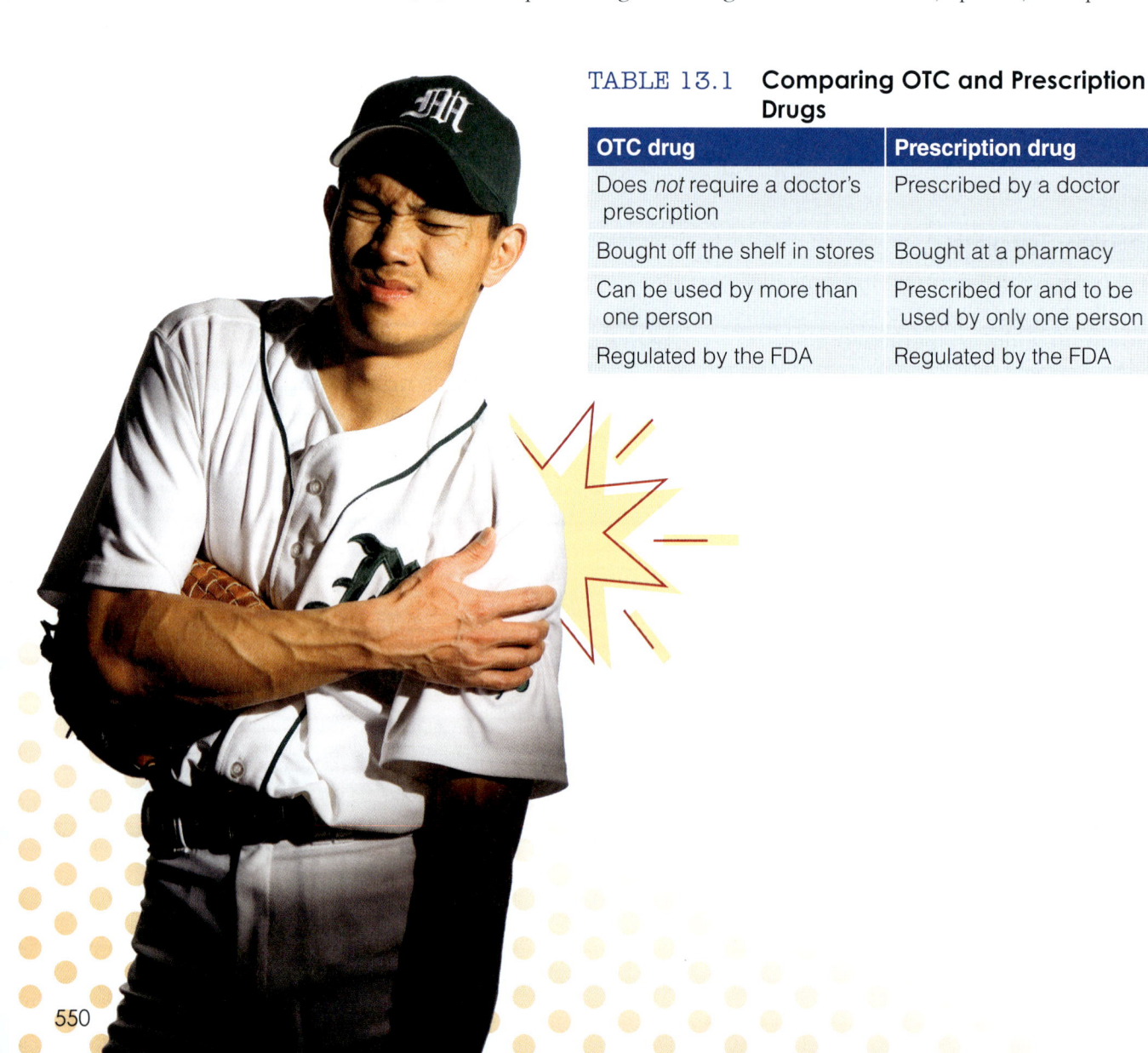

TABLE 13.1 **Comparing OTC and Prescription Drugs**

OTC drug	Prescription drug
Does *not* require a doctor's prescription	Prescribed by a doctor
Bought off the shelf in stores	Bought at a pharmacy
Can be used by more than one person	Prescribed for and to be used by only one person
Regulated by the FDA	Regulated by the FDA

Using OTC and Prescription Drugs Safely

The U.S. Food and Drug Administration (FDA) is the government agency that decides which drugs require a prescription and which drugs may be sold over the counter. The FDA allows new medicines to be used only if they are safe and do what they are supposed to. If the drug's benefits outweigh its risks, the FDA usually approves the sale of the drug. The FDA can take a drug off the market at any time if it is found to cause harmful **side effects**—the effects drugs have on your body that don't help your symptoms.

To use an OTC drug safely means using the drug properly. Proper use includes reading the label of the drug and following the directions for use. While an OTC drug may be helpful for some injuries or illnesses, it is important for you to be able to properly determine when something is minor and when it requires medical attention. The most common OTC medicines are pain relievers such as acetaminophen (Tylenol) and ibuprofen (Advil), cough suppressants, antihistamines for allergies, and antacids for heartburn and acid reflux.

To use prescription drugs safely, it is important you use them as they are prescribed by your doctor. When you use them as prescribed you are at a very low risk for **addiction** or other side effects. Addiction can be a physiological (functions of the body) or psychological (functions of the mind) need for a substance that often has physical or psychological side effects or both. Teens sometimes think that because prescription drugs are prescribed by a doctor, they are safer to use than illicit drugs. Unfortunately, when misused, prescription drugs can be just as dangerous and deadly as illicit drugs.

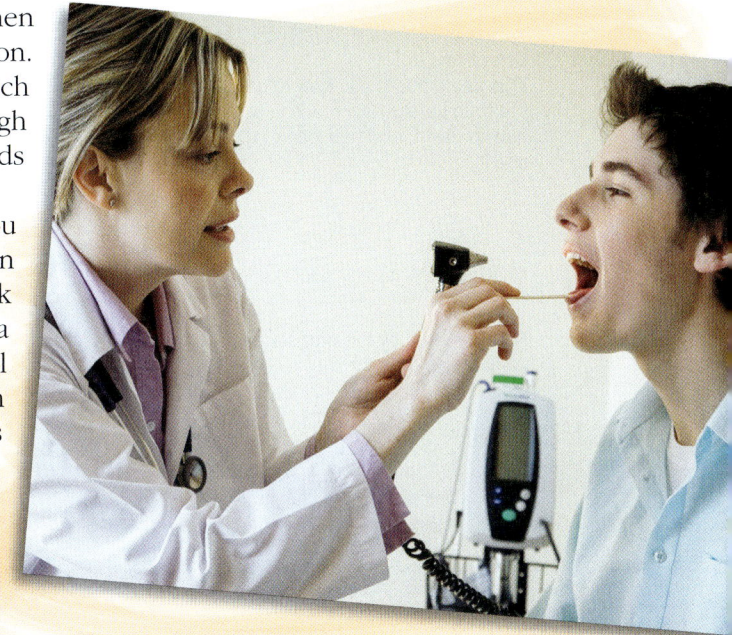

Reading Drug Labels

In the United States, every OTC and prescription drug has a **drug facts label** that tells you what the drug is used for and how to use it safely. Any drug can cause side effects. Following the directions on the label can lower the chance of side effects. Taking a drug as prescribed will ensure that it works the way it is supposed to.

It is important that you understand the different parts of the label and what they mean. Figure 13.1 shows examples of an OTC label and a prescription label. While there are similarities on both labels, there are also sections that are very different. Make sure you understand how to read each label.

Safely Storing and Disposing of OTC and Prescription Drugs

OTC and prescription drugs should be stored in a cool, dry place such as in a drawer or cabinet away from heat and moisture. Heat, air, light, and moisture may damage certain medicines. When exposed to heat and moisture, for example from the shower if kept in the bathroom, medicines can be damaged and lose their

LESSON 13.1 Legal and Illicit Drugs

OTC label

Active ingredients/Purposes
This tells you the part of the medicine that makes it work (known as the active ingredient), what the purpose of the active ingredient is, and how much of each active ingredient is in each pill, tablet, or teaspoon as examples.

Uses
This section tells you the symptoms or disease the medicine will treat or prevent.

Directions
This section tells you how to use the drug safely: how much to use, how to use it, and how often to use it.

Drug Facts

Active ingredient (in each tablet) .... Purpose
Chlorpheniramine maleate 2 mg .... Antihistamine

Uses temporarily relieves these symptoms due to hay fever or other upper respiratory allergies: ■ sneezing ■ runny nose ■ itchy, watery eyes ■ itchy throat

Warnings
Ask a doctor before use if you have
■ glaucoma ■ a breathing problem such as emphysema or chronic bronchitis
■ trouble urinating due to an enlarged prostate gland
Ask a doctor or pharmacist before use if you are taking tranquilizers or sedatives
When using this product
■ drowsiness may occur ■ avoid alcoholic drinks
■ alcohol, sedatives, and tranquilizers may increase drowsiness
■ be careful when driving a motor vehicle or operating machinery
■ excitability may occur, especially in children
If pregnant or breast-feeding, ask a health professional before use.
Keep out of reach of children. In case of overdose, get medical help or contact a Poison Control Center right away.

Directions
adults and children 12 years and over	take 2 tablets every 4 to 6 hours; not more than 12 tablets in 24 hours
children 6 years to under 12 years	take 1 tablet every 4 to 6 hours; not more than 6 tablets in 24 hours
children under 6 years	ask a doctor

Drug Facts (continued)
Other information ■ store at 20-25° C (68-77° F) ■ protect from excessive moisture
Inactive ingredients D&C yellow no. 10, lactose, magnesium stearate, microcrystalline cellulose, pregelatinized starch

Warnings
This tells you conditions that may require advice from a doctor before using, how the medicine might make you feel, when the medicine shouldn't be used, things that shouldn't be done while using the medicine, and when to stop using the medicine.

Other information
This tells you how to store the drug when it isn't being used.

Inactive ingredients
This section tells you the parts of the drug that aren't the active ingredients. These are the ingredients that are added to the active ingredient(s) to help shape the form, to add flavor or color to the drug, or to help the drug last longer.

Prescription label

Pharmacy name and address

Number used by the drugstore to identify this drug for your refills

Person who gets this drug

Instructions about how often and when to take this drug

Name of drug and strength of drug

Number of refills before certain date

℞ **Local Pharmacy**
123 MAIN STREET
ANYTOWN, US 11111   (800) 555-5555
DR J. SMITH
NO 0094021-04153   DATE 04/07/20
JANE SMITH
456 FIRST STREET ANYTOWN, US 11111
TAKE ONE CAPSULE BY MOUTH THREE
TIMES DAILY FOR 10 DAYS UNTIL ALL TAKEN
AMOXICILLIN 500MG CAPSULES
QTY   MRG
NO REFILLS - DR. AUTHORIZATION REQUIRED
USE BEFORE 04/07/21
SLF/SLF

Drugstore phone number

Doctor's name

Prescription fill date

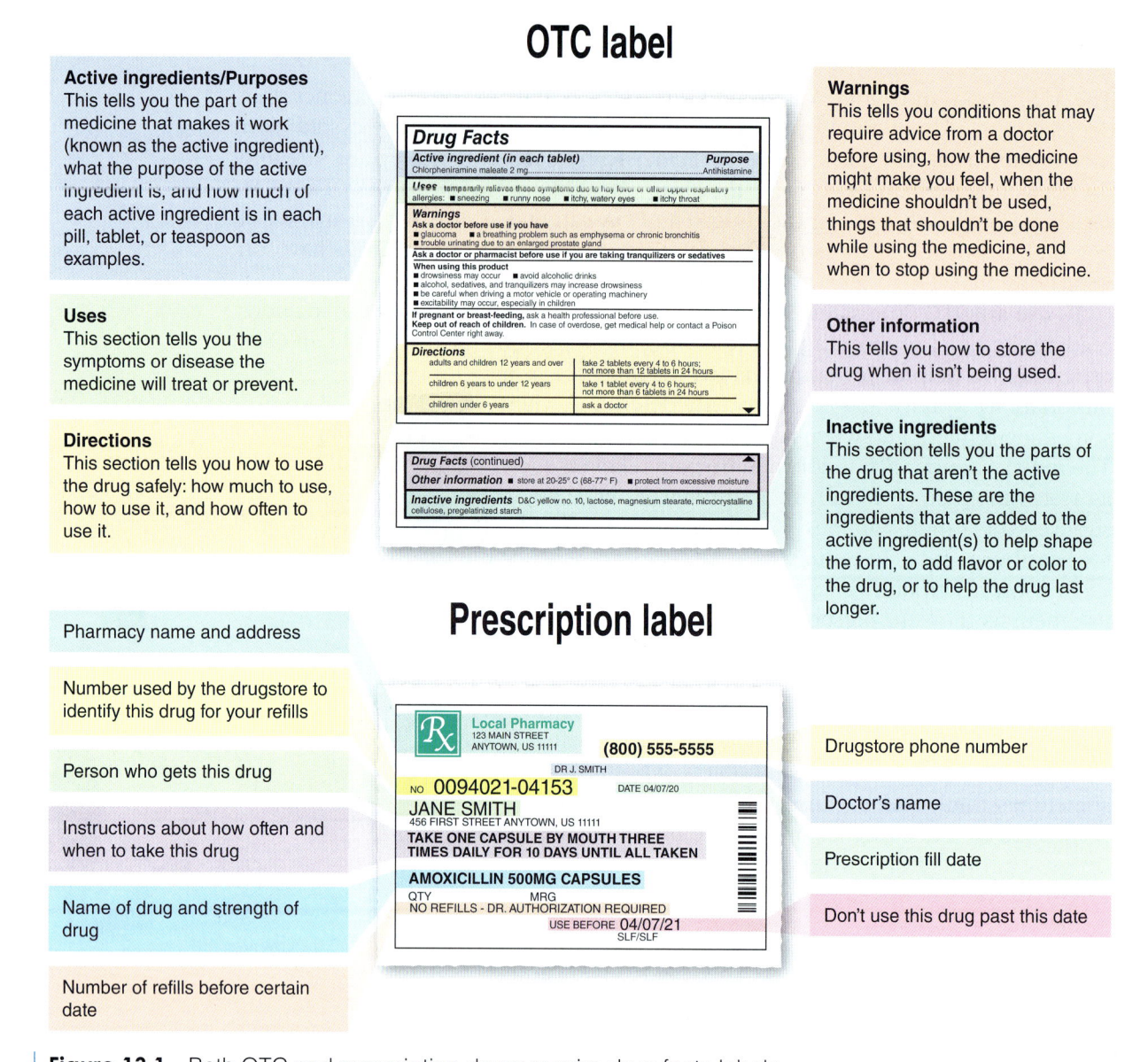

Don't use this drug past this date

Figure 13.1 Both OTC and prescription drugs require drug facts labels.

potency or break down and cause stomach irritation. Prescription and OTC drugs should always be kept in their original containers, so it is clear as to what they are. Some prescription medicines, such as insulin, must be kept in the refrigerator, so it is very important to read the information on how to properly store drugs to make sure they work as they are supposed to.

When OTC and prescription drugs expire or are no longer needed, they should be disposed of properly. Medicines should not be used after their expiration dates. The best ways to dispose of prescription and OTC drugs is to drop off medicines at a drug take-back site where the medicines are destroyed or at local pharmacies that will dispose of them for you. Depending on where you live, there may be a permanent drop off location, or it may be offered at different times during the year. Medicines can also be disposed of directly in your trash at home. To do this, you should scratch out with a permanent marker or take off the prescription label and then mix the medicine in a sealable plastic bag with an unappealing substance such as dirt, coffee grounds, or kitty litter before throwing it into the garbage. People often resort to flushing them down the toilet, but this may harm the water supply, so it's best to avoid disposal of this kind.

Potential Risks of Taking OTC and Prescription Drugs

Although the benefits of taking an OTC or a prescription drug often outweigh the consequences, it is important to be aware of the following four main risks:

1. *Side effects.* Most side effects are unpleasant, and may include nausea, dizziness, diarrhea, dry mouth, skin irritations, and drowsiness. It is important that you read the labels of all drugs before taking them so you know the potential side effects.

2. *Drug–drug interactions.* When two drugs are used together, it affects how your body processes them. When drugs interact, they sometimes make each drug stronger, which could create additional health problems; however, they also can cancel each other out and not work at all. Make sure you always tell your doctor all the medicines you are taking, including herbal supplements, vitamins, and minerals, because even these types of drugs can cause undesirable drug interactions.

3. *Drug–food interactions.* What you eat and drink can affect the ingredients in a drug and prevent it from working the way it should. If your drug should be taken on an empty stomach, you should typically take it an hour before or two hours after eating.

4. *Allergic reactions.* Allergic reactions to medicines are fairly rare. Signs of an allergic reaction may include itching, hives, and breathing problems. Call your doctor or 911 right away if you think you are having an allergic reaction.

HEALTHY LIVING TIP
If you are using a prescription drug, make sure you use it only as directed and that you don't let anyone else use your medicine.

Abuse of OTC and Prescription Drugs

Table 13.2 describes commonly abused OTC and prescription drugs. In the United States, prescription drugs are the fourth most commonly abused substance by teens, after alcohol, marijuana, and tobacco or vaping. Prescription drugs are categorized in the following ways:

- Opioids, which are used primarily to relieve pain
- Depressants, which are mainly used to treat anxiety and sleep disorders
- Stimulants, which are largely used to treat ADHD

The use of prescription drugs, other than as prescribed, by teens is the fastest-growing drug problem in the United States, affecting teens' mental and physical health. Teens abuse prescription drugs for a variety of reasons. Sometimes it is simply out of curiosity, especially when teens have easy access to prescription drugs from their home, family, or friends. Teens may abuse prescription drugs to feel better about themselves and their situations or to decrease physical and emotional pain. Other teens view using prescription drugs as a means to do better in school and sports.

One in four teens reports having misused or abused a prescription drug at least once in their lifetime. Teens are abusing these medicines either by taking more than what is prescribed or by taking someone else's medicine. Teens may also use

LESSON 13.1 Legal and Illicit Drugs

TABLE 13.2 Commonly Misused OTC and Prescription Drugs

Type of drug	Description
Misused OTC drugs	
Cough syrup	Many OTC cough syrups contain dextromethorphan (DXM), which is a cough suppressant. DXM is either swallowed in its original form or mixed with soda for flavor; this is called *Robotripping* or *skittling*. Taking too much DXM can cause hallucinations or slow down brain function, particularly the part of the brain that controls breathing and heart function.
Cold medicine	Pseudoephedrine is a stimulant in many cold medicines used to relieve nasal and sinus congestion from colds and allergies. A stimulant speeds up body systems, especially the brain and central nervous system. Taken in excess, it may cause hallucinations, an irregular heartbeat, shortness of breath, dizziness, or seizures.
Misused prescription drugs	
Adderall and Ritalin	These are stimulants often used to treat ADHD. Teens tend to use them, even if not prescribed to them, as so-called study drugs to feel more awake and alert. These drugs don't increase learning or thinking ability, and the effects last only for a short amount of time.
Vicodin and OxyContin	These opioids contain chemicals that relax the body and relieve pain, especially after severe injuries or surgeries. Opioids are a class of drugs found naturally in the opium poppy plant.
Xanax	Benzodiazepine is a depressant in Xanax that works to calm or sedate a person. It is often used for treating anxiety and panic disorders. Xanax can slow or stop breathing if used with an opioid medication or alcohol.

OTC and prescription drugs to be more alert or to relax after a stressful time over the next day or two. What they don't realize is that they can feel sluggish and tired after the effects of the drugs wear off. These feelings can sometimes trigger the cycle to use again because they want to get the good feeling back. Signs that may indicate abuse of an OTC or prescription drug may include changes in appearance, attitude, grades, or sleep; sudden anger outbursts; and lying or stealing.

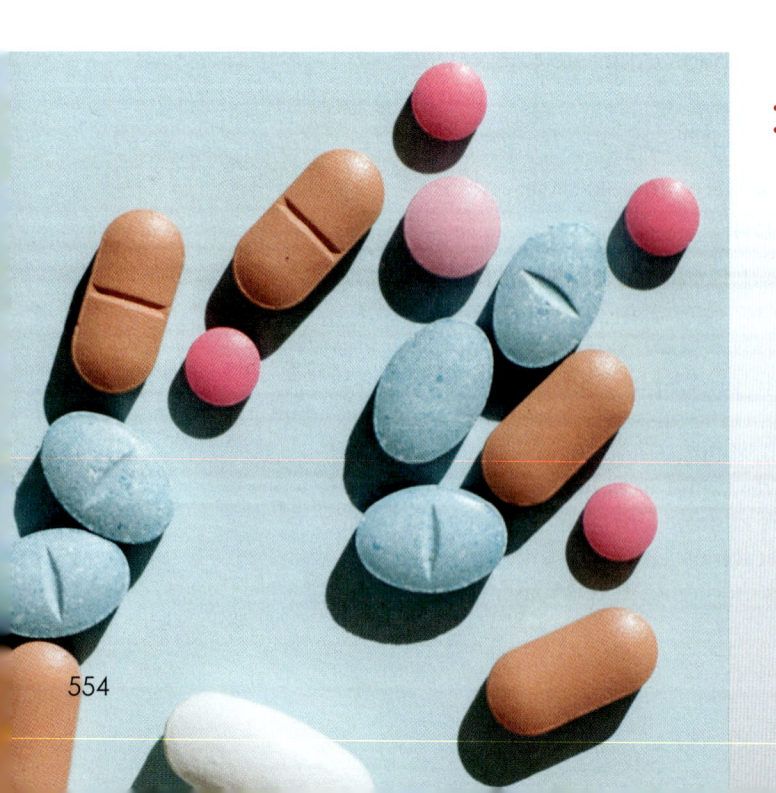

Reasons for abusing OTC and prescription drugs include the following:

- Prescription drugs can be easy to get from friends, family, and acquaintances.
- Some drugs reduce appetite and are often used for weight loss.
- Some drugs increase alertness and improve concentration.
- Some drugs can make people feel good or get high.
- Some drugs can help people relax.

Over-the-Counter and Prescription Drugs **LESSON 13.1**

OTC Performance-Enhancing Drugs

Performance-enhancing drugs are substances used to primarily improve athletic performance. The United States Drug Enforcement Administration (DEA) and athletic governing bodies consider some performance-enhancing drugs legal and others illicit. The two discussed here, caffeine and creatine, are currently legal to use.

Caffeine and Energy Drinks

Caffeine is a stimulant most often found in coffee and energy drinks and may be used by athletes to speed up the central nervous system and increase heart rate and blood pressure. Stimulants can improve endurance, reduce fatigue, suppress appetite, and increase alertness and aggressiveness. Short-term side effects may include trouble sleeping and focusing, shakiness, headaches, and dizziness. Long-term side effects can include irritability, nervousness, and an irregular heart rate. Babies born to women who use caffeine while pregnant may have changes in sleep and movement patterns. While caffeine is not addictive, you can become dependent on it and experience withdrawal when you have less of it.

Caffeine is found in energy drinks and coffee, and while it's not addictive, you can become dependent on it.

Creatine

Your body produces **creatine**, a substance found naturally in muscle cells that helps your muscles produce and release energy during heavy lifting, improves strength, and helps muscles recover more quickly. This may help athletes achieve bursts of speed and energy, especially in sprinting and weightlifting. Creatine is also available as an OTC nutritional supplement often used as a powder that is added to a liquid. Short-term side effects may include anxiety, weight gain, headache, and upset stomach. Caffeine use with creatine can increase the risk of the aforementioned side effects. Creatine is not physically addictive, but it may be psychologically addictive because you may think you *have* to use it if you see benefits in it.

Creatine is an OTC nutritional supplement that can become psychologically addictive.

LESSON 13.1 Legal and Illicit Drugs

Diet Pills

Diet pills often come with a large promise of significant weight loss. While diet pills may help with weight loss, they can also have health risks. The FDA does not review diet pills for safety and effectiveness before they are marketed. If the diet pill contains a new ingredient, manufacturers must notify the FDA about the ingredient prior to marketing the pill. Unfortunately, not all manufacturers follow this requirement.

OTC diet pills are marketed to help you lose weight by increasing your metabolism. Metabolism is how your body converts what you eat and drink into energy your body needs to function. The primary ingredient of most diet pills is caffeine, but they may have other ingredients that may or may not be safe. Without FDA testing, there is no way to know if all the ingredients are safe. Over time, the FDA has banned many of the more popular ingredients in diet pills because of harmful side effects. Side effects include increased heart rate, high blood pressure, agitation, sleeplessness, kidney problems, and liver damage (see figure 13.2). Even with this information, if the manufacturer doesn't list those ingredients on the label, you have no way of knowing what is in the product.

Taking more than the recommended dose, taking diet pills when you are at a normal weight or are underweight, and combining multiple weight loss pills and products are common ways diet pills are misused.

Figure 13.2 Diet pills can have harmful side effects like increased heart rate, high blood pressure, agitation, sleeplessness, kidney problems, and liver damage.

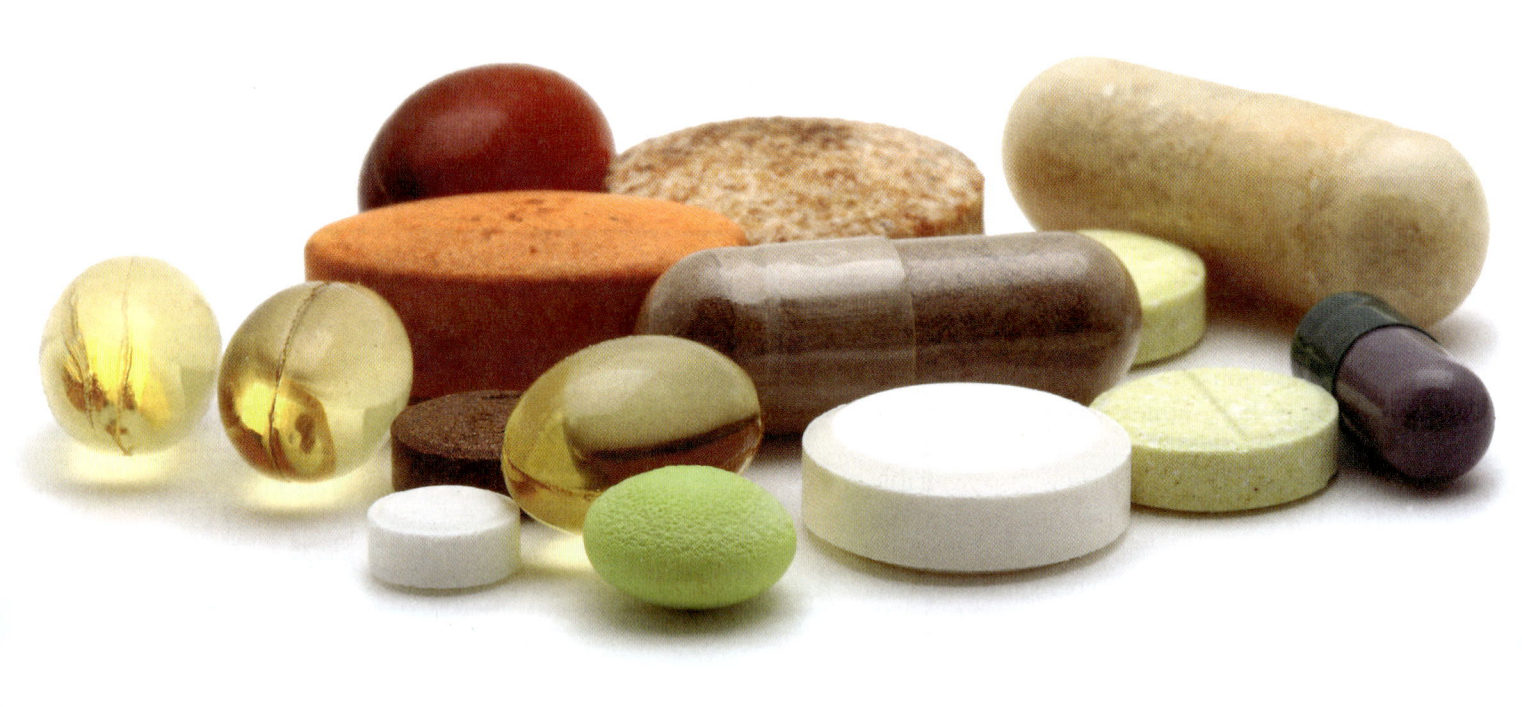

Over-the-Counter and Prescription Drugs **LESSON 13.1**

Skill-Building Challenge

Advocating for the Proper Use of Prescription Medications

You have just heard that one of your classmates got arrested for selling her ADHD pills to some other students at school. The students were buying the pills to help them study for their finals. You read about kids using Adderall to help them focus and stay awake in health class earlier in the year, but you didn't think it would ever happen at your school. Since your classmate's arrest, you've begun hearing about other students also selling their prescription medications at school.

You want to do something to stop the selling of prescription drugs. You talk to a few of your friends and your teacher about what you could do to stop this from happening again. This is a problem that involves families, you realize, because the pills are coming from people's homes, therefore making this an issue you feel your community needs to know about.

You want to advocate for the students and their families to be aware of what is happening and to use prescription medicines properly. Use the Advocacy Skill Cues to complete the challenge.

Healthy Living Skills

This lesson focused on practicing advocacy. Here are some more ways you can develop healthy living skills related to this lesson.

ANALYZING INFLUENCES

Advertisements for all types of medicines are on television and the Internet. Choose two medicines for different illnesses or conditions you think might be helpful. Then answer the following questions about both medicines.
1. What made you choose this medicine? For example, were you influenced by the packaging, by a commercial, or because a friend or family member uses it?
2. Thinking about your answer to question 1, is it a good reason to use this medicine? Explain why or why not.
3. Would you use this? Explain your reasoning.

HEALTHY COMMUNICATION

Your friend admits she has been taking her mom's diet pills and that she has a lot of energy, so she is working out every day, sometimes even twice a day. She offers you a handful of the diet pills and tells you to take them. You refuse, telling your friend you don't want to take the pills. Your friend doesn't back down and counters by saying the diet pills will help you lose weight faster. Use this scenario to practice your refusal skills with a classmate.

LESSON 13.1 Review: Over-the-Counter and Prescription Drugs

LESSON SUMMARY

- OTC (nonprescription) and prescription (prescribed by a doctor) medicines can be used to maintain health or to treat health issues, ease symptoms, prevent or manage diseases, relieve pain, and treat multiple conditions; both are regulated by the FDA.
- A drug facts label tells you what the drug is used for and how to use it safely.
- The reasons why teen misuse and abuse of prescription drugs have become so prevalent in the United States are (1) prescription drugs are easily accessible, (2) teens may be curious about their effects, (3) teens use them to feel better about themselves and their situations or decrease physical and emotional pain, and (4) teens use them to improve their academics and sports.
- The energy and alertness teens can get from various OTC and prescription drugs cause teens to continue using them beyond what they're prescribed for because as the drugs wear off, teens want to get the good feeling back.

REVIEWING CONCEPTS AND VOCABULARY

1. _____ is considered both a science and a drug that is used to maintain health or to treat a health issue.
2. _____, also known as OTC and nonprescription medicines, can be used by anyone.
3. _____ must be bought at a pharmacy and are prescribed by a doctor.
4. A(n) _____ can be a physiological or a psychological need for a substance.
5. The _____ is the government agency that decides which drugs require a prescription and which may be sold over the counter.
6. Nausea and fatigue are possible _____ from using medicine to treat symptoms.
7. _____ tells you what the drug is used for and how to use it safely.
8. _____ is a substance found naturally in muscle cells that helps muscles produce and exert energy.

THINKING CRITICALLY

Alex started taking a friend's prescription medication. Why might Alex be unlikely to tell his doctor or pharmacist about this?

TAKE IT HOME

Talk to a family member about the OTC or prescription medicine they take and the dangers of misusing it. Ask the family member if they have ever asked their doctor or a pharmacist about whether it is safe to take it with other medicines.

LESSON 13.2
Illicit Drugs

Terms to Learn
- cocaine
- edible
- GHB
- hallucinogens
- heroin
- illicit drugs
- inhalants
- marijuana
- MDMA
- methamphetamine (meth)
- opioids
- Rohypnol
- stimulants

The Big Picture
Illicit drugs are drugs that are illegal to have and use. They essentially do one of three things: stimulate your central nervous system, depress your central nervous system, or cause you to hallucinate. Most of the illicit drugs described in this lesson are very addictive. While some of the drugs in this lesson are legal and can be prescribed by a doctor, they can become drugs of abuse when used incorrectly. This lesson will also discuss why teens use illicit drugs, how illicit drugs increase risky behaviors, and the warning signs of illicit drug use.

Learning Targets
- Differentiate between a prescription drug and an illicit drug.
- Identify the different types of drugs based on a description.
- Explain why some teens use illicit drugs.
- Recognize five warning signs of teen drug use.

Write About It
Make three columns on your paper. Label one of the columns "Stimulants," one "Depressants," and one "Hallucinogens." Under each column, list as many illicit drugs as you can think of that would fall into each of the three categories. Compare your answers to the illicit drugs discussed in the lesson to see if you were correct.

Note-Taking Guide

Use this chapter's note-taking guide to help you organize and remember the material in this lesson.

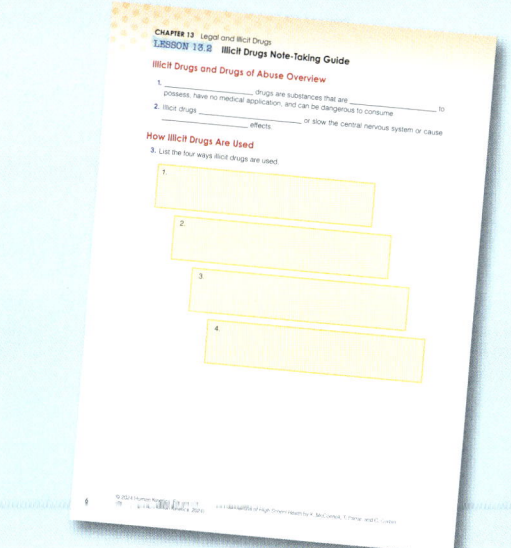

LESSON 13.2 Legal and Illicit Drugs

Teo is at a party with some friends. He knows most of the people there and is having a good time playing video games. Teo finishes his game and goes to the other room to get food. He notices Alicia, a student from his science class, and some guy he doesn't know talking *at* her rather than *to* her. Alicia looks upset. When the guy tries to grab her arm, she pulls away. The guy swipes her soda from her and walks toward the table to fill it up. The guy is looking around suspiciously, and Teo dodges eye contact when the guy looks in his direction. Teo slowly turns back toward the guy and thinks he sees him put some type of powder in Alicia's drink. The guy grins at Teo and takes the drink back to Alicia. Teo isn't positive the guy put something in her drink, but he feels pretty confident about what he saw. What do you think the guy put into Alicia's drink? What should Teo do?

Illicit Drugs and Drugs of Abuse Overview

Illicit drugs are substances that are illegal to possess, have no medical applications, and can be dangerous to consume. They stimulate or slow the central nervous system or cause hallucinogenic effects. Hallucinogenic effects alter a person's awareness of their surroundings, including their own thoughts and feelings. Aside from many being highly addictive, illicit drugs are dangerous: Without regulation, their potency is often unknown because drug dealers may mix illegal substances with other dangerous drugs. Illicit drugs are often injected—adding yet another danger because sharing needles raises users' risks of contracting diseases like HIV and hepatitis. Illicit drug use is associated with child abuse and prison sentences; common effects of using include missing work or school, being violent, and withdrawing from normal activities (see figure 13.3). Eighty percent of all child abuse and neglect cases involve drug or alcohol use.

How Illicit Drugs Are Used

These types of drugs are primarily injected, snorted, smoked, or swallowed. Intravenous injecting of drugs directly into the bloodstream through a vein with a syringe or needle is the fastest method for getting them directly into the bloodstream. This method is also referred to as *mainlining*. With an intravenous injection, the drug goes directly to the brain, resulting in an immediate high. Intravenous injec-

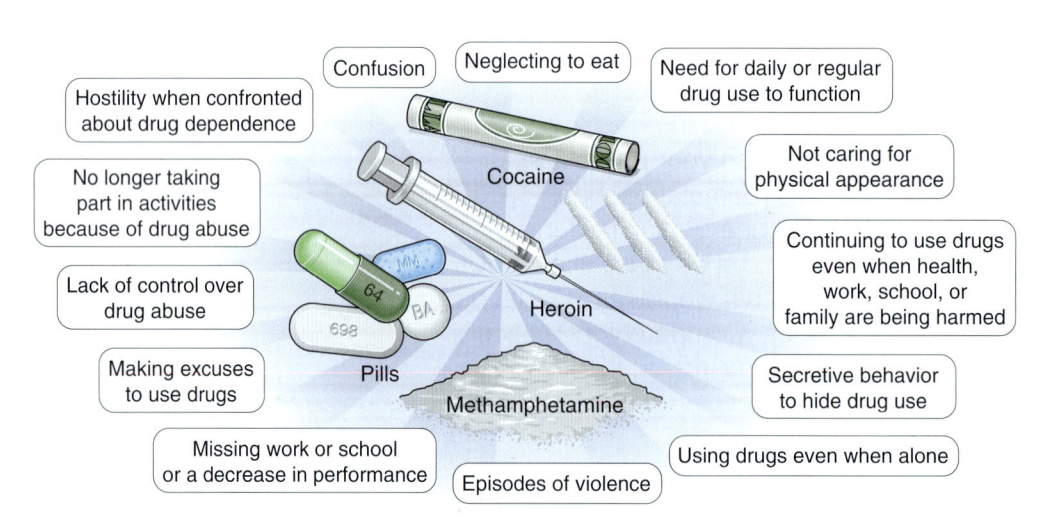

Figure 13.3 Effects of using illicit drugs.

- Confusion
- Neglecting to eat
- Need for daily or regular drug use to function
- Hostility when confronted about drug dependence
- Not caring for physical appearance
- No longer taking part in activities because of drug abuse
- Continuing to use drugs even when health, work, school, or family are being harmed
- Lack of control over drug abuse
- Secretive behavior to hide drug use
- Making excuses to use drugs
- Missing work or school or a decrease in performance
- Episodes of violence
- Using drugs even when alone

(Cocaine, Heroin, Pills, Methamphetamine)

560

tions can result in infections at the site of the injection, the collapsing of veins, and artery damage. If syringes or needles are shared, it can result in bloodborne infectious diseases such as hepatitis B or hepatitis C, which causes chronic liver disease, and HIV.

Ecstasy, cocaine, heroin, and amphetamines can be snorted. Within approximately 15 minutes, a user begins experiencing the high. Snorting drugs can lead to the deterioration of the lining of the nasal cavity. Sharing straws or other items used for snorting can lead to the spread of diseases such as hepatitis C and HIV.

Drugs that are smoked tend to get into the bloodstream rapidly, resulting in a quick sensation or high. Common drugs that are smoked include marijuana, heroin, and crack. Smoking drugs can lead to heart disease, cardiac arrest, stroke, emphysema and bronchitis, and pneumonia among other health issues.

Swallowing drugs is the most common method of drug use. It is also considered the safest way to use a drug because the body is allowed time to absorb the drug. Vomiting as a defense mechanism can occur if something is ingested the body doesn't agree with.

Marijuana

Marijuana is a mind-altering psychoactive drug made from the Cannabis sativa plant. Marijuana (also known as cannabis) is one of the most popular drugs and is the most commonly used illicit drug by high school students in the United States. Often referred to as weed or pot, marijuana is commonly used in a variety of ways: by smoking and vaping, as a blunt (wrapped in cigar paper) or joint (wrapped in cigarette paper), and in a water pipe (bowl) or a bong (hookah). The main psychoactive ingredient in marijuana is delta-9-tetrahydrocannabinol (THC), a chemical that produces the intoxicating effects, or the high. Marijuana can also be consumed as an **edible**, which is food mixed with marijuana or THC. Marijuana edibles are often sold as chocolates and fruit-flavored gummies. Some people who use marijuana regularly may develop marijuana use disorder, which is when they are unable to stop using marijuana even though it's causing health and social problems in their lives.

Marijuana is associated with a number of physical health effects, including respiratory issues similar to those from smoking tobacco or vaping, increased heart rate for up to three hours after smoking, increased weight due to a boost in appetite, weakened immune system, and poor coordination. Children born to women who consume marijuana while pregnant may have a low birth weight, attention problems, and difficulty with problem solving. Mental health effects include an altered sense of time, impaired judgment, memory problems, anxiety, and paranoia. Research has shown that marijuana use also affects brain development. The impact on the brain depends on the amount of THC in the marijuana, how often marijuana is used, a person's age at first use, and whether other substances, such as alcohol, are used simultaneously.

People in the United States have varying viewpoints about the social (recreational) aspect of marijuana use. Those who view it positively cite the connection

Marijuana has several street names, including weed, Mary Jane, pot, and ganja.

LESSON 13.2 Legal and Illicit Drugs

formed with their peers who are also using marijuana and a general acceptance by peers. On the other hand, those with negative views point to the experience of peer disapproval from friends who no longer want to be around them because of their marijuana use. Often people are left with friends who like them only when they are using marijuana. This potentially leads to isolation because they don't have many friends when they aren't using. From a social standpoint, users may also have more family problems and relationship issues than their peers who don't use marijuana. Financial problems may also arise if users have lower-paying jobs, have problems keeping jobs, or lose jobs due to drug-testing requirements.

Marijuana is currently legal in many U.S. states and in the District of Columbia for people over the age of 21. Some states have approved medical marijuana only, and other states have also approved adult-use recreational marijuana. The federal government currently still deems marijuana use illegal.

In states where medical marijuana is legal, it is sold in marijuana stores. Medical marijuana may be prescribed for patients with medical issues such as cancer, chronic pain, HIV, multiple sclerosis, seizure disorders, and glaucoma. Marijuana may also help alleviate nausea, anxiety, and other symptoms in serious medical conditions. The legalization of marijuana in some states has sent a mixed message to teens that marijuana is safe because it has become decriminalized and is used for medicinal purposes.

Cannabidiol (CBD) can be found in both hemp and marijuana plants. Hemp is a specific variety of the *Cannabis sativa* plant that has more CBD and less than 0.3 percent THC. Cannabis is from a different variety of the *Cannabis sativa* plant and contains more THC and less CBD. CBD is non-psychoactive, which means it does not typically cause a high in the user. Hemp-derived CBD is legal in all 50 states and is widely marketed and sold in a variety of products in stores across the United States. However, these products are not approved by the FDA for the cure, treatment, or prevention of any disease. Cannabis-derived CBD is legal in those states in which marijuana is legally sold.

Stimulants

Stimulants speed up the body's systems. This class of drugs includes prescription drugs such as amphetamines—for example, Adderall (described in lesson 13.1)—used to treat ADHD, OTC diet pills (described in lesson 13.1), and illicit drugs such as cocaine and methamphetamine, described as follows:

- **Cocaine** is a white crystalline powder derived from coca leaves. Crack cocaine, which is another common form of cocaine, looks like small, unevenly shaped white rocks. Cocaine has an almost immediate effect, making the user feel energetic, alert, and overly sensitive to sights, sounds, and touch. Tolerance happens quickly, causing users to use cocaine more frequently.

Cocaine, a stimulant. Street names include coke, crack, rock, and snow.

- **Methamphetamine (meth)** is one of the most common illegal drugs in the United States because it is so easy to make. Meth can be made with OTC ingredients including ephedrine or pseudoephedrine, a common ingredient in cold medicines. Meth creates excitement or a pleasurable high that makes people feel good in part due to the high level of dopamine that is released. Common side effects of meth use are meth mouth—a severe dental problem—and intense itching and scratching that leads to skin sores. Meth is extremely addictive and results in ongoing use despite negative outcomes.

Stimulants can be snorted, smoked, injected, or taken as a pill. Effects on the mind include enhanced self-esteem, improved mental performance, reduced appetite, and extended sleeplessness. Effects on the body include headaches, chest pains, shaking, and vomiting. Stimulants can create a psychological dependence, which is a strong craving for the drug being used, in which a person has difficulty thinking about anything else as they depend on the drug to keep feeling a certain way. Women who use cocaine or methamphetamine during pregnancy may have premature babies with low birth weight, and their children may have behavior problems and heart and brain defects.

Methamphetamine, a stimulant. Street names include meth, speed, ice, and crystal.

Opioids

Opioids, or narcotics, occur naturally in the opium poppy plant. This class of drugs includes heroin (illicit), fentanyl (legally used for pain relief but also used illicitly), and prescription pain relievers such as codeine, oxycodone (OxyContin), hydrocodone (Vicodin), and morphine. Some prescription opioids are made directly from the plant; others are synthetically made in labs. Synthetic opioids are manufactured for valid medical purposes and also are produced in illicit labs. Similar to the legal form of the drug, illicit opioids often contain modified ingredients or have enhanced effects.

Opioids can be smoked, injected, or taken as a pill. They relieve pain by stimulating the brain to release endorphins and dopamine. Endorphins reduce pain and increase pleasure, resulting in a positive feeling. Dopamine causes pleasure and increases behaviors that make a person happy. Opioid use can lead to physical and psychological dependence. Women who use opioids during pregnancy may have premature babies with low birth weight, and their babies may have birth defects and withdrawal symptoms.

Examples of opioids include the following:

- **Heroin** is made from morphine, which is a natural substance taken from the seedpod of the opium poppy plant. Heroin can be a white or brown powder or a sticky black substance known as black tar. The initial effects of heroin create a rush of satisfying feelings. Long-term effects may include an inability to make decisions, antisocial behavior, and heart and lung complications. Heroin users develop a tolerance requiring more of the drug, leading to a physical dependence and an addiction to the drug over time.

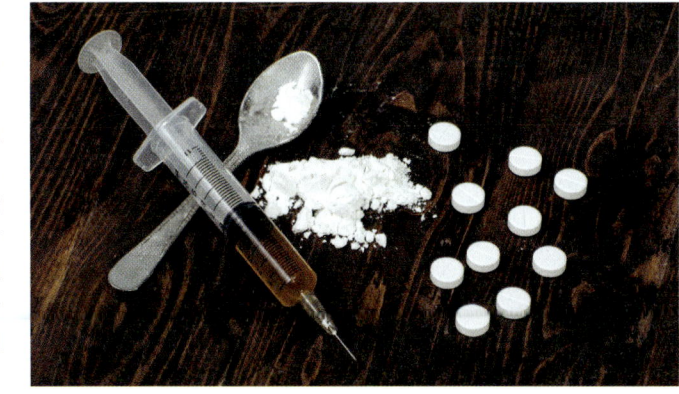

Heroin. Street names include big H, smack, and horse.

- Fentanyl is a synthetic opioid that is used for pain relief. It is 100 times more potent than morphine and 50 times more potent than heroin as a pain reliever. The modifications made to fentanyl in illicit labs and illegal sales of this drug have resulted in a dramatic increase in overdose deaths. Fentanyl's effects include pain relief, relaxation, and happiness. Fentanyl is addictive due to its strength and effectiveness.

- Prescription pain relievers such as codeine, oxycodone, hydrocodone, and morphine may be given to relieve pain after medical and dental surgeries or after athletic injuries, for example. While these types of opioids are highly effective in reducing pain, they can also create a psychological dependence even after a person no longer experiences physical pain. Almost half of all opioid deaths in the United States are caused by a prescription drug containing opioids. When these drugs are taken as prescribed, they provide pain relief, but when they are not used properly, they can result in addiction, overdose, and death.

The misuse of and addiction to opioids is a national crisis that affects people of all ages, ethnicities, and incomes. Opioid use has become such a problem in the United States that naloxone, a medication designed to rapidly reverse opioid overdose, has been created and made available to the public. The OTC version, Narcan, is a nasal spray that is sprayed into one nostril while the patient lies on their back. Narcan is a life-saving medication that can temporarily stop or reverse the effects of an opioid or heroin overdose.

Inhalants

Inhalants are invisible, dangerous substances found in common household products that produce chemical vapors that are inhaled through the nose or mouth to produce mind-altering effects. The high that inhalants produce usually lasts only a few minutes. Examples of inhalants include felt-tip markers, spray paint, hairspray, air freshener, nail polish remover, paint thinner, gasoline, canned whipped cream, helium, canned air, and rubber cement. Effects on the mind may include damage to the parts of the brain that control thinking, moving, vision, and hearing. Effects on the body include a slowing down of the body's overall functions, which can result in uncoordinated movement, general muscle weakness, and dizziness. Inhalant abuse can cause loss of consciousness and even death. It is rare for people to become addicted to inhalants. Children born to women who use inhalants during pregnancy may have delayed brain development and heart defects; as they get older, children also may develop learning disorders and have difficulty getting along with others.

Inhalants. Street names include huff, rush, whippets, and gluey.

Illicit Drugs **LESSON 13.2**

Steroids

Anabolic steroids are the lab-created version of the male hormone testosterone; they are used to promote muscle growth, enhance athletic performance, and improve physical appearance. Anabolic steroids are one of the most widely used performance-enhancing illicit drugs in all sports. Doctors occasionally will legally prescribe anabolic steroids to treat delayed puberty and muscle loss caused by disease as well as low levels of testosterone in men. Anabolic steroids are usually injected into a muscle. They can also be taken as a pill or applied to the skin as a cream or a patch. Effects on the mind include mood swings, aggression (sometimes referred to as *roid rage*), and impaired judgment. Effects on the body depend on the sex of the user. Men may experience shrinking testicles, decreased sperm production, and male-pattern baldness. Women may experience a deepening of the voice, a decrease in breast size, and an increase in facial and body hair. Pregnant women may be given steroids if they are at risk for late preterm births to reduce the risk of severe respiratory problems. Anabolic steroids are neither overly addictive nor result in overdoses.

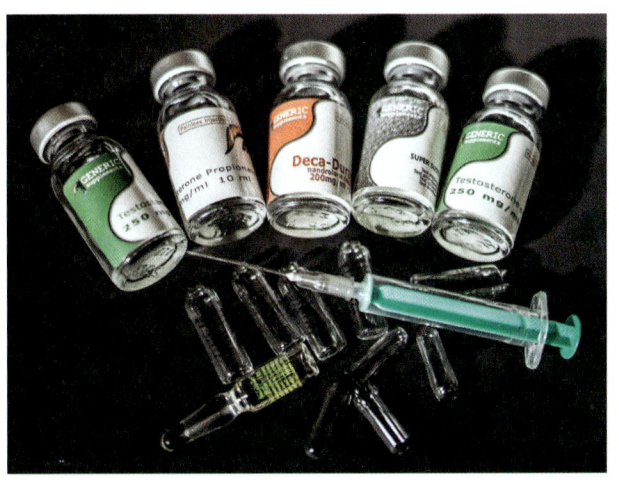

Anabolic steroids. Street names include roids, stackers, arnolds, and gym candy.

Anabolic steroids, if not prescribed, are illegal; if found in possession of them, a person could face a maximum jail time of one year and a minimum fine of $1,000. If a person is caught trafficking steroids, which is a federal offense, they could face up to five years in prison and a fine of up to $250,000.

Hallucinogens

Hallucinogens, which have often been used for cultural rituals, are among the oldest known group of drugs used for their ability to alter human perception and mood. Hallucinogens are found in plants and mushrooms, but they can also be manufactured. They cause hallucinations that seem real—people often say they can see, hear, or feel experiences that are not real. Some people can develop a tolerance to certain hallucinogens such as LSD, while the hallucinogen PCP can be addictive. Women who use hallucinogens during pregnancy may have babies with birth defects, brain damage, and withdrawal symptoms—all of which depend on the hallucinogen used.

The following are examples of three hallucinogens:

• LSD (lysergic acid diethylamide) is an odorless and colorless substance with a bitter taste made from lysergic acid found in a fungus. It is often used on absorbent paper, known as blotter paper, which is divided into small, decorated squares. Each square is one dose and dissolves in the mouth. LSD often alters time and depth perception along with extreme changes in mood. LSD may also cause users to experience flashbacks to a previous LSD experience days or even months after taking the last dose. People using LSD can quickly develop a tolerance requiring a much higher dose.

LSD, a type of hallucinogen. Street names include acid, blotter acid, dots, and window pane.

565

- PCP (phencyclidine), or angel dust, is usually found in the form of a white crystal powder. It is commonly smoked or snorted. PCP in low doses often makes people feel as if they are drunk. In high doses, people can experience hallucinations, seizures, and paranoia. Users may also experience a sense of invulnerability. PCP can be addictive.

Peyote crowns, a type of hallucinogen. Street names include buttons, mesc, and cactus.

- Mescaline is the active ingredient in peyote, a small, spineless cactus. The tops of the peyote cacti, or crowns, look like discs and are often referred to as buttons. Buttons are often chewed or soaked in water to produce an intoxicating liquid. Mescaline causes an altered perception of space and time, hallucinations, and a feeling of euphoria. Individuals who use mescaline can become tolerant quite quickly. Indigenous peoples in northern Mexico and the southwestern United States use peyote as part of their religious ceremonies.

Club Drugs

Club drugs, sometimes referred to as date rape drugs, are primarily used by teens and young adults at parties, concerts, and clubs. They are manufactured in illegal synthetic forms, so the dangers of taking these drugs increase because of the unknown ingredients used in production. Club drugs are primarily taken as a pill or liquid and are often mixed in a beverage. Information on use of club drugs during pregnancy is limited but may lead to premature births and babies with developmental issues.

Examples of club drugs are the following:

- **MDMA** (3,4-methylenedioxymethamphetamine), often referred to as ecstasy or Molly, comes in pill or powder form, with the pills having a variety of logos and colors. It produces feelings of increased energy, distorted perceptions, and an altered understanding of place and time. MDMA causes an increase in the need to be touched, an increase in sexual arousal, and a sense of emotional closeness. These feelings can lead to unsafe sexual behaviors. Further research is needed to determine whether people can develop a tolerance for MDMA.

- **GHB** (gamma-hydroxybutyrate) is a colorless and odorless liquid that is mixed into beverages. GHB can cause people to black out, leaving them completely unaware of what has happened. Taking GHB in high doses can result in loss of consciousness and slowed breathing and heart rate as well as death. Regular use can lead to addiction.

- **Rohypnol** is a central nervous system depressant that is usually smuggled into the United States. Rohypnol is often dissolved in a person's drink without their knowledge, placing the unsuspecting person in a highly vulnerable situation. Rohypnol can cause temporary amnesia, impair judgment, reduce inhibitions, and cause physical dependence when taken regularly over time.

- Ketamine, also known as Special K or K, is an anesthetic that makes people feel detached from their pain and environment. Ketamine comes in a clear liquid or a white or off-white powder and can be easily mixed into beverages. Ketamine takes effect rapidly and makes people feel out of control by causing hallucinations and distorting their perceptions of sight and sound. Regular use may lead to physical and psychological dependence.

MDMA. Street names include ecstasy, Molly, disco biscuit, E, hug drug, X, and XTC.

GHB. Street names include liquid ecstasy, G, and Georgia homeboy.

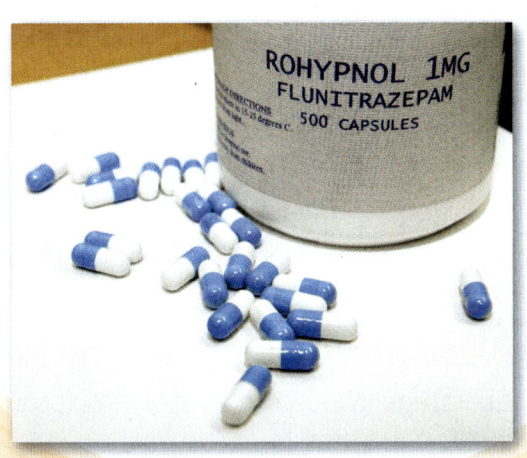

Rohypnol. Street names include roofies, roach, forget-me pill, and R-2.

Depressants

Depressants, which slow down brain activity, are useful for treating anxiety, stress, and sleep disorders. This class of drugs include benzodiazepines (Ativan, Valium, and Xanax), non-benzodiazepine sedative-hypnotics (Ambien and Lunesta), and barbiturates (muscle relaxers). Depressants come in pill or liquid form. Effects on the mind include induced sleep, anxiety relief, and possibly amnesia and confusion. Effects on the body include muscle relaxation, loss of motor coordination, weakness, and slurred speech. Extended use of depressants can lead to a physical dependence on the drug. Some depressants can be used safely during pregnancy.

Examples of depressants include the following:

- Benzodiazepines are legally available only through prescription. The most commonly prescribed benzodiazepines are Ativan, Valium, and Xanax for treating anxiety disorders. They slow down the central nervous system and can cause sleepiness and relaxed mood. The use of benzodiazepines can lead to a physical dependence on the drug.

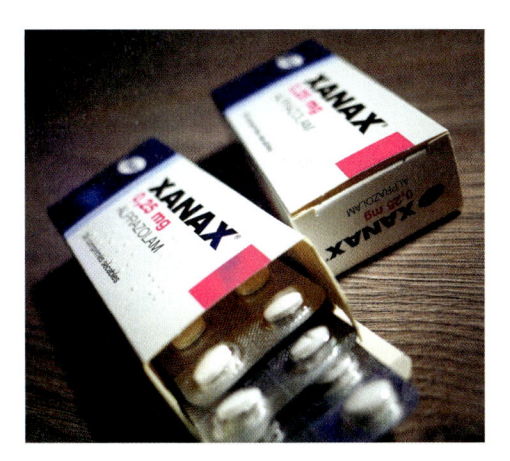

Benzodiazepines are most commonly prescribed as Ativan, Valium, and Xanax.

LESSON 13.2 Legal and Illicit Drugs

HEALTHY LIVING TIP

Using illicit drugs or abusing or misusing drugs of any kind won't help you with your problems. Talk to a trusted adult or friend about your problems and find solutions rather than masking your problems with drugs.

- Non-benzodiazepine sedative-hypnotics are available through prescription and are used for the treatment of insomnia. Two of the most common non-benzodiazepine sedative-hypnotics are Ambien and Lunesta. Both decrease the amount of time it takes to get to sleep while increasing the amount of time spent sleeping. People using Ambien can develop a tolerance, and its use can result in a physical dependence. Lunesta has a high potential for addiction and abuse.

- Barbiturates are available through prescription but are infrequently prescribed because there are similar medications with fewer risks. Barbiturates may be prescribed for anxiety, insomnia, and headaches. Barbiturates are highly addictive and lead to physical dependence and tolerance.

Why Some Teens Use Illicit Drugs

Teens experiment with drugs for a variety of reasons including the following.

Acceptance. A fear of rejection by peers plays a huge role in teen drug use. Teens who think others are doing drugs may perceive experimenting with drugs as their only way to fit in.

Curiosity. Teens may want to know what the effects of drugs feel like.

Pleasure. Drugs interact with the chemicals in the brain to produce feelings of pleasure.

Low self-esteem. Teens may have low self-esteem because of their appearance, lack of friends, peer pressure, social media, bullies, and family, all of which can lead to the self-destructive behavior of using drugs.

Emotional distraction. Teens may use drugs to lessen or forget their feelings of depression, social anxiety, stress, and physical pain.

Performance enhancement. In our competitive society, the constant pressure to be the best may turn some teens to using stimulants to enhance or improve their performance.

Boredom. Teens may seek out drugs as a means for experiencing something thrilling or daring because they have nothing else to do.

Coping mechanism. Teens who feel overwhelmed by problems may perceive drugs as an escape route. Once the drug wears off, however, their initial problems are still there. If they keep avoiding these problems through regular drug use, they risk developing addiction—an additional layer of problems.

How Drug Use Affects School Performance

Teens who misuse and abuse any drug have lower grades and higher absence and dropout rates. Dropping out makes them more likely than their peers to use cigarettes, alcohol, marijuana, and other illicit drugs. Research indicates that drug use not only may change the way the brain processes and retains information but also can have an effect on how well students think, focus, concentrate, and remember.

Marijuana use in the teen years has shown to slow the development of judgment, reasoning, and complex thinking; continued use after high school may accelerate the aging of the brain. It has also been shown to impair emotional development and increase the likelihood of developing depression, anxiety, and other mental health problems. Heavy marijuana use in the teen years has also been shown to continue into adulthood.

How Drug Use Affects Athletic Performance

Whether or not you realize it, drugs take a toll on your mind and body as well as your physical and athletic performance. Using drugs and being physically active or playing sports will affect your abilities and not in a positive way (see figure 13.4).

Trying to perform when using drugs affects you negatively in multiple ways. Depressant drugs, such as marijuana, alcohol, and opioids, slow down your breathing. Marijuana use reduces your lung capacity, making it harder to get oxygen to your muscles. Opioids tend to slow down your breathing and narrow your airway so that breathing becomes much more labored at a time when your body needs extra oxygen. Coordination is important when playing a sport or participating in an activity; by taking a depressant, it reduces your motor coordination so you may not react as you need to.

Stimulants, such as cocaine and caffeine, increase your heart rate and put undue stress on your heart at a time when it is already beating harder than it has to. Cocaine increases your movements but also acts as a painkiller, so being active or playing sports while on cocaine is a bad combination. For example, you may injure yourself without even knowing it and continue playing, thereby causing even more damage. Stimulants can make you irritable and restless, which leads to becoming short-tempered with your teammates and making it difficult to concentrate on the game.

Figure 13.4 The use of drugs can harm your athletic abilities.

How Drug Use Affects Job Performance

Most people who abuse illicit drugs are employed. U.S. companies spend an estimated $81 billion dollars yearly on absenteeism, health care costs, and lost productivity—all related to drug abuse and addiction on the job. Substance use on the job also leads to an increase in physical injuries and fatalities depending on the type of job. Effects on job performance include the inability to focus or concentrate, which leads to the following:

- Being less productive
- Using more sick days
- Needlessly taking risks that cause employer financial and legal impacts
- Selling illicit drugs to coworkers
- Engaging in illicit activities at work
- Causing a decrease in employee morale

LESSON 13.2 Legal and Illicit Drugs

How Illicit Drug Use Increases Risky Behaviors

Using illicit drugs directly correlates to engaging in risky behaviors such as unprotected sex, underage drinking, and dating violence, to name a few examples. According to the CDC, the more often teens use illicit drugs, the more often they engage in sexually risky behaviors, including unprotected sex and a higher number of sex partners. Teens who don't use any substances are the least likely to engage in sexual risk-taking. Several risk factors may lead teens to use illicit drugs and engage in risky behaviors:

- They have a family history of violence, physical or emotional abuse, mental illness, or drug use.
- Guardians don't see a problem with substance use or sexual risk behavior.
- There is a lack of positive guardian influence.
- Friends also use illicit substances and engage in various risk behaviors.
- There is a lack of school or positive peer connectedness.

Warning Signs of Teen Drug Use

Now that we have looked at the different types of drugs and the reasons why teens might use them, it is important to know the warning signs and possible consequences of drug use (see figure 13.5). This way if you ever see these signs in yourself or a friend, you will be able to seek help.

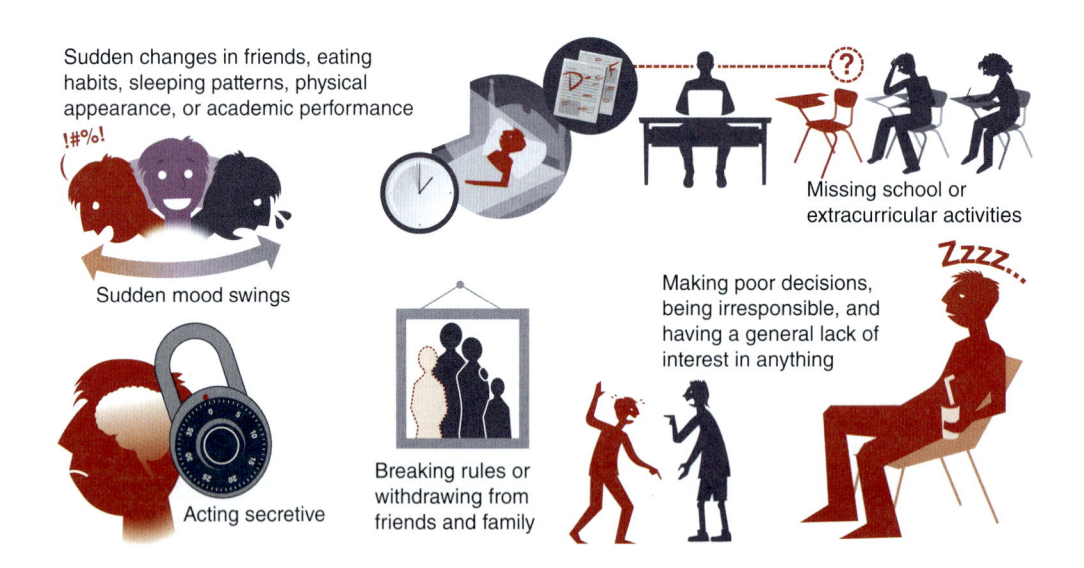

Figure 13.5 Potential signs of drug use.

Illicit Drugs   **LESSON 13.2**

Skill-Building Challenge

Making Healthy Decisions

You and some of your friends heard there was going to be a big party Friday night. You decide to go, and when you get there, it is much bigger than you had imagined. Everyone seems to be having a great time. As you go into another room to find the rest of your friends, you realize they are smoking weed. You knew your friend Emily smoked weed with her older sister now and then, but you didn't know until now that your other friends smoked it too. Your friends all begin encouraging you to smoke weed with them.

You know you shouldn't smoke weed, but your friends are starting to put a lot of pressure on you to give it a try. What do you do?

Use the following decision-making steps and write out your response to each.

- **STEP 1:** What is the problem you are faced with?
- **STEP 2:** What are your options?
- **STEP 3:** What are the consequences based on the options you chose? What would happen if you did smoke weed with your friends? If you didn't?
- **STEP 4:** What is the decision you are going to make?
- **STEP 5:** How do you think your choice will work out for you?

Healthy Living Skills

This lesson focused on making healthy decisions. Here are some more ways you can develop healthy living skills related to this lesson.

ADVOCATING FOR GOOD HEALTH
Create two or three public service announcements about the signs and symptoms of legal and illicit drug use that could be read over the intercom at school. Use the Advocacy Skill Cues to help you organize your work and include at least three realistic alternatives students could do instead of using drugs or other harmful substances as part of your messages.

HEALTHY COMMUNICATION
Write a letter to a middle school student that explains why using marijuana in any form is unsafe. Make sure the letter is appropriate for middle school and include tips on how the student might avoid using marijuana in the future. Include statistics that might be interesting and impactful to the student.

LESSON 13.2 Legal and Illicit Drugs

LESSON 13.2 Review: Illicit Drugs

LESSON SUMMARY

- A prescription drug is legally prescribed by a doctor, bought at a pharmacy, and regulated by the FDA, and it has a low risk for addiction or side effects when used correctly.
- An illicit drug is illegal to possess, has no medical use, can be dangerous to take, has no government regulation, and often is addictive with multiple side effects.
- The following drug categories and drugs were discussed in this lesson: marijuana, stimulants (cocaine, methamphetamine), opioids (heroin, fentanyl, prescription pain relievers), inhalants, anabolic steroids, hallucinogens (LSD, PCP, mescaline), club drugs (MDMA, GHB, Rohypnol, ketamine), and depressants (benzodiazepines, non-benzodiazepine sedative-hypnotics, barbiturates).
- Teens may use illicit drugs to fit in, feel good, forget, do better, relieve boredom, and fulfill their curiosity about the drugs' effects.
- Warning signs of teen drug use include breaking rules, acting secretive, making poor decisions, being absent, and lacking interest in anything.

REVIEWING CONCEPTS AND VOCABULARY

1. _____ drugs stimulate or slow the central nervous system or cause hallucinations.
2. A fruit-flavored gummy mixed with marijuana or THC is known as a(n) _____.
3. When a person's awareness of their surroundings is altered, including their own thoughts and feelings, it is known as a(n) _____ effect.
4. The active ingredient of _____ is THC.
5. A _____ speeds up the body's systems.
6. _____ is made with OTC ingredients including ephedrine or pseudoephedrine, a common ingredient in cold medicines.
7. _____ include heroin and prescription medicines such as oxycodone and hydrocodone.
8. _____ promote muscle growth, enhance athletic performance, and improve physical appearance.
9. _____ produces feelings of increased energy, emotional closeness, and distorted perceptions of surroundings and time.
10. _____ are commonly used for anxiety disorders and insomnia.

THINKING CRITICALLY

Brainstorm with a partner five reasons you think teens use illicit drugs. Then brainstorm one healthy alternative for each reason.

TAKE IT HOME

Ask older family members which illicit drugs were most commonly used when they were in high school. How do the drugs from then compare with today's drugs? Ask your family member if they could give you some reasons why illicit drugs were used when they were in high school and analyze whether the reasons are the same or different now.

LESSON 13.3

Influences on the Use of Drugs

Terms to Learn
advertisement
generic

The Big Picture
You may come across many influences that will try to sway your opinion about using drugs as they are intended and in ways other than what they are commonly used for. Media of various forms are a daily part of most of our lives. Teens regularly use social media, watch streaming media and movies, and use the Internet, which means they may be influenced by advertising for OTC and prescription drugs on a regular basis. Every advertisement is meant to influence your way of thinking about a specific product.

Learning Targets
- Identify three factors that influence teens to use drugs.
- Explain the three pieces of information that drug ads are required to tell consumers.
- Evaluate three techniques marketers use to influence teens to purchase items.
- Devise three healthy alternative activities that are spontaneous and three healthy alternative activities that require planning.

Write About It
Who or what is your most positive influence and why? Who or what is your most negative influence and why? Which external influencing factors have the greatest impact when it comes to making significant decisions in your life? Why are they so important to you?

Note-Taking Guide
Use this chapter's note-taking guide to help you organize and remember the material in this lesson.

LESSON 13.3 Legal and Illicit Drugs

Adam and Gianna have been neighbors and friends since they were little. Now in high school, they have some of the same classes but don't see each other much outside of class. They follow each other on Instagram, and Adam has begun to see Gianna posting pictures at parties on the weekends, sometimes showing handfuls of drugs. Gianna has some new friends who are convincing her to use drugs, which is something she never would have done before. Adam wants to try to help Gianna, so he invites Gianna to go to a movie. Gianna tells Adam she needs to work all weekend on the paper due on Monday. As Adam is looking through Instagram, he sees Gianna is posting selfies at a party that show her using drugs. What can Adam do to help Gianna stop using drugs? Why do you think Gianna has begun to use drugs? Why is Gianna lying to Adam? Do you think Instagram and social media in general have influenced Gianna to use drugs? Explain your answers.

Factors That Influence the Use of Drugs

Many factors will influence your decision about whether to use medications and drugs. External factors may include family, peers, stress, and media; internal factors include how you feel about using or not using drugs.

- *Family influence.* If you have a sibling who uses any type of drug, you will be at a higher risk of using, and the closer in age you are to your sibling increases the chance that you will use.

- *Peer influence.* If you have friends who are using drugs, chances are you will also use because peer pressure can be difficult to resist. It's also important for you to know that not everyone is using drugs and it is okay not to. If your friends really care about you, they will understand and maybe you can even help them not to use.

- *Stress influence.* Teens who are stressed may turn to drugs as a way to cope with what is happening. They may see family members use drugs to "relax" so they may view it as an acceptable coping strategy. Drug use can provide a way to escape what is happening, but it is only temporary and may lead to more stress and has the potential of turning into a drug addiction.

- *Media influence.* TV and movies often contain some use or reference to drugs. Sometimes drugs are portrayed seriously, and drug abuse or addiction is talked about realistically; other times, it is just joked about. Media can include billboards, newspapers, magazines, radio, TV, Internet, and social media, all of which can influence a teen to use substances in an illegal manner.

- *Social media influence.* More teens use Snapchat and TikTok than any other social media platforms. Many teens follow their favorite singers, athletes, and actors and those celebrities often post pictures of themselves in party situations where drugs are being used. You may also see pictures of your friends in party situations where drugs are being used, and that may influence you to use. Teens are able to purchase many types of illicit drugs on a variety of social media platforms.
- *You as an influence.* You have to decide what is best for you. Sometimes you may feel that drugs help you feel better about your problems, but you know that in the end, this is not true.
- *Life influence.* During specific periods of time, you may experience major transitions such as moving from middle school to high school or moving to a new high school. In each case, you will make new friends and experience new academic and social situations. You may also encounter drugs for the first time.

Media and Advertisements

An **advertisement** is the communication of a message about a product or service by means of different types of media. Watch streaming media, read a magazine, or go online for any amount of time and you may see an advertisement for a prescription drug. The United States and New Zealand are the only two countries in the world that allow consumer advertising of prescription drugs. The goal of advertising to consumers is to get them to ask their doctor about a specific drug they have seen in an ad if they have those same symptoms. The goal of advertising to doctors is to get them to prescribe the drug. Drug company sales reps leave doctors with samples they can give to their patients for free with the hope the doctor will like what the medicine does and will prescribe it for their patients.

LESSON 13.3 Legal and Illicit Drugs

Advertising Techniques and Their Influence on Teens

By the time you were eight years old, you began to understand that ads were trying to sell something. Advertisers spend billions of dollars each year ensuring teens view their products on TV, in movies, in apps, and on streaming services and websites that feature music, videos, and games—all the places you spend time. Advertisers also understand that you are still figuring out what your preferences are, and that you have a strong influence on your family's spending.

How Advertisers Employ Techniques to Influence Teens

- *Producing interesting commercials.* Including a variety of situations and actions that appear pleasurable or exciting are fail-safe ways to make commercials memorable and garner viewers' interest.
- *Incorporating engaging, personal experiences.* This is achieved by featuring games, apps, and contests to hold teens' attention. Commercials that include images of families spending and enjoying their time together also draw in teens.
- *Using emotionally appealing music to get teens to identify with a product.* Music can have a powerful way of evoking emotions, so using specific jingles or songs builds interest in not only the product being sold but also the song and artist. Playing off these types of emotions can make a difference in what teens buy.
- *Exploiting teen insecurities.* By appealing to their need to fit in and to be viewed as attractive, athletic, or popular, the messaging implies a person can be cool only if they have the specific product being advertised (very often, a particular brand of clothing).
- *Using celebrity and athlete endorsements.* Teens are more likely to purchase something if their favorite celebrity or athlete is endorsing it than if it is a person who is not famous.
- *Creating messages that imply everyone is doing it.* Teens want to fit in and be part of their peer group, so if the ad can convince them that everyone else has a certain product, they will want it also. For example, a cell phone commercial might show a group of teens looking at their phones and laughing. The implied message is that all teens have their own cell phones and that they are having a great time when they are looking at their phones.
- *Tracking teens' digital footprints.* Ever wonder why certain ads pop up on your phone or computer? Marketers are able to track what you have looked at and use that information to determine your interests, purchases, preferences, and even location. Using privacy settings and being cautious about the information you are sharing online can be helpful in reducing your digital footprint.
- *Having teen followers market their products for them.* In many online stores, you can share items with your friends and upload pictures of yourself with a particular jacket, shoes, or food. This reinforces the idea that the brand "makes" the person. Of course, this isn't true at all, but advertisers are very well aware of how peer influence affects decision making.

Federal law states that advertising must be truthful and backed by scientific evidence. Drug ads are required to tell consumers the following three important pieces of information (see figure 13.6):

1. At least one approved use of the drug must be shared with consumers.
2. The generic name of the drug must be provided. A **generic** drug is simply a copy of the brand name drug. It is the same in dosage, safety, strength, how it is taken, quality, performance, and intended use. Tylenol, for example, is a brand name; the generic name is acetaminophen. Generic medicines are often packaged and labeled under the store brand name and are less expensive than the name brand.
3. All the risks of using the drug must be disclosed.

Figure 13.6 Drug ads must tell consumers three critical pieces of information.

In their ads, drug makers don't tell you how many people the drug has helped, if other treatments with fewer side effects exist, or if the drug is even necessary. Drug ads also give the impression that the drug is better than it really is by showing a person at a party with friends having fun while the narrator reads the side effects in the background. This is done intentionally so that your focus remains on the fun the people are having rather than the side effects. Ads also use terms like *may* or *mild* when they describe a risk or side effect to make it seem less dangerous than it is.

Healthy Alternatives to Substance Use

With all the influences, marketing, and advertising of drugs, it is no wonder teens sometimes get caught up in all the hype and choose to use or misuse legal and illicit drugs. Add to that other times when teens just don't think there's anything else to do, especially if they have older siblings they've seen use drugs. Teens need to realize there are always other options or alternatives to doing drugs; sometimes it is just a matter of thinking about these options ahead of time.

When teens are engaged in productive and healthy activities, such as sports, volunteering, and youth groups, they are much less likely to turn to drugs for recreation. Think outside the normal day-to-day activities and explore other options as alternative activity ideas that will also boost your mental and social health (see figure 13.7).

HEALTHY LIVING TIP

Choose one of the healthy alternative ideas to drugs or add one of your own and go do it.

LESSON 13.3 Legal and Illicit Drugs

Figure 13.7 Some suggestions for healthy alternative activities to drugs. There are many more ideas you can come up with based on where you live and the options you have.

- Go for a walk or hike
- Have a movie marathon
- Make dinner for your friends or family
- Try a new exercise like high-intensity interval training or activity like martial arts
- Volunteer for a cause you think is important

Skill-Building Challenge

Analyzing Influences

Advertisers target teens daily through multiple media outlets in an attempt to make their products appealing to them. Recall that both external and internal factors will influence your purchase of a product. Using at least two different types of media you would typically use to find information, find two advertisements: one for an OTC medication and one for a prescription drug. Then complete the following chart.

	Name of OTC drug: _____	Name of prescription drug: _____
Were you influenced due to an external or internal factor? If so, be specific as to the influence (family, peer, media, yourself).		
What types of media did you use?		
What company or organization is responsible for the advertising?		
What is the ad trying to get you to buy, do, or think?		

Now that you have filled in the chart, answer the following questions.

1. How are the two ads alike?
2. How are the two ads different?
3. Take another look at the two ads. Is the advertiser's point of view different from yours? If so, how is it different?
4. Would either ad influence you to purchase the item? Explain your reasoning.

Healthy Living Skills

This lesson focused on analyzing influences. Here are some more ways you can develop healthy living skills related to this lesson.

HEALTHY COMMUNICATION
Use your conflict resolution skills and your healthy alternatives to communicate a safe alternative to attending a party where the misuse of legal and illicit drugs may take place. What could you say and what steps could you follow if a friend was trying to get you to attend? Write out your options, the consequences of each option, and your decision.

SETTING HEALTHY GOALS
Set a SMART goal to say "no" to peers if they try to influence you to use someone else's prescription drug or an illicit drug. If you plan ahead for something like this to happen, you will be more prepared and less likely to act thoughtlessly. Use the Goal-Setting Skill Cues to set your short-term goals describing how you will deal with peer influences beginning today through the next four weeks.

ACCESSING INFORMATION
There will be times in your life when you need to take safe OTC medicine to treat an illness. Research three different OTC medicines for the same illness. Identify what they are intended to be used for, how to safely use them, and what the potential side effects of using them are. Create a table of your results and indicate which of the three OTC medicines you would use and the reason(s) why you chose that one.

LESSON 13.3 Review: Influences on the Use of Drugs

LESSON SUMMARY

- Factors that influence teens to use drugs include family, peers, media, social media, and teens themselves.
- Drug ads are required to inform consumers of at least one approved use for the drug, the generic name of the drug, and all the risks of using the drug.
- Marketing techniques for teens include showing experiences, producing emotions, promoting a brand as the only way to fit in, using celebrities and athletes, and using peers to influence decision making about a purchase.
- Healthy alternatives to using drugs that don't require much planning include playing a video game, taking a walk, or watching a movie at home. Well-planned healthy alternatives include making dinner for friends or family, volunteering for an important cause, or attending a group exercise class.

LESSON 13.3 Legal and Illicit Drugs

REVIEWING CONCEPTS AND VOCABULARY

1. _____ can include magazines, TV, billboards, newspapers, radio, Internet, and social media.
2. The communication of a message about a product or service is known as a(n) _____
3. A copy of a brand name drug in dosage, safety, strength, how it is taken, quality, performance, and intended use is known as a(n) _____ drug.
4. A(n) _____ is someone who buys a product.

THINKING CRITICALLY

Write down one item you have purchased or something you have done (include both positive and negative choices) for each of the following influencers: (1) family, (2) peers, (3) media, (4) social media, (5) yourself. Draw a star next to the positive choices and an X next to the negative choices.

TAKE IT HOME

Talk to a family member about a purchase they have made because of an advertisement they saw. Referring to the advertisement techniques you learned in this lesson, ask your family member which technique(s) they think persuaded them to purchase the item. Ask the family member how they think advertising influences the purchases they make over time.

LESSON 13.4

Prevention, Treatment, and Being Drug-Free

Terms to Learn
addictive potential
behavioral therapy
relapse
substance use disorder
tolerance
withdrawal

The Big Picture
Substance use disorders happen when you continue to take a drug even though you experience problems as a result of the drug. Being educated from an early age on substance abuse helps prevent substance use from beginning. A substance use disorder can be a lifelong journey filled with tremendous challenges. In general, being drug-free makes friends, school, family, and life much easier.

Learning Targets
- Describe what a substance use disorder is.
- Explain what addictive potential means.
- Select two barriers to being drug-free and assess why they may be barriers.
- Evaluate the importance of behavioral therapy in treating a substance use disorder.
- Examine your school policies about drug use.

Write About It
What would be the consequences if you were found using or possessing marijuana at school? Are you aware of your school's policies related to the use, possession, and sale of illicit drugs? If so, list them. If you don't know what they are, where do you think you could find this information?

Note-Taking Guide
Use this chapter's note-taking guide to help you organize and remember the material in this lesson.

LESSON 13.4 Legal and Illicit Drugs

Kylie began hanging out with people from her art class a while back to work on projects after school. Whenever their instructor left early, a couple of students would smoke a joint, saying it made them more creative and able to produce better art projects. In the beginning, everyone would smoke a little marijuana, and it wasn't a big deal. But then, one of the students, whose older brother is a drug dealer, brought in meth, and that's how they all started snorting meth as well. Kylie had never used it before, but she really loved how it made her feel the first time she did. Since that first time, Kylie's grades have dropped. She craves that high and can't wait to get more meth after school. Kylie is pretty sure she could quit if she actually wanted to. What kind of help might Kylie need and whom could she talk to?

Substance Use Disorder

A **substance use disorder** is a condition in which there is an uncontrolled use of a substance despite the harmful consequences from its use. How people who develop substance abuse disorders live changes through their drug use—they know the drug is causing problems at school or with their family or friends, yet they are still compelled to continue using. The initial classification is determined by the number of criteria a person meets. For example, if you met two or three of the criteria shown in figure 13.8, you would be classified as having a mild substance use disorder; four or five of the criteria classifies you as having a moderate substance use disorder; and six or more criteria indicates a severe substance use disorder.

Addictive Potential of Drugs

A drug's **addictive potential** is determined by the drug's ability to provide the following characteristics: The effects of the drug happen quickly; the feeling of great happiness and excitement go beyond normal expectations; and tolerance and withdrawal are both effects of the drug.

HEALTHY LIVING TIP

If you or someone you know meets any of the substance use disorder criteria, it is important that you take the steps needed to get help. Talk to a trusted adult right away to find out what you need to do for yourself or for your friend.

☐ 1. Hazardous use: Using substances again and again, even when it puts you in danger.

☐ 2. Social and personal problems related to using: Continuing to use, even when it causes problems in relationships.

☐ 3. Neglecting major roles to use: Not managing to do what you should at work, home, or school because of substance use.

☐ 4. Withdrawal: Development of withdrawal symptoms, which can be relieved by taking more of the substance.

☐ 5. Tolerance: Needing more of the substance to get the effect you want.

☐ 6. Using larger amounts or for longer: Taking the substance in larger amounts or for longer than you're meant to.

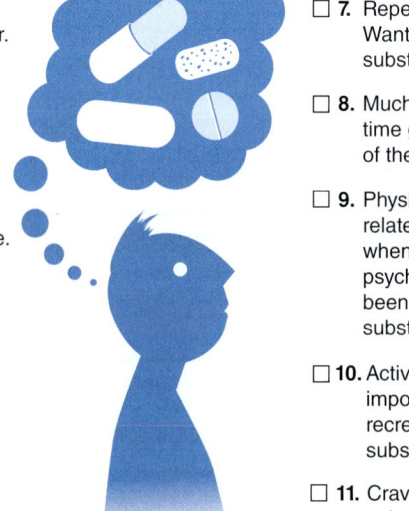

☐ 7. Repeated attempts to control use or quit: Wanting to cut down or stop using the substance but not managing to.

☐ 8. Much time spent using: Spending a lot of time getting, using, or recovering from use of the substance.

☐ 9. Physical or psychological problems related to using: Continuing to use, even when you know you have a physical or psychological problem that could have been caused or made worse by the substance.

☐ 10. Activities given up to use: Giving up important social, occupational, or recreational activities because of substance use.

☐ 11. Cravings: Cravings and urges to use the substance.

Figure 13.8 Substance use disorder criteria.

Prevention, Treatment, and Being Drug-Free **LESSON 13.4**

The more characteristics a drug has, the higher its addictive potential. Tolerance and withdrawal increase the addictive potential of a drug by making it difficult for a person to stop using without experiencing discomfort. If a person develops a **tolerance**, they require higher doses of the drug to have the same effect, and they will want to continue use of the drug to prevent withdrawal symptoms. **Withdrawal** is a group of symptoms that a person experiences when the quantity of the substance is reduced.

Effects of Drugs on the Brain

Drugs that have an addictive potential flood the brain with dopamine, the chemical responsible for feelings of excitement, relaxation, and stress relief. While dopamine is responsible for making people feel good, its real job is to help a person continue important behaviors like sleeping, eating, and forming friendships. When drugs are used, the effects of the increased amounts of dopamine tell the person's brain that it needs more of the drug, which becomes more important than food, sleep, or friendship.

Continued drug use causes the brain to reduce dopamine production, leading to the inability to be happy. To get the happy feeling back, the brain encourages the person to take more drugs in order to feel good again. At this point, the person needs drugs just to feel normal. Teens who use drugs frequently have difficulty with impulse control, judgment, planning, completing tasks, meeting goals, learning, and retaining information.

Being Drug-Free

Being drug-free is a behavior you choose. Sometimes it is difficult because peers and friends may encourage you to use, and in certain circumstances, it may be hard to say "no." Being aware of why someone chooses not to use drugs is an important step in practicing healthy behaviors. Prevention programs are designed to teach teens that there are other options besides using drugs to have fun, make friends, and fit in. Research has shown that if a person delays the first time they use a drug until after the age of 21, their addictive potential chances drop significantly. Teens' addictive potential is seven times greater if they try drugs before the age of 21. To be able to stand up to a peer or a friend and say "no" to using drugs takes belief in your values and confidence to do what is right in a difficult situation. It is being aware of what you want for yourself and having the strength to follow through even when it is challenging. Being drug-free is a way of life, and while it isn't always easy, it is worth the effort. Figure 13.9 shows the benefits and barriers to being drug-free.

LESSON 13.4 Legal and Illicit Drugs

Benefits
Healthier life. People won't have the negative side effects caused by using drugs.
Clean conscience. Drug users no longer have to lie or steal from their family and friends.
Quality friendships. While drug users may think they have good friends, those people are only around if there are drugs. Real friends have mutual respect and are there for each other.
Better educational and employment opportunities. Drug-free teens have a much broader array of options. Their grades will be better, paving the way for more choices of competitive colleges and universities from which to choose. Getting and keeping a job and having a successful career in the future are other opportunities that come with a drug-free lifestyle.
Improved mental health. Teens' minds will be clearer, and they will be able to make plans for their future.

Barriers
A mentality of not needing treatment. Drug users may feel they don't need treatment and believe they can quit whenever they want. In reality, they are in denial of their problem.
Not ready to stop using. When drug users experience uneasiness about quitting, it means they've let their substance use disorder take over their lives.
Financial problems. Cost of treatment is unaffordable for many families, so drug users often face not being able to get the professional help they need.
Adverse impacts on education. Having to go into a treatment facility that requires being out of school for months can adversely affect a person's education (e.g., delaying graduation date, falling so far behind and deciding to drop out, etc.).
Concerns with reputation and friendships. Some users may not want to be seen as having a problem because they are more concerned about what others will think than they are about themselves. Users may also fear that attempts to seek help would only ostracize them from their friends, and no one likes losing friends.
Lack of information. In some cases, drug users may not know where to go or whom to turn to for help, so they don't get the help they need.

Figure 13.9 Benefits and barriers of being drug-free.

Schools can help educate teens about the risks of using different substances: alcohol, nicotine, OTC drugs, prescription drugs, and illicit drugs. While it's important to understand the risk factors of using drugs, it's also important to learn how to make good decisions, become more assertive, stand up to peer pressure, set goals, and build positive relationships.

Families and adult role models can also play a large part in teen substance use prevention. Teens who have an adult to talk to about the dangers of substance use are less likely to develop a substance use disorder. Be sure to always talk to a parent, guardian, or other trusted adult if you suspect someone you know is abusing drugs. It's also important for teens to understand and be able to talk about the mixed messages movies, TV shows, music, video games, and social media show so they can understand that drugs of any kind are not as harmless or fun in real life as media may show them to be.

Getting Help for a Substance Use Disorder

You or a friend should get help for a substance use disorder when you begin to realize you lack energy and don't want to do things you used to like to do. At this same time, you or your friend may also begin breaking promises you've made about the substance you are using. For example, you or your friend may promise to use on weekends only, and then you find yourself using during the week as well. Other examples of when you should get help include when you or your friend begin having problems in school, at home, with other people, or with law enforcement.

- *School.* Not turning in assignments, doing poorly on tests, skipping classes or school, and not being involved in activities you or your friend once enjoyed are signs you need help.
- *Home.* You or a friend may be fighting more with guardians or siblings at home than normal. You've begun distancing yourself from family members by staying in their rooms more than usual.
- *Other people.* You or a friend are having more disagreements with friends, or you no longer want to do things with your friends. You may be distancing yourself from friends you normally hang out with.
- *Law enforcement.* New or ongoing problems with law enforcement may be a sign of a substance use disorder, but is also a sign of personal crisis.

If you are having any of these problems or are seeing them in a friend, it is important you talk with a guardian or trusted adult and get help as soon as possible.

Treating Substance Use Disorders

People with substance use disorders need support from family, friends, and professionals. Sometimes people can stop using drugs on their own or with the help of their family and friends. Other times, they need help from health care professionals such as drug and alcohol counselors, psychotherapists, and medical doctors. Treatment is based on the needs of the person, so no one treatment option works for everyone. Before treatment can begin, the person needs to have a substance use disorder assessment. The result of the assessment determines the appropriate level of treatment.

LESSON 13.4 Legal and Illicit Drugs

Substance use disorder treatment is complex due to the treatment being specifically tailored to each person. Treatment may include individual therapy, family therapy, group therapy, and education. **Behavioral therapy** may be used to help people with withdrawal symptoms along with medication, when appropriate, by teaching them how to handle cravings, avoid situations and people who might trigger the desire to use the drug again, and prevent a relapse. A **relapse** occurs when a person begins using drugs again after they have stopped using. In general, treatment can fall into the following treatment classifications:

- Early intervention education
- Outpatient treatment of one to eight hours of services per week
- Intensive outpatient treatment of nine to 20 hours of services per week
- Residential inpatient treatment—24-hour residential care in which the person lives in a monitored setting
- Medically managed intensive inpatient treatment—a person being admitted into a hospital setting and monitored by medical professionals

School Policies

All schools have specific policies related to the use, possession, and sale of drugs on school grounds and at school functions on or off school grounds. Many schools also have policies for the use, possession, and sale of illicit drugs off school grounds if the teen is an athlete or a representative of the school through their involvement in other clubs or organizations. The school's student handbook describes how schools handle the use, possession, and sale of illicit drugs.

An example of a school policy for the use, possession, and sale of illicit drugs would be contacting the police and possibly enforcing long-term suspension or a short-term suspension with a drug assessment and meetings with a drug counselor. There are often legal consequences for underage use of alcohol, drugs, and other substances, such as juvenile drug counseling, probation, and juvenile detention.

Career Connection

SOCIAL AND HUMAN SERVICES ASSISTANT

Social and human services assistants provide a range of services, including support for families, in a wide variety of fields, such as psychology, rehabilitation, and social work. They assist other workers, such as social workers, by connecting clients to benefits or community services. Social and human services assistants have many job titles, including addiction counselor assistant, social work assistant, case work aide, family service assistant, and human service worker. For people with addictions, human services assistants identify and match rehabilitation centers to the needs of their clients. They can also help find support groups for people who are dependent on alcohol, drugs, gambling, or other substances or behaviors. In addition, social and human services assistants may follow up with clients to ensure that they are receiving the intended services and that the services are meeting their needs. A high school diploma and on-the-job training are required to become a social and human services assistant.

Community Laws

The juvenile justice process is different from the criminal justice process for adults. A juvenile is anyone under the age of 18. Juvenile courts have a much wider range of options when dealing with offenders. Juvenile courts tend to focus on rehabilitating juveniles rather than sending them away to jail or prison. Juvenile court judges may use alternative sentencing options if they determine that a juvenile meets certain requirements. The judge takes into consideration a juvenile's criminal history, their character, the nature and circumstances of the crime committed, the risks and needs of the juvenile, and whether it is necessary to imprison the juvenile to protect the public. Juveniles who commit drug crimes for the first time and who are not charged with transportation or intent to sell illicit drugs have a better chance of qualifying for alternative sentencing.

Juveniles may commit and get charged with a wide variety of drug crimes, including:

- possession of an illicit substance,
- sale of an illicit substance,
- intent to distribute an illicit substance,
- transportation of an illicit substance, and
- cultivation of an illicit substance.

Even a small amount of illicit drugs can result in serious legal charges being filed.

Alternative sentencing programs may include supervised or unsupervised probation, community service, electronic monitoring, Narcotics Anonymous (NA) meetings, behavioral management programs, therapy sessions, and outpatient and drug rehabilitation programs. Some alternative programs, if completed successfully, also allow the lowering or complete dismissal of charges.

Drug-Impaired Driving

Different types of drugs will have different effects on a person's brain. For example, marijuana can slow reaction time and decrease coordination; cocaine and methamphetamine can cause aggressiveness and recklessness; some prescription drugs such as opioids, muscle relaxants, and antidepressants can cause drowsiness and impair thinking and judgment; and some OTC drugs such as cold medicines can cause drowsiness or dizziness.

It is illegal for anyone in the United States to drive under the influence of any potentially impairing drug, no matter if it is prescribed or over the counter or is legal or illegal. At this time, drug-impaired driving is difficult to enforce because it can be difficult to determine if someone has used a specific drug: The only reliable roadside drug test currently available is for alcohol. Some drugs can stay in the body for days or weeks, making it difficult to determine if the drug impaired the driving at all. Many drivers who cause crashes often have both drugs and alcohol in their system, so it is also difficult to determine which substance had the greater impact.

LESSON 13.4 Legal and Illicit Drugs

Yet another challenge to consider that is specific to marijuana is that each state has different standards. Some states have zero tolerance for marijuana drug-impaired driving. Some have zero tolerance for THC. Further complicating matters is that some states designate specific amounts of THC that a person could consume before it's considered illegal to drive. Some states don't even have specific laws for drug-impaired driving, so any legal implications would fall under having possession of a drug.

Skill-Building Challenge

Accessing Information

Search online to locate an outpatient treatment program and a residential treatment program for teens in your area. Make sure they are two different treatment programs and that both work with teens. After you have located the two treatment programs and filled out the following chart, discuss your findings with a classmate.

	Outpatient treatment program	Residential treatment program
Program's name		
Program's location (If it's not in your city or town, about how far away is it?)		
Phone number		
Website		
Do they work with alcohol, tobacco, and drugs? List all that apply.		
How many programs do they have for teens? List at least three.		

Healthy Living Skills

This lesson focused on accessing information. Here is one more way you can develop healthy living skills related to this lesson.

PRACTICING HEALTHY BEHAVIORS

Choosing to be drug-free may be difficult to do at times, so it is important that you have a plan ahead of time to help you. Develop a checklist of ways to stay drug-free: Include people you should spend time with, places you can go after school, activities or clubs you could be involved in, healthy ways to relieve stress, activities you can do if you are bored, and anything else you can think of. Write "Ways I Can Stay Drug-Free" on a piece of paper and list your ideas. Each time you successfully make each choice, put a checkmark, smiley face, or other mark next to the behavior. At the end of the month, reflect on your progress.

LESSON 13.4 Review: Prevention, Treatment, and Being Drug-Free

LESSON SUMMARY

- A substance use disorder is a condition in which there is an uncontrolled use of a substance even though there are harmful consequences from its use (e.g., continuing use while knowing it's causing problems at school or with family or friends).
- Substance use disorders are classified as mild, moderate, or severe, depending on the criteria met.
- Addictive potential is determined by the drug's effects happening quickly, the feeling of great happiness and excitement beyond normal expectations, and whether both tolerance and withdrawal are effects of the drug.
- Barriers to being-drug free for teens can include users feeling they don't need treatment, aren't ready to stop using, can't afford the cost of treatment, worry about the negative impact of being out of school for an extended period of time, concern with what others may think, and don't know where to go for help.
- Behavioral therapy can help with withdrawal symptoms by teaching people how to handle cravings, avoid situations and people who might trigger the desire to use the drug again, and prevent a relapse.
- School policies about teen drug use vary from school to school. Make sure to review your student handbook to know what your policies are.

REVIEWING CONCEPTS AND VOCABULARY

1. A(n) _____ disorder results from the use of a substance that you continue to use even though you experience problems as a result.
2. A drug's _____ is increased by the level of difficulty and discomfort a person will have when trying to stop using the drug.
3. _____ is when a person requires higher doses of a drug to have the same effect.
4. When a drug is no longer being used, or has been reduced substantially, the signs and symptoms a person experiences are known as _____.
5. _____ helps people learn how to modify their attitudes and behaviors related to using drugs.
6. When a person begins using drugs again after they have stopped, it is known as a(n) _____.

THINKING CRITICALLY

Discuss with a classmate the short- and long-term health consequences of substance use disorders. Then discuss what you think your school should do to help prevent substance use.

TAKE IT HOME

Put together a list of resources in your community for people who have substance use problems. Give it to a family member or friend as a resource for themselves or for others they might know who have substance use issues.

Chapter Review

ACTION PLAN: Deciding to Be Drug-Free

Use the My Action Plan worksheet to quit using OTC or prescription products incorrectly. Here is an example.

My Action Plan: Stop Abusing Prescription Drugs

STEP 1: Identify the health behavior you are going to work on.

I am going to stop abusing prescription drugs to help me focus and make myself feel better.

STEP 2: Write SMART goal(s).
Write one or two short-term goals (one day to one month).

I will get a regular amount of sleep each night so I am rested and can focus better.

Write a long-term goal (one to six months or more).

I will not use anyone else's prescription drugs.

STEP 3: Make a plan.
Identify two to four action steps (strategies) you could do to meet your goal.

I will set an alarm on my phone 30 minutes before my bedtime so I can start getting ready for bed. This will help me relax and be ready to fall asleep.

I will chew gum to help me stay focused and alert.

STEP 4: Execute your plan and track your progress.

Short-term goal

☒ Met   ☐ Not met   Date: *November 18*

Long-term goal

☐ Met   ☒ Not met   Date: _____

If you met your goal, what helped you to be successful?

I have gotten eight hours of sleep each night this week. Setting an alarm for 30 minutes before I go to bed has made me aware of the time and has helped me get into a routine, so I am able to fall asleep quickly.

If you did not meet your goal, what made it harder for you to be successful?

For my long-term goal, I have done a lot better this week, but I didn't completely meet it. I have used my friend's prescription drugs twice this week. In the past, I might have used four times a week, so two times is better. It was hard to be successful because I like the way they make me really focused on what I need to do.

Test Your Knowledge

Select the best answer for each question.

1. Which three factors are drug ads required to tell consumers?
   a. prescription name, an approved use, risks of the drug
   b. risks of the drug, how it's advertised, prescription name
   c. generic name, risks of the drug, how it's advertised
   d. an approved use, generic name, risks of the drug

2. Ecstasy is a(n)
   a. stimulant
   b. inhalant
   c. hallucinogen
   d. depressant

3. Using a substance that you continue to take even though you experience problems as a result is called
   a. substance use misuse
   b. substance use abuse
   c. substance use
   d. substance use disorder

4. Which type of drug category should be used by one person only?
   a. generic
   b. OTC
   c. brand name
   d. prescription

5. Heroin is a(n)
   a. stimulant
   b. opioid
   c. hallucinogen
   d. inhalant

6. What is the fastest-growing drug problem in the United States affecting teens' mental and physical health?
   a. OTC drugs
   b. illicit drugs
   c. prescription drugs
   d. hallucinogenic drugs

7. Drugs that stimulate, depress, or cause hallucinations are _____ drugs.
   a. illicit
   b. prescription
   c. stimulant
   d. OTC

8. This category of drugs is composed of both legal and illicit drugs.
   a. inhalants
   b. opioids
   c. club drugs
   d. depressants

9. Meth is a(n)
   a. stimulant
   b. opioid
   c. hallucinogen
   d. depressant

10. Rubber cement, hair spray, gasoline, and nail polish remover are examples of
    a. stimulants
    b. inhalants
    c. hallucinogens
    d. depressants

PROJECT-BASED LEARNING: Reducing Prescription Drug Use in High School Students

What to Remember

Prescription drugs are designed to treat specific illnesses and conditions. Abuse of prescription drugs can be deadly.

Who It Is For

Adult family members, community members, and peers.

Why It Is Important

The use of prescription drugs, other than prescribed, by teens is the fastest-growing drug problem in the United States, affecting teens' mental and physical health.

What to Do

Create a multimedia presentation on the use of prescription drugs in high school to present at a school board meeting.

How to Do It

Work in a small team of three to five students. Conduct online research about prescription drug use by high school students to get the information you will need for your presentation. Remember to use the Checklist for Evaluating Health Websites to ensure you are using valid and reliable websites.

Checklist for Evaluating Health Websites

Who publishes the site? Consider the domain and what it might suggest. Start with .gov, .edu, and .org sites.

What is the purpose of the site? Try to get basic information from sites that are not selling a product or service.

What type of information is on the site? Look for sites that provide data from research and tell you where the data come from.

Is the information reviewed by experts? Use sites that tell you who wrote the information and what credentials they have.

Is the information current? Try to find sites that are no older than five years.

Create a presentation that addresses the following questions, uses multimedia (e.g., PowerPoint), and involves active participation by everyone in your group.

- Where do students get prescription drugs?
- Why are students using prescription drugs?
- Which prescription drugs are most commonly used by students?
- What are the signs you may see if students are using prescription drugs, other than prescribed?
- What are some possible consequences of using prescription drugs, other than prescribed?
- Provide statistics, if possible, on prescription drug use by high school students.
- Note that prescription drug use can lead to a substance use disorder.
- Provide additional resources.
- Add additional information as needed.

Practice your presentation so you can present without reading directly off your slides or notecards. Ask the people at the board meeting to make a plan of action to help reduce the use of prescription drugs in high school students.

CROSS-CURRICULAR CONNECTIONS: Social Studies

Research the history of a prescription drug that you or someone in your family has taken, or that you learned about in this lesson. Include information on how they have been controlled or regulated over the decades. Once you have your information, create a time line that shows how things have changed and evolved over time.

UNIT V

Protecting Yourself and the Environment

CHAPTER 14   **Injury Prevention, Safety, and First Aid**

CHAPTER 15   **Environmental Health**

14

Injury Prevention, Safety, and First Aid

LESSON 14.1   Injury Prevention and Safety at Home
LESSON 14.2   Safety in the Community
LESSON 14.3   Safety Online
LESSON 14.4   First Aid and Emergency Procedures

Understanding My Health

How Prepared Am I for an Emergency?

Having some basic knowledge about what to do in case of an emergency can help keep you and others around you safe in many situations. Answer *yes* or *no* to each question by putting an X in the corresponding box. Add up the total number of *yes* responses and use the guide at the end of the assessment to evaluate your score.

	Yes	No
I know how to reduce the risk of injuries in and around water.		
I know how to prevent sunburns.		
There are smoke alarms installed in my home.		
I always wear a seat belt when I am in a motor vehicle.		
I can be safe when using technology.		
I feel prepared if there is an active shooter situation in my school.		
I know basic first aid procedures.		
I know how to reduce the risk of injuries during sports and recreational activities.		
I know how to protect myself from hackers on social media and my phone.		
I know how to stay safe in a natural disaster if one occurs where I live.		

My score for How Prepared Am I for an Emergency? = _____ (total number of *yes* answers)

If you gave eight or more *yes* responses, you are well prepared to deal with a variety of emergency situations. If you gave six or seven *yes* responses, you are somewhat prepared to deal with a variety of emergency situations. If you gave five or fewer *yes* responses, you may be putting yourself at risk and may not be ready to deal with a variety of emergency situations.

Injury prevention, safety, and first aid are interconnected in your home, your community, and online. In your home and community, you should work at keeping injuries from happening by making your home, school, neighborhoods, and communities as safe as possible. Injury prevention and safety are often focused on your physical well-being, yet we also know mental and emotional safety are just as important. Knowing first aid and emergency procedures will be helpful if you get into a situation in which you or someone else needs help.

LESSON 14.1
Injury Prevention and Safety at Home

Terms to Learn
intentional injuries
natural disasters
safety conscious
unintentional injuries

The Big Picture
In the United States, injuries are the leading cause of death in people 19 years of age and younger. Falls, accidental shootings, poisonings, and fires can all be prevented by paying more attention to what you are doing. Natural disasters can happen anywhere and at any time. Being prepared for the natural disasters in your area can help prevent or lessen injuries, death, and significant property damage.

Learning Targets
- Differentiate between unintentional and intentional injuries.
- Analyze different ways to prevent falls in your home.
- Explain how to keep yourself and others safe from firearms in your home.
- Create a plan of what you should do if there is a fire in your home.
- Design a plan for what you would do if there was a natural disaster in your area.

Write About It
If you have been in a natural disaster, describe what happened. Was there something you wish you had done differently or had with you that you didn't? Why or why not? If you haven't been in a natural disaster, explain what natural disaster could strike where you live and what you are most worried about.

Note-Taking Guide
Use this chapter's note-taking guide to help you organize and remember the material in this lesson.

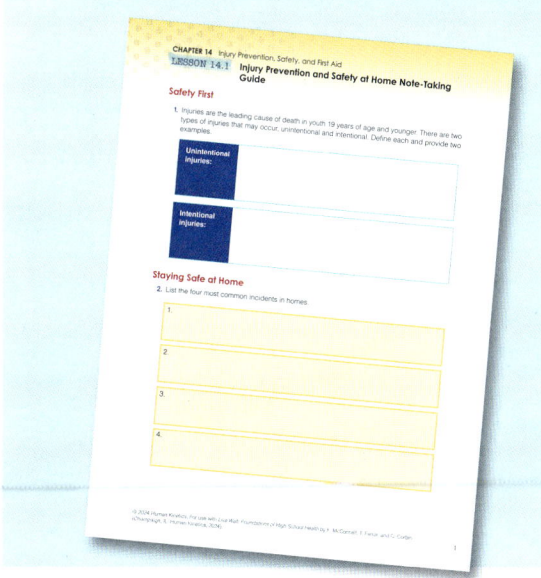

LESSON 14.1 Injury Prevention, Safety, and First Aid

Xander just got his driver's license and is excited to drive to school this morning. It is really cold outside, so he wants his car to be warm before he has to leave. He goes out to the garage to start it so it can warm up and goes back inside to finish getting ready. Xander is in the kitchen packing his lunch and suddenly starts to get a headache and feels dizzy. He's surprised by the suddenness and wonders what is happening. He finishes packing his lunch, and just as he opens the door from the kitchen to the garage, a wall of exhaust hits him. He quickly opens the garage door and scurries out into the fresh air. What do you think is wrong with Xander? Why is it important to open the garage door while the car is warming up?

Safety First

Injuries are the leading cause of death in youth 19 years of age and under. Most injuries are **unintentional injuries**—accidental or unplanned events such as motor vehicle crashes, drowning, poisoning, fires, and falls. Many unintentional injuries happen because people are not paying attention either to themselves or to what others are doing. **Intentional injuries** are caused by another person or are self-inflicted to cause injury such as violence, suicide, self-injury, and homicide. Being more **safety conscious**—trying to be safe and keep yourself and others from getting injured—can help you prevent many unintentional injuries. The benefits of reducing the risks for unintentional injuries in people of all ages include the potential to live free of disability or chronic pain and to avoid loss of productivity in all areas of your life.

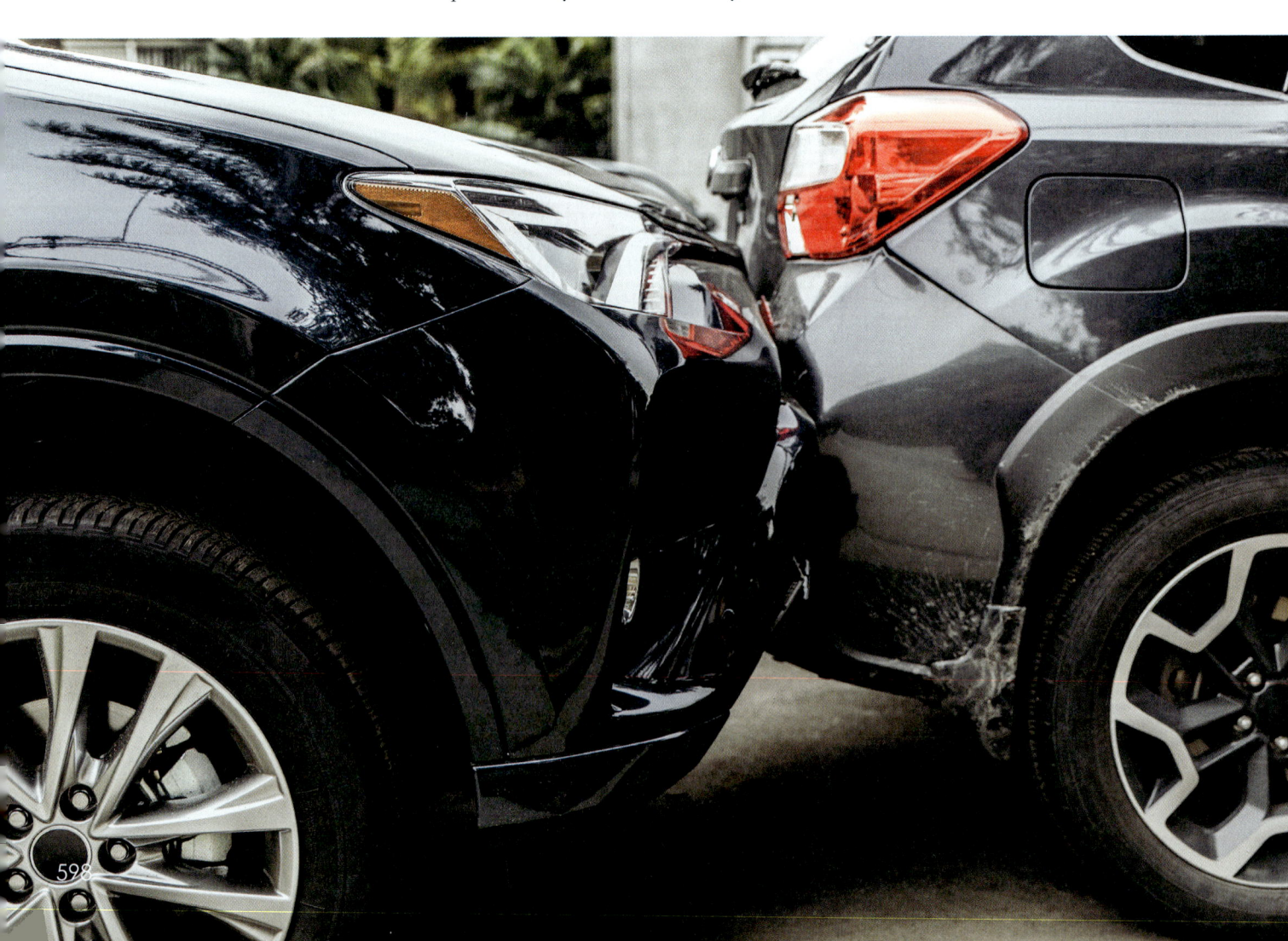

Injury Prevention and Safety at Home **LESSON 14.1**

Staying Safe at Home

Having the tendency to overlook or not think much about safety in our own homes occurs because we are naturally predisposed to feeling safe and comfortable there. Yet injuries and illnesses in our homes are very common. Four of the more common incidents in our home are associated with falls, poisoning, firearms, and fire.

Falls

Falls are the leading cause of nonfatal injuries for children and teens and among the most common, preventable, injury-related deaths in older adults. There are hazards in and around your home you may not even think about that could result in a fall, such as items left on the stairs you may not notice or electrical cords in areas you may trip on, and uneven yards or sidewalks. People can also fall while taking selfies either at home or in various locations. People are more focused on the selfie than on what they are doing and can easily become distracted, resulting in falls and serious injuries. Falls that result in injuries most often happen to children and teens because they tend to run more and are more easily distracted than adults are. Use the following tips for preventing falls in your home.

- Clear items off the floor so they aren't a tripping hazard.
- Make sure there is good lighting, especially outside.
- Use night lights so you don't trip in the dark.
- Don't stand on chairs or tables to reach something high; use a step stool instead.
- If using a ladder, make sure someone else is there to steady it for you.

Poisoning

Eating, drinking, inhaling, injecting, or absorbing through the skin an excessive amount of any substance that causes harm to a person results in poisoning. Children under the age of six tend to be unintentionally poisoned by ingesting personal care products (such as makeup, shampoo, or shaving cream), household cleaning supplies (especially detergent pods for laundry and dishwashers, because they look like candy), and the button batteries used in keyless remote door openers. Preteens and teens tend to be unintentionally poisoned by mixing different prescription medicines unknowingly.

A different kind of poison that you may not think about is carbon monoxide. Carbon monoxide is an invisible, odorless, colorless gas created when fuels such as gasoline, natural gas, or propane burn incompletely. A person can be poisoned by a small amount of carbon monoxide over a long period of time or by a large amount of carbon monoxide over a short period of time. Carbon monoxide poisoning is often heard about when cars are left running in a closed space, like a garage. Carbon monoxide poisoning can lead to severe illness and even death.

LESSON 14.1 Injury Prevention, Safety, and First Aid

If you think poisoning has occurred, you should call the Poison Control Center, 800-222-1222, or 911 immediately. The following are some tips to prevent poisoning.

- Only take prescription medicines that are prescribed to you and take them as prescribed.
- Always keep detergent pod containers closed, sealed, and stored out of the reach of children, as well as button batteries—especially if you have younger siblings who may not know what they are and may try to eat them.
- Have a working carbon monoxide detector in your home. Check with your guardian if you are unsure if you have these in your home.
- If your carbon monoxide detector goes off, immediately move to a fresh air location outdoors and call 911.

Poison Control Center:
800-222-1222

Firearms

Firearm safety is another aspect of staying safe at home. Having an unlocked, loaded gun in your home increases the risk of both intentional and unintentional deaths, including injuries and suicides of children and teens. Most of the guns used by youth under the age of 18 in suicides, unintentional shootings, and intentional school shootings are from their home or the home of a relative or friend. Use the following firearm safety tips to stay safe in your home.

- Keep all firearms unloaded.
- Use a firearm safe or lockbox to store firearms and keep it locked.
- Add gun locks to each firearm in addition to keeping them in a firearm safe.
- Keep the ammunition locked separately from the firearms.
- When using a gun for hunting, keep the safety lock in place until you are ready to fire.
- Treat every gun as if it were real and loaded.

Fire

HEALTHY LIVING TIP
Create a fire escape plan with your family. Make sure to include a gathering place where your family will meet after they are away from the fire.

Fire safety involves both planning to keep fires from ever starting and what to do if a fire does happen. A fire needs oxygen to keep burning. The fire triangle is a simple way to understand the elements of fire (figure 14.1). Each side of the triangle represents one of the elements needed for fire: heat, fuel, and oxygen. If any one of these elements is removed, the fire will go out. By keeping your door closed you cut off the oxygen supply and help contain the fire.

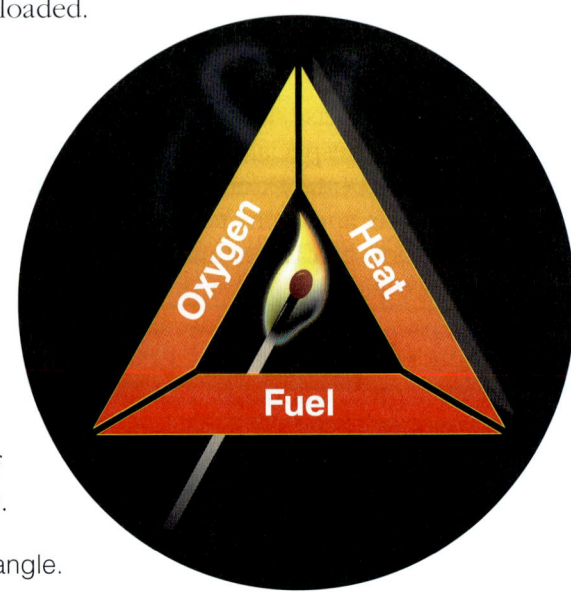

Figure 14.1 The fire triangle.

Fire Safety Tips

Tips to Prevent House Fires

- Change the batteries in the smoke alarms once a year.
- Stay in the kitchen; you should never leave a hot cooking surface unattended. Cooking fires are the number one cause of home fires.
- Electrical cords can produce heat, so don't trap them under a rug or between furniture and the wall.
- Place candles in tip-proof holders and extinguish them before leaving the room or going to sleep.
- Keep items that can catch on fire at least three feet away from anything that gets hot, such as wall heaters, space heaters, and fireplaces.

Make a Fire Escape Plan

- Try to have two ways out of every room in your house.
- The first way out should be a door. Every way needs to be planned and practiced.
- Stay low to the floor when escaping a fire.
- Have a gathering place outside where everyone in your family will meet after they get out.
- After you get out, call 911. Stay outside no matter what; don't go back in for anyone or anything.

Follow these steps if you live in a home:

- Get out quickly.
- If the fire alarm sounds, feel the door before opening and close all doors behind you as you leave. If the door is hot, find another way out.
- If you can't get out of your bedroom because of fire or smoke, stuff wet towels or sheets around the door and vents to keep smoke out.
- If your clothes catch on fire, stop, drop, and roll is the best way to put out the fire.
- If you have a two-story house, have escape ladders to exit through windows.

Follow these steps if you live in a high-rise apartment or condominium building:

- Know the locations of all the exit stairs from your floor in case the nearest one is blocked by fire or smoke.
- If there is a fire, pull the fire alarm on your way out to notify the fire department and your neighbors.
- If you can't get out of your apartment because of fire or smoke, stuff wet towels or sheets around the door and vents to keep smoke out.
- Call 911 and tell them where you are.
- Open a window slightly and wave a bright towel or cloth to signal your location. Be prepared to close the window if it makes the smoke condition worse.

LESSON 14.1   Injury Prevention, Safety, and First Aid

Natural Disasters

Natural disasters include all types of severe weather, and they have the potential to be a significant threat to human health, safety, and property. Severe weather can happen anytime in any part of the country. Natural disasters include winter storms, floods, thunderstorms, tornadoes, hurricanes, and earthquakes. Other natural disasters that may occur where you live include volcano eruptions, wildfires, hurricanes, and tsunamis.

Preparing for Disaster

While natural disasters can't be prevented, you *can* learn how to prepare for them. Winter storms, floods, tornadoes, hurricanes, and thunderstorms are weather phenomena and can be predicted. Earthquakes, volcano eruptions, wildfires, and tsunamis are unpredictable; we can't tell when they may happen. Even though you won't know if an earthquake, volcano eruption, wildfire, or tsunami is going to happen, you can be prepared in case one does. See the Creating a Disaster Preparedness Plan sidebar.

While each natural disaster brings about unique situations, some general ways you can prepare and stay safe regardless of the natural disaster include the following.

- Prepare for power outages and use generators outside only.
- Stay off roads if there is snow, ice, or flooding.
- Always evacuate if told to do so.

Lightning Strikes

- Avoid open areas and stay away from tall objects.
- Unplug appliances and other electric devices such as TVs and computers.

Tornadoes and Hurricanes

- Go to a basement, storm cellar, or small interior room without windows. Cover yourself with blankets or a mattress if possible to help protect you from flying debris or items falling on top of you. Only go to a basement area during a hurricane if flooding is not an issue.
- If in a vehicle:
  - Do not park under an overpass or a bridge because they may collapse.

Career Connection

METEOROLOGIST

A meteorologist studies and predicts the weather and climate and how it may affect our lives and economy. Meteorologists have a bachelor's degree or higher in many different fields, such as physics, chemistry, or math. Many jobs are open to meteorologists, such as forecasting the weather on TV or the radio, teaching at a university, doing atmospheric research, tracking and warning of hazardous weather, and providing forensic services, which means testifying in court cases that involve the weather. The job outlook for meteorologists is very good and is projected to continue growing.

- Stay in the car with the seat belt on and put your head down below the windows. Cover yourself with blankets or coats if possible to help protect you from flying debris or items falling on top of you.
- If there is a ditch that is lower than the roadway, leave your car and lie in the ditch, covering your head with your hands, blankets, or coats.

Earthquakes

- *Drop* to your hands and knees under a desk or table if possible. *Cover* your head and neck with your arms if possible. *Hold* onto any furniture you may be under.
- If you are outdoors, watch out for possible falling objects.

Creating a Disaster Preparedness Plan

Regardless of the natural disaster, it is important that you plan ahead. You can be more prepared for a natural disaster by completing the following steps.

1. With your family, discuss how to prepare and respond to the types of emergencies (winter storms, floods, thunderstorms, tornadoes, hurricanes, earthquakes, volcano eruptions, wildfires, tsunamis, etc.) that are most likely to occur where you live, learn, work, and play.
2. Identify responsibilities for each member of your household and how you will work together as a team. Don't forget about your pets and who will take care of them.
3. Practice as many elements of your plan as possible.

Here are two websites that offer disaster preparedness plans:

1. The Federal Emergency Management Agency (FEMA) has the *Family Emergency Communication Plan*.
2. The American Red Cross has the *Family Disaster Plan Template*.

Here are things you can do to prepare for a natural disaster:

- Listen to a radio or look online for information and instructions as to what is happening and what to do. If you have to try to get to shelter, watch for fallen power lines.
- Sign up for your community's warning system or your state's emergency alert system.
- Make sure you have food that will keep if the power goes out, water, first aid supplies, medicines, flashlights, and batteries in case you are stuck at home for several days. Think about having supplies in your family cars in case you are stuck somewhere and cannot get home.
- Make sure you have food and water for your animals as well.
- Plan how you will communicate with family members after a disaster. Often, the phone lines will be too busy to get through, so texting may be a better option.

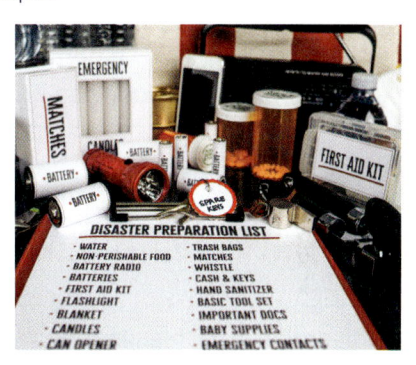

LESSON 14.1 Injury Prevention, Safety, and First Aid

Skill-Building Challenge

Advocating for Gun Safety

Work in a group with other students in your class who have a similar interest in how you want to present this information. You may have seen national news stories about gun violence and want to try to do something to help prevent such an incident in your school and community. People need to know that most guns used by youth and teens are obtained from their home or from a family friend. Gun violence at school is not just about the person with the gun; it starts from where they got the gun to begin with, which involves the home and the community.

You want to persuade family members and community members to lock their guns up so youth and teens cannot get to them. You also want to convince elementary, middle school, and high school students to speak up if they hear of someone having a gun at school or talking about harming others. Use the Advocacy Skill Cues and the following questions to complete the challenge.

1. What is the exact issue you will advocate for? Why is it important? Find research and statistics on your issue so you can show people it is a valid issue. Look at both sides of the issue to make sure you understand other perspectives.

2. What are some realistic solutions to the problem? Think about why people may not agree with your solutions and how you could change their mind.

3. Who will support you in your advocacy? Find other students, teachers, school staff, community members, and family members. You can even reach out to your social media friends for support.

4. Take action. To whom will you present your message? Work with your school district and community groups to help spread your message.

Healthy Living Skills

This lesson focused on advocacy. Here are some more ways you can develop healthy living skills related to this lesson.

ACCESSING INFORMATION

Identify a natural disaster that could happen in your area (e.g., earthquake, tornado, tsunami, hurricane, fire). Conduct online research to determine what steps people in your community should take to stay safe during the disaster and to get the help they may need after the disaster. Use the information you find to create a public service announcement (PSA). Include information on the natural disaster: what it is, how likely it is to occur, how it may affect people in the area, what people may need to survive if they can't leave or get to their home, and a list of community resources as part of your information. Be sure to use valid and reliable sources of information when creating your PSA.

Injury Prevention and Safety at Home **LESSON 14.1**

> **ANALYZING INFLUENCES**
>
> The information in this lesson was on how to keep yourself safe: safety in your home, firearm safety, fire safety, and how to be safe in a natural disaster. There was also information on how to prepare for these situations, such as having gun locks and keeping firearms in a safe or lockbox, creating a fire escape plan, and preparing for a natural disaster. Many people will not take the steps necessary to prepare for these types of situations. Choose one of the three examples—firearm safety, a fire escape plan, or preparing for a natural disaster—and use the Analyzing Influences Skill Cues to respond to the following.
>
> 1. List all possible influences that could cause a person to prepare for the situation you chose.
> 2. Evaluate whether the influences are positive (proactive to the situation) or negative (reactive to the situation).
> 3. What could be the possible positive outcomes if the person was proactive to the situation and what could be the possible negative outcomes if the person was reactive to the situation?

LESSON 14.1 Review: Injury Prevention and Safety at Home

LESSON SUMMARY

- Most teen injuries are unintentional and can be prevented by paying more attention to what you are doing or what other people around you are doing. Intentional injuries are either caused by someone else or are self-inflicted.
- Falls are one of the most common unintentional, preventable injuries. They can be easily prevented by making sure the floor space is clear of items, there is good lighting outside so you can see at night, and paying attention to where you are going and what you are doing.
- Firearms should be kept unloaded and in a locked firearm safe. Locks can be added to individual firearms even in a firearm safe for extra safety. You should never treat a gun as if it were a toy and always assume a gun is loaded.
- The most important things to do if there is a fire in your home are to get out as quickly as possible and call 911 immediately. Know the different ways you can get out of a room and out of the house. If you live in an apartment building, know the locations of all the exit stairs from your floor. If you can't get out of your room or your house because there is smoke or fire, stuff wet towels or sheets around the door and vents to keep smoke out. Hang a brightly colored item out your window to let fire fighters know where you are if you cannot get out.
- A natural disaster is any type of severe weather that has the potential to be a significant threat to human health, safety, and property. General guidelines for preparing for a natural disaster include making sure you have food that will keep if the power goes out, water, first aid supplies, medicines, flashlights, and batteries in case you are stuck at home for several days.

LESSON 14.1 Injury Prevention, Safety, and First Aid

REVIEWING CONCEPTS AND VOCABULARY

1. _____ injuries are caused by accidental or unplanned events.
2. Suicide and homicide are two examples of _____.
3. When you are trying to be safe and prevent yourself and others from getting injured, you are being _____.
4. A(n) _____ includes all types of severe weather that has the potential to be a significant threat to human health, safety, and property.
5. Most guns used by youth under the age of 18 are from their _____ or the home of a _____ or _____.
6. The three elements needed for fire are _____, _____, and _____.

THINKING CRITICALLY

Discuss with a friend or trusted adult what you would do if you heard about a classmate who was talking about bringing a gun to school. Would you tell someone, and if so, whom would you tell? Would you talk to the classmate beforehand? Why or why not? What would you do to protect yourself and others?

TAKE IT HOME

Look around your house and see if you have any smoke alarms and carbon monoxide alarms. Both types of alarms tend to look similar, so you may need to ask a family member to differentiate the two. There should be a smoke alarm in each bedroom, in the hallway of the bedrooms, in the living room, near a stairway if you have one, and on every level of the home including the basement. Carbon monoxide alarms should be located in the hallway of the bedrooms and on every level of the home. Find out from a family member when they were last tested and when the batteries were changed. Smoke alarms and carbon monoxide alarms should be tested every month, and the batteries changed at least once a year.

LESSON 14.2
Safety in the Community

Terms to Learn
active shooter
distracted driving
driving under the influence (DUI)
drowsy driving
public transportation
ride-hailing service

The Big Picture
Your community consists of your school, your neighborhood, where you work, and the public places you may visit such as movie theaters, parks, restaurants, and stores. Staying safe in your community is very important. While we all hope to be safe wherever we are and with whatever we are doing, we need to make sure we are taking precautions to help keep ourselves and those around us safe. This lesson discusses ways to be safe and free of injury: being aware of your surroundings, including who is in the area with you, and being cautious when using any form of transportation.

Learning Targets
- Explain three actions schools are taking to be safer and more prepared for dangerous situations.
- Discuss three ways to stay safe in a public place.
- Analyze why male teens, teens driving with teen passengers, and teens who have just obtained their license are the three groups at the highest risk for a motor vehicle crash.
- Identify three ways to stay free of injuries at a job.

Write About It
Whether it was you driving or being a passenger in a vehicle, have you ever been in an accident or almost in an accident because the person driving was reading or responding to a text? Did it make you rethink your behavior in the situation? For example, if you were driving, has it kept you from using your phone while driving? If you were a passenger, has it made you say something to the person who is driving while checking their phone? Why or why not?

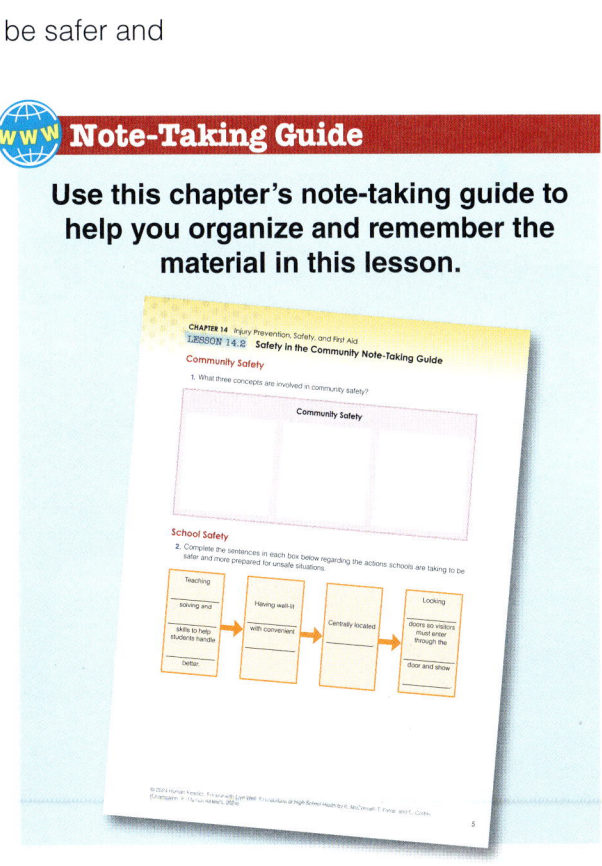

Note-Taking Guide
Use this chapter's note-taking guide to help you organize and remember the material in this lesson.

607

LESSON 14.2   Injury Prevention, Safety, and First Aid

While driving to school one morning, Sydney notices a black SUV behind her is weaving in and out of traffic and speeding. Sydney pulls into the right lane hoping the SUV will get by her safely. As the SUV speeds by, Sydney sees the driver looking at his phone and realizes they go to the same school. Would you call 911 and report the speeding, distracted driver or would you say something when you see him at school?

Community Safety

A community can be described as a group of people with a common interest participating in similar activities or having similar experiences. You have a variety of communities, which include your school, public places you go to, home, and online social media, among others. It is important to be able to stay safe in all your different communities. Community safety involves reducing injuries, practicing safe behaviors, and working to change unsafe situations.

School Safety

In an ideal world, your school would always be a safe place for you, your teachers and classmates would be supportive and encouraging, and your education would be nothing less than a positive experience for you. Unfortunately, that's not a realistic take on life. There have probably been times when you felt picked on or even bullied by other students. Bullying stems from a real or perceived difference in power and occurs multiple times. If you are being bullied, or if you feel threatened or unsafe in any way, you should ask a trusted adult for help.

All schools have rules and policies for keeping students safe. Students are responsible for following the rules and for alerting teachers and school staff about unsafe or dangerous situations, such as a weapon being brought to school, alcohol or drugs being used or sold, or anyone who is being bullied; it is then the teachers' and administrators' responsibility

Safety in the Community   LESSON 14.2

to enforce these rules. Schools should strive to have a safe and welcoming environment where both students and adults feel safe and supported. If you see or hear about something that makes you feel unsafe, report it to an adult. By telling an adult what you saw or heard, you can reduce the chance of injuries and unsafe situations at your school.

Schools are taking actions to do what they can to be safer and more prepared for unsafe situations. Such actions may include teaching problem solving and communication skills to students to help them handle their emotions more effectively. Schools are also working on improving school designs by building well-lit hallways that have convenient exits instead of dead-end hallways. Office areas are centrally located so they are easy to access from all locations in the building. Schools are also locking all outside doors; all visitors must enter through one main door and show identification. Visitors are given a badge to wear to let students and teachers know they have been cleared through the office. While these changes are a good start in helping keep students and teachers safe, everyone has to do their part to speak up when problems exist.

Active Shooter Situations

An **active shooter** is a person who is actively engaged in killing or attempting to kill people in a populated area. In today's schools, an active shooter drill is just as common as a fire drill. While there may be some variations to how you should respond to an active shooter situation, the FBI suggests you run, hide, and fight (see figure 14.2). Make sure you pay attention to what your school policy is for an active shooter and follow directions closely if ever in that situation.

If you hear of someone having a gun at school, either tell a trusted adult you know or call 911. Even if you aren't sure whether someone actually has a gun or not, it is better to be cautious and find out the truth than to not say anything and have people get hurt. If you find a gun, call 911 so it can be safely removed from the area. Do not pick the gun up or play with it because you don't know if it is loaded or not.

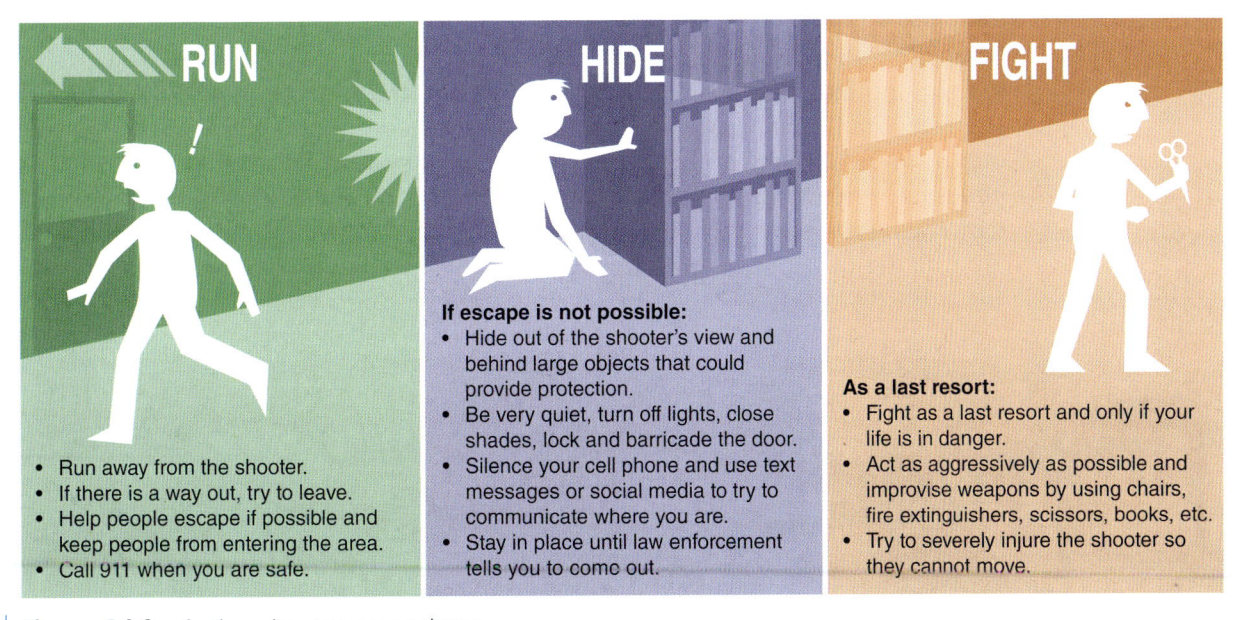

RUN
- Run away from the shooter.
- If there is a way out, try to leave.
- Help people escape if possible and keep people from entering the area.
- Call 911 when you are safe.

HIDE

If escape is not possible:
- Hide out of the shooter's view and behind large objects that could provide protection.
- Be very quiet, turn off lights, close shades, lock and barricade the door.
- Silence your cell phone and use text messages or social media to try to communicate where you are.
- Stay in place until law enforcement tells you to come out.

FIGHT

As a last resort:
- Fight as a last resort and only if your life is in danger.
- Act as aggressively as possible and improvise weapons by using chairs, fire extinguishers, scissors, books, etc.
- Try to severely injure the shooter so they cannot move.

Figure 14.2 Active shooter procedures.

609

LESSON 14.2 Injury Prevention, Safety, and First Aid

Public Safety

You are at an age when you often have the freedom to be out on your own and with your friends in public and private places. With this freedom also comes responsibility to be more aware of your surroundings: both where you are and who is around you. While it may be fun to go to the mall or to the movies and to take different types of transportation, you have to stay aware of your surroundings so you can stay safe.

Tips to Stay Safe in Public Places

- Always tell your guardian where you are going, how you are getting there, and whom you are going with.
- Never accept rides from strangers.
- Be alert for suspicious people or vehicles.
- Avoid walking alone at night.
- Always have your cell phone with you and make sure it is fully charged.
- Carry only as much cash as you need.
- Trust yourself, and if you feel uncomfortable in a location, leave as quickly as you can.

Pedestrian Safety

No matter where you live, you will eventually have to cross a street or get from the parking lot to the store or school as a pedestrian. According to the National Highway Traffic Safety Association (NHTSA), a pedestrian is killed every 85 minutes in traffic crashes in the United States. Most pedestrian deaths occur when a pedestrian tries to cross the road where there is no intersection and when it is dark. Being aware of your surroundings and everything that is going on when you are walking or jogging can help keep you safe (see figure 14.3).

Safety in the Community **LESSON 14.2**

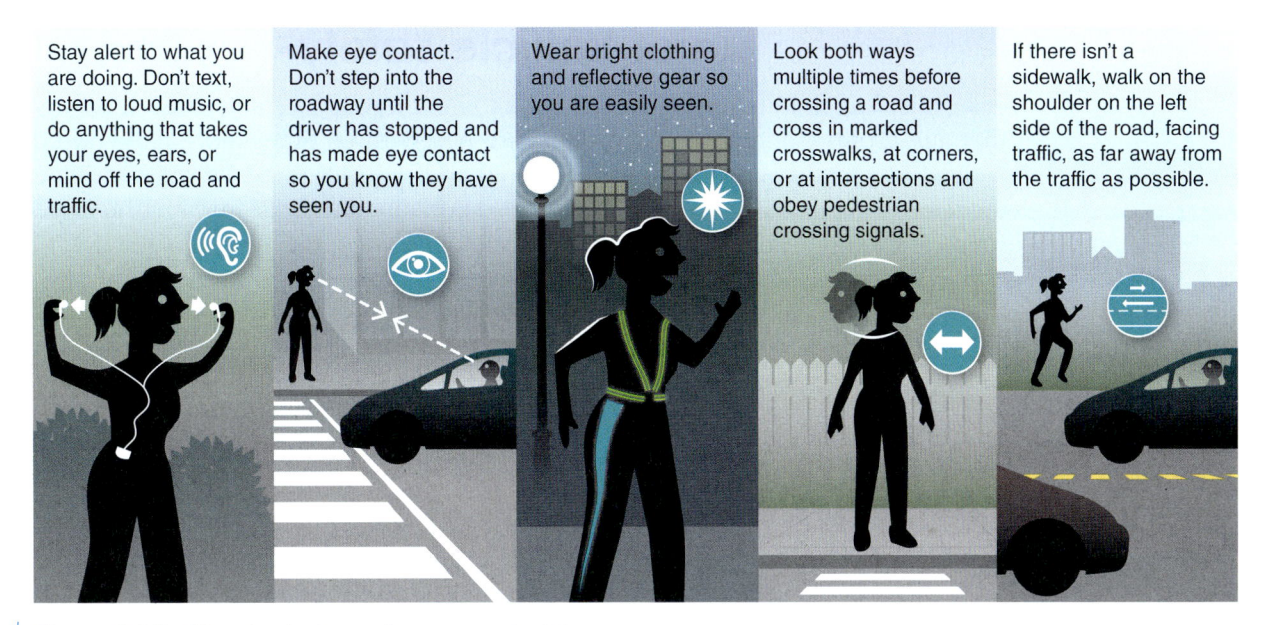

| Stay alert to what you are doing. Don't text, listen to loud music, or do anything that takes your eyes, ears, or mind off the road and traffic. | Make eye contact. Don't step into the roadway until the driver has stopped and has made eye contact so you know they have seen you. | Wear bright clothing and reflective gear so you are easily seen. | Look both ways multiple times before crossing a road and cross in marked crosswalks, at corners, or at intersections and obey pedestrian crossing signals. | If there isn't a sidewalk, walk on the shoulder on the left side of the road, facing traffic, as far away from the traffic as possible. |

Figure 14.3 Tips for being safe as a pedestrian.

Bicycle Safety

Bicycles are a great form of transportation when going to a friend's house, riding to school, or just getting some exercise. Youth ages five to 19 are more likely to get injured or die in a bicycle crash than by being a passenger in a motor vehicle. To help prevent such injuries, it's important to follow the same tips as those for pedestrians in the Pedestrian Safety section of this lesson with one significant difference: You must ride with traffic rather than against it as you would if you were walking. When riding it is important that you ride with traffic and follow all traffic signs and signals just like a motorized vehicle. When riding your bicycle it is also important to always wear a properly fitted bicycle helmet to reduce head and brain injuries in the event of a crash (see figure 14.4). If you are riding at night, make sure you have active lighting, which is a light source, not just a reflector, that transmits light so you can be easily seen: white on the front of your bike and red on the back.

Figure 14.4 Wearing a properly fitted helmet helps reduce injuries.

Motor Vehicle Safety

Teen drivers, ages 15 to 19, are more at risk to have a motor vehicle crash than any other age group (see figure 14.5). Teens are nearly three times more likely to be involved in a fatal crash than drivers ages 20 and older. Male teens, teens driving with teen passengers, and teens who have just obtained their license are the three groups at the highest risk for a motor vehicle crash.

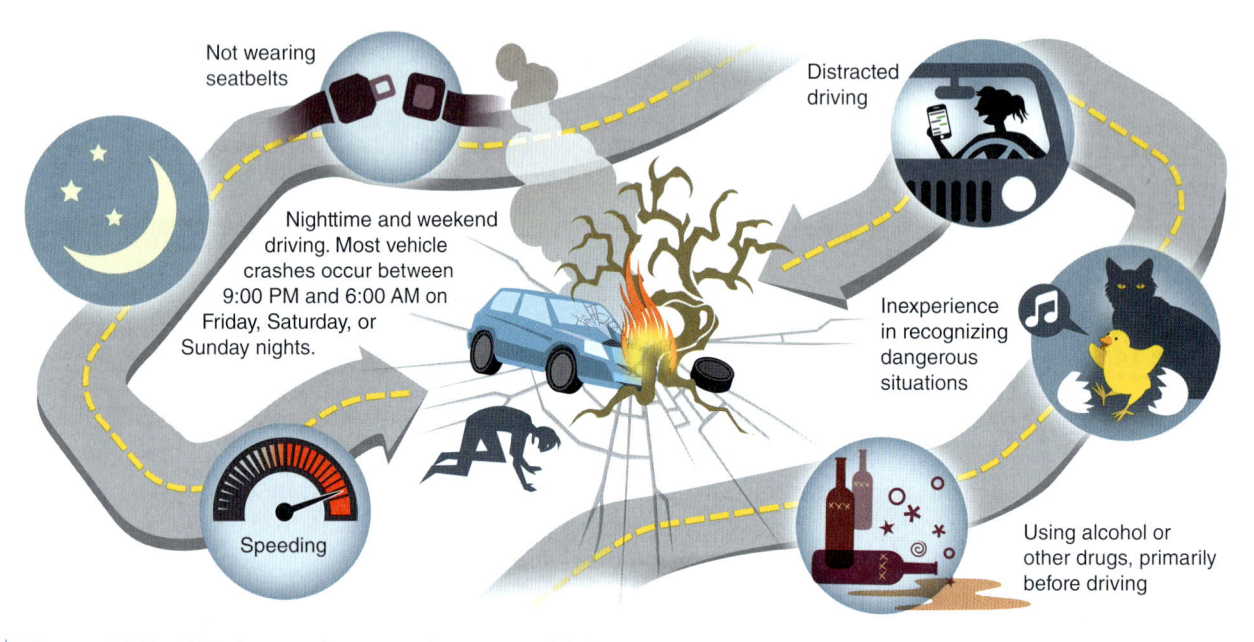

Figure 14.5 Risk factors for teens in motor vehicles.

Graduated Driver Licensing (GDL)

Every state has some type of three-stage graduated driver licensing requirement. The GDL is put in place to provide a longer period of time to practice driving, limit driving at night, and minimize high-risk driving situations overall for new drivers. The two most common examples of GDL laws include the maximum number of passengers that can be in the car and nighttime driving restrictions for new drivers. GDL laws vary state to state, so make sure you know the laws specific to your state.

Seat Belts

Seat belts help save lives when used properly (see figure 14.6). Approximately 47 percent of teen drivers and their passengers who die in vehicle crashes are not wearing a seatbelt at the time of the crash. Wearing a seatbelt is a federal law; it is the easiest way to reduce the chances of serious injuries and death.

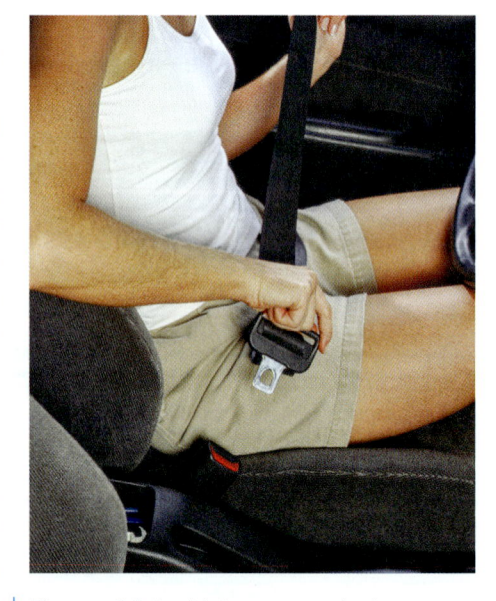

Figure 14.6 Using a seat belt properly can save your life in a car crash. Remember SAFE: **S**eat belts **A**re **F**or **E**veryone.

Distracted Driving

Distracted driving is any activity that takes the driver's attention away from driving. Activities may include using your cell phone to talk or text even if it is hands-free, eating and drinking, talking to people in your vehicle, and adjusting the stereo or navigation system. Sending or reading a text for as little as five seconds, at 55 miles (89 km) per hour, is the same as driving the length of a football field with your eyes closed. Imagine the horrible things that could happen in that amount of time and distance.

Aggressive Driving and Speed

Aggressive driving, described as multiple unsafe driving behaviors with speeding being a leading behavior, is a significant cause of traffic crashes, many of which are fatal. Other behaviors of aggressive driving include tailgating, weaving in and out of traffic, passing where prohibited, and driving too fast for the conditions, such as wet roads. In a study by the Governors Highway Safety Association, U.S. teen drivers and passengers, ages 16 to 19, were involved in more speeding-related fatalities than all other age groups. The study also found that of the speeding-related teen fatalities, the driver was most often male, had run off the road, or had rolled the vehicle without wearing a seatbelt.

Driving Under the Influence

Driving under the influence (DUI) includes operating any type of motorized vehicle—cars, trucks, lawnmowers, mopeds, motorcycles, watercraft, and even bicycles—while being under the influence of drugs or alcohol. A DUI citation can be given to a person who has been drinking alcohol, is under the influence of drugs (OTC, prescription, and illicit), or is driving while drowsy. Alcohol, followed by marijuana, are the two most common DUI-related substances. Both impair judgment, decision making, motor skills, and reaction time. Alcohol impairment can begin after one or two drinks, depending on the person. Marijuana impairment, on the other hand, is more difficult to distinguish in terms of quantity, which is influenced by the method of consumption, quality of the cannabis, and the THC levels in the cannabis. Regardless, any amount of alcohol, marijuana, or any other drug will affect your ability to drive.

Safe Driving Tips for Teen Drivers

- *Buckle up.* Everyone in the vehicle needs to properly wear their seat belt every time they get into a vehicle.
- *Have zero tolerance for drinking or impaired driving.* There is no amount of alcohol or any substance that can be safely used before driving, and it's against the law.
- *Limit the number of passengers in the vehicle.* Many states already stipulate the number of passengers allowed under the GDL laws. Make your own "laws" if the GDL number is too high.
- *Avoid distracted driving.* Put your phone somewhere out of reach or turn it off so it isn't a temptation to check or to respond to messages. If you do need to use your phone, safely pull off the road before answering or texting.
- *Do not speed.* Know what the speed limit is and stick to it. Speeding, especially in neighborhoods where kids may be playing, can prevent a person from stopping in time to prevent an accident.
- *Use extra caution when driving at night or in bad weather.* It can be more challenging to see at night; in rainy or snowy conditions, it can even be more difficult. Slow down and be more attentive to everything around you when driving in challenging conditions.
- *Speak up if you feel unsafe.* If you feel unsafe or uncomfortable as a driver because of your passengers (being loud or disruptive) or road conditions, make sure you let the people in the car know how you are feeling so they can adjust their behavior to help you to feel more comfortable and confident.

Driving While Drowsy

Drowsy driving, which is the combination of driving and sleepiness or fatigue, can cause impaired judgment and delayed reactions in drivers. Drivers with less than five hours of sleep are as dangerous as drunk drivers. People overall tend to overestimate how alert they really are, and turning up the radio or rolling down the window may help for a moment but won't keep a person from falling asleep at the wheel. Being sleepy while driving makes drivers less able to pay attention to the road, slows reaction time if you must brake or steer suddenly, and affects your ability to make good decisions.

Motorcycle Safety

If you are riding on a motorcycle or an ATV, make sure you always wear an approved motorcycle or ATV helmet that fits correctly, no matter how fast or how far you will be going. All helmets should be Department Of Transportation (DOT) compliant and have the DOT sticker on them. Helmets reduce the risk of death by 37 percent and the risk of head injuries by 69 percent.

All states require a motorcycle license of some kind to ride on the street. Completing a motorcycle rider education course is a great way to make sure you have the proper instruction and experience it takes to safely ride a motorcycle.

Riding a motorcycle requires the rider to be more aware of their surroundings, requires more coordination than driving a car, and involves more risks because motorcycles aren't as easily seen as a car. Many motorcycle accidents occur due to other drivers not seeing the motorcyclist: They pull out in front of motorcycles, are distracted while driving, and fail to use their turn signals when changing lanes. Many motorcycle collisions occur because of careless drivers. Motorcyclists who drive defensively and try to anticipate drivers' actions are best at avoiding accidents and serious injuries.

Safety Tips for Motorcyclists

- Always wear proper clothing, shoes, and a helmet.
- Wear brightly colored clothing with reflective material to be more visible to other drivers.
- Go easy on turns to keep from sliding.
- Make sure other drivers can see you.
- Watch the driver in front of you and behind you. Being rear-ended by a distracted driver is a common risk.
- Stay out of bad weather. Wet roads make riding dangerous.
- Never ride under the influence of any type of alcohol or drug.

ATV and UTV Safety

ATVs are all-terrain vehicles and UTVs are utility-terrain vehicles. Both are often used for recreational off-road riding. ATVs are typically built for single riders, and UTVs are designed to hold more people. In a two-seater UTV, people sit side by side. In a four-seater UTV, two people sit in front and two people sit in back, similar to an automobile. UTVs tend to be safer than an ATV in part due to the roll-cage-like enclosure, seat belts, and windscreen. They also have more functionality than an ATV because they can tow larger items and come with storage space to pack extra gear. It is illegal in most states for ATVs and UTVs to be driven on public streets and highways.

There are no federal regulations or age limits for riding an ATV or UTV, but each state has its own guidelines and laws for driving ATVs and UTVs. Some people may view ATVs as less dangerous and easier to handle than a motorcycle. This has the unfortunate effect of giving them a false sense of security, so they feel more confident and less cautious than they should be. The reality is ATVs and UTVs can be unstable and hard to control at times, and rollovers and collisions with rocks, logs, and other objects can result in serious injuries.

LESSON 14.2 Injury Prevention, Safety, and First Aid

Safety Guidelines for ATV and UTV Riding

- Take an ATV or UTV safety training course.
- Always wear proper clothing, shoes, and a helmet.
- Never ride or drive under the influence of any type of alcohol or drug.
- Ride only on designated trails and at a safe speed.
- Never carry a passenger on a single-rider ATV.
- Never carry more than one passenger on an ATV specifically designed for two people.
- Ride an ATV that's the right size for you.
- UTV drivers and passengers should be tall enough to keep their back flat against the seat back, their feet flat on the floor, and their hands on the hand holds as a passenger and the steering wheel as they drive.

Public Transportation Safety

Public transportation, such as buses, light rail, trains, and subways, is transportation that charges a set fare, runs on fixed routes, and is available to the public. If you take public transportation, it is important to be aware of safety procedures while you are waiting and once you are aboard. Consider the following tips:

- Avoid isolated areas to be picked up in.
- Keep the fare amount or pass ready in your hand.
- Stay alert and be aware of the people around you. If someone bothers you, change seats.
- Stay alert to your surroundings and limit your conversation to general topics.
- A legitimate bus, tram, or train driver has a badge or identification of some kind, so look for that before you get in the vehicle.

Ride-Hailing and Ridesharing Services Safety

HEALTHY LIVING TIP
Make sure that anytime you ride in a motor vehicle you wear a seat belt and encourage everyone else in the car to do so also.

Another type of transportation you might take is an Uber or a Lyft ride. These are two examples of a **ride-hailing service** or ridesharing service, which means you hail a driver and car from an app on your phone. This is different from public transportation because it takes you wherever you want to go rather than to designated stops. Uber and Lyft are car-for-hire services, which means you request an Uber or a Lyft, and a driver is dispatched. Uber and Lyft drivers do not have a special license like taxi drivers do. Instead, the drivers use their personal vehicles to offer discounted rides. If you are using an Uber or a Lyft, make sure the car make and model, license plate number, and driver's name and photo match the information on the app. If it doesn't, don't get in.

Staying Safe at Work

Many teens begin working while in high school; some have seasonal or year-round jobs. Teen workplace injuries involve slippery floors, hot grills and fryers, and sharp knives due to often working in the fast-food industry. Workplace injuries also occur because of inexperience and lack of proper training. Regardless of the job you may have, it is important you stay safe while working. Your employer is responsible for keeping the work environment safe. The Occupational Safety and Health Administration (OSHA) is responsible for enforcing laws around safe working environments.

Tips for Staying Safe at Work

- Know the labor laws for your age and state.
- Make sure you are properly trained and ask questions if you don't understand something.
- Be alert and recognize potential hazards in your workspace.
- Wear proper safety gear if applicable.
- Use safety equipment properly.
- Know and follow all safety rules and instructions.
- If working with tools and machines
  - don't remove machine guards,
  - follow maintenance schedules, and
  - never interfere with moving machinery.

Water Safety

Water activities include swimming, boating, water skiing, kayaking, stand-up paddleboarding, and many other fun activities. Injuries can include shoulder, back, and knee injuries from repetitive movements from swimming, kayaking, and stand-up paddleboarding. Water skiing and personal watercraft (e.g., jet skis, waverunners) can also result in collision-related injuries if the skier or driver hits the water at a high rate of speed. Injuries including sprains and fractures often happen to the shoulders, back, and knees. In addition to a variety of injuries, water activities also involve the risk of unintentional drowning. Prevent injuries and drowning by following these tips to stay safe in the water.

- Learn how to swim.
- Always swim with a friend and in areas with lifeguards.
- Make sure you wear a U.S. Coast Guard–approved life jacket when swimming if you are inexperienced or if you are on a boat of any kind.
- Do not dive in shallow water or water you can't see into. Enter the water feet first for your safety.

LESSON 14.2   Injury Prevention, Safety, and First Aid

- When swimming in lakes, rivers, or oceans, avoid swimming in really cold water and watch out for currents.
- If someone starts to struggle in the water or begins to drown, reach out and have them grab your hand or arm so you can pull them to a shallower depth. Make sure someone is also holding onto you so you don't get pulled in. You can also throw a life buoy or extend a pool noodle for the person to grab so you can pull them to the edge.
- Participate in a boater safety course.
- Don't use a personal watercraft or waterski at dusk or later.
- Do not use alcohol or drugs of any kind when swimming, boating, jet skiing, or using other watercraft. Any type of impairment caused by substance use may result in injury or death to yourself or others.

Skill-Building Challenge

Accessing Safe Transportation Information in Your City or Town

Search online to find resources that provide valid and reliable information in your city or town for the following situations:

- Which intersections or areas have the highest and lowest occurrences of accidents involving pedestrians and vehicles? Involving bicycle and vehicles?
- Which times of day and night are the safest and least safe to take public transportation?
- Which ride-hailing service, if your town or city has one, in your area has the best and worst safety records?

Healthy Living Skills

This lesson focused on accessing valid and reliable information. Here are some more ways you can develop healthy living skills related to this lesson.

HEALTHY COMMUNICATION

You are waiting at the bus stop for the 4:30 bus to take you to the mall. There is one other person, a stranger, at the bus stop with you. The bus is still 10 minutes away. A car pulls up with some guys from your school in it. You know one of them is your friend's brother who is meeting up with you at the mall. They are all being loud and laughing, and you can't tell if they are laughing at you or at something else. You feel very uncomfortable. Your friend's brother asks if you want a ride to the mall to meet his sister. You decline, but he persists, and now some of the other guys in the car start telling you to ride with them. Using your refusal skills, write out what you would say to the guys in the car.

PRACTICING HEALTHY BEHAVIORS

If you drive, keep track of how many times you check your phone while you are driving. Do you check it at stop signs and stop lights or sneak a glance when you get a new message or alert? If you don't drive, keep track of how many times the driver checks their phone while driving. Checking the phone may have become a habit for people and they aren't even aware they are doing it. Keep track for one week and then reflect on what you learned about your phone use or that of someone you ride with.

LESSON 14.2 Review: Safety in the Community

LESSON SUMMARY

- Schools are improving building designs to include hallways that have convenient exits and making office areas centrally located so they are easy to access from all locations in the building. Schools are also locking all outside doors so visitors must enter through one main door and show identification to get in. Schools are also developing policies for what to do in an active shooter situation with a focus on run, hide, and fight.
- To stay safe in public places, you should be alert for suspicious people and vehicles, avoid walking alone at night, and always have your fully charged cell phone with you when out in public.
- Male teens, teens driving with teen passengers, and teens who have just obtained their license are at the highest risk for a motor vehicle crash because they are often inexperienced in recognizing dangerous situations, may not wear seatbelts regularly, are often distracted while driving, and tend to speed.
- To avoid workplace injuries, make sure to get the proper training to do your job safely, stay alert for potential hazards in your workspace, wear proper safety gear when applicable, use safety equipment properly, and know and follow the safety rules and instructions.

REVIEWING CONCEPTS AND VOCABULARY

1. A person actively engaged in killing or attempting to kill people in a populated area is known as a(n) _____.
2. Teen workplace injuries are often caused by _____ and lack of proper training.
3. _____ is any activity that takes the driver's attention away from driving.
4. _____ stands for _____, which is when someone who is intoxicated gets behind the wheel of a car.
5. _____ driving is as dangerous as drunk driving.
6. Subways, which charge fares and run on fixed routes, are a type of _____.
7. Using an app on your phone to hail a driver and car to take you exactly where you need to go is a(n) _____.
8. List in order the three steps a person should take in an active shooter situation: _____, _____, and _____.

THINKING CRITICALLY

Do you think teens are more likely to engage in distracted driving? Research information on distracted driving and use it to help you with your answer. Write a paragraph to explain your perspective.

TAKE IT HOME

Whenever your best friend rides with you, he refuses to wear his seatbelt and constantly tries to show you stuff on his phone. You have repeatedly told him he needs to follow the law and wear his seatbelt and to stop showing you his phone, but he just gets mad and tells you to stop being so uptight. You need help with what to say to him so he will respect your requests instead of getting upset. Talk to a family member or trusted adult about ways in which you can talk to your friend.

LESSON 14.3
Safety Online

Terms to Learn
antivirus software
digital footprint
hacker
identity theft
malware
phishing attacks

The Big Picture
While the Internet and smartphones have enriched our lives with conveniences like being able to quickly get in touch with people and find information more easily, they have also led to widespread privacy issues. It is critical that teens understand the need to exercise great caution about sharing personal information on social media. Keeping your personal information secure online is very important not only to your safety but also to the safety others.

Learning Targets
- Evaluate how small or large your digital footprint is based on your online activity.
- Explain why it is important to know your social media privacy settings.
- Describe what identity theft is and how it can affect you.
- Examine the effectiveness of your passwords and change them if needed.

Write About It
List at least three ways you could be safer online in general or on specific social media sites.

Note-Taking Guide
Use this chapter's note-taking guide to help you organize and remember the material in this lesson.

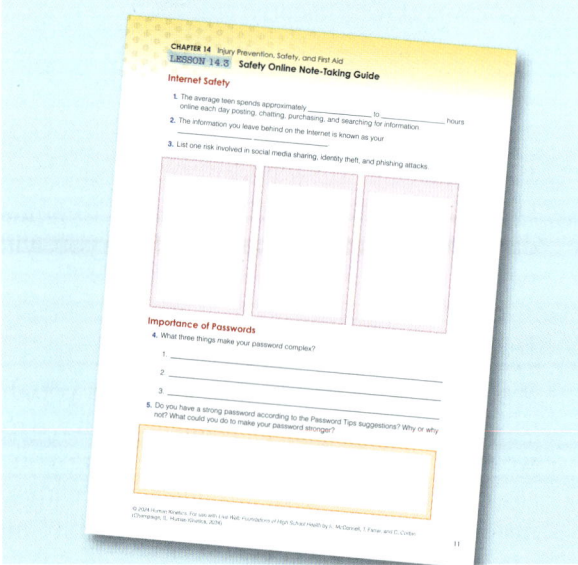

Safety Online LESSON 14.3

Kier often posts selfies of himself with friends drinking and partying as well as memes using inappropriate language and gestures on his social media platforms. Kier thinks all of his posts are hilarious and doesn't care what others think. Kier's ultimate goal is to play sports in college and get a degree in business. Do you think Kier's current social media use will affect his future opportunities and goals? Why or why not?

Internet Safety

It would seem the Internet has something for everyone. You can search for information, get help with homework, listen to music, stream shows and movies, play games, email, interact on different types of social media with friends and people who are new to you, listen to podcasts, go to school online, video conference, and so much more.

The average teen spends approximately seven to nine hours online each day, and, to be clear, this does not include time spent on school or homework. Posting, chatting, purchasing, searching—all the active time you spend online creates your **digital footprint**, or the information you leave behind on the Internet. Each and every time you are online, your digital footprint accumulates. Websites you visit, emails you send, social media you post, online shopping you do, and any personal information (name, address, credit card information) you provide for subscriptions or purchases all comprise your digital footprint. If one other person screenshots something you posted or shares it, even if you delete it, it still exists and is discoverable on the Internet. The Internet can be an amazing source of information, yet it also entails enough risks, such as social media sharing, identity theft, and phishing attacks, that you need to be vigilant about what you share.

HEALTHY LIVING TIP

Use a search engine to check your digital footprint. Enter your first and last names within quotation marks to see what information is publicly available about you. This gives you an idea of the information other people can find about you.

Social Media Sharing

Social media are websites and apps that enable users to electronically share information, ideas, personal messages, and other content and, in a sense, form online communities. Examples of social media sharing are tagging your current location when posting photographs and other content and checking in to a specific building or event. All of this makes it easy for criminals to see and track where you are, the people you are with, and what you are doing. Random strangers can contact, find, and even stalk you because you've led them directly to your location. Social media sharing also allows strangers to know when you're not at home, which could lead to break-ins. Avoid tagging yourself at locations or indicating you will be attending certain events. Check your phone, tablet, laptops, and the different social media platforms and apps you use to make sure location tracking settings are turned off. Often when you are looking for a location of something you will get a pop-up asking if your current location can be used. You should always make sure after you have found what you are looking for and have gotten the address or directions that you turn off the location tracking to keep your location private.

Check your privacy settings on your phone and the different social media platforms you use. Privacy settings allow you to control who can and cannot view information you are posting. While privacy settings still don't make it safe to share personal information online, they do provide another layer of security as to who can see what you are posting.

Identity Theft

Identity theft occurs when someone uses your identity or personal information without your permission to commit a crime. Your identity as a teen can be stolen just like that of an adult. The difference is that you won't necessarily know about it until you are applying for student loans or a credit card and are denied because you have maxed-out credit cards or unpaid bills. Make sure your computer and cell phone are protected with a password, fingerprint scan, or facial recognition. Use only websites and apps you know are trustworthy and make sure you always have the most recent versions of apps and operating system software, which include the latest security updates.

Phishing Attacks

Phishing attacks are fraudulent websites, apps, or emails that appear legitimate. Phishing schemes in the form of an email might ask you to sign into your gaming account because there's a problem that needs to be fixed right away. You click on the link in the email, which takes you to a website that looks just like your game; but, when you log in, all your personal information, including your username and password, has just been given to the attacker. The attacker now has access to your account, and if there is a credit card attached to it, they now have access to the credit card as well.

A phishing attack may also involve you clicking on a link that corrupts your files and causes you to lose all the information on your computer. To protect yourself, do not open emails or text messages from individuals you do not know and do not click on links within messages from anyone you do not know. Just delete the email or message.

Importance of Passwords

Begin your protection by having a strong password (see figure 14.7). Many of the hacks to your social media, email, and other online sites result from weak or stolen passwords. Your password should be complex and have multiple types of characters including numbers, letters, and symbols. Having a different password for each website or app also helps to defend against hacking.

Password:

****

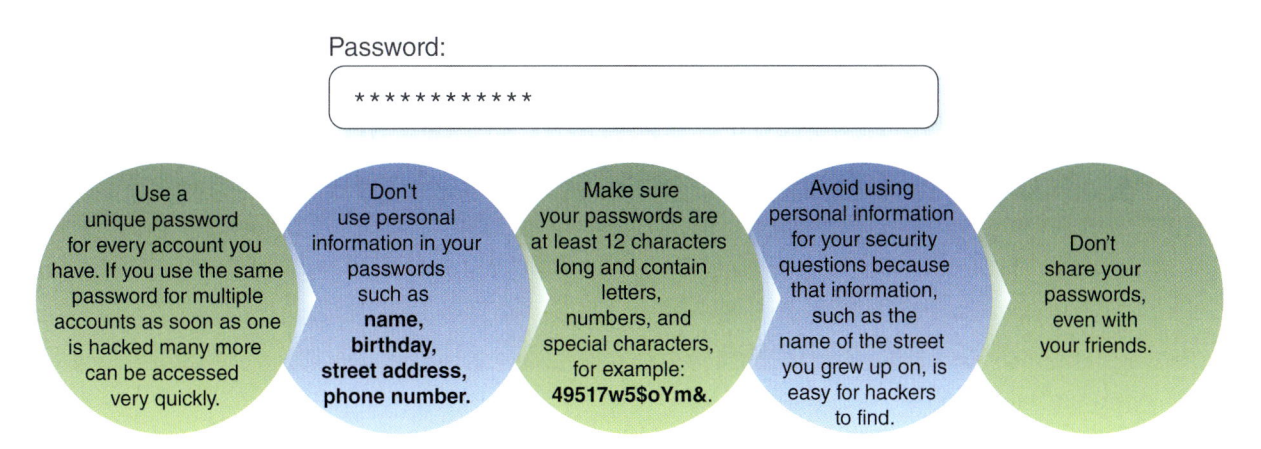

- **Use a unique password** for every account you have. If you use the same password for multiple accounts as soon as one is hacked many more can be accessed very quickly.
- **Don't use personal information in your passwords** such as **name, birthday, street address, phone number.**
- **Make sure your passwords are at least 12 characters long and contain letters, numbers, and special characters,** for example: **49517w5$oYm&.**
- **Avoid using personal information for your security questions** because that information, such as the name of the street you grew up on, is easy for hackers to find.
- **Don't share your passwords, even with your friends.**

Figure 14.7 Tips for creating a strong password.

Technology Safety Tips

1. Think before clicking on any links or apps on social media. If a link seems fake, don't click on it. Suspicious links, when clicked on, are intended to spread **malware**, a virus designed to invade your computer system and perform damaging actions to change the way it works. As soon as you click on a fake app or link, it can collect all your personal information including cell numbers, email IDs, passwords, home address, and other personal details. This is how your identity is stolen.

2. Think before you share your location; this includes double-checking with the people you are with if you can tag them in your post. Sharing inappropriate selfies and photos of you or friends or sharing personal details may not be a good idea because that information is out there for everyone to see.

3. Know your social media friends and don't accept friend requests from people you don't know in real life. Most **hackers** try to create a rapport with you by acting as if they know you. A hacker is a skilled computer programmer who hacks your password or gains remote access to your computer system to alter or steal information.

4. Adjust your privacy controls to limit the people who see your information, including your location. Don't always post where you are by sending pictures or tagging images with your live location displayed for all to see. Customize your setting or uncheck the box while installing a new app that asks your permission to access location details.

5. Use **antivirus software**, which is designed to detect, prevent, and remove malware. Make sure you also update it regularly to remain protected from the most current threats.

6. If you receive a message that makes you uncomfortable, do not delete the message and do not respond; instead, tell your guardian or another trusted adult.

7. Don't meet people in person you only know from being online.

8. Anything you upload, email, post, or message has the potential to remain online indefinitely. Even if you delete it, someone else may have saved a copy of it. Don't share anything you wouldn't want your guardians, teachers, future employers, potential colleges, or military branches to see.

9. Be careful about whom you give your cell number to and how you use your GPS or other apps that can pinpoint your physical location.

10. Secure your phone with a PIN, fingerprint swipe, or facial recognition.

LESSON 14.3 Injury Prevention, Safety, and First Aid

Skill-Building Challenge

Practicing Healthy Behaviors: Keeping Myself Safe on Social Media

Reflect on your own social media habits. If you are not allowed to use social media, partner up with someone who does and help them. Answer the following questions and then complete the final task.

1. How often do you use social media?
2. What social media do you use?
3. Why do you use social media?
4. What actions do you take to help you stay safe on social media? What things do you do that might not be safe?
5. What steps could you take to change your behavior so that it is safer? Identify as many specific actions as you can.
6. Create a way to track your social media behaviors (e.g., a daily checklist you can fill out). Include everything you already do that keeps you safe as well what you should be doing differently.

Final task: Log your social media behaviors for one or two weeks and reflect on how, or if, your behaviors improved and became healthier. If you are working with a partner, check in with them each day to see how they are doing with their behaviors.

Healthy Living Skills

This lesson focused on practicing healthy behaviors. Here are some more ways you can develop healthy living skills related to this lesson.

HEALTHY COMMUNICATION

If you find yourself in a situation where you are feeling unsafe at school, at home, or online, it is important to be able to tell a trusted adult what is happening so they can help you. Practice asking for help by using an *I* message. Use the following steps to create an *I* message you could use for asking a trusted adult for help.

1. Take responsibility for your feelings: "I feel . . ."
2. State the behavior that is the problem: "when . . ."
3. State what it is about the behavior or its consequences you don't like: "because . . ."
4. Suggest a preferred alternative: "I would really like it if . . ."

ADVOCATING FOR GOOD HEALTH

You know that you and many of your friends spend too much time online, and you want to have more face-to-face interactions with them. You're advocating for teens in your school to leave their phones in their lockers at lunch and spend quality time with their friends rather than looking at social media posts. Identify three to five reasons why face-to-face interactions are important. Put together a short presentation for your health class advocating for less time on social media and more time in person, face to face.

LESSON 14.3 Review: Safety Online

LESSON SUMMARY

- Your digital footprint is all the information you share online about what you are doing, who you are with, where you are, and the history of your online purchases and websites you've visited.
- The privacy settings on your social media accounts allow you to control who can and cannot see the information you are posting. Making sure your privacy settings allow only your known friends to see what you are doing can make your online presence safer. Make sure to also turn off location tracking information to keep your location private as well.
- Identity theft occurs when someone uses your identity or personal information without your permission to commit a crime. Use only websites and apps you know are trustworthy and make sure you always have the most recent versions of apps and operating system software so that you have the latest security updates.
- Passwords should be complex and unique, and you should have a different password for each website and app you use. Passwords should be 12 characters long and include letters, numbers, and special characters.

REVIEWING CONCEPTS AND VOCABULARY

1. Your _____ accumulates every time you are active online.
2. Having strong passwords and the latest security updates can prevent the crime known as _____.
3. Fraudulent websites, apps, texts, or emails that appear legitimate are known as _____.
4. _____ is another word for a virus designed to invade your computer system and perform damaging actions on it to change the way it operates.
5. A(n) _____ is a skilled computer programmer who gains remote access to a computer system to alter or steal information.
6. _____ is software designed to detect, prevent, and remove malware.
7. People should have strong passwords for their social media, email, and online resources, which include _____, letters, and _____.

THINKING CRITICALLY

Take time to check to make sure your identity hasn't been used by someone else. You could use a consumer credit report company to see if someone else has used your identity to open a credit card or get a car loan. Make sure to check with your guardian before doing this because they may already have the ability to check for you.

TAKE IT HOME

Talk to your family members about the importance of strong passwords and review the password tips from this lesson to strengthen their passwords, if needed.

LESSON 14.4

First Aid and Emergency Procedures

Terms to Learn

anaphylaxis
cardiac arrest
cardiopulmonary resuscitation (CPR)
cold-related emergency
concussion
first aid
heat-related emergency
shock
wounds

The Big Picture

Medical emergencies can happen anytime and anywhere. When a medical emergency does happen, it is important to know basic first aid so you can provide medical care. Being able to recognize that an emergency exists and, at the very least, call 911 can save someone's life.

Learning Targets

- Practice each of the emergency action steps.
- Explain why you should use universal precautions.
- Describe the steps to giving cardiopulmonary resuscitation (CPR).
- Identify the common signs of a sudden illness.
- Distinguish the differences between closed and open wounds.
- Describe two memory and thinking issues of a person with a concussion.

Write About It

What steps would you take if your guardian said they weren't feeling well and suddenly collapsed onto the floor?

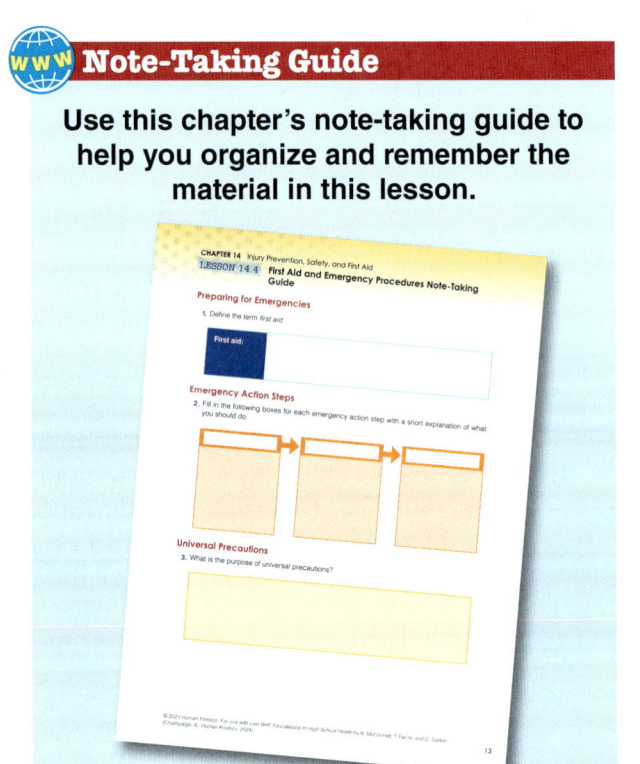

Note-Taking Guide

Use this chapter's note-taking guide to help you organize and remember the material in this lesson.

First Aid and Emergency Procedures **LESSON 14.4**

Bryce is playing volleyball with his friends on a Saturday morning. Craig spikes the volleyball hard, and it hits Bryce in the face. Now Bryce's nose and lip are bleeding, and it appears that two of his teeth are missing. What should Craig do to help Bryce?

Preparing for Emergencies

An emergency is an unexpected situation that requires immediate action. One of the first things you can do to prepare for an emergency is to have a first aid kit ready in your home and in your vehicles. If an emergency does happen, make sure the first thing you do is call 911. The sooner emergency medical services (EMS) arrives, the better chances the patient has for a positive recovery. In an emergency, you may be able to provide **first aid**, basic medical care to someone experiencing a sudden injury or illness.

Having a first aid kit on hand is one thing you can do to be prepared for emergencies. You can either buy one or assemble one. See figure 14.8 for the basic supplies recommended in a first aid kit. You should encourage your family members to put a list of any medications they take into the first aid kit, so everyone knows where the information is in case it is ever needed in a medical emergency.

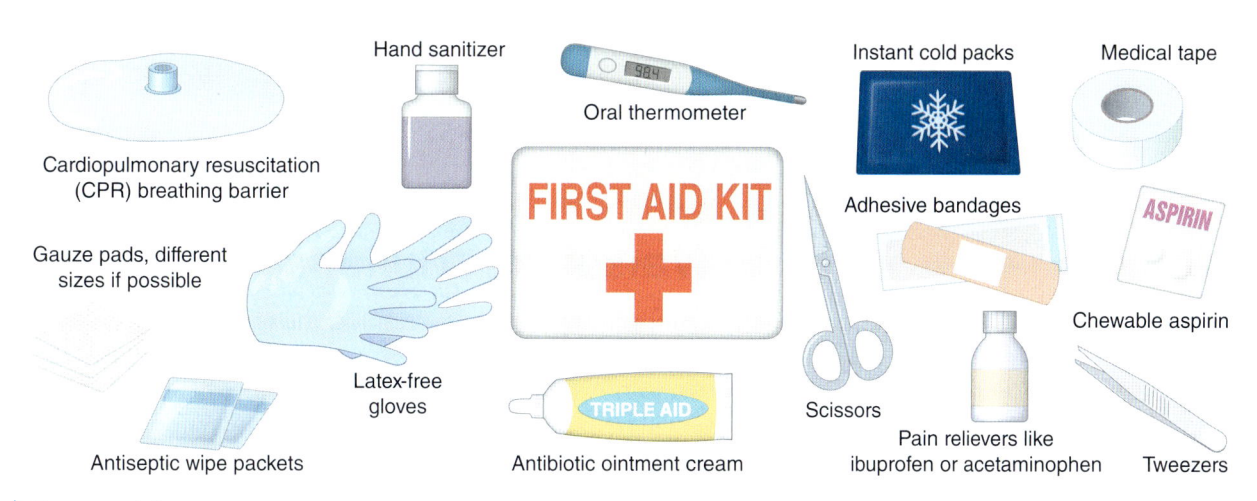

- Cardiopulmonary resuscitation (CPR) breathing barrier
- Hand sanitizer
- Oral thermometer
- Instant cold packs
- Medical tape
- Gauze pads, different sizes if possible
- Adhesive bandages
- Latex-free gloves
- Antiseptic wipe packets
- Antibiotic ointment cream
- Scissors
- Chewable aspirin
- Pain relievers like ibuprofen or acetaminophen
- Tweezers

Figure 14.8 First aid kit basics.

Emergency Action Steps

In any emergency situation, use the emergency action steps of check, call, and care:

1. Check the scene to make sure it is safe to enter and check the person to determine what the illness or injury might be.
2. Call 911 or have another person who is there with you place the call. See figure 14.9 for what you should tell the 911 dispatcher.
3. Care for the person according to the conditions that you find and your level of knowledge and training until EMS arrives.

Even if you are afraid to give care to the person, you can still be helpful by calling 911.

LESSON 14.4 Injury Prevention, Safety, and First Aid

Tips for Calling 911

When calling 911, be prepared with the following information:

- *Location of the emergency.* If you don't know the address, look for nearby intersections or landmarks you can refer to.
- *Number of the phone being used.* If you get disconnected, they can call you back.
- *Type of emergency.* Describe what happened.
- Number of injured or ill people
- What help, if any, has been given so far, and by whom
- Be prepared to follow the dispatcher's directions for giving care.
- Stay on the phone with the 911 dispatcher until EMS arrives.

Figure 14.9 Information to give the 911 dispatcher.

Universal Precautions

Universal precautions are steps people take to reduce the risk of transmitting pathogens from one person to another through close physical contact or through a contaminated surface or object. A pathogen is an organism that causes disease. Using universal precautions will help protect you from bloodborne pathogens such as human immunodeficiency virus (HIV) infection and hepatitis B, C, and D. You may also be exposed to airborne pathogens when an infected person breathes, coughs, or sneezes. Universal precautions may include wearing gloves, masks, gowns, and other personal protection equipment as deemed necessary based on the situation.

Cardiac Emergencies

The two most common cardiac emergencies are heart attack and cardiac arrest. A heart attack occurs when blood flow to part of the heart muscle is blocked. With **cardiac arrest**, the heart stops beating or beats too ineffectively to circulate blood to the brain and other vital organs. If a person is having a heart attack or is in cardiac arrest, call 911 right away. Monitor the victim until EMS arrive and be ready to perform CPR or use an automated external defibrillator (AED) if they stop breathing or no longer have a heartbeat. See figure 14.10 for how to use an AED.

First Aid and Emergency Procedures **LESSON 14.4**

Steps to Using an AED

▶ Turn the AED on and follow the voice prompts.

▶ Remove or adjust clothing of the person as the pads need to be placed directly on the skin.
  a. Place one pad on the upper right side of the chest.
  b. Place the other pad on the lower left side of the chest.
    • If the pads are touching due to the small size of the person, place one pad in the middle of the chest and the other pad on the back between the shoulder blades.

▶ Plug the pad connector cable into the AED, if necessary.

▶ Let the AED analyze the heart's rhythm.
  a. Make sure no one is touching the person.
  b. Say CLEAR in a loud voice to move everyone away from the person.

▶ Deliver a shock, if the AED determines one is needed.
  a. Push the shock button to deliver the shock.

▶ After the AED delivers the shock, or if no shock is advised, immediately start CPR beginning with compressions.

Figure 14.10 Steps to using an AED.

STEM in Health

AUTOMATED EXTERNAL DEFIBRILLATOR

An automated external defibrillator (AED) delivers an electrical shock to the heart, helping it to return to a normal beating rhythm. When an AED is used on a victim, the chance of saving their life increases by 75 percent. The first AED that looks similar to what you may see on TV was used successfully in 1947 on a 14-year-old boy. The paddles then were gauze-covered spoons with wooden handles. In 1966, the first portable defibrillator was installed in an ambulance. A car battery was used for the current, and the machine weighed a total of 150 pounds (68 kg). Starting CPR immediately and using an AED as soon as possible gives the person the best chance for surviving cardiac arrest. Portable AEDs are found in all public buildings, now weigh about three pounds (2 kg), and are fully automated so that anyone can use them.

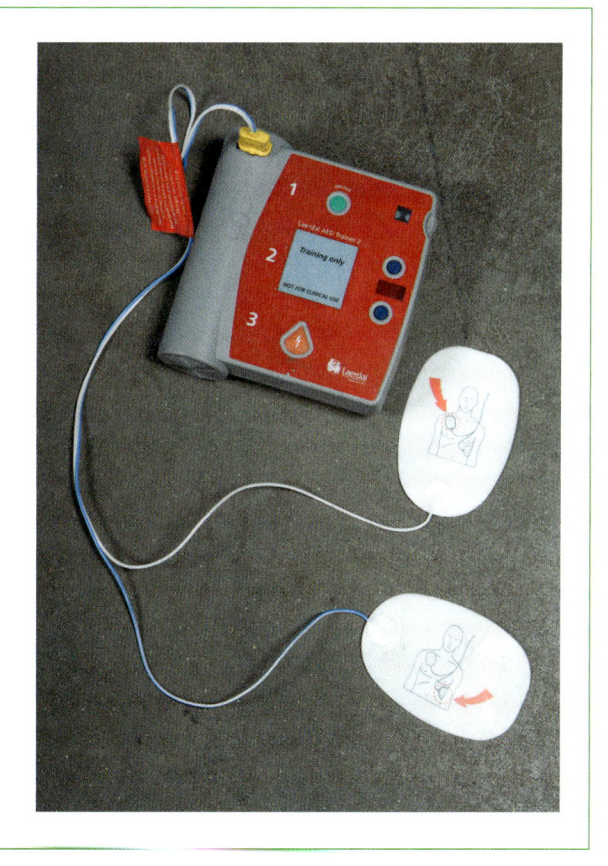

LESSON 14.4 Injury Prevention, Safety, and First Aid

Cardiopulmonary Resuscitation

Cardiopulmonary resuscitation (CPR) uses chest compressions and rescue breaths to keep oxygenated blood moving to the brain and other vital organs until advanced medical help arrives (see figure 14.11). The chest compressions squeeze the heart between the breastbone and the spine, which moves blood out of the heart to the brain and other vital organs. The rescue breaths deliver a fresh supply of oxygen into the person's lungs.

If you are not comfortable giving chest compressions and rescue breaths, you can give compression-only CPR instead. In compression-only CPR, you give continuous chest compressions, which is better than doing nothing and can save a person's life.

Steps to Giving CPR

Look, listen, and feel for breathing. Monitor them. If the person is not breathing,

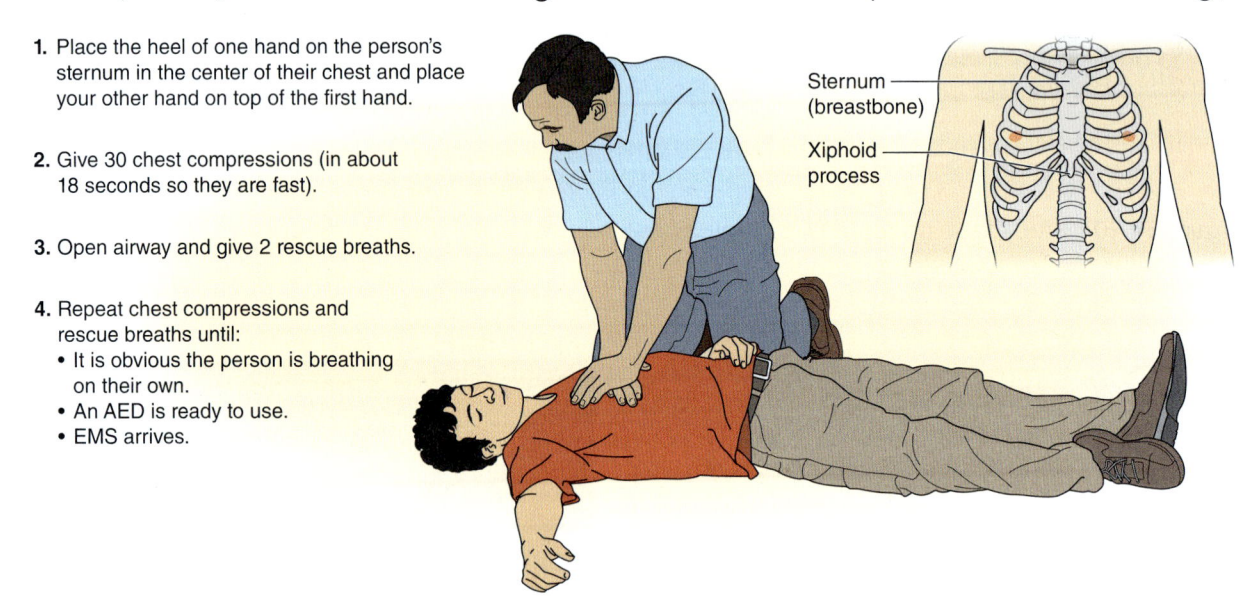

1. Place the heel of one hand on the person's sternum in the center of their chest and place your other hand on top of the first hand.

2. Give 30 chest compressions (in about 18 seconds so they are fast).

3. Open airway and give 2 rescue breaths.

4. Repeat chest compressions and rescue breaths until:
   - It is obvious the person is breathing on their own.
   - An AED is ready to use.
   - EMS arrives.

Figure 14.11 Steps for performing CPR.

Sudden Illness

A sudden illness often strikes with little to no warning. Examples of sudden illnesses include the following.

- *Asthma.* Asthma is a chronic illness in which certain substances or conditions cause inflammation and narrowing of the airways, making breathing difficult. A person who has been diagnosed with asthma may use an inhaler to take their medication.

- *Allergic reactions and anaphylaxis.* People can be allergic to almost anything. A person who is having a mild to moderate allergic reaction may develop a skin rash, stuffy nose, or red and watery eyes. **Anaphylaxis** is when a person has a severe, life-threatening allergic reaction. Symptoms include breathing difficulties, swelling of the face or tongue, and feeling a tightness in the chest or throat within minutes of contact with the allergy trigger. People with allergic reactions may carry an EpiPen that contains epinephrine, a drug that slows or stops the effects of anaphylaxis.

- *Diabetic emergencies.* Diabetes is a chronic condition characterized by the body's inability to process glucose (sugar) in the bloodstream. The two kinds of diabetic emergencies are hypoglycemia (excessively low blood glucose levels) and hyperglycemia (excessively high blood glucose levels). For hypoglycemia, you may be able to give the person a small amount of sugar by mouth if they are responsive and able to swallow. Acceptable forms of sugar include fruit juice, regular (not diet or zero sugar) soda, or a spoonful of sugar mixed into a glass of water. Hyperglycemia is typically treated by taking an extra dose of insulin. Extreme cases of hyperglycemia must be treated in a hospital. Drinking water can help manage the symptoms of hyperglycemia in the short term.

- *Seizures.* Seizures occur when the brain experiences abnormal electrical activity. They can happen for different reasons, including epilepsy, high fevers, and brain injuries. The two types of seizures are grand mal seizure, in which the person loses consciousness and has convulsions, and absence seizure, in which the person is silent and has a blank stare. If a person is having a seizure, let the seizure run its course; don't try to hold the person down or stop the seizure.

- *Fainting.* Fainting is caused by a sudden decrease in blood flow to the brain. A person who may suddenly lose consciousness, and then comes to after about a minute or less, is likely to have fainted. Dehydration, being too hot, being in a crowded room, or feeling intense emotion can lead to fainting.

> **If someone has a sudden illness, use the following general care steps:**
>
> 1. Call 911 if appropriate. *Not all illnesses need 911 help.*
> 2. Help the person rest in a comfortable position and reassure them to keep them calm.
> 3. Monitor the person's breathing and level of consciousness.
> 4. Keep the person from getting too hot or too cold.
> 5. Continue to watch for changes in the person's condition.

Other Types of Emergencies

Other types of emergencies, such as choking, shock, heat- and cold-related emergencies, and burns, are often the result of an external factor.

Choking

Choking occurs when an obstruction (e.g., a piece of food) blocks the airway either partially or completely. Some signs and symptoms of choking include placing one or both hands on the throat (the most common sign), gagging, being unable to cough, and skin turning bluish. If the airway is fully blocked, the person will not be able to speak, cry, or cough. To care for a choking child or adult, see figure 14.12.

LESSON 14.4 Injury Prevention, Safety, and First Aid

1. **Give 5 back blows:**
   a. Stand to the side and just behind the person.
   b. Place one arm diagonal across the person's chest for support and bend the person over at the waist so their upper body is parallel with the ground.
   c. Give 5 back blows between the person's shoulder blades with the heel of your hand.

2. **Give 5 abdominal thrusts:**
   a. Stand behind the person with one foot slightly between their feet for balance.
   b. Wrap your arms around the person making a fist with one hand and place it thumb side against the person's body just above their navel. Cover your fist with your other hand.
   c. Pull inward and upward to perform the 5 abdominal thrusts.

3. **Continue to alternate between the 5 back blows and 5 abdominal thrusts until the blockage is dislodged.**

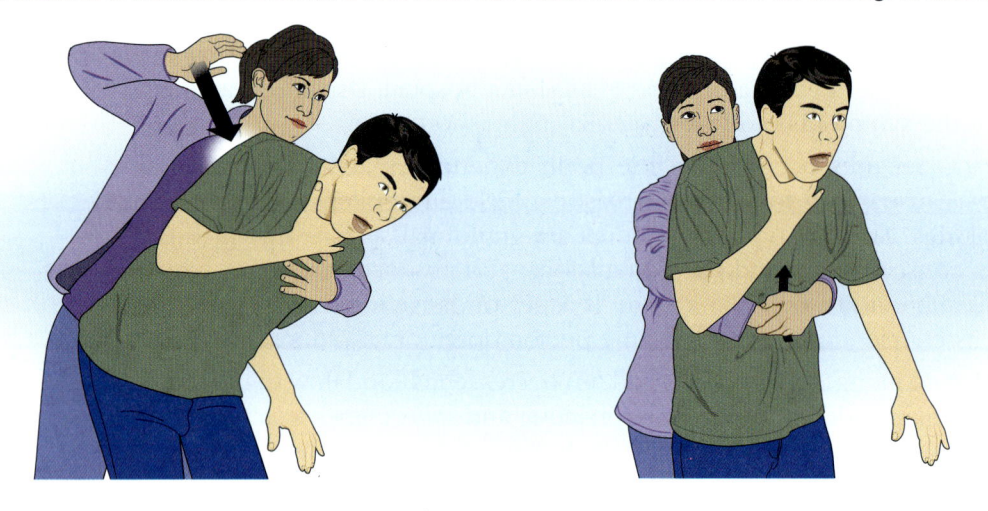

* You may do chest thrusts instead of abdominal thrusts if a person is too large to wrap your arms around, is pregnant or in a wheelchair.
* For a child you may need to get down on one knee to be in a better position to perform back blows and abdominal thrusts.

Figure 14.12 Guidelines for helping someone who is choking.

Shock

Shock is a life-threatening condition in which the circulatory system fails to deliver enough oxygen-rich blood to the rest of the body. Common causes of shock include severe bleeding, allergic reactions (anaphylaxis), and potentially the aftereffects of any serious injury or illness. Signs and symptoms of shock may include restlessness, an altered level of consciousness, pale or grayish skin color, and rapid breathing. A person who is showing signs and symptoms of shock needs immediate medical attention.

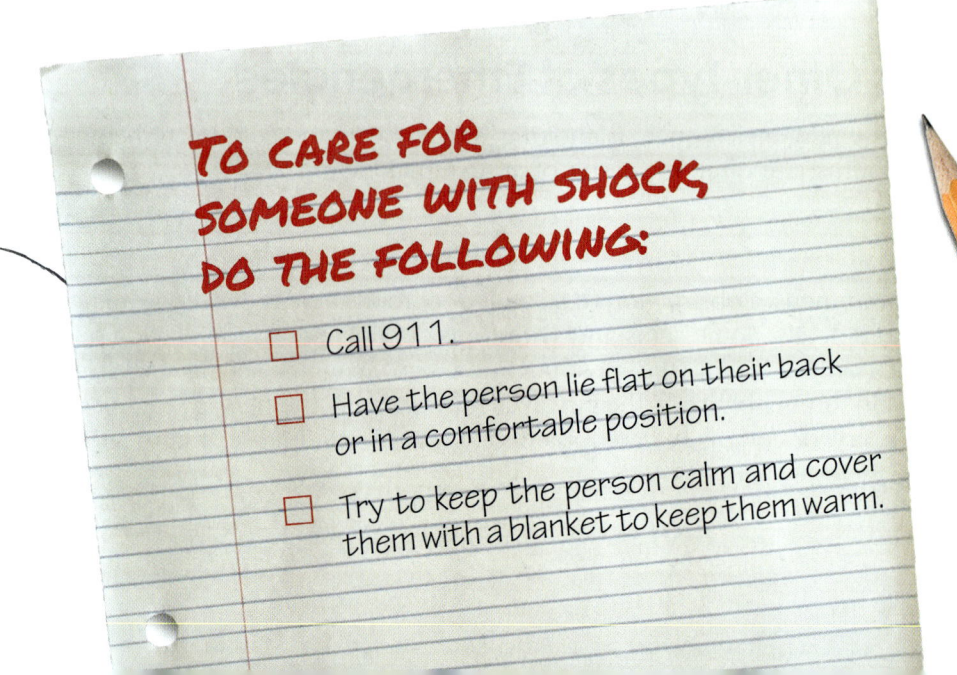

TO CARE FOR SOMEONE WITH SHOCK, DO THE FOLLOWING:

- ☐ Call 911.
- ☐ Have the person lie flat on their back or in a comfortable position.
- ☐ Try to keep the person calm and cover them with a blanket to keep them warm.

First Aid and Emergency Procedures — LESSON 14.4

Heat-Related Emergencies

A **heat-related emergency** is caused by overexposure to heat and by dehydration. The three types of heat-related emergencies are heat cramps, heat exhaustion, and heat stroke.

Heat cramps are painful muscle spasms, usually in the legs or abdomen. To care for heat cramps, move the person to a cool place and give them cool water to drink. Stretch the muscle and gently massage.

Heat exhaustion is more severe than heat cramps. Symptoms may include nausea, weakness, headache, and dizziness. To care for heat exhaustion, move the person into the shade or indoors with air conditioning and let the person rest. Apply cool, wet towels to try to cool the person down.

Heat stroke is the most severe and least common. Heat stroke causes a person to have an extremely high body temperature, but they won't be sweating and they may be unconscious. To care for heat stroke, call 911 and take steps to rapidly cool the person's body by immersing them in cold water or placing ice water–soaked towels or bags of ice over the person's entire body.

Cold-Related Emergencies

A **cold-related emergency** occurs from an overexposure to cold. The two types of cold-related emergencies are frostbite and hypothermia.

Frostbite is the freezing of the skin and underlying tissues resulting from prolonged exposure to freezing or below-freezing temperatures. The affected body part is numb, and the skin is cold to the touch. To care for frostbite, remove any wet clothing, rewarm the affected body part using skin-to-skin contact with warm hands, or soak the frostbitten area in warm water.

Hypothermia is the lowering of the body's core temperature to a point where body function becomes impaired. Hypothermia results from exposure to cold air, cold water, or both. Signs of hypothermia include intense shivering, overall numbness, confusion, and possible loss of consciousness. To care for hypothermia, call 911, move the person to a warm place, and have them put on dry clothing including a hat and gloves. Wrap the person in blankets, warm them slowly near a heat source, and treat for shock if needed.

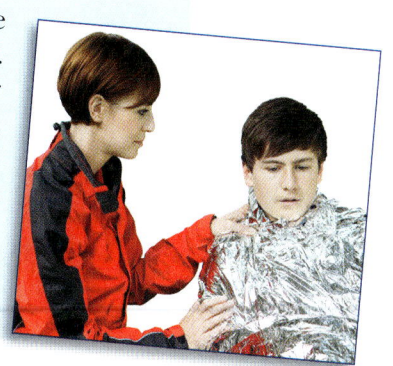

LESSON 14.4 Injury Prevention, Safety, and First Aid

Burns

Burns are caused by contact with extreme heat, chemicals, radiation, or electricity. Burns range in severity from minor to critical. A critical burn is life threatening or potentially disfiguring and requires immediate medical attention. Burns can be classified according to how deep they are: the deeper the burn, the greater the severity (see table 14.1).

TABLE 14.1 Types and Characteristics of Burns

Degree or thickness of burn	Depth of burn	Characteristics of burn
First-degree or superficial burns	Epidermis	Pain, redness, mild swelling
Second-degree or partial thickness burns	Epidermis and dermis	Pain, blisters, splotchy skin, severe swelling
Third-degree or full thickness burns	Epidermis, dermis, and the subcutaneous tissue (fat, muscle, bone, nerves)	White or charred skin. Nerve endings are destroyed, so there may be no pain at the site; however, surrounding tissue that has superficial or partial thickness burns will still be painful.

HEALTHY LIVING TIP
Prevent sunburns by avoiding being in the sun between 10 a.m. and 2 p.m., wear sunglasses with UV protection, use a sunscreen with an SPF of 30 or higher, and reapply the sunscreen every two hours.

Follow these general steps in caring for burns:
1. Stop the burning by removing the source of the injury if it is safe to do so.
2. Cool the burn and relieve pain using clean cool or cold water. Never use ice or ice water because that can cause more damage to the skin.
3. Cover the burn loosely with a sterile dressing.

First Aid and Emergency Procedures **LESSON 14.4**

Call 911 if the person has trouble breathing or has burns that cover more than one body part or a large surface of the body. Make sure you monitor for shock. Do not remove pieces of clothing that may be stuck to the burned area.

A sunburn is both a heat-related emergency and a type of burn. Sunburns occur when skin has an overexposure to the sun. Many sunburns are classified as superficial (first-degree) or partial thickness (second-degree) burns.

To protect yourself from potential damage from the sun, do the following:

- ☐ Stay in the shade to limit your sun exposure.
- ☐ Put on sunscreen and reapply it throughout the day.
- ☐ Wear a hat with a brim that shields your face and neck.
- ☐ Wear sunglasses to protect your eyes.

Wounds

Wounds are injuries that result when the skin or other tissues of the body are damaged. The two types of wounds are closed and open. Closed wounds consist of bruises and internal bleeding. Bruises usually result from blunt trauma such as running into something like a table. Bruising occurs when the small blood vessels under the surface of the skin are damaged and blood leaks into the surrounding tissues. More severe blunt trauma, such as falling from a ladder onto the cement or being struck by a vehicle, can cause internal bleeding, which typically occurs in the abdomen, chest, or skull and may be life threatening.

Open wounds involve the skin being broken apart and typically result in some bleeding. The four types of open wounds are abrasions (scrapes), lacerations, avulsions or amputations, and punctures (see table 14.2). In mass trauma situations such as natural disasters, active shooters, and multiple vehicle accidents, the most common injury is often a life-threatening bleeding emergency. Knowing how to recognize and stop a life-threatening bleeding emergency by properly taking care of the victim can be the difference between life and death.

LESSON 14.4 Injury Prevention, Safety, and First Aid

TABLE 14.2 Types of Open Wounds

Wound type	Description
Abrasion (scrape) 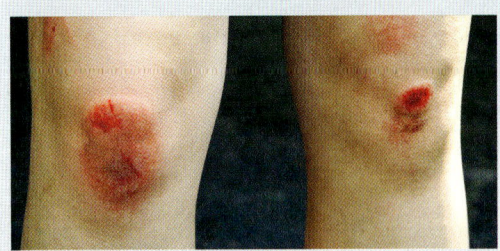	An abrasion occurs when something rubs roughly against your skin.
Laceration 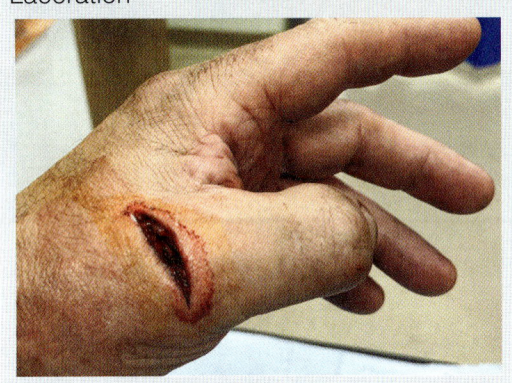	A laceration is a cut, usually from a sharp object, through layers of skin, fat, and muscle.
Avulsion or amputation 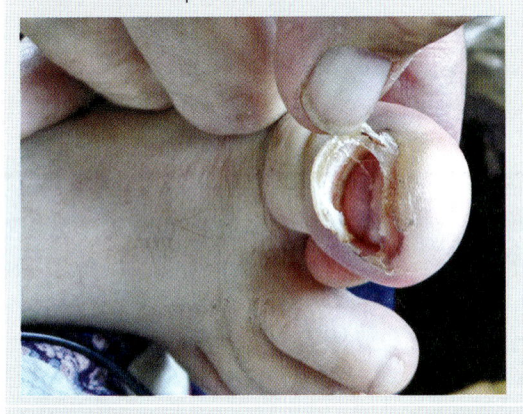	Avulsion means that a portion of the skin and sometimes the underlying tissue is partially or completely torn away; amputation refers to the loss of part or all of a body part, such as a finger.
Puncture 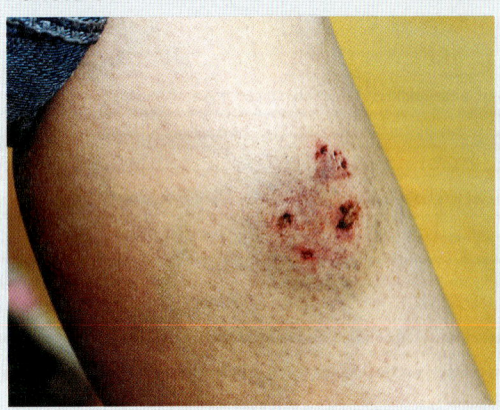	Punctures occur when an object, such as a nail, pierces the skin.

Caring for Open and Closed Wounds

To care for a minor open wound, use gloves so you don't come in direct contact with another person's blood. Apply direct pressure with a gauze pad to stop the bleeding. If blood soaks through the dressing, place another dressing on top of the first and continue applying direct pressure. Do not remove the blood-soaked dressing because that might restart the bleeding. After the bleeding stops, wash the area with soap and water, apply antibiotic ointment, and cover with a bandage. If blood is spurting from the wound or the wound is a very deep gash you won't be able to control the bleeding of, call 911 instead of trying to care for the open wound yourself.

To care for a closed wound, apply an ice pack to a bruise. The ice will help to decrease the bleeding and reduce the pain and swelling. For internal bleeding, call 911 immediately and be prepared to treat for shock until help arrives.

Injuries to the Face

Facial injuries frequently occur when people are active and usually involve the nose and teeth. Injuries can range from minor cuts, bloody noses, and knocked-out teeth to more severe injuries, such as broken bones. Two of the more common facial injuries are nosebleeds and knocked-out teeth. To stop a nosebleed, pinch the nostrils together with the head tilted slightly forward. Keep the nostrils pinched shut until the bleeding has stopped. If the bleeding is severe or gushing, call 911. If a tooth is knocked out, control the bleeding by placing a rolled gauze pad into the space left by the missing tooth and have the person gently bite down to maintain pressure. If possible, put the knocked-out tooth into whole milk or into the injured person's saliva in a small cup or baggie. The sooner the person can get to the dentist, the better chance that the tooth will survive and be able to be put back into place.

Muscle, Bone, and Joint Injuries

Injuries to the muscles, bones, and joints include sprains, strains, dislocations, and fractures. Sprains occur when a ligament is stretched or torn and typically take place in the ankle, knee, wrist, or finger joints. Strains are stretched or torn tendons or muscles that happen most frequently in the back or hamstring. Dislocations happen when the bones that meet at a joint move out of their normal position. This usually happens in the fingers, knees, and collarbone. Fractures are a complete break, chip, or crack in a bone. Fractures can be open or closed. In open fractures, the end of the broken bone breaks through the skin. Closed fractures are when the broken bone does not penetrate the skin. While arm and leg fractures are the most common to occur, other bones can be broken.

If calling 911 is necessary, help the injured person to rest in a position that is comfortable for them without moving or straightening the body part. Apply a cold pack, wrapped in a thin towel, to the injured area if the person can tolerate it to help reduce swelling and pain. If you don't need to call 911, use the reminder RICE—rest, immobilize, cold, elevate—to help care for a muscle, bone, or joint injury (see figure 14.13).

Rest by limiting the use of the injured body part.

Immobilize the injured body part to limit movement.

Cold - apply a cold pack wrapped in a thin towel to the injured area.

Elevate the injured body part to help reduce swelling unless it causes more pain.

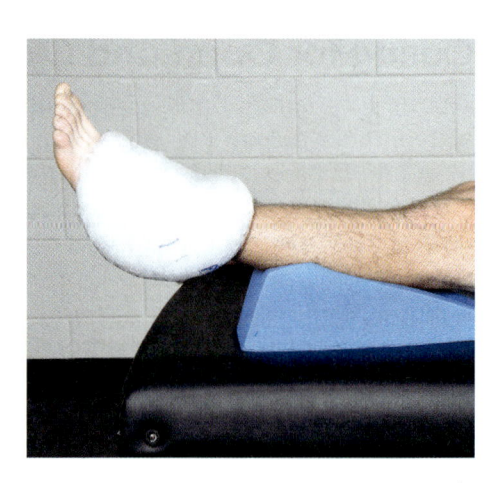

Figure 14.13 The acronym RICE can help you remember how to care for a muscle, bone, or joint injury.

Head, Neck, and Spinal Injuries

Head, neck, or spinal injuries are serious; depending on how severe they are, they can leave a person with a permanent disability. Head injuries can occur from a blow to the head or from a motor vehicle accident that causes the head to snap forward and then back. A blow to the head can lead to concussion (a traumatic brain injury that alters the way the brain functions), brain contusion (bruising of the brain tissue), or brain hematoma (bleeding into the space between the brain and the skull).

Spinal cord injuries can result from trauma that causes one or more vertebrae (the bones that surround and protect the spinal cord) to break. The bone fragments can press into the soft tissue of the spinal cord, damaging it. Damage can also result if the injury causes the soft tissue of the spinal cord to swell, compressing it against the vertebrae. Depending on the location and severity of the spinal cord injury, the person may develop paralysis (the loss of movement, sensation, or both) in body parts below the level of the injury.

Signs and Symptoms of Head, Neck, and Spinal Injuries

Signs and symptoms depend on the type of injury and the location of the injury, and may include

- changes in level of consciousness;
- blood or other fluids in the ears or nose;
- partial or complete loss of movement of any body part;
- severe pain or pressure in the head, neck, or back; and
- a broken or damaged safety helmet (from riding a bicycle, motorcycle, skateboard, or scooter).

If you think someone has suffered a head, neck, or spinal injury, call 911. As long as the person is breathing normally, they should stay in the position they are in. If the person is wearing a helmet, do not remove it unless you must perform CPR. If a child is strapped in a car seat, do not remove the child unless you need to perform CPR.

Concussions

A **concussion** is a common type of traumatic brain injury that involves a temporary loss of brain function. Concussions are common sports-related injuries. Many people who experience a concussion do not lose consciousness, or they may lose consciousness only very briefly. See table 14.3 for signs and symptoms of a concussion.

TABLE 14.3 **Signs and Symptoms of Concussion**

Memory and thinking issues	Physical issues	Emotional issues	Behavioral issues
• Difficulty remembering new information • Difficulty thinking clearly • Difficulty concentrating • Difficulty remembering events that occurred just prior to and just after the incident	• Headache • Blurry vision • Nausea or vomiting • Dizziness • Sensitivity to noise or light • Balance problems • Lack of energy	• Irritability • Sadness • Overwhelming emotions • Nervousness or anxiety	• Sleeping more or less than usual • Difficulty falling asleep

If you think a person has a concussion, have them stop what they are doing and follow up with a health care provider.

LESSON 14.4 Injury Prevention, Safety, and First Aid

Skill-Building Challenge

Healthy Communication

Practice what you would say if you had to call 911 in each of the following situations.

- A friend suddenly stands up at lunch and grabs her throat. She isn't speaking or making any noise.
- You and a friend are out for a jog when he begins complaining he is having difficulty breathing and experiencing pain in his stomach and chest. He suddenly falls to the ground.
- Your teammate passes out at practice on a hot day in summer. You notice that her skin is pale and feels clammy.

After you have practiced your call to 911, explain to a classmate the steps you would take in each situation while waiting for EMS to arrive. Then determine what could have been done to prevent each scenario from happening.

Healthy Living Skills

This lesson focused on healthy communication. Here are some more ways you can develop healthy living skills related to this lesson.

ACCESSING INFORMATION

You have just learned about first aid in your health class, and you want to know how to get a first aid and CPR card. Using the steps for Accessing Information decide whom you can ask or where you can look to get more information on how to get a first aid and CPR card.

ANALYZING INFLUENCES

Aiyden and Jayshawn are driving home from school when they suddenly hear tires screeching and a huge bang and Aiyden has to slam on the brakes to keep from hitting the car in front of them. They both are okay, but they hear a car horn blaring and people yelling. They can see the two cars that ran into each other and decide to go see if they can help. They get to the cars and see that one person is lying on the ground bleeding badly and two other people are still in their cars; one seems to be unconscious, and the other is yelling in pain. There are other bystanders looking at the scene, but no one is helping any of the victims. Aiyden and Jayshawn have both taken first aid training and know what to do, but they wonder if they should help when none of the bystanders who are adults are helping the victims. How are Aiyden and Jayshawn being influenced by the other bystanders? If you were Aiyden or Jayshawn, what would you do in this situation? Explain your decision.

LESSON 14.4 Review: First Aid and Emergency Procedures

LESSON SUMMARY

- Know and practice the emergency action steps: Check the scene and the victim, call 911, and care for the victim.
- Universal precautions are taken to reduce the risk of transmitting pathogens. You should protect yourself from bloodborne illnesses and other infectious diseases.
- To administer CPR, do sets of 30 chest compressions followed by two rescue breaths. The chest compressions squeeze the heart between the breastbone and the spine, which moves blood out of the heart to the brain and other vital organs. The rescue breaths deliver a fresh supply of oxygen to the person's lungs.
- Common symptoms of a sudden illness include trouble breathing, dizziness, chest pain, changes in levels of consciousness, blurred vision, and numbness or weakness.
- Closed wounds consist of bruises and internal bleeding and open wounds involve the skin being torn apart and typically involve some bleeding.
- Concussions often cause a person to have difficulty remembering new information, thinking clearly, and concentrating or remembering what just happened.

REVIEWING CONCEPTS AND VOCABULARY

1. Keeping oxygenated blood moving to the brain and other vital organs until advanced medical help arrives is known as _____.
2. A(n) _____ delivers an electrical shock to the heart's electrical activity long enough to allow the heart to spontaneously develop an effective rhythm on its own.
3. _____ is a life-threatening allergic reaction.
4. A progressive, life-threatening condition in which the circulatory system fails to deliver enough oxygen-rich blood to the body's tissues and organs is called _____.
5. An injury that results when the skin or other tissues of the body are damaged is called a _____.
6. _____ is a common type of traumatic brain injury that involves a temporary loss of brain function.
7. _____ are steps people take to reduce the risk of transmitting pathogens from one person to another.

THINKING CRITICALLY

Choose a medical emergency discussed in the lesson and explain the steps, in the proper order, you would take to help the victim.

TAKE IT HOME

Check your first aid kit or whatever medical supplies you have at home to see if you have dressings and bandages you could use if someone cut themselves and had severe bleeding. Make a list of items you need to create or improve your first aid kit.

Chapter Review

MY ACTION Plan: Staying Safe and Injury-Free

Use the My Action Plan worksheet to develop a plan to stay safe and injury-free. Here is an example.

My Action Plan: Learn First Aid and CPR

STEP 1: Identify the health behavior you are going to work on.

I want to take a first aid and CPR class.

STEP 2: Write SMART goal(s).

Write one or two short-term goals (one day to one month long).

I will do a Google search to find out where I can take a first aid and CPR class.

Write a long-term goal (one to six months or more).

I will sign up for a first aid and CPR class.

STEP 3: Make a plan.

Identify two to five action steps (strategies) you could do to meet your goal.

I am always busy, so I will block out one hour to look up information on where I can take a first aid and CPR class.

I will have my calendar with me so I can schedule a class when I find one I can take. I know if I don't sign up for it right away, then I may not get around to it again.

STEP 4: Execute your plan and track your progress.

Short-term goal

☒ Met   ☐ Not met   Date: *May 31*

Long-term goal

☐ Met   ☒ Not met   Date: _____

If you met your goal, what helped you to be successful?

I met my short-term goal because I set aside one hour and found a first aid and CPR class I could take at the YMCA.

If you did not meet your goal, what made it harder for you to be successful?

I did not meet my long-term goal because even though I found a class, I decided not to sign up for it until a friend could go with me. I am working on trying to get my friend to go with me.

Test Your Knowledge

Select the best answer for each question.

1. The correct order of the emergency action steps are
   a. call, check, care
   b. care, call, check
   c. check, call, care
   d. check, care, call

2. Which natural disaster includes staying safe by dropping, covering, and holding?
   a. thunderstorm
   b. tornado
   c. earthquake
   d. hurricane

3. How many characters should your password be?
   a. 6
   b. 8
   c. 10
   d. 12

4. When the bones that meet at a joint move out of their normal position, this is known as a
   a. sprain
   b. dislocation
   c. strain
   d. fracture

5. An example of an intentional injury is
   a. suicide
   b. drowning
   c. motor vehicle crash
   d. fall

6. A virus designed to invade your computer system and perform damaging actions on it to change the way it operates is known as
   a. antivirus
   b. phishing
   c. hacker
   d. malware

7. What is the correct order of heat-related emergencies from least critical to most severe?
   a. heat cramps, heat stroke, heat exhaustion
   b. heat stroke, heat cramps, heat exhaustion
   c. heat cramps, heat exhaustion, heat stroke
   d. heat stroke, heat exhaustion, heat cramps

8. When doing CPR, what is the ratio of chest compressions to rescue breaths?
   a. 1 to 15
   b. 30 to 2
   c. 15 to 1
   d. 2 to 30

9. An example of an unintentional injury is
   a. self-injury
   b. homicide
   c. fall
   d. suicide

10. RICE stands for
    a. rest, immobilize, compress, evaluate
    b. raise, ice, cold, elevate
    c. raise, immobilize, cold, evaluate
    d. rest, immobilize, cold, elevate

PROJECT-BASED LEARNING: Keeping You Safe and Injury-Free

What to Remember

There are many areas of your life to think about when you are told to keep safe. It could be at your home, at school, on the Internet, in your social media, during a natural disaster, during a fire, on public transportation, riding your bike, and so many others. Staying safe can be as simple as being aware of your surroundings and the people around you—acquaintances and strangers alike. Keep your head up and keep looking around at all that is happening instead of burying your head in your phone and making yourself vulnerable.

Who It Is For

This is intended for students in your class or school specifically, but it could also be posted to your social media account or your school's, which could even influence students in other countries with your amazing ideas.

Why It Is Important

While no one wants to think about bad things happening or about getting injured, these things do happen, so it is important to have a plan to try to stay safe and injury-free.

What to Do

You and your partner will plan 31 days of ways to keep yourself safe and injury-free that you could post on a social media platform, or if you don't have a social media option it could be used as part of the school's daily announcements. Develop a series of posts that provide one tip per day to keep yourself safe and free of injuries. Each day must include written information and a picture or short video. Work with your teacher to decide how they want your materials collected and if they want you to post directly to social media or not.

How to Do It

- Plan your 31 days using information from this chapter as well as other original ideas you have that we haven't already discussed. Remember that each social media post must include a picture or short video of what you are doing that will keep you safe and injury-free as well as an explanation of what you did and how it is important in your life as a high school student. Make sure your pictures, videos, and explanations are all school appropriate.
- If both of you have social media, then you should agree on a time of day when you will both make the post at about the same time. This way you can reach twice as many people, especially if you and your partner post on different social media platforms.
- Make sure your teacher can see your social media posts and find out if other students in the class would also like to see your posts if you aren't already friends with them.

CROSS-CURRICULAR CONNECTIONS: Music

Create a song that teaches younger kids about how to stay safe during different natural disasters. Make a different verse for each disaster you teach about and use a common chorus between verses. Make sure your song has a strong beat and that the lyrics are clear and easy for a younger person to learn and remember.

15

Environmental Health

LESSON 15.1 Air, Water, and Noise Pollution

LESSON 15.2 Chemicals, the Environment, and Your Health

LESSON 15.3 Conservation and Green Living

Understanding My Health

How Environmentally Aware Am I?

There are simple actions everyone can take to help support the health of the environment and the people who live in it. This assessment asks you to reflect on your choices and behaviors to see how environmentally aware you are. Respond to each statement in the following chart by selecting the response that is most accurate for you. When you are done, add up your points. The closer your score is to 21, the more environmentally aware you are in your choices.

	Always	Sometimes	Never
I do not leave the water running when I am washing dishes or brushing my teeth.	3	2	1
I carry a water bottle with me to school or work.	3	2	1
I participate in recycling at home, work, and school.	3	2	1
I bring my own bags when I go shopping.	3	2	1
I volunteer for projects, organizations, or school activities that help protect or clean up the environment.	3	2	1
I turn off my personal device at night or whenever I am not using it.	3	2	1
I walk, ride a bike, or use public transportation (including the school bus).	3	2	1

My score for How Environmentally Aware Am I? = _____ (total number of points)

The health of our environment determines how healthy we can be, from the air we breathe to the water we drink. Taking care of our environment is an important part of our individual, community, and global health.

LESSON 15.1
Air, Water, and Noise Pollution

Terms to Learn

acid rain
air pollution
air quality index
built environment
environment
natural environment
noise pollution
smog

The Big Picture

The environment you live in affects your health and well-being. The pollution of air and water is among the most significant crises this and future generations must face. Becoming knowledgeable about the many ways different factors cause air, water, and noise pollution is critical to making healthy decisions for yourself and finding solutions to the challenges that lie ahead.

Learning Targets

- Explain how air pollution can affect personal and community health.
- Understand influences on health by identifying four common sources of indoor air pollution.
- Analyze two causes of water pollution and how individual actions influence community health.
- Explain how individual choices can affect health risks associated with noise pollution.
- Analyze influences on air and water pollution.

Write About It

In what ways do air, water, and noise pollution affect your health? Provide specific examples in your explanation.

Note-Taking Guide

Use this chapter's note-taking guide to help you organize and remember the material in this lesson.

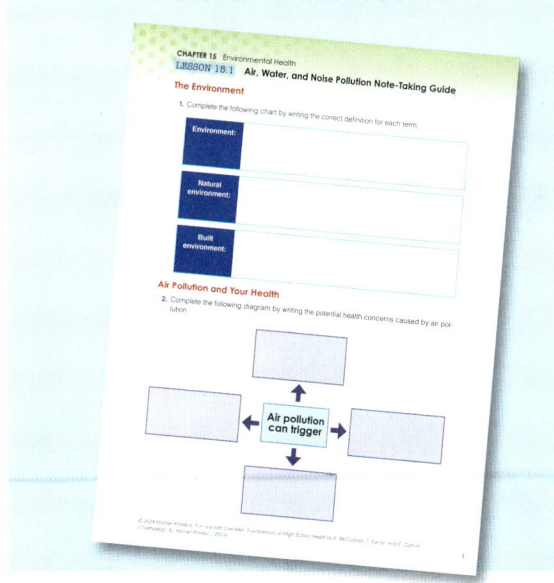

647

LESSON 15.1 Environmental Health

Last year, Jamal began experiencing dizziness and headaches and didn't know why. At first, he assumed the culprit was poor air quality since his city has high levels of smog. Not long after, his symptoms started getting worse—he began feeling fatigued, and his muscles ached. A couple of his friends from school had similar symptoms.

When Jamal kept complaining, his aunt took him to the local health clinic where a blood test was done. It turned out that Jamal had lead poisoning. Several of his friends were diagnosed with the same thing. The results were alarming, and officials launched an investigation. They determined that the school's pipes were old and leaking lead into the drinking water. Jamal, like most of the school's student population, usually carried an empty water bottle to school and filled it at the drinking fountains. He and his family were shocked to learn that the water was contaminated. How would you feel if something in your environment was making you sick? Have you ever considered how your environment at home, work, and school might be influencing your health?

The Environment

The **environment** comprises the surroundings and conditions in which you live. It includes the air you breathe; the water you drink; and the parks and buildings where you work, study, and hang out. The **natural environment** includes all living species, climate, weather, and natural resources, whereas the **built environment** includes all human-made spaces. Each environment affects your health.

Air, Water, and Noise Pollution **LESSON 15.1**

Air Pollution and Your Health

Air is an essential part of human life. We breathe an average of 12 to 20 times per minute, and the oxygen we take in supports all of the vital functions of our bodies. It should come as no surprise that the quality of the air you breathe can affect your health. **Air pollution** occurs when the air contains dangerous particles such as particulates, carbon monoxide, and carbon dioxide. Human activities are a major contributor to air pollution. Pollutants can come from mobile sources (cars, buses, planes, trucks, and trains), stationary sources (power plants, refineries, and factories), area sources (fireplaces, cities, and agricultural areas), and natural sources (dust, wildfires, and volcanos). Mobile sources contribute more than half of all air pollution in the United States.

Air pollution can trigger asthma and allergy attacks; sleepiness; headaches; and irritation of the eyes, nose, throat, and skin. The quality of the air we breathe affects the health of all people at all stages of life (see figure 15.1). Air pollution is particularly dangerous for some groups of people, including children; older adults (over age 65); and people with existing health conditions, including respiratory infections, respiratory diseases including asthma and COPD, heart or circulatory disease, diabetes, and a history of stroke.

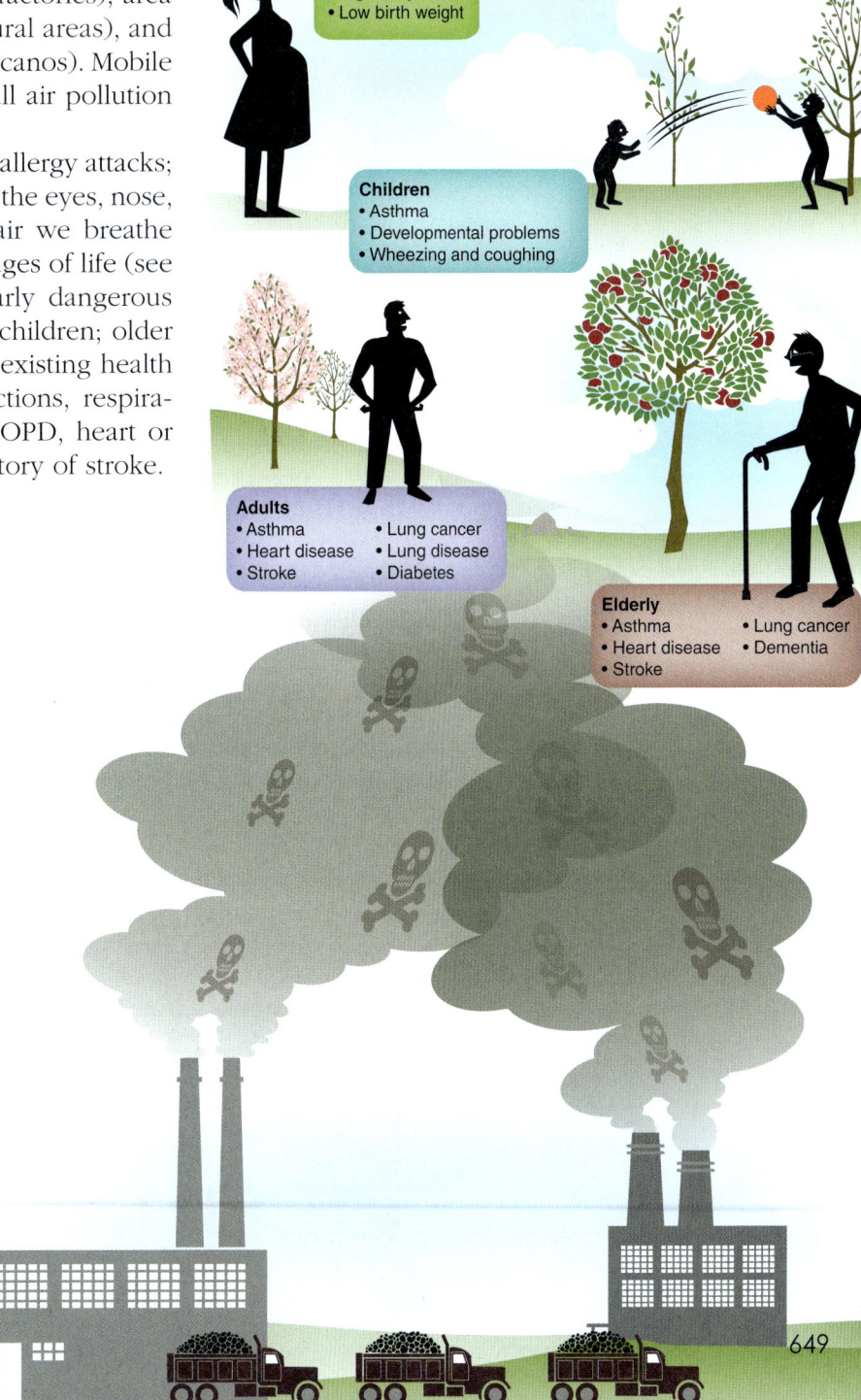

Pregnancy
- Low birth weight

Children
- Asthma
- Developmental problems
- Wheezing and coughing

Adults
- Asthma
- Heart disease
- Stroke
- Lung cancer
- Lung disease
- Diabetes

Elderly
- Asthma
- Heart disease
- Stroke
- Lung cancer
- Dementia

Figure 15.1 Air pollution can contribute to health problems at all stages of life.

LESSON 15.1 Environmental Health

Outdoor Air Quality

Human activity is not the only factor to influence outdoor air quality; natural forces in the environment have an impact as well. Natural events, such as large wildfires, can release carbon monoxide and smoke (see figure 15.2). Volcanic eruptions release carbon dioxide, sulfur dioxide, and ash. Dust storms, particularly in desert environments, also dramatically affect air quality. Winds can carry these air pollutants for thousands of miles. Naturally occurring pollens from trees and flowers also factor in to outdoor air quality: Many people suffer from seasonal allergies when these pollens are at high levels in the air.

Figure 15.2 Air pollution comes from a variety of different sources.

Human activities, such as driving motor vehicles and burning coal and oil for fuel, contribute to air pollution. The quality of air in large metropolitan areas can be especially problematic where industrial processes create high levels of pollution. **Smog** is the combination of moisture in the air that has mixed with smoke and chemical fumes. Regular exposure to smog has harmful effects on the lining of the lungs and the respiratory tract; it also causes irritation to the eyes. In addition, smog damages plants, buildings, and other materials. When weather conditions are just right, smog can hang over a city for weeks or months. When the smog is bad enough, cities sometimes place temporary restrictions on driving and burning fuel.

Chemicals that are released into the air can mix with water and oxygen to form acids, which fall to the ground in the form of rain, snow, or ice. This **acid rain** eventually enters the ground, waterways, and oceans and damages plant and animal life as well as our food and water supplies (figure 15.3).

Figure 15.3 Forest damaged from acid rain.

Air, Water, and Noise Pollution **LESSON 15.1**

Indoor Air Quality

Indoor air quality refers to how polluted the air is inside buildings and structures. Ventilation (access to outdoor air), humidity, mold, chemicals, tobacco smoke, dust, and other allergens like pollen and pet dander are major factors in indoor air quality (see figure 15.4). Sometimes it is difficult to know the quality of indoor air. Everyday activities such as cooking can add smoke and other pollutants to the air. Unless people are actively smoking, we usually can't see air pollution when we are inside the way we might when we are outside.

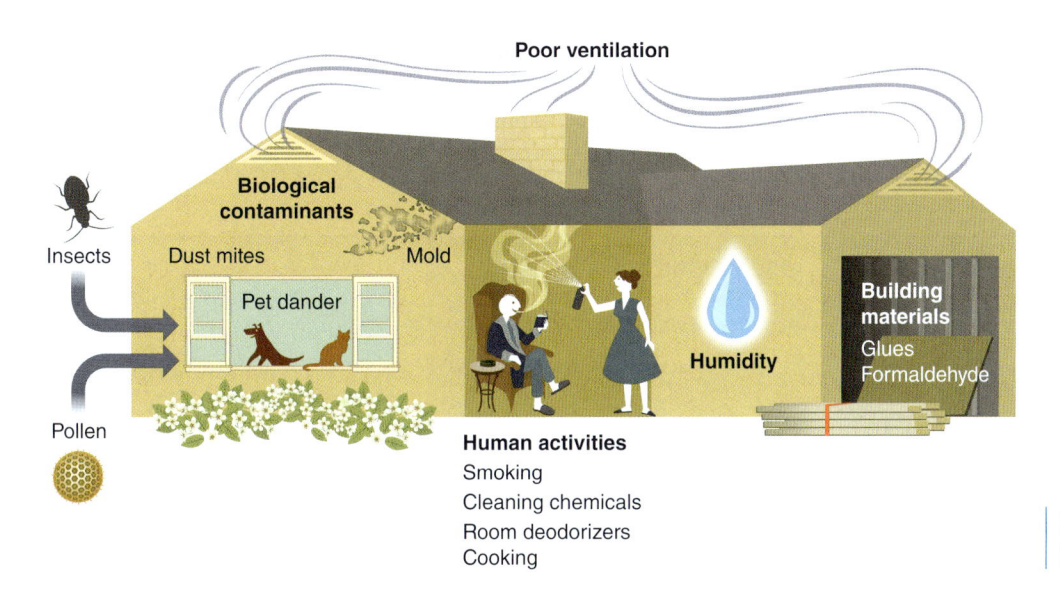

Figure 15.4 Sources of indoor air pollution.

> **The best ways to improve indoor air quality are to**
>
> - keep things clean, including bedding, clothing, curtains, and furniture;
> - keep air filters clean in heating and cooling units;
> - use chemical-free cleaning products when possible;
> - use air purifiers; and
> - let fresh air in when outdoor air quality is good.

Determining Air Quality

Air quality is measured and reported as the **air quality index**, or AQI, which measures ozone, particulate matter, carbon monoxide, sulfur dioxide, and nitrogen dioxide levels in the air (see figure 15.5). Many weather apps include an AQI score for your local area. There are also apps that feature maps of air quality across the United States. When the air quality is unhealthy, people are advised to avoid spending long periods of time outside. Those with respiratory conditions like asthma should pay close attention to the air quality when working or playing outdoors.

651

LESSON 15.1 Environmental Health

Air quality index	Levels of health concern	Color	
0-50	Good	Green	Safe for most people
51-100	Moderate	Yellow	
101-150	Unhealthy for sensitive groups	Orange	
151-200	Unhealthy	Red	
201-300	Very unhealthy	Purple	
301-500	Hazardous	Maroon	Everyone should avoid physical activity outside.

Figure 15.5 The air quality index is used to communicate the quality of the air in a region on any given day.

Water Pollution and Your Health

Water is one of the most important natural resources we have, and it supports all forms of life on planet Earth. It covers nearly two thirds of Earth's surface. Oceans, alone, comprise 97 percent of Earth's water. However, it isn't limited to just the surface; water also exists below the surface in the planet's interior. How can it be, then, that our access to safe drinking water has reached such a critically low level?

Saline, or salt, makes up around 3 percent of ocean water. This may seem like a relatively insignificant portion, but our bodies, as well as other animals' bodies, are not designed to process this much salt. Therefore, drinking salt water continuously would result in dehydration and ultimately death. Fresh water, on the other hand, generally contains much lower concentrations of saline—generally under 1 percent—so it is safe for us to consume. However, only about 3 percent of the water found on Earth is fresh water, much of which is essentially locked away, frozen in glaciers and ice caps. This leaves an even smaller amount of water—just under 1 percent—that is readily accessible to humans and other animals for drinking. This is why our lakes are so vital—a majority of them are fresh-water lakes. The continuously rising human global population only exacerbates (worsens) the accessibility to safe drinking water for all life on Earth, making this one of the world's most challenging issues.

The Water Cycle

Water moves around earth in a cycle (see figure 15.6). As the sun shines on bodies of water, the water evaporates into the air. The air travels inland and moves upward. Eventually water in the air concentrates into clouds. When the clouds become

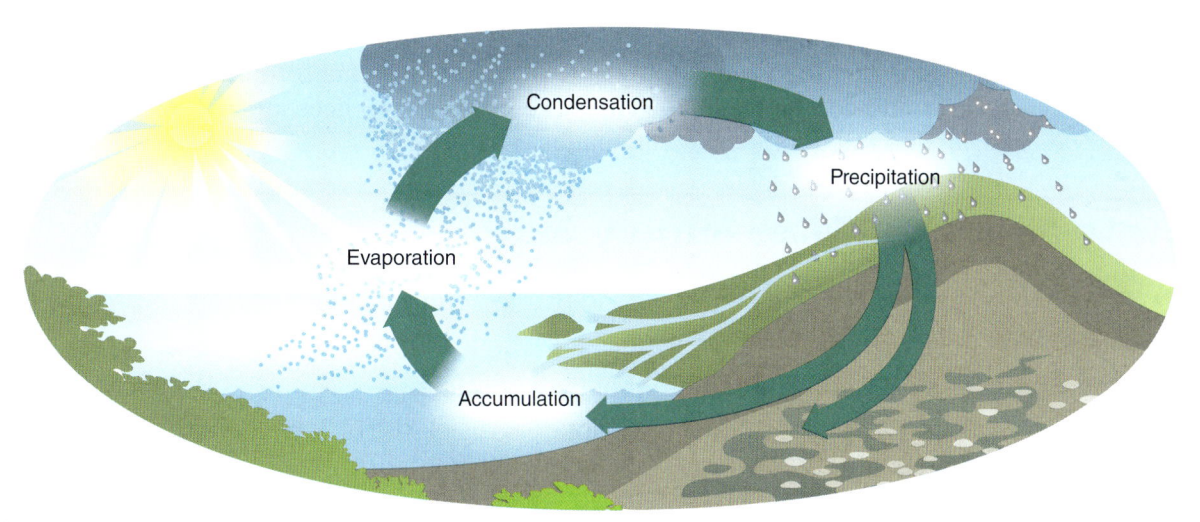

Figure 15.6 The water cycle.

dense enough with water, precipitation in the form of rain, snow, or ice will occur. The water lands on the earth's surface and travels downhill in streams and rivers until it eventually finds its way to the oceans and lakes where the process repeats. Water pollution occurs along this process as water picks up chemicals and debris from the atmosphere and the land.

How Humans Contaminate the Water

Human activity is a major cause of water pollution. The agricultural industry, which uses herbicides and pesticides on a large scale, is the top polluter and consumer of water both worldwide and in the United States. Whenever it rains, residual toxins mix with the water and seep into the cracks and pores of rock below the earth's surface where groundwater is located. Half of the U.S. population uses groundwater in various ways, including for drinking.

Other industry giants, such as the manufacturing sector, involve processes that combine water with chemicals. Discharge from this wastewater travels via streams and rivers, eventually entering larger bodies of water: for example, lakes, most of which are sources of fresh water, and oceans. As you can imagine, the effects are far reaching. From massive die-offs of marine life to unsafe drinking water supplies, excessive pollution levels can even make water unfit for swimming and other water-based recreational activities.

At the individual level, there are several ways in which people contaminate water. When we do ordinary, seemingly harmless things like apply chemical treatments to our lawns or wash our cars in the driveway on nice summer days, the chemicals we use enter the water cycle. When we do not properly dispose of household products containing chemicals, such as paint, batteries, and medicines, we contribute to water pollution. When it comes to chemicals, it's our individual responsibility to give pause and think about what choices we make.

In addition to chemicals, other microorganisms from animal and human waste and improper disposal of garbage and food waste can get into the water supply. When this happens, the water may contain potentially dangerous pathogens that infect our water and food supplies, resulting in illnesses. Water-borne illnesses can cause a variety of health problems including gastrointestinal and reproductive problems, nervous system damage, and even death.

HEALTHY LIVING TIP
Help keep the environment safe by properly disposing of unused medicines. Participate in National Prescription Drug Take Back Day or check with your local law enforcement officials to find a safe disposal location near you. You can also consult a pharmacist about medicine drop boxes or mail-back programs.

LESSON 15.1   Environmental Health

Government regulations and oversight over the proper disposal of waste can help to protect the water supply and Earth's ecosystem. Corporate and company policies and commitments to safe waste disposal practices are also critical to the health and safety of local communities.

How to Keep the Water Supply Safe

- Don't dump hazardous waste on the ground or into storm drains.
- Avoid using pesticides and chemical fertilizers whenever possible.
- Choose nontoxic household products whenever possible.
- Don't flush unused medicines down the toilet or in a sink drain. Take them to a proper disposal site or secure them in a sealed container (zipper bag or plastic container with a lid) before discarding. Always remove labels and identifying information before disposing.

STEM in Health

WATER TREATMENT

More than 85 percent of drinking water in the United States is sourced from surface water like streams, ponds, rivers, and lakes or groundwater. The remaining population sources groundwater from private wells. The public water supply is treated in large water treatment facilities. The water purification process involves removing all pollutants from the water. The first step is to get rid of solid particles in the water. To do this, chemicals called coagulants are added to the water, which cause the solids to stick together (coagulate) and settle to the bottom so that they can undergo filtration.

After solids are removed, other contaminants such as chemicals, bacteria, or viruses may still remain. The second step in the process is to remove these by passing the water through filters made of sand, gravel, and charcoal. The final step is to disinfect the water by adding chlorine to kill all remaining pathogens. Most cities have codes as to what the maximum and minimum chlorine levels must be at service points throughout a water network. The treated water is used for homes, farms, and industries in the United States. The goal of water treatment is to protect people and animals from drinking polluted water and becoming ill as a result.

Air, Water, and Noise Pollution LESSON 15.1

Other Causes of Water Pollution

Natural disasters can also contaminate the earth's water. During hurricanes and floods, the chemicals and garbage that are normally properly stored can be swept into the floodwater and eventually into the runoff. Earthquakes can damage pipes in homes or city sewage systems and disrupt water treatment plants. If you live in an area where any natural disaster occurs, it is important to remember that the water supply is potentially contaminated.

Noise Pollution and Your Health

Sound is a significant part of our environment as well. You are almost always exposed to some sort of noise from cars, planes, trains, televisions, music, video games, and machinery as well as from natural events like wind and rain. **Noise pollution**, or sound that is unwanted, excessive, or bothersome, can damage hearing and cause high blood pressure, difficulty sleeping, and poorer performance at school and work. People who are exposed to constant noise can also become irritable and suffer from depression or anxiety.

A major source of noise comes from the earbuds and headphones worn with personal devices. The use of earbuds is leading to record rates of hearing loss among teenagers. In fact, it is estimated that one in five teenagers has developed mild hearing loss. This can interfere with the ability to accurately hear conversation. Hearing loss is permanent and is also likely to get worse with age. Most smartphones provide warnings when volume is increased above safe levels. It is important to reduce the volume on your personal device to protect your hearing now and in the future.

CASE STUDY

Lamar's Music Habit

Lamar loves to dance and loves the music he and his troop dance to. He also plays the drums, so he really enjoys finding new songs that have prevalent beats and fresh drum solos. Most of the time, Lamar uses headphones to listen to music from his phone while he is dancing or creating his choreography. His friends Jackson and Roberto give him a hard time because the music is loud enough to hear it coming from Lamar's headphones when they are standing next to him. He likes to have the music loud because it helps him pick up the different sounds and rhythms, and it gives him more energy to dance.

Think About It

1. Do you think Lamar is risking his hearing by listening to music? Why or why not?
2. What could Jackson and Roberto say to Lamar to help him make a healthier choice when it comes to his listening habits?

LESSON 15.1 Environmental Health

Skill-Building Challenge

Analyzing Influences on Air and Water Pollution

Think about the different ways people might pollute the air and water in your community. Write down as many examples as you can think of. For example, do people contribute to air pollution by driving everywhere they go instead of walking or taking public transportation? Try to focus on what you notice in your school, neighborhood, community, or town or city. Once you have made your list, compare it with another student's list. Identify where your ideas are the same and where they are different. Combine your lists and then rank-order them. Put the behavior that you think is most common at the top of the list and the behavior that is least common at the bottom. Once you are finished, answer the following questions together:

- Why do you think people make choices that pollute the environment? How might the choices people make be influencing the health of other people in your community?
- What might you do to be a positive influence on others to help them change these behaviors? Provide some specific suggestions.

Healthy Living Skills

This lesson focused on analyzing influences. Here are some more ways you can develop healthy living skills related to this lesson.

HEALTHY COMMUNICATION
What would you do if you saw a relative pouring leftover cleaning products into a street drain? How would you get that person to understand that they are polluting the water? Practice what you would say to this person to try to get them to stop and to properly dispose of the cleaner. Use I messages in your approach.

ADVOCATING FOR GOOD HEALTH
Consider the ways in which technology may help or hinder physical activity levels in your community. Create a short public service announcement about your findings. Be sure to include ways to use technology to help people become and stay active so that you can have a positive impact on the health of your community.

LESSON 15.1 Review: Air, Water, and Noise Pollution

LESSON SUMMARY

- Air pollution can trigger asthma and allergy attacks, sleepiness, headaches, and irritation of the eyes, nose, throat, and skin; it contributes to heart disease, cancers, and dementia. The quality of the air we breathe affects the health of all people at all stages of life.
- Indoor air quality is affected by ventilation (access to outdoor air), cooking, humidity, mold, chemicals, tobacco smoke, dust, and other allergens, like pollen and pet dander.
- Water pollution occurs when rainwater that mixes with the residual chemicals from agricultural products seeps into groundwater or washes out to bodies of surface water. Natural disasters can also cause water pollution, especially when sewer lines are damaged and sewage escapes.
- People exposed to constant noise pollution or who choose to listen to music too loudly in their earbuds can damage their hearing, get high blood pressure, have difficulty sleeping, and suffer from depression or anxiety.

REVIEWING CONCEPTS AND VOCABULARY

1. The _____ is the surroundings and conditions in which you live. It includes the air you breathe, the water you drink, and the places you go.
2. The natural environment includes all living species, _____, weather, and natural resources.
3. The _____ environment includes all the human-made spaces where you work, live, and go to school.
4. A form of air pollution that happens in cities is called _____.
5. When the _____ is high, people are advised to stay inside.
6. Excessively loud jackhammers at a construction site or blaring car horns are examples of _____.
7. Acid rain occurs when _____ that are released into the air mix with water and oxygen and fall to the ground.

THINKING CRITICALLY

You noticed some discolored water in the river near a manufacturing plant in your neighborhood. When you walked closer to the area, you also noticed a chemical smell. Write a short letter to a local government official explaining your concerns. Be sure to address why you think this may be a problem for your community and for the environment.

TAKE IT HOME

Pay attention to the noise in your environment. Keep track of the types of noises you encounter over a typical week. Once you have made your list, come up with ways to reduce your exposure to the noises. For example, if you hear construction noise on your walk to school, could you take a different route?

LESSON 15.2

Chemicals, the Environment, and Your Health

Terms to Learn
chemical
hazardous materials
synthetic chemical
toxic chemical

The Big Picture
Chemicals cause air and water pollution and are harmful to our environment. Chemicals can also be harmful to human health. Products we use daily contain a range of chemicals, some of which may be dangerous. Becoming familiar with where dangerous chemicals are found and how they may affect your health will allow you to make healthier decisions.

Learning Targets
- Explain the dangers of toxic chemicals.
- Explain how to identify toxic chemicals in personal care products.
- Explain three ways to reduce your exposure to toxic chemicals found in household items.
- Explain what to do if you are exposed to toxic chemicals.

Write About It
Have you ever considered whether the personal care products you use are safe? How would you feel if you found out that your shampoo, soap, or sunscreen contained dangerous ingredients? Would you try to change the products you use?

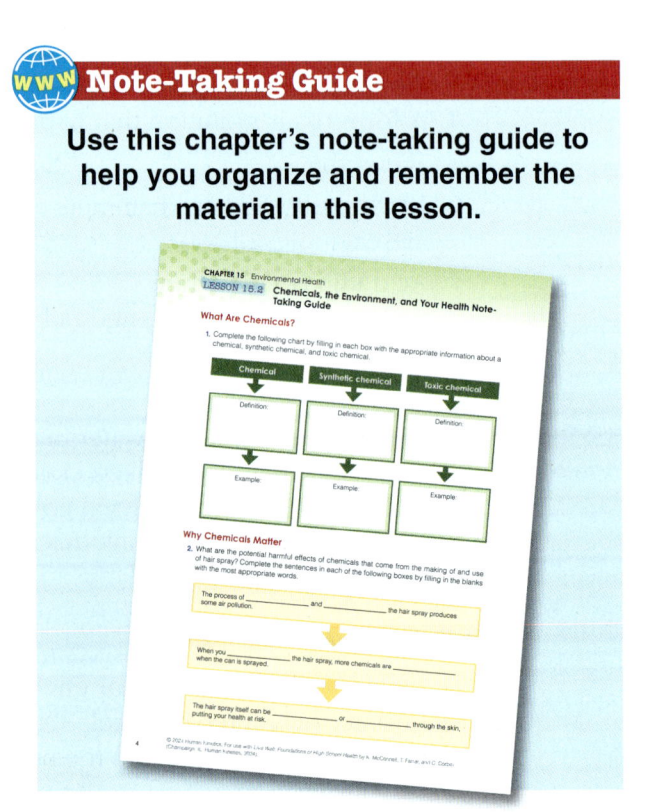

Note-Taking Guide
Use this chapter's note-taking guide to help you organize and remember the material in this lesson.

Chemicals, the Environment, and Your Health **LESSON 15.2**

Darnell lives in a home that has a lot of chemicals sitting around. His parents are both artists. One works with paints, including spray paints, and has different paint thinners and solvents lying around. The other works with metals and wood and is always using stains and acids. Even though one parent works in the basement and the other works in the garage, Darnell can smell the fumes in the house when they are both finishing projects. He also notices that chemicals are poured down the drains almost every day. Darnell wonders whether his parents' work will negatively influence their health and wishes they would be more aware of the environmental impact of their work. What could Darnell say to his parents to try to improve the health of their household environment?

What Are Chemicals?

A **chemical** is a substance that cannot be broken down without changing into something else. Chemicals can occur naturally, like the gold found in rocks or the vitamin C found in citrus fruits. A **synthetic chemical** is human-made for a particular purpose. For example, aspirin is a chemical compound that people make from substances found in tree bark. Aspartame is another synthetic chemical that is used to sweeten beverages like diet sodas. We are all in contact with natural and synthetic chemicals every day. Chemicals are everywhere: in the air you breathe, the food you eat, the paper you write on, and the plastic that holds your lunch.

Chemicals serve very different purposes. Some are designed to kill microorganisms on surfaces to help keep people safe from infectious diseases. Other chemicals are designed to protect fabric or building supplies from rain and sun. We use chemicals to make building materials like adhesives and plastics and to preserve everything from food to body lotion. Many chemicals are safe when used properly and in appropriate amounts. A **toxic chemical** is dangerous no matter how carefully we use it and can make you pass out for a period of time or worse—permanent harm and even death.

LESSON 15.2 Environmental Health

Why Chemicals Matter

Chemicals not only create air and water pollution but also are potentially dangerous to your health (see figure 15.7). Let's consider a can of hair spray as an example. To begin, the process itself of creating and packaging the product produces air pollution. Each use of the product also releases additional chemicals into the air. The final factor, the hair spray itself, puts your health at risk if you inhale it or absorb it through your skin. Chemicals in household products like cleaners also have the same effects. It is important to consider the ways in which you can reduce the dangers chemicals pose to you and the environment.

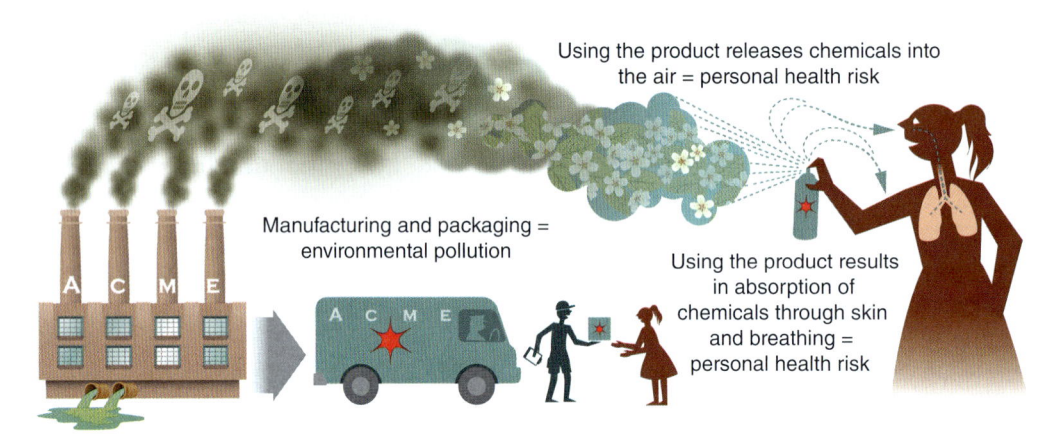

Figure 15.7 Chemicals are linked to both environmental and personal health risks.

Chemicals and Your Health

People have different perspectives on the use of synthetic chemicals in common household and personal products. On one side of the spectrum are people who trust that the chemicals found in foods and personal products are safe; they don't worry much about using them. On the other end are people who have serious concerns about the dangers that chemical exposures can cause; they avoid using products with any unnecessary synthetic chemicals in them as much as possible. Everyone else falls somewhere in between these opposing perspectives.

Chemicals in Personal Care Products

HEALTHY LIVING TIP

Research the ingredients in the personal care products you use most often. Use the information you gather to help you make informed consumer decisions.

Your body absorbs chemicals through your lungs and skin. When you breathe, bathe, eat, drink, and use personal care products like shampoo, toothpaste, deodorant, sunscreen, and makeup, you are exposing yourself to chemicals that could have a negative effect on your health (see figure 15.8). While a single product may have a chemical level that is considered safe, the use of multiple products over many years may be dangerous. For example, a recent study showed that people who used sunscreen as directed for four days absorbed dangerous chemicals through their skin into their blood. More research is needed to fully understand the health risks of using products containing chemicals.

Chemicals, the Environment, and Your Health **LESSON 15.2**

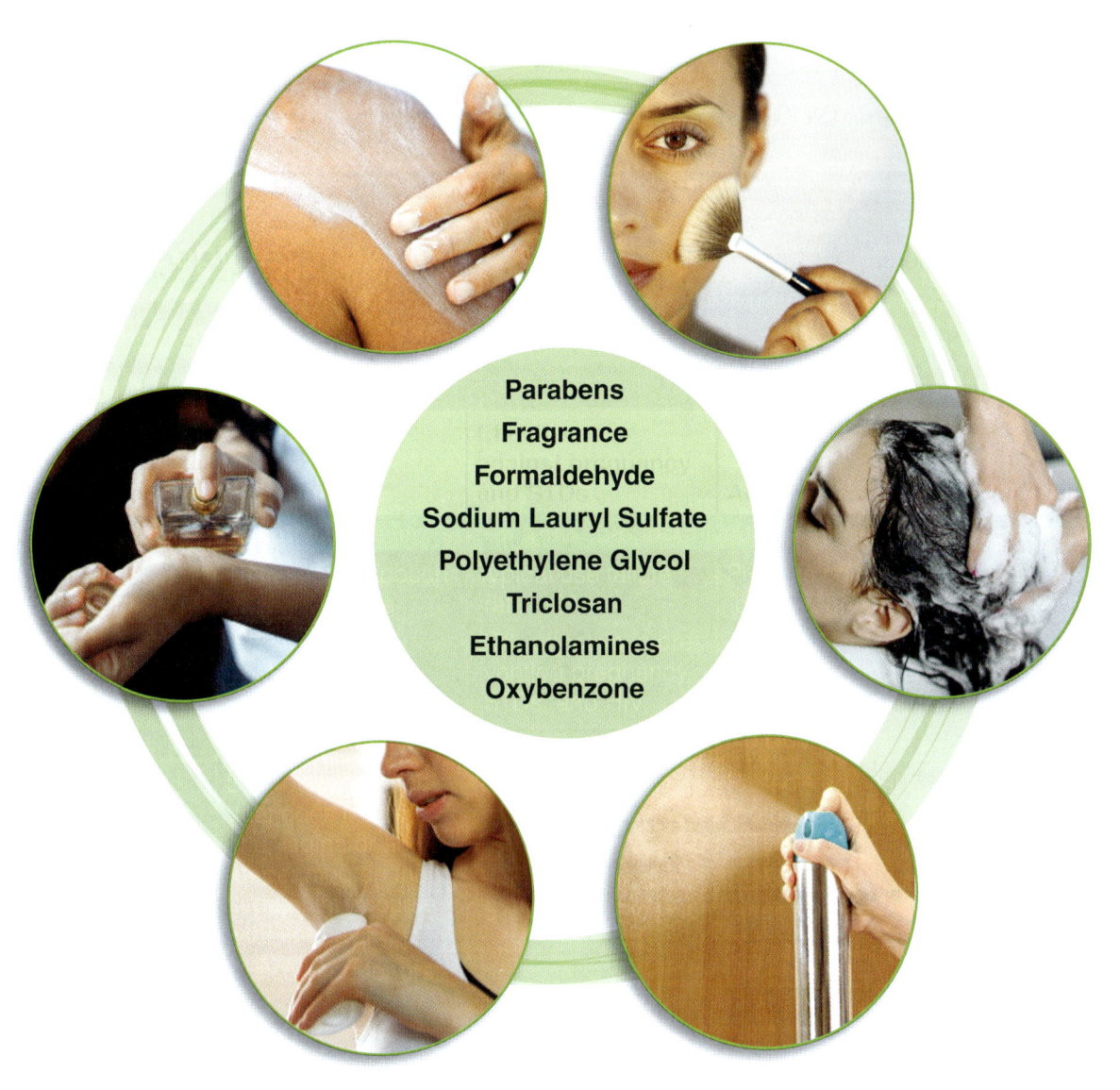

Parabens
Fragrance
Formaldehyde
Sodium Lauryl Sulfate
Polyethylene Glycol
Triclosan
Ethanolamines
Oxybenzone

Figure 15.8 Personal care products like perfume and shampoo often contain potentially dangerous chemicals.

Chemicals in Household Items

Household products and materials that we use to build our homes and communities also contain toxic chemicals (see figure 15.9). Solvents, paints, batteries, pool cleaners, antifreeze, and bug and weed killers are examples of common products that can be dangerous. People can become sick if they touch, inhale, or accidentally ingest the chemicals in these products. Whether a person gets seriously ill from a chemical depends on their general health and the amount of exposure. Groups with highest risk are babies, young children, and pregnant women. Babies and young children are small and still growing, which makes their risk higher. Contact with dangerous chemicals or other environmental hazards during pregnancy can cause harm to the fetus such as increased risk of birth defects or future health problems.

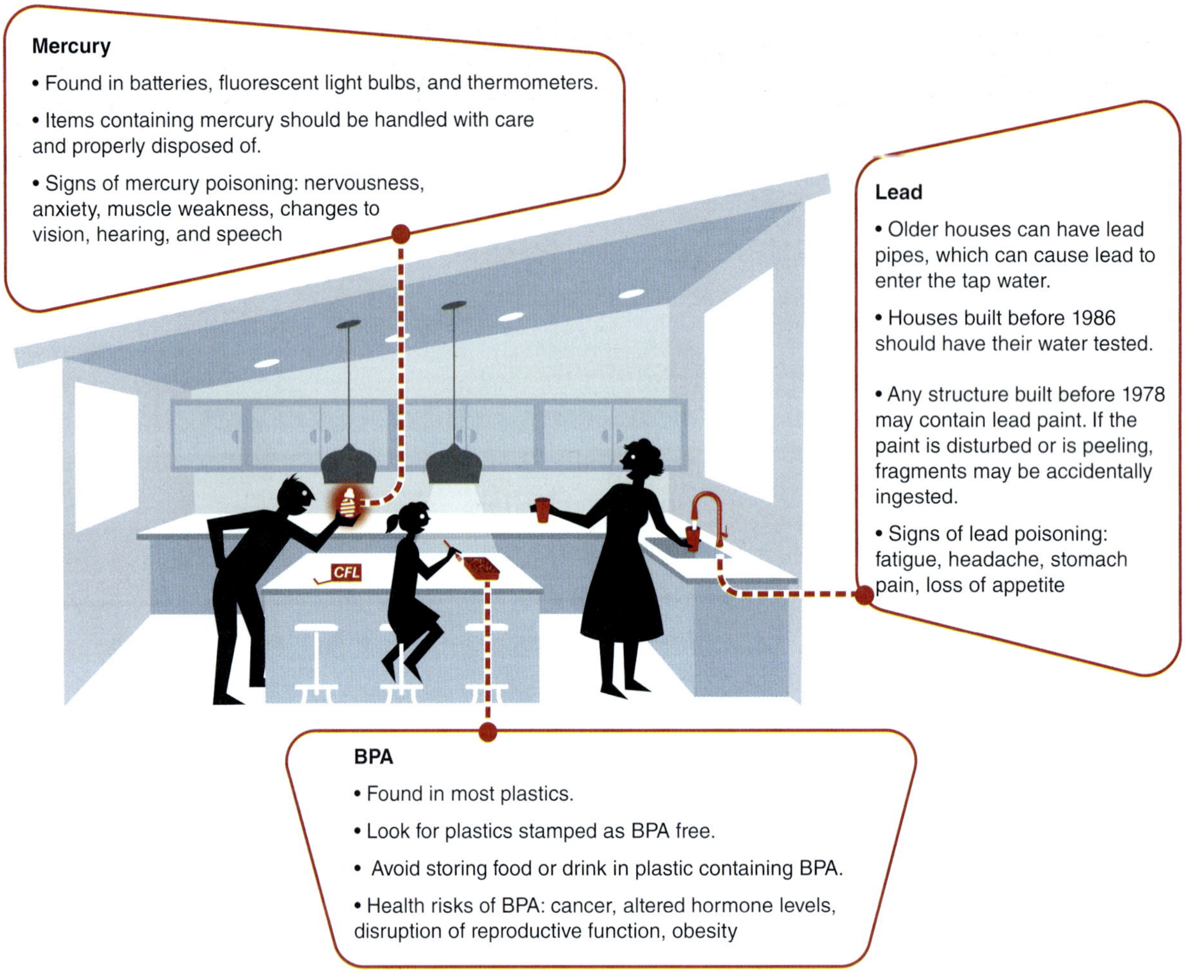

LESSON 15.2 Environmental Health

Mercury
- Found in batteries, fluorescent light bulbs, and thermometers.
- Items containing mercury should be handled with care and properly disposed of.
- Signs of mercury poisoning: nervousness, anxiety, muscle weakness, changes to vision, hearing, and speech

Lead
- Older houses can have lead pipes, which can cause lead to enter the tap water.
- Houses built before 1986 should have their water tested.
- Any structure built before 1978 may contain lead paint. If the paint is disturbed or is peeling, fragments may be accidentally ingested.
- Signs of lead poisoning: fatigue, headache, stomach pain, loss of appetite

BPA
- Found in most plastics.
- Look for plastics stamped as BPA free.
- Avoid storing food or drink in plastic containing BPA.
- Health risks of BPA: cancer, altered hormone levels, disruption of reproductive function, obesity

Figure 15.9 Examples of hazardous chemicals in household items.

How to Get Help When You Might Be Poisoned

All products containing dangerous chemicals are labeled toxic or health hazard according to the danger they pose. If you inhale or ingest a dangerous chemical, or if your skin is exposed to it, tell your doctor, school nurse, or other trusted adult right away. You can also call the national Poison Control Centers toll-free at 800-222-1222 to ask for advice. Be sure you know the name of the product or chemical so they can best help you.

Poison Control Center:
Call toll free:
1-800-222-1222

Chemicals, the Environment, and Your Health   **LESSON 15.2**

Proper Disposal of Chemical Waste

Chemicals harm the environment when they enter our air and water supply system. You can help reduce the impact of chemicals on the environment, and keep yourself and others safer, when you properly dispose of chemical-containing products. All products containing chemicals include specific instructions on the label about proper disposal. Most cities also support the proper disposal of chemicals by providing designated drop-off areas for hazardous materials. **Hazardous materials** include all items that could cause damage to human or animal life or to the environment.

Skill-Building Challenge

Making Responsible Decisions

If you come into contact with a dangerous or toxic chemical, it is important to act quickly in order to lessen the damage the chemical might cause. Develop a short story about what you would do if you accidentally came into contact with a toxic chemical. The story should focus on what you would say and do in the situation. Use the information from this chapter to build the details of your story so that it is accurate and results in a positive outcome. Be sure to include the Poison Control Centers toll-free number as part of your story and use the Decision-Making Skill Cues to demonstrate how you would make a healthy decision in this scenario.

Healthy Living Skills

This lesson focused on making healthy decisions. Here are some more ways you can develop healthy living skills related to this lesson.

ANALYZING INFLUENCES
How do the media and the social norms of your peer group influence the types of personal care products you use? Do you think this influence will stay with you even as you graduate from school and become more independent? Why or why not?

ACCESSING INFORMATION
Use the Internet to shop for three personal care products that don't contain any of the toxic ingredients listed in this lesson. Choose a shampoo, a lotion or skin care product, and a deodorant. Write down the name of the products you selected and their price. Compare the price to other products that do contain toxic ingredients. Describe which products you would buy and explain why.

ADVOCATING FOR GOOD HEALTH
Develop a handout that you can give to your peers. It should explain some of the chemicals found in common household items and potential health risks. Include information on how to handle and dispose of these products safely.

LESSON 15.2 Environmental Health

LESSON 15.2 Review: Chemicals, the Environment, and Your Health

LESSON SUMMARY

- A toxic chemical is any chemical that can cause death, temporary incapacitation, or permanent harm to humans or animals.
- Toxic chemicals can be found in personal care items and common household items, such as shampoo, hair spray, deodorant, lotion, batteries, and cleaning products.
- Lead, BPA, and mercury are common toxins found in household items like pipes, paint, fluorescent light bulbs, and plastics.
- If you have come into contact with something that could be toxic, it is important to seek immediate medical attention. You can also call the national Poison Control Centers at 800-222-1222.

REVIEWING CONCEPTS AND VOCABULARY

1. A(n) _____ is a substance that cannot be broken down without changing into something else.
2. Aspirin is an example of a human-made chemical or a(n) _____ chemical.
3. If a chemical is dangerous enough to cause death or permanently harm a person or animal, that chemical is known as a _____ chemical.
4. Chemicals can be found in personal care products and in _____ items like paint, batteries, and bug killer.
5. _____ include all items that could cause damage to human or animal life or to the environment.

THINKING CRITICALLY

Why do you think chemicals are used in personal care products like shampoo if they are known to be potentially dangerous? Do you think products containing potentially dangerous chemicals should be sold in the United States? Explain your response, using specific examples when possible.

TAKE IT HOME

Pick out three products that contain chemicals in your home. Study the label and its list of ingredients and determine whether they would be harmful to a pregnant woman or her fetus. Identify the potentially harmful effects of each product.

LESSON 15.3

Conservation and Living Green

Terms to Learn

biodegradable
biodiversity
composting
conservation
living green
recycling
renewable energy source

The Big Picture

The environmental issues we face are enormously challenging. Solving them involves families, communities, laws, and regulations working together. While that can feel overwhelming, as an individual, you do have a real impact. Understanding the preservation and conservation of natural resources, and the sustainable use of materials will help you, and hopefully others around you, to make healthy choices. Making a commitment to live green is one of the most impactful things you can do to protect the environment.

Learning Targets

- Explain five ways to protect the environment.
- Provide two examples of commonly recycled products and what they are used for.
- Explain what it means to live green and identify four related actions.

Write About It

What does it mean to live green? Do you think about the environmental impact of your daily life? Why or why not?

Note-Taking Guide

Use this chapter's note-taking guide to help you organize and remember the material in this lesson.

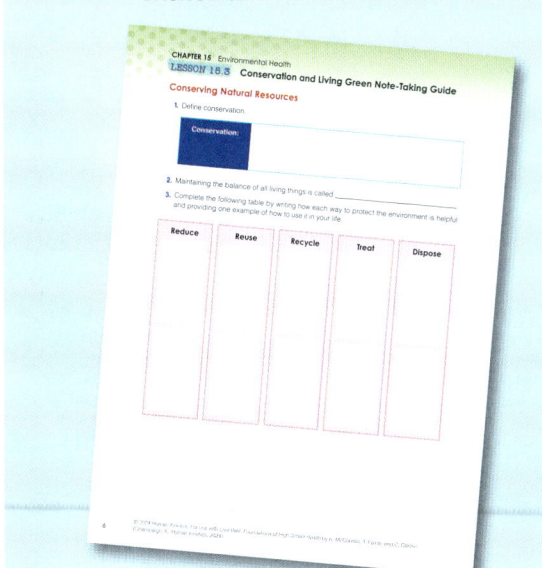

665

LESSON 15.3 Environmental Health

George is an environmentally conscious person. He joined the Save the Planet club at his school, and together, the members planted and care for the school garden. They're also working on getting additional recycling bins to place in convenient locations inside the school building and in areas around the school's outdoor campus. They put up signs to help other students know what to recycle and why it is important.

At home, no one seems to care about any of it—his parents don't even recycle. He wishes they would buy environmentally friendly products, but they seem to care more about saving money than saving the environment. George created his own recycling system in his room and carries bottles and cans to a local store where they let him use the recycling bins. He is proud of his efforts but wishes he could do more. What could George do to help his family make changes to their habits? What challenges do you think he would face?

Conserving Natural Resources

Conservation is the steps people take to prevent the exploitation, destruction, or neglect of natural resources. Through conservation efforts, we can preserve and maintain the **biodiversity**, or variety, of life in particular habitats and ecosystems. Another benefit of these conservation efforts is they maintain our food supply and help protect against natural disasters like landslides and wildfires.

In order to take better care of the environment, policymakers create and pass laws and policies that govern our behaviors and help support conservation efforts. The U.S. Environmental Protection Agency (EPA) is the federal agency that establishes these laws and regulations. In addition to establishing laws, the EPA also regulates the disposal of chemical pollutants and enforces laws that protect human health. See figure 15.10 for the work the EPA does.

Conservation and Living Green **LESSON 15.3**

The Environmental Protection Agency (EPA)

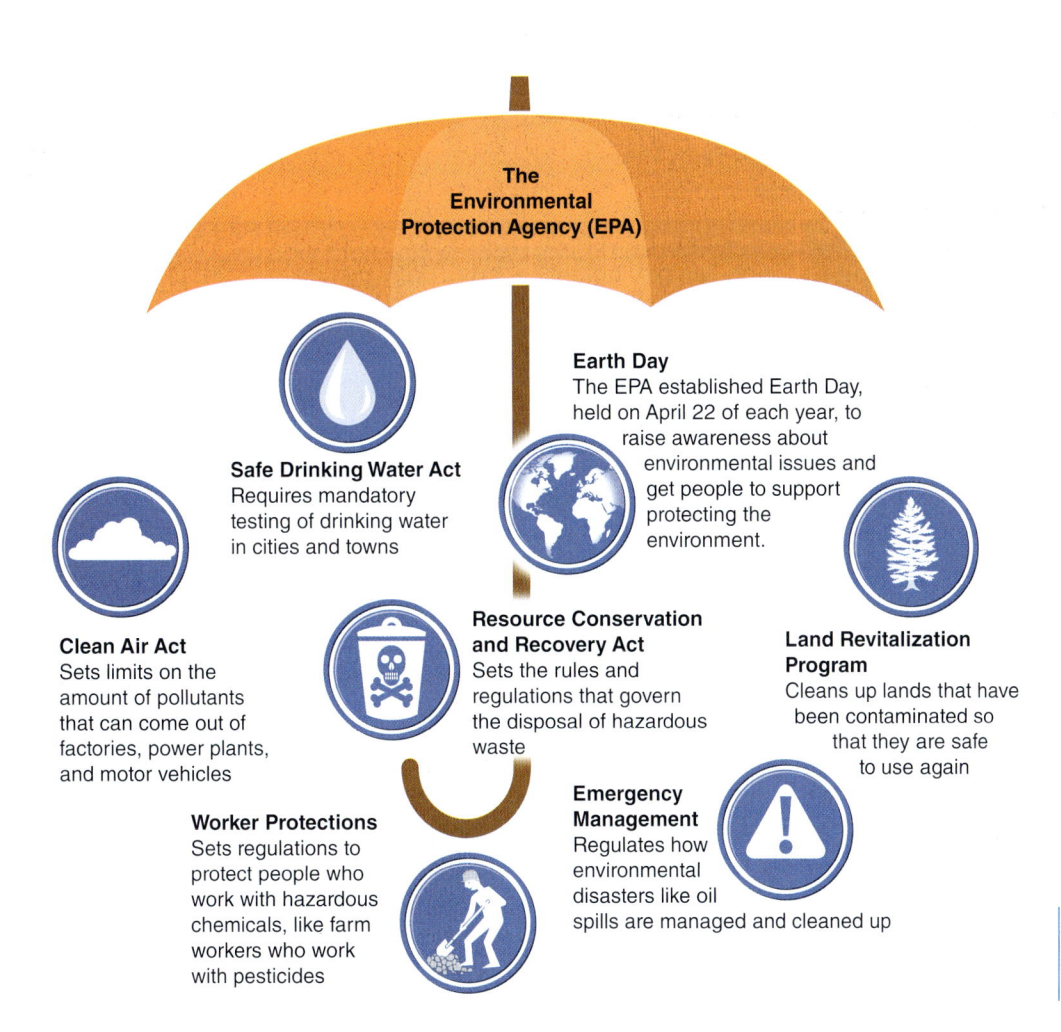

Safe Drinking Water Act
Requires mandatory testing of drinking water in cities and towns

Earth Day
The EPA established Earth Day, held on April 22 of each year, to raise awareness about environmental issues and get people to support protecting the environment.

Clean Air Act
Sets limits on the amount of pollutants that can come out of factories, power plants, and motor vehicles

Resource Conservation and Recovery Act
Sets the rules and regulations that govern the disposal of hazardous waste

Land Revitalization Program
Cleans up lands that have been contaminated so that they are safe to use again

Worker Protections
Sets regulations to protect people who work with hazardous chemicals, like farm workers who work with pesticides

Emergency Management
Regulates how environmental disasters like oil spills are managed and cleaned up

Figure 15.10 How the EPA works to protect the environment.

Protecting the Environment

You can make individual choices every day that can help conserve resources and protect the environment. The EPA cites five ways to protect the environment: reduce, reuse, recycle, treat, dispose.

Reduce

The most impactful way to protect the environment is to reduce the amount of trash and pollution we create in the first place. This involves changing the way we make and use energy. Focusing on energy sources that create less pollution is one approach. We can also use renewable energy sources. A **renewable energy source** is any type of energy that will never run out. Energy generated from the sun and from the wind are two examples of renewable energy. Reducing our consumption of nonrecyclable and nonbiodegradable products can also help keep pollutants out of circulation and can help reduce their impact.

Reuse

On average, each person in the United States produces five pounds (2 kg) of waste materials every day. It is very common for people in our society to buy a product

HEALTHY LIVING TIP
Get an insulated reusable water bottle and use it for the school year. Be sure to pick a BPA-free bottle. Properly clean the bottle every day and deep clean it once a week. To deep clean the bottle, rinse the interior with diluted distilled white vinegar. Use about a teaspoon in two to three cups of water and let it sit in the bottle overnight. Rinse the bottle well in the morning and you will be good to go!

LESSON 15.3   Environmental Health

and throw it away before it is used up or worn out. The stuff we collect contributes to environmental pollution when it is manufactured and when it is thrown out. To help protect the environment, buy fewer things you don't need and find ways to reuse the things you have. You can reuse something yourself, like finding a new use for a plastic shopping bag, or you can reuse something by giving it to someone who will use it if you no longer will. When you reuse items, you help reduce the need for more to be made and sold.

Recycle

Another way to protect the environment is to recycle items whenever you can. **Recycling** is the process of collecting and processing materials that would otherwise be thrown away as trash and turning them into new products (see figure 15.11). When we recycle items, we reduce the amount of trash that goes into landfills. Most communities have recycling services for some plastics, paper products, and glass. Recycling can help to reduce the amount of new materials that need to be produced. This conserves natural resources and saves energy. It is important to realize that not all plastics can be recycled, so reducing the consumption of plastics is also an important element to conserving resources.

Treat

The fourth step to protecting the environment is to treat potentially dangerous substances. The goal is to protect people and the environment from the damage the substances cause. Treating contaminated water so that it is safe to use is an example. We also treat land that is contaminated so that it can be used for future projects. For example, land near old factories might contain high levels of lead, arsenic, or other contaminants. In order for that land to be safe for kids to play

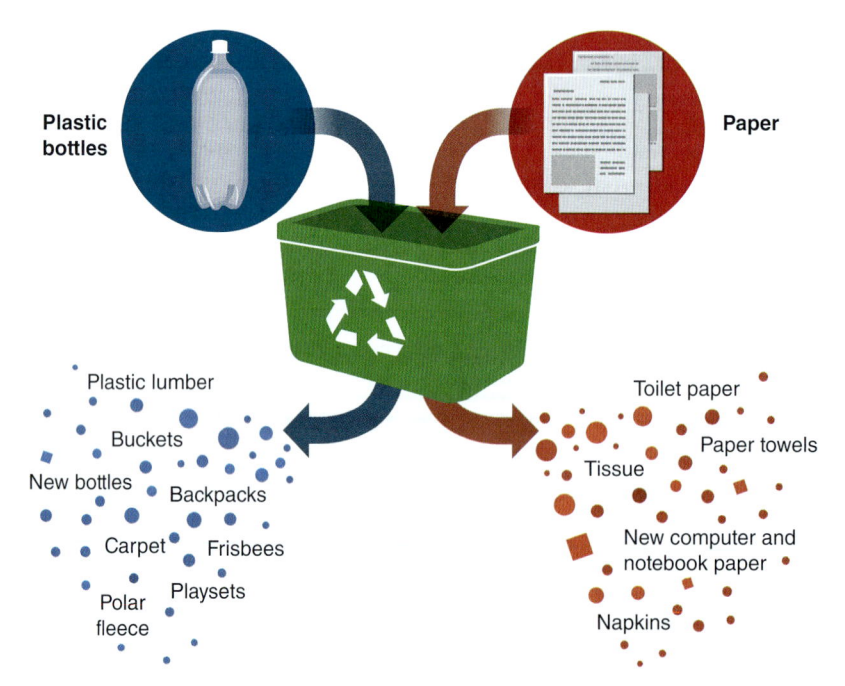

Figure 15.11   What happens to commonly recycled items.

on or for people to garden in, the top layers of the soil need to be removed and replaced with soil that is safe. The removed contaminated soil is typically disposed of in a landfill.

Dispose

The last step we can take is to properly dispose of materials that can't be recycled or otherwise treated. This can be as simple as not littering. It also includes properly disposing of any item containing toxic or dangerous substances so that they don't contaminate the water, soil, or air. Batteries are an example of a product that is hazardous and should be disposed of properly.

What Does Living Green Mean?

When we choose to be aware of how our choices impact our environment and when we change our behaviors as a result of that knowledge, we are **living green**. Living green may involve a series of small choices like buying products based on their packaging or manufacturing practices, or it can involve larger decisions like choosing to live within walking or bicycling distance from work in order to avoid commuting. When people choose to live green, they are choosing to protect the environment. In general, living green involves considering how to reduce our environmental impact while also reusing and recycling everyday products and items as much as you can.

LESSON 15.3   Environmental Health

Tips for Being a Green Student

Now is a great time to develop green habits. You can start by thinking about what you already do as a student and what you can change. You can also think about your habits at home. Here are a few ideas to help you be green.

Take Notes Electronically
If you are able to use an electronic device to take notes and study, you will reduce usage of not only ink but also paper (notebooks, flashcards, sticky notes).

Carry a Water Bottle With You
Reuse old water bottles several times, or purchase water bottles that you can refill. We can reduce the impact of plastics on the environment by taking this effort seriously. It is estimated that close to 80 percent of water bottles in the United States are not recycled. This is alarming because it takes more water to make a water bottle than it can hold! Some schools and universities even ban the sale of bottled water in order to encourage students to carry a reusable water bottle.

Use a Reusable Lunch Bag
Avoid using a paper or plastic bag by using a reusable lunch bag to carry your lunch. Many of these bags are insulated so they have the added benefit of helping to keep your food fresh.

Power Down
When you're not using your computer or device, put it to sleep or power it down. At the end of the day make sure all computers at school are powered all the way off. Also be sure to turn off the lights any time you leave a room and no one else is there, even if you will only be gone a few minutes.

Recycle Your Paper
School usually involves paper. When you use paper for class or for your studies, recycle it when you are done.

Walk, Bike, Carpool, or Use Public Transportation
In addition to helping you live a healthier lifestyle, when you walk or bike, you will help cut down on the use of gasoline and reduce air pollution. You can also help the environment by carpooling with others or using public transportation if your school is too far to walk or bike to. Remember to always make smart decisions when walking or biking to school. Walk with someone, avoid isolated roads and spaces, and follow all traffic laws.

Take Only What You'll Eat
Help reduce food waste by taking only food you are going to eat when you go through the cafeteria line. When we take less and throw out less, we help to create a more sustainable food market for everyone.

Being Green at Home

You may live in a home that recycles and is careful of its consumer habits, or maybe your family needs to make changes to become more environmentally friendly. Here are some green behaviors you and your family could adopt.

Reuse Bags
Take reusable bags to the store with you to grocery shop instead of opting for paper or plastic. It's easy once you are in the habit. Using fewer bags per trip will add up to a lot of saved energy over a lifetime.

Buy Less
Only buy what you actually need. We live in a consumer culture and people often buy things to display success and wealth. If you only purchase what you absolutely need, you'll be going green and saving money, too.

Borrow More
If you have the option, borrow items instead of buying them. This is especially important if you need to use an item only once or twice.

Use Energy-Efficient Light Bulbs
Try to switch your bulbs to energy-efficient compact fluorescent (CFL) or LED bulbs. These types of bulbs may be a little more expensive, but they last up to five times longer than regular light bulbs and provide brighter light.

Save Energy and Sleep Better
Turn down the heat when you go to bed. People sleep better if the environment is slightly cooler, and you'll save energy and money.

Eat Sustainable Seafood
If your family eats seafood, consider including options that are labeled as sustainable. Seafood that is sustainable has the least impact on the environment and on the balance of fish populations.

Eat Less Meat
Cows produce more greenhouse gases than cars and other transportation. Raising cattle contributes to damaging the environment. Eating less meat can have a significant influence on the environment. Consider choosing free-range, organic, and hormone- and antibiotic-free options when you eat meat.

Watch Your Water Usage
Take simple steps to use less water at home. Turn off the water when you are not using it. This can mean turning it off while you brush your teeth or scrub the dishes. Take shorter showers—each person who shortens their shower by four minutes a day will save 3,650 gallons of water each year.

Buy Eco-Friendly Products
A truly eco-friendly product keeps both environmental and human safety as a priority. Eco-friendly products are always nontoxic. Sometimes they include the use of sustainably grown or raised ingredients, are made from recycled materials, or are biodegradable products. A **biodegradable** product breaks down through natural decomposition, meaning less waste entering the environment.

LESSON 15.3   Environmental Health

Giving Back to the Environment

You can also think about ways to give back to the natural environment. One way to do that is to plant a tree. Trees add beauty to our yards, schools, and streets. Trees also provide much-needed shade, plus they help clean carbon dioxide out of the air and produce oxygen. People who live around green spaces that include trees and people who walk and exercise in greener environments report higher levels of happiness and lower levels of depression. Trees are good for the environment and they are good for us.

Another way to give back to the environment is to compost your food waste. **Composting** involves gathering food scraps and waste into outdoor bins and letting it decompose. When these materials decompose you can mix them into the soil of a garden or yard. The compost helps the soil be as healthy as it can be and supports the life of microbes, worms, and insects, which in turn help the plants to grow and thrive.

Skill-Building Challenge

Living Green Challenge

Living green is both a social and a personal responsibility. Part of deciding to live green is thinking about your own values and strengths. To help protect the environment, you need to make choices every day that will help, or at least not harm, the environment. This lesson provided you with examples of ways you can live green. Select three to five of the ideas presented and try to do them consistently over a week or longer (depending on what your teacher says). Select ideas that you value and that are realistic. Write down—or better yet, type out—your choices and create a log to track your progress. Here is an example.

Action or behavior	Log of progress
Bring a reusable water bottle to school every day.	I did this every day except when I forgot to on Wednesday.
Walk or ride my bike to school every day.	I walked four days. When it rained my mom gave me a ride.
Put my used papers in the right recycling bin.	I did this every day!

Healthy Living Skills

This lesson focused on demonstrating healthy behaviors. Here are some more ways you can develop healthy living skills related to this lesson.

ACCESSING INFORMATION

Research a company that makes eco-friendly products. Discuss the products the company makes and explain how they are different from traditional products. Compare and contrast production, manufacturing and consumer costs, and company mission statements.

> **HEALTHY COMMUNICATION**
> Talk to a friend, family member, or classmate about their commitment to living green. Use active listening skills and try to appreciate their point of view. Take a side for or against an environmental topic like electric cars and engage in a healthy debate on this topic.

LESSON 15.3 Review: Conservation and Living Green

LESSON SUMMARY

- Conservation refers to the steps people take to prevent the exploitation, destruction, or neglect of natural resources. Biodiversity refers to maintaining the balance of all living things in a given area.
- We can protect the environment by reducing the amount of trash and pollution we create, by reusing and recycling products whenever possible, by carefully treating toxins so they do the least harm possible, and by safely disposing of environmentally dangerous substances.
- Many products can be recycled and used in the manufacturing of other products.
- Living green means being aware of the impact your lifestyle and choices have on the environment. In general, living green involves reducing, reusing, and recycling everyday products and items as much as you can.

REVIEWING CONCEPTS AND VOCABULARY

1. The sun and the wind are examples of _____ energy sources.
2. When we _____ items, we reduce the amount of trash that goes into landfills.
3. A(n) _____ product is something that will decompose naturally.
4. Living green involves making choices on a daily basis to reduce, _____, and recycle.
5. _____ involves gathering food scraps and waste into outdoor bins and letting it decompose.

THINKING CRITICALLY

Do you think it is appropriate to require people to individually change their behaviors in order to protect the environment? For example, should people be fined if they don't properly sort their personal garbage into appropriate recycling bins? Explain your thoughts and support them with facts when possible.

TAKE IT HOME

In what ways does your home environment support or detract from living green? Make a list of the ways your family lives green and the ways it doesn't.

Chapter Review

ACTION PLAN: Setting Green Goals

Use the My Action Plan worksheet to set goals for living green. Here is an example.

My Action Plan: Living Green

STEP 1: Identify the health behavior you are going to work on.

I am going to be greener in my choices.

STEP 2: Write SMART goal(s).
Write one or two short-term goals (one day to one month long).

I will recycle 90 percent of the time.

Write a long-term goal (one to six months or more).

I will help my family create recycling bins and a recycling plan for the house.

STEP 3: Make a plan.
Identify two or three action steps (strategies) you could do to meet your goal.

I will put all of my used paper into the paper recycling bin at school.

I will separate plastic bottles from the garbage at home and take them to the plastic recycling bin at the grocery store on the weekends.

If I can't find a recycling bin when I am in a public place, I will carry my bottle and bring it home with me so that I can recycle it later.

STEP 4: Execute your plan and track your progress.

Short-term goal

☒ Met　　　☐ Not met　　　Date: *January 17*

Long-term goal

☐ Met　　　☒ Not met　　　Date: _____

If you met your goal, what helped you to be successful?

Having a paper recycling bin in the classroom at school helped me recycle my papers.

If you did not meet your goal, what made it harder for you to be successful?

I didn't meet my long-term goal. My family did not want to have extra garbage cans around the house, and I couldn't come up with another way to make my recycling bin.

Test Your Knowledge

Select the best answer for each question.

1. The combination of moisture in the air that has mixed with smoke and chemical fumes is called
   a. acid rain
   b. smog
   c. fog
   d. dew

2. Which of the following might contribute to water pollution?
   a. the manufacturing of products
   b. the use of chemical products on lawns
   c. earthquakes and other natural disasters
   d. all of the above

3. Noise pollution is when sound is
   a. unwanted
   b. excessive
   c. bothersome
   d. all of the above

4. A chemical made by humans is
   a. synthetic
   b. toxic
   c. hazardous
   d. biodegradable

5. Any chemical that can cause death, temporary incapacitation, or permanent harm to humans or animals is called
   a. a synthetic chemical
   b. a toxic chemical
   c. a base chemical
   d. an organic chemical

6. Wind and sun energy are examples of
   a. recycled energy
   b. treated energy
   c. renewable energy
   d. all of the above

7. Common toxic chemicals found in household items include
   a. lead and mercury
   b. mercury and sulfate
   c. BPA and sorbitol
   d. lead and chlorine

8. When you are aware of the impact your lifestyle and choices have on the environment you are
   a. living green
   b. living red
   c. living yellow
   d. none of the above

9. Taking steps to prevent the exploitation, destruction, or neglect of natural resources is called
   a. preservation
   b. conservation
   c. manipulation
   d. filtration

10. An area that has a good balance of plant and animal life has
    a. biodiversity
    b. environmentalism
    c. composting
    d. renewable energy

PROJECT-BASED LEARNING: Advocating for the Environment

What to Remember
Our environmental health depends on both the individual and collective choices we make each day. Advocating for environmental issues is one way to help others understand the choices they have and to help them make smarter choices.

Who It Is For
Your campaign will be directed at the audience you select.

Why It Is Important
Learning how to advocate for issues you care about is an important health skill that can help you stand up for yourself and others when you are in need.

What to Do
Develop an advocacy campaign on an environmental issue you care about.

How to Do It

Complete the following steps to develop your campaign.

1. *Develop your message.* Work in a small group identified by your teacher. Remember to keep your message clear and simple and to decide who your audience is. How will you get your message to the people who most need to hear it? Should you use social media? If so, which platform might work best? What other options do you have? Brainstorm messaging and delivery ideas and work together with your group to build your message. Remember to be creative. Keep notes as you work.

2. *Do the campaign.* Once you have settled on your message and know how you want to deliver it, share it with your teacher. If they approve your campaign, work together as a group to decide when you should start and end your campaign. As the campaign progresses, watch it unfold and see if it is working.

3. *Reflect on your work.* Did the campaign work? What worked best? What part or parts weren't as successful? What did you learn about protecting the environment by doing this campaign? What did you learn about yourself and your ability to work with others on complex challenges?

CROSS-CURRICULAR CONNECTION: Math

Eating less meat is an option some people use to reduce the impact cows have on the environment. Answer the math questions in the following list to help you understand the impact of their choices.

- Going meatless one day a week helps reduce your meat consumption by one seventh, or _____ percent.
- Around 1,850 gallons of water are required to produce one pound (0.5 kg) of beef, while one pound of vegetables can be produced with only 39 gallons of water. What is the percentage of water used to produce vegetables versus meat? If you ate two pounds (2 kg) less meat each month, how many gallons of water would you save each month?
- One pound (0.5 kg) of beef produces 13.6 pounds (6 kg) of greenhouse gas. One pound of rice produces 0.6 pounds (0.3 kg) of greenhouse gas. How many pounds of rice could be grown before 13.6 pounds of greenhouse gases were produced?

Appendix

Supplemental Information for Reproductive Health

Complete lessons on these and other topics are available in *Live Well: Reproductive and Sexual Health*.

Contraceptives

While abstinence is the preferred choice for teens, it is important to be aware of other methods of preventing unintended pregnancy (see table 1).

TABLE 1 **Contraceptives**

Contraceptive	Description	Effectiveness against pregnancy and STDs	Advantages	Disadvantages
Barrier contraceptives prevent sperm from entering a woman's uterus and may prevent STDs.				
Male latex condom	Thin, stretchy pouch that covers the penis. Best material is latex. Collects semen.	Typical use failure rate: 13%. 87% effective in preventing pregnancy, STDs, and HIV.	Protects against both pregnancy and STDs. Easy to get and easy to use. No side effects.	Must be used correctly to be effective. A new one must be used every time you have sex.
Female, or internal, condom	Soft, plastic pouch that goes inside the vagina or anus, depending on the type of intercourse you are having. Is also used for oral sex.	Typical use failure rate: 21%. 79% effective in preventing pregnancy, STDs, and HIV.	Protects against both pregnancy and STDs. Easy to use. No side effects. Can be made more effective if used with the pill.	A new one must be used every time you have sex. Do *not* use with a male latex condom at the same time. May not stay in place during intercourse.
Diaphragm (female use)	A shallow cup made of soft silicone that inserts into the vagina to cover the cervix. Must be used with a spermicide.	Typical use failure rate: 17%. 83% effective in preventing pregnancy. No protection against STDs.	Effective as soon as it is in place. Easy to take with you, reusable, and hormone free. Can be used with a condom.	May be difficult to insert and must be used every time you have vaginal sex. Spermicide may have the side effect of irritating the vagina. Must be fit by a doctor.
Cervical cap (female use)	A small cup, shaped like a sailor's hat, made from soft silicone that is inserted into the vagina to cover the cervix. Must be used with a spermicide.	Typical use failure rate: 17%. 83% effective in preventing pregnancy if you have never given birth. Is 71% effective in preventing pregnancy if you have given birth. No protection against STDs.	Effective as soon as it is in place. Easy to take with you, reusable, and hormone free. Can be used with a condom.	May be difficult to insert and must be used every time you have vaginal sex. Spermicide may have the side effect of irritating the vagina. Must be fit by a doctor.

>continued

Appendix

Table 1 >continued

Contraceptive	Description	Effectiveness against pregnancy and STDs	Advantages	Disadvantages
Sponge (female use)	Small, round sponge made from soft, squishy plastic that covers the cervix and contains a spermicide.	Typical use failure rate: 17% if you have never had a baby and 27% if you have had a baby. 83% effective in preventing pregnancy if you have never given birth and 73% effective if you have given birth. No protection against STDs.	No prescription needed. Effective as soon as it is in place. Easy to take with you and hormone free. Can be used with a condom.	Good for only 24 hours and then needs to be replaced. May be difficult to insert and must be used every time you have vaginal sex. Spermicide may have the side effect of irritating the vagina.
Spermicide (female use)	A chemical that is put in the vagina right before sex to prevent sperm from getting past the cervix and reaching an ovum. Can be used by itself or with other birth control methods. Most commonly used with a male latex condom.	Typical use failure rate: 21%. 79% effective in preventing pregnancy when used by itself. No protection against STDs.	Is affordable, convenient, easy to use, and hormone free. No prescription needed.	Must use it every time you have sex. May have side effects.
Hormonal contraceptives contain progestin, with or without estrogen, which works to prevent ovulation.				
Birth control pill (female use)	Taken once a day. May also be used to ease menstrual pain or regulate the menstrual cycle. Prevents ovulation.	Typical use failure rate: 7%. 93% effective in preventing pregnancy. No protection against STDs.	Safe, simple, and convenient. Makes periods lighter and more regular and eases menstrual cramps. Can get pregnant right after you stop taking the pill.	No STD protection. May be difficult to remember to take the pill on a daily basis. May have negative side effects, but they usually go away in 2-3 months. May have spotting or bleeding between periods.

Appendix

Contraceptive	Description	Effectiveness against pregnancy and STDs	Advantages	Disadvantages
Patch (female use)	A contraceptive patch that is worn on certain parts of your body. Releases hormones through the skin that prevent pregnancy. Prevents ovulation.	Typical use failure rate: 7%. 93% effective in preventing pregnancy. No protection against STDs.	Safe, simple, and convenient. Change the patch once a week.	May be hard to remember to change the patch once a week. May have some side effects, such as spotting between periods.
Depo-Provera shot (female use)	A shot a female gets every 3 months to prevent ovulation.	Typical use failure rate: 4%. 96% effective in preventing pregnancy. Is 0% effective in preventing STDs.	Safe, simple, and convenient. Highly effective in preventing pregnancy. Must get the shot only 4 times a year. Period may be lighter or stop altogether. May help protect you from uterine cancer. Shot is temporary, so individual can become pregnant after stopping it.	No STD protection. Must be sure to get the shot every 3 months. May decrease bone density. May cause depression, migraines, or heavy bleeding from vagina, or bleeding for longer than usual may happen for up to the first year after beginning the shot. May take up to 10 months after stopping the shot to get pregnant.
Intrauterine device (female use) (IUD)	A small piece of flexible T-shaped plastic put into the uterus to prevent pregnancy. Two types: copper and hormonal.	Typical use failure rate: Less than 1%. More than 99% effective in preventing pregnancy. No chance for a mistake since it is always in place. No protection from STDs.	Lasts for years but is not permanent. Doctor must insert and remove it. Can get pregnant right after the IUD is removed. Hormonal IUDs can help prevent cramps and make the period lighter.	May have side effects initially, but they usually go away within 3-6 months.

>continued

Appendix

Table 1 >continued

Contraceptive	Description	Effectiveness against pregnancy and STDs	Advantages	Disadvantages
Permanent contraceptives				
Tubal ligation (female sterilization)	Surgical procedure to permanently block the fallopian tubes.	Typical use failure rate: 0.5%. More than 99% effective against pregnancy. No protection from STDs.	Is effective in preventing pregnancy and convenient and permanent.	Is permanent, so it is difficult to reverse if you change your mind. All surgeries have some risks, and there may be some pain and discomfort after the procedure.
Vasectomy (male sterilization)	Surgical procedure to permanently block the vas deferens tube so sperm can't get to the semen.	Typical use failure rate: 0.15%. More than 99% effective against pregnancy but not right away. Can take up to 3 months for semen to become sperm free. No protection from STDs.	Is effective in preventing pregnancy and convenient and permanent.	Is permanent, so it is difficult to reverse if you change your mind. All surgeries have some risks, and there may be some pain and discomfort after the procedure.

Reducing the Risk of Infection From an STD

Abstinence is the only way to eliminate the risk of infection from an STD. If you choose to be sexually active, you can reduce your chances of getting an STD by being in a long-term, mutually monogamous relationship with a partner who has negative STD test results. It is important to be checked or screened for STDs periodically, especially during yearly physicals or any time there is a concern. Early detection and treatment can help prevent the complications of STDs. Table 2 lists symptoms of and treatment for STDs.

TABLE 2 Symptoms of and Treatment for STDs

Sexually transmitted disease	What is the STD?	How is the STD spread?	Symptoms	Treatment
Chlamydia	A bacterial infection. Can infect all humans. Can cause serious, permanent damage to the female reproductive system. One of the most common STDs among 14- to 24-year-olds.	By having unprotected vaginal, anal, or oral sex with someone who has chlamydia. Can infect the penis, vagina, cervix, anus, urethra, eyes, and throat.	Most people do not show any symptoms. Women may notice an abnormal vaginal discharge or a burning sensation when urinating. Men may notice a discharge from their penis, burning sensations when urinating, or pain and swelling in one or both testicles. If infected in the rectum, symptoms may include rectal pain, a discharge, and bleeding.	Can be cured with antibiotics to treat the infection.

>continued

Appendix

Table 2 >continued

Sexually transmitted disease	What is the STD?	How is the STD spread?	Symptoms	Treatment
Gonorrhea	A bacterial infection. Very common STD, especially for teens and people in their 20s. Also called "the clap" or "the drip."	By having unprotected vaginal, anal, or oral sex with someone who has gonorrhea. Can infect the penis, vagina, cervix, anus, urethra, eyes, and throat. Can also be spread to a baby during birth if the mother has it. Not spread through casual contact, such as kissing, hugging, holding hands, coughing, and sneezing.	Most people do not show any symptoms. Women may notice an abnormal vaginal discharge or a pain or burning sensation when urinating and may have bleeding between periods. Men may notice a yellow, white, or green discharge from their penis; pain or burning sensations when urinating; or pain and swelling in one or both testicles. If infected in the anus, symptoms may include itching in or around your anus, pain when you defecate, and discharge from your anus.	Can be cured with antibiotics to treat the infection.
Hepatitis B (HBV)	A very contagious infection that can cause liver disease.	Through semen, vaginal fluids, and blood when having unprotected vaginal, anal, or oral sex; sharing toothbrushes and razors because any blood on them can carry hepatitis B; or sharing needles or getting stuck with a needle that has hepatitis B on it. Can also be passed to babies during birth if mother has it.	Often has no symptoms. Symptoms can occur between 6 weeks and 6 months after getting the virus. Symptoms are similar to the flu and can stick around for months.	No cure once you have it but it usually goes away on its own in 4 to 8 weeks. One in 20 people who get hepatitis B become carriers, which means they have a chronic infection and are contagious for the rest of their lives. Hepatitis B infections that last a long time may lead to liver disease, such as cirrhosis and liver cancer. There are medications that can help with a chronic case.

Appendix

Sexually transmitted disease	What is the STD?	How is the STD spread?	Symptoms	Treatment
Genital herpes and oral herpes	Caused by two viruses: HSV-1 and HSV-2. Oral herpes is caused by HSV-1 and can result in cold sores around the mouth. Oral herpes can be spread from the mouth to the genitals through oral sex. Genital herpes is primarily caused by HSV-2 virus but can be caused by HSV-1 through oral sex. Very common in the United States because 1 out of every 6 people aged 14 to 49 has genital herpes.	By having unprotected vaginal, anal, or oral sex with someone who has herpes. You can come in contact with the herpes virus through a herpes sore, saliva (if partner has oral herpes), or genital secretions (if partner has genital herpes). Partners do not have to have visible sores or even know they are infected for you to contract it.	Most people with genital herpes have no symptoms or very mild symptoms. Herpes sores appear as blisters on or around the genitals, rectum, or mouth.	No cure for herpes. There are medicines that can prevent or shorten the outbreaks.
HIV (human immunodeficiency virus) and AIDS (acquired immunodeficiency syndrome)	HIV is the virus that causes AIDS. HIV damages the immune system, making it easier to get sick and even die because your body can't fight off the infections it normally can. Over time, the damage to the immune system from HIV leads to AIDS. AIDS is when you get opportunistic infections or types of cancer due to your damaged immune system. The damaged immune system cannot fight off the infections.	Through unprotected vaginal or anal sex; sharing needles; getting stuck with an HIV-infected needle; or getting HIV-infected blood, semen, or vaginal fluids into open cuts or sores on your body.	Can take 10 years or even longer if you are taking HIV medicines for HIV to show any symptoms. Initial HIV symptoms may be flu-like and last for only a few days.	No cure. Once you have HIV, the virus stays in your body for life. Medicines can help you stay healthy and lower your chances of spreading the virus to other people.

>continued

Appendix

Table 2 >continued

Sexually transmitted disease	What is the STD?	How is the STD spread?	Symptoms	Treatment
Human papillomavirus (HPV) infection HPV is a common virus. HPV can lead to 6 types of cancers later in life. Children should get the HPV vaccine at the ages of 11-12 to help protect them from ever developing any of the cancers from HPV.	HPV is the most common STD. It is so common that almost every sexually active person will contract HPV at some time in their life if they don't get the HPV vaccine.	By having unprotected vaginal, anal, or oral sex with someone who has the virus. Can be spread whether or not the infected person has signs or symptoms.	There is no test to find out whether you have HPV. There are HPV tests used to screen for cervical cancer, which is a common health problem caused by HPV. There are health problems related to HPV, rather than symptoms of HPV. Genital warts and cervical cancer are the two most common health problems associated with HPV.	No treatment for HPV but there are treatments for the health problems that HPV can cause. Genital warts are treated by a health care provider or prescription medication. Cervical cancer can be treated when diagnosed early.
Pelvic inflammatory disease (PID)	An infection in the uterus, fallopian tubes, or ovaries. Can lead to chronic pain and other problems, such as infertility.	Happens when bacteria spread from the vagina and cervix to the uterus, fallopian tubes, or ovaries. Is usually caused by chlamydia or gonorrhea.	May include longer, heavier, or more painful periods; being very tired; or fever or chills.	Can be cured with antibiotics but people don't know they have the disease.
Genital warts	Show up on the skin around the genitals and anus. Caused by certain types of HPV. A wart you may get on your hand is not the same as a genital wart.	By having unprotected vaginal, anal, or oral sex with someone who has genital warts. Can be passed during vaginal childbirth but this is rare. Can be spread even when a person doesn't have any visible warts.	Skin-colored or whitish bumps that appear on your genitals or anus. Look like little pieces of cauliflower. May itch but most of the time don't hurt.	No cure. You will always have the virus, but genital warts can be treated. Doctor can remove by putting a chemical on them to make them go away or stop growing. Can get a prescription for a cream that you put on the warts yourself. Can be frozen off, burned off, or removed with a knife or electricity.

Appendix

Sexually transmitted disease	What is the STD?	How is the STD spread?	Symptoms	Treatment
Syphilis	A common bacterial infection spread through sex. Causes sores on the genitals called chancres. Chancres show up between 3 weeks and 3 months after you get the infection. Chancres last for 3 to 6 weeks and then go away on their own.	By having unprotected vaginal, anal, or oral sex with someone who has syphilis. A mother can pass it to a baby during pregnancy and childbirth. You get syphilis from contact with the sores or chancres.	Symptoms can be so mild that you don't notice them. The sores may not hurt and can be confused for pimples or rashes. Symptoms vary by stage: • Primary stage is when a chancre pops up. Chancres are very contagious. • Secondary stage includes a rash on palms of hands and other parts of the body, which can last for 2 to 6 weeks and may come and go for up to 2 years. • Late stage includes tumors, blindness, and paralysis.	Curable with antibiotics in early stages. If treatment is started later, it can still cure the infection and stop future damage but can't change what has already happened.
Trichomoniasis (Trich)	Caused by a parasite that is spread during sex.	By having unprotected vaginal, anal, or oral sex with someone who has Trich.	Most people don't know they have Trich because symptoms are so mild. Most common symptom is vaginitis, which happens when the vulva and vagina are irritated. Can also infect the urethra, which can result in pain and burning when peeing.	Cured with antibiotics. Without treatment, can be passed to partners even if you don't have any symptoms.

>continued

Table 2 >continued

Sexually transmitted disease	What is the STD?	How is the STD spread?	Symptoms	Treatment
Pubic lice (crabs)	Different from head lice. Small parasites that attach to the skin and hair near the genitals.	By having sexual contact since they like to live in pubic hair. May also get in beards and mustaches if having oral sex. Pubic lice can also be spread by sharing clothes, bed linens, blankets, or towels. Condoms will not protect a person from crabs.	Symptoms start about 5 days after you get them. Symptoms include intense itching in pubic area, small crabs in pubic hair, nits or crab eggs on the base of pubic hairs, dark spots on the skin from the crab bites, and feeling feverish and run down.	Can buy over-the-counter treatment without a prescription.
Scabies	Caused by scabies mites, which are tiny, insect-like parasites that infect the top layer of a person's skin.	Through skin-to-skin contact, usually during sex.	Can take from 3 to 6 weeks before symptoms begin if you have never had scabies. May take only a few days for symptoms to appear if you have had scabies before. Symptoms can include intense itching; rashes with tiny blisters; and small, raised, crooked lines on your skin from where the scabies mites burrow under the skin.	Treated with a prescription medication that kills scabies mites and eggs, which is often a cream you put all over your body and leave on for several hours.

Getting Tested for an STD

People who are sexually active should get tested for STDs regularly, at least yearly. Many STDs do not have any signs or symptoms, so an individual may have an STD but not know it and may spread it to their partner. STDs are tested for through blood samples, urine samples, swabbing the inside of the penis or cervix, or swabbing a genital sore. There are also some at-home STD tests that can be purchased and the urine sample or oral or genital swab is sent to a lab for analysis. At-home testing may have a higher rate of false-positive results due to human error. If an at-home test comes back positive or comes back negative but symptoms are being experienced, see a medical doctor or go to a public health clinic for further testing and to learn your treatment options.

Glossary/Glosario

English

absorption—Getting nutrients into the cells of the body.

abstinence—Avoiding all forms of sexual activity and genital contact including vaginal, oral, or anal sex.

abuse—Consistent and violent mistreatment of a person.

acid rain—When chemicals are released into the air and then combine with water and fall back down in rain, snow, or ice.

acne—A condition that affects the oil glands and hair follicles on the skin.

acquaintance—A person you don't know very well.

active ingredient—The chemical or drug in a product that causes the desired effect.

active listening—Giving your full attention to the speaker and actively showing verbal and nonverbal signs of listening.

active shooter—An individual actively engaged in killing or attempting to kill people in a populated area.

addiction—A physiological (functions of the body) or psychological (functions of the mind) need for a substance.

addictive potential—Determined by how quickly the drug takes effect, the experience of a feeling of happiness and excitement beyond expectation; tolerance and withdrawal are both effects of the drug.

adequacy—Getting enough calories and nutrients each day to function and stay healthy.

advertisement—Communication of a message about a product or service by means of different types of media.

advocacy—The act or process of supporting or promoting a cause or an issue.

aerobic—Term often used to describe moderate to vigorous physical activity that can be sustained for a long time because the body can supply adequate oxygen to continue activity; means "with oxygen."

Español

absorción—Hacer llegar nutrientes a las células del cuerpo.

abstinencia—Evitar toda forma de actividad sexual y contacto genital, incluido el sexo vaginal, oral o anal.

abuso—Maltrato constante y violento hacia una persona.

lluvia ácida—Cuando se liberan productos químicos al aire y luego se combinan con agua y vuelven a caer en forma de lluvia, nieve o hielo.

acné—Un trastorno que afecta las glándulas sebáceas y los folículos capilares de la piel.

conocido—Una persona a quien no conoces muy bien.

ingrediente activo—El producto químico o droga contenido en un producto que causa el efecto deseado.

escucha activa—Prestar plena atención al orador y demostrar activamente señales verbales y no verbales de estar escuchando.

tirador activo—Una persona dedicada activamente a matar o intentar matar personas en un área poblada.

adicción—La necesidad fisiológica (funciones del cuerpo) o psicológica (funciones de la mente) de consumo de una sustancia nociva.

potencial adictivo—Determinado por cuánto demora la droga en hacer efecto, la experiencia de una sensación de felicidad y excitación superior a la esperada; la tolerancia y la abstinencia son ambos efectos de la droga.

adecuación nutricional—Obtener suficientes calorías y nutrientes a diario para funcionar y mantenerse saludable.

anuncio—Comunicación de un mensaje acerca de un producto o servicio a través de diferentes tipos de medios.

apoyo—El hecho o proceso de apoyar o promover una causa o un asunto.

aeróbico—Un término utilizado frecuentemente para describir la actividad física moderada a vigorosa que se puede mantener durante un tiempo largo ya que el cuerpo puede aportar el oxígeno adecuado para continuar la actividad; significa "con oxígeno".

Glossary/Glosario

English

aggression—Engaging in a forceful action with the intent to dominate or control another person or a situation.

aggressive communication—A communication style in which people express their feelings and opinions in an intimidating manner without regard to how it makes others feel.

air pollution—A condition in which the air contains dangerous chemicals.

air quality index—Measurement of the ozone, particulate matter, carbon dioxide, sulfur dioxide, and nitrogen levels in the air.

alcohol overdose—Occurs when a person has drunk so much alcohol that the areas of the brain controlling basic life-support functions begin to shut down.

alcohol treatment program—Professional help for an alcohol use disorder.

alcohol use disorder (AUD)—A medical condition that is diagnosed when an individual's drinking causes distress or harm.

allergen—Something in the environment that causes the immune system to react.

Alzheimer's disease—A particular type of dementia.

anabolic steroids—A class of hormones that can stimulate muscle growth.

anaphylaxis—A severe, life-threatening allergic reaction.

anemia—A disease caused by a shortage of red blood cells.

antibody—A cell that can remember and recognize pathogens that have been in the body before.

antioxidant—Substances found in fruits and vegetables that work to rid the body of dangerous chemicals.

antivirus software—Software designed to detect, prevent, and remove malware from computers.

anxiety—An emotion that includes tension, worried thoughts, and physical changes such as increased blood pressure.

Español

agresión—Participar de una acción enérgica con la intención de dominar o controlar a otra persona o una situación.

comunicación agresiva—Un estilo de comunicación en el que las personas expresan sus sentimientos y opiniones de manera intimidatoria, sin considerar cómo hacen sentir a los demás.

contaminación del aire—Una condición en que el aire contiene productos químicos nocivos.

índice de calidad del aire—Una medición de los niveles de ozono, material particulado, dióxido de carbono, dióxido de azufre y nitrógeno en el aire.

sobredosis de alcohol—Ocurre cuando una persona ha bebido tanto alcohol que las áreas del cerebro que controlan las funciones vitales básicas comienzan a desconectarse.

programa de tratamiento del alcoholismo—La ayuda profesional para un trastorno por consumo de alcohol.

trastorno por consumo de alcohol (en inglés AUD)—Una afección médica diagnosticada cuando el consumo de alcohol de una persona provoca sufrimiento o causa daños.

alérgeno—Algún elemento del ambiente que hace reaccionar al sistema inmunológico.

enfermedad de Alzheimer—Un tipo particular de demencia.

esteroides anabólicos—Una clase de hormonas que pueden estimular el crecimiento muscular.

anafilaxia—Una reacción alérgica grave y mortal.

anemia—Una enfermedad provocada por la falta de glóbulos rojos.

anticuerpo—Una célula que puede recordar y reconocer patógenos que ya han existido en el organismo.

antioxidantes—Sustancias que se encuentran en frutas y verduras y que trabajan para liberar al cuerpo de agentes químicos nocivos.

software antivirus—Software diseñado para detectar, prevenir y eliminar software malicioso (malware) de las computadoras.

ansiedad—Una emoción que incluye tensión, ideas angustiantes y cambios físicos, tales como un aumento en la presión arterial.

Glossary/Glosario

English

anxiety disorder—A disorder in which people have intense, excessive, and persistent worry and fear about everyday situations.

appetite—The desire to eat whether hungry or not.

arteriosclerosis—A condition in which the arteries are hardened and lose their flexibility.

arthritis—A set of more than 100 diseases in which the joints become swollen or damaged.

assertive—Being able to communicate your feelings and needs directly without offending others.

assertive communication—A communication style in which people express their own needs, feelings, and goals while being respectful of others.

assertiveness—A nonviolent and confident way of expressing your needs and point of view.

atherosclerosis—Clogged arteries.

bacteria—A single-cell organism found in the environment that can carry disease.

balance—The proper amount of carbohydrates, fats, and proteins to meet your daily need.

behavioral therapy—Used to help people learn how to handle withdrawal symptoms (cravings, situations, and people) that might trigger the desire to use again.

bereavement—The period of time when one mourns the loss of a loved one.

bias—Treating a person, thing, or group differently based on how you think about them.

biased information—Information based on feelings and opinions more than on facts.

bile—A yellow-green fluid that helps break down and absorb the fat you eat.

binge drinking—Considered to be males consuming five or more drinks or females consuming four or more drinks within about two hours.

biodegradable—Able to break down through natural decomposition.

biodiversity—Maintaining the balance of all living things (plant and animal) in a given area.

blood alcohol content (BAC)—Amount of alcohol in the bloodstream that indicates how intoxicated an individual is.

Español

trastorno de ansiedad—Un trastorno en el que las personas sienten una preocupación y un temor intenso, excesivo y persistente acerca de situaciones de la vida diaria.

apetito—El deseo de comer, con o sin hambre.

arterioesclerosis—Una afección en la que las arterias se endurecen y pierden flexibilidad.

artritis—Un conjunto de más de 100 enfermedades en las que las articulaciones se inflaman o lesionan.

asertivo—Poder comunicar los sentimientos y necesidades directamente sin ofender a los demás.

comunicación asertiva—Un estilo de comunicación en el que las personas expresan sus propias necesidades, sentimientos y metas de manera respetuosa con los demás.

asertividad—Una manera no violenta y segura de expresar necesidades y puntos de vista.

ateroesclerosis—Arterias obstruidas.

bacteria—Un organismo unicelular que se encuentra en el ambiente y puede transmitir enfermedades.

equilibrio—La cantidad adecuada de carbohidratos, grasas y proteínas para satisfacer las necesidades diarias.

terapia conductual—Usada para ayudar a las personas a manejar síntomas de abstinencia (apetencias, situaciones y personas) que pueden desencadenar el deseo de volver a consumir.

duelo—El período en que se llora la pérdida de un ser querido.

sesgo—Tratar a una persona, cosa o grupo de manera diferente en base a lo que piensas acerca de ellos.

información sesgada—Información basada en sentimientos y opiniones más que en datos.

bilis—Un líquido amarillo verdoso que ayuda a disolver y absorber la grasa que se come.

consumo excesivo de alcohol—Consumir cuatro bebidas alcohólicas o más (mujeres) o cinco bebidas alcohólicas o más (hombres) dentro de un plazo de aproximadamente dos horas.

biodegradable—Capaz de disolverse a través de descomposición natural.

biodiversidad—Mantener el equilibrio de todos los seres vivos (plantas y animales) en una zona determinada.

contenido de alcohol en sangre (en inglés BAC)—Cantidad de alcohol en el torrente sanguíneo que indica el grado de ebriedad de una persona.

English

body composition—The ratio of lean tissue to fat tissue in the body.

body image—Thoughts, feelings, and behaviors related to body size, shape, and appearance.

body mass index (BMI)—A person's height-to-weight ratio.

body shaming—Making cruel comments about someone's body or appearance.

boundaries—Determining what behavior you will and will not accept from others.

bruxism—Grinding the teeth.

built environment—All human-made spaces where people work, live, and play.

bully—A person who engages in unwanted aggressive behavior toward another.

bullying—Any unwanted aggressive behavior by a person who is not the victim's sibling or dating partner.

caffeine—A substance found in certain foods and drinks that stimulates the nervous system.

calcium—A mineral that helps bones to grow.

calorie—The form of energy found in food.

cancer—Uncontrolled growth of abnormal cells in one or more parts of the body.

carbohydrate—The main source of energy for the body.

carcinogen—A chemical or other substance that causes cancer.

cardiac arrest—Heart stops beating or beats too ineffectively to circulate blood to the brain and other vital organs.

cardiac muscle—Found only in the walls of the heart. Cardiac muscles contract automatically and regularly so the heart can pump blood throughout the body.

cardiopulmonary resuscitation (CPR)—A procedure used to keep oxygenated blood moving to the brain and other vital organs when a person is not breathing and doesn't have a heartbeat.

cardiorespiratory endurance—The ability to exercise your entire body for an extended period of time without stopping.

Español

composición corporal—La relación de tejido magro contra tejido graso en el cuerpo.

imagen corporal—Pensamientos, sentimientos y comportamientos relacionados con el tamaño, forma y aspecto del cuerpo.

índice de masa corporal (IMC)—La relación entre altura y peso de una persona.

humillación corporal—Hacer comentarios crueles sobre el cuerpo o apariencia de una persona.

límites—Determinar qué comportamientos de los demás aceptarás o no aceptarás.

bruxismo—Rechinar los dientes.

ambiente construido—Todos los espacios fabricados donde las personas trabajan, viven y juegan.

hostigador—Una persona que se comporta de manera agresiva no deseada para con el otro.

hostigamiento—Cualquier comportamiento agresivo no deseado por parte de una persona que no sea hermano o hermana de la víctima ni su pareja sentimental.

cafeína—Una sustancia hallada en ciertos alimentos y bebidas que estimula el sistema nervioso.

calcio—Un mineral que ayuda al crecimiento de los huesos.

caloría—La forma de energía encontrada en los alimentos.

cáncer—Crecimiento descontrolado de células anormales en una o más partes del cuerpo.

carbohidrato—La fuente principal de energía para el cuerpo.

carcinógeno—Una sustancia química o cualquier otra que provoque cáncer.

paro cardíaco—El corazón deja de latir o late demasiado ineficazmente para que la sangre circule hacia el cerebro y hacia otros órganos vitales.

músculo cardíaco—Encontrado únicamente en las paredes del corazón. Los músculos cardíacos se contraen de manera automática y regular para que el corazón pueda bombear sangre hacia todo el cuerpo.

reanimación cardiopulmonar (RCP)—Un procedimiento usado para que la sangre oxigenada siga llegando al cerebro y a otros órganos vitales cuando una persona no está respirando y no tiene pulso.

resistencia cardiorrespiratoria—La capacidad de ejercitar todo el cuerpo durante un largo período sin detenerse.

English

cardiovascular disease—Any of several chronic diseases that affect the cardiorespiratory system.

cartilage—Connective tissue that cushions joints and helps them move smoothly and easily.

cavity—A hole in a tooth caused by plaque.

chemical—A substance that cannot be broken down without changing into something else.

chronic disease—A disease that lasts longer than three months.

chyme—Partially digested and mixed-up food.

circulatory system—Controls the flow of blood in the body; it consists of the heart, blood vessels, and blood.

cirrhosis of the liver—Irreversible scarring of the liver, which keeps it from working properly.

cocaine—A stimulant in the form of a white, crystalline powder, derived from coca leaves.

coercion—The act or process of persuading someone to do something that they do not want to do.

cold-related emergency—Emergency caused by overexposure to cold.

cold sore—A common infection caused by the herpes simplex virus.

communication—The exchange of information between two or more people.

community—A group of people who share the same characteristics and interests.

community health—A form of public health that is focused on a particular group of people or a geographic area.

complete protein—A food that contains all nine essential amino acids.

composting—Gathering food scraps into outdoor bins and allowing it to decompose.

concussion—Type of traumatic brain injury that involves a temporary loss of brain function.

conductive hearing loss—When sound isn't transferred into the inner ear; often results from damage to the eardrum.

conflict—When two or more people disagree on an issue and feel threatened in some way.

conflict resolution—The formal or informal process that two or more individuals or groups use to find a peaceable solution to a disagreement.

Español

enfermedad cardiovascular—Cualquiera de las enfermedades crónicas que afectan al sistema cardiorrespiratorio.

cartílago—Tejido conectivo que amortigua las articulaciones y las ayuda a moverse suave y fácilmente.

caries—Un orificio en un diente causado por placa.

sustancia química—Una sustancia que no se puede descomponer sin transformarse en otra cosa.

enfermedad crónica—Una enfermedad que dura más de tres meses.

quimo—Alimentos parcialmente digeridos y mezclados.

sistema circulatorio—Controla el flujo de sangre en el cuerpo; está formado por el corazón, los vasos sanguíneos y la sangre.

cirrosis hepática—Cicatrices irreversibles del hígado, que le impiden funcionar correctamente.

cocaína—Un estimulante en forma de polvo blanco cristalino, derivado de las hojas de la coca.

coerción—El acto o proceso de persuadir a alguien a hacer algo que no desea.

emergencia relacionada con el frío—Una emergencia causada por sobreexposición al frío.

herpes labial—Una infección común causada por el virus herpes simple.

comunicación—El intercambio de información entre dos o más personas.

comunidad—Un grupo de personas que comparten las mismas características e intereses.

salud comunitaria—Una forma de salud pública orientada hacia un grupo particular de personas o hacia una zona geográfica.

proteína completa—Un alimento que contiene los nueve aminoácidos esenciales.

compostaje—Recolectar restos de alimentos en contenedores de exterior y permitir su descomposición.

conmoción cerebral—Tipo de lesión cerebral traumática que incluye una pérdida temporal de la función cerebral.

pérdida auditiva conductiva—Cuando el sonido no se transfiere al oído interno; suele ser el resultado de un daño en el tímpano.

conflicto—Cuando dos o más personas discrepan sobre un tema y se sienten de alguna manera amenazadas.

resolución dc conflictos—El proceso formal o informal por el cual dos o más personas o grupos encuentran una solución pacífica a un desacuerdo.

Glossary/Glosario

English	Español
conservation—The steps people take to prevent the exploitation, destruction, or neglect of natural resources.	**conservación**—Las medidas que toman las personas para prevenir la explotación, la destrucción o el abandono de los recursos naturales.
consumer—Someone who uses a product or service.	**consumidor**—Alguien que usa un producto o servicio.
contagious—Describes a disease that spreads from person to person.	**contagioso**—Describe una enfermedad que se transmite de una persona a otra.
cool-down—A time to slow the body down and give it time to adjust when ending an activity.	**enfriamiento**—Un tiempo para desacelerar el cuerpo y darle tiempo para adaptarse al finalizar una actividad.
coronary heart disease—When the arteries in the heart are clogged, and blood cannot deliver enough oxygen to the heart muscle.	**enfermedad coronaria**—Cuando las arterias del corazón están obstruidas y la sangre no puede llevar suficiente oxígeno al músculo cardíaco.
creatine—Substance produced by the body to help muscles release energy, improving strength and helping muscles to recover quickly.	**creatina**—Sustancia producida por el cuerpo que ayuda a los músculos a liberar energía, lo que mejora la fuerza y ayuda a los músculos a recuperarse rápidamente.
cultural norm—Standards lived by and shared expectations and rules that guide the behavior of people within a specific culture.	**norma cultural**—Estándares adoptados y expectativas y normas compartidas que rigen el comportamiento de las personas dentro de una cultura específica.
custom—A traditional and widely accepted way of behaving or doing something that is specific to a particular society, place, or time.	**costumbre**—Una forma tradicional y ampliamente aceptada de comportarse o de hacer algo que es específica de una sociedad, lugar o momento en particular.
cyberbullying—Aggressive behavior using technology such as social media.	**acoso cibernético**—Comportamiento agresivo mediante el uso de tecnología, como las redes sociales.
daily energy need—The number of calories a person needs every day.	**necesidad energética diaria**—La cantidad de calorías que necesita una persona a diario.
dating—Spending time with someone you are interested in romantically.	**salir con alguien**—Pasar tiempo con alguien con quien compartes un interés romántico.
deficiency—An inadequate (not enough) amount of a needed nutrient.	**deficiencia**—Una cantidad inadecuada (insuficiente) de un nutriente necesario.
dehydration—Occurs when you lose more fluid than you take in.	**deshidratación**—Ocurre cuando pierdes más líquidos de los que ingieres.
dementia—A loss of brain function over time that impacts memory, judgment, behavior, thinking, and language skills.	**demencia**—La pérdida de una función cerebral a lo largo del tiempo que afecta las habilidades de la memoria, el juicio, el comportamiento, el pensamiento y el lenguaje.
depressant—A substance that slows down the functions of the central nervous system.	**depresor**—Una sustancia que desacelera las funciones del sistema nervioso central.
depression—A serious mood disorder that affects the way someone thinks, feels, and handles daily activities.	**depresión**—Un trastorno emocional grave que afecta la manera en que alguien piensa, se siente y maneja las actividades diarias.
dermis—The middle layer of the skin.	**dermis**—La capa media de la piel.
designated driver—The person who agrees not to drink any alcohol so they can safely drive their friends.	**conductor designado**—La persona que acepta no beber ninguna bebida alcohólica para poder conducir con seguridad al resto de sus amigos.

Glossary/Glosario

English

diabetes—A chronic disease related to having too much glucose (sugar) in the blood.

diagnosis—A decision reached by a medical professional when a person has a disease or illness.

diet—The combinations of nutrients you consume and the way you eat.

Dietary Guidelines for Americans—A government document updated every five years that helps Americans know what they need to eat to stay healthy.

dietitian—An expert in nutrition with a university education and a professional license.

digestion—The mechanical and chemical process of breaking down food in the body.

digital footprint—The information you leave behind on the Internet as a result of your online activity.

disability—A physical or mental condition that limits a person's movements, senses, or activities.

disability inclusion—Understanding the relationship between the way people function and how they are able to participate in society and making appropriate adjustments as a result.

disease—Something that causes the body to not function properly.

disordered eating—A range of irregular eating behaviors such as skipping meals, stress eating, or periodic fasting.

distracted driving—When an activity takes the driver's attention away from driving.

distress—Negative stress from situations that cause worry, sorrow, anger, or pain.

domestic violence—Violence between people in a romantic relationship, or between the members of a married couple.

drama—Often involves untruthful gossiping about another person.

driving under the influence (DUI)—Operating any type of motorized vehicle while being under the influence of drugs or alcohol.

drowsy driving—The combination of driving and sleepiness or fatigue.

Español

diabetes—Una enfermedad crónica relacionada con la presencia de demasiada glucosa (azúcar) en la sangre.

diagnóstico—Una decisión a la que llega un profesional médico cuando una persona padece una enfermedad o dolencia.

dieta—La combinación de nutrientes que consumes y la forma en que te alimentas.

Pautas alimentarias para estadounidenses (Dietary Guidelines for Americans)—Un documento gubernamental que se actualiza cada cinco años y ayuda a los estadounidenses a saber qué deben comer para mantenerse saludables.

dietista—Un experto en nutrición con educación universitaria y licencia profesional.

digestión—El proceso mecánico y químico de descomponer los alimentos dentro del organismo.

huella digital—La información que vas dejando en Internet como resultado de tu actividad en línea.

discapacidad—Un trastorno físico o mental que limita los movimientos, sentidos o actividades de una persona.

inclusión de la discapacidad—Comprender la relación entre la forma en que funcionan las personas y cómo pueden participar en la sociedad y entonces hacer las adaptaciones correspondientes.

enfermedad—Algo que hace que el cuerpo no funcione correctamente.

alimentación desordenada—Un rango de conductas irregulares de alimentación, como saltarse comidas, comer por estrés o ayunar periódicamente.

conducción distraída—Cuando una actividad desvía la atención del conductor de la tarea de conducir.

angustia—Estrés negativo por situaciones que causan preocupación, pena, enfado o dolor.

violencia doméstica—Violencia entre personas que están en una relación amorosa o entre miembros de una pareja casada.

dramatismo—Suele incluir chismes falsos sobre otra persona.

conducir bajo la influencia (DUI, por sus siglas en inglés)—Operar cualquier tipo de vehículo motorizado estando bajo los efectos de drogas o alcohol.

conducción somnolienta—La combinación de conducir y somnolencia o fatiga.

Glossary/Glosario

English | ## Español

drug facts label—Tells what the drug is used for and how to use it safely.

dual sport—A sport where two people compete against each other.

dynamic stretching—Performing dynamic movements of the muscles through the full range of motion in the joints.

eating disorder—A type of serious, diagnosable mental illness that affects the person's relationship with food and eating.

e-cigarette—A battery-operated device that heats a liquid and produces an aerosol.

eczema—Dry, itchy skin. Also called dermatitis.

edible—Food mixed with marijuana or its active ingredient of THC. Marijuana edibles are often sold as chocolates and fruit-flavored gummies.

e-liquid—The liquid used by an e-cigarette, which usually contains nicotine, flavoring, and other chemicals.

elder abuse—The mistreatment of older adults in their home, in nursing homes, in hospitals, or in some other setting.

elimination—The removal of waste products from the body.

emotional attraction—A connection individuals feel based on personality, sense of humor, the way they share and care for things, and loyalty to their family and friends.

emotional awareness—The ability to recognize and make sense of your own emotions and those of others.

emotional connection—A deep bond with a friend whom you can trust, respect, and share anything with.

emotional health—Having a positive state of well-being that allows you to function in society and meet the demands of daily life.

emotional intelligence—The ability to identify and use emotions in productive ways.

emotional intimacy—A sense of closeness with your partner through empathy, respect, and communication.

emotional needs—The emotional security needed in order to feel accepted, supported, and loved.

---

prospecto de un medicamento—Indica para qué se usa la droga y cómo se la usa de manera segura.

deporte dual—Un deporte en el que dos personas compiten entre sí.

estiramiento dinámico—Realizar movimientos dinámicos de los músculos a través de todo el rango de movimiento de las articulaciones.

trastorno alimentario—Un tipo de enfermedad mental diagnosticable grave que afecta la relación de una persona con la comida y la alimentación.

cigarrillo electrónico—Un dispositivo a batería que calienta un líquido y produce un vapor.

eczema—Piel seca e irritada. También conocida como dermatitis.

comestibles—Alimentos mezclados con marihuana o su ingrediente activo THC. Los comestibles de marihuana a menudo se venden como chocolates y gomitas con sabor a frutas.

e-líquido—El líquido usado por un cigarrillo electrónico, que generalmente contiene nicotina, saborizantes y otros productos químicos.

abuso de ancianos—El maltrato hacia adultos mayores en sus hogares, en asilos, hospitales o en algún otro ámbito.

eliminación—La expulsión de desechos del cuerpo.

atracción emocional—Una conexión que sienten las personas basada en la personalidad, el sentido del humor, la forma en que comparten y se interesan por las cosas y la lealtad a sus familias y amigos.

conciencia emocional—La capacidad de reconocer y darle sentido a tus emociones y a las de los demás.

conexión emocional—Un lazo profundo con un amigo en quien puedes confiar, a quien puedes respetar y con el que puedes compartir cualquier cosa.

salud emocional—Tener una sensación positiva de bienestar que te permita funcionar en sociedad y cumplir con las exigencias de la vida diaria.

inteligencia emocional—La capacidad de identificar y usar las emociones de manera productiva.

intimidad emocional—Un sentido de cercanía con tu pareja a través de la empatía, el respeto y la comunicación.

necesidades emocionales—La seguridad emocional necesaria para sentirte aceptado, apoyado y amado.

Glossary/Glosario

English

emotional violence—Psychological injury or injury to another person's emotional or social well-being.

empathy—The ability to understand and appreciate the feelings and emotions of others.

empty-calorie food—A food with no nutritional value that still contains calories.

enamel—A hard, white substance made of calcium that is found on the outside of teeth.

energy balance—The relationship between the calories you eat and the calories you burn off.

environment—The surroundings and conditions in which you live.

epidemiologist—A person who researches and investigates patterns of disease.

epidermis—The outermost layer of the skin.

epinephrine—A hormone that causes blood pressure and heart rate to increase.

equilibrium—The sense of balance regulated by the inner ear.

escalate—Making a conflict more intense.

esophagus—A muscular tube leading from the mouth to the stomach.

exercise—Planned, structured, and repetitive physical activity for the purpose of improving or maintaining one or more components of fitness.

external influence—Family, friends, environment, social media, and the like that guide your decisions.

family—People you are related to by blood, marriage, adoption, or other emotional and social ties.

farsightedness—Being able to see farther away but not up close. Also called hyperopia.

fat—The greasy parts of foods; a good source of energy for the human body.

fat distribution—The location of fat on the body, particularly comparing upper to lower body.

fetal alcohol spectrum disorder (FASD)—A group of conditions that can cause physical, behavioral, and learning problems.

fetal alcohol syndrome (FAS)—Most severe FASD results in delayed development, poor coordination, behavior problems, and poor social skills.

fiber—A type of carbohydrate found in plant foods that is hard for the body to digest.

Español

violencia emocional—Daño psicológico o daño hacia el bienestar emocional o social de otra persona.

empatía—La capacidad de comprender y apreciar los sentimientos y emociones de los demás.

alimento de calorías vacías—Un alimento sin valor nutricional que aun así contiene calorías.

esmalte—Una sustancia blanca y dura formada por calcio que recubre el exterior de los dientes.

equilibrio energético—La relación entre las calorías que ingieres y las calorías que quemas.

ambiente—Los entornos y condiciones en las que vives.

epidemiólogo—Una persona que busca e investiga patrones de enfermedades.

epidermis—La capa exterior de la piel.

epinefrina—Una hormona que aumenta la presión arterial y la frecuencia cardíaca.

equilibrio—La sensación de equilibrio regulado por el oído interno.

escalar—Intensificar un conflicto.

esófago—Un tubo muscular que conecta la boca con el estómago.

ejercicio—Actividad física planificada, estructurada y repetitiva con el fin de mejorar o mantener uno o más de los componentes de la aptitud física.

influencia externa—Familia, amistades, ambiente, redes sociales y cosas por el estilo que influyen sobre tus decisiones.

familia—Personas con las que estás emparentado por sangre, matrimonio, adopción u otros lazos emocionales y sociales.

hipermetropía—Poder ver bien a la distancia, pero no de cerca. También conocida como hiperopía.

grasa—Las partes grasas de los alimentos; una buena fuente de energía para el cuerpo humano.

distribución de grasas—La ubicación de las grasas en el cuerpo, comparando especialmente entre la parte superior y la parte inferior del cuerpo.

trastornos del espectro alcohólico fetal (TEAF)—Un grupo de afecciones que pueden causar problemas físicos, conductuales y de aprendizaje.

síndrome alcohólico fetal (SAF)—Un TEAF más severo que provoca atraso madurativo, falta de coordinación, problemas conductuales y escasas habilidades sociales.

fibra—Un tipo de carbohidratos encontrado en alimentos de origen vegetal que son difíciles de digerir.

Glossary/Glosario

English | ## Español

fight-or-flight response—The initial reaction to a stressor causing heart rate to increase, pupils to dilate, and muscles to tense up.

first aid—Providing basic medical care to someone experiencing a sudden injury or illness.

fitness plan—Detailed plan using the FITT formula that serves as a guide for meeting your fitness and activity goals.

FITT formula—Used to determine how much physical activity you should be doing for each of the health-related fitness components. FITT stands for frequency, intensity, time, and type.

fixed mindset—The belief that you were born with a certain skill or ability and that it cannot be changed or improved.

flexibility—The ability to use your joints fully through a wide range of motion.

food additive—A substance added to food to improve freshness, add nutrition, or improve texture, taste, or appearance.

Food and Drug Administration (FDA)—A government agency responsible for protecting public health by ensuring the safety of various products through regulating manufacturing, marketing, and distribution.

foodborne illness—Any symptom or disorder people get from eating or drinking contaminated food or beverages.

food chain—The steps involved in bringing food from farm to plate, including production, processing, distribution, and preparation.

food insecurity—Not having enough food to support an active, healthy life.

food log—A list of all of the foods you ate and the amount of each food eaten over a set period of time.

food preservative—A food additive used to prevent food from spoiling too quickly.

food recall—Happens when a particular food or food item becomes contaminated and is pulled from shelves or restaurants in order to keep people from becoming ill.

---

reacción de lucha o huida—La reacción inicial a un factor estresante que hace aumentar el ritmo cardíaco, provoca dilatación de las pupilas y tensa los músculos.

primeros auxilios—Brindar atención médica básica a alguien que esté padeciendo una lesión o enfermedad repentina.

plan de aptitud física—Un plan detallado que usa la fórmula FITT y que sirve de guía para cumplir tus metas de actividad y aptitud física.

fórmula FITT—Usada para determinar cuánta actividad física debes realizar por cada uno de los componentes de la aptitud física relacionada con la salud. FITT es la sigla en inglés para frecuencia, intensidad, tiempo y tipo.

mentalidad fija—La creencia de haber nacido con cierta habilidad o destreza que no se puede modificar ni mejorar.

flexibilidad—La capacidad de usar las articulaciones a través de un rango amplio de movimientos.

aditivo alimentario—Una sustancia agregada a un alimento para mejorar la frescura, agregar nutrición, o mejorar la textura, el sabor o la apariencia.

Administración de Alimentos y Medicamentos (Food and Drug Administration—FDA)—Una agencia gubernamental responsable de proteger la salud pública y garantizar la seguridad de varios productos a través de la regulación de la elaboración, la comercialización y la distribución.

intoxicación alimentaria—Cualquier síntoma o trastorno que sufren las personas por comer o beber alimentos o bebidas contaminados.

cadena alimentaria—Los pasos incluidos en traer los alimentos del campo a la mesa, incluida la producción, el procesamiento, la distribución y la preparación.

inseguridad alimentaria—No contar con alimentos suficientes para llevar adelante una vida activa y saludable.

registro de comidas—Un listado de todos los alimentos que comiste y la cantidad de cada uno durante un período determinado.

conservante alimentario—Un aditivo alimentario para impedir que los alimentos se deterioren demasiado pronto.

retiro de alimentos—Ocurre cuando un alimento en particular resulta contaminado y se lo retira de las góndolas o restaurantes para evitar que las personas se enfermen.

English

food-toxic environment—An environment where food is easily accessible and cheap but unhealthy.

frequency—How often you exercise.

fungus—A single- or multiple-cell plantlike organism that thrives in warm, humid environments.

gang—A group of three or more people who share an identity and commit violent and illegal acts.

gastroenterologist—A medical professional who specializes in the digestive system.

generic—A copy of the brand name product but is often less expensive. Same dosage, safety, strength, how it is taken, and the intended use of the brand name drug.

genetically modified food—A food that has been altered by having its genetic makeup changed.

GHB—A hallucinogen that can cause hallucinations and blackouts.

gingivitis—A disease of the gums caused by bacteria.

good quality sleep—Sleep that is long, peaceful, and deep.

gossip—Sharing details of a person's life they don't want shared.

gratitude—Being thankful and showing kindness and an appreciation for kindness from others.

grief—A deep sadness caused by the loss of a loved one or a pet.

grit—Having the dedication and passion needed to achieve long-term goals.

growth mindset—Being able to learn and grow through any situation.

gut health—The balance of good and bad bacteria in the digestive system.

habit—Something you do automatically without thinking about it.

hacker—A skilled computer programmer who steals passwords or gains remote access to computer systems to alter or steal information.

halitosis—Bad breath.

hallucinogen—A drug used to alter your perception of your surroundings, thoughts, and feelings.

Español

ambiente de toxicidad alimentaria—Un ambiente donde los alimentos son de fácil acceso y baratos, pero insalubres.

frecuencia—Cada cuánto te ejercitas.

hongo—Un organismo unicelular o pluricelular similar a las plantas que se desarrolla en ambientes cálidos y húmedos.

pandilla—Un grupo de tres o más personas que comparten una identidad y cometen actos violentos e ilegales.

gastroenterólogo—Un profesional médico especializado en el sistema digestivo.

genérico—Una copia de un producto de marca generalmente más económica. Es la misma dosis, seguridad, concentración, manera de administrar y uso previsto que el medicamento de marca.

alimento genéticamente modificado—Un alimento alterado a través de cambios en su composición genética.

GHB—Un alucinógeno que puede provocar alucinaciones y desvanecimientos.

gingivitis—Una enfermedad de las encías causada por bacterias.

buena calidad de sueño—Sueño largo, tranquilo y profundo.

chismes—Compartir detalles de la vida de una persona que no quiere que se compartan.

gratitud—Ser agradecido y demostrar amabilidad y aprecio por la amabilidad de los demás.

duelo—Una tristeza profunda causada por la pérdida de un ser querido o de una mascota.

perseverancia—Tener la dedicación y pasión necesarias para alcanzar metas de largo plazo.

mentalidad de crecimiento—Ser capaz de aprender y crecer ante cualquier situación.

salud intestinal—El equilibrio entre bacterias buenas y malas dentro del sistema digestivo.

hábito—Algo que se hace automáticamente sin pensar en ello.

pirata informático—Un programador informático avezado que roba contraseñas u obtiene acceso remoto a sistemas informáticos para alterar o robar información.

halitosis—Mal aliento.

alucinógeno—Una droga usada para alterar la percepción del entorno, las ideas y los sentimientos.

English

hazardous material—Any material that could cause damage to human or animal life or to the environment.

hazing—Any activity expected of someone joining or participating in a group that humiliates, degrades, abuses, or endangers them.

health—The state of being free of illness or disease.

health care consumer—Anyone who uses medical services, buys health-related products, or selects a medical professional.

health care system—All available medical services, the ways in which medical care is paid for, and the programs and services that prevent disease and disability.

health disparity—A preventable difference in disease, injury, violence, or opportunities to achieve optimal health.

health equity—The absence of unfair and avoidable or addressable differences in health among population groups defined socially, economically, demographically, or geographically.

health literacy—The ability to find and understand basic health information.

health-related fitness—The physical fitness components that help you to stay healthy. Includes cardiorespiratory endurance, muscular strength, muscular endurance, flexibility, and body composition.

healthy relationship—A relationship that allows both people in the relationship to feel supported and connected.

healthy weight—A weight that a person is comfortable with and that can be maintained by following basic nutrition and physical activity guidelines.

heart attack—Damage to the heart muscle that occurs when a clot or blockage reduces blood flow and oxygen delivery to the heart tissue.

heat-related emergency—Emergency caused by overexposure to heat and dehydration.

heredity—The passing of characteristics from parent to child.

heroin—An illicit opioid drug made from morphine.

Español

material peligroso—Cualquier material que pueda causar daño a la vida humana o animal o al ambiente.

novatada—Cualquier actividad esperada de alguien que se incorpora o participa en un grupo que humilla, degrada, abusa o pone en peligro a esa persona.

salud—El estado de estar libre de enfermedades o dolencias.

consumidor de atención médica—Cualquier persona que usa servicios médicos, compra productos relacionados con la salud o selecciona un profesional médico.

sistema de atención médica—Todos los servicios médicos disponibles, las formas en que se paga la atención médica, y los programas y servicios para prevenir enfermedades y discapacidades.

disparidad de salud—Una diferencia evitable en enfermedades, lesiones, violencia u oportunidades para alcanzar una salud óptima.

equidad en salud—La ausencia de diferencias injustas y evitables o remediables en salud entre grupos de población definidos por factores sociales, económicos, demográficos o geográficos.

conocimientos sobre la salud—La capacidad para encontrar y comprender información básica de salud.

aptitud física relacionada con la salud—Actividades de aptitud física que deben realizarse regularmente para mantenerse sanos. Incluye resistencia cardiorrespiratoria, fortaleza muscular, resistencia muscular, flexibilidad y composición corporal.

relación saludable—Una relación que permite a ambas personas sentirse apoyadas y conectadas.

peso saludable—El peso con que una persona se siente cómoda y que se puede mantener cumpliendo pautas básicas de nutrición y actividad física.

ataque cardíaco—Daño al músculo cardíaco que ocurre cuando un coágulo o una obstrucción reduce el flujo sanguíneo y el suministro de oxígeno al tejido cardíaco.

emergencia relacionada con el calor—Una emergencia causada por sobreexposición al calor y deshidratación.

herencia—El traspaso de características de un padre a su hijo.

heroína—Un opioide ilícito hecho de morfina.

English

hospital—An institution that provides advanced medical care and surgical treatment.

human immunodeficiency virus (HIV)—A virus that attacks the immune system and can lead to acquired immunodeficiency syndrome (AIDS).

human trafficking—Forcing people to perform a service or job against their will or in exchange for a basic human right like food or water.

hunger—The communication inside the body that tells you when you need to eat.

hygiene—The practice of keeping yourself in good health by maintaining personal cleanliness.

hypertension—High blood pressure.

hypodermis—The inner layer of skin that connects skin to the muscles and bones underneath.

identity theft—Someone using another person's identity or personal information without their permission to commit a crime.

illicit drug—A substance used to increase or slow the central nervous system or to cause hallucinations. Illicit drugs are illegal to have or use, and have no medical application.

illness—The state of not feeling well or not being fully healthy.

immune system—The body's defense system.

immunization—Preventative measures, often shots, taken to help build antibodies against particular diseases such as the flu.

impairment—A loss of function that happens with a disability.

impulsiveness—Acting suddenly without regard for consequences.

incomplete protein—A food that contains proteins but not all nine essential amino acids.

individual sport—A sport that you compete in by yourself against others.

influence—To have an effect on the decisions you make in life.

inhalant—A dangerous substance found in common household products; it produces chemical vapors that are inhaled through the nose or mouth to produce mind-altering effects.

insomnia—The state of being unable to sleep through the night almost every night.

intensity—How hard you exercise.

Español

hospital—Una entidad que brinda atención médica avanzada y tratamiento quirúrgico.

virus de inmunodeficiencia humana (VIH)—Un virus que ataca el sistema inmunológico y puede derivar en el síndrome de inmunodeficiencia adquirida (SIDA).

trata de personas—Obligar a personas a realizar un servicio o trabajo contra su voluntad o a cambio de un derecho humano básico, como agua o alimentos.

hambre—La comunicación dentro del cuerpo que te avisa cuando necesitas comer.

higiene—La práctica de mantenerse en buena salud mediante la limpieza personal.

hipertensión—Presión arterial alta.

hipodermis—La capa interior de la piel que conecta la piel con los músculos y huesos que están debajo.

robo de identidad—Alguien que usa la identidad de otra persona o su información personal sin su permiso para cometer un delito.

droga ilegal—Una sustancia usada para aumentar o ralentizar el sistema nervioso central o para provocar alucinaciones. Es ilícito poseer o usar drogas ilegales, y no tienen ninguna aplicación médica.

enfermedad—El estado de no sentirse bien o no estar plenamente sano.

sistema inmunológico—El sistema de defensa del cuerpo.

inmunización—Medidas preventivas, generalmente vacunas, tomadas para generar anticuerpos contra enfermedades en particular, como la gripe.

impedimento—La pérdida de una función que ocurre con una discapacidad.

impulsividad—Actuar repentinamente sin medir las consecuencias.

proteína incompleta—Un alimento que contiene proteínas pero no todos los nueve aminoácidos esenciales.

deporte individual—Un deporte en el que compites tú solo contra otros.

influenciar—Tener impacto sobre las decisiones que tomas en la vida.

inhalante—Una sustancia peligrosa que se encuentra en productos comunes del hogar; produce vapores químicos que se inhalan a través de la nariz o boca y producen efectos que alteran la mente.

insomnio—El estado de no poder dormir toda la noche, casi todas las noches.

intensidad—La fuerza con la que te ejercitas.

Glossary/Glosario

English | ## Español

intentional injury—An injury caused by another person or one that is self-inflicted.

internal influence—Your own thoughts and opinions that guide your decisions.

intimacy—A one-on-one closeness and connectedness with another person that includes trust, acceptance, honesty, safety, compassion, affection, and communication.

intolerance—An inability or unwillingness to examine prejudices and biases.

intoxicated—The state where alcohol has made it difficult for a person to do simple tasks; they may also be happier or sadder than usual.

iron—A mineral that helps the blood carry oxygen to the body.

jealousy—A strong negative emotion that usually occurs when a person perceives a threat to a valued relationship from a third person.

joint—The place where two or more bones meet.

keratin—A hard protein that makes up the nails.

kidney dialysis—A machine used to filter blood for the body when the body cannot do so.

kidney disease—Occurs when the kidneys gradually lose their ability to function.

large intestine—A large, tubelike organ that absorbs water and prepares waste for elimination.

ligaments—Strong bands of tissue that connect bones.

living green—Being aware of the effect your lifestyle choices have on the environment; being earth friendly in your choices.

longevity—The length or duration of life.

long-term goal—A target for behaviors that you can achieve over one to six months.

love—A complex emotion that involves intense feelings of affection.

lung disease—A variety of conditions that can affect the lungs and the ability to breathe normally.

malnutrition—Having inadequate (not enough) or unbalanced nutrition.

lesión intencional—Una lesión causada por otra persona o por ti mismo.

influencia interna—Tus propias ideas y opiniones que guían tus decisiones.

intimidad—Una cercanía y conexión individual con otra persona que incluye confianza, aceptación, honestidad, seguridad, compasión, afecto y comunicación.

intolerancia—Una falta de capacidad o voluntad para examinar prejuicios y sesgos.

ebrio—El estado en que el alcohol hace que sea difícil para una persona realizar tareas simples; también pueden verse más felices o más tristes que lo habitual.

hierro—Un mineral que ayuda a la sangre a llevar oxígeno al cuerpo.

celos—Una fuerte emoción negativa que habitualmente ocurre cuando una persona percibe una amenaza a una relación preciada por parte de un tercero.

articulación—El lugar donde se encuentran dos o más huesos.

queratina—Una proteína dura que conforma las uñas.

diálisis renal—Una máquina usada para filtrar la sangre del cuerpo cuando el cuerpo no puede hacerlo.

enfermedad renal—Ocurre cuando los riñones pierden gradualmente su capacidad para funcionar.

intestino grueso—Un órgano largo con forma de tubo que absorbe agua y prepara los desechos para su eliminación.

ligamentos—Bandas fuertes de tejido que conectan los huesos.

vida verde—Ser consciente del efecto que tu estilo de vida tiene sobre el ambiente; ser ecológico en tus elecciones.

longevidad—La extensión o duración de la vida.

meta a largo plazo—Objetivos más grandes de comportamientos que puedes alcanzar dentro de uno a seis meses.

amor—Una emoción compleja que incluye sentimientos intensos de afecto.

enfermedad pulmonar—Una variedad de afecciones que pueden afectar los pulmones y la capacidad de respirar normalmente.

desnutrición—Tener una nutrición inadecuada (insuficiente) o desbalanceada.

Glossary/Glosario

English

malware—A virus designed to invade a computer system and perform damaging actions on it to change the way it works.

marijuana—Mind-altering drug made from the dry, shredded, green or brown flowers, stems, seeds, and leaves of the Cannabis sativa plant.

marketing—Promoting, selling, and distributing products in stores and online.

maximum heart rate—The highest the heart rate should be when exercising.

MDMA—A hallucinogen that produces feelings of increased energy, distorted perceptions, and an altered understanding of place and time.

medicine—A drug used to maintain health or treat a health issue.

mental disorder—A serious and ongoing problem involving how a person thinks and manages their emotions.

mental health—When a person has successful thinking and mental processes, including staying focused, processing information, and storing and retrieving information.

mental health therapist—A medical professional who helps people achieve emotional wellness.

mental needs—Family members and friends helping you develop self-esteem and confidence in yourself.

mental toughness—The ability to resist, manage, and overcome doubts, worries, concerns, and circumstances that prevent you from succeeding or excelling.

metabolic rate—The number of calories burned to keep the basic body functions working.

methamphetamine (meth)—A stimulant made with common ingredients including ephedrine, a common cold medicine ingredient.

minerals—Naturally occurring substances found in foods that are essential for life.

minor in possession (MIP)—An individual under 21 in possession of alcohol.

moderate drinking—Considered to be one drink per day for women and two drinks per day for men.

Español

software malicioso (malware)—Un virus diseñado para invadir un sistema informático y ejecutar acciones dañinas para cambiar la forma en que funciona.

marihuana—Una droga que altera la mente; hecha de flores, tallos, semillas y hojas verdes o marrones, secas y trituradas de la planta Cannabis sativa.

comercialización—Promocionar, vender y distribuir productos en tiendas y en línea.

frecuencia cardíaca máxima—La frecuencia cardíaca más alta que se debería alcanzar al hacer ejercicio.

MDMA—Un alucinógeno que produce sensaciones de energía aumentada, percepciones distorsionadas y una comprensión alterada del tiempo y el espacio.

medicamento—Una droga utilizada para mantener la salud o tratar un problema de salud.

trastorno mental—Un problema grave y permanente que implica la forma en que una persona piensa y controla sus emociones.

salud mental—Cuando una persona tiene pensamientos y procesos mentales acertados, incluido permanecer concentrado, procesar información, y almacenar y recordar información.

terapeuta de salud mental—Un profesional médico que ayuda a las personas a alcanzar el bienestar emocional.

necesidades mentales—Miembros de la familia y amigos que te ayudan a desarrollar autoestima y confianza en ti mismo.

fortaleza mental—La capacidad de resistir, manejar y sobreponerse a dudas, preocupaciones, inquietudes y circunstancias que te impiden triunfar o destacarte.

índice metabólico—La cantidad de calorías quemadas para mantener en funcionamiento las funciones básicas del organismo.

metanfetamina (meta)—Un estimulante hecho con ingredientes comunes que incluyen la efedrina, un ingrediente común de los medicamentos para tratar los resfríos.

minerales—Sustancias naturales que se encuentran en los alimentos y son esenciales para la vida.

menor en posesión (en inglés MIP)—Una persona menor de 21 años en posesión de alcohol.

beber con moderación—Considerado como una bebida alcohólica por día para mujeres y dos bebidas alcohólicas por día para hombres.

Glossary/Glosario

English

moderation—Not eating too much of any one nutrient while still getting enough of all nutrients.

mood disorder—A group of mental disorders that affect a person's emotional state.

mourning—The external process and behaviors associated with grieving the loss of a loved one.

multigrain—A food that contains two or more grains.

muscular endurance—The ability of the muscles to perform continuously without tiring.

muscular strength—The amount of force a muscle can produce.

muscular system—Responsible for all movement.

MyPlate—A graphic tool and website designed to help people make healthy food choices.

natural disaster—Any type of severe weather that has the potential to be a significant threat to human health, safety, and property.

natural environment—Includes all living species, climate, weather, and natural resources.

nearsightedness—Being able to see things up close but not farther away. Also called myopia.

negative body image—Having a distorted view of your appearance or feeling bad about your appearance.

negative energy balance—Burning off more calories than are taken in.

neglect—The failure of adults to meet the basic physical, emotional, medical, or educational needs of a child or other dependent.

nervous system—Provides all the electrical signals that control your movements.

nicotine—An addictive chemical; the main ingredient in tobacco.

nicotine replacement therapy (NRT)—A common way to quit smoking. Includes the patch, gum, inhalers, lozenges, and nasal sprays to help reduce nicotine withdrawal feelings.

noise pollution—Unwanted, excessive, or bothersome sound.

Español

moderación—No comer demasiado de ningún nutriente en particular y a la vez obtener suficiente de todos los nutrientes.

trastorno del estado de ánimo—Un grupo de trastornos mentales que afectan el estado emocional de una persona.

luto—El proceso externo y los comportamientos asociados con llorar la pérdida de un ser querido.

multicereal—Un alimento que contiene dos o más cereales.

resistencia muscular—La capacidad de los músculos de funcionar de forma continua sin cansarse.

fuerza muscular—La cantidad de fuerza que puede producir un músculo.

sistema muscular—Responsable de todos los movimientos.

MiPlato—Una herramienta gráfica y sitio web diseñado para ayudar a las personas a tomar decisiones alimentarias saludables.

desastre natural—Cualquier tipo de condición climática severa que tiene el potencial de ser una amenaza considerable para la salud, seguridad y propiedad de las personas.

ambiente natural—Incluye todas las especies vivientes, el clima, las condiciones meteorológicas y los recursos naturales.

hipometropía—Poder ver objetos que están cerca pero no los alejados. También conocida como miopía.

imagen corporal negativa—Tener una visión distorsionada de tu apariencia o sentirte mal por tu apariencia.

equilibrio energético negativo—Quemar más calorías que las que se consumen.

negligencia—El incumplimiento de los adultos de atender las necesidades físicas, emocionales, médicas o educativas básicas de un niño o de otro dependiente.

sistema nervioso—Provee todas las señales eléctricas que controlan tus movimientos.

nicotina—Un producto químico adictivo; el ingrediente principal del tabaco.

terapia de reemplazo de nicotina (en inglés NRT)—Una forma común de dejar de fumar. Incluye el parche, goma de mascar, inhaladores, pastillas y aerosoles nasales que ayudan a reducir sensaciones de abstinencia de nicotina.

contaminación sonora—Sonido no deseado, excesivo o molesto.

Glossary/Glosario

English

noncommunicable disease—A disease that cannot be transmitted from person to person.

nonnutritious drink—A drink that contains calories without providing vitamins or minerals.

nonprescription or over-the-counter (OTC) drug—A type of drug that does not require a doctor's prescription, is bought off the store shelf, and can be used by more than one person.

nonverbal communication—Using facial expressions, body language, hand gestures, tone of voice, and how loud or soft the voice is to express the information being shared.

nutrient—The substance found in food that the body needs to survive.

nutrition facts label—The label on all food products that provides important information.

nutritious drink—A drink that contains essential nutrients like vitamins, minerals, and carbohydrates.

obese—Having too much body fat per unit of weight, often described as a BMI of 30 or higher.

offender—The person who commits a violent crime; also called a perpetrator.

opioid—A class of drugs used legally as pain relievers and available by prescription, such as oxycodone, hydrocodone, and morphine. This class of drugs also includes the illicit drug heroin.

optimal stress—A stress response that helps a person perform better under pressure, sometimes called butterflies.

optimistic—Having a generally positive outlook and positive emotions.

organic food—A food that is grown or produced on an organic-certified farm without chemical pesticides and that contains no synthetic ingredients and is not bioengineered or treated with radiation.

osteoporosis—A chronic disease in which the bones become weak.

outpatient treatment—Treatment that allows a person to attend counseling while still going to school and living at home.

overload—Needing to do more physical activity than you normally do.

overweight—Having too much weight per unit of height, often described as a BMI of 25.0-29.9.

pandemic—The worldwide spread of a disease.

Español

enfermedad no contagiosa—Una enfermedad que no se puede transmitir de una persona a otra.

bebida no nutritiva—Una bebida que contiene calorías sin aportar vitaminas o minerales.

medicamento sin receta o de venta libre (en inglés OTC)—Un tipo de droga que no requiere la receta de un médico, se encuentra en las góndolas de las tiendas, y la puede usar más de una persona.

comunicación no verbal—Usar expresiones faciales, lenguaje corporal, gestos con las manos, tono de voz y volumen de voz para expresar la información que se comparte.

nutriente—La sustancia que se encuentra en alimentos que el cuerpo necesita para sobrevivir.

etiqueta de información nutricional—La etiqueta de todos los productos alimentarios que brinda información importante.

bebida nutritiva—Una bebida que contiene nutrientes esenciales como vitaminas, minerales y carbohidratos.

obeso—Tener demasiada grasa corporal por unidad de peso, también llamado IMC de 30 o más.

delincuente—La persona que comete un delito violento; también conocido como perpetrador.

opioide—Una clase de droga usada legalmente como analgésico y disponible con receta médica, como la oxicodona, la hidrocodona y la morfina. Esta clase de drogas también incluye la droga ilegal heroína.

estrés óptimo—Una respuesta al estrés que ayuda a las personas a desempeñarse mejor bajo presión, también conocido como mariposas.

optimista—Tener una mirada generalmente positiva y emociones positivas.

alimento orgánico—Un alimento cultivado o producido en una granja con certificación orgánica, sin pesticidas químicos y que no contiene ingredientes sintéticos y no está modificado por bioingeniería ni tratado con radiación.

osteoporosis—Una enfermedad crónica en la que los huesos se debilitan.

tratamiento ambulatorio—Tratamiento que le permite a la persona asistir a terapia y seguir yendo a la escuela y viviendo en su casa.

sobrecarga—Necesidad de realizar más actividad física de la que realizas normalmente.

sobrepeso—Tener demasiado peso por unidad de altura, a veces definido como IMC de 25.0-29.9.

pandemia—La propagación mundial de una enfermedad.

Glossary/Glosario

English	Español
passive communication—A communication style in which people avoid expressing their opinions or feelings.	**comunicación pasiva**—Un estilo de comunicación en el que las personas evitan expresar sus opiniones o sentimientos.
passive-aggressive communication—A communication style in which people appear to be passive yet will act out in indirect ways such as spreading rumors or giving people the silent treatment rather than confronting the person.	**comunicación pasivo-agresiva**—Un estilo de comunicación en el que las personas aparentan ser pasivas pero actúan de maneras indirectas, por ejemplo difundiendo rumores o ignorando a alguien en lugar de confrontarlo.
pathogen—Anything foreign that enters your body and can cause disease.	**patógeno**—Cualquier elemento extraño que ingresa a tu cuerpo y puede causar una enfermedad.
pediatrician—A medical doctor who specializes in working with children.	**pediatra**—Un médico especializado en trabajar con niños.
peripheral artery disease—A disease in which the arms or legs do not get enough blood.	**enfermedad arterial periférica**—Una enfermedad en la que los brazos o las piernas no reciben sangre suficiente.
personal boundaries—The limits set with other people, including intellectual, emotional, physical, social, and spiritual boundaries.	**límites personales**—Los límites establecidos con otras personas, incluidos los intelectuales, emocionales, físicos, sociales y espirituales.
pessimistic—A tendency to see the worst aspect of things or believe that the worst will happen; a lack of hope or confidence in the future.	**pesimista**—Una tendencia a ver el peor aspecto de las cosas o creer que ocurrirá lo peor; una falta de esperanza o confianza en el futuro.
pesticide—A chemical used in the production of food that protects a crop from insects, weeds, and infections.	**pesticida**—Un producto químico usado en la producción de alimentos que protege un cultivo contra insectos, malezas e infecciones.
pharmacy—A store that sells legal prescription and nonprescription drugs.	**farmacia**—Una tienda que vende drogas legales con receta y de venta libre.
phishing attack—When you log into a website, app, text, or email that looks legitimate but is not, and all of your personal information such as username and password has just been given to the attacker.	**ataque de phishing**—Cuando ingresas a un sitio web, aplicación, texto o correo electrónico que parece legítimo pero no lo es, y toda tu información personal, como tu nombre de usuario y contraseña, le ha sido entregada al atacante.
phobia—A persistent, excessive, or unrealistic fear of an object, person, animal, activity, or situation.	**fobia**—Un temor persistente, excesivo o poco realista a un objeto, persona, animal, actividad o situación.
physical activity—Movement using the large muscles of the body.	**actividad física**—Movimiento que usa los músculos largos del cuerpo.
physical fitness—Refers to the body systems being able to work together efficiently to allow someone to be healthy and be able to perform all the necessary daily activities needed.	**aptitud física**—Se refiere a los sistemas corporales que tienen la capacidad de trabajar juntos de manera eficiente para permitir que alguien esté sano y pueda realizar todas las actividades necesarias para la vida diaria.
physical intimacy—The physical sharing, giving, and getting through touch.	**intimidad física**—Compartir físicamente, dar y recibir a través del tacto.
physical needs—Shelter, food, clothing, and medical care.	**necesidades físicas**—Refugio, comida, vestimenta y atención médica.
physical violence—The use of bodily force, including hitting or kicking someone, forcing someone to do something against their will, or destroying property.	**violencia física**—El uso de la fuerza corporal, incluido pegar o patear a alguien, para forzar a alguien a hacer algo en contra de su voluntad, o para destruir una propiedad.

English

plain language—Language that makes written or oral information easier to understand, especially in relation to complex health information.

positive body image—A person's realistic sense of how they look and feel good about their appearance.

positive energy balance—Taking in more calories than are burned off.

prebiotic—A food that helps feed the healthy bacteria in the gut.

prejudice—Having an opinion about someone or something that is not based on reason or actual experience.

prescription drug—A drug that is prescribed by a doctor, bought at a pharmacy, and meant to be used only by the person it was prescribed for.

preventive screening—Medical tests done to check for early signs of disease.

primary prevention—Actions and services that reduce risk and avoid health problems, such as efforts to keep underage people from drinking.

probiotic—Living bacteria found in food.

processed food—A food that was changed before being sold or eaten.

progression—As workouts become easier, gradually increasing the amount or the intensity of the exercise in order to continue to see progress.

protein—A substance found in foods that provides energy and helps repair body tissues.

protozoan—A large single-celled organism that can move through the body in search of food.

psychotherapy—Talking with a psychiatrist, psychologist, or other mental health provider in order to help treat a mental disorder.

public health—The art and science of protecting and improving the health of individuals and large populations.

public transportation—Transportation that charges a set fare, runs on fixed routes, and is available to the public.

quality of life—How healthy, happy, and fulfilling your daily life is.

Español

lenguaje sencillo—Lenguaje que hace que la información escrita u oral sea más fácil de entender, especialmente en relación con información compleja de salud.

imagen corporal positiva—El sentido realista de una persona sobre cómo se ve y cómo se siente bien acerca de su apariencia.

equilibrio energético positivo—Ingerir más calorías que las que se queman.

prebiótico—Un alimento que ayuda a nutrir las bacterias saludables del intestino.

prejuicio—Tener una opinión acerca de alguien o algo que no se basa en la razón o en experiencias reales.

medicamento recetado—Una droga recetada por un médico, comprada en una farmacia y destinada a ser usada únicamente por la persona para quien fue recetada.

análisis preventivos—Pruebas médicas realizadas para detectar señales tempranas de una enfermedad.

prevención primaria—Medidas y servicios que reducen el riesgo y evitan problemas de salud, como los esfuerzos por impedir que los menores de edad beban alcohol.

probiótico—Bacterias vivas encontradas en los alimentos.

alimentos procesados—Un alimento que fue modificado antes de venderse o consumirse.

progresión—A medida que los ejercicios se hacen más fáciles, aumentar gradualmente la cantidad o intensidad de los mismos para seguir viendo progresos.

proteína—Una sustancia encontrada en alimentos que provee energía y ayuda a reparar los tejidos del organismo.

protozoario—Un organismo grande unicelular que puede viajar dentro del cuerpo en busca de alimento.

psicoterapia—Hablar con un psiquiatra, psicólogo u otro prestador de salud mental para ayudar a tratar un trastorno mental.

salud pública—El arte y ciencia de proteger y mejorar la salud de las personas y de grandes poblaciones.

transporte público—Transporte que cobra una tarifa establecida, circula por rutas fijas y está disponible al público.

calidad de vida—Cuán saludable, feliz y gratificante es tu vida diaria.

English

rating of perceived exertion (RPE) scale—An easy way to determine if you are working at a moderate- or vigorous-intensity level based on the numbers or pictures that relate to how easy or difficult you feel the aerobic activity you are doing is.

reasonable accommodation—A change, exception, or adjustment to a rule, policy, practice, or service that ensures equal access and opportunity for an individual with a disability.

recycling—The process of collecting and processing materials that would otherwise be thrown away as trash and turning them into new products.

refusal skills—Techniques you use to say no to something you don't want to do.

relapse—Going back to using drugs again after having stopped.

relationship—The connection between people.

relaxation technique—Specific strategies that are used to help reduce the fight-or-flight response.

reliable information—Information that is consistent and similar across multiple sources.

renewable energy source—A type of energy that will never run out, such as solar and wind energy.

residential treatment center—A place where the patient lives full time for the length of treatment while participating in individual and group counseling sessions and other therapeutic and educational activities.

resilience—The ability to bounce back from a difficult or stressful situation.

respiratory system—Controls the flow of oxygen in the body; consists of the mouth, nose, trachea, diaphragm, and lungs.

ride-hailing service—A service by which a driver and car are hailed from an app on the phone to take customers exactly where they need to go.

ritual—A religious or solemn ceremony consisting of a series of actions performed according to a prescribed order.

Rohypnol—A depressant that can impair motor coordination and judgment as well as cause temporary amnesia.

sadness—A normal human emotion felt as a result of a situation or event.

safety conscious—Trying to prevent yourself and others from getting injured.

Español

escala de índice de esfuerzo percibido (en inglés RPE)—Una forma sencilla de determinar si estás trabajando a un nivel de intensidad moderada o vigorosa, en base a números o imágenes que se relacionan con lo fácil o difícil que sientes la actividad aeróbica que estás realizando.

adaptación razonable—Un cambio, excepción o ajuste a una norma, política, práctica o servicio que garantiza la igualdad de acceso y oportunidades a una persona con una discapacidad.

reciclado—El proceso de recoger y procesar materiales que de otro modo se descartarían como basura, y convertirlos en productos nuevos.

habilidades de rechazo—Técnicas que utilizas para decir que no a algo que no quieres hacer.

recaída—Volver a consumir drogas después de haberlas dejado.

relación—La conexión entre personas.

técnica de relajación—Estrategias específicas usadas para ayudar a reducir la reacción de lucha o huida.

información confiable—Información consistente y similar en múltiples fuentes.

fuente de energía renovable—Un tipo de energía que nunca se agota, como la energía solar y la eólica.

centro residencial de tratamiento—Un lugar donde el paciente vive a tiempo completo durante un tratamiento mientras participa de sesiones de terapia individuales y grupales y de otras actividades terapéuticas y educativas.

resiliencia—La capacidad de recuperarse de una situación difícil o estresante.

sistema respiratorio—Controla el flujo de oxígeno dentro del cuerpo; está conformado por la boca, nariz, tráquea, diafragma y pulmones.

servicio de movilidad a demanda—Un servicio en el que se llama a un conductor y su vehículo desde una aplicación del teléfono para que lleve a los clientes exactamente adonde necesitan ir.

ritual—Una ceremonia religiosa o solemne que consiste en una serie de acciones realizadas de conformidad con un orden establecido.

Rohypnol—Un depresor que puede afectar la coordinación motora y el juicio, además de causar amnesia temporal.

tristeza—Una emoción humana normal que se siente como resultado de una situación o evento.

consciente de la seguridad—Intentar prevenir que tanto tú como otros se lesionen.

English

satiated—When the body is full and hunger is satisfied.

saturated fat—A type of fat found in food that can lead to heart attack and heart disease.

secondary prevention—A public health effort that involves recognizing risks for problems and intervening before serious illness or effects arise.

secondhand aerosol—The vapor that originates from the e-cigarette along with the vapor exhaled by the vaper.

secondhand smoke—The smoke or vape breathed out by a smoker or vaper.

self-awareness—Having a sense of your personality, including strengths and weaknesses, thoughts, beliefs, motivation, and emotions.

self-care—All of the decisions made and the actions taken to maintain health.

self-confidence—The trust you have in yourself to manage challenges, seize opportunities, and deal with difficult situations.

self-esteem—How much you like and admire yourself.

self-harm—Hurting yourself on purpose, often as a way to cope with overwhelming emotion or circumstances.

self-image—How you view yourself.

self-talk—The messages you send to yourself; your inner conversation.

sensorineural hearing loss—A type of hearing loss resulting from damage to the auditory nerve itself, keeping sound from being passed properly from the inner ear to the brain.

sex trafficking—Requiring a person to perform sexual acts against their will in exchange for basic human rights like food or water.

sexting—Sending photos and/or videos containing nudity or semi-nudity or that show or simulate sex acts.

sexual assault—Any forced or unwanted sexual contact; it can occur between romantic partners as well as between strangers.

sexual coercion—Using pressure, alcohol, drugs, or force to have sexual contact with another person against their will.

Español

saciado—Cuando el cuerpo está lleno y el apetito está satisfecho.

grasa saturada—Un tipo de grasa encontrada en alimentos que puede derivar en un ataque cardíaco y enfermedad coronaria.

prevención secundaria—Un esfuerzo de salud pública que implica reconocer riesgos de problemas e intervenir antes de que surja una enfermedad o efectos graves.

aerosol de segunda mano—El vapor que se origina del cigarrillo electrónico junto con el vapor exhalado por el vapeador.

humo indirecto—El humo o vapor exhalado por un fumador o vapeador.

conciencia de sí mismo—Tener un sentido de tu personalidad, incluidas fortalezas y debilidades, ideas, creencias, motivación y emociones.

autocuidado—Todas las decisiones y acciones para mantener la salud.

autoconfianza—La confianza que tienes en ti mismo para manejar desafíos, aprovechar oportunidades y enfrentar situaciones difíciles.

autoestima—La medida en que te agradas, te admiras y te valoras a ti mismo, sin tener en cuenta las opiniones de los demás.

autolesión—Lesionarte a propósito, muchas veces como forma de manejar emociones o circunstancias abrumadoras.

autoimagen—Cómo te ves a ti mismo.

diálogo interno—Los mensajes que te envías a ti mismo; tu conversación interior.

pérdida de audición neurosensorial—Un tipo de pérdida de audición que resulta de un daño en el nervio auditivo, que impide que el sonido pase adecuadamente del oído interno al cerebro.

tráfico sexual—Requerir que una persona realice actos sexuales contra su voluntad a cambio de derechos humanos básicos, como alimentos o agua.

sexting—Enviar fotos o videos que contengan desnudez o semidesnudez o que muestren o simulen actos sexuales.

agresión sexual—Cualquier contacto sexual forzado o no deseado; puede ocurrir entre parejas y también entre extraños.

coerción sexual—Usar presión, alcohol, drogas o fuerza para tener contacto sexual con otra persona contra su voluntad.

English

sexual violence—Any sexual activity done against a person's will or without their consent.

sexually transmitted diseases—Infections passed from one person to another during vaginal, anal, or oral sex.

shock—A condition in which the circulatory system fails to deliver enough oxygen-rich blood to the body's tissues and organs.

short-term goal—A small target for behaviors that can be reached in a day to a month.

sibling abuse—The mistreatment of one sibling by another.

sibling rivalry—The competition between siblings that can lead to anger or jealousy.

side effect—Negative effect of a drug on your body.

skeletal muscles—Muscles attached to the bones that enable movement. They are voluntary muscles.

skeletal system—Made up of bones and the tendons, ligaments, and cartilage that connect the bones together. Gives the body support and protection and allows movement.

skill—Something that can be developed and improved over time with effort.

skill-related fitness—Includes activities used to help a person perform well in sports and other activities that require specific skills. Includes speed, agility, balance, power, coordination, and reaction time.

sleep debt—Happens when a person loses sleep night after night and can't catch up.

sleep-deprived—Not getting enough good quality sleep each night, which reduces the ability to function during the day.

small intestine—A long, tubelike organ responsible for most of the body's digestion and absorption.

smog—Air pollution caused by a combination of moisture in the air mixed with smoke and chemical fumes.

smooth muscle—Found in the walls of hollow organs; smooth muscles are involuntary, so they contract automatically.

Español

violencia sexual—Cualquier actividad sexual realizada contra la voluntad de una persona o sin su consentimiento.

enfermedades de transmisión sexual—Infecciones que se transmiten de una persona a otra durante el sexo vaginal, anal u oral.

shock—Una afección en la cual el sistema circulatorio deja de suministrar suficiente sangre oxigenada a los tejidos y órganos del cuerpo.

meta a corto plazo—Un objetivo pequeño de comportamientos que puedes alcanzar en el término de un día a un mes.

abuso fraternal—El maltrato de un hermano hacia otro.

rivalidad entre hermanos—La competencia entre hermanos que puede derivar en ira o celos.

efecto secundario—Efecto negativo de una droga en tu organismo.

músculos esqueléticos—Músculos adheridos a los huesos que permiten el movimiento. Son músculos voluntarios.

sistema esquelético—Formado por los huesos y los tendones, ligamentos y cartílagos que conectan los huesos entre sí. Le dan soporte y protección al cuerpo, y permiten el movimiento.

habilidad—Algo que puede desarrollarse y mejorarse a lo largo del tiempo y con esfuerzo.

aptitud relacionada con la habilidad—Incluye actividades usadas para ayudar a una persona a desempeñarse bien en los deportes y otras actividades que requieren habilidades específicas. Incluye velocidad, agilidad, equilibrio, fuerza, coordinación y tiempo de reacción.

deuda de sueño—Ocurre cuando una persona pierde horas de sueño noche tras noche y no las puede recuperar.

privado del sueño—No obtener suficientes horas de sueño de buena calidad todas las noches, lo que reduce la capacidad de funcionar durante el día.

intestino delgado—Un órgano largo con forma de tubo responsable de la mayor parte de la digestión y absorción del cuerpo.

esmog—Contaminación del aire provocada por una combinación de humedad en el aire mezclada con humo y vapores químicos.

músculo liso—Encontrado en las paredes de órganos huecos; los músculos lisos son involuntarios, de modo que se contraen automáticamente.

Glossary/Glosario

English

social comparison—Comparing yourself to others or to media images.

social health—The ability to get along with people.

social media—Any form of electronic communication in which information, ideas, and personal messages are shared.

social needs—Strong communication, getting along with others, and respecting others' rights and individuality.

social norm—When a behavior is so common in a group or society that it is considered standard or expected.

socioecological model—A model that helps to explain the interrelationship between individual, relationship, community, and societal factors on health.

sodium—A mineral the body needs; it is found in salt.

specificity—Describes specific kinds of exercise to improve specific muscles or specific types of fitness.

static stretching—Being able to maintain an extended stretching position.

stigma—A distinguishing characteristic or personal trait that is thought to be, or actually is, a disadvantage.

stimulant—A class of drugs that speed up the central nervous system.

stomach—A hollow organ that holds food and prepares it for digestion.

stress—The body's reaction to a demanding or difficult situation.

stress management technique—Any strategy used to control how much stress affects a person.

stressor—Something that triggers a feeling of stress.

stroke—A condition in which the brain does not get enough oxygen and a portion of it dies or is damaged.

student assistance program—A program designed to help students and families by bringing a substance abuse counselor into the school to meet with students individually or as a group on a regular basis.

Español

comparación social—Compararte con otras personas o con imágenes de los medios.

salud social—La capacidad de llevarse bien con las personas.

redes sociales—Cualquier forma de comunicación electrónica en la que se comparte información, ideas y mensajes personales.

necesidades sociales—Comunicación sólida, llevarse bien con los demás y respetar sus derechos e individualidades.

norma social—Cuando un comportamiento es tan común en un grupo o sociedad que se considera estándar o esperado.

modelo socio-ecológico—Un modelo que ayuda a explicar la interrelación entre los factores individuales, de relación, comunitarios y sociales en la salud.

sodio—Un mineral que el cuerpo necesita; se encuentra en la sal.

especificidad—Describe tipos específicos de ejercicios para mejorar músculos específicos o tipos de aptitud física específicos.

estiramiento estático—Poder mantener una posición de estiramiento extendida.

estigma—Una característica distintiva o rasgo personal que se considera, o realmente es, una desventaja.

estimulante—Una clase de drogas que aceleran el sistema nervioso central.

estómago—Un órgano hueco que contiene el alimento y lo prepara para la digestión.

estrés—La reacción del cuerpo a una situación difícil o exigente.

técnica de manejo del estrés—Cualquier estrategia usada para controlar cuánto afecta el estrés a una persona.

factor estresante—Algo que dispara una sensación de estrés.

derrame cerebral—Una afección en la que el cerebro no recibe suficiente oxígeno y una porción muere o resulta dañada.

programa de asistencia estudiantil—Un programa diseñado para ayudar a los estudiantes y las familias que consiste en llevar a las escuelas un consultor de abuso de sustancias tóxicas para reunirse regularmente con los estudiantes de manera individual o en grupo.

English

substance abuse counselor—A person who works specifically with people dealing with an alcohol use disorder or other substance abuse disorder.

substance use disorder—Symptoms resulting from the use of a drug that you continue to take even though you experience problems as a result.

suicide—Self-directed violence, by someone who intends to end their life, that results in the person dying because of their actions.

suicide attempt—Serious self-harm resulting from someone's attempt to take their own life.

suicide cluster—When there are several suicide attempts or suicides within a community in a relatively short period of time.

suicide contagion—When a person is influenced by other people's suicides and they become more likely to attempt suicide themselves.

suspicious activity—A behavior or action that causes a feeling that something is wrong or that someone is doing something wrong.

symptom—A sign experienced in the body that tells you that something is not right with your health.

synthetic chemical—A human-made chemical.

target heart rate zone—A range of two numbers, 60 to 75 percent of maximum heart rate, for a person to ideally stay in when exercising to get the most benefit from their workout.

team sport—A sport played by a group of people working toward a common goal.

tendons—Tough bands of tissue that connect bones to muscles and can shorten or lengthen just like a muscle.

tertiary prevention—The treatment and rehabilitation of a person who is already sick to avoid death.

thirdhand smoke—The nicotine and chemical residue that can remain on furniture, walls, clothing, carpets, and all other surfaces for months after someone smokes.

Español

consultor de abuso de sustancias tóxicas—Una persona que trabaja específicamente con individuos con problemas de consumo de alcohol u otros trastornos por abuso de sustancias tóxicas.

trastorno por consumo de sustancias tóxicas—Síntomas que resultan del consumo de una droga que continúas usando a pesar de experimentar problemas por las consecuencias.

suicidio—Violencia dirigida a sí mismo por alguien que intenta poner fin a su vida, que resulta en la muerte de la persona como consecuencia de sus acciones.

intento de suicidio—Autolesión grave resultante del intento de una persona de poner fin a su vida.

foco de suicidios—Cuando se producen varios suicidios o intentos de suicidio dentro de una comunidad en un período relativamente corto.

contagio del suicidio—Cuando una persona está influenciada por los suicidios de otros y es más probable que intente suicidarse.

actividad sospechosa—Una conducta o acción que da la impresión de que algo está mal o de que alguien está haciendo algo malo.

síntoma—Una señal que se experimenta en el cuerpo y que te informa que algo no está bien con tu salud.

producto químico sintético—Un producto químico elaborado por el hombre.

zona de frecuencia cardíaca deseada—Un rango de dos números, 60 a 75 por ciento de la frecuencia cardíaca máxima, en el que una persona debería mantenerse idealmente cuando se ejercita para obtener el máximo beneficio de su entrenamiento.

deporte en equipo—Un deporte jugado por un grupo de personas que trabajan por una meta común.

tendones—Bandas resistentes de tejido que conectan los huesos con los músculos y se pueden acortar o estirar igual que un músculo.

prevención terciaria—El tratamiento y rehabilitación de una persona que ya está enferma para evitar la muerte.

humo de tercera mano—La nicotina y los residuos de sustancias químicas que pueden permanecer sobre los muebles, paredes, la ropa, alfombras y todas las demás superficies durante meses después de que alguien fume.

English

time—How long you exercise. The first "T" in the FITT formula.

tinnitus—A ringing, buzzing, or other sound in the ear.

tobacco—Plant grown for its leaves, which are dried and put into tobacco products.

tolerance—Requiring higher doses of a drug to have the same effect.

tooth decay—The destruction of some part of the tooth.

toxic chemical—Any chemical that can cause death, a loss of consciousness, or permanent harm to humans or animals.

toxin—A poisonous substance given off by bacteria.

trait—A characteristic you are born with, like eye color and hair color.

trigger—Something that affects your emotional state, often overwhelmingly, by causing extreme distress.

type—The actual exercise you choose to do based on the fitness component you are working on.

unconscious—A state during which the body is inactive and without awareness, such as during sleep.

underage drinking—Consuming alcohol under the age of 21.

unhealthy relationship—A relationship that leaves a person feeling uncomfortable, sad, or afraid.

unintentional injury—An injury caused by accidental or unplanned events.

universal design—Refers to creating and designing an environment so that it can be accessed, understood, and used to the greatest degree possible by all people regardless of their age, size, ability, or disability.

universal precautions—Very specific steps taken to prevent the spread of disease through blood and other body fluids.

unsaturated fat—Fat found in plant foods that is generally healthier for the human body.

valid information—Logical and factually accurate information.

Español

tiempo—Durante cuánto tiempo te ejercitas. La primera "T" de la fórmula FITT.

tinnitus—Un zumbido o timbre u otro sonido dentro del oído.

tabaco—Una planta cultivada por sus hojas, que se secan y se usan para productos de tabaco.

tolerancia—Requerir una dosis mayor de una droga para lograr el mismo efecto.

deterioro dental—La destrucción de una parte del diente.

producto químico tóxico—Cualquier producto químico que pueda causar la muerte, una pérdida de conciencia o una lesión permanente a humanos o animales.

toxina—Una sustancia venenosa producida por las bacterias.

rasgo—Una característica con la que naces, como el color de los ojos y del cabello.

desencadenante—Algo que afecta tu estado emocional, muchas veces de manera abrumadora, y causa una angustia extrema.

tipo—El verdadero ejercicio que eliges hacer en base al componente de aptitud física sobre el que estás trabajando.

inconsciente—Un estado durante el cual el cuerpo está inactivo y sin conciencia, como durante el sueño.

consumo de alcohol en menores de edad—Consumir alcohol antes de los 21 años.

relación tóxica—Una relación que hace sentir incómoda, triste o asustada a una persona.

lesión involuntaria—Una lesión causada por eventos accidentales o no planificados.

diseño universal—Se refiere a crear y diseñar un ambiente para que todas las personas, cualquiera sea su edad, tamaño, capacidad o discapacidad, puedan acceder, comprenderlo y usarlo en la mayor medida posible.

precauciones universales—Pasos muy específicos que se dan para prevenir la transmisión de una enfermedad a través de la sangre y otros fluidos corporales.

grasa insaturada—Grasa que se encuentra en alimentos vegetales que generalmente es más saludable para el cuerpo humano.

información válida—Información lógica y objetivamente correcta.

English

values—Principles that describe what is most important to an individual.

vaping—The act of inhaling and exhaling aerosol produced by an e-cigarette.

variety—A diet with a lot of different types of foods.

verbal communication—Using spoken and written words to express the information being shared.

victim—The person on the receiving end of violent behavior.

violent behavior—The intentional use of words or actions that cause or threaten to cause injury to someone or something.

virtual friend—A person you know only online through social media or gaming.

virus—A small bundle of infectious material that invades the cells and multiplies.

vitamins—Organic compounds found in foods that are essential for life.

warm-up—An activity that includes large muscle movements that get the whole body moving.

water—A tasteless liquid that is essential for life.

weight cycling—Repeatedly losing and regaining weight over time.

weight prejudice—The presence of negative beliefs, attitudes, and behaviors toward individuals who appear to be overweight or obese.

wellness—Positive component of health that involves having a good quality of life and a good sense of well-being.

whole food—Food that has not been processed or changed.

whole grain—A grain that has not had fiber removed.

withdrawal—A group of symptoms experienced when the quantity of a substance is reduced.

witness—Someone who sees a violent act but does not participate in it.

wound—An injury that results when the skin or other tissues of the body are damaged.

youth violence—Violent behavior by young people ages 10 to 24.

Español

valores—Los principios que describen qué es lo más importante para una persona.

vapear—El hecho de inhalar y exhalar aerosol producido por un cigarrillo electrónico.

variedad—Una dieta con muchos tipos diferentes de alimentos.

comunicación verbal—Usar palabras orales y escritas para expresar la información que se comparte.

víctima—La persona que recibe la acción de una conducta violenta.

conducta violenta—El uso intencional de palabras o acciones que causan o amenazan causar lesión a alguien o a algo.

amigo virtual—Una persona que conoces únicamente en línea a través de redes sociales o videojuegos.

virus—Un pequeño paquete de material infeccioso que invade las células y se multiplica.

vitaminas—Un compuesto orgánico encontrado en alimentos que son esenciales para la vida.

calentamiento—Una actividad que incluye movimientos de los músculos largos que hacen mover todo el cuerpo.

agua—Un líquido sin sabor que es esencial para la vida.

ciclo de peso—Perder y recuperar peso reiteradamente a lo largo del tiempo.

prejuicio de peso—La presencia de creencias, actitudes y comportamientos negativos hacia personas que parecen tener sobrepeso o ser obesas.

bienestar—Componente positivo de la salud que implica tener una buena calidad de vida y sentirse bien.

alimento integral—Un alimento no procesado ni modificado.

cereal integral—Un cereal al que no se le ha extraído la fibra.

abstinencia—Un grupo de síntomas que se experimentan cuando se reduce la cantidad de una sustancia nociva.

testigo—Alguien que ve un hecho violento pero no participa del mismo.

herida—Una lesión que ocurre cuando se daña la piel u otros tejidos del cuerpo.

violencia juvenil—Comportamiento violento de personas jóvenes de 10 a 24 años de edad.

Credits

p. 3: gradyreese/E+/Getty Images

p. 4: FatCamera/E+/Getty Images

p. 5: fstop123/Getty Images/Getty Images

p. 10: Oliver Rossi/Digital Vision/Getty Images

p. 13: Robert Daly/OJO Images RF/Getty Images

p. 15: JulieanneBirch/E+/Getty Images

figure 1.4: Adapted from CDC.

p. 26: JUAN GAERTNER/SCIENCE PHOTO LIBRARY/Science Photo Library RF/Getty Images

photos in figure 1.12: KATERYNA KON/SCIENCE PHOTO LIBRARY/Getty Images

photo in "HIV and AIDS" graphic, p. 31: KATERYNA KON/SCIENCE PHOTO LIBRARY/Getty Images

p. 33 (top): © Cathy Stancil - Fotolia.com

p. 37: BSIP/UIG/Collection Mix: Subjects RF/Getty Images

p. 38: Lambert And Young/Digital Vision/Getty Images

photos in figure 1.17: Westend61/Getty Images (direct); Kasipat Phonlamai/EyeEm/Getty Images (indirect); John M Lund Photography Inc /DigitalVision/Getty Images (airborne); iStockphoto.com/Viktor Kitaykin (host)

figure 1.18: Juanmonino/E+/Getty Images

figure 1.21: ViDi Studio/iStock/Getty Images

figure 1.22: Carroteater/iStock/Getty Images

p. 44 (bottom): Halfdark/fStop/Getty Images

p. 49: Suriyo Hmun Kaew/EyeEm/EyeEm/Getty Images

p. 52: Ivan-balvan/iStockphoto/Getty Images

p. 54: iStockphoto/Ina Peters

p. 55: kali9/E+/Getty Images

p. 56: LEA PATERSON/SCIENCE PHOTO LIBRARY/Science Photo Library RF/Getty Images

p. 57: Jeffrey Collingwood/fotolia.com (top); © Mark Bowden/iStockphoto (bottom)

p. 63: Marc Romanelli/Tetra images RF/Getty Images

p. 64: SDI Productions/E+/Getty Images

p. 65: Fuse/Corbis RF Stills/Getty Images

p. 66: Primorac91/iStockphoto/Getty Images

p. 69 (top): Boyloso/iStockphoto/Getty Images

figure 2.2: Gokhanilgaz/E+/Getty Images

figure 2.3: Reprinted from National Cancer Institute (1990).

p. 71 (top): ultramarinfoto/iStockphoto/Getty Images

photos in figure 2.4: Science Photo Library - E. GRAY/Brand X Pictures/Getty Images (head lice); FatCamera/E+/Getty Images (hair loss); Powerofforever/E+/Getty Images (dandruff); Zlisjak/iStock/Getty Images (infections); Apomares/E+/Getty Images (ingrown nails); Dmitry Epov/iStock/Getty Images (warts)

p. 73: BFG Images/Gallo Images ROOTS Collection/Getty Images

p. 74: FGorgun/iStockphoto/Getty Images

p. 75: gerenme/iStockphoto/Getty Images

p. 79: Photodisc

p. 81: Alex Potemkin/iStockphoto/Getty Images

p. 88: Yasser Chalid/Moment RF/Getty Images

p. 90: Tetra Images/Getty Images

photos in figure 2.13: JGI/Jamie Grill/Getty Images (weight gain); Jayk7/Moment/Getty Images (mood swings); Yuichiro Chino/Moment/Getty Images (impaired memory); Aslan Alphan/E+/Getty Images (heart disease)

p. 92: SDI Productions/iStockphoto/Getty Images (top); Goodboy Picture Company/E+/Getty Images (bottom)

p. 95: eggeeggjiew/iStockphoto/Getty Images

p. 97: Monkey Business/Getty Images

p. 98: mihailomilovanovic/Getty Images

p. 99: Huntstock/DisabilityImages/Getty Images

p. 101: Courtney Hale/E+/Getty Images

p. 102: Kingfisher Productions/Digital Vision/Getty Images

p. 109: jarenwicklund/iStockphoto/Getty Images

p. 110: JohnnyGreig/E+/Getty Images

p. 111: LumiNola/E+/Getty Images

p. 112: Ben Gingell/iStockphoto/Getty Images

p. 115: Marius Faust/EyeEm/EyeEm/Getty Images

p. 116: ampueroleonardo/E+/Getty Images (top); Oliver Rossi/Digital Vision/Getty Images (bottom)

p. 119: kali9/E+/Getty Images

p. 120: Tempura/E+/Getty Images

p. 121 (bottom): Kali9/E+/Getty Images

p. 122: BuildPix/Construction Photography/Avalon/Getty Images

p. 123 (top): RonBailey/E+/Getty Images

p. 124: Ryan McFadden/MediaNews Group/Reading Eagle via Getty Images

p. 127: Pakorn Kumruen/EyeEm/EyeEm/Getty Images

p. 128: REB Images/Tetra images RF/Getty Images

photos in figure 3.7: Reprinted from "Campaign Materials," United States Federal Trade Commission, last modified September 2013, https://consumer.ftc.gov/articles/0393-campaign-materials (primary); Photodisc (tertiary)

p. 132 (bottom): Jamie Grill/Tetra Images/Getty Images

p. 133: Courtney Hale/E+/Getty Images

p. 141: Kingfisher Productions/Digital Vision/Getty Images

p. 142: Tom Werner/Digital Vision/Getty Images

p. 143: Steve Debenport/iStockphoto/Getty Images

photos in figure 4.3: xxmmxx/Getty Images (apples); Etiennevoss/iStock/Getty Images (applesauce)

figure 4.4: burwellphotography/E+/Getty Images

photos in figure 4.5: egal/Getty Images/iStockphoto (nuts/seeds); iStock / Getty Images Plus (olive oil); gbh007/iStockphoto/Getty Images (fish); Eyewave/iStock/Getty Images (avocados)

photos in figure 4.6: IgorDutina/iStockphoto/Getty Images (seeds); Elena Schweitzer/Getty Images/iStockphoto (grains); popovaphoto/Getty Images/iStockphoto (beans); conejota/Getty Images/iStockphoto (nuts)

photos in figure 4.7: Creative Crop/DigitalVision/Getty Images (bottle); Thomas Barwick/DigitalVision/Getty Images (boy drinking)

p. 150: imagestock/E+/Getty Images (top); VICTOR DE SCHWANBERG/Science Photo Library RF/Getty Images (bottom)

photos in figure 4.8: Magnetcreative/E+/Getty Images (energy drink); Perch Images/Photodisc/Getty Images (iced coffee); Scanrail/iStock/Getty Images (soda)

p. 151: Daniel Grill/Tetra Images/Getty Images

p. 154: margouillatphotos/iStockphoto/Getty Images

Credits

photo in figure 4.13: Lite Productions/Lite Productions RF/Getty Images

photos in figure 4.14: Ivan/Moment Open/Getty Images (Spain); Edwin Remsberg/The Image Bank/Getty Images (Morocco); Luchezar/E+/Getty Images (Italy); MagicBones/iStock /Getty Images (Ethiopia); Jose Gerardo San Miguel/EyeEm/Getty Images (Philippines); Martin Puddy/Stone/Getty Images (Indonesia); Jordan Lye/Moment/Getty Images (China); Sumit Pandit/EyeEm/Getty Images (India); Aeril01/iStock/Getty Images (Argentina); Fitopardo/Moment/Getty Images (Ecuador); Sonia Tapia/Moment/Getty Images (Cuba); Claudia Totir/Moment/Getty Images (USA)

p. 160: Jasmin Merdan/Moment RF/Getty Images

p. 163: Oscar Wong/Moment RF/Getty Images

p. 166: Juanmonino/Getty Images/iStockphoto

figure 4.18: USDA's Center for Nutrition Policy and Promotion (MyPlate graphic)

p. 167: YinYang/E+/Getty Images

photos in figure 4.19: fcafotodigital/Getty Images/iStockphoto (dairy); Elena Schweitzer/Getty Images/iStockphoto (grains); Tetra Images/Getty Images (protein); nezabudka123/Getty Images/iStockphoto (fruit); AlinaMD/Getty Images/iStockphoto (vegetables)

Tetra Images

p. 172: krisanapong detraphiphat/Moment RF/Getty Images

p. 176: Jurgita Vaicikeviciene/EyeEm/EyeEm/Getty Images

p. 177: BoValentino/iStock/Getty Images

figure 4.25: Esdelval/iStock/Getty Images; spxChrome/E+/Getty Images (inset)

p. 179: Picsfive/iStockphoto/Getty Images

p. 182: JGI/Jamie Grill/Tetra images RF/Getty Images

photos in figure 4.26: paci77/E+/Getty Images (olives); Yevgen Romanenko/Moment RF/Getty Images (bread); Brian Hagiwara/The Image Bank RF/Getty Images (frozen dinners)

figure 4.27: Caspar Benson/Getty Images

figure 4.28: Kristin Lee/Getty Images

figure 4.29: SCIENCE PHOTO LIBRARY/Science Photo Library RF/Getty Images (left); margouillatphotos/iStockphoto/Getty Images (right)

photos in table 4.5: Juanmonino/E+/Getty Images (chips); R.Tsubin/Moment RF/Getty Images (chocolate); popovaphoto/Getty Images/iStockphoto (beans)

p. 187: Natalia Ganelin/Moment RF/Getty Images (cereal); LauriPatterson/E+/Getty Images (peanut butter); LauriPatterson/iStockphoto/Getty Images (eggs); Nkisu Machona/EyeEm/EyeEm/Getty Images (avocado toast); LauriPatterson/E+/Getty Images (yogurt); Arx0nt/Moment RF/Getty Images (oatmeal)

photo in figure 4.30: YinYang/E+/Getty Images

p. 190: AlasdairJames/Getty Images (mushrooms); Fotosearch (cauliflower); Roy Morsch/Corbis/Getty Images (turnips); Santiago Urquijo/Moment/Getty Images (onions); Science Photo Library/Getty Images (lemons); PhotoDisc (corn, peaches, kiwi, green beans, blueberries, berries); Art Explosion (peppers, carrots, cabbage, cherries); margouillatphotos/Getty Images/iStockphoto (sweet potatoes); tanuha2001/iStock/Getty Images (broccoli); getsaraporn/iStockphoto/Getty Images (lettuce); Philippe Intraligi/EyeEm/Getty Images (eggplant); Selektor/Getty Images (plums); vitalssss/Getty Images/iStockphoto (beets)

p. 197: SDI Productions/E+/Getty Images

p. 198: Anthony Lee/OJO Images RF/Getty Images

p. 199: Indeed/ABSODELS RF/Getty Images

p. 200: MoMo Productions/DigitalVision/Getty Images

photos in figure 5.1: R.Tsubin/Moment/Getty Images (dark chocolate); Roberto Machado Noa/Moment/Getty Images (white beans); Melanie Hobson/EyeEm/Getty Images (lentils); Popovaphoto/iStock/Getty Images (shellfish); Bdsp/iStock/Getty Images (liver); Paci77/E+/Getty Images (green olives); Maribee/E+/Getty Images (Swiss chard); Westend61/Getty Images (beef); R.Tsubin/Moment/Getty Images (apricots); Diana Taliun/iStock/Getty Images (pinto beans); Ranasu/E+/Getty Images (lima beans); Magone/iStock/Getty Images (quinoa); Melanie Hobson/EyeEm/Getty Images (pumpkin seeds); Kevin Dyer/E+/Getty Images (tofu)

photos in figure 5.3: LauriPatterson/E+/Getty Images (yogurt); David Crockett/Moment RF/Getty Images (broccoli smoothie); skaman306/Moment RF/Getty Images (edamame); popovaphoto/Getty Images/iStockphoto (beans); gbh007/iStockphoto/Getty Images (salmon); Natalia Ganelin/Moment RF/Getty Images (cereal)

p. 205: ShutterOK/iStockphoto/Getty Images

p. 206: Ryasick/E+/Getty Images

p. 209: Image Source/Getty Images

p. 210: Feverpitched/iStock/Getty Images

p. 212: Adam Gault/OJO Images/Getty Images

photos in figure 5.6: Creativ Studio Heinemann/Westend61/Getty Images (strawberry); tanuha2001/iStock/Getty Images (broccoli)

p. 217: Kohei Hara/Digital Vision/Getty Images

p. 218: Microgen/iStock/Getty Images

p. 225: SolStock/E+/Getty Images

p. 228: puhhha/iStockphoto/Getty Images

figure 5.10: nemchinowa/iStockphoto/Getty Images

p. 232: Jeff Greenough/Tetra Images/Getty Images

p. 235: AndreyPopov/iStockphoto/Getty Images

p. 237: Valentinrussanov/E+/Getty Images

p. 245: PamelaJoeMcFarlane/E+/Getty Images

p. 246: YinYang/E+/Getty Images

p. 247: Fran Polito/Moment RF/Getty Images

photo in figure 6.1: MichaelDeLeon/E+/Getty Images (left)

p. 249: coffeekai/iStockphoto/Getty Images

figure 6.2: © C.B. Corbin, from *Fitness for Life*, 7th ed. (Champaign, IL: Human Kinetics, 2021).

p. 254: otlphoto/iStockphoto/Getty Images

figure 6.8: Vladimir Vladimirov/E+/Getty Images

photo in figure 6.11: Image Source/Getty Images

photo in figure 6.14: Terry Vine/Digital Vision/Getty Images (top center: balance)

p. 264: Petri Oeschger/Moment RF/Getty Images

p. 267: Jordi Salas/Moment RF/Getty Images

p. 268: RyanJLane/E+/Getty Images

p. 270: Maskot/Maskot/Getty Images

p. 271: Christine Kohler/iStock/Getty Images

p. 278: oleg66/iStockphoto/Getty Images

p. 281: AndreyPopov/Getty Images/Getty Images (top); Maskot/Maskot/Getty Images (bottom)

p. 289: kali9/iStockphoto/Getty Images

p. 290: Egoitz Bengoetxea Iguaran/iStockphoto/Getty Images

p. 291: Hibatallah Khawaja/EyeEm/EyeEm/Getty Images

p. 292: ThitareeSarmkasat/iStock/Getty Images

photo in figure 7.5: Fstop123/E+/Getty Images

p. 298: Francesco Carta fotografo/Moment RF/Getty Images

714

Credits

p. 299: SDI Productions/E+/Getty Images

p. 302: eleonora galli/Moment RF/Getty Images

p. 303: Weedezign/iStock/Getty Images

figure 7.8: NPHOTOS/Moment/Getty Images

p. 305: SDI Productions/E+/Getty Images

p. 306: Burak Karademir/Moment/Getty Images

p. 307: FatCamera/E+/Getty Images

p. 310: Ridofranz/iStockphoto/Getty Images

p. 311: Oliver Rossi/DigitalVision/Getty Images

p. 315: Nick David/Stone/Getty Images

p. 318: g-stockstudio/iStockphoto/Getty Images

p. 321: SDI Productions/E+/Getty Images (top); Skynesher/E+/Getty Images (bottom)

p. 326: quavondo/E+/Getty Images

p. 327: Bymuratdeniz/E+/Getty Images

p. 328: Arman Zhenikeyev/Corbis/Getty Images

p. 330: Steve Smith/Tetra Images/Getty Images

p. 331: Westend61/Getty Images

p. 337: monkeybusinessimages/iStockphoto/Getty Images

p. 338: Layland Masuda/Moment RF/Getty Images

p. 339: Ridofranz/iStockphoto/Getty Images

"Mental Disorders and Youth by the Numbers", p. 341: Adapted from "New CDC Data Illuminate Youth Mental Health Threats During the COVID-19 Pandemic," Centers for Disease Control and Prevention, accessed August 3, 2022, https://www.cdc.gov/media/releases/2022/p0331-youth-mental-health-covid-19.html.

p. 341: catscandotcom/E+/Getty Images (top); DebbiSmirnoff/E+/Getty Images (bottom)

p. 342: Maskot/Getty Images

p. 343: Mordolff/E+/Getty Images (top); Tassii/E+/Getty Images (bottom)

p. 348: Kentaroo Tryman/Moment RF/Getty Images

p. 349: Westend61/Getty Images

p. 353: FangXiaNuo/E+/Getty Images

p. 356: Rebecca Smith/Moment RF/Getty Images

p. 357: Justin Paget/Stone/Getty Images

photos in figure 8.4: Paula Daniëlse/Moment RF/Getty Images (top); SCIEPRO/SCIENCE PHOTO LIBRARY/Science Photo Library RF/Getty Images (center); Francesco Carta fotografo/Moment RF/Getty Images (bottom)

p. 360: Monkeybusinessimages/iStock/Getty Images

p. 363: mdurson/iStockphoto/Getty Images

p. 365: Harpazo hope/Moment/Getty Images

p. 367: Juanmonino/E+/Getty Images

p. 373: kali9/E+/Getty Images

p. 374: The Good Brigade/Digital Vision/Getty Images

p. 375: kali9/E+/Getty Images

p. 377: Johner Images/Getty Images

p. 379: Andy Sack/The Image Bank/Getty Images

p. 381: Viviana Loza/EyeEm/Getty Images

p. 384: Willie B. Thomas/Digital Vision/Getty Images

p. 386: MoMo Productions/DigitalVision/Getty Images

p. 387: Ferrantraite/E+/Getty Images

p. 389: Jose Luis Pelaez Inc/DigitalVision/Getty Images

p. 390: MoMo Productions/DigitalVision/Getty Images

p. 393: kali9/E+/Getty Images

p. 394: Maladrino/Stone/Getty Images

p. 397: Daisy-Daisy/iStock/Getty Images

p. 400: Klaus Vedfelt/Digital Vision/Getty Images

p. 401: www.davingphotography.com/Moment/Getty Images

p. 402: Egoitz Bengoetxea Iguaran/iStock/Getty Images

p. 404: Mayur Kakade/Moment/Getty Images

p. 407: Izusek/E+/Getty Images

p. 409: Stock-Eye/E+/Getty Images

p. 419: MachineHeadz/iStockphoto/Getty Images

p. 420: praetorianphoto/E+/Getty Images

p. 421: thianchai sitthikongsak/Moment RF/Getty Images

p. 422: Sean De Burca/The Image Bank/Getty Images

p. 426: Kali9/iStock/Getty Images

p. 430: Andrew Holt/The Image Bank RF/Getty Images

p. 431: Wendy Connett/Moment/Getty Images

p. 434: Sturti/E+/Getty Images

p. 437: Courtney Hale/E+/Getty Images

photos in figure 10.8: Constantinis/E+/Getty Images (physical); SDI Productions/E+/Getty Images (emotional); FatCamera/E+/Getty Images (social); AIM-STOCK/E+/Getty Images (cyberbullying)

p. 439: Elva Etienne/Moment/Getty Images

p. 440: Motortion/iStock/Getty Images

p. 441: FluxFactory/E+/Getty Images

p. 447: juanestey/E+/Getty Images

"Youth Violence" statistics, p. 448: Adapted from "The State of America's Children® 2021: Gun Violence," Children's Defense Fund, accessed August 3, 2022, https://www.childrensdefense.org/state-of-americas-children/soac-2021-gun-violence/.

p. 448: Filadendron/E+/Getty Images

p. 450: George Doyle/Stockbyte/Getty Images

p. 452: amanalang/iStockphoto/Getty Images

p. 455: Pascal Broze/Onoky/Getty Images

p. 456: CareyHope/E+/Getty Images

p. 459: Martin Novak/Moment/Getty Images (top); Kittisak Jirasittichai/EyeEm/Getty Images (bottom)

Table 10.2: Adapted from "Myths and Facts About Sexual Violence," Georgetown Law, accessed October 31, 2022, https://www.law.georgetown.edu/your-life-career/health-fitness/sexual-assault-relationship-violence-services/myths-and-facts-about-sexual-violence/

p. 462: filadendron/E+/Getty Images

p. 471: BrianAJackson/iStockphoto/Getty Images

p. 472: fstop123/iStockphoto/Getty Images

p. 473: Gerasimov174/iStockphoto/Getty Images

p. 476: Sturti/E+/Getty Images

p. 478: powerofforever/E+/Getty Images

figure 11.7: Used with permission of Susan Tapert, University of California, San Diego.

p. 483: VICTOR DE SCHWANBERG/Science Photo Library/Getty Images

p. 484: Creatingmore/E+/Getty Images

p. 488: SolStock/E+/Getty Images

p. 489: Fotosearch

p. 492: HRAUN/E+/Getty Images

p. 497: Kemal Yildirim/E+/Getty Images

p. 498: skaman306/Moment RF/Getty Images

p. 500: Georgijevic/E+/Getty Images

p. 501: NoSystem Images/E+/Getty Images

p. 509: AndreyPopov/iStockphoto/Getty Images

p. 510: Rob Lewine/Tetra images RF/Getty Images

p. 511: NengLoveyou/iStockphoto/Getty Images

Credits

p. 513: Rouzes/E+/Getty Images (cigarette); Rouzes/E+/Getty Images (cigar); Douglas Sacha/Moment RF/Getty Images (snuff and snus); VICTOR DE SCHWANBERG/Science Photo Library RF/Getty Images (e-cigarette); victoriya89/iStockphoto/Getty Images (pipe); InkkStudios/E+/Getty Images (chewing tobacco)

p. 516: Natnan Srisuwan/Moment/Getty Images

photo in figure 12.6: Maskot/Getty Images

p. 521: HAZEMMKAMAL/iStockphoto/Getty Images (top); Morsa Images/DigitalVision/Getty Images (bottom)

p. 522: ClarkandCompany/E+/Getty Images

p. 525: VisualArtStudio/iStockphoto/Getty Images

p. 526: Duel/Image Source/Getty Images

p. 527: mikroman6/Moment RF/Getty Images

p. 530: JGI/Tom Grill/Tetra Images/Getty Images

p. 532: Mikroman6/Moment/Getty Images

p. 536: Jesus Calonge/Moment/Getty Images

p. 539: Tetra Images/Getty Images

p. 540: JGI/Tom Grill/Tetra Images/Getty Images

p. 547: MARHARYTA MARKO/iStockphoto/Getty Images

p. 548: monkeybusinessimages/iStockphoto/Getty Images

p. 549: Photodisc

p. 550: PM Images/Stone/Getty Images

p. 551: Ron Levine/Stone/Getty Images

p. 554: Tanja Ivanova/Moment/Getty Images

figure 13.2: rudchenko/Getty Images/iStockphoto

p. 559: FotoMaximum/iStockphoto/Getty Images

p. 561: Thanasis/Moment/Getty Images

p. 562: mikroman6/Moment/Getty Images

p. 563: Daniel Kaesler/EyeEm/Getty Images (top); seksan Mongkhonkhamsao/Moment (bottom)

p. 564: James Marshall/Corbis/Getty Images

p. 565: Simon Hausberger/Getty Images (top); RapidEye/E+/Getty Images (bottom)

p. 566: ALFREDO ESTRELLA/AFP via Getty Images

p. 567: Silas Stein/picture alliance via Getty Images (top left); VictorZwiers/iStockphoto/Getty Images (top right); MERJA OJALA/AFP via Getty Images (center); BSIP/Universal Images Group via Getty Images (bottom)

figure 13.4: lzf/Getty Images/iStockphoto

p. 573: MoMo Productions/Digital Vision/Getty Images

p. 574: Maskot/Getty Images

p. 575: Karen Moskowitz/The Image Bank RF/Getty Images

p. 576: Witthaya Prasongsin/Moment/Getty Images

p. 581: Luis Alvarez/Digital Vision/Getty Images

p. 583: Kali9/E+/Getty Images

p. 585: Feverpitched/iStockphoto/Getty Images

p. 587: Timurlaykov/iStock/Getty Images

p. 595: SDI Productions/iStockphoto/Getty Images

p. 596: sturti/E+/Getty Images

p. 597: Valeriy_G/iStockphoto/Getty Images

p. 598: Peter Stark/fStop/Getty Images

p. 599: Klaus Vedfelt/Digital Vision/Getty Images

p. 601: Photodisc (top); wsmahar/E+/Getty Images (bottom)

p. 603: Kevin J Salisbury/Moment (top left); Chris Kridler/Cultura RF/Getty Images (top center); Warren Faidley/The Image Bank RF/Getty Images (top right); CatLane/iStockphoto/Getty Images (bottom)

p. 607: ajr_images/iStockphoto/Getty Images

p. 608: RealPeopleGroup/E+/Getty Images

p. 610: John Giustina/The Image Bank RF/Getty Images (top); Brandon Colbert Photography/Moment/Getty Images (bottom)

figure 14.4: Nattakorn Maneerat/EyeEm/Getty Images

figure 14.6: Bill Crump/Brand X Pictures

p. 613: SoCalShooter/E+/Getty Images

p. 615: Brook Pifer/DigitalVision/Getty Images

p. 616: Ascent/PKS Media Inc/Stone/Getty Images

p. 620: d3sign/Moment RF/Getty Images

p. 621: Maskot/Getty Images

p. 626: Tonywestphoto/Corbis Documentary RF/Getty Images

photo in figure 14.9: Douglas Sacha/Moment/Getty Images

p. 633: THOMAS SAMSON/AFP via Getty Images (top); Science Photo Library/Science Photo Library RF/Getty Images (bottom)

photos in table 14.1: Jason Todd/The Image Bank/Getty Images (first-degree); Nadya Tkach/iStockphoto/Getty Images (second-degree); ROBERTO SCHMIDT/AFP via Getty Images (third-degree)

p. 635: Tatiana Kulyashina/EyeEm/Getty Images

photos in table 14.2: iStockphoto.com/Judith Bicking (abrasion); jax10289/iStockphoto/Getty Images (laceration); Randy Tyler/EyeEm/Getty Images (avulsion); RapidEye/iStockphoto/Getty Images (puncture)

p. 639: IndiaPix/IndiaPicture/Getty Images

p. 645: Alistair Berg/Digital Vision/Getty Images

p. 646: Alistair Berg/Digital Vision/Getty Images

p. 647: Herianus Herianus/EyeEm/EyeEm/Getty Images

p. 648: Francesco Carta fotografo/Moment RF/Getty Images

figure 15.2: ByoungJoo/iStockphoto/Getty Images (left); Dermot Conlan/Tetra images RF/Getty Images (left center); Daniel Stein/iStockphoto/Getty Images (right center); Patrick Orton/Aurora Open/Getty Images (right)

figure 15.3: Will & Deni McIntyre/Corbis Documentary RF/Getty Images

p. 654: BNBB Studio/Moment RF/Getty Images

p. 655: FatCamera/E+/Getty Images

p. 658: tunart/E+/Getty Images

p. 659: Dorling Kindersley/Dorling Kindersley RF/Getty Images

photos in figure 15.8: PhotoDisc (makeup); Stevica Mrdja/EyeEm/Getty Images (shampoo); belchonock/iStock/Getty Images (air freshener); artursfoto/ iStock/Getty Images (deodorant); Visoot Uthairam/Moment/Getty Images (perfume); Image Source/Getty Images (sunscreen)

p. 665: Anna Blazhuk/Moment RF/Getty Images

p. 666: Daisy-Daisy/iStockphoto/Getty Images

p. 669: Peter Zelei Images/Moment RF/Getty Images

p. 670: Dougal Waters/DigitalVision/Getty Images

p. 671: somchaisom/iStockphoto/Getty Images

Index

Note: The italicized *f* and *t* following page numbers refer to figures and tables, respectively.

A

ABCDE method 70
abdominal fat 219
abrasion 636*t*
absent grief 329*t*
abstinence 408, 410, 411
abuse 423*f*, 456-459, 463
accommodations 122
acid rain 650
acne 68-69
acquaintances 395
acquired immunodeficiency syndrome (AIDS) 31
active, being 269-270
active ingredient 98
active listening 265, 298, 378-379, 381
active shooter 609
acute stressors 320
added sugars 184, 186*f*
addiction 536, 551, 564
addictive potential 582-583
adequate diet 164
adoptive family 385
advertising 529-530, 575-577
advocacy 22-23, 117, 382
aerobic activities 249, 255
aggression 430-431, 432*f*
aggressive communication 102, 380
aggressive driving 613
agility 263*f*
airborne transmission 39*f*
air pollution 647, 649-651, 656, 657
air quality 650-651
air quality index (AQI) 651, 652*f*
alcohol
 alternatives to using 494
 brain effects of 482
 communication skills to avoid use of 493-494
 consequences of using 481-483
 consumption of 475-478
 definition of 474
 driving and 483-484, 613
 effects of 479-481
 emotional reasons for using 476-477
 influences and 488-495
 minor in possession of 483
 overdose of 475, 479*f*
 in pregnancy 481
 use of 473, 476-478, 481-483, 491-494
alcohol-free 494, 505
Alcoholics Anonymous (AA) 502
alcohol treatment programs 501-503
alcohol use disorders (AUD) 497-504
allergens 33
allergies 33, 80, 553, 630-631

alopecia 71*f*
alpha hydroxy acids 68
Alzheimer's disease 57
amputation 636*t*
anabolic steroids 221, 565
anaphylaxis 630
anemia 147, 202, 203*f*
anger 298, 420, 430-431
animal abuse 423*f*
anorexia 231*f*
anti-anxiety medications 344
antibodies 29
anticipatory grief 329*t*
antidepressants 343
antioxidants 185, 186*t*
antipsychotic medications 344
antivirus software 623
anxiety/anxiety disorders 338, 340*f*, 348-353
appendix 175
appetite 158-160, 162
arteriosclerosis 51
arthritis 55
assertive communication 46, 102, 380, 440
assertiveness 431, 432*f*
asthma 30, 56, 514, 630
astigmatism 82
atherosclerosis 51
athlete's foot 43-44
athletic performance 569
attention deficit hyperactivity disorder 340*f*
ATVs 615-616
autoimmune disorders 32-33
automated external defibrillator (AED) 628-629
avoidant restrictive food intake disorder (ARFID) 231*f*
avulsion 636*t*

B

bacteria 28
bacterial infections 41, 71*f*
bad breath 74
balance 263*f*
balanced diet 164
ball-and-socket joint 261*t*
barbiturates 567-568
beauty 75-76
behavior(s) 9-10, 16, 21, 387
behavioral therapy 586
behavior contracts 57-58
benzodiazepines 567
benzoyl peroxide 68
bereavement 329-331
best friends 395

beverages 149-151
bias 165, 424-425
bicycle safety 611
bile 175
binge drinking 115, 475
binge eating 231*f*
biodegradable 671
biodiversity 666
bioelectrical impedance (BIA) 220*t*
bipolar disorder 358*f*
blended family 385
blood alcohol content (BAC) 478, 484-485
bloodshot eyes 82
body composition 219, 220*t*, 262
body image 225-234, 241, 304
body mass index (BMI) 219
body piercings 45
body shaming 229
body weight 218-224
bone 260, 637
boundaries 408, 463, 464*f*
brain 259, 296, 342, 482*f*, 583
breakfast 187, 210
breaking up 409, 410*f*
breast cancer 55*t*
breast self-examination 97
breathalyzer 478
bronchitis 56, 514
bruises 635
bruxism 75
built environment 648
bulimia 231*f*
bully/bullying 229, 423*f*, 437-444, 438*f*, 439*f*
burns 634-635

C

caffeine 150-151, 204, 321, 555, 569
calcium 203-205
calories 145, 155-157
cancer 53-54, 55*t*, 56, 70, 115, 177*t*
cancer researcher 521
cannabidiol (CBD) 562
cannabis 562
carbohydrates 145, 147
carbon monoxide poisoning 599-600
carcinogens 522
cardiac arrest 628
cardiac muscle 258
cardiopulmonary resuscitation (CPR) 630, 638, 642
cardiorespiratory endurance 255-258, 276-277
cardiovascular diseases (CVD) 51-52
careers 132, 133*t*
cartilage 260

Index

casual friends 395
cavity 74
centers 100-101
Centers for Disease Control and Prevention (CDC) 34, 68, 129, 477, 531
central nervous system (CNS) 259
certified health education specialist (CHES) 22
character 314
chemical peels 76
chemicals 659-664
chemistry 403
chewing 174
chewing tobacco 513*f*, 517
child abuse 423*f*, 457, 458*t*
childless family 385
child pornography 444
choking 631-632
chronic diseases 50
chronic obstructive pulmonary disease (COPD) 56, 515
chronic stressors 320
chyme 175
circulatory system 255
cirrhosis 177*t*, 480
clinics 100-101
closed wounds 635, 637
close friends 395, 396*f*
closeness 403
club drugs 566, 567*f*
cocaine 562, 569
cochlear implant 84
coercion 461
coercive relationships 461
cognitive impairments 121*f*
cold-related emergencies 272, 633
cold sores 74
colitis 177*t*
collagen 67
colon cancer 55*t*, 177*t*
color blindness 82
commitment 403
common cold 41-43
communicable diseases 37-45, 39*f*, 132
communication
 aggressive 380
 alcohol refusal and 493-494
 assertive 46, 102, 380
 definition of 378
 of emotions 294
 of health needs 18
 healthy 24, 86, 391
 for healthy eating 205-207
 mental disorders and 345-346
 nonverbal 378
 online relationship 404-407
 passive 380
 passive-aggressive 380
 social media 380-381
 styles of 379-380

 of support 331-332
 text messages 380-381
 verbal 378
community
 advocacy for 23
 definition of 23, 608
 food and 160
 health resources 134
 safety in 607-619
 violence in 427
community health 128, 132, 133*t*
comparison shopping 98
competence 314
complete proteins 147
complicated grief 329*t*
composting 672
concussion 638-639
conductive hearing loss 84
confidence 304*f*, 307, 314
conflict 420, 430, 432-436
conjunctivitis 43
conservation 665, 666
constipation 177
consumer 97, 101, 102
contagious 38
contusion 638
convenience foods 189
cool-down 269
coordination 263*f*
coping skills 350, 370
coronary heart disease 51
coronavirus 130
counseling 342-343, 501
COVID-19 43, 352, 359
creatine 555
Crohn's disease 177*t*
crooked teeth 73-74
crowded teeth 73-74
cultural beliefs 159
cultural norms 386
culture 490
customs 330
cyberbullying 423*f*, 438, 441-444

D

daily energy need 156
dandruff 71*f*
dating 400-412, 459
death 327-328, 390
decay, tooth 74
decision making 19, 189, 191-193, 308, 361, 523, 571, 663
deficiency 156
dehydration 272, 631
delayed grief 329*t*
dementia 57, 115
dentist 75
depressants 474, 553, 567-568
depression 338, 356-362
dermatitis 69
dermis 67

designated driver 484
determinants 7-8, 113*f*
diabetes 53-54, 133, 156, 184, 631
diagnosis 7
dialysis 179
diet 142, 164, 184
dietitian 169
diet pills 556
digestion 174-175
digestive system 172-177, 179-181
digital citizen 443
digital footprint 621
direct contact 39*f*
disability 119-124, 389-390
disasters 602-603
discrimination 425
disease 7
disenfranchised grief 329*t*
dislocation 637
disordered eating 230
disruptive mood dysregulation disorder 358*f*
distracted driving 613
distraction 298
distress 321, 322*f*
disulfiram 502
domestic violence 459-460
dopamine 516, 563, 583
drama 397
drinking 475-478, 483-484. *See also* alcohol
driving
 alcohol and 483-484, 613
 distracted 613
 drowsy 614
 drug-impaired 587-588
driving under the influence (DUI) 483, 613
driving while intoxicated (DWI) 483
drowsy driving 614
drug/drug use
 addictive potential of 582-583
 advertisements and 575-577
 alternatives to 577, 578*f*
 athletic performance and 569
 brain effects 583
 driving and 587-588
 illicit 559-572
 influences on 573-580
 over-the-counter 548-556, 558
 prescription 548-558, 564, 587, 590
 school and 568, 586
 tolerance to 583
 warning signs of 570
 withdrawal from 583
drug crimes 587
drug facts label 551, 552*f*
drug-free 583-584
dual sports 270
dynamic stretching 262, 277

E

ear(s) 82-85
earthquakes 603
eating behaviors 198
eating disorders 230-231
eating out 187, 188f
e-cigarettes 511, 513f, 516, 518-521, 529f, 530, 541
ecommerce 98
eczema 69
edibles 561
education 113f
elastin 67
elder abuse 423f, 459
electronic bullying 438
e-liquids 518-519, 526
emergencies 596, 626-641
emergency contact card 100
emotional abuse 423f, 458t
emotional attraction 401
emotional connection 394
emotional health 290-301, 312, 317, 334
emotional impairments 121f
emotional intelligence 293, 294f
emotional intimacy 407
emotional needs 386
emotional violence 422
emotions
 anxiety and 338
 communicating of 294
 controlling of 296-300
 dating 403-404
 definition of 292
 influences on 295-296
 managing of 298-299
 sexual activity and 411
empathy 85, 294-295, 299
emphysema 56
empty-calorie food 150
enamel 72
endorphins 563
energy balance 154-156, 162
energy drinks 150-151, 555
energy needs 157t
environment 646-674
environmental determinants 8
epidemiologists 132, 133t
epidermis 67
epinephrine 536, 631
equilibrium 82
equity 111-112
escalate 433
esophagus 174
exaggerated grief 329t
exercise 248
extended family 385
external influences 527, 528t
eyes 81-82

F

face masks 271, 273
facial injuries 637
fad diets 222
fainting 631
falls 599
family
 advocacy for 23
 alcohol use disorder in 500-501
 appetite and 158-159
 changes to 389-390
 dating and 404
 definition of 385
 drug use and 574
 health disparities 115
 needs of 386
 roles in 387-389
 types of 385
farsightedness 82
fat distribution 219, 220t
fats 146, 185, 186t
fat soluble vitamins 149
fee-for-service care 99t
fentanyl 564
fetal alcohol spectrum disorder (FASD) 481, 486
fetal alcohol syndrome (FAS) 481
fiber 145, 186t
fight-or-flight response 319, 320f, 321, 324
fire 600, 601
firearms 449, 600
first aid 626-627, 642
fitness. *See* physical fitness
fitness plan/planning 275-276, 279-281, 284
fitness tests 276
FITT formula 276-279
fixed mindset 312, 313f
flexibility 262, 268, 277
flu. *See* influenza
food
 access to 209-211, 215
 healthy choices 206
 lessons on 143
 preparation of 213
 processed 183
 religion and 160
 safety of 211-216
food additives 213-214
Food and Drug Administration (FDA) 530, 556
foodborne illnesses 211-212
food chain 211
food handling 213
food insecurity 210
food labels 98, 165, 166f
food log 236
food preservatives 213-214
food recall 211
food science 237
food toxic environment 184

foster family 385
fractures 637
frequency, of exercise 276, 279
fresh water 652
friendships 393-399, 482
frostbite 633
fruits 214f
fungal infections 43-44, 71f

G

gang violence 423f, 447, 450-452
gardens 211
gas 177
gastroenterologist 179
general anxiety disorder 351t
genetically modified foods 215
genetic engineering 215
genetics 8, 30, 341, 357
gestational diabetes 53
GHB 566, 567f
gingivitis 74
gliding joints 261t
global public health 130
goals 20, 237-238, 324
goggles 271, 273
gossip 397
government health insurance 99-100
graduated driver licensing (GDL) 612
grains 145, 146f
grandparents-as-parents family 385
gratitude 353-354
grief 326, 328, 329f, 329t
grinding, of teeth 75
grit 315
growth mindset 312, 313f
guardian 387-388, 388t, 404, 413
gum disease 74
guns 449, 604
gut bacteria 176

H

habit 14, 21f, 65
hackers 623
hair 70-71, 76f
halitosis 74
hallucinogens 565-566
hate crimes 423f
hazardous materials 663
hazing 423f, 437, 444-446
head injuries 638-639
health
 advocacy for 22-23
 community 128, 132, 133t
 culture of 113
 determinants of 7-8, 113f
 digestive 177, 179-180
 disability and 121
 emotional 290-301, 312, 317, 334
 physical activity benefits 248-249
 public. *See* public health
 self-esteem and 306

Index

health *(continued)*
  social 377
  socioecological model of 114
  stress and 323
  urinary 179
health behaviors 9-10, 16, 21
health care consumer 97, 103
health care products 97-98
health care system 99-101
health disparities 115-117
health educator 22
health equity 111-112, 136
health habits 65, 78
health inequities 113
health information 16-18
health inspector 133*t*
health insurance 99-100
health knowledge 15, 19
health literacy 14-15
health maintenance organization (HMO) 99*t*
health needs 18
health prevention 131-132
health promotion 131-132
health-related fitness 255-262, 266, 276
health resources 16-18
healthy communication 24
healthy dating relationships 401-402
healthy decision making 19
healthy eating 205-206
healthy food choices 206
healthy goals 20
healthy lifestyle 8-9, 31
healthy living skills 11, 13-14, 24, 35
healthy relationships 374-377, 382-383
healthy weight 220-221
hearing 79, 82-84, 87, 121*f*. *See also* ear(s)
hearing loss 83-84
heart 255
heart attack 51
heartburn 177
heat-related emergencies 272, 633
helmets 271, 273, 611, 614
hematoma 638
hemorrhoids 177
heredity 8
heroin 563
herpes simplex virus (HSV) 74
high blood pressure 52, 185
hinge joints 261*t*
homicide 423*f*
hospital 100-101
host transmission 39*f*
household products 661, 662*f*
housing 113*f*
human immunodeficiency virus (HIV) 31, 38, 628
human trafficking 423*f*, 461-462
hunger 157, 162
hurricanes 602-603

hygiene 66-67, 71, 73
hyperglycemia 631
hypertension 52, 185
hypodermis 67
hypoglycemia 631
hypothermia 633

I

identity theft 622
illicit drugs 559-572
illness
  definition of 7
  in family 389-390
  sudden 630-631
  vector-borne 45-46
image alterations 75-76, 229
I messages and statements 46, 102, 265, 379, 381, 493
immune deficiency disorders 32
immune response 29, 31*f*
immune system 26-27, 29-33, 36
immunizations 29
impairment 120, 121*t*
impulsiveness 297
inactivity 251
inclusion, disability 122-124
income 113*f*
incomplete proteins 147
indigestion 177
indirect contact 39*f*
individual determinants 8
individual sports 270
indoor air quality 651
infant mortality 115
influenza 41-43, 130
information access 125
ingrown nails 71*f*
inhalants 564
inhibited grief 329*t*
injuries 271-272, 597-598, 605-606
insomnia 91
insulin 53
intensity, of exercise 276, 279
intentional injuries 598
internal influences 527, 528*t*
Internet safety 621-622
intimacy 407-408
intolerance 424-425
intoxicated 484-486
iron 147, 202-203
irritable bowel syndrome (IBS) 177*t*

J

jealousy 397
job performance 569
joints 260, 261*t*, 637
journal 299
juvenile justice process 587
juvenile rheumatoid arthritis 55

K

keratin 71

ketamine 566
kidney dialysis 179
kidney disease 179
kidney stones 178
kissing disease. *See* mononucleosis
knives 449

L

labels 98
laceration 636*t*
lactose intolerance 177*t*
large intestine 175
laser eye surgery 85
lasers 85
laughter 299
leukemia 53, 55*t*
leukopenia 32
leukoplakia 517
lice 71*f*
licensed marriage and family therapist (LMFT) 390
lifespan 199-200, 201*t*, 208
ligaments 260
lightning 602
listening, active 265, 298, 378-379, 381
literacy, health 14-15
living green 665, 669-671, 674
longevity 200
long-term goals 20
loss 326, 329*f*, 367
love 397-398, 403
LSD 565
lunch programs 210
lung cancer 55*t*, 56
lung disease 56
lymphoma 33, 53

M

mainlining 560
major life events 320
malnutrition 156, 210
malware 623
managed care 99*t*
mandatory reporter 457
mania 344
marginalized groups 117
marijuana 561-562, 568, 587, 613
marriage and family therapist, licensed 390
maximum heart rate 257
MDMA 566, 567*f*
media
  alcohol use and 490-491
  body image and 228-229, 233
  drug use and 574
  self-image and 76*f*, 77
  targeting of teens by 160
Medicaid 99-100
medical history 96
medical screenings 97
Medicare 99-100

Index

melanoma 55*t*
menstruation 203
mental disorders
   anxiety/anxiety disorders 338, 340*f*, 348-353
   causes of 341-342
   communication and 345-346
   definition of 340
   depression 356-362
   facts about 341
   medications for 343-344
   mood disorders 356-362
   social stigma and 344, 345*f*
   treatment of 342-344
   types of 340*f*
mental health 249, 292, 515-516
mental health therapist 501
mental needs 386
mental toughness 311, 315-317
mescaline 566
metabolic rate 155
meteorologist 602
methamphetamine 563
microbiologist 133*t*
mindset 312, 313*f*
minerals 147-149, 202-205
minor in possession (MIP) 483
mobility impairments 121*f*
moderate diet 164
moderate drinking 475
mononucleosis 43
mood disorders 340*f*, 356-362
mood stabilizers 344
mortician 332
motorcycle safety 614-615
motor vehicle safety 612-616
mourning 329-331
mouth 72-75
mouth guards 271, 273
multigenerational family 385, 387
multigrain 145
muscle 258
muscle injuries 637
muscle mass 221
muscular endurance 259
muscular strength 259, 277
muscular system 258
MyFitnessPal 236, 281
MyPlate 166-168, 236

N

nails 70-71
naloxone 502
Narcan 564
narcolepsy 91
natural disasters 602-603, 655
natural environment 648
nearsightedness 82
neck injuries 638
negative body image 226-227
negative energy balance 155

negative self-talk 315, 316*t*
neglect 423*f*, 457, 458*t*, 459
neighborhood 113*f*
nervous system 259
neuroleptics 344
never-married family 385
nicotine 512, 515-516, 518-519, 536, 537*f*
nicotine replacement therapy (NRT) 541
nicotine use disorder 539
night blindness 82
911 627, 628*f*
noise-canceling earphones 83
noise pollution 647, 655, 657
noncommunicable diseases 50-58. *See also specific diseases*
nonnutritious drinks 150
nonverbal communication 378
nuclear family 385, 387
nurse practitioners (NPs) 133
nutrients 143-147
nutrition 165, 169, 183, 192-193, 200, 201*t*
nutrition facts label 165, 166*f*
nutritionists 169
nutrition plan 236-240
nutritious drinks 151

O

obesity 218-219
obsessive compulsive disorder 340*f*
offender 424
online relationship 404-407
online safety 620-625
online shopping 98
open wounds 635-637
opioids 553, 563-564, 569
optimal stress 322
optimistic 312
oral cavity 72
organic food 214
orthorexia 231*f*
osteoporosis 54-55, 147, 204
out-of-pocket insurance limit 100
overload 278
over-the-counter (OTC) drugs 548-556
overweight 219-220

P

pandemics 43, 130
panic attacks 351*t*
panic disorder 351*t*
passive-aggressive communication 380
passive communication 102, 380
passwords 622, 623*f*
pathogens 28, 38, 628
patient advocates 101
PCP 566
pedestrian safety 610, 611*f*
peer pressure 489-490, 574
pepper spray 450
performance-enhancing drugs 555

peripheral artery disease 52
peripheral nervous system (PNS) 259
persistent depressive disorder 358*f*
personal care products 660, 661*f*
personal health habits 65, 78, 105
personality disorders 340*f*
personal protective equipment 40*f*
personal trainer 264
pessimistic 312
pesticides 214
pharmacy 97
phishing attacks 622
phobia 349, 351*t*
physical abuse 423*f*, 458*t*
physical activity
   benefits of 248-249
   definition of 246, 248
   disease prevention and 249
   dressing for 271-272
   emotions and 299
   guidelines 249-251
   injury prevention during 271-272
   preparing for 267-274
   protective equipment for 271
   self-assessments 246
Physical Activity Pyramid 249, 250*f*
physical fitness
   definition of 248
   health-related 255-262, 266, 276
   skill-related 262-264, 266
physical intimacy 407-408
physical needs 386
physical violence 422
phytochemicals 190
piercings 45
pink eye. *See* conjunctivitis
pivot joint 261*t*
plain language 24
pneumonia 56, 514
point-of-service care 99*t*
poisoning 599-600, 662
pollution 647, 649-657
positive body image 226
positive energy balance 155
postpartum depression 358*f*
post-traumatic stress disorder 340*f*
poverty 115
power 263*f*
prebiotics 176
preferred provider organization (PPO) 99*t*
pregnancy 115, 410, 481, 516, 517*f*
prejudice 228, 344, 424-425
presbyopia 82
prescription drugs 548-558, 564, 587, 590
preservatives 213-214
prevention 131-132
preventive screening 97
primary care physician 100

Index

primary prevention 131, 132f
private health insurance 100
probiotics 176
processed foods 183
product labels 98
progression 278
prostate cancer 55t
protective equipment 271
protective spray devices 450
protein 147, 221
protozoan infections 45
psychotherapy 342-343
psychotic depression 358f
puberty 189, 203
public health 127-132, 133t, 135
public health analyst 133t
public health educator 133t
public health insurance 100
public health nurse 133t
public health organizations 129t
public safety 610
public transportation 616, 670
puncture 636t

Q
quality of life 8

R
rabies 38
rating of perceived exertion (RPE) scale 256, 257f
reaction time 263f
reasonable accommodations 122
Recommended Daily Allowance (RDA) 147
recycling 668
red eyes 82
refusal skills 409, 493-494, 538, 542
relapse 586
relationships
  coercive 461
  dating 400-412, 459
  definition of 376
  family 384-391
  friendships 393-399, 482
  guardian 387-388, 388t
  healthy 374-377, 382-383
  sibling 388-389
  unhealthy 377, 378f
  violence in 426, 455-466
relaxation techniques 324
reliable information 16
religion 160
renewable energy source 667
reproductive health 410-411
residential treatment center 502-503
resilience 313-315
respect 427, 428
respiratory system 256
rest 89
retina 80
rheumatoid arthritis 55
RICE 637, 638f

ride-hailing/ridesharing service 616-617
risk-taking 476
risky behaviors 570
rituals 330
Rohypnol 566, 567f
roid rage 565

S
sadness 360
safety
  bicycle 611
  community 607-619
  at home 599-600
  motorcycle 614-615
  motor vehicle 612-616
  online 620-625
  pedestrian 610, 611f
  public 610
  public transportation 616
  school 608-609
  water 617-618, 654
  at work 617
safety conscious 598
salicylic acid 68
salivary glands 174
salt 185, 652
satiated 157
saturated fats 185, 186t
schizophrenia 340f
school
  counseling services 342
  food choices 160
  health clinics 100
  health services 110, 130
  norms in 386
  safety in 608-609
  sports in 270
  substance use and grades 483, 568, 586
  tobacco product policies of 532-533
  violence in 423f, 452-453
school counselors 360
screening 97
seasonal affective disorder 358f
seat belts 612
secondary prevention 131, 132f
secondhand aerosol 522
secondhand smoke 522
sedative-hypnotics 567-568
seeking help 299, 366-367
seizures 631
selective mutism 351t
self-awareness 302-309
self-care 64, 95-97, 103, 361
self-confidence 304f, 307, 314
self-control 314
self-esteem 304f, 305-306, 306f
self-examinations 97
self-harm 363-365
self-image 77, 304, 304f
self-talk 315, 316t
sensorineural hearing loss 84

separation anxiety 351t
sexting 406-407, 444
sex trafficking 461-462
sexual abuse 423f, 458t
sexual activity 410-411
sexual assault 460-461
sexual coercion 461
sexually transmitted diseases (STDs) 408, 410, 476
sexual violence 422
sharps 40
shock 632
shoes 271
short-term goals 20
sibling abuse 423f, 459
sibling rivalry 389
side effects 551
simple phobia 349, 351t
single-parent family 385, 387
skeletal muscle 258
skeletal system 260, 261f
skill 313-314
skill-related fitness 262-264, 266
skin 28, 66-69, 76f
skin cancer 53, 70
skinfold calipers 220t, 262f
sleep 89-94, 296
sleep apnea 91
sleep deprivation 91
small intestine 175
SMART goals 20, 237-238, 279, 282, 324
smog 650
smokeless tobacco 513f, 517, 529
smoking. *See* tobacco products
smooth muscle 258
social and human services assistants 586
social anxiety disorder 351t, 352
social comparison 228
social determinants 8
social health 377
social media
  alcohol use and 491
  anxiety and 352
  body image and 229, 233
  communication using 380-381
  definition of 491
  drug use and 575
  emotions and 296
  friendships and 396-397
  influences of 75-77
  safety 621-622, 624
  self-image and 77
social needs 386
social norms 85-86, 386-387
social stigma 344, 345f
social worker 133t, 434
socioecological model of health 114
sodium 185
specificity 278
speed 263f
speeding 613

722

Index

spinal cord 259
spinal injuries 638
sports 270
sprain 637
static stretching 262, 277
steroids 221, 565
stigma 344, 345*f*
stimulants 553, 554*t*, 562-563, 569
stomach 174-175
STOP tool 344, 345*f*
strain 81-82, 637
strep throat 41
stress
  anxiety and 349
  body effects of 321-323
  definition of 319
  drug use and 574
  health and 323
  high blood pressure and 52
  immune system affected by 30, 31*f*
  management of 323-325
  optimal 322
  performance and 322
stressors 319-321
stretching 262, 277
stroke 51*f*, 52
student assistance program 502
Students Against Destructive Decisions (SADD) 485
substance abuse counseling 344, 501
substance use disorders 390, 581-589
sudden illness 630-631
sugar 150, 184, 186*t*, 631
suicide 363, 365-366, 600
sunburn 69, 635
sunglasses 80
sunscreen 67, 70
supplements 221-222
support 331-332
suspicious activity 452-453
swallowing 174
symptoms 40-41
synthetic chemical 659

T

target heart rate zone 257
tattoos 44
team sports 270
technology 75-76, 296
teenagers 200
teen dating violence (TDV) 459
teeth 72-75, 92
tendons 260
terrorism 423*f*
tertiary prevention 132
testicular self-examination 97
tetrahydrocannabinol (THC) 561
text messages 380-381, 406-407, 540
thirdhand smoke 522
time, of exercise 276, 279
time-out 298

tinnitus 85
tobacco-free 537-539
tobacco products
  advertising of 529-530
  avoiding 535
  e-cigarettes 511, 513*f*, 516, 518-521, 529*f*, 530, 541
  effects of 514-516
  influences on use of 525-534
  ingredients of 512
  marketing of 529-530
  nicotine 512, 515-516, 518-519, 536, 537*f*
  norming of 529-530
  pregnancy and 516, 517*f*
  prevention of use 530-532, 537
  quitting of 535, 538*f*, 540-541
  refusal skills 538, 542
  regulation of 530-532
  school policies on 532-533
  smokeless 513*f*, 517, 529
  types of 513*f*
  vaping 511, 516, 518-521, 520*f*, 524, 526, 533, 544
tolerance 583
tooth decay 74
top-level domains 17
tornadoes 602-603
toxic chemical 659
toxins 41
training principles 278
trait 313
trauma 321, 635
traumatic brain injury (TBI) 341
trigger 364
tuberculosis 56
type, of exercise 276, 279
type 1 diabetes 53, 184
type 2 diabetes 53, 144, 156, 184

U

ulcers 177
ultraviolet (UV) rays 80
unconscious 89
underage drinking 474
underwater weighing 220*t*
underweight 220
unhealthy relationships 377, 378*f*, 402-403
unintentional injuries 598
universal design (UD) 123
universal precautions 40, 628
unsaturated fats 185, 186*t*
urinary system 172, 178-179, 181
urinary tract infections (UTIs) 178
UTVs 615-616

V

vaccinations 33, 43
valid information 16
values 491

vaping 511, 516, 518-521, 520*f*, 524, 526, 533, 544
varied diet 164
vector-borne illnesses 45-46
vegetables 214*f*
verbal communication 378
victim 424, 439*f*
violence 421-429, 447-454, 455-467
violent behavior 421-429
viral infections 41-43
virtual friends 395
virtual reality 343
viruses 28
vision 79-80, 82, 87, 121*f*
vitamins 147-149, 203-205
vomiting 177, 561

W

waist-to-hip ratio 220*t*
warm-up 269
warts 71*f*
water 149-151, 175
water cycle 652-653
water pollution 647, 652-657
water safety 617-618
water treatment 654
weapons 447, 449-450
wearable technology 281
web domains 17
websites 17-18, 34
weight 218-224
weight cycling 222
weight loss 221-223
weight prejudice 228
well-being 4
wellness 6, 11
wet weather 272
whole foods 145
whole grains 145, 146*f*
wisdom teeth 73-74
withdrawal 583
witness 425-426
workplace safety 617
World Health Organization 6
wounds 635-637

Z

zero tolerance 483, 588